# AMERICAN LAW YEARBOOK 1998

AN ANNUAL SOURCE PUBLISHED
BY GALE RESEARCH AS A
SUPPLEMENT TO
WEST'S ENCYCLOPEDIA OF
AMERICAN LAW

GALE

DETROIT · LONDON

Kris E. Palmer, *Editor*

Dawn R. Barry, Ashyia N. Henderson, and Rebecca Parks, *Associate Editors*

Linda S. Hubbard, *Managing Editor*

Elsa Peterson Ltd., *Photographic Research*

Keasha Jack-Lyles, *Permissions Assistant*

Mary Beth Trimper, *Production Director*

Evi Seoud, *Assistant Production Manager*

Cynthia Baldwin, *Product Design Manager*

Barbara J. Yarrow, *Graphic Services Manger*

Randy Bassett, *Imaging Supervisor*

Robert Duncan, *Senior Imaging Specialist*

Pamela A. Reed, *Photography Coordinator*

Eleanor Allison, *Manager, Data Entry Services*

# CONTENTS

The need for a layperson's comprehensive, understandable guide to terms, concepts, and historical developments in U.S. law has been well met by *West's Encyclopedia of American Law* (*WEAL*). Published at the end of 1997 by the foremost legal professional publisher, *WEAL* has proved itself a valuable successor to *The Guide to American Law: Everyone's Legal Encyclopedia* from the same publisher, West Group, in 1983.

Now, in cooperation with West Group, Gale Research, a premier reference publisher, extends the value of *WEAL* with the publication of *American Law Yearbook*. The *Yearbook* both adds entries on emerging topics not covered in the main set and provides updates through May 1998, on cases, statutes, and issues documented there. A legal reference must be current to be authoritative, so the *Yearbook* is a vital companion to a key reference source. Uniform organization and cross-referencing make it easy to use the titles together, while inclusion of key definitions and summaries of earlier rulings in supplement entries, whether new or continuations, make it unnecessary to refer constantly to the main set.

## Understanding the American Legal System

The legal system of the United States is admired around the world for the freedoms it allows the individual and the fairness with which it attempts to treat all persons. On the surface, it may seem simple. Yet, those who have delved into it know that this system of federal and state constitutions, statutes, regulations, and common law decisions is elaborate and complex. It derives from the English common law, but includes principles older than England, along with some principles from other lands. Many concepts are still phrased in Latin. The U.S. legal system, like many others, has a language all its own. Too often it is an unfamiliar language.

*West's Encyclopedia of American Law* (*WEAL*) explains legal terms and concepts in everyday language. It covers a wide variety of persons, entities, and events that have shaped the U.S. legal system and influenced public perceptions of the legal system.

## FEATURES OF THIS SUPPLEMENT

### Entries

This supplement contains 180 entries covering individuals, cases, laws, and concepts. Entries are arranged alphabetically and, for continuation entries, use the same entry title as in *WEAL*. There may be several cases discussed under a given topic. Entry headings refer to decisions of the U.S. Supreme Court by case name; other cases are identified by their subject matter.

Profiles of individuals cover interesting and influential people from the world of law, government, and public life, both historic and contemporary. All have played a part in creating or shaping U.S. law. Each profile includes a time-line highlighting important moments in the subject's life.

### Definitions

Each entry on a legal term is preceded by a definition, which is easily distinguished by its sans serif typeface.

## Cross References

To facilitate research, two types of cross-references are provided within and following entries. Within the entries, terms are set in small capital letters (e.g. DISCLAIMER) to indicate that they have their own entry in *WEAL*. Cross references at the end of an entry refer readers to additional relevant topics in *WEAL*.

## In Focus Pieces

In Focus pieces present complex and controversial issues from different perspectives. These pieces, which are set apart from the main entries with boxed edges and their own logo, examine some of the difficult legal and social questions that confront attorneys, judges, juries, and legislatures. The Independent Counsel Act and election campaign financing are among the high-interest topics in this yearbook.

## Appendix: Lobbying Organizations

The appendix to this volume features listings for 30 of the most prominent lobbying organizations in the country on a wide variety of subjects. Lobbying organizations influence the law by disseminating information to legislatures and the public and by providing funding to support their agendas.

## Table of Cases Cited and Index

These features make it easy for users to quickly locate references to cases, people, statutes, events, and other subjects. The Table of Cases Cited traces the influences of legal precedents by identifying mentions of cases throughout the text. In a departure from *WEAL*, references to individuals have been folded into the general index to simplify searches. Litigants, attorneys, justices, historical and contemporary figures, as well as topical references are included in the Index.

## Citations

Wherever possible, *American Law Yearbook* includes citations to cases and statutes for readers wishing to do further research. The citation refers to one or more of the series called "reporters" that publish court opinions and related information. Each citation includes a volume number, an abbreviation for the reporter, and the starting page reference. Underscores in a citation indicate that a court opinion has not been officially reported as of publication. Two sample citations, with explanations, are presented below.

*Miranda v. Arizona*, 384 | U.S. | 436, | 86 S.Ct. 1602, | 16 L.Ed. 2d 694 | (1966)

   1         2   3   4      5             6       7

1. *Case title*. The title of the case is set in italics and indicates the names of the parties. The suit in this sample citation was between Ernesto A. Miranda and the state of Arizona.

2. *Reporter volume number*. The number preceding the reporter abbreviation indicates the reporter volume containing the case. (The volume number appears on the spine of the reporter, along with the reporter abbreviation.)

3. *Reporter abbreviation*. The suit in the sample citation is from the reporter, or series of books, called *U.S. Reports*, which contains cases from the U.S. Supreme Court. (Numerous reporters publish cases from the federal and state courts; consult the abbreviations list at the back of this volume for full titles.)

4. *Reporter page*. The number following the reporter abbreviation indicates the reporter page on which the case begins.

5. *Additional reporter citation*. Many cases may be found in more than one reporter. The suit in the sample citation also appears in volume 86 of the *Supreme Court Reporter*, beginning on page 1602.

6. *Additional reporter citation*. The suit in the sample citation is also reported in volume 16 of the *Lawyer's Edition*, second series, beginning on page 694.

7. *Year of decision*. The year the court issued its decision in the case appears in parentheses at the end of the cite.

*Brady Handgun Violence Prevention Act*, Pub. L. No. 103-159, 107 Stat. 1536 (18 U.S.C.A. § § 921-925A)

     1            2      3  4  5  6  7    8

1. *Statute title.*

2. *Public law number.* In the sample citation, the number 103 indicates this law was passed by the 103d Congress, and the number 159 indicates it was the 159th law passed by that Congress.

3. *Reporter volume number.* The number preceding the reporter abbreviation indicates the reporter volume containing the statute.

4. *Reporter abbreviation.* The name of the reporter is abbreviated. The statute in the sample citation is from *Statutes at Large.*

5. *Reporter page.* The number following the reporter abbreviation indicates the reporter page on which the statute begins.

6. *Title number.* Federal laws are divided into major sections with specific titles. The number preceding a reference to the U.S. Code stands for the section called Crimes and Criminal Procedure.

7. *Additional reporter.* The statute in the sample citation may also be found in the *U.S. Code Annotated.*

8. *Section numbers.* The section numbers following a reference to the *U.S. Code Annotated* indicate where the statute appears in that reporter.

## COMMENTS WELCOME

Considerable efforts were expended at the time of publication to ensure the accuracy of the information presented in *American Law Yearbook 1998.* The editors welcome your comments and suggestions for enhancing and improving future editions of this supplement to *West's Encyclope-* *dia of American Law.* Send comments and suggestions to:

*American Law Yearbook*
Gale Research
27500 Drake Rd.
Farmington Hills, MI 48331-3535

## SPECIAL THANKS

The editors wish to acknowledge the contributions of the writers, copyeditors, assistant, and photo researcher who aided in the compilation of *American Law Yearbook*. In particular, the editors gratefully thank Richard J. Cretan, Susan L. Dalhed, Frederick Grittner, James Heiberg, Ann Laughlin, Mary J. Scarbrough, and Scott Slick for their writing contributions; Deborah Drolen Jones, Cheryl Wilms, and Ann Laughlin for copyediting; Sheri James for her administrative assistance; and Nancy D'Antonio for her photo research expertise.

## PHOTOGRAPHIC CREDITS

The editors wish to thank the permission managers of the companies that assisted us in securing reprint rights. The following list acknowledges the copyright holders who have granted us permission to reprint material in this edition of *American Law Yearbook*:

**AP/Wide World Photos**: pages 7, 8, 14, 15, 17, 31, 53, 55, 60, 94, 108, 119, 147, 177,194, 206, 214, 235, 242, and 245; **Archive Photos**: pages 29, 34, 78, 110, 111, 176, 220, 241, 243, 247, 255, 274, and 277; **Corbis-Bettmann**: pages 1, 30, 170, 195, 217, and 272; **Gamma Liaison Network**: pages 24, 27, 69, 93, 113, 127, 209, 222, 232, 256, and 271; **The Image Works**: pages 5, 169, 188, and 270; **PhotoEdit**: pages 18, 46, 50, 57, 79, 118, 145, 155, 208, 229, and 263; **Photo Researchers, Inc.**: pages 56, 100, 105, 124, 182, and 250; **The Picture Cube**: pages 70, 72, 103, and 131; and **Stock Boston**: pages 74, 148, 260, and 262.

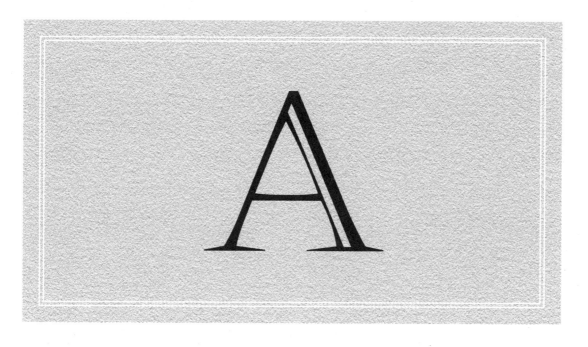

## ABERNATHY, RALPH DAVID

In the long battle for civil rights, few leaders had as an important a role as Ralph David Abernathy. From the late 1950s until 1968, Abernathy was the right-hand man of Martin Luther King, Jr. Together in 1957 they founded the Southern Christian Leadership Conference (SCLC), the organization chiefly responsible for the nonviolent protest movement whose gains over the next decade included major legal and social reforms for black Americans. Abernathy often shared a place next to King in meetings, marches, and jail, yet despite his considerable contributions to the civil rights movement, he labored largely in King's shadow. Later becoming SCLC president, he watched the transformation of the movement as his influence weakened and his politics changed, until controversy ultimately divided him from its mainstream.

Born on March 11, 1926, in Marengo County, Alabama, Abernathy was the grandson of a slave. His family members were successful farmers, and his father's leadership in the county's black community inspired him. Upon graduating from Linden Academy, he served in the army in World War II. He was ordained as a Baptist minister in 1948. He earned a B.A. in mathematics from Alabama State College in 1950, an M.A. in sociology from Atlanta University in 1951, and later a law degree from Allen University in 1960.

The defining moment in Abernathy's life was meeting King. As a student in Atlanta, he had heard King preach in church. From there, they began a friendship that would shape both men's futures. In 1955, while both were pastors in Montgomery, Alabama, they began the first of many local protest actions against racial discrimination. They organized a boycott of city buses by black passengers that led to the successful desegregation of local bus lines one year later. To build on this triumph, the pastors called a meeting of black leaders from ten southern states in January 1957 at an Atlanta church. This meeting marked the founding of the SCLC, which was devoted to the goal of furthering civil rights throughout the south. King was appointed the group's president, Abernathy its secretary-treasurer. The civil rights movement had begun.

Although the SCLC had committed itself to nonviolent protest, the forces they opposed were far from gun-shy. Segregationists bombed Abernathy's home and church. As opposition from individuals as well as government and law enforcement mounted, Abernathy continued to stress nonviolence. He said, "violence is the weapon of the weak and nonviolence is the weapon of the strong. It's the job of the state troopers to use mace on us. It's our job to keep marching. It's their job to put us in jail. It's our job to be in jail."

For nearly a decade, this philosophy was a clarion call answered by thousands. Through sit-down strikes, marches, arrests and jailings, and frequently at great personal danger, King and Abernathy led a mass of nonviolent protesters across the south, working together to devise strategy and put it into action. The enactment of federal civil rights legislation in 1964 marked a major success. But tragedy followed with King's assassination in May 1968, after which Abernathy replaced him as SCLC presi-

*Ralph David Abernathy*
CORBIS-BETTMANN

## RALPH DAVID ABERNATHY

**1926**  Born in Marengo County, Alabama

**1948**  Ordained Baptist minister

**1955**  Along with Martin Luther King, Jr., began local protests and bus boycott in Montgomery, Alabama

**1957**  Co-founded SCLC with King and other area black leaders

**1968**  Became SCLC president upon the assassination of King

**1977**  Forced from leadership of SCLC amid a feud with Coretta Scott King

**1980**  Supported presidential campaign of Ronald Reagan

**1989**  Memoir, *And the Walls Came Tumbling Down*, released

**1990**  Died in Atlanta, Georgia

dent. He now added a new aggressiveness to the group's goals, notably organizing a week-long occupation of Potomac Park in Washington, D.C., by five thousand impoverished tent-dwellers in what was called the Poor People's Campaign. This effort to dramatize poverty was quickly crushed by federal law enforcement.

By the end of the 1960s, Abernathy's influence was in decline. The civil rights movement had splintered as younger, more militant members gravitated toward groups such as the Black Panthers and the Committee on Racial Equality (CORE). In 1977 Abernathy was forced from leadership of the SCLC amid a feud with King's widow, Coretta Scott King, and made an unsuccessful bid for Congress. In 1980, he supported the presidential campaign of conservative Republican Ronald Reagan, which further divided him from former friends and associates. References to Martin Luther King, Jr.'s, marital infidelities in Abernathy's 1989 memoir *And the Walls Came Tumbling Down* provoked more criticism. Politically and personally isolated, Abernathy died one year later of a heart attack on April 17, 1990, at the age of 64. In death,

however, the criticism faded and was replaced by praise for his contributions to civil rights.

**CROSS REFERENCES**
Civil Rights Movement; King, Martin Luther, Jr.; Southern Christian Leadership Conference

# ABORTION
The spontaneous or artificially induced expulsion of an embryo or fetus. As used in legal context, usually refers to induced abortion.

### Partial-Birth Abortion
In 1997 Congress attempted to impose a ban on partial-birth abortions, but President Bill Clinton vetoed the measure, the second time he had done so in less than two years. HR 1122, entitled the Partial-Birth Abortion Act of 1997, was introduced on March 19, 1997, and was vetoed on October 10, 1997. A similar bill was vetoed in April 1996 by Clinton. An attempt to override the first bill failed; Congressional Republicans stated they would attempt to override the veto of HR 1122 in 1998.

HR 1122 would have amended 18 U.S.C.A. § 1531. The bill defined partial-birth abortion as "an abortion in which the person performing the abortion partially vaginally delivers a living fetus before killing the fetus and completing the delivery." "Vaginally delivers a living fetus before killing the fetus" was defined as "deliberately and intentionally deliver[ing] into the vagina a living fetus, or a substantial portion thereof, for the purpose of performing a procedure the physician knows will kill the fetus, and kills the fetus."

The statute would have applied to doctors of medicine or osteopathy legally authorized to perform abortions, other medical personnel authorized to perform abortions, or anyone who "directly performs" a partial-birth abortion. The law provided for fines or imprisonment of not more than two years, with exceptions in cases where a partial-birth abortion is necessary to "save the life of a mother whose life is endangered by a physical disorder, illness, or injury."

Civil damages available under the statute included money damages for all psychological and physical injuries occasioned by the partial-birth abortion, and statutory damages equal to three times the cost of the abortion. Anyone accused of an offense under the statute was entitled to a hearing before the appropriate state medical board to determine whether the procedure was necessary to save the life of the mother.

Findings from such a hearing would be admissible at the trial of the defendant.

HR 1833, passed and vetoed in 1996, was remarkably similar to HR 1122. In vetoing HR 1833 Clinton stated that he supports a woman's right to chose, believes that abortions should be "safe and rare," and that he has long opposed late-term abortions except when necessary to protect the life or the health of the mother. HR 1833 used much of the same language found in the successor bill, but did not apply the ban where a partial-birth abortion was necessary because the mother's life is endangered by a physical disorder, illness, or injury, "provided that no other medical procedure would suffice for that purpose." In addition, the 1996 bill did not provide for a defendant's right to a hearing on the question of the necessity of the procedure to save the life of the mother. Clinton stated the bill was deficient because it did not cover cases where serious health consequences, such as losing the ability to have more children, were likely to occur absent the procedure. In vetoing HR 1122 Clinton stated he was doing so for exactly the same reasons he had vetoed HR 1833, in that the bill was "consistent neither with the Constitution nor sound public policy."

State-imposed restrictions on the method of abortions fared a little better in the courts than did the vetoed federal legislation of 1997. As with HRs 1122 and 1833, Ohio House Bill 135 provided for civil and criminal consequences for its violation. The Ohio legislature devised a statute banning an abortion procedure known as D&X, or dilation and extraction. This procedure involves "purposely inserting a suction device into the skull of a fetus to remove the brain." The Ohio statute would have forbidden the use of this procedure in all abortions. The statute also prohibited abortions of a viable fetus unless a physician makes a good faith determination in the exercise of reasonable medical judgment that the abortion is required to prevent the mother's death or a "serious risk of the substantial and irreversible impairment of a major bodily function of the pregnant woman." The ban also would not apply for late-term abortions where the physician determined in good faith and in the exercise of reasonable medical judgment that the fetus is not viable. Viability is rebuttably presumed for any fetus of at least twenty-four weeks gestational age.

The Ohio statute contained a number of requirements that must be met before a physician could perform a post-viability abortion: (1) written certification by the physician of the necessity of the abortion; (2) certification by a second physician of its necessity; (3) the abortion must be performed in a facility having access to neonatal services for premature infants; (4) the physician is required to choose the abortion method that provides the best opportunity for the fetus to survive, unless it would impose a significantly greater risk of death or serious risk of substantial and irreversible impairment to a major bodily function of the pregnant woman; and (5) a second physician must be present at the abortion to care for the unborn human. These requirements are waived in cases of a defined medical emergency.

Ohio House Bill 135 was never implemented. A lawsuit in U.S. federal district court challenged the act and resulted in a temporary restraining order, and ultimately an injunction, prohibiting its enforcement (*Women's Medical Professional Corp. v. Voinovich*, 911 F.Supp. 1051 [S.D. Ohio 1995]). Plaintiffs, operators of a number of clinics and abortion services, as well as a doctor affiliated with the clinics, charged that the statute imposed an undue burden on the rights of pregnant women who choose an abortion. They also argued that the law was unconstitutionally vague and violated rights to privacy, liberty, and due process, as guaranteed by the Fourteenth Amendment.

Ohio Governor George Voinovich and other defendants appealed to the Sixth Circuit Court of Appeals. The Sixth Circuit affirmed the lower court and ruled the statute was fatally flawed because it did not permit an exception for women who might suffer psychological or emotional injury without termination of their pregnancies. In addition, the wording of the law also prohibited the most commonly used second-trimester procedure, D&X. To prohibit these abortions would place an unacceptable, "substantial obstacle" in the path of women seeking abortions. The Sixth Circuit also found the law unconstitutionally vague as it related to a physician's culpability. The court found that a physician might act in good faith according to his or her best medical knowledge, but still be found criminally liable if other doctors determined that the judgment was not reasonable.

Defendants in *Voinovich* sought U.S. Supreme Court review. In a 6-3 decision on March 23, 1998, the Supreme Court refused to hear the appeal (*Voinovich v. Women's Medical Professional Corp.*, ___U.S.___, 118 S. Ct. 1347, ___ L.Ed.2d___ [1998]). Justice Clarence Thomas, joined by Chief Justice William H. Rehnquist and Justice Antonin Scalia, wrote a dissenting

these peaceful efforts would often give way to "in your face" yelling, and sometimes pushing, shoving, and grabbing.

The district court found that for a number of reasons, the local police were unable to control the protests. The protests were constant and overwhelmed police resources, protesters would disperse when police arrived and then return later, and prosecution of protesters was difficult because patients were often reluctant to cooperate for fear of making their identity public. In addition, the protesters harassed orally and by mail the police officers and persons who testified against them.

The court issued the TRO, setting restrictions on how close protesters could come in proximity to the clinics. Though the protesters abided by the restrictions for a short time, they again started to blockade clinic entrances. In February 1992 the district court issued a preliminary injunction that retained some features of the TRO but made some significant changes.

The court placed three major restrictions on protesters. First, the injunction banned demonstrating within fifteen feet of doorways or doorway entrances, parking lot entrances, and driveways and driveway entrances of clinic facilities. This provision created "fixed buffer zones" between clinics and protesters. Second, the injunction banned demonstrating within fifteen feet of any person or vehicle entering or leaving the clinics. These were called "floating buffer zones." Finally, the injunction allowed two sidewalk counselors inside the buffer zones but required them to stop their counseling if the person asked them to stop.

Two individual defendants, Paul Schenck and Dwight Saunders, appealed to the Second Circuit Court of Appeals, arguing the injunction violated their First Amendment rights. On a closely divided vote, the full appeals court upheld the district court injunction (67 F.3d 377 [1995]).

The Supreme Court ruled that the fixed buffer zones and sidewalk counseling provisions were constitutional but struck down the floating buffer zone restriction. Chief Justice William H. Rehnquist, in his majority opinion, noted that the Court's decision in *Madsen v. Women's Health Center, Inc.*, 512 U.S. 753, 114 S. Ct. 2516, 129 L. Ed. 2d 593 (1994), bore some factual similarities to this case. More importantly, *Madsen* articulated a test for evaluating the constitutionality of content-neutral injunctions that restrict free speech. The test is "whether the challenged provisions ... burden no more speech than necessary to serve a significant government interest."

Rehnquist rejected Schenck and Saunder's contention that no significant government interest supported the injunction. As in *Madsen*, the facts of the case demonstrated there were sufficient government interests at stake, including public safety and order, the free flow of traffic on streets and sidewalks, protecting property rights, and protecting a woman's freedom to seek reproductive services. Therefore, the Court needed to determine if the three provisions burdened "no more speech than necessary."

The Court struck down the provision for floating buffer zones, stating the zones imposed a greater burden on speech than was necessary to achieve the government interests. Rehnquist concluded that this prohibition was too broad, preventing defendants from communicating their message "from a normal conversational distance or handing out leaflets on the public sidewalk." Noting that leafleting and commenting on matters of public concern are "classic forms of speech that lie at the heart of the First Amendment," Rehnquist ruled it would be difficult for protesters to know whether they have encroached on the fifteen-foot floating zone around people. This lack of certainty "leads to the substantial risk that much more speech will be burdened than the injunction by its terms prohibits."

The Court found, however, that the fixed buffer zone was constitutional. Noting the efforts of protesters to block entrances and driveways, Rehnquist deferred to the district court's judgment that a fifteen-foot buffer zone was required to ensure access to the clinics. Likewise, the Court upheld the provision that allowed two sidewalk counselors, to be within the fixed buffer zone, saying that this provision was an effort by the court to enhance the protesters' speech rights. However, the Court also ruled in favor of the "cease and desist" provision for counselors within the fixed buffer zone. Rehnquist pointed out that counselors remain free to spread their message outside the fixed buffer zone and that the restriction itself was the result of the counselors' previous harassment and intimidation of patients.

**CROSS REFERENCES**

First Amendment; Freedom of Speech; Rehnquist, William Hubbs; Temporary Restraining Order; Women's Rights

## ABZUG, BELLA SAVITSKY

Bella Savitsky Abzug served as a Democratic congresswoman in the 1970s and became one of the most outspoken advocates for women's rights in the United States. After leaving Congress in 1976, she remained involved in political and social issues both nationally and internationally. With her raspy voice, New York accent, and trademark floppy hat, Abzug was one of the most recognizable public figures in recent U.S. history.

Bella Savitsky was born on July 24, 1920, in New York City and was raised in the Bronx. The daughter of Russian immigrant Jews, her father was a butcher who operated the "Live and Let Live" meat market. As a young girl, she raised and collected money on behalf of Zionism. After graduating from high school, she attended Hunter College, where she was president of the student government. Following graduation in 1944, she attended Columbia University Law School. In 1946 she married Martin Abzug, who would go on to be a successful stockbroker. At Columbia, Abzug was the editor of the law review and an outstanding student.

After graduating in 1947, Abzug concentrated her legal practice in the fields of labor law and civil rights, while becoming active in left-wing politics. As an attorney for the American Civil Liberties Union, Abzug went to Mississippi in 1950 to argue the appeal of Willie McGee, an African American man convicted of raping a white woman. She also defended individuals who were accused of Communist subversion by Wisconsin Senator Joseph R. McCarthy. During the 1950s, Abzug managed to juggle her legal and political careers, while being a mother to two daughters.

In the 1960s Abzug organized opposition to nuclear arms testing by founding Women's Strike for Peace. In 1970 she was elected as a Democratic congresswoman from New York City. She was an outspoken critic of the Vietnam War and the policies of President Richard M. Nixon. After the Watergate scandals erupted in 1973, Abzug was the first public official to call for Nixon's impeachment.

Though Abzug antagonized many of her male colleagues in Congress by insisting on gender equality inside and outside of the Capitol, in 1974 she served as an assistant whip to House Speaker Thomas P. ("Tip") O'Neill, Jr. She chaired a subcommittee on government information and individual rights and coauthored the Freedom of Information Act and the Privacy

## BELLA SAVITSKY ABZUG

| | |
|---|---|
| **1920** | Born in New York City |
| **1947** | Graduated from Columbia University Law School |
| **1960s** | Founded Women's Strike for Peace |
| **1970** | Elected to the U.S. House of Representatives |
| **1974** | Served as assistant whip to House Speaker Thomas P. ("Tip") O'Neill, Jr. |
| **1976** | Lost Democratic nomination for the Senate |
| **1995** | Played major role in world conference on women's issues in Beijing, China |
| **1998** | Died in New York City |

*Bella Savitsky Abzug*
AP/WIDE WORLD PHOTOS

Act. Abzug also worked on behalf of the ill-fated Equal Rights Amendment, which failed to acquire the necessary number of states for ratification.

A national figure by the mid-1970s, Abzug sought the Democratic party nomination for the Senate in 1976. She lost a close race to Daniel Patrick Moynihan. Several campaigns for New York City mayor and Congress followed, but Abzug never served in elective office again. Despite these defeats, she remained active in efforts for women's rights. She was president of the National Commission on the Observance of International Women's Year, cofounder of the National Women's Political Caucus, and the founder of the International Women's Environmental and Development Organization. In 1995 she played a major role in a world conference on women's issues held in Beijing, China.

Abzug remained active in the women's movement despite numerous health problems that began in the mid-1980s. She died on March 31, 1998, in New York City following heart surgery.

**CROSS REFERENCES**
Equal Rights Amendment

## ADULTERY

Voluntary sexual relations between an individual who is married and someone who is not the individual's spouse.

### Lieutenant Kelly Flinn Case

The prosecution of a young female pilot, Lt. Kelly Flinn, embroiled the Air Force in a national debate over its handling of adultery. Praised for becoming the first woman to fly the nuclear-equipped B-52 bomber, Flinn underwent an intense public investigation for her affair with the civilian husband of another military woman. In May 1997 the Air Force threatened her with court-martial on charges of adultery, lying, and disobedience; if convicted, she faced more than nine years in prison. When Flinn ultimately accepted a discharge along with financial penalties, the charges were dropped, but not before critics in the media and Congress attacked the Air Force and collateral damage from the case claimed two other military careers.

Prior to December 1996, Flinn had enjoyed a stellar career. Her accomplishments were touted in Air Force training films. Secretly—or so the 26-year-old single woman thought—she was having an extramarital affair with Marc Zigo, a married civilian sports coach at Minot Air Force Base in South Dakota. Zigo's wife, Gayla Zigo, discovered Flinn's love letters to her husband and informed her commander. On December 13, Flinn's superiors served her with a written order to terminate the relationship. In a written statement, she denied the affair. Meanwhile, as Mr. Zigo had already left Mrs. Zigo and moved in with Flinn, she disobeyed the order and let the affair continue.

The Air Force charged Flinn with five offenses: (1) disobeying the order to end the relationship; (2) lying about ending the relationship; (3) committing adultery; (4) fraternizing, based on a separate relationship Flinn had in 1996 with an Air Force enlisted man; and (5) conduct unbecoming of an officer. The penalties carried up to nine years and six months in prison as well as a so-called bad conduct discharge, the second worst discharge in the service.

Flinn fought back in the court of public opinion. Her family hired a public relations team, she got a lawyer, and by May, her version of the story was well known. She alleged that Marc Zigo had deceived her by saying he was legally separated at the time of their affair. Her lawyer, Frank Spinner, argued that the Air Force had put his client between a rock and a hard place with its December 1997 order not to communicate with Zigo. Since the two were already living together, he said, the order was based on incorrect factual circumstances and therefore impossible to obey.

The question at how much attention the Air Force should pay to extra-marital affairs prompted nationwide debate. The number of people the Air Force court-martialed for adul-

Lieutenant Kelly Flinn, the nation's first female pilot to fly a nuclear-equipped B-52, accepted a discharge with financial penalties from the Air Force.

tery had more than tripled from 20 in 1986 to 67 in 1996, and a total of 305 people had been court-martialed since 1990. Politicians as ideologically distinct as Senate Majority Leader Trent Lott (R-Miss.) and Senator Tom Harkin (D-Iowa) criticized the Air Force's zeal. At Senate hearings Senator Harkin asked Air Force chief of staff Gen. Ronald Fogelman how many attorneys the Air Force had "running around, trying to find out how many people are committing adultery?" But other critics denounced Flinn and supported the Air Force in its apparently frustrated effort to insist that lying and disobedience—not adultery—were what really concerned it. If Flinn could not be trusted to tell the truth or follow orders, they asked, how could she be trusted with nuclear weapons?

Ultimately, on May 22, Flinn avoided court-martial by accepting a so-called general discharge under honorable circumstances. Not the same as an honorable discharge, it meant, in practical terms, the end of her military flying career. She could not now become a pilot in the Air National Guard as she had hoped. Additionally, she was required to repay up to $19,000 to the Air Force Academy for her training.

Following the Flinn matter, the Clinton Administration put forward Air Force Gen. Joseph Ralston as a candidate for Chairman of the Joint Chiefs of Staff, the nation's top military position. It emerged that the four-star general had had an adulterous affair thirteen years earlier, but Defense Secretary William Cohen stood by the nomination. This led critics to charge that the service had a double standard for men and women; Flinn's career was ruined by adultery but the secretary of defense was willing to overlook adultery by a male officer. Ralston withdrew his name from consideration.

The following month, Chief of Staff General Fogelman announced his retirement one year ahead of schedule. Though he gave another reason for early retirement, it was widely speculated that bitterness over the Flinn case was part of the decision.

**CROSS REFERENCES**
Armed Services; Court-Martial; Military Law

# AFFIRMATIVE ACTION

Employment programs required by federal statutes and regulations designed to remedy discriminatory practices in hiring minority group members; i.e. positive steps designed to eliminate existing and continuing discrimination, to remedy lingering effects of past discrimination, and to create systems and procedures to prevent future discrimination; commonly based on population percentages of minority groups in a particular area. Factors considered are race, color, sex, creed, and age.

## Board of Education of the Township of Piscataway v. Taxman

The political and legal debates over the legitimacy of affirmative action that began with the passage of the Civil Rights Act of 1964 (42 U.S.C.A. § 2000e et seq.) remain contentious. Proponents of affirmative action contend that it is necessary to remedy past discrimination, whereas opponents claim that such policies are no more than unfair preferences based on race.

The U.S. Supreme Court was scheduled to hear the case of *Board of Education of the Township of Piscataway v. Taxman* during its 1997 term. Many observers expected the Court to issue a ruling that would fundamentally alter the use of racial preferences in the workplace, severely limiting the use of affirmative action. In a stunning move, however, the school board settled the lawsuit, with the help of civil rights organizations that provided seventy percent of the settlement costs. Because the case was settled, the Supreme Court struck it from its calendar. For opponents of affirmative action, the settlement was viewed as both a delaying tactic and an admission that the days of legal support for affirmative action are numbered.

The case began in 1989, when the Board of Education of the Township of Piscataway decided to eliminate a position in the business education department of the Piscataway High School. New Jersey law required that the board first look to the teacher with the least amount of seniority. In this case, however, the two most junior teachers, Sharon Taxman and Debra Williams, were hired on the same day and therefore had equal seniority. After considering various factors, the board determined that the two teachers were equally qualified in all respects.

For the first time in twenty years, the board used its affirmative action plan for a layoff decision. The plan provided that "when candidates appear to be of equal qualification, candidates meeting the criteria of the affirmative action program will be recommended." The board accordingly retained Williams, who is black, and laid off Taxman, who is white. At the time of the layoff, Williams was the only African American teacher in the business department, but black teachers were not under-represented in the Piscataway School District as a whole. The board justified its decision not as a remedial measure (to correct discriminatory conduct in the past), but on the ground that a diverse faculty provides educational benefits to students.

The Bush administration filed suit under Title VII of the Civil Rights Act of 1964, challenging the legality of the layoff under the board's affirmative action plan. Taxman intervened in the lawsuit, claiming violations of Title VII and New Jersey state law. The federal district court found the board liable for violating Title VII and state law and awarded damages to Taxman.

The Third Circuit Court of Appeals affirmed the lower court (*Taxman v. Piscataway Township Board of Education*, 91 F.3d 1547 [3d. Cir. 1996]). Relying on two Supreme Court cases (*Johnson v. Transportation Agency, Santa Clara County*, 480 U.S. 616, 107 S. Ct. 1442, 94 L. Ed. 2d 615 [1987], and *United Steelworkers v. Weber*, 443 U.S. 193, 99 S. Ct. 2721, 61 L. Ed. 2d 480 [1979], the court ruled, in an 8-4 decision, that an affirmative action plan is valid under Title VII only if it has a purpose that mirrors that of the statute and does not unnecessarily trammel the interests of nonminority employees. It found that the board's policy failed the first prong of this test because it did not have a remedial purpose. The policy failed the second prong because it was too unstructured and not sufficiently temporary, and because it was applied in a layoff context.

The case received national attention during the presidential debates between Senator Robert J. Dole (the Republican nominee) and President Bill Clinton. Dole called for an end to affirmative action and used the *Taxman* case as an example of unfair, preferential treatment given to a person merely on account of race. He noted that the Clinton administration had withdrawn the U.S. government from the lawsuit as a party, which suggested that Clinton favored the school board's decision. Clinton defended affirmative action and the need to ensure diversity in the workplace.

When the Supreme Court agreed in 1997 to hear an appeal by the school board, legal commentators predicted that the Court would use the case to severely restrict affirmative action. Many groups with an interest in the case filed amicus curiae (friend of the court) briefs that sought to illuminate the legal, economic and social ramifications of affirmative action.

By this time Taxman's job was no longer an issue. She was rehired by the school district in 1993, but she was still seeking $144,000 in back pay. Fearing that the Supreme Court would end affirmative action, civil rights leaders proposed that the school board settle the back pay issue and end the case before the Court heard oral argument. The Black Leadership Forum, a confederation of seventeen prominent civil rights organizations, agreed to pay seventy percent of the $433,500 settlement. Taxman agreed to accept $188,000, representing her back pay with interest, and her attorneys received the remainder.

On November 20, 1997, the Piscataway School Board voted 5-3 in favor of the settlement and agreed with civil rights leaders to drop its appeal. David Rubin, the school board's attorney, defended the settlement, saying that the notoriety, of the case was distracting the students and that concern for their welfare was part of the reason for the settlement. The presence of local and national news media around the school and, in Rubin's view, "the prospect of even more intense media coverage" had created additional concerns.

Even supporters of affirmative action conceded that the settlement may only briefly delay another Supreme Court decision on affirmative action. The American Civil Liberties Union (ACLU) pointed out that the settlement came two weeks after the Supreme Court had refused to hear another affirmative action case. The Court rejected an appeal brought by the ACLU challenging the constitutionality of California's Proposition 209, which forbids the use of race in hiring and school admissions.

## AGE DISCRIMINATION

### Oubre v. Entergy Operations, Inc.

Since the 1960s Congress has enacted numerous laws that seek to prevent discrimination in employment, whether on the basis of race, gender, age, or disability. These statutes prescribe procedures that employees must follow to initiate a discrimination lawsuit. Conversely, these laws also spell out what employers must do to protect themselves from such lawsuits.

In *Oubre v. Entergy Operations, Inc.*, ____ U.S.____, 118 S. Ct. 838, ____L. Ed. 2d____ (1998), the U.S. Supreme Court ruled that an employee who, as part of a termination agreement, signed a release of claims against her employer in return for severance pay could sue the employer for age discrimination because the release did not comply with the requirement of federal law on age discrimination. The former employee could proceed, even though she had not returned or offered to return the severance pay she received for signing the release.

Dolores Oubre worked as a scheduler at a power plant in Killona, Louisiana, which was operated by Entergy Operations, Inc. After Oubre received a poor performance rating, her supervisor gave her the option of either improving her performance or accepting a voluntary arrangement for her severance. She received a packet of information about the severance agreement and had fourteen days to consider her options, during which she consulted with attorneys. On the fourteenth day, Oubre decided to accept. She signed a release, which stated, "[I] agree to waive, settle, release, and discharge any and all claims, demands, damages, actions, or causes of action … that I may have against Entergy …." In exchange, she received six installment payments over the next four months, totaling $6,258.

After she received the severance payments, Oubre filed a charge of age discrimination with the Equal Employment Opportunity Commission (EEOC), which dismissed her charge but issued a right-to-sue letter. She then filed suit in federal district court, alleging constructive discharge on the basis of her age, in violation of the Age Discrimination in Employment Act of 1967 (ADEA) (81 Stat. 602, 29 U.S.C.A. § 621 et seq.). Before she filed suit, Oubre had not offered or attempted to return the severance payments. Entergy asked the court to dismiss the case, claiming Oubre had ratified the release by failing to return or offer to return the monies she had received. The court agreed and entered judgment for Entergy. On appeal, the Court of Appeals for the Fifth Circuit affirmed the decision (112 F. 3d 787 [1996]).

The Supreme Court disagreed with the lower courts, reversing the decision. Justice Anthony M. Kennedy, writing for the majority, found that the release that Oubre had signed did not comply with specific requirements contained in the Older Workers Benefit Protection Act (OWBPA) (29 U.S.C.A. § 626(f)(1)(B),(F), (G)). He noted that Congress had enacted the OWBPA in 1990 to ensure that older workers do not waive age discrimination claims under the ADEA unless specific procedures are followed.

The OWBPA was forthright in its intent, stating, "An individual may not waive any right or claim under [the ADEA] unless the waiver is knowing and voluntary … [A] waiver may not be considered knowing and voluntary unless at a minimum" it satisfies certain enumerated requirements.

In Oubre's case, the Court concluded that Entergy's release did not comply with the OWBPA in three respects. Entergy had not given Oubre enough time to consider her options, it did not give her seven days after she signed the release to change her mind, and the release made no specific reference to claims under the ADEA. Kennedy characterized the OWBPA as a "strict, unqualified statutory stricture on waivers," concluding that the Court was compelled to follow the clear language and intent of Congress. This meant that the waiver was unenforceable against her "insofar as it purports to waive or release her ADEA claim. As a statutory matter, the release cannot bar her ADEA suit, irrespective of the validity as to the other claims."

In making this ruling, Kennedy rejected Entergy's argument that general principles of state contract law barred Oubre's lawsuit. Entergy contended that contract law required Oubre to tender back any benefits that she received under her severance agreement within a reasonable time after learning her rights. Her failure to do so, therefore, meant she had ratified the contract and made it binding on her. Kennedy found, however, that the federal statutory requirements contained in OWBPA made state contract principles irrelevant.

In a dissenting opinion, Justice Clarence Thomas sided with Entergy. Thomas argued prior Court decisions had established the rule that statutes, which invade the common law "are to be read with a presumption favoring the retention of long-established and familiar principles, except when a statutory purpose to the contrary is evident." He concluded that the OWBPA did not supplant the common law doctrine of ratification. Therefore, Oubre's retention of the severance payments should have prevented her from proceeding with the age discrimination lawsuit.

## Stratton v. New York City Department for the Aging

In a case brimming with irony, a federal appeals panel upheld a verdict of age discrimination against a city department that is supposed to help the elderly (*Stratton v. New York City*

*Department for the Aging*, 132 F.3d 869 [2nd Cir. 1997]). The decision affirmed a trial award of $1.5 million in damages to Joyce Stratton, who sued after she was fired by the New York City Department for the Aging (DFTA) in 1991. Stratton was 61-years-old and had 21 years of experience, an outstanding work record, and a recent award for service. The department laid her off and later gave her job to a younger person. After she sued for discrimination, DFTA retaliated by refusing to rehire her for new positions created in the department. On October 16, 1997, a three-judge panel of the Second Circuit Court of Appeals unanimously rejected the department's appeal.

Stratton began working in 1970 for the DFTA, which coordinates a broad range of services for elderly citizens in New York City. For most of her 21 years of service, she was the director of its Central Information and Referral Bureau, distributing technical information to 2,600 agencies that serve the city's poorest residents. According to the department's own evaluations, Stratton, a senior staff member, consistently performed at a "very good" or "outstanding" level in her job.

Stratton began to notice that her supervisors were treating her differently after a new department commissioner, 39-year-old Prema Mathai-Davis, was appointed in January 1990. As Mathai-Davis reorganized the department, the average age of its senior staff fell from 50.3 to 45.9 years. Soon Stratton was directed to stop sending out technical information. She was told not to participate on task forces and committees on which she had previously served. She was not consulted about organizational changes or invited to the commissioner's retreat for senior staff members—or even made privy to closed-door meetings held with her own staff. Then her staff was cut. And in her first performance evaluation under Mathai-Davis's regime, her rating was downgraded to "good."

In February 1991, the DFTA laid off Stratton and 35 other employees, citing a budget crisis. Stratton had pleaded not to be let go, fearing the harm to her pension as she approached retirement, but was told by a supervisor that Mathai-Davis had responded, "What about young mothers who are being fired?" Officially, Stratton's job was deemed too expensive in an era of budget cutting. But later in the year, after she had filed an age discrimination lawsuit, the department changed its mind: it hired a new employee for the position who was some 26 years younger than Stratton. It also began re-calling the laid-off employees—but not Stratton. Although she applied for one of two newly created positions, candidates younger than her by 17 and 21 years were chosen instead.

In 1995 a jury ruled for Stratton. The jury found that the DFTA had violated the Age Discrimination in Employment Act of 1967 (29 U.S.C.A. § 621 et seq.) and the New York State Human Rights Law (Exec. Law § 296 et seq.). It found that the department's excuse of budget cuts was merely a pretext to get rid of older employees who were soon replaced. The jury also found that the department had retaliated against Stratton for filing a claim by not hiring her for the new positions. Finally, the jury determined that the department had acted willfully in its discriminatory behavior, showing reckless disregard for Stratton's rights under the law. U.S. District Judge Shira A. Scheindlin awarded Stratton the sum of $1,559,359 in salary, benefits, attorneys' fees, and compensatory damages.

On appeal, the DFTA made three principal arguments. First, it contended that the district court erred by allowing Stratton to submit evidence in the form of charts showing the decline in the average ages of senior staff under Commissioner Mathai-Davis. Second, it argued that the evidence was insufficient to support the jury's findings. Third, it complained that the compensatory damages were excessive.

The appeals panel ruled that Stratton's charts were reliable because they were the department's own documents. No expert was required to evaluate them because only "simple arithmetic" was used. The DFTA could have offered its own charts or statistical evidence, but did not. Moreover, the evidence was relevant and formed only part of Stratton's overall proof. The appeals panel noted that the district judge had properly cautioned the jury that the charts were not conclusive proof.

Although the panel considered the second claim at greater length, it again ruled against the department. Stratton had provided sufficient evidence to prove her claim. This included Mathai-Davis's remark about young mothers being fired, which the panel ruled could reasonably have been viewed "as evidencing a preference for young mothers over older workers." Additionally, the evidence was sufficient to support the jury's finding of pretext: "There simply was no plausible reason why DFTA would cast aside and mistreat a 21-year veteran in the manner the jury found that it did," wrote the panel, "or why DFTA would refuse to meaningfully consider her for new positions for which she was qualified or available." Finally, the panel concluded that the evidence supported the jury's findings of retaliation and willfulness by the department.

In considering the department's claim that damages were excessive, the panel stated that it had only to decide if the trial judge had abused her discretion. Judge Scheindlin had actually reduced damages when setting the award, and the panel found she had no reason to reduce them further. It dismissed the department's assertions that the salary figure used to compute damages—$70,000 annually, the amount given to Stratton's successor—was too high because Stratton was not qualified to earn that amount. "The short answer to this argument," concluded the panel, "is that the jury rejected it." The panel affirmed the full $1.5 million award.

**CROSS REFERENCES**
Equal Employment Opportunity Commission

# AIRLINES

### Airline Passenger Violence

At a time when violence on airlines appeared to be increasing, the U.S. Court of Appeals for the Eleventh Circuit issued a ruling that eases federal prosecutions of unruly passengers (*United States v. Grossman*, 131 F.3d 1449 [11th Cir. 1997]). Federal law has long prohibited interfering with the performance of a flight attendant's duties (49 U.S.C.A., § 46504). Congress revised the law and toughened penalties in 1994. In *United States v. Grossman*, the Eleventh Circuit heard an appeal by an airline passenger convicted for an in-flight fracas in which he swore at and pushed a flight attendant. On appeal was the question of intent: how stringent are the law's requirements for proving that a defendant intended to commit an offense? On December 29, 1997, the appeals court ruled that the law only requires prosecutors to prove general intent—a standard that is easier to prove than specific intent.

In 1997 the media reported that flight crews were increasingly faced with belligerent or violent passengers. The scope of the problem was unclear, however, because of disparities in the collection of data. According to the Federal Aviation Administration (FAA), such attacks decreased between 1995 and 1996 from 139 to 119 recorded incidents. But the FAA only records incidents handled by federal law enforcement. Because local police and airline security personnel deal with the vast majority of cases, data compiled by airlines themselves may be more representative. United Airlines, for example, showed an increase of incidents from 226 in 1995 to 404 in 1996. American Airlines reported 296 incidents in 1994 and 836 in 1996. Unions representing pilots and flight attendants have complained that the problem is out of control, allegedly because airlines fear losing business in a competitive market if they press charges.

In *United States v. Grossman*, Howard A. Grossman appealed his conviction for assaulting and intimidating Carnival Airlines flight attendant Peggie Lee Hatten. While on a flight from New York to Fort Lauderdale, Florida, Grossman ran up the aisle yelling obscenities, ignored Hatten's instructions to sit down, and pushed her twice. Convicted by a jury in the Southern District Court of Florida, he was sentenced to five years reporting probation along with the special conditions that he pay a $10,000 fine, pay $8,761 in prosecution expenses, perform 2,000 hours of community service, and be placed on community confinement for a period of four months. Grossman's six-point appeal argued that the district court committed several procedural errors and that his conviction violated his First Amendment rights.

After rejecting five points of the appeal without comment, the appeals court chose only to analyze one point: Grossman's claim about the prosecution's burden to prove intent. This argument involved an important distinction in criminal law between *general intent* and *specific intent*. General intent means that the defendant intended to do what the law forbids. As a lower evidentiary standard, it does not require prosecutors to prove that the defendant intended the precise harm that resulted. By contrast, specific intent means the intent to accomplish the precise act that the law prohibits, and it is harder to prove. Grossman asserted that his conviction should be overturned because the district court did not require prosecutors to prove his specific intent to violate federal law.

The appeals court disagreed. On its face, the law contained nothing to indicate that it required proving specific intent. The court noted the "plain language" of (49 U.S.C.A. § 46504), which states:

> An individual on an aircraft in the special aircraft jurisdiction of the United States who, by assaulting or intimidating a flight crew member or flight attendant of the aircraft, interferes with the performance of the du-

*Madeleine Korbel
Albright*

AP/WIDE WORLD PHOTOS

## MADELEINE KORBEL ALBRIGHT

| | |
|---|---|
| **1937** | Born in Prague, Czechoslovakia |
| **1969–1972** | Counselor for economic affairs at the U.S. embassy in Belgrade, Yugoslavia |
| **1976–1978** | Chief legislative assistant under Senator Edmund S. Muskie |
| **1978–1981** | Member of the National Security Council |
| **1982–1993** | Taught at Georgetown University's School of Foreign Service |
| **1983** | Published *Poland, the Role of the Press in Political Change* |
| **1989–1993** | President of the Center for National Policy |
| **1992–1996** | Chief U.S. representative to the United Nations |
| **1997** | Became U.S. Secretary of State |

ties of the member or attendant or lessens the ability of the member or attendant to perform those duties, shall be fined under title 18, imprisoned for not more than 20 years, or both.

The law replaced (49 U.S.C.A. § 1472(j)), which had prohibited assaulting, intimidating or threatening any crew member or flight attendant. There was no indication that Congress wanted to change the meaning of the statutory language in 1994 as it related to intent, the court said.

In a review of the case law, the court found no appellate decisions addressing the intent issue with respect to the current statute. But two circuits had addressed the old statute, and both held that it described general intent. In 1975 the Ninth Circuit had reasoned that, if Congress had intended to legislate a specific intent crime, lawmakers would have used different language (*United States v. Meeker*, 527 F.2d 12). Moreover, it concluded that viewing the statue as requiring only general intent was in harmony with

the law's compelling purpose—safeguarding flight personnel. Later, in 1992, the Fifth Circuit had essentially followed this reasoning in *United States v. Hicks*, 980 F.2d 963. Based on the decisions in *Meeker* and *Hicks*, the appeals court ruled that current law does not require any showing of specific intent. Grossman's conviction was upheld.

## ALBRIGHT, MADELEINE KORBEL

Madeleine Korbel Albright is a U.S. diplomat who has served since 1997 as U.S. Secretary of State, the government's highest-ranking foreign relations officer. She also has the distinction of being the first woman to serve in this position. Albright, who has also taught international affairs, has had a long association with Democratic party presidential candidates, advising them on foreign policy.

Albright was born on May 15, 1937, in Prague, Czechoslovakia, the daughter of a Czech diplomat. In 1939 her family left Czechoslovakia for London, arriving shortly before the outbreak of World War II. After the war ended in 1945, the family returned to their homeland but left again in 1948 following the Communist takeover of the Czech government. The family settled in the United States in 1949.

Albright earned a bachelor's degree in political science from Wellesley College in 1959 and then studied at the School of Advanced International Studies at Johns Hopkins University. She then entered the graduate program at Columbia University, receiving her master's degree and doctorate from the university's Department of Public Law and Government. While working on her advanced degrees, Albright served in the diplomatic corps, acting as counselor for economic affairs at the U.S. embassy in Belgrade, Yugoslavia, from 1969 to 1972. She also worked for the Export-Import Bank.

After receiving her doctorate in 1976, Albright joined the staff of Democratic Senator Edmund S. Muskie of Maine, serving as his chief legislative assistant until 1978. She became a staff member of the National Security Council in 1978, serving President Jimmy Carter until he left office in 1981.

Albright shifted her focus in 1981 to academia. From 1981 to 1982, she was awarded a fellowship at the Woodrow Wilson International Center for Scholars at the Smithsonian, following an international competition in which she wrote about the role the press played in the political changes that occurred in Poland during the early 1980s. Her findings were published in *Poland, the Role of the Press in Political Change* (1983). Albright also served as a Senior Fellow in Soviet and Eastern European Affairs at the Center for Strategic and International Studies, conducting research in developments and trends in the Soviet Union and Eastern Europe. From 1982 to 1993, Albright taught at Georgetown University's School of Foreign Service, lecturing on international affairs, U.S. foreign policy, Russian foreign policy, and Central and Eastern European politics. She was also responsible for developing and implementing programs designed to enhance women's professional opportunities in international affairs. From 1989 to 1993, Albright was president of the Center for National Policy, a nonprofit research organization formed in 1981 by representatives from government, industry, labor, and education to promote the study and discussion of domestic and international issues.

Albright began working with Democratic presidential candidates in 1984 when she advised Walter F. Mondale on foreign policy. She served in a similar role for 1988 nominee Michael Dukakis and did the same for Bill Clinton in 1992. After Clinton was elected president, he named Albright chief U.S. representative to the United Nations, a cabinet-level position.

After President Clinton was reelected in 1996, he made changes in his cabinet. In December 1996 Clinton nominated Albright as secretary of state. After being unanimously confirmed by the U.S. Senate, she was sworn in as secretary of state on January 23, 1997.

## ALIENATION OF AFFECTION

The removal of love, companionship, or aid of an individual's spouse.

### Million Dollar Judgment in North Carolina

In August 1997 a broken heart led to an extraordinary damage award. The case of Dorothy Hutelmyer of Burlington, North Carolina against the woman who wrecked her marriage resulted in a $1 million judgment. Hutelmyer sued for *alienation of affection*, an eighteenth-century common-law remedy that allows a husband or wife to sue a third party who lures away a spouse. Nationally, these lawsuits have become rare; for social, political, and practical reasons, all but twelve states have abolished them. In North Carolina, however, an estimated two

*Dorothy Hutelmyer was awarded $1 million in her lawsuit against Margie B. Cox for breaking up her marriage to Joseph Hutelmyer.*

KAREN TAM/AP/WIDE WORLD PHOTOS

hundred cases are initiated annually. The size of the judgment in the Hutelmyer case prompted debate over the legitimacy of such suits in modern courtrooms.

The common-law remedy of alienation of affection originated in the 1700s. Designed to serve jilted spouses whose husband or wife ran off with a third person, it allowed the abandoned party to sue the third party for monetary damages. Hence it was called the "heart-balm" suit, the legal term for civil claims where financial rewards were sought for loss of romantic love. These claims came into existence in an era when wives were legally considered the property of their husbands, and thus the remedies were designed not to protect romantic love as much as a man's property interests. By the middle to late twentieth century, when this outlook no longer fit modern concepts of marriage and divorce, state legislators and courts restricted monetary damages, then abolished the claim entirely.

In fact, North Carolina, where Hutelmyer sued, briefly joined this trend. In 1984 the state's court of appeals abolished alienation of affection as a cause of action in *Cannon v. Miller*, 71 N.C. App. 460, 322 S.E.2d 780 (1984), vacated 313 N.C. 324, 327 S.E.2d 888 (1985). But the state Supreme Court overruled *Cannon* for procedural reasons, and plaintiffs have continued to sue. Today the claim is equally available to men and women. To prevail, plaintiffs must prove that: (1) the parties to the marriage were happily married and genuine love and affection existed between them; (2) this love and affection was alienated and destroyed; and (3) the wrongful and malicious acts of the defendant caused that loss.

As such cases go, Hutelmyer's was hardly unusual. At trial she asserted that her marriage to Joseph Hutelmyer, the president of a maritime insurance company, was a happy one as proven by his love poems to her. However, she claimed that his secretary, Margie B. Cox, had an affair with him that led to the Hutelmyers' divorce and his subsequent marriage to Cox. In testimony Cox admitted to the affair, but she claimed that the Hutelmyers' marriage had been unhappy because they had not had sex in more than seven years. On August 5, 1997, the jury sided with Dorothy Hutelmyer.

Hutelmyer declared that the decision had morally vindicated her. Cox (who took the name Hutelmyer) told *Time* magazine that on her monthly salary of $425, her husband's ex-wife would have a hard time collecting the $1 million judgment. Commentators debated the validity of alienation of affection suits in light of current attempts to reform no-fault divorce laws. Conservatives viewed alienation of affection suits favorably, arguing that they protect marriages by making affairs less likely. Liberals derided the suits as anachronisms that squander limited court resources. Most experts believe that the suits will not stage a comeback outside of the states where they are currently legal.

## AMISTAD

In 1839 a group of Africans were kidnapped from their homeland and transported to Cuba as slaves. While being transported from one port in Cuba to another, the Africans revolted, killed the captain and cook, and steered for the coast of Africa. The ship was eventually boarded by U.S. authorities in U.S. waters, and the Africans were imprisoned. Fierce legal battles ensued regarding entitlement to the Africans and the ship's cargo. In 1997 Steven Spielberg's company, DreamWorks, released a movie based upon the uprising. *Amistad* engendered its own legal furor amid charges that the screenplay had been plagiarized from a 1989 novel.

### The Ship and Slavery

In April 1839 a Spanish slaving brig with kidnapped Africans aboard sailed from the West African coast to Havana, Cuba. Jose Ruiz, a Spaniard living in Puerto Principe, Cuba, bought 49 males for $450 each. Another Spanish planter living nearby, Pedro Montes, bought four children, including three girls. In late June 1839 the ship *Amistad* sailed from Havana to Puerto Principe. On the third night out, two Africans named Cinque and Grabeau managed to free and arm themselves. During the uprising, the captain and cook were killed, but Montes and Ruiz were spared and forced to assist in navigation. The *Amistad* sailed east toward Africa by day, but at night Montes and Ruiz steered the ship north.

On August 26, 1839, the ship anchored off Long Island and was discovered by the U.S. brig *Washington*. The vessel, the cargo, and the Africans were taken into the District of Connecticut.

Montes and Ruiz filed suit in federal court to recover some of the cargo and the Africans, asserting ownership of the Africans as their slaves. The U.S. district attorney for the District of Connecticut appeared on behalf of the Spanish government and demanded that the Africans be handed over for trial in Cuba on murder and piracy charges.

Rallying on behalf of the Africans, New York abolitionists hired attorney Roger Sherman Baldwin. Baldwin argued that because Spain had outlawed the African slave trade, the Africans could use whatever means possible to attain freedom after their illegal kidnapping and enslavement. The abolitionists sought a writ of habeas corpus relief to free the Africans pending charges of piracy or murder that might be brought. The writ was denied and the Africans remained in custody, but were not indicted on any criminal charges.

The trial proceeded in the U.S. district court of New Haven, Connecticut, on what should be done with the Africans, the cargo, and the ship. Anticipating that U.S. District Judge Andrew Judson would order the Africans turned over for criminal proceedings in Cuba, President Martin Van Buren ordered that the *U.S.S. Grampus* wait in the New Haven harbor to transport the Africans to Cuba immediately upon such a ruling.

The *U.S.S. Grampus* waited in vain. Judge Judson ordered that the kidnapping and enslavement had been illegal and that the United States must return the Africans to their homeland. The United States, now acting on behalf of the Spanish government and the claims of Montes and Ruiz, appealed to the U.S. circuit court, where Judge Judson's ruling was upheld. The United States appealed again, to the U.S. Supreme Court.

Former U.S. president John Quincy Adams, now a member of the U.S. House of Representatives on behalf of Massachusetts, and sympathetic to the abolitionist movement, joined Baldwin in representing the Africans before the Supreme Court. Adams and Baldwin contended that the Africans should be granted their freedom because they had exercised their natural rights in fighting to escape illegal enslavement. The U.S. Supreme Court opinion, delivered by Justice Joseph Story, affirmed the rulings by the lower courts, but instead of ordering the United States to return the Africans to Africa, declared them to be free and ordered them to be immediately discharged from custody (*U.S. v. Amistad*, 40 U.S. [15 Pet.] 518, 10 L. Ed. 826 [1841]).

While the *Amistad* case essentially presented questions of international law and did not involve any legal attacks on U.S. slavery, it was important in U.S. history because of the attention and support it garnered for the abolitionist movement.

### The Movie and Plagiarism

The 1997 movie by Steven Spielberg and his company, DreamWorks SKG, is a fictitious rendering of the real events that ensued in 1839–1841. But before the movie was released, an author who had written a historical novel about the uprising attempted to halt the film's release, charging the moviemakers with copyright infringement. Filing suit in October 1997,

Barbara Chase-Riboud sought $10 million in damages and screenwriting acknowledgment, based upon alleged plagiarism of her novel, *Echo of Lions*. In December, a federal district judge declined to delay the movie's opening, ruling that the similarities between the movie and the novel did not establish a probability of success for Chase-Riboud, but did raise serious questions for trial.

The plagiarism suit took a strange turn in December 1997 when the *New York Times* reported that Chase-Riboud had plagiarized several passages of her 1986 book, *Valide: A Novel of the Harem*, from a nonfiction book published 50 years earlier. Chase-Riboud admitted to the *New York Times* that she had used material for *Valide* without attribution. DreamWorks also charged that Chase-Riboud had taken passages for *Echo of Lions* from a 1953 novel, *Slave Rebellion*, by William A. Owens, the book optioned by *Amistad* producers for the movie.

In early 1998 Chase-Riboud and DreamWorks settled the lawsuit for an undisclosed amount. In dropping the lawsuit, Chase-Riboud stated that she and her attorneys had concluded that neither Spielberg nor DreamWorks had done anything improper.

**CROSS REFERENCES**
Adams, John Quincy; Copyright; Kidnapping

*Director Steven Spielberg, left, discusses a scene with actors Anthony Hopkins, center, and Morgan Freeman, right, on the set of DreamWorks' Amistad.*

ANDREW COOPER, DREAMWORKS, HO/AP/WIDE WORLD PHOTOS

## ANTITRUST LAW

Legislation enacted by the federal and various state governments to regulate trade and commerce by preventing unlawful restraints, price-fixing, and monopolies, to promote competition, and to encourage the production of quality goods and services at the lowest prices, with the primary goal of safeguarding public welfare by ensuring that consumer demands will be met by the manufacture and sale of goods at reasonable prices.

### State Oil Company v. Khan

When Congress enacted the Sherman Anti-Trust Act (15 U.S.C.A. § 31 et seq.) in 1890, the law's vague and ambiguous language indicated that Congress was passing on to the Supreme Court the work of defining and refining the scope of government regulation of trusts and monopolies. Since the late nineteenth century, the court has established often-controversial legal precedents about antitrust issues. In *State Oil Co. v. Khan*, ___U.S.___, 118 S. Ct. 275, 139 L. Ed. 2d 199 (1997), the Court overruled a prior decision and held that vertical maximum price fixing is not a *per se* violation of the Sherman Act.

The case arose out of a dispute between Illinois businessman Barkat U. Khan and State Oil Co. Khan entered into an agreement with State Oil to lease a gas station and convenience store owned by the company. The agreement pro-

*Small businesses leased to individuals by larger corporations, such as gasoline stations, may be subject to vertical price fixing.*

MICHAEL NEWMAN/PHOTOEDIT

vided that Khan would purchase the station's gasoline supply from State Oil at a price equal to the suggested retail price set by State Oil, less a margin of 3.25 cents per gallon. Under the agreement, Khan could charge any amount for gasoline sold to the station's customers, but if the price charged was higher than State Oil's suggested retail price, the excess was to be rebated to State Oil. Khan could sell gasoline for less than State Oil's suggested retail price, but any such decrease would reduce his margin of 3.25 cents per gallon.

Khan fell behind in his lease payments to State Oil after operating the station for about a year. State Oil then gave notice that it was terminating the agreement and started a proceeding to evict Khan from the station. At the company's request, the Illinois state court appointed a receiver to operate the station. The receiver operated the station for several months without being subject to the price restraints in Khan's agreement with State Oil. According to Khan, the receiver obtained an overall profit margin in excess of 3.25 cents per gallon by lowering the price of regular-grade gasoline and raising the price of premium grades.

Khan then sued in federal district court, alleging that State Oil had engaged in price fixing in violation of section one of the Sherman Act by preventing him from raising or lowering retail gas prices. Khan contended that if he had not been bound by State Oil's terms, he could have charged different prices based on the grades of gasoline, in the same way that the receiver had, thereby achieving increased sales and profits.

On State Oil's motion the district court dismissed Khan's case, concluding that Khan had failed to demonstrate antitrust injury or harm to competition. However, the Court of Appeals for the Seventh Circuit reversed the lower court, noting that the agreement did fix maximum gasoline prices by making it "worthless" for Khan to exceed the suggested retail price (93 F.2d 1358 [1996]). Despite overturning the district court, the court of appeals had deep misgivings about the merit of its decision. It reversed the district court's ruling because the 1968 U.S. Supreme Court case of *Albrecht v. Herald Co.*, 390 U.S. 145, 88 S. Ct. 869, 19 L. Ed. 2d 998, held that vertical maximum price fixing is a per se violation of the Sherman Act. As a court of appeals, it could not overturn a Supreme Court decision, even though it characterized *Albrecht* as "unsound when decided" and inconsistent with later decisions of the Supreme Court.

The Supreme Court took the case to consider whether State Oil's conduct constituted a per se violation of the Sherman Act. Justice Sandra Day O'Connor, writing for a unanimous court, concluded that the company had not committed a per se violation and that the *Albrecht* case must be overruled. O'Connor noted that the Court has analyzed antitrust claims under either the rule of reason or the per se rule. Most antitrust actions are analyzed by the rule of reason, which takes into account a variety of factors, including specific information about the relevant business, its condition before and after the restraint was imposed, and the restraint's history, nature, and effect. However, some types of restraints have such predictable and harmful anticompetitive effect, and such limited potential for competitive benefit, that they are found to be unlawful per se. O'Connor stated that per se treatment is appropriate when the Supreme Court can "predict with confidence that the rule of reason will condemn it."

*Albrecht* involved a newspaper publisher who had granted exclusive territories to independent carriers subject to their adherence to a maximum price on resale of the newspapers to the public. The Court ruled that it was per se unlawful for the publisher to fix the maximum retail price of his newspaper, condemning maximum price fixing for "substituting the perhaps erroneous judgment of a seller for the forces of the competitive market."

O'Connor acknowledged that legal commentators had vigorously attacked the *Albrecht* decision for many years. They challenged the Court's assumptions that vertical maximum price fixing could allow distributors to discriminate against certain dealers, restrict the services that dealers could afford to offer customers, or disguise minimum price fixing schemes. These commentators also argued that the per se rule had been imposed prematurely and that this type of price fixing should be subjected on a case-by-case basis, using the rule of reason standard.

Other antitrust decisions by the Supreme Court had weakened the credibility of the *Albrecht* precedent. O'Connor concluded that the time had come to abandon the precedent, finding it "difficult to maintain that vertically-imposed maximum prices could harm consumers or competition to the extent necessary to justify their per se invalidation."

O'Connor cited Chief Judge Richard A. Posner's court of appeals decision, in which he questioned whether maximum resale price fixing was an antitrust violation. Posner found it unlikely that State Oil could squeeze its dealers' margins below a competitive level, because an attempt to do so would drive the dealers to another supplier. More importantly, Posner thought that a supplier might fix a maximum resale price to prevent its dealers from exploiting a monopolistic position. The supplier would do so out of commercial self-interest: "The higher the price at which gasoline is resold, the smaller the volume sold, and so the lower the profit to the supplier if the higher profit per gallon at the higher price is being snared by the dealer."

Posner's argument was buttressed by the argument that the *Albrecht* decision had been counterproductive. Though the decision had banned maximum, resale price limitations in the name of "dealer freedom," *Albrecht* had led many suppliers to abandon independent resellers, choosing instead to set up their own company-owned and -managed stores. O'Connor also read *Albrecht* as expressing a concern that maximum prices may be set too low for "dealers to offer consumers essential or desired services." She found this concern uncompelling, because such conduct, "by driving away customers, would seem likely to harm manufacturers as well as dealers and consumers, making it unlikely that a supplier would set such a price as a matter of business judgment." Finally, she dismissed the fear implied in *Albrecht* that maximum price fixing could be used to disguise arrangements to fix minimum prices. If such conduct occurred, it could be "recognized and punished under the rule of reason."

The Court concluded that the *Albrecht* rule "may actually harm consumers and manufacturers." It found insufficient economic justification for the per se invalidation of vertical maximum price fixing. In addition, the Court acknowledged that the precedent had "little or no relevance to ongoing enforcement of the Sherman Act."

In overturning *Albrecht*, O'Connor defended the Court's right to overrule one of its precedents. This was especially true with respect to the Sherman Act, because Congress "expected the courts to give shape to the statute's broad mandate by drawing on common-law traditions." O'Connor was quick to point out, however, that this decision did not hold that all vertical maximum price fixing is per se lawful. This type of commercial arrangement must be subjected to the antitrust law under the rule of reason.

## United States v. Microsoft

In October 1997, Microsoft faced new federal antitrust charges only two years after narrowly avoiding prosecution. The Department of Justice accused the software giant of breaking an agreement to stop anticompetitive practices in the marketing of its Windows software, twice asking a federal judge to fine the company $1 million per day. Microsoft vigorously denied the charges, struck a deal to avoid paying fines, and meanwhile fought the Justice Department in an escalating war of words and court documents.

The current dispute had roots in 1995, when federal authorities seemed ready to sue the company after four years of investigations. Microsoft's competitors had charged that it illegally dominated the software market. The key to these complaints was the company's licensing agreements with computer manufacturers (known as original equipment manufacturers, or OEMs), which, as an essential part of their business, contract with software companies, to proved programs on new personal computers (PCs). By 1995 nearly 75 percent of the world's PCs used Microsoft's MS-DOS and Windows operating systems. Competitors blamed exclusive licensing agreements between computer manufacturers and Microsoft for shutting them out of the market.

To avoid prosecution, Microsoft entered a deal simultaneously with U.S. and European authorities. It signed a broadly-worded *consent decree*, a legally binding agreement that essentially changed how it would do business in the future with OEMs. Microsoft agreed not to require exclusive licensing agreements and not to tie the purchase of one product to the purchase of another.

In October 1997, the Justice Department accused Microsoft of violating the consent decree. The allegations this time focused on how the company was marketing its Internet Explorer software, a program known as a web browser that is used for accessing the World Wide Web, e-mail, and other Internet media. The government claimed Microsoft was forcing OEMs that purchased Windows 95 to also license and distribute Internet Explorer, thus illegally tying together requirements to purchase two separate products. "Microsoft is unlawfully taking advantage of its Windows monopoly to protect and extend that monopoly and undermine consumer choice."

The government asked the court to do three things: (1) bar Microsoft from requiring OEMs to simultaneously license Windows 95 and Internet Explorer; (2) order Microsoft to inform OEMs that they could ship Windows 95 with a competitor's web browser, such as the Netscape Communications Corp.'s Navigator software; and (3) fine Microsoft $1 million a day in civil contempt charges for breaking the consent decree. Federal attorneys also accused Microsoft of hindering their investigation through its nondisclosure agreements with OEMs, which require the companies not to reveal technical details about Microsoft products.

In response, Microsoft denied doing anything wrong. Noting that the 1995 consent decree allowed it a free hand to create "integral" features for its operating systems software, the company argued that Internet Explorer was just such an integral feature of Windows 95, not a separate product. "A fundamental principle at Microsoft," founder and chairman Bill Gates told reporters, "is that Windows gets better and makes the PC easier to use with each new version." In court papers, company attorneys attacked the government for interfering with Microsoft's right to compete, complained that it did not understand software, and accused it of punishing Microsoft for being successful.

The first round of the case ended with mixed results (*United States v. Microsoft Corp.*, 980 F.Supp. 537). In a blow to Microsoft on December 11, 1997, U.S. District Judge Thomas Penfield Jackson issued a preliminary injunction ordering it to stop requiring OEMs to license both products; the decision effectively told the company to separate its web browser from its operating system. However, Jackson refused to strike nondisclosure agreements between Microsoft and OEMs. More significantly, he also refused to hold the company in civil contempt or level the $1 million fine wanted by the government. Prosecutors, he ruled, had not yet proved their case. In order to help address the many technical and legal questions in the case, Judge Jackson appointed Harvard Law School professor Lawrence Lessig, a computer and Internet law expert, as "special master"—an expert appointed by the court and given quasi-judicial powers.

Although both sides declared victory in the short term, Microsoft immediately appealed Judge Jackson's preliminary injunction to the U.S. Court of Appeals for the District of Columbia. Microsoft also accused Professor Lessig of being biased, on the basis of an e-mail he sent to Netscape Communications, and argued that Microsoft should be allowed to help select a different special master. The Justice Department called the allegation unfounded.

Federal prosecutors swiftly returned to court in December 1997 claiming that Microsoft had already violated the preliminary injunction. The company had offered OEMs three options for licensing, which included a crippled version of Windows 95 (without Internet Explorer) that was commercially useless or inoperable. Arguing that this option sidestepped Judge Jackson's order, the Justice Department renewed its request for the court to levy a $1 million a day contempt fine. This issue was settled in late January 1998. The government agreed to drop contempt charges in return for Microsoft providing OEMs with the most up-to-date, functioning version of Windows 95 without a clickable button for Internet Explorer.

The case touched off widespread commentary by legal and technical experts. Almost everyone agreed that Microsoft—with a market value of nearly $200 billion—dominates the computer software industry. There was also agreement that Netscape was the only viable competition Microsoft faced in the web browser market. But as to the question of whether Internet Explorer was actually integrated with Windows 95, there was little consensus. Some observers pointed out that removing Internet Explorer 4.0 could make Windows 95 and some other programs malfunction—a point that seemed to underscore Microsoft's position. Others pointed out that this was true primarily of programs installed by OEMs, a contention supporting the government's argument about tying products illegally. Some expected the government's case to become more complex when Microsoft launched its new operating system, Windows 98, in mid-summer. Windows 98 is expected further to blur the lines between an operating system and a web browser.

On the broader question of monopoly control, conservatives and liberals were surprisingly close in outlook. In November 1997, liberal consumer activist Ralph Nader held a conference in Washington, D.C., to weigh Microsoft's threat to free competition as it expands into markets such as banking, media, and even used car sales. In February 1998, conservative Senator Orrin Hatch (R-Utah), praised Microsoft but warned that it could soon dominate commerce on the Internet and called for effective antitrust action in the short term in order to head off the necessity of government regulations later.

In the spring of 1998, the Justice Department issued subpoenas to national companies that provide Internet access to consumers. Officials met with state attorneys general in San Francisco to consider combining their legal efforts against Microsoft. Twenty-seven states filed a brief in court supporting the Justice Department's position. Meanwhile, European authorities were simultaneously conducting their own antitrust investigations.

On March 3, 1998, Gates testified in his company's defense before a public hearing of the Senate Judiciary Committee. Denying any monopolization, Gates declared that the Internet represented an open territory to all entrepreneurs. Afterwards, Hatch and other senators said their inquiry would continue, possibly including an effort to seek waivers from Microsoft that would allow its licensees to speak freely to the committee without violating their nondisclosure agreements.

On June 23, 1998, a federal appeals court struck a blow to the government's antitrust suit against Microsoft by ruling that the company did not have to alter the way it sold its Internet navigation software, contrary to a lower court's previous decision. The court's ruling supported Microsoft's right to determine what features and functions to include in its operating system.

**CROSS REFERENCES**
Sherman Anti-Trust Act

## AUTOMOBILES

### Negligent Entrustment

On June 9, 1993, Anthony D. Routt arrived at Credit Car Center in Nebraska, intending to purchase a white Oldsmobile Ninety-eight. Routt, whose driver's license was suspended, asked if he could test drive the car, and Jerry Epperson, an employee of Credit Car Center, gave him the keys. Epperson did not ask Routt for a driver's license, and Epperson did not accompany Routt on the test drive. The words "ICE COLD AIR" were written across the windshield of the car in white shoe polish. "[W]e just tell them to be careful," Epperson testified at trial, "and cross your fingers," *Suiter v. Epperson*, 6 Neb.App. 83, 571 N.W.2d 92 (1997).

Routt drove north on a primary thoroughfare, reaching a speed of approximately 50 miles per hour in a 35 miles per hour zone. Harry E. Wolstencroft was driving with his wife, Lillian, from east to west on a street that crossed the thoroughfare. Wolstencroft was stopped at a stop sign; traffic on the thoroughfare did not have to stop at the intersection. As Routt approached the intersection, Wolstencroft sped in front of Routt. Although Routt saw Wolstencroft and swerved and hit the brakes, he was unable to avoid hitting Wolstencroft's car. The collision killed Lillian instantly and Wolstencroft died a few hours later.

Diana J. Suiter, the Wolstencrofts' only child and the representative of her father's estate, sued Credit Car Center for negligently entrusting the vehicle to Routt, and sued Routt for negligence. Specifically, Suiter alleged that Routt failed to keep a proper lookout, failed to exercise reasonable control, and operated the Oldsmobile Ninety-eight at a speed greater than was reasonable and prudent under the conditions.

At trial, a jury returned a verdict in favor of both defendants, finding that Suiter had failed to carry her burden-of-proof. Suiter appealed, charging that the trial court made various errors in the jury instructions. Suiter claimed, in part, that it was error for the trial court to: (1) instruct the jury that one does not forfeit his right of way by driving at an unlawful speed; (2) instruct the jury that Wolstencroft was negligent, and not instructing the jury about allocating that negligence; (3) refuse to instruct the jury on Epperson's negligence in entrusting a vehicle to Routt, whose license was suspended; and (4) omit all mention of Wolstencroft's wife in the case. The appeals court disagreed with Suiter on all the issues and affirmed the judgment of the trial court.

According to the appeals court, it was not error for the trial judge to instruct the jury that a person does not forfeit his right-of-way by driving at an unlawful speed because it was a correct statement of the law in Nebraska. It likewise was not error for the trial court to instruct the jury that Wolstencroft was negligent in entering the intersection because, in the court's opinion, the facts supported such a conclusion. Furthermore, the trial judge had mentioned the possible negligence of the defendants and had issued instructions on the law of comparative negligence, under which each party to the accident is assigned an appropriate percentage of fault.

The appeals court also ruled that it was permissible for the trial court to omit from the trial any reference to Lillian Wolstencroft. Suiter argued in part that witnesses were forced to testify about Wolstencroft awkwardly, as if Wolstencroft's wife had not existed. The court noted that Lillian's estate had already filed and settled a separate action for damages and held that the trial court had not abused its discretion in so ruling because references to Lillian may have been overly prejudicial to the defendants.

On the issue of negligent entrustment, the trial judge had instructed the jury about negligent entrustment on the basis of the shoe polish on the windshield. Suiter argued, however, that the trial judge erred by failing to instruct the jury that part of Epperson's negligence was giving the Oldsmobile Ninety-eight to a person whose license was suspended. Under Nebraska law, however, Epperson was under no duty to ask for Routt's license. In Nebraska, there are two basic elements to imposing liability on a car dealer for negligent entrustment of a vehicle. First, the dealer must know, or should know, that the driver is incompetent. The court declared that there was no way for Epperson to know that Routt was incompetent, and the court was not prepared to hold "that the absence of a license equates with incompetency." Second, the victim's injuries must be a result of such incompetence. The appeals court observed that the jury had found the sole proximate cause of the accident to be Wolstencroft's negligence in pulling in front of Routt and that no Nebraska statute required a car dealer to examine the driver's license of a person who takes a test drive.

**CROSS REFERENCES**
Negligence; Negligent Entrustment

## BANKRUPTCY

A federally authorized procedure by which a DEBTOR—an individual, CORPORATION, or municipality—is relieved of total LIABILITY for its DEBTS by making court-approved arrangements for their partial repayment.

### Cohen v. De La Cruz

Although the U.S. Bankruptcy Code, 11 U.S.C.A. § 101 et seq., prevents the discharge of debts that are based on fraudulent activities, the federal courts have been divided over whether the law prevents the discharge of all liability arising from fraud, including punitive and treble (triple) damages, or is limited to only the actual value of the money, property, services, or credit the debtor obtained through fraud. In *Cohen v. De La Cruz*, ___U.S.___, 118 S. Ct. 1212, ___ L. Ed. 2d___ (1998), the U.S. Supreme Court resolved the issue, ruling that punitive and treble damages cannot be discharged as debts in bankruptcy where fraud was involved.

Edward S. Cohen owned residential properties in the Hoboken, New Jersey area, one of which was subject to rent control. In 1989 the Hoboken rent control administrator determined that Cohen had been charging rents above the level permitted by the rent control ordinance. Though the administrator ordered Cohen to refund almost $32,000 in excess rents, he refused. Cohen filed for bankruptcy under Chapter Seven of the Bankruptcy Code, but the tenants filed suit in bankruptcy court claiming that the debt of $32,000 was barred from discharge by 11 U.S.C.A. § 523(a) (2) (A) since the debt was the result of Cohen's fraudulent actions. The tenants also sought treble damages and attorney's fees and costs, based on a provision of the New Jersey Consumer Fraud Act (N.J. Stat. Ann. §§ 56:8-2, 56:8-19 [West 1989]).

The bankruptcy court ruled in the tenants' favor and awarded them treble damages totaling almost $95,000, plus attorney fees and costs. Cohen appealed, arguing that the original debt of $32,000 was not dischargeable, but the treble damages and attorney fees and costs were dischargeable. The Court of Appeals for the Third Circuit affirmed the bankruptcy court, finding that in section 523(a)(2)(A), the term "debt" meant a right to payment, which clearly encompassed all liability for fraud, whether in the form of compensatory or punitive damages (106 F. 3d 52 [1997]). The court did acknowledge that if other circuit courts and bankruptcy courts took Cohen's position that only compensatory damages were not dischargeable.

The Supreme Court affirmed the Third Circuit's position. Justice Sandra Day O'Connor, writing for a unanimous court, found support for this interpretation from the text of section 523(a)(2)(A), the historical basis for the fraud exception, the meaning of parallel provisions in the statute, and the general policy underlying the exceptions to discharge. Justice O'Connor noted that the "most straightforward reading of section 523(a)(2)(A) is that it prevents discharge of 'any debt' respecting 'money, property, services or … credit' that the debtor has fraudulently obtained, including treble damages assessed on account of fraud." Reviewing a series of definitions in the statute, O'Connor

concluded that a debt is an "enforceable obligation" of the debtor that encompasses treble damages.

Justice O'Connor rejected Cohen's interpretation that the word "debt" in section 523 (a)(2)(A) meant only liability for the base amount, thus imposing a ceiling on the "extent to which a debtor's liability for fraud is nondischargeable." The judge found this interpretation at odds with a plain reading of the statute. In addition, she noted other sections of the code that use language similar to section 523 (a)(2)(A), and which have not been interpreted to limit the amount of a debt that is not dischargeable. These parallel provisions all connote "broadly any liability arising from the specified object." Thus, when "construed in the context of the statute as a whole," section 523 (a)(2)(A) was "best read to prohibit the discharge of any liability arising from a debtor's fraudulent acqui-

sition of money, property, etc., including an award of treble damages for the fraud."

Justice O'Connor also relied on the history of the bankruptcy fraud exception. Since 1898 federal bankruptcy law has honored this exception and nothing in the legislative record since then altered this viewpoint. Moreover, the general policy of the bankruptcy laws disfavored Cohen's position. If Cohen's position prevailed, the "objective of ensuring full recovery by the creditor would be ill served." Justice O'Connor also emphasized that limiting the exception to the value of the property or money that was fraudulently obtained might prevent even a compensatory recovery for losses due to fraud. If, for example, a debtor sold $5,000 of steel bolts to an airplane manufacturer after fraudulently claiming the bolts were aircraft quality, and the plane later crashed because of defective bolts, Cohen's theory would allow the debtor to escape a multimillion dollar judgment through bankruptcy. Such a scenario, according to O'Connor, did not agree with the policy of the Bankruptcy Code to afford relief only to an "honest but unfortunate debtor." Congress could not have intended to favor "the interest in giving a perpetrator of a fraud a fresh start over the interest in protecting victims of fraud."

## Couple Could Not Put Church Before Creditors

In July 1997, the U.S. Bankruptcy Court in Massachusetts ruled that charitable contributions to churches are not allowed under Chapter Thirteen bankruptcy requirements (*In re Saunders*, 214 B.R. 524). The ruling applied to tithing, a practice in some religious faiths in which church members give, or "tithe", a percentage of their income to the church. Since the early 1990s, tithing has caused considerable controversy in bankruptcy law: Creditors complain that it deprives them of money they are owed, and debtors argue that tithing is required by their faith. Although courts have been divided over the legality of tithing in bankruptcy plans, the court in *Saunders* refused to allow a couple to tithe income that was owed to their creditors. Judge William C. Hillman ruled that the practice fails to satisfy key requirements under federal bankruptcy law.

The case involved a bankruptcy plan proposed by Alan J. Saunders and Della C. Randall-Saunders. The couple filed for bankruptcy under chapter thirteen of the federal bankruptcy code (11 U.S.C.A.), which is designed to give insolvent wage earners additional time to pay their debts. Under the law, debtors must submit to the court a plan for allocating their future earnings, subject to the supervision and control of a trustee, until the debt is paid. The Saunders proposed monthly payments to their creditors of $215 for two years. During the same period, however, they intended to contribute $400 a month to their church. Although their church did not require tithing, the Saunders regarded the practice as being "mandated by Scripture."

Objecting to the proposed tithing, the trustee filed a motion with the court to dismiss the Saunders' chapter thirteen plan. The trustee argued that tithing is not reasonably necessary for the debtors' maintenance and support as defined under 11 U.S.C.A § 1325(b). This section of the federal bankruptcy code allows debtors to keep a reasonable amount of their wages for survival, but it does not allow them to keep so-called disposable income. Similar objections have been made in several other chapter thir-

teen cases. Additionally, the trustee's motion asserted that, because the Religious Freedom Restoration Act (RFRA) (42 U.S.C.A. § 2000bb) allowed for tithing, the court should hold it to be unconstitutional. Enacted in 1993, the RFRA was intended to restore protections for religion that Congress believed had been eroded by various court decisions. The Saunders couple relied largely on this law in their response to the trustee's motion.

Because the case involved the RFRA, the federal government intervened. By 1997 a case challenging the constitutionality of RFRA was pending before the U.S. Supreme Court, and the Justice Department wanted the bankruptcy court to wait until the higher court had ruled on the matter. On June 25, 1997, the Supreme Court ruled that Congress had exceeded its authority in passing the RFRA (*City of Boerne v. Flores*) 117 S. Ct. 2157, 138 L. Ed. 2d 624).

Judge Hillman delivered his eight-page opinion in *Saunders* on July 17, 1997. Permitting tithing in chapter thirteen cases would excessively entangle church and state, he wrote, and he observed that this opinion comported with Justice John Paul Stevens' concurring opinion in *City of Boerne*. The chapter thirteen system is neutral with regard to religion, Hillman opined. As such, a religious practice such as tithing cannot be a reasonable expense for the maintenance or support of a debtor but must be considered disposable income. The Saunders couple's tithing therefore failed to satisfy the federal bankruptcy code's disposable income requirement and was impermissible.

In a final round to the case, the Justice Department filed a motion for the court to reconsider. It argued that Hillman had misapplied the ruling in *City of Boerne*. The Supreme Court had struck down the RFRA only as it applies to the states, but the statute continued to apply to the federal government and to federal laws, such as the bankruptcy code. On December 1, 1997, Hillman rejected the government's motion and reaffirmed his decision. He held that the RFRA, if it authorizes tithing, is unconstitutional because it violates the Free Exercise Clause of the First Amendment. The judge noted that his decision was a "harsh result" for bankrupt debtors who want to tithe, but said "I find myself compelled to it by the mandate of the Constitution."

## Kawaauhau v. Geiger

The federal bankruptcy code (11 U.S.C.A. § 101 et seq.) gives debtors an opportunity to discharge their debts through a legal proceeding. However, code provisions state that certain types of debts cannot be discharged. These statutory exceptions are often open to interpretation, leading to court decisions that clarify the code. In *Kawaauhau v. Geiger*, ___U.S.___, 118 S. Ct. 974, ___L. Ed. 2d____ (1998), the U.S. Supreme Court ruled that a debt arising from a medical malpractice judgment attributable to negligent or reckless conduct did not fall within one of these statutory exceptions. Therefore, the doctor escaped paying the full amount of damages to the victim of his malpractice.

In 1983 Dr. Paul Geiger treated Margaret Kawaauhau for a foot injury. He admitted her to a hospital out of concern that the injury had led to an infection. He prescribed oral penicillin rather than intravenous penicillin, explaining at his malpractice trial that he understood Kawaauhau wished to minimize the cost of her treatment. Geiger then left on a business trip, leaving Kawaauhau in the care of other doctors, who decided she should be transferred to an infectious disease specialist. When Geiger returned, he canceled the transfer and discontinued all antibiotic treatment because he believed the infection had subsided. Kawaauhau's condition deteriorated over the next few days, requiring the amputation of her right leg below her knee.

Kawaauhau and her husband sued Geiger for malpractice. Though the jury awarded them $355,000 in damages, Geiger did not carry malpractice insurance, and the Kawaauhaus were forced to garnish his wages. Geiger then filed for bankruptcy. The Kawaauhaus requested that the bankruptcy court find that the malpractice judgment was non-dischargeable because, under section 523(a)(6) of the code, it was a debt "for willful and malicious injury" that was excepted from discharge. The bankruptcy court agreed that Geiger's treatment fell far below the appropriate standard of care and therefore was "willful and malicious." The federal district court agreed, but the U.S. Court of Appeals for the Eighth Circuit reversed, 113 F. 3d 848 (1997). The appeals court ruled that the section 523(a)(6) exemption from discharge was confined to debts "based on what the law has for generations called an intentional tort." Therefore, a debt for malpractice that is based on conduct that is negligent or reckless, rather than intentional, remains dischargeable.

The Supreme Court agreed to hear the Kawaauhaus' appeal because the Sixth and Tenth Circuit Courts of Appeals had ruled contrary to the Eighth Circuit court on the same issue in other cases. Justice Ruth Bader Ginsburg, writing for a unanimous Court, upheld the Eighth Circuit court's interpretation of section 523(a)(6). The central question for the Court concerned the scope of the "willful and malicious" exception. Did it cover acts done intentionally that cause injury, or only acts done with the actual intent to cause injury?

The Kawaauhaus contended that the exception covered acts done intentionally that caused injury. Geiger had intentionally provided inadequate medical care that led to the amputation of part of Kawaauhau's leg. His deliberate choice of less effective treatment, done because he wanted to cut costs, demonstrated that he knew he was providing substandard care.

Ginsburg was not persuaded by this argument. She noted that the words of the statutes supported the Eight Circuit court's ruling. The word *willful* modified the word *injury* "indicating that non-dischargeability takes a deliberate or intentional injury, not merely a deliberate or intentional act that leads to injury." If Congress had wanted to exempt debts resulting from unintentionally inflicted injuries, it could have written the phrase "willful acts that cause injury." The language of section 523(a)(6) was clearly meant to address the category of "intentional torts" as distinguished from negligent or reckless torts. This meant that the actor intended the consequences of an act, not simply the act itself.

To depart from the intentional tort interpretation would mean expanding the scope of section 523(a)(6) in ways that could disturb congressional intent. Ginsburg stated that "every traffic accident stemming from an initial intentional act," such as intentionally turning the wheel to make a turn without first checking oncoming traffic, would fit the description put forward by the Kawaauhaus. In addition, the Court was hesitant to adopt an interpretation that would make other sections of the code superfluous. Section 523(a)(9) specifically exempted debts for "death or personal injury caused by the debtor's operation of a motor vehicle if such operation was unlawful because the debtor was intoxicated from using alcohol, a drug, or another substance." This section would not be needed if an intentional act causing injury were enough to prevent the discharge of a debt.

The Kawaauhaus also argued that, as a policy matter, malpractice judgments should be excepted from discharge, at least when the debtor acted recklessly or carried no malpractice insurance. Ginsburg rejected this argument, noting that it is up to Congress to make such policies. The Court, therefore, had to follow the direction of the statute as currently written.

**CROSS REFERENCES**
Damages; Fraud; Medical Malpractice; Religion

## BANKS AND BANKING

Authorized financial institutions and the business in which they engage, which encompasses the receipt of money for deposit, to be payable according to the terms of the account; collection of checks presented for payment; issuance of loans to individuals who meet certain requirements; discount of commercial paper; and other money-related functions.

### Evasion of U.S. Banking Laws

Ghaith R. Pharaon , a central figure in the savings and loan scandals involving the Bank of Credit and Commerce International (BCCI), a multinational financial institution based in Luxembourg, was fined $37 million and barred permanently from participation in the U.S. banking industry. He appealed the fine and in *Pharaon v. Board of Governors*, the U.S. Court of Appeals for the District of Columbia Circuit, in February of 1998, affirmed the penalties, fines, and sanctions levied against him.

In the 1980s, BCCI was operating in almost 70 different nations, but it was losing money. Additionally, BCCI was facing pressure from Luxembourg officials to find a new home country with the resources to regulate it. BCCI proceeded to seek control of various banks in the United States without actually declaring its control in order to avoid banking regulations. According to federal prosecutors and the board of governors of the federal reserve system (the board), Pharaon was one of the persons used by BCCI to accomplish the bank takeovers.

In 1991 the board issued a Notice of Assessment in which it charged Pharaon with participating in a scheme with BCCI to obtain control of Independence Bank, a thrift located in California. The notice stated that the annual reports BCCI was required to submit to the board as a foreign bank with U.S. branches concealed BCCI's control of the bank. Pharaon, a major shareholder in BCCI, was used as an undisclosed nominee or front person for BCCI's secret control. According to the board, Pharaon and a BCCI-owned company, International Credit

and Investment Company (Overseas) Ltd. (ICIC) together purchased all of the voting stock in Independence in May 1985. All of the voting stock was held in Pharaon's name, but 85 percent of that stock was held in a fiduciary capacity for ICIC. Essentially, BCCI had become a holding company for Independence Bank without the approval of the board, in violation of the Bank Holding Company Act (12 U.S.C.A. § 1841 et seq).

In making its findings, the board relied on a signed agreement between Pharaon, Swaleh Naqvi, a BCCI official, and Independence Bank, titled "Acquisition of Shares of Independence Bank," *Pharaon v. Board of Governors of the Federal Reserve System*, 135 F. 3d 148 (D.C. Cir 1998). In addition to the shareholder arrangement, the agreement revealed that ICIC had the right to possess Independence's share certificates, that ICIC was able to collect dividends on the stocks held by Pharaon, and that Pharaon could not sell the shares held for ICIC. The notice issued by the board asked an administrative law judge for the imposition of a fine of $37 million against Pharaon and an order barring Pharaon from participating in the affairs of any federally insured depository.

Shortly after the notice was issued, Pharaon was indicted on criminal charges in Florida, New York, and Washington, D.C. Pharaon remained at his home in Saudi Arabia, but answered the board's notice through a U.S. attorney and denied all charges. The administrative law judge proceeded against Pharaon and, after a 19-day hearing, approved the board's recommendations on Pharaon. Pharaon appealed to the board, which adopted the judge's recommendation. Pharaon then appealed to the D.C. Circuit Court of Appeals, which affirmed the judgment of the board.

The appeals court rejected all of Pharaon's arguments. Pharaon attacked the factual findings of the board, arguing that BCCI had not violated the Bank Holding Company Act, and that even if it had, he could not be held personally liable for the violation. Pharaon noted that Congress had changed the law respecting holding companies to omit the word "individual" in connection with liability. The appeals court found ample evidence to support the finding that BCCI had violated the act, and it rejected Pharaon's argument on personal liability, stating that "we cannot imagine that Congress would have exempted individuals from liability for false reports without saying so."

The appeals court also dismissed Pharaon's procedural arguments. Pharaon argued that he was denied discovery of evidence and that the administrative law judge improperly excluded testimony by misapplying the fugitive disentitlement doctrine. Under this court-created doctrine, a person who is a fugitive from legal proceedings may be sanctioned. The administrative law judge, however, had acted pursuant to his discretion to exercise procedural powers to ensure that Pharaon's fugitive status did not disrupt the proceeding. The court impatiently dispatched with Pharaon's other procedural complaints. Pharaon had argued that the board failed to address all the exceptions he made to the administrative law judge's findings and rulings, but the appeals court rejected this contention, recalling that at oral argument it had asked Pharaon's counsel to name an exception that the board did not address and that the attorney was unable to offer one.

Finally, the appeals court turned to Pharaon's constitutional and statutory challenges to the fine and the lifetime exclusion from the U.S. banking industry. Pharaon argued that the board did not reveal how it arrived at the figure of $37 million, but the appeals court refused to strike down the fine under precedent holding that the court may uphold unclear decisions by an agency "if the agency's path may reasonably be discerned." The appeals court reminded Pharaon that the fine was still less than $111 million, the maximum allowed in the case under 12 U.S.C.A. § 1847(b), a figure recom-

mended to the board by the board's own enforcement counsel.

**CROSS REFERENCES**
Federal Reserve Board

## BLACK PANTHER PARTY

### Elmer Pratt Released

On May 29, 1997, a California court ended the twenty-seven-year ordeal of convicted black activist Elmer ("Geronimo") Pratt. Formerly a leader of the radical Black Panther Party, Pratt was convicted of murder in 1972 and sentenced to life in prison. For nearly three decades, mounting evidence suggested that had been denied a fair trial. His claim that federal, state, and local law enforcement agencies had framed him for political reasons won support from members of the U.S. Congress and the human rights group Amnesty International.

Pratt's legal woes began in 1970. He was a Vietnam War veteran who had joined the Black Panthers. The black nationalist political group, formed in Oakland, California, in the late 1960s, became one of the most prominent radical organizations of the era. Although Pratt had brushes with police before December 1970, that month he was suddenly indicted for murder. Los Angeles police charged him with killing Caroline Olson, a young teacher, on a Santa Monica tennis court two years earlier. At the trial in July 1972, Pratt testified that he had been four hundred miles away from Santa Monica at the time of the murder, attending a Black Panther meeting. But the jury convicted him, and he received a life sentence.

The conviction was largely based on testimony from a former Black Panther member and involved the curious passage of a letter through the Los Angeles Police Department (LAPD). In 1969 Julius C. Butler had written a letter stating that Pratt had confessed to him to committing the tennis court murder. He gave the letter to the LAPD with the understanding that it would be opened in the event of his death. One year later it surfaced during an internal affairs investigation and swiftly led to Pratt's arrest and indictment. At trial Butler was the prosecution's star witness. He denied, however, being a police informant.

During the 1970s and 1980s, Pratt gathered evidence for an appeal. Through information secured under the Freedom of Information Act, his defense team learned that the Federal Bureau of Investigation (FBI) had targeted him in

*Former Black Panther leader Elmer "Geronimo" Pratt pumps his fist at a news conference after being released on bail from a 27-year imprisonment for the 1968 robbery-slaying of a teacher. Pratt's wife, Ashaki, is at his side.*

SAM MIRCOVICH/REUTERS/ARCHIVE PHOTOS

its covert campaign to spy on and destabilize the Panthers. FBI documents also showed that the bureau and the LAPD had used Julius Butler as an informant for at least three years. Moreover, they revealed that informants spied on Pratt's legal defense team and that the FBI suppressed wiretap evidence that would have supported his claim that he was not in the city where the murder occurred. At the very least, these revelations suggested that prosecutors had misled the defense team. Under well-established U.S. Supreme Court doctrine, they had a legal duty to disclose their witness' identity as a police informant to the defense. The revelations also implied that Pratt had been framed.

Although Pratt received public support, progress on his case inched along while he remained in prison. He received backing from members of the U.S. Congress, the American Civil Liberties Union, the National Association for the Advancement of Colored People Legal Defense and Educational Fund, and Amnesty International, which declared him a prisoner of conscience in 1981. Yet federal and state courts rejected four petitions for a new trial, and Pratt was denied parole 16 times.

No significant breakthrough occurred until the mid 1990s, when Los Angeles District Attorney Gil Garcetti agreed to informally review the case. Garcetti subsequently released files that contained more damaging evidence against the prosecution. Then in 1996 Pratt received powerful legal help. His original defense attorney, Johnnie L. Cochran, Jr., who had since become famous for his defense of O. J. Simpson, rejoined the defense team. Cochran vowed that he would not retire from law until he saw Pratt released.

Early in 1996 the case cleared an important hurdle. Pratt's latest request for a retrial stood before the Los Angeles Superior Court, which ruled that it did not have jurisdiction and transferred it to the California Supreme Court. In May the state supreme court provided the break sought by the defense, ordering the superior court to review the case.

On May 29, 1997, Superior Court Judge Everett W. Dickey overturned Pratt's conviction. In ruling that Pratt had been denied a fair trial, Dickey cited the U.S. Supreme Court's 1972 decision in *Giglio v. United States*, 405 U.S. 150, 92 S. Ct. 763, 31 L. Ed. 2d 104, which shored up an earlier doctrine holding that prosecutors have a duty to disclose substantial material evidence favorable to an accused. That evidence, the Supreme Court said, must include not only evidence directly related to the question of guilt but also to the credibility of a material witness. Judge Dickey ruled the prosecution had suppressed that evidence in denial of Pratt's constitutional rights. If defense attorneys and the jury had known about Butler's status as a police informant, his credibility could have been called into question. This would have "permitted potentially devastating cross-examination or other impeachment evidence" that might have resulted in a different verdict, the judge wrote.

After a new trial was ordered, Los Angeles District Attorney Garcetti declined to retry the case. On June 10, 1997, Pratt was released from custody at the age of 49, having spent more than half his life behind bars.

**CROSS REFERENCES**
Evidence; Witnesses

## BOND, HORACE JULIAN

In the annals of the civil rights movement, the career of the politician, activist, and educator (Horace) Julian Bond holds a unique place. Bond's work on behalf of social justice spans the

*Horace Julian Bond*
UPI/BETTMANN

# HORACE JULIAN BOND

| | |
|---|---|
| **1940** | Born in Nashville, Tennessee |
| **1960** | Formed the Committee on Appeal for Human Rights |
| **1960** | Co-founded the Student Nonviolent Coordinating Committee (SNCC) |
| **1965** | Elected to Georgia House of Representatives; legislature voted not to seat him |
| **1966** | U.S. Supreme Court ruled the legislature's actions violated the First Amendment |
| **1967–1974** | Member of the Georgia House of Representitives |
| **1968** | Nominated for vice president at the Democratic Convention, withdrew name |
| **1971** | Became first president of the Southern Poverty Law Center |
| **1972** | Author of *A Time to Speak, A Time to Act* |
| **1974–1987** | Served as state senator of Georgia |
| **1998** | Elected national board chairman of the NAACP |

period from the 1960s to the late 1990s. As a college organizer in 1960, he helped found the Student Nonviolent Coordinating Committee (SNCC), arguably the most important group channel for the young people who expanded and radicalized the movement. In 1965, he became one of the first members of his generation to make the transition from activism to political office, subsequently serving for nearly two decades in Georgia state government. Through his legislation, writing, teaching, and planning for legal affairs groups, he is widely recognized as an intellectual leader of the contemporary civil rights movement.

Born on January 14, 1940, in Nashville, Tennessee, Bond was the son of black educators. His childhood was steeped in the intellectual life of Lincoln University in Pennsylvania, where his father, Horace Mann Bond, served as president. The family's accomplishments—Bond was the descendant of a freed slave—did not insulate him from prejudice. While at the George School, a Quaker prep school at which he was the only black student in the 1950s, Bond was told by the headmaster not to wear his school jacket on dates with white girls. The experience scarred him, yet awakened him politically. At this time he also began developing a philosophy of racial awareness and pacifism, along with the witty, penetrating style for which he later became known.

In 1957, Bond entered Morehouse College in Atlanta, Georgia. He would not receive his bachelor of arts degree in English until fourteen years later, but in the interim, he would make history. The civil rights movement and particularly Martin Luther King, Jr.'s philosophy of nonviolent change, inspired him. In 1960, Bond helped found two influential student groups. The first of these, the Committee on Appeal for Human Rights, succeeded in integrating Atlanta businesses and public places. The second group, SNCC, grew into a national phenomenon, becoming the leading civil rights organization among young people in the mid-1960s. SNCC's activities ranged from voter registration drives in the South to opposition to the Vietnam War, and Bond, in addition to joining SNCC in the field, edited its newsletter.

Dropping out of college in 1961 to become a full-time activist, Bond soon established himself as a national figure through this work and his subsequent political career. In 1965, he was elected to the Georgia House of Representatives. But lawmakers voted not to seat him, ostensibly because of his anti-war activities, particularly his signing of a SNCC statement that supported men who chose not to respond to their draft summons. Bond's supporters argued that the real reason he was not seated was racism. After the legislature called a new election, Bond won again, but was still refused office. His lawsuit claiming the right to be seated went to the U.S. Supreme Court, which ruled unanimously in December 1966 that the legislature's actions violated the First Amendment (*Bond v. Floyd*, 385 U.S. 116, 87 S. Ct. 339, 17 L. Ed. 2d 235). Bond took office in January 1967.

Bond's success led to his name being placed in nomination for vice president at the 1968 Democratic Convention, a first for a black man. The nomination was symbolic; he was too young to serve, and so withdrew his name. In Georgia he served as a state representative until 1974 and as a state senator from 1974 to 1987. During this period, he introduced some sixty bills aimed at helping minorities and low-income citizens; he also led a successful drive to create a new congressional district in Atlanta representing a black majority. He made an unsuccessful bid for the U.S. House of Representatives in 1987.

During Bond's career, he has written and taught about civil rights and has served in many civil rights organizations. He is the author of the essay collection *A Time to Speak, A Time to Act*, as well as numerous articles; he has also frequently delivered commentary on television. In 1971, he became the first president of the Southern Poverty Law Center, a nonprofit legal organization based in Montgomery, Alabama, devoted to ending discrimination. In the 1990s, in addition to serving a fourth term on the board of the National Association for the Advancement of Colored Persons (NAACP), he was a visiting professor at Derail University, Harvard University, and Williams College, and a faculty member at the University of Virginia. In February 1998 Bond was elected national board chairman of the NAACP.

**CROSS REFERENCES**
Civil Rights Movement

## BONO, SONNY

The accidental death of Representative Sonny Bono (R-Ca.) ended one of the more unusual careers in modern politics. Famous as half of the 1960s-era duo Sonny and Cher, the singer-songwriter and comedian entered politics as a Republican in the late 1980s. After a successful term as the mayor of Palm Springs, California, he was elected to Congress in 1994 and 1996. In Washington, he won respect among

### SONNY BONO

| 1935 | Born in Detroit, Michigan |
|------|---------------------------|
| 1964 | First hit song as co-writer of "Needles and Pins" |
| 1965 | Married Cher; their recording of "I Got You Babe" reached Top 40 |
| 1971 | "Sonny and Cher Comedy Hour" debuted on prime-time television |
| 1974 | Divorced; television show ended |
| 1988 | Elected mayor of Palm Springs, California |
| 1991 | Unsuccessful candidacy for U.S. Senate |
| 1994 | Elected to U.S. House of Representatives |
| 1998 | Died in Lake Tahoe, California |

politicians of both parties for his wit and self-deprecating style, while steering a course between social conservatism and policies that favored the entertainment industry. His untimely death brought an outpouring of eulogies from leaders in government and business.

Born on February 16, 1935, in Detroit, Salvatore Bono was the son of Sicilian immigrants. While working as a truck driver following high school, he launched a song writing career by making unscheduled stops to drop off his compositions at record companies. He had a hit in 1964 as co-writer of the song "Needles and Pins," and fame followed after he and his girlfriend Cherilyn Sarkisian began recording his duets. The couple married, adopted the stage name of Sonny and Cher, and recorded ten Top 40 songs, including "I Got You Babe" in 1965. "The Sonny and Cher Comedy Hour," which aired from 1971 to 1974, was a highly-rated weekly TV show. The show featured the duo singing and clowning in hippie-era style, with Bono playing the fall guy and Cher the put-down artist.

After they divorced in 1974 and he made an unsuccessful comeback bid two years later, Bono disappeared from the public eye to become a restaurateur in West Hollywood. In 1988 he reinvented himself as a conservative politician.

*Sonny Bono*
MARK WILSON/AP/WIDE WORLD PHOTOS

# BOUNTY HUNTERS: LEGITIMATE LAW ENFORCEMENT OR DANGEROUS ANACHRONISM?

**M**ost citizens do not realize bounty hunters still exist in modern society and that these agents have few limitations placed on them by state laws. Concerns have been raised about the failure of many states to regulate the actions of bounty hunters. In general, bounty hunters are not subject to civil liability for the injuries they may cause in recapturing a person who has been released on bond and fled. Critics contend that the legal privileges granted to bounty hunters in the nineteenth century make no sense today, and that it might be prudent to outlaw bounty hunters. Defenders reply that bounty hunters serve an important role in the criminal justice system and should not be forced to follow regulations that will prevent them from carrying out their responsibilities.

Defenders of bounty hunters note that the common law right of recapture dates back to the constitutional begin-

IN FOCUS

nings of the United States. They contend that critics have ignored the underlying legal relationship between the bail bonding company and the principal, the person who is bailed out of jail. When the bonding company bails a defendant out of jail, the defendant waives his rights when he signs the bail bond contract. Then, if a defendant fails to appear in court, the bail bond company may have to forfeit the bond it posted with the court. If this system was not available, many defendants would not be able to post bond themselves; and they would have to remain in jail, driving up the cost for local governments to house defendants awaiting trial. In addition, the bail bonding company serves as guarantor that the defendant will appear in court. This system also removes from public law enforcement the responsibility of tracking down many defendants who fail to appear in court.

Defenders also point out the significant difference between free-lance bounty hunters and agents who work directly for the bail bonding company. These agents, commonly known as bail agents, are involved from just after arrest to the disposition of the case. They are familiar with the workings of the local criminal courts and are trained by the bail bonding company. In contrast, freelance bounty hunters cause most of the problems. Defenders of bounty hunting believe that the occasional public outcries over violent recapture of a bail-skipper are the result of a few irresponsible freelancers.

Finally, defenders rely on the U.S. Supreme Court decision in *Taylor v. Taintor*, 83 U.S. 366, 21 L. Ed. 287, 16 Wall. 366 (1872). The *Taylor* ruling gives bounty hunters authority to seize and imprison a principal at any time. The decision also allows bounty hunters to pursue a person to another state and arrest the pursued person without legal

---

Bono credited this career move to frustration with poor leadership and government bureaucracy in the wealthy desert community of Palm Springs, California, where he won the mayoral election by the largest margin in the city's history. His accomplishments in office included cutting red tape, expanding the revenue base, and launching the annual Palm Springs International Film Festival in 1990. He made a failed bid for the U.S. Senate in 1991, but won election to the 104th Congress three years later.

Washington was unsure at first what to make of the congressional freshman, who acknowledged that he was widely perceived as a lightweight. He soon turned heads with his trademark humor, telling a roomful of politicians in 1995: "I am so pleased that we are all so dedicated to mankind, unlike show business, where there you have egomaniacs, and you have power-mongers and you have elitists. And here, I am now part of this wonderful institution that is going to move mankind forward." This light touch endeared him to GOP leaders, who put

him to work at fund-raisers. It played well with the voters, too, who reelected him in 1996.

Politically, Bono's philosophy veered between conservative social attitudes and what was good for the entertainment industry. He opposed gay and lesbian rights, despite having a lesbian daughter, Chastity Bono. He voted against federal funding for the National Endowment for the Arts (NEA) in 1997, arguing that it had never produced valuable art. But at a time when many Republicans routinely criticized the social mores of popular entertainment, Bono stood squarely behind industry interests. His opposition to censorship and his work on behalf of strengthening copyright protection met with high approval from the music, film, and television industries; and, in an unlikely tribute for a Republican politician, he even received favorable mention in a song by the controversial rap band Public Enemy.

On January 5, 1998, Bono died after hitting a tree on a ski slope in South Lake Tahoe. Hun-

process. *Taylor* concludes that the bail bonding company has the "principal on a string," and "may pull the string" whenever it pleases. Defenders conclude, therefore, that the Court has given bounty hunters authority under the U.S. Constitution to practice their trade. This authority has never been revoked.

Finally, defenders point out that defendants who skip bail do not want to be found and do not want to surrender, if discovered. Bounty hunters do not seek to inflict injuries on principals or damage property, but in many situations surprise entry into a dwelling is required to effect the arrest. Physical resistance by the principal leads to most of the violence associated with bounty hunters.

Critics of bounty hunters contend that the time has long passed for bounty hunters. The *Taylor* decision was rendered a few years after the Civil War, at a time when the United States was relatively unpopulated and the West was just beginning to be settled. Moreover, police departments in urban areas were inadequate, ill-equipped, and ill-trained. Cooperation between jurisdictions was minimal, and there was no organization

similar to the Federal Bureau of Investigation (FBI) with the power to cross state borders in pursuit of escaped felons. In addition communication between points separated by great distances was poor. At that time, therefore, it made sense to allow bounty hunters to track down persons who jumped bail. The critics argue that these considerations no longer make sense in the 1990s, when modern law enforcement has the benefit of the FBI, electronic communication, and cooperation between jurisdictions.

Critics believe that allowing bounty hunters to use questionable, and often violent, methods to recapture principals does not promote respect for the administration of justice. In addition, since the 1960s the Supreme Court has recognized that criminal defendants are entitled to numerous constitutional rights. The "due process revolution" runs counter to the methods of bounty hunters, who can commit acts that law enforcement officers are prohibited from committing. Critics contend that it is unwise to allow private law enforcement to run roughshod over the rights of persons, merely because they have entered into a contractual relationship.

While some critics believe bounty hunters should be banned, others believe that states should regulate bail agents. Some states, such as Florida, require bounty hunters to be licensed and to be employed by only one bail bonding company that will supervise and be responsible for the agents. Florida imposes age and residence requirements on licensed bounty hunters, who must also demonstrate they are of high moral character. Some states also require bounty hunters to complete a certification course in criminal justice within a few years of obtaining their license. Some jurisdictions mandate that bounty hunters take continuing education courses in their field every year. Many of these reforms have been proposed by the National Institute of Bail Enforcement, which seeks to professionalize its membership and enhance its public reputation.

Critics also believe it essential that bounty hunters be held liable for injuries to persons and property. State laws must, they argue, be amended to impose civil liability. Such legislation would deter bounty hunters from taking dangerous actions that may injure innocent people.

dreds of mourners paid their last respects at his flag-draped coffin as industry and government leaders issued eulogies. Jack Valenti, president of the Motion Picture Association of America, said "the movie industry had no larger supporter." House Speaker Newt Gingrich (R-Ga.) told the Cable News Network that Bono had "brought both wisdom and a joy of life" to Congress. And President Bill Clinton expressed sadness and praised Bono's ability to "make us laugh even as he brought his own astute perspective to the work of Congress."

## BOUNTY

A subsidy paid to a category of persons who have performed a public service.

### Bounty Hunters

In August 1997 the brutal slaying of a young couple in their Phoenix, Arizona, home raised concerns about the legal powers of bounty

hunters. The man and woman were killed when five armed men burst into their bedroom at night, allegedly in search of a criminal fugitive whom they hoped to capture in exchange for a fee. The shooting deaths of Chris Foote, age twenty-three, and his girlfriend, Spring Wright, age twenty, in an apparent case of mistaken identity that escalated into tragedy, provoked outrage. Critics called for regulating the trade of semiprofessional manhunters, who are an important, if controversial, part of the criminal justice system.

Bounty hunting is a practice dating to medieval England. It reached violent heights in the era of the Wild West, when bounty hunters pursued outlaws who were wanted dead or alive. Contemporary bounty hunting is somewhat more limited: it is directly related to the system of posting bail, whereby criminal defendants pay courts in order to leave jail until trial. Because bail figures run in the thousands of dollars, defendants often must ask private businesses known as bail bondsmen or bonding companies

*Chris Foote, left, and Spring Wright, right, were shot to death August 31, 1997, when five men burst into their Phoenix home looking for a California man who had jumped bail.*

REUTERS/HO/ARCHIVE PHOTOS

to post bail for them. Because the bondsman stands to lose the investment if the defendant fails to appear for trial, and because criminal defendants routinely skip out, bondsmen hire bounty hunters to track down, capture, and return fugitives. According to the National Institute of Bail Enforcement in Tucson, Arizona, bounty hunters catch 23,000 "bail jumpers" per year.

This work occupies an unusual place on the spectrum between law enforcement and crime. Bounty hunters, who may be ex-felons themselves, have extraordinary legal powers that exceed the constitutional restrictions on police. Unlike police, they can legally enter the residence of fugitives without a search warrant. This broad power derives from the contract that criminal defendants enter into with bail bondsmen: it specifies that any force necessary may be used to apprehend them if they break their pledge to appear in court. The U.S. Supreme Court upheld this power in 1872 in *Taylor v. Taintor*, 83 U.S. 366, 21 L. Ed. 287, 16 Wall. 366, recognizing that bounty hunters are not arresting suspects but fugitives from law. Their authority, it said, "is a continuance of the original imprisonment." Contemporary state laws impose few restrictions, chiefly by way of vague admonitions to bounty hunters to use reasonable force. Licensing is required only in Indiana, Nevada, and North Carolina. Texas has the toughest requirements: bounty hunters must first procure warrants and then make arrests only in the presence of licensed security officials.

The Arizona tragedy occurred on August 31, 1997. Some time around 4:00 A.M., police said, at least five armed men wearing body armor and ski masks used sledge hammers to break down the door of a Phoenix house. They bound and held one couple and their children at gunpoint and then kicked in the door to Foote and Wright's bedroom. Foote opened fire with his 9-mm pistol, wounding two of the men before he and his girlfriend were killed. Police arrested and charged with second-degree murder Brian Robbins, age twenty-eight; Ronald Timms, age twenty-eight; Michael Sanders, age forty; Matthew Brackney, age twenty; and David Brackney, age forty-five. The case initially baffled police. Neither Foote nor Wright was a fugitive, and neither knew the fugitive being sought—a man wanted by a California bonding company for skipping out on a $25,000 bail. Moreover, the California company denied that the men were working for it.

Further investigation led police to believe that the bounty hunter claim was simply a ruse and that the defendants' real intent was to rob a drug dealer. A small amount of methamphetamine was found in Foote's blood, but no drugs were found in the house. Timms had asked a friend if he knew any drug dealers and Sanders, a convicted felon, had bragged about killing a man in Tucson during another bounty hunter raid.

Despite the murkiness of the case, critics demanded regulation of bounty hunters, denouncing them as a dangerous anachronism from an era of near-lawlessness. As a petition drive led by Foote's family attracted national media attention, Arizona state senator John Kaites promised to introduce legislation. His bill would require background checks and licensing of bounty hunters and mandate that bounty hunters notify police before apprehending a fugitive. Arizona bonding companies announced their support of reform efforts.

Nationally, the likelihood of stringent regulations seemed remote. Public outcry over bounty hunting is not new; in the late 1980s, for example, similar demands for regulation followed the shooting death of a fugitive by a nineteen-year-old bounty hunter. Yet legal critics acknowledge that bounty hunting plays a key role in the criminal justice system, because the bail system, bonding companies, and bounty hunting are inextricably linked. Traditionally, bail has existed to provide defendants time to prepare for trial; it is premised on the notion that they *will* appear rather than risk forfeiting their bail. But, as the high incidence of skipping bail shows, the financial incentive to appear is diminished when the money at stake is not one's own. Law enforcement lacks the resources to track down fugitives, and, moreover, the onus is on bonding companies to prevent a loss of their investment. These reasons combine to give bounty hunters job security for the forseeable future.

## CAPITAL PUNISHMENT

The lawful infliction of death as a punishment; the death penalty.

### Buchanan v. Angelone

Although the U.S. Supreme Court has held that capital punishment is not a violation of the Eighth Amendment's prohibition against cruel and unusual punishments, the Court has developed standards of due process that seek to ensure that the death penalty is fairly imposed. In *Buchanan v. Angelone*, ___U.S___, 118 S. Ct. 757, 139 L. Ed. 2d 702 (1998), however, the Court declined to require juries to be instructed on the concept of mitigating evidence for the defendant or on particular statutory mitigating factors. The Court was satisfied that the jurors in this case had understood they could consider mitigating evidence even without specific jury instructions to that effect.

In 1987 Douglas Buchanan murdered his father, stepmother, and two younger brothers. A Virginia jury convicted Buchanan of capital murder. A separate sentencing hearing was held, in which the prosecutor sought the death penalty on the basis of Virginia's aggravating factor that the crime was vile. In his opening statement at the sentencing hearing, the prosecutor admitted that Buchanan had endured a troubled childhood and that the jury would have to balance the factors in Buchanan's favor against the crimes he had committed. The defense attorney told the jurors that he would present mitigating evidence that he hoped would convince them not to sentence Buchanan to death.

The defense presented seven witnesses and the prosecution eight during the two-day hearing. Buchanan's witnesses recalled the early death of his mother, his father's remarriage, and his parents' attempt to prevent him from visiting his maternal relatives. A psychiatrist testified that Buchanan had been under extreme emotional disturbance at the time of the murders. Two mental health experts testified for the prosecution, agreeing with the factual events of Buchanan's life but disputing their effect on his commission of the crimes. During final arguments, Buchanan's attorney explained to the jury the concept of mitigation, which allows a jury to reduce the severity of a sentence because of certain factors or circumstances. He contended that Buchanan's lack of prior criminal activity, his extreme emotional disturbance, his severely impaired capacity to appreciate the criminality of his conduct, and his youth were factors that mitigated against the death penalty. The attorney argued that these four mitigating factors were recognized in the Virginia Code (Va. Code Ann., § 19.2-264.4(B) [Michie 1995]).

The legal dispute in the case centered on the jury instructions. The judge instructed the jury that before it could sentence Buchanan to death, the state had to prove beyond a reasonable doubt that the conduct was vile. If the jury found that condition met, the jury could "fix punishment of the Defendant at death or if you believe from all the evidence that the death penalty is not justified, then you shall fix the punishment of the Defendant at life imprisonment." The judge refused Buchanan's request that the jury be instructed on each of the four particular mitigating factors cited by his counsel and be told that if it found the factor to exist, "then that is a fact which mitigates against imposing the death penalty." Buchanan also proposed an instruction that would have told the jury that it must consider "the circumstances surrounding the offense, the history and background of [Buchanan] and any other facts in mitigation of the offense." The judge refused to give the instruction, ruling that under Virginia case law it is not proper to give instructions singling out certain mitigating factors to the sentencing jury. The jury sentenced Buchanan to death. Buchanan challenged the sentence, arguing that the Eighth Amendment requires states to adopt specific standards for instructing jurors on mitigating circumstances so that the death penalty is not administered in an arbitrary and capricious manner. Because his jury was not properly guided on the concept of mitigation, Buchanan contended, his sentence was unconstitutional. The U.S. Court of Appeals for the Fourth Circuit rejected this argument, holding that by allowing the jury to consider all relevant mitigating evidence, Virginia's sentencing procedure satisfied the Eighth Amendment requirement of individualized sentencing in capital cases (103 F.3d 344 [1996]).

The U.S. Supreme Court agreed with the court of appeals. Chief Justice William H. Rehnquist, writing for the majority, stated that the Court in prior cases had distinguished between two different aspects of the capital sentencing process: the eligibility phase and the selection phase. In the eligibility phase, the jury narrows the class of defendants eligible for the death penalty, often through consideration of aggravating circumstances. In the selection phase, the jury determines whether to impose a death sentence on an eligible defendant. Buchanan agreed that only the selection phase was at stake in his case.

Rehnquist rejected Buchanan's contention that the jury at the selection phase must both have discretion to make an individualized determination and have that discretion limited and channeled. He noted that "no such rule has ever been adopted by this Court" and that such channeling and limiting of a jury's discretion had been applied only to the eligibility phase. As for the selection phase, Rehnquist wrote that the Court has "emphasized the need for a broad inquiry into all relevant mitigating evidence to allow an individualized determination." The Court refused, however, to go further and direct the state to "affirmatively structure in a par-

ticular way the manner in which juries consider mitigating evidence."

Turning to Buchanan's case, Rehnquist concluded that the jury instruction was not unconstitutional because it "did not foreclose the jury's consideration of any mitigating evidence." The instruction's broad command that the jury base its decision on "all the evidence" gave the jurors an opportunity to consider Buchanan's life and emotional problems. Even if there was doubt about the clarity of the instructions, the entire context of the sentencing hearing revealed that the jury had been expressly informed about mitigation and the fact that it could be considered in sentencing Buchanan. Therefore, the absence of an instruction on the concept of mitigation and of instructions on particular statutorily defined mitigating factors did not violate the Eighth Amendment.

Justice Stephen G. Breyer, in a dissenting opinion, contended that the jury instruction was poorly written and could have led jurors to believe they could not consider the mitigating factors Buchanan had put into evidence. Breyer noted that most states have model jury instructions that explicitly state the jury's consideration of mitigating evidence. Virginia had itself changed its model instructions in 1993 to require the jury to consider "any evidence presented of the circumstances which do not justify or excuse the offense but which in fairness or mercy may extenuate or reduce the degree of moral culpability and punishment" (Virginia Model Jury Instructions, Criminal, Instruction No. 34.127 [1993 and Supp. 1995]).

Breyer also disputed the majority's conclusion that the entire context in which the instructions were given made up for their lack of clarity. Though the defense may have presented considerable evidence about Buchanan's background, this presentation "does not tell the jury that the evidence presented is relevant and can be taken into account." Moreover, Breyer said, the defense attorney's statement to the jury that the evidence was relevant could be interpreted by the jury as "advocacy which it should ignore or discount." Because of these limitations, Breyer concluded that counsel's statements "cannot make up for so serious a misinstruction, with such significant consequences as are present here. The jury will look to the judge, not to counsel, for authoritative direction about what it is to do with the evidence that is here." Absent a proper instruction on mitigating factors, opined Breyer, there was a reasonable likelihood that the jury did not consider "constitutionally relevant evidence."

### Karla Faye Tucker Execution

On February 3, 1997, the state of Texas executed Karla Faye Tucker, the first woman prisoner to be put to death in that state since the Civil War. Tucker's gender, religion, and widely televised pleas for mercy made her case an international *cause celebre*. Her story was one of self-transformation. A former drug-addicted prostitute who confessed to a grisly pickax murder in 1983, she converted to Christianity while in prison. In 1997, as her execution date neared, she began asking that her sentence be reduced to life in prison. This plea was taken up by opponents of the death penalty, then by conservative TV preachers, and finally by world leaders, human rights activists, and even the Pope—to no avail. With her appeals rejected in the state and federal courts, Tucker was killed by lethal injection in the Huntsville state prison.

Tucker received the death penalty for her role in a double murder. In 1983 she and her boyfriend, Daniel Garret, took drugs for three days and then decided to steal motorcycle parts from Jerry Lynn Dean, age twenty-seven. They entered Dean's Houston apartment, where Garret battered him with a hammer. Tucker grabbed a three-foot-long pickax and repeatedly plunged it into him. Nearby, the killers discovered Deborah Thornton, age thirty-two, cowering under a sheet in a corner. Tucker killed her and later told friends she experienced orgasm with each swing of the ax. After she confessed to the crimes, she and Garret received the death sentence; he later died in prison of liver disease.

Nearly fourteen years later, Tucker professed herself a changed woman. She was a born-again Christian, she said, and wanted her sentence commuted. Interviews with her appeared on "The 700 Club," the TV program run by televangelist and former presidential candidate Pat Robertson, during which she urged Christians to believe in mercy. Previously a supporter of the death penalty, Robertson took up Tucker's case as did other religious conservatives as well as liberal opponents of the death penalty. In early 1998, her supporters included the European Parliament, the United Nations, Amnesty International, Italian Prime Minister Romano Prodi, and Pope John Paul II. Calling for Tucker's execution was Richard Thornton, the estranged husband of her murder victim Deborah Thornton, along with other death penalty advocates.

As Tucker's attorneys pursued every legal avenue available to stay her execution, their appeals underscored the near-futility of such efforts in the U.S. legal system. In December 1997 and twice in February 1998, the U.S. Supreme Court declined their requests to intervene. The Court did not explain its reasoning. Each year it receives several dozen emergency appeals from death-row inmates, delays the execution of only a handful, and rejects without comment the majority. One of Tucker's appeals to the High Court argued that the Texas clemency system through which inmates ask the Texas Board of Pardons and Paroles for stays of execution, was unconstitutional because it never results in a stay of execution. In fact, the parole board voted 16-0 to reject her request just as it had rejected seventy-six other requests since 1993. The Supreme Court was not moved by this argument. Tucker's appeal also failed before the U.S. Court of Appeals for the Fifth Circuit in New Orleans, Louisiana.

Tucker found no help in Texas, which has been the site of more than one fourth of the 431 executions carried out in the United States since the Supreme Court held in 1976 that a state may constitutionally deprive a person of life. On February 2, 1998, the parole board declined Tucker's request because it was skeptical of her rehabilitation and repentance. Chairman Victor Rodriguez told reporters that he did not believe Tucker, and that, moreover, the horrific nature of her crime "carried a lot of weight" in the board's decision. This left Tucker's fate in the hands of Texas Governor George W. Bush. On February 3, the governor, who had never stopped an execution, sealed Tucker's fate with these words: "I have concluded judgment about the heart and soul of an individual on death row are [sic] best left to a higher authority." Less than an hour later, Tucker was executed.

In terms of gender, the case was historically significant. The last execution of a woman in Texas occurred in 1983, when convicted ax murderer Chipita Rodriguez was hanged. Nationwide, the last woman put to death was Velma Barfield, executed in North Carolina in 1984 for killing her boyfriend with rat poison.

### Ohio Adult Parole

An individual who has been convicted of a crime may appeal the decision through the courts. If the conviction if affirmed, the individual may request clemency from the state governor (or in the case of a federal crime, the president), seeking either a pardon or a commutation of the sentence. The governor has complete discretion to grant or deny clemency, and the decision cannot be contested in a court of law. Questions have arisen, however, as to whether a convict sentenced to death is entitled to certain constitutional protections during clemency proceedings.

The U.S. Supreme Court, in *Ohio Adult Parole Authority v. Woodard*, ___U.S.___, 118 S. Ct. 1244, ___L. Ed. 2d___ (1998), ruled that an inmate does not have a protected life or liberty interest in clemency proceedings and that giving an inmate the option of voluntarily participating in an interview as part of the clemency process does not violate the inmate's Fifth Amendment rights. However, four members of the Court stated that there may be circumstances where a court must review clemency proceedings to insure minimal procedural safeguards have been applied.

Eugene Woodard was sentenced to death by the state of Ohio for aggravated murder committed in the course of a car-jacking. The Ohio courts upheld his conviction and sentence, and forty-five days before his scheduled execution date, the state's clemency review began. The Ohio Adult Parole Authority carried out the review, which is conducted according to the terms of Ohio law (Ohio Revised Code Ann. § 2967.07 [1993]). The procedure for inmates under death sentence requires the Authority to conduct a clemency hearing within forty-five days of the scheduled date of execution. Prior to the hearing, the inmate may request an interview with one or more parole board members. Legal counsel for the inmate is not allowed at this interview. The Authority must hold the hearing, complete its clemency review, and make a recommendation to the governor, even if the inmate subsequently obtains a stay of execution. If additional information later becomes available, the Authority may in its discretion hold another hearing or alter its recommendation.

Woodard did not request an interview, objecting to the short notice of the interview and the fact that his attorney could not attend and participate in the interview and hearing. He filed suit in federal court, alleging that Ohio's clemency process violated his Fourteenth Amendment right to due process and his Fifth Amendment right to remain silent. The district court dismissed his case, but the Sixth Circuit Court of Appeals affirmed in part and reversed in part this ruling (107 F.3d 1178 [1997]). The appeals court agreed with the state that there was no liberty interest in clemency that gave Woodard a due process claim. However, the court held that using a due process analysis centered on the "role of clemency in the entire punitive scheme" demonstrated that Woodard's "original" life and liberty interests that he possessed before trial at each proceeding remained with him during the clemency process. The court did note that the amount of due process could be minimal at the clemency stage. Finally, the court agreed with Woodard that the voluntary interview procedure was unconstitutional, because it forced him to make a choice between asserting his Fifth Amendment rights and participating in the clemency review process. Woodard had a strong interest in avoiding incrimination in ongoing post-conviction proceedings, as well as with respect to possible charges for other crimes revealed during the interview.

The Supreme Court rejected the Sixth Circuit decision. Chief Justice William H. Rehnquist noted that a "death row inmate's petition for clemency is . . . a 'unilateral hope.' The defendant in effect accepts the finality of the death sentence for purposes of adjudication, and appeals for clemency as a matter of grace." There was no life or liberty interest implicated in this process because clemency was completely dependent on the discretion of the governor. Justice Rehnquist reemphasized prior rulings of the Court that pardon and commutation proceedings have not traditionally been the business of courts and are rarely, if ever, appropriate subjects for judicial review.

Turning to the Ohio clemency process, Rehnquist concluded that it did not violate due process. He rejected the Sixth Circuit's holding that clemency is an integral part of Ohio's system of adjudicating the guilt or innocence of a defendant, and therefore subject to due process protection. Rehnquist stated that clemency proceedings "are not part of the trial—or even of the adjudicatory process." Instead, the executive branch "independent of direct appeal and collateral relief proceedings" conducted clemency proceedings.

Finally, Chief Justice Rehnquist concluded that giving the inmate the option of voluntarily participating in an interview did not violate the Fifth Amendment. The Fifth Amendment protects a person against compelled self-incrimination, but nothing in the clemency process grants inmates immunity for what they might say. Woodard faced a choice similar to one made by a criminal defendant in the course of a criminal proceeding. For example, a defendant who chooses to testify in his own defense "abandons the privilege against self-incrimination when the prosecution seeks to cross-examine him." In the Ohio clemency process, Woodard had a choice of providing information—at the risk of damaging his case for clemency or for post-conviction relief—or of remaining silent. The pressure on him to speak did not, however, make the interview compelled.

Justice Sandra Day O'Connor wrote a separate opinion, which was joined by Justices Souter, Ginsburg, and Breyer. Justice O'Connor agreed that in Woodard's case he had failed to allege any constitutional violations, but concluded that in some circumstances the Due Process Clause of the Fourteenth Amendment could provide constitutional safeguards. Judicial intervention might be warranted, for example, "in the face of a scheme whereby a state official flipped a coin to determine whether to grant clemency, or in a case where the State arbitrarily denied a prisoner any access to its clemency process."

**CROSS REFERENCES**
Cruel and Unusual Punishment; Due Process of Law; Fifth Amendment; Fourteenth Amendment; Sentencing

# CHILD ABUSE

Physical, sexual, or emotional mistreatment or NEGLECT of a child.

### Abuse of Unborn Child

In August 1997, the Supreme Court of South Carolina affirmed the criminal conviction of a woman who had ingested cocaine while pregnant (*Whitner v. State*, 328 S.C.I, 492 S.E. 2d 777 [1997]). The court's decision extended the definition of "person" under South Carolina's child neglect criminal statute and made South Carolina the first state to uphold a woman's conviction for endangering the health of her own unborn child.

In April 1992, Cornelia Whitner pleaded guilty in South Carolina state court to criminal child neglect. At that time under the state's criminal child abuse and endangerment statute, a person was guilty of a misdemeanor (now a felony) if he or she had custody of a child or helpless person and refused or neglected to provide to that person the proper care and attention needed, thereby endangering the person's life. Whitner had caused her baby to be born with cocaine in its system through her own use of cocaine, and the state charged her with violation of the child neglect statute. After she entered her plea in the lower court, Whitner petitioned for post-conviction relief, arguing that she had received ineffective assistance of counsel because her court-appointed lawyer failed to advise her that the statute under which she was being prosecuted might not apply to prenatal drug use. The petition was granted, and the state appealed to the state's highest court.

In a 3–2 decision, the Supreme Court of South Carolina reversed the decision of the lower court. The main question in the case was whether, for the purposes of the criminal child neglect statute, a viable fetus (a fetus capable of living outside the womb, usually six months old) was considered a "person." The majority noted that the court had already recognized that viable fetuses hold certain legal rights and privileges, such as the right to be free from harm.

The majority observed that a person has the right to sue another person for causing the death of a fetus (*Fowler v. Woodward*, 244 S. C. 608, 138 S.E.2d 42 [1964]), and that a person who stabs a pregnant woman and causes the death of the unborn fetus may be held criminally liable for the death of the fetus, even though the fetus was never alive outside of the woman's womb (*State v. Horne*, 282 S. C. 444, 319 S.E.2d 703 [1984]). The court reasoned that, given the protections that fetuses already receive, there was no rational basis for failing to define a fetus as a person under the criminal child neglect statute. "Although the precise effects of maternal crack use during pregnancy are somewhat unclear," the majority reasoned, "it is well documented and within the realm of public knowledge that such use can cause serious harm to the viable unborn child."

Whitner argued that most other states refused to hold a woman responsible for injuries she inflicts on her own fetus and that South Carolina should follow suit, but the majority disagreed. Failure to hold a mother responsible for harm she does to her own fetus means that "the viable fetus lacks rights of its own that deserve vindication." The majority closed its opinion by methodically rejecting all of Whitner's arguments, including ineffective assistance of counsel, the unconstitutional vagueness of the criminal child neglect statute, certain interpretations of South Carolina case precedent, and invasion of privacy. "It strains belief," the majority wrote, "for Whitner to argue that using crack cocaine during pregnancy is encompassed within the constitutionally recognized right of privacy."

The dissenters concentrated on the definition of "person." They opined that a plain reading of the entire child neglect statute made it clear that the South Carolina legislature was referring to a child in being, and not a fetus. The dissent pointed out that the South Carolina legislature, while the child endangerment statute was on the books, had tried and failed to pass legislation making it a discrete criminal offense for a pregnant woman to ingest illegal drugs during pregnancy. This suggested that the child endangerment statute did not cover such acts.

The dissent also criticized the apparent absurdity of the statute's construction and warned against prosecutorial abuses because of the decision. "Is a pregnant woman's failure to obtain prenatal care unlawful?" the dissent asked. "Failure to quit smoking or drinking?" The majority had virtually ignored this slippery slope, but "the impact of today's decision is to render a pregnant woman potentially criminally liable for myriad acts which the legislature has not seen fit to criminalize."

Historically, courts in the United States have refused to hold a pregnant woman liable for injuries she caused to her fetus, courts refused to hold anyone liable for injuries to a fetus, holding that the mother and the fetus were a single entity. In time, courts recognized that fetuses could survive the death of the mother or removal from the mother prior to end of the pregnancy, and did away with the single entity theory. Courts began to hold persons liable for injuries they caused to a mother's fetus.

Until the *Whitner* case, courts held that a woman who causes injuries to her own fetus is not criminally liable for the injuries. However, unborn children are gaining rights in more and more states. In the 1990s, some state courts and legislatures created laws that allow lawsuits for the wrongful death of a fetus that is not yet viable. No court has held that a pregnant woman is responsible for injuries she caused to the fetus when the fetus was not viable.

Advocates of female reproductive rights fear that the trend of awarding "person" status to fetuses will undermine the reproductive privacy rights given to women in *Roe v. Wade*, 410 U.S. 113, 93 S. Ct. 705, 35 L. Ed. 2d 147 (1973). Critics of the decisions also contend that the decisions will lead to investigations of every miscarriage in an effort to detect some shortcoming in the mother's care. Supporters of the decision countered that no law should give immunity to a mother who causes harm to a viable fetus.

**CROSS REFERENCES**
Privacy; Reproduction; Roe v. Wade; Void for Vagueness Doctrine

# CIVIL RIGHTS
Personal liberties that belong to an individual owing to his or her status as a CITIZEN or resident of a particular country or community.

## Board of County Commissioners of Bryan County, Oklahoma v. Brown
Since the 1960s, 42 U.S.C.A. § 1983 has been an important federal civil rights law. Originally enacted in 1871 as part of the Reconstruction-era Ku Klux Klan Act, section 1983 took on new life after the Supreme Court, in *Monroe v. Pape*, 365 U.S. 167, 81 S. Ct. 473, 5 L. Ed. 2d 492 (1961), held that police officers and other municipal employees could be held civilly liable for violating an individual's civil rights as long as the officers had acted "under color of law." Before the *Monroe*, case, the courts had limited section 1983 actions to deprivations of constitutional rights based on unconstitutional state laws.

Thousands of section 1983 actions were filed in the years after *Monroe*, yet plaintiffs had difficulty collecting damages they were awarded. The Supreme Court enhanced the collection of damages in 1978 in *Monell v. New York City Department of Social Services*, 436 U.S. 658, 98 S. Ct. 2018, 56 L. Ed. 2d 611, when it ruled that municipalities were "persons" within the meaning of section 1983. The recognition of municipal liability in *Monell* was tempered by the Court's rejection of the theory of *respondeat superior*, a common-law doctrine that makes an employer strictly liable for the actions of an employee when the actions take place within the scope of employment.

Instead, the Court in *Monell* required a plaintiff seeking to impose liability on a municipality under section 1983 to identify a municipal "policy" or "custom" that caused the plaintiff's injury. The Court justified the policy requirement as a way of holding the municipality liable for only those deprivations resulting from the decisions of a municipal legislative body or of those officials whose acts can be attributed to the municipality.

In a series of decisions that followed *Monell*, the Court struggled to define what constituted a policy and a policy maker. In addition, the Court held in *Canton v. Harris*, 489 U.S. 378, 109 S. Ct. 1197, 103 L. Ed. 2d 412 (1989), that a municipality is liable for a municipal action, which on its face is lawful, only when the action is taken with "deliberate indifference" as to its known or obvious consequences.

This intertwined set of precedents came before the Supreme Court in *Board of County Commissioners of Bryan County, Oklahoma v. Brown*, No. 95-1100, 117 S. Ct. 1382, 137 L. Ed. 2d 626 (1997). The Court, still opposed to the application of *respondeat superior*, placed more stringent requirements on plaintiffs seeking to prove that a single act that itself neither violates nor commands a violation of federal law triggers municipal liability. The 5–4 vote revealed, however, that the dissenters were troubled by the increasing complexity of section 1983 jurisprudence and that they believed the Court should reconsider its opposition to the *respondeat superior* doctrine.

The case arose out of a traffic stop conducted by Bryan County, Oklahoma, sheriff's deputy Stacy Burns. Following a traffic chase, Burns twice ordered a passenger, Jill Brown, to exit the vehicle. When she did not leave the car, Burns grabbed Brown's arm at the wrist and elbow, pulled her from the car, and spun her to the ground. Brown's knees were severely injured: they required corrective surgery and may need to be replaced.

Brown sued Burns, Bryan County Sheriff B. J. Moore, and the county itself under section 1983. Brown argued that the county was liable for Burns's excessive force based on Sheriff Moore's decision to hire Burns, the son of his nephew. Brown alleged that Moore had failed to adequately review Burns's driving record and his criminal record, which included convictions for assault and battery, resisting arrest, and public drunkenness.

At trial Moore claimed he had obtained the background information on Burns but had not looked closely at it. The trial court ruled that Moore was a policy maker for the Bryan County sheriff's department and that the hiring and training policies instituted by Moore were "so inadequate as to amount to deliberate indifference to the constitutional needs" of Brown. The jury found Bryan County liable for Brown's injury.

On appeal the Fifth Circuit Court of Appeals upheld the trial decision (67 F. 3d 1174 [1995]). The appeals court focused on the county's argument that it was improper to hold the county liable for Brown's injuries based on Moore's single decision to hire Burns. The court ruled that a single decision was sufficient to trigger municipal liability.

The Supreme Court disagreed. Justice Sandra Day O'Connor, writing for the majority, reiterated the Court's opposition to the doctrine of *respondeat superior* and the need for a plaintiff to identify a municipal policy. O'Connor noted that "it is not enough for a section 1983 plaintiff merely to identify conduct properly attributable to the municipality. The plaintiff must also demonstrate that, through its *deliberate* conduct, the municipality was the 'moving force' behind the injury alleged." Of critical importance was the plaintiff's demonstration of a "direct causal link between the municipal action and the deprivation of federal rights."

O'Connor did not find the causal link between Moore's hiring decision and Burns's use of excessive force on Brown. In addition, O'Connor said, Brown could not identify any pattern of injuries linked to the sheriff's hiring decisions, and at trial it was established that Moore had adequately screened all previous deputies he hired. Thus, Brown's claim of municipal liability was based, in O'Connor's view, on a "deviation from Sheriff Moore's ordinary hiring practices." This claim troubled O'Connor, because "the danger that a municipality will be held liable without fault is high."

The majority concluded that basing municipal liability on hiring decisions would risk collapsing this theory into *respondeat superior* liability. O'Connor stated that "every injury suffered at the hands of a municipal employee can be traced to a hiring decision in a 'but-for' sense: but for the municipality's decision to hire the employee, the plaintiff would not have suffered the injury."

O'Connor pointed out that establishing deliberate indifference on the basis of a single hiring decision is extremely difficult. To establish it, the plaintiff must prove that "a municipal actor disregarded a known or obvious consequence of his action." In Moore's case, there was insufficient evidence to support a finding that in hiring Burns, Moore disregarded a known or obvious risk of injury. Burns's traffic and criminal record may have made him a poor candidate for a deputy but it had not been shown that this record, if reviewed by Moore, would have made Burns's excessive use of force "a plainly obvious consequence of the hiring decision." Therefore, the Court reversed the lower court decisions.

Justice Stephen G. Breyer in a dissenting opinion joined by Justices John Paul Stevens and Ruth Bader Ginsburg, argued that section 1983 municipal liability case law had become too complicated: "The original principle has generated a body of interpretive law that is so complex that the law has become difficult to apply," making the "original distinction, not simply wrong, but obsolete and a potential source of confusion."

Breyer questioned the *Monell* conclusion that Congress did not intend to apply *respondeat superior* to municipal employees. Therefore, he urged the Court to reexamine the "continued viability of *Monell*'s distinction between vicarious municipal liability [*respondeat superior*] and municipal liability based upon policy and custom."

**CROSS REFERENCES**
Breyer, Stephen G.; Ku Klux Klan Act; O'Connor, Sandra Day; Section 1983

## CIVIL SERVICE

The designation given to government employment for which a person qualifies on the basis of merit rather than political PATRONAGE or personal favor.

### LaChance v. Erickson

A person who lies under oath is guilty of the crime of perjury. If a person makes a false statement not under oath, he or she commits no crime, but may be required to pay damages to an injured party in a civil action. Courts ruled that under federal and state civil service systems, a government agency could not sanction employees for making false statements to the agency regarding alleged employment-related misconduct. The U.S. Supreme Court, however, reversed this holding in *LaChance v. Erickson*, No. 96-1579, 118 S. Ct. 753, 139 L. Ed. 2d 695 (1998), finding that neither federal law nor the Due Process Clause of the Fifth Amendment forbade a government agency to discipline its employees for making false statements.

Lester E. Erickson, Jr., and four other federal employees were the subject of adverse actions by the various agencies for which they worked. Each employee made false statements to agency investigators about the misconduct with which they were charged. In each case, the agency disciplined the employee for making a false statement as well as for the underlying mis-

conduct. The employees separately appealed the actions taken against them to the Merit Systems Protection Board, a federal body that reviews civil service disciplinary decisions. The board upheld that part of the penalty based on the underlying charge in each case but ruled that the employee's false statement could not be used to impeach the employee's credibility nor could it be considered in setting punishment for the employee's underlying misconduct.

Janice R. LaChance, acting director of the Office of Personnel Management, appealed the five decisions to the Court of Appeals for the Federal Circuit. The appeals court affirmed the board decision, holding that the Due Process Clause of the Fifth Amendment prohibited penalizing an employee for making a false denial of the underlying claim (89 F. 3d 1575 [1996]). The court also agreed with the board that false statements could not be used for purposes of discrediting the employee's other statements.

The Supreme Court reversed. Writing for a unanimous Court, Chief Justice William H. Rehnquist found the court of appeals' decision out of step with Supreme Court precedents, specifically *Bryson v. United States*, 396 U.S. 64, 90 S. Ct. 355, 24 L. Ed. 2d 264 (1969). Rehnquist quoted the following passage from *Bryson*: "a citizen may decline to answer the question, or answer it honestly, but he cannot with impunity knowingly and willfully answer with a falsehood."

Rehnquist noted that no provision of the Civil Service Reform Act (5 U.S.C.A. § 1101 et seq.) precluded a federal agency from sanctioning an employee for making false statements. Furthermore, section 7513(a) of the act provided that an agency may impose penalties "for such cause as will promote the efficiency of the service." This broad grant of authority, however, is accompanied by four procedural rights accorded to the employee against whom adverse action is proposed. The employee must be given advance written notice, a reasonable time to answer orally and in writing, the opportunity to be represented by an attorney or other representative, and a written decision that gives specific reasons for the adverse action.

Rehnquist found that these procedural rights satisfied the Due Process Clause, because "the core of due process is the right to notice and a meaningful opportunity to be heard." A "meaningful opportunity to be heard", however, does not include the right to make false statements regarding the charged conduct. Though the employees had not been under oath, this was not persuasive. The employees had not been charged with perjury but were charged with making false statements during an investigation. This charge does not require that the statements be made under oath. The Court failed to see how the "presence or absence of an oath is material to the due process inquiry."

The Court rejected the court of appeals' supposition that if employees were not allowed to make false statements, they could be coerced into admitting misconduct, whether or not they believed they were guilty, to avoid the more severe penalty of removal that might result from a falsification charge. Rehnquist found this supposition uncompelling. If answering an agency's question might expose an employee to a criminal prosecution, the employee could invoke the Fifth Amendment right to remain silent. Rehnquist acknowledged that an agency, in determining the truth or falsity of a charge, would take into consideration the failure of the employee to respond, but he stated that "there is nothing inherently irrational about such an investigative posture."

**CROSS REFERENCES**
Due Process of Law; Perjury

## CLASS ACTION

A lawsuit that allows a large number of people with a common interest in a matter to sue or be sued as a group.

### Amchem Products, Inc. v. Windsor

When a company produces a dangerous or defective product that injures an individual, that person may sue the company in a tort action, demanding compensation for the injuries. If many individuals have been injured by the same product, the courts may permit the filing of a class action lawsuit, in which a small number of plaintiffs represent the entire group of injured victims. Most large-scale class actions are filed in federal court and are governed by Rule 23 of the Federal Rules of Civil Procedure. The U.S. Supreme Court, in *Amchem Products, Inc. v. Windsor*, ___U.S. ___, 117 S. Ct. 2231, 138 L. Ed. 2d 689 (1997), placed limits on how far Rule 23 and class actions may be extended in dealing with mass tort actions.

Rule 23 contains guidelines that plaintiffs must meet in order to have their lawsuit certified as a class action. Class actions can simplify the gathering of information during litigation, reduce the demand on judicial resources by eliminating hundreds, if not thousands, of trials by individual plaintiffs, and give plaintiffs more leverage with powerful and well-financed corporate defendants.

The class action lawsuit has become particularly attractive for parties involved in mass tort actions involving silicone breast implants, birth control devices, and asbestos. Though the danger of asbestos was known in the 1930s, millions of people in the United States were exposed in the 1940s and 1950s. Injuries from exposure to asbestos began to appear in the 1960s, and a flood of lawsuits began in the 1970s. By the 1990s state and federal courts were clogged with asbestos litigation. Because the latency period may last as long as forty years for some asbestos-related diseases, claims are projected to be filed into the twenty-first century. As many as 265,000 people may die of asbestos disease deaths by the year 2015.

Though the Judicial Conference of the United States has requested Congress to establish a national asbestos dispute-resolution system, which would take the litigation out of the courts and into an administrative agency, Congress has not responded. In the face of this inaction, federal courts have tried to use the procedural tools available to improve management of federal asbestos litigation. In 1991 all asbestos cases that had been filed but not tried were consolidated and transferred to a single judge in Pennsylvania. Once this consolidation occurred, the plaintiffs and defendants met to discuss settlement.

The defendants were unwilling to settle the cases, which involved persons claiming asbestos-related injuries, unless the parties established an administrative plan for the disposing of asbestos claims not yet filed. Thus, the attorneys representing injured plaintiffs were forced to represent the interests of the anticipated future claimants if they were to obtain compensation for their clients. Once negotiations seemed likely to produce such an agreement, the defendants agreed to settle the claims. In one agreement a defendant promised to pay more than $200 million to plaintiffs claiming injuries.

Once agreement was reached, the parties went into court. On January 15, 1993, the parties presented to the district court a complaint, answer, a proposed settlement agreement, and a joint motion for certification of a class action. The complaint identified nine plaintiffs and their families as representing a class comprised

of all persons who had not filed an asbestos-related lawsuit against the defendants as of January 15, 1993, but who had been exposed to asbestos or products containing asbestos attributable to the defendants, or whose spouse or family member had been so exposed.

The settlement agreement submitted to the court was a comprehensive effort to control and manage asbestos claims. The agreement proposed to prevent all class members from litigating their claims, detailed an administrative procedure and schedule of payments to compensate members of the class, described four types of compensable cancers and nonmalignant conditions, specified the range of damages to be paid to qualifying claimants, capped the number of claims payable annually for each disease, denied compensation for claims involving a host of alleged injuries, including loss of consortium and

emotional distress, and made no adjustment in payments based on inflation.

The district court approved the certification of the class action and the settlement. However, many persons in the class objected to the settlement and appealed to the Third Circuit Court of Appeals. The appeals court concluded that the district court had misapplied the criteria for approving class actions contained in rule 23. The Third Circuit ruled that though a class action can be certified for settlement only, the certification requirements of rule 23 must be met as if the case were going to be litigated, without taking the settlement into account (83 F.3d 610 [1996]). Therefore, it decertified the class and vacated the district court's orders.

On appeal to the U.S. Supreme Court, the Court ruled that the Third Circuit's reasoning was incorrect but nevertheless upheld the appeals court's ruling. Justice Ruth Bader Ginsburg, writing for the majority, held that a district court could take the settlement into account when determining whether to certify a class action. Ginsburg concluded that the Third Circuit did not ignore the settlement in rendering its decision and had "homed in" on settlement terms in several vital areas.

Ginsburg analyzed the provisions of rule 23 and their application to the proposed settlement. She concluded that the "sprawling class" that had been certified did not satisfy Rule 23 requirements. Rule 23(b)(3) permits judgments for money that bind all class members unless they opt out of the class. To qualify for this type of certification, a class must satisfy the requirements of Rule 23(a), including that the named class representatives will protect class interests. Rule 23(b)(3) also requires that common questions "predominate over any questions affecting only individual members" and that class resolution be "superior to other available methods for the fair and efficient adjudication of the controversy."

Applying these provisions, Ginsburg found major problems with certifying this particular class. The Court was troubled that attorneys of current victims stood to receive compensation from the defendants and thus bind future victims to a settlement that greatly restricted their ability to receive compensation. In this case, Ginsburg stated, "parties with diverse medical conditions sought to act on behalf of a single giant class rather than on behalf of discrete subclasses." Ginsburg concluded that representatives of the class could not adequately protect all members of the proposed class.

Another concern was that the proposed class did not have sufficient unity so that the future claimants could "fairly be bound by class representatives' decisions." The current plaintiffs, who had asbestos injuries and wanted immediate compensation, had agreed to terms that future claimants would find unacceptable. These included the lack of inflation adjustment, the limitation on the number of payable claims each year, and the prohibitions against asking for damages based on emotional distress and loss of consortium. Ginsburg acknowledged that it was understandable that current litigants wanted their compensation packages, yet it was unfair to allow these litigants to dictate what future claimants might receive.

The Court found that the proposed class was not "sufficiently cohesive." Though all members of the class shared experience of asbestos exposure, this did not meet the predominance requirement under Rule 23(b)(3). In fact, there were many individual issues and many categories of persons who were exposed and injured, or exposed but not yet injured. Ginsburg noted that no settlement class brought to the Court's attention was "as sprawling as the one certified here." It would be difficult for all members of the proposed class to know they were part of the class and have the opportunity to opt out in time. The Court expressed its skepticism that sufficient notice could ever be given to proposed class members to satisfy constitutional due process requirements.

Ginsburg noted that a "nationwide administrative claims processing regime" would be the best way of compensating asbestos victims, yet that solution remained with Congress. She stated that the provisions of rule 23 could not be stretched to certify a large class that would hurt the interests of future asbestos victims.

### Breast Implant Litigation

On August 18, 1997, a Louisiana jury ruled against Dow Chemical Co. in the early stages of the nation's first breast-implant class action suit (*Spitzfaden v. Dow Chemical*, 92-2589 [Orleans Parish Civ. Dist. Ct. *See* 1998 WL 56944]). In the legal battlefield over the health effects of breast implants in the 1990s, the closely watched lawsuit by 1,700 women is unique: it targets not the manufacturer of the implants, Dow Corning Corp., but the manufacturer's parent company, Dow Chemical. Concluding the first of four phases in the trial, jurors ruled that Dow Chemical hid negative information about silicone from consumers. The verdict represented a setback for the company, but legal analysts remained skeptical about the plaintiffs' long-term chances of success.

The *Spitzfaden* class action came to trial after several complicated turns in breast implant litigation. In the early 1990s, several hundred thousand women pursued lawsuits against breast-implant manufacturers following the emergence of allegations that silicone-gel implants posed serious health risks: plaintiffs said the implants ruptured up to 70 percent of the time, allowing silicone to travel to other organs where it caused autoimmune diseases. Implant manufacturer Dow Corning offered a $4.25 billion global settlement of claims against it in 1994. But after 440,000 women registered for the settlement, the corporation filed for chapter-eleven bankruptcy protection in 1995. This move plunged the future of its litigation and set-

# SHOULD CLASS ACTIONS BE RESTRICTED?

C lass action lawsuits have become a controversial topic in the 1990s. Once seen as a way of empowering individuals with small claims to have their day in court, class actions are viewed by many lawyers, legislators, and government officials as a vehicle for plaintiffs' lawyers to make millions of dollars on issues of dubious merit. Other critics charge that class actions have been used by defendants in mass tort cases, such as asbestos litigation, to frustrate the large and legitimate claims of individual victims.

Defenders of class actions argue that this type of lawsuit has a legitimate social purpose. A lawyer who prosecutes a class action can be viewed as a "private attorney general" who aggressively enforces various regulatory laws or who alerts the public to fraud, health, and safety problems. In a time when government is seeking to reduce government regulation, class action lawsuits provide an opportunity for the private sector to take up the oversight function.

IN FOCUS

Defenders note that the class action format has most often been used to aggregate small claims that were not worth litigating separately. A class action is an effective means for holding defendants accountable for widespread harm that would otherwise go unchecked. There is public value in allowing this type of class action to go forward, even if the amount payable to each member of the class is small. The deterrent effect of a class action can be substantial, forcing the defendant to change its product or procedures.

Supporters of class actions contend that trivial cases are rare and that neither high settlement rates nor small individual recoveries demonstrate frivolous litigation. Moreover, criticism of multimillion-dollar attorney fees ignores the risk that class action attorneys take in starting such lawsuits. Not every class action will be successful and the costs of litigation can be substantial. Without a financial incentive, attorneys will not take on and plaintiffs will not

find redress for certain types of injury. Defenders also point out that personal injury attorneys receive large portions of the awarded damages through contingent fee agreements. Class action attorneys should not be treated differently.

Defenders of large claim class actions believe that mass tort cases benefit from using a class action structure. When victims of mass torts seek substantial compensation for injuries caused by a defective product, such as asbestos, breast implants, and birth control devices, it makes sense to aggregate the claims. It is more economical for attorneys and the courts to manage hundreds or even thousands of similar claims as a group rather than on a case-by-case basis. The courts would be tied up for years if each case had to be handled individually, and the duplication of evidence and expert witnesses would generate needless expense. A class action, on the other hand, can resolve the central issues and develop rational compensation schedules for the victims. Settlement also becomes a more attractive

tlements into uncertainty. Simultaneously, several thousand more women who did not accept the 1994 settlement offer continued to pursue their own suits in federal and state courts, including the Louisiana case.

In this context, the suit is unique in one critical respect. Previously, Dow Chemical succeeded in having cases against it dismissed in California, Michigan and New York and in having other suits against it effectively joined to the bankruptcy proceedings of its subsidiary, Dow Corning. The Louisiana case became the first class action suit to successfully advance the claim that the parent company has liability for the breast implants manufactured by its subsidiary. Three phases of the trial remain: determining whether the implants actually caused the illnesses alleged by the plaintiffs, notifying other members of the class represented in the suit, and determining damages, if any.

The first phase of *Spitzfaden* dealt with the relationship between the two companies. Nearly a decade before Dow Corning marketed sili-

cone-gel implants, Dow Chemical tested silicone for health risks on its behalf. The plaintiffs alleged that this testing was improperly conducted and, even so, revealed certain risks about which the company failed to warn Louisiana consumers. They cited internal Dow Chemical memos: some referred to "cover-ups," and others condemned the marketing of the implants as "inexcusable." In its defense Dow Chemical offered scientific evidence from a wide range of respected sources—including studies by Harvard University, the Mayo Clinic, and the American Medical Association—that flatly rejects a link between silicone implants and autoimmune diseases.

Although jurors sided with the plaintiffs in the initial round, the trial is far from over. Dow Chemical expects to appeal the verdict in phase one of the trial on several grounds. Defense attorneys were highly critical of Judge Yada T. Magee. On July 17, Judge Magee declared a mistrial on the ground that a member of the defense team had ignored her warnings about

option for defendants when the victims are members of a class.

Critics of class actions remain unconvinced about the social and legal value of group lawsuits. In small claims class actions, critics question the value of supporting litigation in which individual class members have very small stakes. For example, does it make sense to permit a lawyer to initiate a class action where a utility company overcharged two million customers two cents per month? Such filings demonstrate to the critics the lawyer-driven nature of most small claims class actions. The individual claimants, because they have so little at stake, do not exercise any control over the litigation or elect to opt out of the class and pursue individual claims. With the plaintiffs' lawyer in total control, the dynamics of the lawsuit change. The lawyer has the largest economic stake in the outcome, leading to settlements that guarantee high attorney fees and minimal payouts to the class members.

Critics also dispute the value of the private attorney general role. Most class action attorneys, they contend, are seeking lucrative financial awards rather than social justice. Moreover, class actions may interfere with the regulatory and oversight functions of the appropriate government agency. The agency may conclude that the injuries attributed to the defendant are insignificant and do not warrant prosecution. A class action substitutes the judgment of the private attorney for that of the public's elected officials.

As to the deterrence value of class actions, the critics maintain that state and federal law enforcement organizations have the ability to investigate and punish cases involving widespread small-scale fraud and offer an alternative means of addressing wrongful conduct. Private enforcement through a class action reduces the accountability of the law enforcement effort and delegates to the plaintiffs' attorney control over enforcement priorities.

As to large claim class actions, critics believe that the victims may not be fairly served. They contend that large claim cases raise concerns about the capacity of the class action format to provide individualized justice, the ability of class attorneys to effectively represent the various needs of class members, and the impact on future class members who do not, at the time of litigation, have a ripe claim (their injury is not yet apparent).

Critics argue that in these large claim cases, defendants have sought class action status as a way of limiting liability. In some cases, the parties propose a settlement before a complaint has ever been filed, suggesting the possibility of collusion between the attorneys for the two sides. Finally, defendants in mass tort class actions have an incentive to search for and negotiate with the plaintiffs' attorney for the lowest settlement amount.

Critics of class actions propose that legislation and court rules be changed to give more power to the courts to examine class action applications. Courts should carefully review the applications and deny class status to small claims cases with little social value in the adjudicating the claims. Another alternative is to sharply reduce attorney fees, which would reduce the incentive for frivolous actions.

using improper gestures, body language, and eye contact with the jury; a day later, she reversed herself. Lead defense attorney Herb Zarov said that the case might be appealed on this and other grounds, including improper jury instructions.

Legal analysts viewed the verdict as a troubling, but not fatal, development for Dow Chemical. Phase two of the trial represents the most difficult part of the case, and here scientific evidence is on the side of the defense. That evidence has not prevented a few juries from awarding large judgments. But the trend in individual suits has favored breast implant manufacturers. Dow Corning, for example, won fourteen out of nineteen cases in 1997. Moreover, the venue for the next phases of the *Spitzfaden* trial remains uncertain. The U.S. Circuit Court of Appeals was expected to rule in late 1997 on whether the case would continue to be tried in New Orleans or be joined to consolidated implant litigation against Dow Chemical and Dow Corning in Michigan.

**CROSS REFERENCES**
Mistrial; Negligence; Product Liability; Tort Law; Torts

# COMMERCE CLAUSE

The provision of the U.S. Constitution that gives Congress exclusive power over trade activities between the states and with foreign countries and Indian tribes.

## Camps Newfound/Owatonna, Inc. v. Town of Harrison

The Commerce Clause of the U.S. Constitution, Article I, Section 8, Clause 3, authorizes Congress to pass laws regulating interstate commerce. The Framers of the Constitution considered the clause a vital provision because it overcame the limitations of the Articles of Confederation, which gave each state the right to regulate commerce and trade. The thirteen states had responded to the Articles by enacting conflicting and restrictive trade regulations, in-

*A camp worker instructs junior high students on life-jacket safety.*
PHOTOEDIT

cluding taxes on goods imported from other states. Thus, the Constitution's Commerce Clause placed an important limitation on the power of the states.

The U.S. Supreme Court has recognized Congress's right to regulate interstate commerce through legislation. However, the Court has also developed a position on interstate commerce that is referred to as either "dormant" or "negative" Commerce Clause jurisprudence. This jurisprudence recognizes that the Commerce Clause curtails state power involving interstate commerce even without congressional legislation and that therefore the federal courts may strike down state laws that violate the Commerce Clause.

In *Camps Newfound/Owatonna, Inc. v. Town of Harrison*, ___U.S.___, 117 S. Ct. 1590, 137 L. Ed. 2d 852 (1997), the Supreme Court ruled that a state real estate tax violated the Commerce Clause because its exemption for property owned by charitable institutions excluded organizations operated principally for the benefit of nonresidents. Under its dormant Commerce Clause doctrine, the Court viewed the denial of a tax exemption for a nonprofit organization, based on the fact that the organization served nonresidents, as discriminatory against interstate commerce.

The case arose when Camps Newfound/Owatonna, a nonprofit corporation that operates a summer camp in Harrison, Maine, for the benefit of the Christian Science faith, protested the town's assessment of more than $20,000 in annual property taxes. Harrison officials taxed the camp on the basis of a Maine property tax

statute (Me. Rev. Stat. Ann. tit. 36, § 652 (1) (A) [Supp. 1996]) that provided a general exemption for real estate and property taxes for "benevolent and charitable institutions incorporated" in the state. The Statute stated, however, that if an institution "operated principally for the benefit of persons who are not residents of Maine," the charity could only qualify for a more limited tax benefit, and then only if the weekly charge for services did not exceed $30 per person. The camp operated by Camps Newfound/Owatonna drew 95 percent of its children from outside Maine and charged $400 per week per child. Therefore, Harrison imposed the property taxes on the camp.

The corporation camp filed suit in Maine state court, alleging that the denial of the tax exemption violated interstate commerce and must be ruled unconstitutional. Although the trial court agreed, the Maine Supreme Judicial Court reversed its decision, ruling the law constitutional (655 A.2d 876 [1995]).

The Supreme Court, on a 5–4 vote, reversed the Maine court. Justice John Paul Stevens, writing for the majority, placed great emphasis on the historical and constitutional importance of the Commerce Clause. He noted the problems the national government had under the Articles of Confederation in attempting to regulate interstate commerce and the fact that states adopted measures "fostering local interests without regard to possible prejudices to non-residents." In his view the need to correct the problem of interstate commerce led to the call for a Constitutional Convention and the writing of the Constitution. Stevens reiterated the Commerce Clause's broad grant of authority to override restrictive and conflicting commercial regulations, and the power of the federal courts to strike down state laws absent congressional legislation.

Turning to the Maine law, Stevens was unpersuaded by the town's argument that the dormant Commerce Clause was inapplicable. The town argued that because the campers were not "articles of commerce," and that the tax exemption statute did not affect interstate commerce, the Court could not invoke the Commerce Clause. Stevens concluded, however, that the camp was "unquestionably engaged in commerce," not only as purchaser of goods and services but also as a provider of goods and services similar to a hotel. He cited *Heart of Atlanta Motel, Inc. v. United States*, 379 U.S. 241, 85 S. Ct. 348, 13 L. Ed. 2d 258 (1964), which recognized that hotels are part of interstate commerce.

Though *Heart of Atlanta* dealt with racial discrimination that impeded interstate commerce, Stevens found that the Maine law was official discrimination that created "similar impediments" that limited the access of nonresidents to summer camps.

The town also argued that the dormant Commerce Clause was inapplicable because a real estate tax was at issue. The Court rejected this argument as well, finding that a tax on real property, "like any other tax, may impermissibly burden interstate commerce." Even assuming the town's argument that Congress could not impose a national real estate tax, Stevens found no basis to conclude that a state could levy taxes in a way that discriminated against interstate commerce. To permit the state to levy the tax this way "would destroy the barrier against protectionism that the Constitution provides."

Stevens pointed out that there was "no question" that a similar law that targeted profit-making entities would violate the dormant Commerce Clause. Prior case law indicated that state laws that discriminated against interstate commerce on their face are "virtually *per se* invalid." In this case, Stevens said, the Maine law expressly distinguished between entities that serve primarily interstate and intrastate clientele, "singling out camps that serve mostly in-staters for beneficial tax treatment." The tax policy penalized the "principally nonresident customers of businesses catering to a primarily interstate market." In effect, the Maine law functioned as an export tariff "that targets out-of-state customers by taxing the businesses that principally serve them." Therefore, the statute, on its face, discriminated against interstate commerce.

Stevens found no basis to create a rule to apply to tax exemptions for charitable institutions that was different from the rule for profit-making entities. Prior Court decisions applied laws regulating commerce, including federal labor and antitrust laws, to not-for-profit corporations. A nonprofit entity differs from a for-profit organization principally because it is prohibited from distributing its net earnings, if any, to individuals who exercise control over it. Stevens concluded that "nothing intrinsic to the nature of nonprofit entities prevents them from engaging in interstate commerce." Any "categorical distinction" between the two types of entities was, therefore, "wholly illusory."

The Court rejected the town's contention that the exemption statute should be viewed as an expenditure of government money designed to lessen its social service burden and to foster the societal benefits provided by charitable organizations. The town contended that, portrayed in this way, the tax exemption provision was either a legitimate discriminatory subsidy of only those charities that concentrated on local concerns, or a government "purchase" of charitable services, both of which fall within an exception to the dormant Commerce Clause. Stevens was unpersuaded by these claims, holding that there are significant differences between tax exemptions and subsidies.

Stevens acknowledged that the case, viewed by itself, did not appear to "pose any threat to the health of the national economy" but stated that the historical record suggested that "even the smallest discrimination invites significant inroads on national solidarity."

### Recent Developments

The U.S. Supreme Court altered the landscape of Commerce Clause jurisprudence in *United States v. Lopez*, 514 U.S. 549, 115 S. Ct. 1624, 131 L. Ed. 2d 626 (1995), by invalidating the Gun-Free School Zones Act of 1990 (18 U.S.C.A. § 921). This act prohibited possession of firearms within one thousand feet of school property. The case represented the first time in more than a half century that the Supreme Court scrutinized the evidence presented by Congress in justifying the exercise of its power to regulate interstate commerce.

Before the *Lopez* case, the Supreme Court had permitted Congress to regulate activity that even remotely touched upon interstate commerce, including legislation that regulated wheat grown and consumed entirely on a family farm (*Wickard v. Filburn*, 317 U.S. 111, 63 S. Ct. 82, 87 L. Ed. 122 [1942]). But the Court in *Lopez* emphasized that the Constitution does not authorize Congress to use relatively trivial impacts on interstate commerce as an excuse for broad regulation of state or private activities. At the same time, *Lopez* did not draw a bright line separating trivial impacts from more substantial impacts that Congress may regulate under the Commerce Clause.

Over the last two years, litigants have tested the boundaries of *Lopez* by bringing various actions in federal court to see how closely judges would examine congressional laws regulating local activities under the guise that they substantially affect interstate commerce. The challenged legislation has ranged from laws regulating domestic violence and abortion clinic protests, to laws regulating the environment and possession of machine guns. Federal courts took the opportunities presented by these cases to flesh out the parameters of congressional Commerce Clause power in the wake of *Lopez*.

In two cases federal courts had occasion to consider whether a law governing the possession of machine guns (18 U.S.C.A. § 922) exceeded Congress's power to regulate interstate commerce. In the first case, *United States v. Rybar*, 103 F.3d 273 (1996), the U.S. Court of Appeals for the Third Circuit upheld the legislation, ruling that federal regulation of machine guns was intended to decrease interstate commercial traffic in such weapons. The Third Circuit said that, although the federal machine gun law may not achieve its intended goal, the Constitution allows Congress to pass legislation it deems appropriate in this area without interference from the federal courts.

The federal machine gun law was also upheld in *United States v. Kirk*, 105 F.3d 997 (1997), but the U.S. Court of Appeals for the Fifth Circuit relied on a different rationale. The Fifth Circuit contrasted the federal machine gun law with the Gun-Free School Zone Act that was overturned in *Lopez*. The Gun-Free School Zone Act, the Fifth Circuit noted, attempted to regulate a small geographic area finitely circumscribed and related to education, which was a uniquely local concern. In *Kirk*, however, the Fifth Circuit chronicled the extensive history of federal firearm regulation that underscores its national character. The Fifth Circuit also stressed that the federal machine gun law not only governs the possession of machine guns but governs their manufacture and transportation as well, two activities traditionally linked to interstate commerce.

The Violence Against Women Act (VAWA) (18 U.S.C.A. § 2261 et seq.) also withstood a number of challenges to its constitutionality under the Commerce Clause in 1997. The VAWA makes it a federal crime to cross state lines with the intent to violate a protective order (an order restraining a defendant from having any contact with a specific person whom he has harassed, stalked, or otherwise threatened or injured) and then to violate it. In *Doe v. Hartz*, 970 F. Supp. 1375 (N.D. Iowa 1997), the court observed that Congress, in passing the VAWA, had made significant findings showing that gender-motivated violence has a substantial effect on interstate commerce.

Evidentiary findings were also important to the court's holding in *National Association of Home Builders of United States v. Babbitt*, 130 F.3d 1041 (D.C. Cir. 1997), a case in which the secretary of interior applied the Endangered Species Act of 1973 (ESA) (16 U.S.C.A. 1531 et seq.) to protect a species of fly found only in California. The court said that legislation enacted under the Commerce Clause may be invalidated only if there is clearly no rational basis for finding that a regulated activity affects interstate commerce. Although the ESA had been originally enacted under the Commerce Clause in 1973, the court said that the secretary of the interior made sufficient findings to support its regulatory action in this case. The findings revealed that the fly was on exhibit in at least three museums outside California, the species had been the subject of interstate trade among insect collectors before being declared endangered, and people visited California from around the world just to study the species.

Evidentiary findings will not be as important in cases where the regulated activity's effect on interstate commerce is more evident. In *United States v. Bramble*, 103 F.3d 1475 (9th Cir. 1996), a federal court of appeals upheld the Bald and Golden Eagles Protection Act (16 U.S.C.A. § 668 et seq.), without the aid of congressional findings. The court made its own findings that extinction of bald and golden eagles would substantially affect interstate commerce by foreclosing any possibility of certain commercial activities, including future commerce in these eagles, their parts, or their genetic material.

In *Terry v. Reno*, 101 F.3d 1412 (D.C. Cir. 1996), *cert. denied, Terry v. Reno*, ___U.S.___, 117 S. Ct. 2431, 138 L. Ed. 2d 193 (1997), another federal court of appeals made the same point more bluntly, ruling that Congress need not make formal findings of the substantial effect that regulated activities will have on interstate commerce when such a conclusion is clear from the nature of the activity involved. Based on this ruling, and without the benefit of detailed legislative findings, the court concluded that Congress had not exceeded its power under the Commerce Clause by enacting the Freedom of Access to Clinic Entrances Act (18 U.S.C.A. § 248), which prohibits the use of violence as a tool in preventing access to abortion clinics. Despite the lack of legislative findings on the subject, the court said it had "no doubt" that Congress understood the adverse relationship between violent and obstructive activity outside abortion clinics and the availability of reproductive services in interstate commerce.

**CROSS REFERENCES**

Interstate Commerce; Taxation

## COMMITMENT

Proceedings directing the confinement of a mentally ill or INCOMPETENT person for treatment.

### John Hinckley, Jr., Release Petitions

In 1997 presidential assailant John W. Hinckley, Jr., lost again in his ongoing legal battle to gain temporary release from a federal mental hospital. Hinckley shot and wounded President Ronald W. Reagan in 1981. He has tried unsuccessfully for ten years to be allowed briefly outside St. Elizabeth's Hospital in Washington, D.C., where he was committed following his acquittal for reasons of insanity in 1982. The U.S. District Court for the District of Columbia has repeatedly denied his petitions. In June 1997 the court again refused to grant him a monthly twelve-hour supervised pass (*United States v. Hinckley*, 967 F. Supp. 557). Six months later it denied his request to make a six-hour holiday visit with his parents (*United States v. Hinckley*, 984 F. Supp. 35). As in previous decisions, the court held that Hinckley was still dangerous.

Although Hinckley's acquittal surprised much of the legal community, his legal struggle is ordinary. In 1982 many people expected him to be convicted for trying to kill the president and wounding three others. After his acquittal, states hurried to tighten laws that permit the insanity defense. But when Hinckley began petitioning for "conditional release" from the hospital only six years later, he was merely exercising his rights under District of Columbia law. The district's law provides patients in mental hospitals with legal recourse to see the outside world again. Insanity acquittees like Hinckley may file court petitions under District of Columbia Code 1981 section 24–301(k). If successful, they are allowed to be taken off the hospital grounds for a short time and then returned.

To be successful, the petition must show that release will benefit the patient and be safe for the public. The petition is decided by the court without a jury. The law gives the court broad reviewing power to make all findings of fact and conclusions of law, while being free to consider any evidence in the patient's legal and psychiatric history and to accept or reject expert testimony. The law requires that a preponder-

*John Hinckley, Jr., attempted to assassinate President Ronald Reagan on March 31, 1981.*

AP/WIDE WORLD PHOTOS

ance of evidence favor the patient's petition. Not once in five attempts has Hinckley succeeded in gaining a release.

Hinckley's June 1997 petition made two separate requests. First, he wanted to be released into the care of his parents for twelve hours each month, with no other supervision. Second, he wanted the court to vacate its order from April 24, 1987, which requires that the hospital give two weeks' notice to the court and to the U.S. Attorney's Office prior to letting him off its grounds with supervision. The federal government filed a motion opposing the petition.

During four days of hearings in June, the court heard conflicting expert testimony about Hinckley's mental condition. Hinckley presented the diagnoses of two psychologists and two psychiatrists. They testified that he presented a very low risk of danger to himself or others, chiefly because his major mental illnesses were in remission and any recurrence of symptoms could be detected by the hospital before a scheduled release.

Opposing this view was the government's sole expert witness, Dr. Raymond F. Patterson. Although also diagnosing remission, Dr. Patterson reached a different assessment about the risks. Hinckley's behavior in the hospital was secretive, deceptive, and bore "striking similarities" to the stalking behavior that he had exhibited in the past. In particular, he had violated a hospital order to stay away from a female staff employee. Dr. Patterson testified that this resembled the patient's stalking of President Jimmy Carter, President Reagan, and the actress Jody Foster, which ultimately led to the assassination attempt on Reagan.

On June 19, 1997, the court ruled that Hinckley still presented a danger to himself or to others. Hinckley appealed. Nearly six months later, the hospital requested that Hinckley be released into his parents' custody for six hours in December for a holiday visit. It had taken steps to ensure the public's safety during the proposed supervised visit. Once again, the federal government opposed the petition. In motions, both sides contested the standard of review that the court should use. The government argued that the hospital's petition should be regarded as another request for conditional release; Hinckley contended that the request was an internal matter of patient treatment.

Declaring that this was "not an easy question," the court accepted the government's position that the controlling case law was *United States v. Ecker II*, 543 F.2d 178 (D.C. Cir. 1976). *Ecker II* established the standard of review for hospital-sponsored petitions as they relate to the court's obligations to protect the public. It said that courts have "far heavier responsibilities" when determining if patients should be allowed to leave hospital grounds. Hinckley maintained that he would be in the custody of hospital staff and therefore not be released at all, but the court rejected this argument as disingenuous. Left with the question of determining whether he presented a danger to the public, the court cited its June 1997 decision and denied the request on December 15, 1997.

## COPYRIGHT

An intangible right granted by statute to the author or originator of certain literary or artistic productions, whereby, for a limited period, the exclusive privilege is given to the person to make copies of the same for publication and sale.

### Astaire v. Best Film & Video Corp.

Though federal copyright law provides the most comprehensive system of protecting intellectual property, the states are free to enact laws that offer persons other protections. In 1984 the state of California enacted a law that restricts the commercial exploitation of the name, voice, signature, photograph, or likeness of a deceased celebrity or public figure in the marketing of goods and services (Cal. Civ. Code § 990 [1997]). The law sought to prohibit the use of a deceased celebrity's name or likeness on posters, T-shirts, porcelain plates, and other collectibles. With its enactment, the estate of the deceased celebrity gained a valuable benefit, because companies could only use a celebrity likeness by paying the estate for a license.

The scope of the statute was tested in a lawsuit filed by Robyn Astaire, the widow of the legendary dancer, singer, and actor, Fred Astaire. In *Astaire v. Best Film & Video Corp.*, 116 F.3d 1297 (1998), the Ninth Circuit Court of Appeals rejected Astaire's claim that Best Film must pay her for the use of film clips of Fred Astaire in a series of dance instructional videotapes. In so ruling, the court interpreted the statute as allowing the use of the film clips because the videotapes were exempt from the statute. In addition, the court found that even if film clips constituted an advertisement, the advertisement was for the videotapes themselves rather than for another commercial product. Under the law this use was also permitted.

The case originated in 1965, when Fred Astaire granted the Ronby Corporation an exclusive license to use his name in connection with the operation of dance studios. Astaire also granted Ronby the right to use certain pictures, photographs, and likeness of him. Astaire died in 1987. In 1989 Ronby entered into an agreement with Best film to produce a series of dance instructional videotapes using the Fred Astaire Dance Studios name and licenses. Best Film began marketing a series of five videotapes in 1989, using the phrase "Fred Astaire Franchised Dance Studios" on the videotape boxes, along with quotes from Astaire about dancing. Each of the videotapes contained an introductory sequence that showed still photographs of Astaire and ninety seconds of footage from two of his films, *Second Chorus* and *Royal Wedding*. Both films were in the public domain. After the introduction, the remainder of each videotape dealt with teaching viewers how to dance in a particular style.

Robyn Astaire sued Best Film in 1989, alleging that under section 990 of the California Civil Code, she, as the widow of Astaire, succeeded to all rights in his name, voice, signature, photograph, likeness, and persona. Astaire argued that Best Film violated her rights by using her late husband's image in the two film clips. She agreed that Ronby had legally authorized Best Film to use Astaire's name and the still photographs, so she did not challenge that part of the videotapes.

The federal district court found in Astaire's favor, but a three-judge panel of the Ninth Circuit court overturned that decision. Judge Charles E. Wiggins, writing for the majority, concluded that Best Film's use of the film clips came within either of two exceptions found in section 990(n). Clause (n)(1) allows the use of a deceased personality's name, likeness, voice, or photograph in a "play, book, magazine, newspaper, musical composition, film, radio, or television program, other than an advertisement or commercial announcement." Wiggins construed videotape to be analogous to film, thus putting the dance videotape on the same footing as a film released to theaters or television.

Wiggins concluded that a second provision of the statute, also protected Best Film. Wiggins held that under sections 990(n)(4), the film clips served as an advertisement or commercial announcement for the "videotapes themselves rather than some other product." Reviewing the legislative history of section 990, Wiggins concluded that the legislature wished to prohibit the use of deceased personalities to market other goods. For example, the use of the two film clips in a television commercial for dance shoes would be prohibited. In this case, however, the introductory section of the videotapes merely served to increase the marketability of the learn-to-dance videos that followed. Therefore, Astaire was not entitled to damages.

In a dissenting opinion, Judge Mary M. Schroeder disagreed with the majority's statutory interpretation. Schroeder concluded that the use of the Astaire film footage was an impermissible advertisement or commercial announcement. The clips were not an integral part of the instructional videos that followed. If the clips had been used in an announcement "physically separated from the rest of the video, the use of the clips would clearly not have been exempt." Using the majority's reasoning, Schroeder said, a person could "with impunity hawk a videotape on fashion for the next century by introducing it with footage of Jacqueline Kennedy."

### No Electronic Theft (NET) Act

On December 16, 1997, President Bill Clinton signed into law the No Electronic Theft (NET) Act. The NET Act substantially enhances existing federal copyright law. Aimed primarily at the rampant theft of computer soft-

*Dancer Fred Astaire's widow sued Best Film & Video Corp. for using footage of Astaire in a series of instructional videotapes.*

AP/WIDE WORLD PHOTOS

ware, it allows the prosecution of anyone who violates the copyright of materials worth more than $1,000 in a six-month period by copying, distributing, or receiving software. Congress passed the law in November 1997 after the software and entertainment industries, strongly lobbied for it, complaining of losses amounting to more than $2 billion in 1996 in the United States alone. In particular, the law closed a narrow loophole in existing federal law, which allowed criminal prosecution for copyright violation only possible if the violation resulted in financial gain. Under the NET Act, individuals face fines and jail sentences even if they do not profit financially from the violation. It was enacted over protests by scientists who feared it would hinder their research.

Lobbying on behalf of the law was fierce. Industry representatives testified in congressional hearings that copyright has not fared well in the age of the Internet. Existing federal laws did not envision the rise of a communications medium that would make the mass violation of copyright so simple. Piracy on the Internet has become commonplace for everything from computer games to high-priced business software and commercial music recordings. In testimony before the House Subcommittee on Courts and Intellectual Property, representatives from the computer and entertainment industries and the Motion Picture Association told lawmakers that such piracy robbed them of profits and threatened their existence.

*A man reads the copyright screen of an Internet bulletin board on his computer.*

JERRY MASON/PHOTO RESEARCHERS, INC.

Lobbyists pointed repeatedly to what has become known as the "*LaMacchia* loophole." This term refers to an unforeseen weakness in federal law that was exposed by the failed federal prosecution of computer hacker David LaMacchia in 1994 (*United States v. LaMacchia*, 871 F.Supp. 535). At that time a twenty-one-year-old student at the Massachusetts Institute of Technology, LaMacchia had used an electronic bulletin board to freely distribute countless commercial software programs. Although he was indicted for wire fraud under 18 U.S.C.A. § 1343 for allegedly causing software companies losses of more than $1 million, the case was dismissed, U.S. District Court Judge Richard Stearns ruled that criminal sanctions did not apply because LaMacchia had not profited from his actions.

According to the software industry, the decision paved the way for piracy of material through Web pages and other commonly used Internet sites. Software manufacturers were not only concerned about deliberate piracy by computer hackers; they wanted to stop the casual lending and copying of computer software between consumers and within offices, too. Joining them in this effort were the music and film industries, which have increasingly become partners of software companies in the production of multimedia CD-ROMs. Additionally, the music industry viewed with alarm the widespread distribution of commercial recordings by fans, which became popular over the Internet in 1997 with the development of new software technology for digitally copying songs.

In July 1997, Representative Robert Goodlatte (R-Va.) introduced the NET Act (H.R.2265) with the intent of closing the *LaMacchia* loophole. Swiftly passed by the House and subsequently approved by the Senate, the act accomplishes this by amending two key parts of federal copyright law: title 17 and title 18 of the United States Code. These laws previously defined copyright violation strictly in terms of financial gain. The NET Act broadens them to include the reproduction or distribution of one or more copies of copyrighted works and considers financial gain simply to be the possession of a copyrighted work. It defines a misdemeanor violation as occurring when the value of the copied material exceeds $1,000 over a 180-day period; a felony occurs if the value exceeds $2,500. Penalties range from a one–year jail sentence and up to $100,000 in fines for first-time offenders, to five years imprisonment and up to $250,000 in fines for repeat offenders.

A leading group of scientists opposed the legislation. The Association for Computing, an international group with 80,000 members, wrote to President Clinton asking him to veto the NET Act on the ground that it would threaten scientific research. The group feared new limits on the fair use doctrine, which permits limited use of copyrighted materials without payment of royalties to the copyright holder. In particular, the association noted that many scientific publications on the Internet quote widely from papers whose copyright is owned by scientific journals. The NET Act, it said, could hamper the free flow of such information. After lawmakers downplayed such fears and Clinton signed the law, the group said it would closely monitor how the law is applied.

The NET Act arms prosecutors with new ammunition against pirates. Congress primarily intended for prosecutors to target the owners of Web pages and other Internet sites where trafficking in copyrighted materials is conducted openly on a large scale. Although the law does not create liability for services that connect users to the Internet, analysts expect these companies to respond by shutting down access to areas online where piracy occurs.

### Quality King Distributors, Inc. v. L'Anza Research International, Inc.

U.S. producers often sell their products at high discounts in foreign countries, sometimes in hopes of building a new market and sometimes as a way of testing a product before its introduction to the U.S. market. Because of these steep discounts, U.S. distributors and retailers find it more profitable to buy these products in overseas markets than to buy them from the U.S.

producer. It is estimated that $130 billion worth of goods are bought in this "gray market" and re-imported annually for sale in the United States.

The U.S. Supreme Court, in *Quality King Distributors v. L'Anza Research International* ___U.S.___, 118 S. Ct.1125, ___L. Ed. 2d___ (1998), reversed an appellate decision that gave U.S. producers the ability to control some gray market practices through provisions of the federal Copyright Act of 1976 (17 U.S.C.A. § 101 et seq.). The Supreme Court held that copyright owners do not have the exclusive right to control the marketing of their products. Once the copyright owner sells the product, the owner loses the ability to prevent other companies from re-importing the product for sale in the United States.

L'Anza Research International, Inc., a California corporation that manufactures and sells shampoos, conditioners, and other hair care products, sued Quality King Distributors, Inc., alleging that Quality King had violated copyright law by importing L'Anza products originally sold to a company in the United Kingdom. L'Anza used the copyright law because it had copyrighted the labels that are affixed to all its hair care products. The company sells its products in the United States to domestic distributors who have agreed to resell within limited geographic areas and only to authorized retailers such as barber shops, hair salons, and professional hair care colleges. L'Anza promotes its domestic sales through extensive advertising in trade magazines and at point of sale and by providing special training to authorized retailers. It contended that its higher-priced, high-quality products did not compete well when sold at supermarkets and drug stores that carried lower-priced, lower-quality hair care products.

L'Anza also marketed its products in foreign markets, with prices to its foreign distributors 35 to 45 percent lower than the prices charged to domestic distributors. L'Anza claimed that the reason for this price disparity was that its overseas advertising and promotion was not comparable to the advertising and promotion it used in the United States. The lower prices led a United Kingdom distributor in 1992 and 1993 to sell shipments of L'Anza products to a distributor in Malta, who resold them to Quality King. Quality King then sold the products in California to unauthorized resellers, who were able to charge lower prices than those found at authorized retailers.

*Makers of some beauty products attempt to restrict their distribution to authorized retailers.*

DAVID YOUNG-WOLFF/PHOTOEDIT

The federal district court entered judgment in favor of L'Anza, and the Ninth Circuit Court of Appeals affirmed the decision (98 F.3d 1109 [1996]). The U.S. Supreme Court reversed the appellate court in a unanimous decision. Justice John Paul Stevens, writing for the Court, acknowledged that this was "an unusual copyright case because L'Anza does not claim that anyone has made unauthorized copies of its copyrighted labels." The real purpose was to "protect the integrity of its method of marketing the products to which the labels are affixed." Stevens concluded that despite the "limited creative component" found in the labels, the copyright provisions applied whether the material at issue was a book, a sound recording, or a label.

Turning to the merits of the case, Stevens held that the "first sales" doctrine applied. This doctrine, first announced *Bobbs-Merrill Co. v. Straus*, 210 U.S. 339, 28 S. Ct. 722, 52 L. Ed. 1086 (1908), and codified in the 1976 Copyright Act as section 109, gives the copyright owner the ability to control only the first sale of the product. The act states that once the product is sold, the new owner "is entitled, without the authority of the copyright owner, to sell or otherwise dispose of the possession or that copy …." Stevens concluded that other provisions of the copyright law did not override the first sales limitation and give L'Anza the right to control subsequent sales of its products. Once it sold its hair care products to the United Kingdom distributor, it lost its right under copyright law to control further distribution.

Stevens noted the problem of gray market re-importation of goods but declined to be swayed by policy arguments proffered by L'Anza

# COURTS: SHOULD COURT RECORDS BE SEALED?

Since the early 1980s, there has been a sharp increase in the number of civil cases in which the court orders the record sealed. These cases typically involve product liability and mass torts. The result is that when the parties settle their case, the public has no way of knowing the case existed, the outcome, or the specific witnesses and evidence that were produced. Legal commentators have engaged in a spirited debate concerning whether and when court records should be sealed. Proponents of sealing court records argue that it promotes the settlement of cases, thereby reducing the workload of the court. Opponents contend that sealing records violates both the First Amendment and the common law right of the public to know what the courts are doing.

IN FOCUS

Proponents of sealing court records believe that the issuance of a sealing order is sometimes an essential part of a proposed settlement. Public access to the record that had been developed up to that point could seriously impair the settlement process. Without a sealing order, parties might prefer to go to trial, electing to expose themselves to the misleading or incorrect implications that often arise from settlement in order to vindicate their innocence. This course of action would be more time-consuming and costly to the parties and the judicial system. In the end, the public would suffer, as an already overburdened court system would have to use its resources to try the case.

Supporters of sealing orders also point out that these orders offer something to all participants. The court finds the issuance of a sealing order a small price to pay for encouraging settlement. Plaintiffs' attorneys exploit the sealing order to negotiate larger settlements for their clients, while defense attorneys take advantage of the order to limit public discussion about their client's products.

Defenders of sealing orders contend that civil litigation is a dispute resolu-

tion process between private parties, in which a large number of disputes are settled without the intervention of a court. Viewed as a purely private dispute, settlement resolves the matter with much less expense to society than a full trial. Moreover, a pretrial settlement demonstrates the parties' desire to end the litigation and does not support any inferences as to the merits of the claim or the amount of damages.

Sealing orders also protect the privacy interests of individuals and corporations. Defenders of sealing orders believe that persons should not have to surrender their privacy in exchange for using the court system. Court pleadings are addressed to the court and the parties, not to other readers. Until some court action takes place, the public has no right to become involved. Defenders argue that the more removed the information becomes from the actual litigation and the more the process is distanced from judicial supervision, the more the balance tips in favor of litigant privacy.

---

and the U.S. government, stating that whether the Court thought "it would be wise policy to provide statutory protection for such price discrimination is not a matter that is relevant to our duty to interpret the text of the Copyright Act."

**CROSS REFERENCES**
Internet

# CREDIT UNION

A CORPORATION formed under special statutory provisions to further thrift among its members while providing CREDIT for them at more favorable rates of INTEREST than those offered by other lending institutions. A credit union is a COOPERATIVE association that utilizes funds deposited by a small group of people who are its sole borrowers and beneficiaries. It is ordinarily subject to regula-

tions by state banking boards or commissions. When formed pursuant to the Federal Credit Union Act (12 U.S.C.A. § 1751 et seq. [1934]), credit unions are chartered and regulated by the NATIONAL CREDIT UNION ADMINISTRATION.

## National Credit Union Administration v. First National Bank & Trust Co.

The competition between banks and credit unions has intensified since the 1980s. Credit unions were created after the bank failures of the Great Depression of the 1930s. Organized as tax-exempt cooperatives, credit unions encouraged savings and provided an alternative to banks, which refused to lend small amounts of money without security. By 1997 credit unions had become a major force in the financial industry, boasting thirty-two million members in 3,600 organizations that hold $376 billion in loans, deposits, and member shares.

Those who support the use of sealing orders also note that the disclosure of information can have an adverse effect on defendants in certain circumstances. For example, if information gets out that a large number of lawsuits has been filed and settled, the defendant will likely be exposed to adverse publicity that will make the selection of untainted juries difficult in future cases involving the same product. This exposure, the defenders say, will also lead to sharp declines in stock prices, even though the information distributed is false or misleading. Sealing orders help avoid this situation.

Opponents of sealing orders view civil litigation as a public, rather than a private process, at least when the complaint is filed with the court. Once filed, the case should be a matter of public record, and the public should have the right to attend any proceedings and read all relevant court documents that are filed. When a sealing order is filed, the case is simply listed on the docket sheet with an entry such as "Sealed v. Sealed." Though the parties may both get what they want, a public court system has been used to solve a private dispute without giving the public information about the outcome.

Critics believe that judges should have uniform standards concerning when sealing a court record is permitted. Moreover, the critics think a court must err on the side of openness, sealing records only in circumstances when evidence is strong that public disclosure would be very damaging to a party.

As to the contention that sealing orders promote judicial economy, critics lament that modern judicial case management has placed too much emphasis on quickly disposing of civil cases. Faced with granting a request for a sealing order that facilitates a settlement or denying the request, which might lead to an extended trial, judges usually sign the sealing order. This dynamic encourages a judge to issue sealing orders as a matter of course, without taking the time to assess whether there is good cause to issue the order.

Critics base their opposition to sealing orders on the First Amendment and the common law right of access to the court and court records. The Framers of the Constitution did not want to allow secret court proceedings, as had existed in England, because secrecy encouraged the abuse of authority and trampled on an individual's basic

human rights. Though the Framers concerned themselves with criminal law, civil law should be held to the same principles.

Opponents argue that a total sealing of the record makes the judicial system mysterious and undercuts its legitimacy. Secrecy also diminishes the public's understanding of the legal process and undermines the public's belief in the overall fairness of the judicial system. The public sees a double standard of justice, where rich individuals and large corporations and organizations obtain sealing orders, while the poor must see all their matters made public.

Finally, opponents believe that public health and safety can be injured by total sealing orders. A corporation can avoid public disclosure of a defective and dangerous product by quietly paying individual victims large sums of money in return for a sealing order that prevents future victims from knowing about the defect. While courts have the inherent authority to unseal records, such authority is rarely used. Therefore, opponents want the courts held to a standard that makes the total sealing of court records exceptional, rather than commonplace.

The banking industry, which saw credit unions become a strong competitor for consumer loans and deposits, contended that the growth of federal credit unions was due to a 1982 ruling by the National Credit Union Administration (NCUA) that misinterpreted federal law. The banking industry filed suit in 1990, challenging the NCUA's interpretation of section 109 of the Federal Credit Union Act (FCUA) (12 U.S.C.A. § 1759). The U.S. Supreme Court, in *National Credit Union Administration v. First National Bank & Trust Co.*, No. 96-843, 118 S. Ct. 927, ___ L. Ed. 2d___ (1998), agreed with the banks, ruling that the NCUA had exceeded its authority in changing credit union membership rules. The decision sent shock waves through the credit union industry because it was unclear whether the ruling would require credit unions to force members out of their organizations.

Section 109 provides that federal credit union membership "shall be limited to groups having a common bond of occupation or association, or to groups within a well-defined neighborhood community, or rural district." Until 1982 credit unions could only sign up employees of a specific company. For example, the AT&T Family Federal Credit Union was limited to AT&T employees and their families. Then the NCUA changed the ground rules, reversing its long-standing policy in order to permit federal credit unions to be composed of multiple unrelated employer groups. It interpreted the "common bond" requirement of section 109 to apply only to each employer group in a multiple-group credit union, rather than to every member of that credit union. The AT&T credit union soon took advantage of this change in policy, and by 1997 it had 110,000 members in all 50 states, including employees of a Coca-Cola bottler, a television station, an auto supply chain, an apparel firm, the Black and Decker Corporation, Duke Power Company, and the American Tobacco Company. Only 35 percent of its members worked for AT&T.

The banks filed their lawsuit by invoking the judicial review provisions of the Administrative Procedure Act (APA) (5 U.S.C.A. § 702), which sets standards for the activities and rulemaking of all federal regulatory agencies. They claimed that the NCUA's interpretation of section 109 was contrary to law because members of credit unions must share a common bond of occupation. The federal district court dismissed the complaint because the banks did not have standing under the APA. To have standing, a plaintiff must show that the defendant has invaded some personal legal interest. It is not enough that a plaintiff is merely interested as a member of the general public in the resolution of the dispute. The plaintiff must have a personal stake in the outcome of the controversy. In the case of the APA, the Supreme Court has held that a plaintiff must be within "the zone of interest" that the relevant law was intended to protect. The district court ruled that the banks were not within the zone of interest because the Federal Credit Union Act was not intended to protect banks or foster competition (772 F. Supp 609 [D.C. 1991]). The Court of Appeals for the District of Columbia reversed (988 F.2d 1272 [1992]). On remand the district court considered the merits of the case but upheld the NCUA's interpretation (863 F. Supp. 9 [D.C. 1994]), and again the Court of Appeals for the District of Columbia reversed (90 F.3d 525 [1996]). The appellate court concluded that because the concept of a "common bond" is implicit in the term "group," the term "common

bond" would be surplus language if it applied only to the members of each constituent "group" in a multiple-group federal credit union.

The Clinton administration appealed the ruling to the Supreme Court. The Court, on a 5–4 vote, upheld the appellate court. Justice Clarence Thomas, writing for the majority, addressed both the standing issue and the issue of whether section 109 permitted multiple-group credit unions.

Thomas concluded that the banks had standing to bring the legal challenge. The banks had an interest in limiting the markets that federal credit unions can serve. Moreover, that interest "is arguably within the zone of interests that can be protected by section 109." Thomas admitted that prior Supreme Court cases "have not stated a clear rule for determining when a plaintiff's interest" is within the zone of interests protected by statute. Nevertheless, he rejected the government's contention that there must be a "congressional intent to benefit the would-be plaintiff." It was enough for the plaintiff (the banks) to show that their interests were affected by the agency action to meet the standing requirement.

Turning to the merits of the case, Thomas applied the analysis given in *Chevron U.S.A. Inc. v. Natural Resources Defense Council, Inc.*, 467 U.S. 837, 104 S. Ct. 2778, 81 L. Ed. 2d 694 (1984). Under that analysis, the court first asks whether Congress has "directly spoken to the precise question at issue. If the intent of Congress is clear, that is the end of the matter; for the court, as well as the agency, must give effect to the unambiguously expressed intent of Congress." If the court determines that Congress has not directly spoken to the precise question at issue, the court then asks whether the agency's interpretation is reasonable. In this case Thomas concluded that because Congress had made it clear that "the same common bond of occupation must unite each member of an occupationally defined federal credit union, we hold that the NCUA's contrary interpretation is impermissible under the first step of *Chevron*."

Thomas advanced three reasons for this conclusion. First, the Supreme Court agreed with the appeals court that the NCUA's interpretation of the phrase "common bond" made it surplus usage when applied to federal credit unions with multiple unrelated employer groups, because each "group" in such a credit union already had its own "common bond." The NCUA interpretation limited federal credit union membership to occupational groups, but that was not what the statute provided.

NCUA's interpretation also violated the established canon of construction (judicial rules of statutory interpretation) that "similar language contained within the same section of the statute must be accorded a consistent meaning." In this case the second clause of section 109 limits membership "to groups within a well-defined neighborhood, community, or rural district." The NCUA has never read this geographic limitation to allow "a credit union to be composed of members from an unlimited number of unrelated geographic units" because to do so would render the geographic limitation "meaningless." Therefore, Thomas held that "we must interpret the occupational limitation in the same way."

Finally, Thomas concluded that, by its terms, section 109 requires that membership in federal credit unions "shall be limited." The NCUA's interpretation of the common bond requirement "has the potential to read these words out of the statute entirely." Under the current interpretation, Thomas believed that it would be permissible to charter a "conglomerate credit union whose members included the employees of every company in the United States." Section 109 cannot permit "such a limitless result." Therefore, under the *Chevron* analysis, the NCUA's interpretation of section 109 was "contrary to the unambiguously expressed intent of Congress and is thus impermissible."

Justice Sandra Day O'Connor, in a dissenting opinion, argued that the Court had abandoned its prior case precedents on the standing issue. She contended that the Court's new rule would make it very easy to file similar lawsuits challenging agency decisions. Requiring the banks simply to have an interest in enforcing the law "amounts to hardly any test at all." She and the other dissenters concluded that the banks should not have been allowed to sue.

In the wake of the decision, Congress began reviewing ways of dealing with the issue. Credit unions announced efforts to change the law to permit the membership rules that had been struck down, while Congress sought to ensure that no member of a credit union would have to leave it because of the Court's decision.

**CROSS REFERENCES**
Banks and Banking; Standing

# CRIMINAL LAW

A body of rules and statutes that defines conduct prohibited by the government because it threatens and harms public safety and welfare and that establishes punishment to be imposed for the commission of such acts.

### Brogan v. United States

In *Brogan v. United States*, ___U.S.___, 118 S. Ct. 805, ___L. Ed. 2d___ (1998), the U.S. Supreme Court overturned an interpretation of federal criminal law that had existed since the 1930s. The Court ruled that a federal statute imposing criminal liability for making false statements to federal investigators does not include an exception for a false statement that consists of mere denial of wrongdoing. The Court struck down the "exculpatory no" exception that had been affirmed by many of the circuit courts of appeals.

James Brogan was a union officer who accepted cash payment from a real estate company whose employees were represented by the union. In 1993 federal agents from the Department of Labor and the Internal Revenue Service went to Brogan's home and explained that they were seeking his cooperation in an investigation of the real estate company and various individuals. The agents asked Brogan if he would answer some questions and he agreed. When the agents asked Brogan whether he had accepted any cash or gifts from the real estate company when he was a union officer, Brogan answered "no." He was then told that a search of the real estate company's headquarters had produced company records showing that he had received cash and gifts. In addition, the agents warned him that lying to federal agents in the course of an investigation is a crime. Brogan did not change his answers and the interview ended.

Brogan was indicted for accepting unlawful cash payments from an employer and for making a false statement within the jurisdiction of a federal agency in violation of federal law (18 U.S.C.A. § 1001). He was tried and found guilty. On appeal, Brogan argued that his denial to the agents was an "exculpatory no," which a number of circuit courts of appeals had ruled did not violate the statute. The U.S. Court of Appeals for the Second Circuit, which did not endorse the exculpatory no doctrine, affirmed his conviction (96 F.3d 35 [1996]). Brogan then appealed to the Supreme Court.

The Supreme Court affirmed the decision. Justice Antonin Scalia, writing for the majority, noted that 18 U.S.C.A. § 1001 covers any false statement. The word "no" in response to a question makes a "statement." Brogan admitted that under a literal reading of the statute he was guilty, yet he contended that the "exculpatory no" doctrine adopted by many of the circuits exempted him from the statute. The central feature of the doctrine is that "a simple denial of guilt does not come within the statute."

Brogan argued that the doctrine was based on two premises: that the statute criminalizes only those statements to government investigators that "pervert governmental functions," and that simple denials of guilt to government investigators do not pervert governmental functions. Scalia rejected both premises. He reasoned that the purpose of an investigation is to uncover the truth and that any falsehood pertinent to the investigation perverts the function. A simple "no" is as damaging as an elaborate false statement in the conduct of an official investigation.

Scalia also rejected Brogan's contention that the exculpatory no doctrine is inspired by the Fifth Amendment. Brogan argued that a literal reading of section 1001 violated the spirit of the amendment because it places a "cornered suspect" in the "cruel trilemma" of admitting guilt, remaining silent, or falsely denying guilt. Scalia found no merit in this argument, because the trilemma "is wholly of the guilty suspect's own making, of course." To validate the exculpatory no doctrine, the Court would have to make the right to remain silent "a cruelty."

Scalia rejected the idea, concluding that "we are not disposed to write into our law this species of compassion inflation."

Brogan contended that silence was an "illusory" option because a suspect may fear that his silence will be used against him later, or may not even know that silence is an option. Scalia found these arguments uncompelling. It is well established that the fact that a person's silence can be used against him "does not exert a form of pressure that exonerates an otherwise unlawful lie." As to the possibility that a person may be unaware of his right to remain silent, Scalia found it unlikely: "In the modern age of frequently dramatized 'Miranda' warnings, that is implausible."

The Court also rejected Brogan's argument that the exculpatory no doctrine is necessary to eliminate the risk that the statute will be abused by prosecutors, who will punish the denial of wrongdoing more severely than the wrongdoing itself. Scalia concluded that it was beyond the authority of the Court to limit the reach of the statute. Moreover, Scalia thought that clever prosecutors could avoid the doctrine, because "it is easy enough for an interrogator to press the liar from the initial simple denial to a more detailed fabrication that would not qualify for the exemption."

Scalia wrote that courts may not "create their own limitations on legislation, no matter how alluring the policy arguments for doing so, and no matter how widely the blame may be spread." Because the plain language of section 1001 made no exception for an exculpatory no, the Court could not create one.

In a concurring opinion, Justice Ruth Bader Ginsburg agreed that the Court had no authority to create such a doctrine but suggested that Congress might wish to revise the statute. She wished "to call attention to the extraordinary authority Congress, perhaps unwittingly, has conferred to prosecutors to manufacture crimes." Moreover, Ginsburg concluded that the doctrine was "far removed" from the problems Congress originally sought to address.

In a dissenting opinion, Justice John Paul Stevens agreed with Ginsburg that the application of section 1001 went beyond the original intent of Congress. However, Stevens thought that the Court should have upheld the doctrine because it had been a "well-settled interpretation of that statute." He pointed out that the Court had in prior decisions concluded that "the literal text of a criminal statute is broader than the coverage intended by Congress."

## United States v. Lanier

One of the cardinal rules of criminal law is that a criminal statute must adequately describe the offensive conduct it seeks to prohibit, so that persons know that behavior is proscribed. This fair warning requirement has been the subject of much analysis by the courts. Justice Oliver Wendell Holmes, Jr., described the requirement as "fair warning ... in language that the common world will understand, of what the law intends to do if a certain line is passed. To make the warning fair, so far as possible the line should be clear" (*McBoyle v. United States*, 283 U.S. 25, 51 S. Ct. 340, 75 L. Ed. 816 [1931]).

The U.S. Supreme Court, in *United States v. Lanier*, ___U.S.___, 117 S. Ct. 1219, 139 L. Ed. 2d 432 (1997), had to determine whether a federal criminal civil rights statute gave fair warning to a judge charged with sexual assault. The Sixth Circuit Court of Appeals had ruled that fair warning was lacking, but the Supreme Court reversed, deciding that the appeals court had applied incorrect standards in determining whether the fair warning requirement was satisfied.

The case arose out of the conduct of David W. Lanier, formerly a trial court judge for two rural counties in western Tennessee. From 1989 to 1991, while Lanier was a judge, he sexually assaulted five women in his judicial chambers. Two of the assaults were against a woman whose divorce case had come before Lanier. The custody of the woman's daughter remained subject to Lanier's jurisdiction. When the woman applied for a secretarial job at Lanier's courthouse, Lanier interviewed her, suggested he might reexamine the issue of her daughter's custody and then sexually assaulted her. Several weeks later he talked the woman into returning to the courthouse to discuss a job and again sexually assaulted her. On five other occasions he sexually assaulted four other women, all of whom worked in the local criminal justice system.

Lanier was charged with eleven violations of 18 U.S.C.A. § 242, a federal statute that makes it criminal to act willfully and under color of state law to deprive a person of rights protected by the Constitution or laws of the United States. The indictment alleged that he had violated section 242 by depriving the women of their "right not to be deprived of liberty without due process of law, including the right to be free from willful sexual assault."

Prior to trial, Lanier moved to dismiss the charges on the ground that section 242 is void for vagueness. The district court denied the motion and the case went to trial. The jury returned verdicts of guilty on seven counts and not guilty on three counts. One count was dismissed at trial. Lanier was sentenced to consecutive maximum terms on each count, totaling twenty-five years.

Lanier appealed his convictions to the Sixth Circuit Court of Appeals. After a three-judge panel of the court affirmed the convictions, the full court vacated that decision and reheard the case en banc (all members of the Sixth Circuit participated). On rehearing, the court set aside Lanier's convictions for "lack of any notice to the public that this ambiguous criminal statute includes simple or sexual assault crimes within its coverage" (43 F. 3d 1033 [1995]). The court went on to hold that criminal liability may be imposed under section 242 only if the constitutional right said to have been violated is first identified in a decision of the Supreme Court and only when the right has been held to apply in "a factual situation fundamentally similar to the one at bar." In Lanier's case there was no Supreme Court decision identifying sexual assault as protected under section 242 in a situation "fundamentally similar" to the former judge's. Therefore, the Sixth Circuit reversed the conviction and ordered the trial court to dismiss the indictment.

On appeal to the Supreme Court, the Court rejected the Sixth Circuit's interpretation of section 242 and the fair warning requirement, setting its own standard for determining whether particular conduct falls within the range of criminal liability under section 242. Justice David H. Souter, writing for a unanimous Court, noted that the general language of section 242 incorporates constitutional law by reference. The courts have incorporated many constitutional guarantees, yet many of these references do not "delineate the range of forbidden conduct with particularity." Therefore, Souter said, the question was whether Lanier received fair warning that his sexual assaults violated section 242.

Souter pointed out that there are three related issues concerning the fair warning requirement. First, the vagueness doctrine prohibits enforcement of a law that forbids or requires the doing of an act in terms so vague that persons of common intelligence would guess at its meaning and differ as to its application. Second, the canon of strict construction (how a court reads a law) of criminal statutes, known as the rule of lenity, ensures fair warning by resolving ambiguity in a criminal statute so that it applies only to conduct clearly covered. Third, due process allows a court to supply a "judicial gloss on an otherwise uncertain statute," but the court may not apply a "novel construction of a criminal statute to conduct that neither the statute nor any prior judicial decision has fairly disclosed to be within its scope." In all three cases, the "touchstone is whether the statute, either standing alone or as construed, made it reasonably clear at the relevant time that the defendant's conduct was criminal."

Souter cited *Screws v. United States*, 325 U.S. 91, 65 S. Ct. 1031, 89 L. Ed. 1495 (1945), as controlling precedent in the case. The Court in *Screws* limited the coverage of section 242 to rights fairly warned of, having been made specific by the time of the charged conduct. Souter found nothing in *Screws* or later cases that justified the Sixth Circuit's conclusion that the rights had to be declared by the Supreme Court and then only when the Court had applied its ruling in a case "fundamentally similar" to the case being prosecuted. There was no need, in Souter's view, to require "the extreme level of factual specificity" envisioned by the Sixth Circuit as necessary to give fair warning.

Souter rejected the idea that only Supreme Court decisions could provide the required warning. The *Screws* decision referred in general terms to rights made specific by "decisions interpreting" the Constitution. Souter could find no later case that confined interpretive decisions to Supreme Court opinions, pointing to the Court's use of courts of appeal decisions on whether a right was clearly established under section 242.

The Court also rejected the "fundamentally similar" factual situation requirement of the Sixth Circuit. Souter found that the Court had upheld section 242 convictions "despite notable factual distinctions between the precedents relied on and the cases then before the Court, so long as the prior decisions gave reasonable warning that the conduct then at issue violated constitutional rights." In addition, Souter saw the Sixth Circuit requirement as impractical, leading "trial judges to demand a high degree of certainty at once unnecessarily high and likely to beget much wrangling." It is enough, Souter concluded, to rely on whether the prohibited conduct has been "clearly established."

Souter found that "general statements of the law are not inherently incapable of giving fair and clear warning." Criminal liability under section 242 may be imposed for deprivation of a constitutional right only if in the light of pre-existing law the unlawfulness under the Constitution is apparent. Souter concluded that where the unlawfulness is apparent, "the constitutional requirement of fair warning is satisfied."

The Supreme Court remanded the case to the court of appeals for further consideration. In August 1997, before the appeals court had had a chance to reconsider, Lanier fled the country. He was apprehended two months later in Mexico. In addition to the twenty-two years that remain on his sentence of twenty-five years, he could face an additional five years for fleeing from justice.

## DISABLED PERSONS

Persons who have a physical or mental impairment that substantially limits one or more major life activities. Some laws also include in their definition of disabled persons those people who have a record of or are regarded as having such an impairment.

### Casey Martin Sues PGA

In *Martin v. PGA Tour* a disabled golfer became the first professional athlete to sue for the right to play a competitive sport. Casey Martin, who suffers from a birth defect in one leg, won the right to ride in a motorized golf cart on the Professional Golfers Association (PGA) tour. The PGA bans the use of carts in tournaments, and it vigorously opposed making an exception for Martin. But he successfully sued under the Americans with Disabilities Act of 1990 (ADA), a federal law enacted to prevent discrimination against disabled persons in public accommodations (42 U.S.C.A. § 12100 et seq.). Held in January 1998, the trial featured arguments about the nature of competition in professional golf, the power of courts to change the rules of professional sports, and the rights of the disabled. Legal observers predicted that Martin's groundbreaking victory could open the door to similar lawsuits.

Martin was born with a rare disease known as Klippel-Trenaunay-Weber Syndrome. It curtails blood circulation in his right leg, which is half the size of his other leg. The condition causes him substantial pain when walking or even standing for long periods of time; he testified that his leg often feels as if it were about to explode. Nonetheless, he overcame the disability and became a successful golfer during college, traveling golf courses in a motorized cart. In 1997, at the age of twenty-five, he qualified for the PGA Tour—the highest level of professional golf, with an annual $90 million in prize money awarded over forty-two events. PGA rules allowed him to use a cart during the qualifying rounds (known as the qualifying school) but forbade him from doing so in the tournament itself. When tour officials denied Martin's request to change the rules, he brought suit under the ADA.

The lawsuit faced two hurdles. First, Martin had to prove that a professional golf tournament came under the ADA's scope. The ADA was specifically designed to make public venues accessible to persons with disabilities. It applies broadly to public accommodations—those places such as hotels, restaurants, theaters, and stores that are open to the public—but only in limited ways to private institutions. Second, Martin had to prove that the application of the ADA would not have far-reaching effects on the golf tour itself. This hurdle had to do with a limitation that Congress built into the law as a safeguard: in any use of the ADA, the courts must not fundamentally alter the nature of the institution to which it is applied.

The first part of the case chiefly concerned the tour's status as a legal entity. Martha Walters, one of Martin's attorneys, made three arguments. First, conceding that the PGA was a private entity, she argued that it operates a place of public accommodation—a golf course, which is specifically listed in the law (42 U.S.C.A.

§ 12182). Second, she argued that the PGA was subject to the law because it offered examinations related to certification, as specified under 42 U.S.C.A. § 12189. Third, she contended that the PGA was an employer as defined under 42 U.S.C.A. § 12111(5) and therefore forbidden to discriminate in hiring. In reply, PGA attorney William Maledon asserted that the tour was a private nonprofit group exempt from the ADA under 42 U.S.C.A. § 12187. He moved for summary judgment asking the court to dismiss the case because there were no material facts in dispute and his client was entitled to prevail according to law.

Both sides hotly contested the issue of whether Martin's use of a golf cart would fundamentally alter the nature of the tournament. Martin's attorneys argued that golf essentially involved swinging a club to sink balls in a hole; walking was not important to this feat. The PGA countered with testimony by golfing champions Ken Venturi, Arnold Palmer, and Jack Nicklaus, who said walking caused fatigue and that a cart gives a golfer an advantage.

There were emotional moments in the trial. Over defense objections, Judge Thomas W. Coffin allowed the introduction of videotaped testimony in which Martin exposed his malformed leg, causing gasps in the packed courtroom. In a terse statement, Maledon cautioned Coffin that the judge's views of walking on a golf course were irrelevant because the ADA forbids fundamental changes to a defendant's program. Maledon said, "You don't get to make the policy decisions."

Before deciding the case, Coffin had issued a temporary order that permitted Martin to ride in a cart. In January 1998, Martin won the Nike Tour's Lakeland Classic and, as a result, landed an endorsement contract with the athletic goods manufacturer.

On January 30, 1998, Martin also won the first round of his lawsuit. Coffin ruled that the PGA Tour was a public accommodation subject to the ADA's antidiscrimination provisions (*Martin v. PGA Tour*, 984 F. Supp. 1320 [D. O.]). He rejected the PGA's claim that it only offered public accommodation on the edges of the golf course, where spectators watch, but not on the actual fairways and greens, where professionals golf. Calling the argument flawed, Coffin dismissed the notion that places of public accommodation have "zones" where the law applies and those where it does not apply. He scoffed at the PGA's example of a professional baseball stadium, which, it had argued, contained public areas subject to the law—the bleachers where fans sit—and private areas not subject to the law—the dugout where players sit).

"What about a disabled manager of a team?" wrote Coffin, rhetorically. "May the St. Louis Cardinals refuse to construct a wheelchair ramp to the visitor's dugout to accommodate a disabled manager of the Chicago Cubs simply because spectators cannot go into the dugout?" He rejected the defense motion for summary judgment but did not rule on whether the PGA was an employer.

On February 11, Coffin ordered the PGA to lift its ban. Walking, he ruled in an unpublished opinion, was not significantly taxing to golfers; instead, it was as natural as breathing. But because of his disability, Martin experienced much greater fatigue from walking than did the other golfers. Therefore, his use of a cart would not fundamentally alter the tour by giving him an advantage. Notably, the decision applied only to Martin; the judge did not order the PGA to change its rules.

The PGA appealed the case, but it decided against asking for an expedited appeal, thereby giving Martin some two years of professional golfing before returning to court.

Some legal analysts believe that the decision could lead to similar lawsuits. By broadly defining public accommodations, Coffin provided a precedent for viewing professional sports in this context. His emphasis on evaluating ADA arguments on a case-by-case basis offered hope to other disabled athletes.

**CROSS REFERENCES**
Disabled Persons; Discrimination

# DOUBLE JEOPARDY

A second prosecution for the same offense after ACQUITTAL or CONVICTION or multiple punishments for same offense. The evil sought to be avoided by prohibiting double jeopardy is double trial and double conviction, not necessarily double punishment.

### Hudson v. United States

The Fifth Amendment's Double Jeopardy Clause prohibits the government from imposing multiple criminal punishments for the same offense. The Supreme Court has had to consider, however, whether additional sanctions may be imposed that are not technically "criminal," but which are clearly punishment. The Supreme Court, in *Hudson v. United States*, ___U.S.___, 118 S.Ct. 488, 139 L. Ed. 2d 450 (1997), ruled that the government could impose both civil and criminal sanctions on persons without violating double jeopardy. In doing so, the Court overruled its own precedent, one that the current Court believed had blurred the analysis of double jeopardy claims.

John Hudson was the chairman and controlling shareholder of two small Oklahoma banks. Hudson and two of his bank associates were found by federal bank regulators to have used their bank positions to arrange a series of loans to third parties, in violation of various federal banking statutes and regulations. While the loans were nominally made to third parties, they were in reality made to Hudson to enable him to redeem bank stock that he had pledged as collateral on defaulted loans.

The federal Office of Comptroller of the Currency (OCC) issued a "Notice of Assessment of Civil Money Penalty" to Hudson and his associates. The OCC alleged that the loans were unlawfully made to Hudson and that the illegal loans resulted in losses to the banks of almost $900,000 and contributed to the failure of the banks. The OCC sought substantial monetary penalties. The OCC also issued a "Notice of Intention to Prohibit Further Participation" against the three men, with the intent of barring them from participating in any "insured depository institution." Hudson and his associates negotiated a stipulated settlement, agreeing to pay substantially reduced monetary penalties and not to participate in any banking institution without written authorization of the OCC and all other relevant regulatory agencies.

Three years later, Hudson and his associates were charged in a 22-count indictment with conspiracy, misapplication of bank funds, and making false bank entries. The violations were based on the same lending transactions that formed the basis of the OCC administrative actions. The three defendants moved to dismiss the indictment on double jeopardy grounds. The district dismissed the charges, but the Tenth Circuit Court of Appeals reversed them (92 F. 3d 1026 [1996]). The Court of Appeals used the test for double jeopardy found in *United States v. HalperHalper, United States v.*, 490 U.S. 435, 109 S. Ct. 1892, 104 L. Ed. 2d 487 (1989), to reach its decision.

On appeal, the Supreme Court affirmed the decision but did so on different grounds. It announced it was disavowing the test found in *Halper*. Chief Justice William H. Rehnquist, writing for the majority, stated that the Double Jeopardy Clause "protects only against the imposition of multiple criminal punishments for the same offense." In deciding whether a particular punishment was criminal or civil, the Court must first look to the statute to determine whether the legislature indicated a preference for "one label or the other." Even if the legislature indicated an intention to establish a civil penalty, the Court may inquire as to whether the statute was so punitive in purpose or effect as to transform a civil remedy into a criminal penalty.

In determining whether a penalty is criminal in nature, the Court has looked at various "guideposts," including whether the penalty has historically been regarded as a punishment, whether its aims will "promote the traditional aims of punishment—retribution and deterrence," whether the behavior to which it applies is already a crime, and whether "it appears excessive in relation to the alternative purpose assigned." Justice Rehnquist emphasized, however, that "only the clearest proof" will allow the Court to override legislative intent and change a civil remedy into a criminal remedy.

Turning to *Halper*, Justice Rehnquist noted that in this decision the Court for the first time applied the Double Jeopardy Clause to a sanction without first deciding whether it was criminal in nature. *Halper* announced that the imposition of "punishment" of any type was subject to double jeopardy constraints. Whether a sanction constituted "punishment" depended primarily on whether it served the traditional goals of punishment, namely retribution and deterrence. Any sanction that was so "overwhelmingly disproportionate" to the injury caused that it did not solely serve a remedial purpose of compensating the government for its loss, must serve either "retributive or deterrent purposes."

Justice Rehnquist concluded that *Halper* had departed from traditional double jeopardy doctrine in two ways. First, *Halper* had bypassed the threshold question of "whether the successive punishment at issue is a 'criminal' punishment." Second, it had assessed the character of the actual sanction imposed rather than evaluating the statute on its face to determine whether it provided for what amounted to a criminal sanction. Because of these deviations, Rehnquist stated that Halper was "ill-considered" and "unworkable." Since *Halper*, the Court had decided that all civil penalties have some deterrent effect. If a sanction must be "solely" remedial to avoid "implicating the Double Jeopardy Clause, then no civil penalties are beyond the scope of the clause."

In light of these problems, the Court discarded the *Halper* precedent. Justice Rehnquist noted that other constitutional provisions addressed the concerns found in *Halper*. The Due Process and Equal Protection Clauses protect individuals from "sanctions which are downright irrational." In addition, the Eighth Amendment protects against excessive civil fines, including forfeitures.

Having removed *Halper* from the analysis, Justice Rehnquist applied traditional double jeopardy principles to the facts of the case. He concluded that the criminal prosecution of Hudson and his associates did not violate the Double Jeopardy Clause. It was clear that Congress intended the money penalties and debarment sanctions to be civil in nature. There was little evidence to suggest the penalties were so punitive as to make them criminal despite congressional intent.

In addition, the sanction that prohibited the defendants from participating in the banking industry did not approach the punishment of imprisonment. Justice Rehnquist concluded that while the penalties may serve to deter others from similar conduct, deterrence may serve civil as well as criminal goals. The sanctions in this case also "serve to promote the stability of the banking industry." To adopt the defendant's position that the civil penalties were in fact criminal "would severely undermine the Government's ability to engage in effective regulation of institutions such as banks." Therefore, the Double Jeopardy Clause was not implicated and the three defendants could be tried on the pending criminal charges.

In a concurring opinion, Justice John Paul Stevens agreed that the prosecution of the banking officials was not prohibited by the Double Jeopardy Clause. Stevens did object to the Court's abandonment of *Halper*, arguing that neither the disposition of the case nor the Court of Appeals' opinion required the Court to overturn a precedent that was contained in a unanimous opinion.

Stevens contended that "this is an extremely easy case" to decide. He pointed to the holding in *Blockburger v. United States*, 284 U.S. 299, 52 S. Ct. 180, 76 L. Ed. 2d 306 (1932), which stated that the Double Jeopardy Clause is not implicated simply because a criminal charge involves "essentially the same conduct" for which a defendant has previously been punished. Unless a second proceeding involves the "same offense" as the first, there is no double jeopardy. In this case, the two proceedings involved different offenses. The civil and criminal statutes contained different elements that required different types of proof. Therefore, under *Blockburger*, there was no double jeopardy.

**CROSS REFERENCES**
Banks and Banking; Conspiracy; Fifth Amendment

## DRUGS AND NARCOTICS

*Drugs* are articles intended for use in the diagnosis, cure, mitigation, treatment, or prevention of disease in humans or animals, and any articles other than food intended to affect the mental or body function of humans or animals. *Narcotics* are any drugs that dull the senses and commonly become addictive after prolonged use.

### Controlled Substance Tax

The U.S. Court of Appeals for the Fourth Circuit ordered North Carolina to give defendants all the safeguards of a criminal trial when assessing its so-called Controlled Substance Tax, which was intended to tax drug dealers (N.C. Gen. Stat. §§ 105-113.105 through 105-113.113). The appeals court ruled that the tax was actually a criminal penalty, and, as such, could not be assessed like a normal tax.

In the 1990s, North Carolina enacted its Controlled Substance Tax as a measure in the so-called "war on drugs." Federal law, as well as laws in every state, makes it a crime to possess or sell illegal drugs. The Controlled Substance Tax supplemented these laws by imposing a special excise tax on illegal drug dealing: if dealers possessed a sufficient quantity of a controlled substance, they were required to declare the amount and pay taxes on it. Following this action, the state would send stamps to the dealers, who would affix them to the drugs before sale. Not surprisingly, no one came forward to pay the tax. Funds collected by the state—a reported $26 million between 1990 and 1994—came only following the arrest of drug dealers.

On March 1, 1993, state and federal law enforcement agents seized 970 grams of cocaine worth $25,000 at the residence of David Lynn, Jr., in Reidsville, North Carolina. One day later,

*U.S. Customs seized 3.3 tons of cocaine in one raid.*

JON LEVY/GAMMA LIAISON

North Carolina assessed Lynn for failure to pay the state drug tax. The state Department of Revenue ruled that he owed a tax of $200 per gram on the 970 grams of confiscated cocaine, which came to $194,000. It also charged him a 100% penalty for failure to pay the tax on time, plus interest of $1,125.20, thus bringing his total tax liability to $389,125.20. Next, the department obtained a writ of execution in Rockingham County for the seizure of Lynn's property to satisfy the assessment. He was also later convicted on federal drug charges.

Along with relatives, Lynn sued the state and lost. His challenge to the constitutionality of the drug tax argued that it was in reality a criminal penalty, not a tax. Disagreeing, the federal district court ruled that the drug tax was indeed a true tax under state law, and, as such, it had no jurisdiction over Lynn's complaint. It invoked the Tax Injunction Act, which prevents federal district courts from hearing lawsuits when 1) the plaintiff seeks to stop collection of a state tax; 2) that tax is a true tax under state law; and 3) state courts provide a fast, speedy, and efficient remedy of their own (28 U.S.C.A. § 1341). The court also dismissed the plaintiffs' claims for monetary damages, ruling that they had failed to state a claim and that state employees were protected from liability by the Eleventh Amendment.

On appeal, the Fourth U.S. Circuit Court of Appeals reversed a key part of the decision (*Lynn v. West*, 134 F.3d 582). Ruling that the district court had erred in evaluating the nature of the drug tax, it cited a 1994 U.S. Supreme Court decision in which a similar tax in Montana was found to be a criminal penalty (*Department of Revenue v. Kurth Ranch*, 511 U.S. 767, 114 S. Ct. 1937, 128 L. Ed. 2d 767). Like Montana's, North Carolina's drug tax had enough punitive features that its nature was that of criminal penalty: it featured a high rate of taxation, served a deterrent purpose, was conditioned on the commission of a crime, and had no relationship to lawful possession of a drug.

As such, the appeals court ruled, imposing the drug tax as a civil sanction was unconstitutional. Enforcement of the tax had to give defendants all the constitutional safeguards that accompany criminal proceedings, which North Carolina was ordered to do in the future. But the appeals court saw no need to send the case back to the district court. Moreover, it upheld the remainder of the lower court's decision denying damages to Lynn and the other plaintiffs.

### Louisiana Drug Testing Laws

In the summer of 1997, the Louisiana legislature passed a set of laws that mandated drug tests for state welfare recipients, state government contractors and vendors, elected officials (H.B. 646), state employees, and anyone else who receives anything of economic value from the state. The laws placed approximately one in four Louisiana residents under its purview and

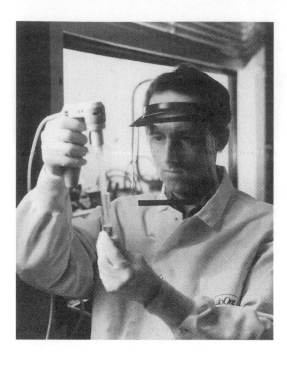

*Drug testing of people who receive money from the government, such as welfare recipients, has become the focus of recent legislative debate.*

EDWARD L. LALLO/THE PICTURE CUBE, INC.

gave Louisiana the broadest drug-testing rights in the nation and the world.

The sponsor of the bill that gave rise to the laws, Representative Heulette "Clo" Fontenot, introduced it as a measure to drug-test welfare recipients. The bill was criticized as unfairly targeting indigent persons, so the legislature expanded it. Ultimately, the legislature decided to authorize drug testing for anyone who receives "anything of economic value" from the state.

Louisiana's drug-testing laws specify that testing is mandatory for "certain adult participants" in the Temporary Assistance for Needy Families Block Grant Program. The secretary of the Department of Social Services in consultation with the secretary of the Department of Health and Hospitals and the commissioner of administration determine the identity of these

persons. Testing of other persons is conducted in a random fashion.

Under the new laws, drug-testing procedures are devised and implemented by the commissioner of administration. Any person who fails a drug test must complete a drug education and rehabilitation program. Failure to complete a drug education and rehabilitation program can result in the loss of benefits and government contracts.

The main bill that authorized the widespread drug testing in Louisiana cited the governmental interest in promoting the safety and welfare of its citizens as justification for the laws. Governor M. J. "Mike" Foster, a strong supporter of the new laws, asserted that the laws are necessary to stop drug use. "You are either serious about drugs or you are not. Until we test, we are not going to stop it," remarked Foster. Cheney Joseph, executive counsel to Foster, stated that the governor has "a real interest in trying to help people who may be disadvantaged avoid the use of illegal drugs."

Representative Arthur Morrell of New Orleans, one of the few Louisiana House members who opposed the bill, called the laws "crazy" and pointed out some possible flaws in the laws, such as the possibility that the state could start drug-testing priests, nuns, and rabbis. "I don't know if this bill is even restricted to humans," Morrell said.

The ACLU vowed to challenge the laws as soon as it could find plaintiffs in each class that must undergo the tests. A challenge to the law likely would postpone its implementation. This means that even if Louisiana successfully defends the laws, it could be years before the laws take effect.

**CROSS REFERENCES**
Eleventh Amendment; Fourth Amendment; Search and Seizure

## EDUCATION LAW

The body of state and federal constitutional provisions; local, state, and federal statutes; court opinions; and government regulations that provide the legal framework for educational institutions.

### Alabama School Prayer Laws

Alabama lawmakers have long sought to legalize prayer in their state's public schools. In 1977 the Alabama Legislature passed the first of four school prayer statutes. The statute, Ala. Code § 16-1-20 (1995), provided for a moment of silence to be observed at the beginning of the school day. The second statute, enacted in 1981, provided that this moment of silence "shall be observed for meditation or voluntary prayer." (Ala. Code § 16-1-20.1 [1995]). In 1982 the legislature passed a third statute, which stated that "the Lord God is one" and allowed public school teachers to lead students in prayer (Ala. Code § 16- 1-20.2 [1995]). The federal courts eventually struck down both the 1981 and 1982 statutes because they violated the Establishment Clause of the First Amendment to the U.S. Constitution *Jaffree v. Wallace*, 705 F.2d 1526 [11th Cir. 1983], *aff'd*, 472 U.S. 38, 105 S. Ct. 2479, 86 L. Ed. 2d 29 [1985]; *Jaffree v. Wallace*, 705 F.2d 1526 [11th Cir. 1983], *aff'd*, 466 U.S. 924, 104 S. Ct. 1704, 80 L. Ed. 2d 178 [1984]).

In 1993 the Alabama Legislature made a fourth attempt to enact a law legitimizing school prayer. Alabama Code § 16-1-20.3 states, in part, "On public school, other public, or other property, non-sectarian, non-proselytizing student-initiated voluntary prayer, invocations and/or benedictions, shall be permitted during compulsory or non-compulsory school-related student assemblies, school-related student sporting events, school-related graduation or commencement ceremonies, and other school-related student events."

For many years Michael Chandler, an assistant principal at Valley Head High School in DeKalb County, Alabama, had complained to school officials about what he considered to be coercive religious practices such as prayer sessions before athletic events, prayers at graduation ceremonies, and distribution of Bibles to students in the schools by representatives of Gideon International. Chandler, who was raised as a Baptist, lived with his wife and their teenage son, Jesse, in the town of Fyffe in DeKalb County, where Jesse attended Fyffe School.

Despite Chandler's complaints, the religious practices continued. In 1996 Chandler, along with several organizations including the ACLU and Americans United for Separation of Church and State, sued the DeKalb County Board of Education, the Alabama State Board of Education, and the governor of Alabama, among others, in federal court, claiming that Ala. Code § 16-1-20.3 was unconstitutional. They argued that the law had resulted in practices such as teachers allowing students to pray aloud in class, with students who objected being told to leave the classroom and stand in the hall.

In March 1997 a federal district court struck down the 1993 statute, holding that it violated the Establishment Clause and the Free Exercise Clause of the Constitution (*Chandler v. James*, 958 F. Supp. 1550 [M.D. Ala]). These two provisions appear in the First Amendment and read

as follows: "Congress shall make no law respecting an establishment of religion, or prohibiting the free exercise thereof."

The Establishment Clause prevents the majority from legislating preferential treatment for those of a particular religious faith. The Free Exercise Clause ensures that the government will not unnecessarily burden the practice of any religious faith. Together, these clauses require the government to remain strictly neutral both among religions and between religion and non-religion. It is the courts' responsibility to ensure the government's neutrality, particularly when government actions affect public schools. School children are especially susceptible to peer-pressure, school attendance is mandatory, and students' behavior while in school is strictly regulated. When prayer is added to the school curriculum, students who find it offensive are not able to leave or object to it.

The court first examined the statute in light of the Free Exercise Clause. The court noted that the legislature had attempted to assure the public that the statute had no effect on the constitutional rights of public school students, including the rights of free speech and prayer, by adding subsection (c) to the statute, which stated that the law "shall not diminish the right of any student or person to exercise his or her rights of free speech and religion … at times or events other than those stated in subsection (b). The "times and events" referred to include compulsory or non-compulsory school-related student assemblies, student sporting events, and graduation or commencement exercises. However, the court said that instead of "saving" the statute, subsection (c) had the opposite effect, diminishing the students' free speech and prayer rights during the times listed. According to the court, the legislature defined the students' rights too narrowly by limiting their definition, to school-related student events. As a result, section 16-1-20.3 infringed those rights.

The court then analyzed the statute under the Establishment Clause, applying the three-part test set forth by the U.S. Supreme Court in *Lemon v. Kurtzman*, 403 U.S. 602, 91 S. Ct. 2105, 29 L. Ed. 2d 745 (1971): (1) does the statute have a secular purpose, (2) is the primary effect of the statue to advance or inhibit religion, and (3) does the statute foster excessive entanglement with religion?

Although the statute's statement of purpose stated that it was intended to protect freedom of speech, the court found that the only speech protected was religious speech. Singling out religious speech and informing school officials and the public that students have an unqualified right to engage in this one type of speech does not constitute a secular purpose, according to the court. Instead, by singling out religious speech, the statute endorsed religion. In addition, the court noted that a letter from the Alabama attorney general to the statute's legislative sponsor, who had asked the attorney general to evaluate its constitutionality, evidenced the statute's non-secular purpose. The attorney general's letter stated: "You ask: What is the strongest, clearest constitutional language which Alabama might enact restoring student prayer to public schools?"

The court found that even if the statute were enacted for a secular purpose, it violated the second part of the *Lemon* test in that its primary effect was to endorse religion. The statute singled out prayer as the one form of student speech that had to be permitted at school events, and it forced non-consenting students to listen to or participate in that prayer.

The court also found that the statute resulted in excessive entanglement between the state and religion, violating the third part of the *Lemon* test. Because the student speech permitted in subsection (b) was limited to non-sectarian, non-proselytizing prayer, school officials would be forced to oversee the student prayers to determine which ones were permissible and monitor the conduct of dissenting students to prevent them from interfering with those students who were exercising their right to pray.

The court noted that the U.S. Supreme Court has repeatedly stated that religion should be a part of the public school curriculum. According to the Supreme Court, schools are allowed to teach students about the influence of religion on such subjects as art, music, and literature, and the Bible can be used in the study of history, civilization, ethics and comparative religion. However, the Bible and similar religious materials may not be used in public schools when the purpose of such use is to advance a particular religious belief, according to the Court.

The district court set out various types of student religious activity that it found to be constitutionally permissible. These activities included individual or group prayer outside of organized classes or school-sponsored events; individual silent prayer that does not interfere with schoolwork; appropriate distribution of religious literature and display of religious symbols provided the school permits students to distribute other literature not related to the school curriculum and display non-religious symbols in an appropriate manner.

Several months after the district court's decision, Alabama Governor Forrest H. "Fob" James, Jr., wrote to U.S. District Judge Ira DeMent, the author of the opinion, asking him to reverse his decision striking down the school prayer statute. James argued that the Supreme Court exceeded its authority in separating church and state and said that the federal courts have no jurisdiction over the states on First Amendment issues. According to James, federal courts have no right to interfere in a state's decision to allow prayer in public schools. DeMent responded that the Supreme Court's authority to interpret the Constitution was established in 1803 and was well settled.

Following its March 1997 decision, the court asked the parties to the lawsuit to address the steps that should be taken to end the religiously coercive activities in the DeKalb County School System. Based on evidence submitted by the plaintiff, the court determined that despite its March 1997 order, the defendants had continued their coercive practices, including allowing mass vocal prayer in the classroom, using the public address system to deliver prayers, and offering student-led prayer at graduation ceremonies. In addition, the court found that Chandler's son, Jesse, had been harassed by fellow students, who often stood up and prayed when he entered the school lunchroom. Although school officials were aware of these activities, the court found that they had done nothing to stop this harassment.

The court found that without permanent injunctive relief, it was substantially likely that the DeKalb County Board of Education would continue to ignore the court's order. On October 29, 1997, the court issued a permanent injunction prohibiting the defendants from allowing school-organized or officially sanctioned religious activity in the DeKalb County schools, including vocal prayer, religious readings, distribution of religious materials including Bibles, discussions of a devotional nature, and announcements of religious messages over the public address system during the school day or in connection with any school-sponsored event. The court also ordered the defendants to stop the harassment of Jesse Chandler.

The defendants have appealed the district court's decision to the U.S. Court of Appeals for the Eleventh Circuit. As of early 1998, the appellate court had not issued an opinion.

### School Regulation of Hair Length

At the beginning of the 1990-91 school year, eight-year-old Zachariah Toungate showed up to class at Mira Elementary School sporting a "rattail," a thin variation of a ponytail that extended beyond his shirt collar. Under the Bastrop Independent School District grooming regulations, Zachariah's ponytail was too long, and school officials notified Zachariah and his mother, September Toungate, that Zachariah had to cut his ponytail to a length that did not reach below his collar. Toungate met with the school's principal, who explained that the reason for the regulation was "to enforce the notion that boys should look like boys and girls should look like girls" (*Board of Trustees of Bastrop Independent School District v. Toungate*, 958 S.W.2d 365 [Tex. 1997]).

Zachariah did not cut his ponytail, and he was suspended from school for three days. Still wearing his ponytail, Zachariah returned to school and was placed on "in-school suspension." Under this status, Zachariah spent the school day in a small room darkened by heavy paper over the windows, alone except for the supervision of a substitute teacher. Zachariah was not allowed to have lunch or take recess with the other children, and he was not allowed to participate in choral activities or the school's Christmas program. After four months of in-school suspension, Toungate removed her son from Mira Elementary, arranged home schooling for Zachariah, and brought suit against the Bastrop Independent School District.

Toungate argued that the school district's hair length regulations violated the Texas Equal Rights Amendment incorporated into the state constitution (Texas Constitution, Article, I, Section 3a) as well as Texas' Civil Practice and Remedies (Code § 106.001(a)(4)-(6)). These provisions prohibited the deprivation of rights

*The imposition of hair length regulations by school boards could violate a student's equal rights.*

BOB DAEMMRICH/STOCK BOSTON, INC.

based on certain characteristics, such as race, ethnicity, and sex. Because the hair length rules did not apply to girls, Toungate asserted, the school's hair length rules were contrary to the equal rights provisions in the state's constitution and statutory code.

The trial court granted summary judgment to the school district. That judgment was reversed in part on appeal, and the case continued to trial. The trial court initially awarded nothing to Toungate, but later reversed itself and held that the school district had in fact violated both the state equal rights amendment and section 106.001. The trial court ordered the school district to permanently refrain from enforcing the hair length regulation, and it also ordered the school district to pay Toungate's attorney fees.

The Bastrop Independent School District appealed, and the appeals court affirmed the judgment on the strength of the statutory claim, but denied the constitutional claim under recent precedent from the Supreme Court of Texas, 922 S.W.2d 650 (1996). In *Barber v. Colorado Independent School District*, 901 S.W.2d 447 (Tex. 1995), the Supreme Court of Texas had essentially declared that constitutional challenges to hair length rules were non-justiciable, or unworthy of judicial review.

The school district appealed to the Supreme Court of Texas, arguing, in part, that the state statute in question was not intended to govern the hair length regulations of a school district. The statute, originally enacted in 1967, declared that it was a prohibited act for an officer or employee of the state to discriminate against a person on the basis of race, religion, color, or national origin. In pertinent part, the statute stated that a state officer or employee could not, when acting in an official capacity, "refuse to permit the person to participate in a program owned, operated, or managed by or on behalf of the state," "refuse to grant a benefit to a person," or "impose an unreasonable burden on the person" because of that person's race, religion, color, or national origin. In 1971 the legislature amended the statute to prevent discrimination on the basis of a person's sex.

The majority agreed with the school district, citing state cases that had upheld hair length regulations. Most of the cases dealt with hair length rules for adults in the workplace, but the majority dismissed this discrepancy by comparing the responsibilities that school officials have for children with the responsibilities that employers have to their employees. The majority reasoned that "[g]rooming requirements do not elevate the status of one sex over another," and they do not deny educational opportunities to students any more than similar workplace regulations foreclose opportunities to adults.

The majority noted that the statute provided for criminal penalties. This feature militated against a construction that would place school officials at risk of prosecution and incarceration for the enforcement of grooming codes.

Two justices concurred with the majority opinion, writing separate opinions to express the belief that the court should not involve itself in school hair length rules, regardless of whether the right is asserted under a statutory provision or a constitutional provision. One justice dissented, acknowledging that some dress and grooming rules were acceptable and even necessary for an orderly, functional school, but criticizing the position "that school districts have a license to impose unjustified, discriminatory standards." The dissent maintained that a plain reading of the statute did not indicate it intended to exempt schools from its provisions, and an analysis of the facts and the statute indicated that the statute had been violated.

The dissent opined that the hair length regulations were based on sex because they applied only to boys, and not to girls. The distinction made between boys and girls was used to impose an unreasonable burden on Zachariah by depriving him of his right to participate in school activities. The school district had claimed that it had not burdened Zachariah because the school district's legitimate goals justified the in-school suspension. The dissent addressed each of the school district's arguments on this topic and concluded that discipline, security, gender identification, or socialization goals were not achieved or promoted by the hair length regulation and that therefore the regulations were not justified.

### Students Strip Searched at School

On May 1, 1992, a second-grade student reported to her teacher, Hilda Fannin, at Graham Elementary School in Talladega, Alabama, that seven dollars were missing from her purse. Although some of the facts are in question, it is certain that at least one student proceeded to allege that two eight-year-old classmates, Cassandra Jenkins and Oneika McKenzie, had stolen the money.

After searching McKenzie's backpack and finding no money, Fannin questioned Jenkins and McKenzie in the hallway outside the classroom. Each accused the other of the theft. Another teacher, Susannah Herring, then suggested that Jenkins and McKenzie remove their socks and shoes, but no money was found. Herring and a guidance counselor, Melba Sirmon, then escorted Jenkins and McKenzie to the girls' rest room, where the girls were instructed to remove their clothes. The search yielded no money.

Jenkins and McKenzie were then taken to the principal's office along with Anthony Jamerson, another student implicated in the theft. At the principal's office, Jamerson stated that the money was hidden behind a file cabinet. A search of that area turned up no money. According to Jenkins and McKenzie, Herring then escorted them to the rest room and performed a second fruitless strip search.

The parents of Jenkins and McKenzie subsequently sued Herring, Sirmon, the superintendent of the Talladega City School District and others. In their complaint the plaintiffs cited violations of McKenzie's and Jenkins' rights to be free from unreasonable search and seizure under the Fourth and Fourteenth Amendments to the U.S. Constitution. They also alleged that the defendants had violated provisions of 42 U.S.C.A. § 1983, title VI of the Civil Rights Act of 1964 (42 U.S.C.A. § 2000d) title IX of the Education Amendments of 1972 (20 U.S.C.A. § 1681), and Alabama law. The U.S. District Court for the Northern District of Alabama granted summary judgment for the defendants on the grounds that they were immune from the suit as state actors acting within their official capacities.

The plaintiffs appealed to the U.S. Court of Appeals for the Eleventh Circuit, which affirmed part of the district court's decision but reversed the Fourth Amendment claims based on 42 U.S.C.A. § 1983, (*Jenkins v. Talladega City Board of Education*, 95 F.3d 1036 [1996]. After a rehearing *en banc*, the court, by a vote of eight to three, reversed its earlier decision on the Fourth Amendment claims, thereby affirming the dismissal of all claims *Jenkins v. Talladega City Board of Education*, 115 F.3d 821 [1997].

Judge Stanley F. Birch, Jr., writing for the majority, began the opinion by stating the law on qualified immunity for a state actor: Qualified immunity applies if a state actor's conduct violates no "clearly established statutory or constitutional rights of which a reasonable person would have known." The majority also noted that the court had to take into account the law as it existed in 1992, at the time of the defendants' conduct. This law was the U.S. Supreme Court's 1985 decision in *New Jersey v. T. L. O.*, 469 U.S. 325, 105 S. Ct. 733, 83 L. Ed. 2d 720 (1985).

According to the majority, the law on searches in school as expressed in *T. L. O.* was not clearly enough defined to put the defendants on notice that their actions were unconstitutional or contrary to the law. Under *T. L. O.* a search of a student at school must be "reasonably related to the objectives of the search" and it must not be "excessively intrusive in light of the age and sex of the student and the nature of the infraction."

In *T. L. O.* a teacher caught a student smoking cigarettes in a bathroom. In the principal's office, the vice-principal searched the student's purse and discovered a pack of cigarettes. When he removed the cigarettes from the purse, he noticed a pack of cigarette rolling papers. This prompted him to make a further search of the purse, which uncovered a small quantity of marijuana and drug paraphernalia. The Supreme Court upheld both searches.

Judge Birch wrote that the *T. L. O.* opinion lacked detailed guidance to school officials. For example, *T. L. O.* did not clarify whether a search of a younger student was more intrusive than one of an older student; whether a search of a girl was more intrusive than a search of a boy; or what kind of infraction is serious enough to warrant a strip search. Without this information, held the *Jenkins* majority, the defendants could not have known that their actions were unconstitutional. They were therefore immune from suit.

Writing for the dissent, Senior Circuit Judge Phyllis A. Kravitch agreed with the majority that state actors should be shielded from liability for actions that they reasonably could not have known were unconstitutional. Kravitch opined, however, that *T. L. O.* "sufficiently forewarns teachers that strip-searching eight-year-olds in pursuit of a few dollars violates the Fourth Amendment."

The dissent attacked the majority's conclusion that *T. L. O.* was too general to provide notice to school officials and employees. Kravitch opined that it is not enough simply to label preexisting law 'general,' or to identify factual distinctions in relevant precedent." Instead, the dissent maintained, the court should engage in further analysis of the factual distinctions and the precedent to determine whether the conduct was permissible. To support its proposition that *T. L. O.* was sufficiently instructive, the dissent cited several cases in which courts had found certain school conduct, including strip searches for the purpose of finding money, to violate of the standard enunciated in *T. L. O.*

The dissent also focused on the majority's view that each strip search was justified because the school employees had ample reason to believe that Jenkins and McKenzie had, in fact, stolen the money. According to the majority, "several students" implicated Jenkins, McKenzie, and Jamerson in the theft. The dissent noted, however, that the employees conducting the strip search were not aware of allegations from other students until after they had conducted the first strip search. Testimony differed on the topic of the employees' knowledge of accusations, but, viewing the testimony in a light most favorable to the plaintiffs, the dissent suggested that the employees who conducted the strip search knew only that one student had accused the girls of stealing the money. Moreover, only two other students made subsequent accusations against the girls to the employees.

The dissent found that strip-searches violated the Fourth Amendment; they were excessively intrusive given the nature of the infraction and the personal characteristics of the students. Neither of the girls had ever been accused of theft. Jamerson, on the other hand, had been accused of theft in the past and had actually admitted to taking the money and hiding it behind a cabinet. Jenkins stated that she saw Jamerson open the victim's purse, yet Jamerson was not strip searched.

Upon a search of McKenzie's backpack and both girls' shoes and socks, no money was found. There was no evidence, the dissent pointed out, that the girls had hidden the money under their clothing. The dissent felt that the defendants should have obtained additional information after the initial fruitless searches before conducting more intrusive searches.

Some commentators attached the *Jenkins* case as reinforcing discriminatory conduct. The student who accused Jenkins and McKenzie, and the persons who conducted the searches, are white. Jenkins and McKenzie, who are black, were represented by the National Association for the Advancement of Colored People's Legal Defense and Educational Fund.

CROSS REFERENCES
Civil Rights; Fourth Amendment; Searches and
Seizures

# ELECTION CAMPAIGN FINANCING

## 1996 Campaign Finance Scandal

Amid allegations that President Bill Clinton, Vice President Albert Gore, Jr., and the Democratic National Committee (DNC) had violated federal campaign election financing laws during the 1996 presidential campaign, committees in both houses of Congress conducted investigations during 1997 and 1998. Though some in Congress believed that revelations about illegal political fund-raising would create a demand from the public for election finance reform, the hearings soon became partisan battlegrounds that generated virtually no public outcry. The latest incarnation of the McCain-Feingold reform proposal was defeated in the Senate in February 1998, signaling an end to current attempts to restrict the flow of money into political campaigns.

The problems uncovered concerning Democratic party fund-raising centered on the soliciting of "soft money," which is money that individuals and corporation contribute to political parties rather than direct to candidates. The allowance of these contributions is the biggest loophole in federal campaign laws. Contributions to political parties, rather than to political candidates, are referred to as soft money because, as one observer stated, "It is so squishy." Although soft money clearly is used to support the candidates, it is difficult to track closely where the money goes. Political parties have used soft money to cover the costs of such activities as registering voters, printing brochures, advertising in the media, and fund-raising events.

The soft money loophole means that there are no limits to the amount of money an individual or corporation can contribute to a party. Although the loophole had been around since the passage of a 1979 amendment to the federal election laws, it was little known or used until the 1990s. By 1996 soft money had become the main source of campaign money in the presidential campaign, with the Republicans raising nearly $300 million and the Democrats raising more than $200 million.

Though both major parties sought soft money, 1996 Republican presidential nominee Bob Dole accused the Democrats of accepting large soft money contributions from foreign sources, even though federal law prohibits foreign contributions to U.S. campaigns. Though the Clinton campaign was able to deflect the issue during the closing weeks of the campaign, media and legal scrutiny about Asian political contributions intensified after Clinton's election in November 1996.

In early 1997 Senator Fred D. Thompson (R-Tenn.), as chair of the Senate Governmental Affairs Committee, began hearings into campaign fund-raising improprieties. In his opening statement, Thompson alleged that the Chinese government had made a concerted effort to influence the U.S. election by funneling money through various Asian business executives. Representative Dan Burton (R-Ind.), chair of the House Government Reform and Oversight Committee, initiated a similar investigations. However, Thompson's committee drew the most attention and conducted the more far-reaching investigation.

The committee soon confirmed that the DNC had targeted the Asian American community as a potentially lucrative soft money source. The DNC released papers that showed, that it had a "National Asian Pacific American Campaign Plan," which had as its goal the raising of $7 million from the Asian American community. At the center of this fund-raising was John Huang, who had once served as the head of U.S. operations for the Lippo Group, an Indonesian conglomerate, which includes the Lippo Bank, U.S.A.

While working for Lippo in the 1980s, Huang became active in Democratic politics and fund-raising. After Clinton's 1992 victory, Huang secured a mid-level appointment in the Commerce Department, where he was responsible for Asian trade matters. In 1995 he moved to a fund-raising job at the DNC, where he courted Asian American donors. The records suggest that in return for a sizable soft money contribution to the DNC, Huang arranged for the donors to have, at a minimum, a face-to-face meeting with President Clinton.

Clinton's meetings with donors was in keeping with similar actions by President Ronald Reagan and President George Bush, but the number of meetings outpaced those of his predecessors. Numerous White House coffee meetings were arranged for donors, who were given a few minutes to chat with the president. In addition, large contributors were invited to stay as overnight guests in the Lincoln bedroom.

*This photo showing President Clinton shaking hands with John Huang at a White House coffee on June 18, 1996, was introduced into evidence at the Senate Governmental Affairs hearing on September 16, 1997.*

RICK WILKING/REUTERS/ARCHIVE PHOTOS

As the Thompson hearings revealed, many of the donors who came to the White House had questionable pasts and should never have been given clearances. The DNC, however, encouraged the Clinton campaign to use these visits to increase the soft money coming into the campaign.

Vice President Gore came under scrutiny for making telephone solicitations from his office. A more serious problem arose out of his appearance at a 1996 election event at a California Buddhist temple. Maria Hsia, a DNC fund-raiser, was indicted in February 1998 for allegedly using the event to route funds from the International Buddhist Progress Society, commonly known as the Hsi Lai Temple, to the DNC and several Democratic candidates. All of the supposed individual contributors were allegedly reimbursed later with temple funds, which is illegal because nonprofit religious organizations are not allowed to make political donations.

As the Thompson hearings proceeded, the DNC announced that it had returned or would return $2.8 million in questionable or illegal contributions raised by John Huang and two other fund-raisers, Yah Lin ("Charlie") Trie and Johnny Chung. Trie had gotten to know Clinton in Little Rock, Arkansas, while Clinton served as governor. Trie ran a Chinese restaurant that Clinton frequented but moved to Washington in 1994, where he opened an office and became a Democratic fund-raiser. That same year he became a business partner with a Macao businessman, whom Trie encouraged to contribute to the Democrats. Trie also arranged for a Chinese arms-trading executive to be in-

vited to a White House coffee meeting. Trie left the United States in late 1996 and was believed to have resided in China. Indicted by a federal grand jury in January 1998 for collecting money from foreign businessmen not eligible to contribute to U.S. campaigns, Trie returned to the United States in February 1998 to face the charges.

Johnny Chung, who delivered a $50,000 campaign contribution to the White House and escorted Chinese businessmen to a presidential radio address, visited the White House forty-nine times in 1995 and 1996. From 1994 to 1996, Chung made twelve personal or corporate donations to the DNC totaling $366,000. The DNC, which had suspicions that Chung was illegally handing money over from Chinese businessmen, nevertheless accepted the money. Only in 1997 did the DNC return the funds, stating it had "insufficient information" as to the source of the funds. In March 1998, Chung made a plea agreement with federal prosecutors. He was charged with funneling illegal contributions to the Clinton-Gore campaign by asking friends and employees of his business to make donations for which they were later reimbursed. In his plea agreement, Chung promised to cooperate with the investigation into the 1996 campaign financial abuses.

Despite the involvement of Huang, Trie, and Chung, Thompson's committee was unable to conclusively prove that the Chinese government was behind the illegal contributions. The committee's Republican majority issued its final report in March 1998, declaring that the Democrats' 1996 presidential campaign "eviscerated federal fund-raising laws," "debased the White House and the presidency itself," and showed that "nothing was sacred in the President's search for campaign funds." The majority also excused the conduct of former Republican National Committee chair Haley Barbour, who is under investigation by the Justice Department for his alleged involvement in a complex arrangement that indirectly provided foreign money to the Republican National Committee.

The Democrats issued a minority report. The report reiterated the comments of Senator John Glenn (D-Ohio), the ranking minority member, who questioned the alleged "plan" of the Chinese government to influence the 1996 presidential election. The minority report criticized the majority's report for making "a series of speculative assertions" and suggested that the China connection was "a conclusion looking for supporting information that was not available."

As the Thompson committee concentrated on the China connection, another campaign finance scandal developed in 1997 involving Secretary of the Interior Bruce Babbitt. Allegations were made that Babbitt lied to Congress about whether the White House pressured him in 1995 to stop a proposed Wisconsin Indian gambling casino because tribes opposed to the new casino had contributed $350,000 to the Democrats for the 1996 campaign. Babbitt admitted to Congress in the fall of 1997 that he had told a lobbyist who supported the casino—on the day the casino application was rejected—that Harold Ickes, then a White House deputy chief of staff, had called him and directed him to make a decision that day. In addition, the lobbyist claimed that Babbitt told him that the tribes opposed to the casino had contributed $500,000 to the DNC. Babbitt testified, however, that the statements were not true but were merely a way of getting the persistent lobbyist, a former friend, out of his office. In February 1998, Attorney General Janet Reno requested that an independent counsel be appointed to investigate these allegations.

### Campaign Finance Reform

Campaign finance reform was a hot topic in 1997, but lawmakers have not been able to agree on how implement it. The most comprehensive proposal for reform failed to pass the U.S. Senate. As proposed by Senators John McCain (R-Ariz.) and Russ Feingold (D-Wisc.), the so-called McCain-Feingold bill would have enacted sweeping changes—chiefly by banning certain contributions and forcing candidates to more fully disclose their finances. Opinion polls showed broad public support for reform, and both parties spent the year denouncing the current system. Yet the parties remained divided over the issue of money. In October, Republican leaders killed the McCain-Feingold bill, most likely dooming reform chances for the near future.

The bill addressed long-standing complaints about federal campaign financing. Throughout the 1990s, critics charged that big money makes elections unfair. They argued that it creates unfair advantages for some candidates and leads to selling influence to corporations and wealthy donors. It was a similar charge that led Congress to impose limits on individual donations to candidates in 1974, the last time major reform was enacted. But in the 1980s, this scheme came undone. A series of rulings by the Federal Campaign Finance Election Commis-

sion created a new kind of unlimited donation, so-called soft money. Intended only for the activities of political parties, soft money is not supposed to fund elections. Yet both parties regularly pour it into campaigns.

*A woman signs a petition for campaign finance reform.*
JAMES SHAFFER/PHOTOEDIT

McCain-Feingold proposed four reforms aimed at politicians and their parties. First, the bill banned both from raising soft money. Second, it imposed tougher disclosure requirements on fund-raising and spending. Third, it sought to take away advantages held by wealthy candidates: they would only be able to receive financial support from their parties if they agreed to a voluntary personal spending limit. Fourth, it limited independent expenditures on campaign advertisements. This last measure attacked a 1990s trend in which unions and corporations purchased ads that ostensibly promoted issues, but actually advanced certain candidates. Under McCain-Feingold, any mention of a candidate's name in an advertisement within sixty days of an election would have subjected the advertisement to spending regulations.

The bill attracted chiefly liberal and moderate support. It won the backing of most Democratic senators, the White House, and special interest groups such as the League of Women Voters and Common Cause, that have long criticized the influence of money on federal elections. Democrats have consistently been less successful than Republicans at raising soft money. In the first half of 1997, for example, the Federal Election Commission reported that Democrats raised $21.7 million, while Republicans raised $35 million, in soft money contributions.

# SHOULD CAMPAIGN FINANCING BE REFORMED?

The 1996 presidential and congressional elections revealed the growing amount of private money that businesses, unions, and individuals contribute to political campaigns. Congressional hearings in 1997 revealed that the Democratic National Committee had solicited and received contributions from questionable sources. Despite these revelations, many members of Congress did not see any reason to reform federal campaign finance laws. Nevertheless, campaign finance reform proposals will continue to be debated.

The debate over campaign financing is framed by the Supreme Court's decision in *Buckley v. Valeo*, 424 U.S. 1, 96 S. Ct. 612, 46 L. Ed. 2d 659 (1976). The Court ruled that provisions of the Federal Election Campaign Act of 1971 (FECA), (2 U.S.C.A. §§ 431-456), which set mandatory limits on the amount of money a candidate may spend in a campaign, violated the First Amendment. Though the Court upheld the provisions of FECA that set disclosure requirements, private contribution limits, and provide public funding of qualified presidential candidates, the elimination of mandatory spending limits has meant that campaign costs and the funds to pay for them have steadily escalated.

**PAC Reform** Many advocates of reform, including liberal public interest groups, President Clinton, and former senator and 1996 presidential candidate Bob Dole argue that a ban or strict limitations be placed on money that comes from Political Action Committees (PACs). One of the reasons for limiting or banning PAC money is that PAC campaign contributions are biased towards incumbents, which has serious implications for competitiveness in elections. PAC contributors are more likely to give to incumbents because they want to preserve an existing relationship or create a new one. Because of the high cost of campaigns, PACs give the

IN FOCUS

incumbent a head start over the challenger.

Critics of placing more restrictions on PACs, or banning them completely, contend that such "reform" would further concentrate power in the hands of government, particularly those already in office. Campaign contributions can be viewed as "protection" money, according to these observers. Individuals, businesses, and unions should be able to avail themselves of using PAC money to protect themselves from legislators, agencies, and bureaucrats. Without PAC dollars, politicians would have less incentive to look at issues put forward by individuals and interest groups.

**Foreign Contributions** Reformers also seek better ways to prevent the possible influence of foreign business interests on the federal government. The disclosures about the way foreign contributions were obtained during the 1996 election cycle have led reformers to seek a complete ban on foreign gifts.

With a distinct advantage in fund-raising, Republicans gave the bill little support. Only four Republican senators said they would vote for it. Moreover, the GOP leadership attacked the bill's most dramatic change—the soft money ban—on principle. Along with conservative organizations, they characterized soft money as a form of speech protected by the First Amendment. They also criticized President Bill Clinton for raising soft money for the Democratic National Committee only two months earlier. At best, GOP leaders would only accept the provision tightening funding disclosures. In October, Republicans used a legislative maneuver to kill the bill. They attached an amendment that imposed limits on the use of union members' dues for political purposes, a measure unpopular with Democrats, who then abandoned Mc-Cain-Feingold.

With the 1998 midterm elections looming, the timing of the bill's defeat was critical. Tra-ditionally, Congress is unwilling to tinker with election laws during an election year; thus further reform efforts were unlikely until 1999 or even after the 2000 presidential elections. Further lessening the short-term chances of reform was bitter partisan politics. Throughout 1997, Republicans had hammered away at the Clinton administration in Senate hearings for alleged campaign abuses in the 1996 elections. The result, according to most observers, was that politicians would continue to blast the current system without changing it.

**CROSS REFERENCES**
Elections

## ELECTIONS

The processes of voting to decide a public question or to select one person from a designated group to perform certain obligations in a government, corporation, or society.

Critics of an outright ban on foreign contributions point out that this complex issue was considered and rejected by the Federal Election Commission (FEC) in 1991. The FEC rejected a proposal to prohibit companies that were more than 50 percent foreign owned from establishing corporate PACs. The commission reasoned that with businesses becoming more global, it is difficult to judge whether a company is foreign or domestic. U.S. companies may have ownership in a foreign business, which then has a U.S. subsidiary, making it unclear whether the subsidiary is a foreign or domestic company. Enforcement would be difficult and a ban would raise a constitutional issue. U.S. citizens working for a foreign subsidiary in the United States are entitled to participate as fully in the U.S. political process as their colleagues working for a company that is completely U.S.-owned. Workers at a U.S. Ford plant should not have more rights than workers at a U.S. Honda plant.

**Soft Money** The most troubling issue for reformers is the growing importance of soft money (money given to a party to further the party rather than a particular candidate). U.S. corporations and unions provided unprecedented amounts of soft-money contributions during the 1996 election cycle. At the same time, the Federal Election Commission had its budget cut, making the commission virtually helpless to prevent the parties from skirting existing campaign finance laws. In light of the impact soft money has made on elections, reformers believe soft money must either be eliminated or severely limited. They recognize, however, that *Buckley v. Valeo* may have to be overturned in order to gain soft-money reform.

Despite the perceived excesses of soft money, critics of soft-money reform contend that it would be unfair and unconstitutional to restrict or ban it. These critics point to *Buckley v. Valeo*, arguing that the contribution of money to political parties is a form of free speech protected by the First Amendment. If a person or group believes strongly in an issue or position supported by a political party, they have a legitimate right to give as much as they want to help the party.

**Campaign Spending Limits**
Expenditures for advertisements on television and radio have steadily increased. Some reformers believe that government-licensed forms of communication should provide significant amounts of free air time to candidates. Free air time, reformers argue, would reduce the cost of campaigns and dramatically ease the need to raise millions of dollars. Television and radio stations are adamantly opposed to such a proposal, contending that it would be unfair to place the burden of reform on their industry.

Some reformers believe limiting private campaign contributions or spending is not the best way to improve the political system. Limitations imposed by the Federal Election Campaign Act of 1971 should be repealed. These reformers advocate a full disclosure of all funding sources. Politicians would have to document on a daily basis the source and size of every contribution, including donated labor and equipment.

Most reformers, however, believe such an approach is unrealistic, because it would create a serious record-keeping problem. Documenting all contributions would cost time and money, and would be particularly hard on smaller groups that could not afford to hire legal advisers and support staffs to track donations on a daily basis.

### Foster v. Love

The U.S. Constitution gives the states the authority to establish procedures for congressional elections. However, the Constitution also gives Congress the option of making or altering these election procedures. The U.S. Supreme Court, in *Foster v. Love*, __U.S.__, 118 S. Ct. 464, 139 L. Ed. 2d 369 (1997), ruled unconstitutional a Louisiana election statute that established an "open primary" system for congressional elections. The Court found that the open primary, which took place in October, violated federal statutes that mandate a November election date.

In 1975 Louisiana enacted a new procedure for electing U.S. senators and representatives (La. Rev. Stat. Ann. § 18: 402(B)(1) ([West Supp. 1997]). In October of a federal election year, the state held what was popularly known as an "open primary" for congressional offices, in which all candidates, regardless of party, appeared on the same ballot and all voters were entitled to vote. If no candidate for a given office received a majority, the state held a runoff (called a "general election") between the top two vote-getters on the November federal election day. However, if one such candidate did get a majority in October, that candidate was elected, and citizens did not vote for a candidate on federal election day to fill the office in question. Since this system went into effect in 1978, more than 80 percent of the contested congressional elections in Louisiana ended as a matter of law with the open primary.

A group of Louisiana voters sued the state in federal court, charging that the open primary law violated federal law. The district court dismissed the lawsuit, but the Fifth Circuit Court of Appeals reversed, concluding that the open primary system was in conflict with federal statutes that establish a uniform federal election day (90 F.3d 1026 [1996]).

The Supreme Court agreed with the court of appeals. Justice David Souter, writing for the Court, noted that the Constitution's Election Clause (art. I, sec. 4, cl. 1) provides that "[t]he Times, Places and Manner of holding elections for Senators and Representatives, shall be prescribed in each State by the Legislature thereof; but the Congress may at any time by Law make or alter such Regulations." The clause invests the states with responsibility for the mechanics of congressional elections, yet only so far as Congress declines to preempt state legislative choices. Prior court precedents make clear that Congress may override state regulations by enacting uniform rules for federal elections that are binding on the states.

Congress had, in fact, passed such uniform rules. Souter pointed out that Congress sets the date of the biennial election for federal offices (2 U.S.C.A. § 1, 7; 3 U.S.C.A. § 1), providing that "[t]he Tuesday next after the 1st Monday in November, in every even numbered year, is established as the day for the election, in each of the States and Territories of the United States, of Representatives and Delegates to the Congress commencing on the 3d day of January next thereafter." Similar provisions include senatorial and presidential elections, thus mandating elections for Congress and the presidency on a single day throughout the United States.

Louisiana argued that state sovereignty permitted it to modify the rule. The Supreme Court disagreed, holding that the federal election statutes did not exceed the Election Clause's grant of authority to Congress. Instead, Souter found that the issue before the court was a narrow one, "turning entirely on the meaning of the state and federal statutes." When the federal statutes speak of "the election … they plainly refer to the combined actions of voters and officials meant to make a final selection of an officeholder." By establishing "the day" on which these actions must take place, "the statutes simply regulate the time of the election, a matter on which the Constitution explicitly gives Congress the final say."

Souter acknowledged that there was a legitimate argument over "what may constitute the final act of selection within the meaning of the law," but he concluded that it "is enough to resolve this case to say that a contested selection of candidates for a congressional office that is concluded as a matter of law before the federal election day, with no act in law or in fact to take place on the date chosen by Congress" clearly violates the federal law. Souter was careful, however, to qualify the Court's decision, noting that the case did not present the question of whether a state must always employ the conventional mechanics of an election. He stated that "we hold today only that if an election does take place, it may not be consummated prior to federal election day."

Louisiana contended that because it provided for a "general election" on federal election day when one was needed, the open primary system concerned only the "manner" of electing federal officials, not the "time" at which the elections took place. The state argued that Congress only intended to alter the time in which elections were conducted, not their manner. The open primary, therefore, changed only the manner of election and not the timing of the general election.

Souter dismissed this argument, finding it "merely wordplay, and wordplay just as much at odds with the Louisiana statute as that law is at odds" with the federal statute. The Louisiana statute "straightforwardly provides" that a candidate who receives a majority of the votes in a primary election is elected. After a declaration that a candidate received a majority in the open primary, "state law requires no further act by anyone to seal the election; the election has already occurred." Therefore, Souter stated, the open primary does affect the timing of federal elections.

Finally, Souter noted that strong policy reasons were behind the federal statutes. Congress insisted upon a uniform federal election day because it was "concerned both with the distortion of the voting process threatened when the results of an early federal election in one State can influence later voting in other States, and with the burden on citizens forced to turn out on two different election days to make final selections of federal officers in presidential election years."

### Timmons v. Twin Cities Area New Party

U.S. politics has been dominated by the two-party system. Although many minor political parties have always existed, in the twentieth century candidates of the Democratic and Republican parties usually win local, state, and federal elections. Minor political parties have complained that the two major parties have written the election laws to ensure that they remain in power.

The U.S. Supreme Court resolved the constitutionality of one such election law in *Timmons v. Twin Cities Area New Party*, __U.S.__, 117 S. Ct. 1364, 137 L. Ed. 2d 589 (1997), holding that states may lawfully prohibit a candidate from appearing on the ballot as the candidate of more than one political party. In upholding "anti-fusion" laws, the Court rejected the argument of a minor political party that the prohibition violated the party's associational rights under the First and Fourteenth Amendments.

The term *fusion* in this context means the electoral support of a single set of candidates by two or more political parties and is also called "cross-filing" or "multiple-party nomination." The practice was popular between the 1870s and 1900, particularly in the West and Midwest where candidates of issue-oriented parties like the Populists and the Grangers were elected through fusion with the Democratic party. In the South, Republicans sometimes used fusion with these parties as a way to divide the Democrats.

Fusion worked during a time when political parties rather than state or local governments prepared election ballots. These ballots contained the names of only a particular party's candidates, so a voter could deposit the party's ticket in the ballot box without knowing that other parties supported the party's candidates as well. After the 1888 presidential election, which was marred by allegations of voter fraud, many states adopted the "Australian ballot system." Under this system the government prepared and distributed an official ballot containing the names of all the candidates legally nominated by all the parties. By 1900 the Australian ballot had gained widespread acceptance, and state legislatures had enacted election reform laws, including bans on fusion candidates. Most states now prohibit fusion candidacy, the most notable exception being New York.

*Timmons* arose out of the 1994 attempt of the Twin Cities chapter of the national New Party to create a fusion candidacy. Minnesota State Representative Andy Dawkins was running unopposed as the Minnesota Democratic-Farmer-Labor (DFL) party candidate in the primary election. The New Party chose Dawkins as its candidate as well. Dawkins and the DFL party did not object, and Dawkins signed the required affidavit of candidacy for the New Party. Local election officials, however, refused to accept the New Party's nomination petition because Minnesota law (Minn. Stat. § 204B.06 [1994]) prohibits fusion candidates.

The New Party filed suit in federal court, arguing that the Minnesota anti-fusion law violated the party's associational rights under the First and Fourteenth Amendments. The district court dismissed the suit, finding that the law was valid and nondiscriminatory. However, the Eighth Circuit Court of Appeals reversed the trial court, holding that the law severely burdened the New Party's freedom to choose the best candidate and its right to "broaden the base of public participation in and support for [its] activities" (73 F.3d 196 [1996]). The appeals court concluded that the law was too broad to serve the state's interests in avoiding intra-party discord and party splintering, maintaining a stable political system, and avoiding voter confusion.

The Supreme Court disagreed with the Eighth Circuit and reversed the decision on a 6–3 vote. Chief Justice William H. Rehnquist, writing for the majority, noted the history of anti-fusion legislation and the fact that only a few states permit multiple-party candidates. He acknowledged that under the First Amendment, states may not intrude on political parties' government or structure and that their activities enjoy constitutional protection. On the other hand, states have the right to "enact reasonable regulations of parties, elections, and campaign-related disorder."

In examining the constitutionality of state election laws under the First and Fourteenth Amendments, the Court applied a test that first weighs the "character and magnitude" of the burden the state's law imposes on those constitutional rights against the state's interests in creating the burden. The Court then "considers the extent to which the State's concerns make the burden necessary." Laws that impose severe burdens on plaintiffs' rights must be narrowly tailored and advance a compelling state interest. The Court defers more to laws that create lesser burdens, however. The state must assert "important regulatory interests" to justify "reasonable, nondiscriminatory restrictions."

Rehnquist concluded that in *Timmons*, the Minnesota anti-fusion law did not impose a severe burden on the New Party and therefore the state need only assert "important regulatory interests." He found unpersuasive the New Party's assertion that it has a right to select its own candidate. A party does not have an absolute right to have its nominee appear on the ballot as its candidate. A nominee may be ineligible for office (because of her age, residency, or conviction for a felony) or may be another party's candidate. In the Court's view, these restrictions do not severely burden a party's associational rights. The Court suggested that the New Party was free to convince Representative Dawkins to forsake the DFL party and be its candidate.

Rehnquist dismissed the Eighth Circuit view that Minnesota had interfered with the ability of minor political parties to develop, organize, or take part in the election process. In his view the "New Party remains free to endorse whom it likes, to ally itself with others, to nominate candidates for office, and to spread its message to all who will listen." He also pointed out that members of the New Party may "campaign for, endorse, and vote for their preferred candidate even if he is listed on the ballot as another party's candidate."

Having established that the anti-fusion law was not a severe burden on the New Party's associational rights, Rehnquist then examined the reasonableness of the state's justification for the restriction. He concluded that states have the right to ensure the integrity and fairness of their election processes and agreed with Minnesota's contention that a candidate or party could exploit fusion by forming bogus parties that used popular catchwords and slogans such as "No New Taxes" or "Stop Crime Now" for their names. Such methods, in the Court's view, would transform the purpose of the ballot "from a means of choosing to a billboard for political advertising."

In addition, the Court held that Minnesota had a "valid interest in making sure that minor and third parties who are granted access to the ballot are bona fide and actually supported, on their own merits." Minor parties that do not receive a minimum number of votes at an election must submit a nominating petition with a certain number of signatures before being placed on the ballot at the next election. By attaching themselves to major party candidates, minor parties might "bootstrap their way to major-party status in the next election and circumvent" the nominating-petition requirement.

The Court concluded, therefore, that the burden on the New Party's First Amendment rights was relatively light and that the state's interest in banning fusion candidates was reasonable. The state had a legitimate interest in preserving "ballot integrity and political stability."

In a dissenting opinion, Justice John Paul Stevens contended that the burdens on the First Amendment were severe and that the state had failed to show a compelling interest in banning fusion candidates. He found the concerns about ballot manipulation "farfetched."

**CROSS REFERENCES**
First Amendment; Fourteenth Amendment; Freedom of Association; Rehnquist, William H; Stevens, John Paul

# ELEVENTH AMENDMENT

The Eleventh Amendment to the U.S. Constitution reads:

> The Judicial power of the United States shall not be construed to extend to any suit in law or equity, commenced or prosecuted against one of the United States by Citizens of another State, or by Citizens or Subjects of any Foreign State.

## Enforcing the Eleventh Amendment

In 1997 federal courts continued to shape the contours of the states' Eleventh Amendment sovereign immunity. In so doing, federal courts have helped lawyers, litigants, and other members of the public to understand the U.S. Supreme Court's groundbreaking decision in *Seminole Tribe of Florida v. Florida*, 517 U.S. 44, 116 S. Ct. 1114, 134 L. Ed. 2d 252 (1996), where the Court held that Congress may not abrogate a state's Eleventh Amendment sovereign immunity to federal court jurisdiction by enacting legislation pursuant to the Indian Commerce Clause contained in Article I of the U.S. Constitution, and suggested that the only legitimate basis for such legislation is the Enforcement Clause of the Fourteenth Amendment.

The Eleventh Amendment grants states immunity from being sued in federal court, with four limited exceptions. First, the Eleventh Amendment does not apply to lawsuits brought against a state's political subdivisions. Second, the amendment permits a state government to waive its constitutional protection by consenting to a lawsuit against it in federal court. Third, it permits citizens of any state to seek an injunction against state officials in federal court to end a continuing violation of federal law. Fourth, the amendment permits Congress to abrogate a state's immunity from being sued in federal court by enacting appropriate legislation.

After the Supreme Court's decision in *Seminole Tribe*, the abrogation exception came to the fore of litigation involving the Eleventh Amendment. In *Seminole Tribe* the Court said that Congress has the power to abrogate state sovereign immunity under the Eleventh Amendment if two requirements are satisfied: Congress must unequivocally express its intent to abrogate the states' sovereign immunity when enacting a piece of legislation, and Congress must enact such legislation pursuant to a valid exercise of constitutional power.

Overturning a prior decision in which the Interstate Commerce Clause was advanced as the constitutional grounds for a piece of legislation that attempted to abrogate the states' sovereign immunity (*Pennsylvania v. Union Gas Co.*, 491 U.S. 1, 109 S. Ct. 2273, 105 L. Ed. 2d 1 [1989]), the Supreme Court in *Seminole Tribe* suggested that the only lawful grounds for congressional action in this area was the Enforcement Clause of the Fourteenth Amendment, which grants Congress the power to enforce the Fourteenth Amendment against the states. In 1997 federal courts began to flesh out the meaning of the Court's holding in *Seminole Tribe*.

In *In re Rose*, 214 B.R. 372 (Nov. 10, 1997), the U.S. Bankruptcy Court for the Western District of Missouri held that Congress may not rely on the Bankruptcy Clause in Article I, section 8, Clause 4, in abrogating the states' Eleventh Amendment sovereign immunity. In 1994 Congress enacted the Bankruptcy Reform Act, Pub. L. No. 103-394, HR 5116 (codified in part at 11 U.S.C.A. § 106), to amend provisions of the federal bankruptcy code relating to the dischargeability of student loans. The bankruptcy court said that when a state has loaned money to a student, the student debtor may not initiate an action in federal court to determine the dischargeability of her student loans without first obtaining the state's consent to federal jurisdiction. The bankruptcy court intimated that the Enforcement Clause of the Fourteenth Amendment is the sole constitutional basis upon which Congress may act in attempting to abrogate a state's sovereign immunity.

In reaching the same conclusion regarding section 106 of the bankruptcy code, the U.S. Court of Appeals for the Fifth Circuit ruled that Congress may not rely on any power enumerated in Article I of the Constitution when attempting to expand the jurisdiction of federal courts over lawsuits naming a state as a party (*Matter of Estate of Fernandez* 123 F.3d 241 [1997]). Quoting *Seminole Tribe*, the Fifth Circuit said that "it has not been widely thought that the federal antitrust, bankruptcy, or copyright statutes abrogated the States' sovereign immunity. This Court never has awarded relief against a state under any of those statutory schemes."

Even where Congress relies on the Enforcement Clause of the Fourteenth Amendment when enacting a piece of legislation that purports to abrogate the states' sovereign immunity under the Eleventh Amendment, federal courts will closely scrutinize the legislation to make sure it is a valid exercise of constitutional power. For example, in *College Savings Bank v. Florida Prepaid Postsecondary Education Expense Board Bonds* 131 F.3d 353 (1997), the U.S. Court of Appeals for the Third Circuit determined that Congress had passed section 43 of the Lanham Trademark Act (15 USCA § 1125) in an effort to enforce the due process guarantees of the Fourteenth Amendment. The Third Circuit noted that the Lanham Act's protection against unfair advertising was intended to secure certain property rights of business competitors. However, the Third Circuit held that these types of property rights are not protected by the Due Process Clause of the Fourteenth Amendment. Consequently, the Third Circuit concluded that any attempt by Congress to abrogate the states' sovereign immunity to be sued for violating section 43 must fail.

At the same time, Congress need not expressly rely on the Enforcement Clause of the Fourteenth Amendment to effectively abrogate the states' sovereign immunity, as long as its reliance may be reasonably inferred from the historical evidence. In *Carmen v. San Francisco Unified School District*, 982 F. Supp. 1396 (1997), the U.S. District Court for the Northern District of California ruled that Congress permissibly abrogated the states' sovereign immunity in passing the Age Discrimination in Employment Act of 1967 (ADEA), Pub. L. No. 90-202, 81 Stat 602 (codified as amended at 29 U.S.C.A. § 623 [1994]). In a case of first impression in the Ninth Circuit, the district court observed that other federal circuits had examined the legislative history of the ADEA and determined that it had been enacted pursuant to the Enforcement Clause of the Fourteenth Amendment, though Congress had not expressly mentioned this clause in the ADEA. The legislative history and debates surrounding its passage provided sufficient evidence linking the ADEA and the equal protection guarantees of the Fourteenth Amendment. As a result, the district court concluded that Congress had not contravened the Eleventh Amendment by enacting this piece of legislation and that states could be sued in federal court without their consent for alleged ADEA violations.

Before a federal court will examine the constitutional basis for a piece of legislation under the Eleventh Amendment, there must be "unmistakable evidence" that the legislation even purports to abrogate the states' sovereign immunity from federal jurisdiction. For example, in *Commack Self-Service Kosher Meats Inc. v. New York*, 954 F. Supp. 65 (1997), the U.S. District Court for the Eastern District of New York held that Congress, by passing the Religious Freedom Restoration Act of 1993 (RFRA) (42 U.S.C.A. § 2000bb et seq.) did not abrogate the states' immunity from federal jurisdiction because neither RFRA nor its textual declaration refers to sovereign immunity, its abrogation or the Eleventh Amendment. The general statutory authorization to assert freedom of religion claims in federal court, the district court said, does not amount to unmistakable evidence that Congress has unequivocally abrogated sovereign immunity.

**CROSS REFERENCES**
Native Americans; Sovereign Immunity

# EMPLOYMENT LAW

The body of law that governs the employer-employee relationship, including individual employment contracts, the application of TORT and CONTRACT doctrines, and a large group of statutory regulation on issues such as the right to organize and negotiate COLLECTIVE BARGAINING AGREEMENTS, protection from DISCRIMINATION, wages and hours, and health and safety.

### Robinson v. Shell Oil Company

The Civil Rights Act of 1964 (42 U.S.C.A. § 2000e et seq.) contains broad prohibitions against discrimination on the basis of race, color, religion, national origin, or sex. Title VII of the act defines discrimination in employment as including failure or refusal to hire, discrimination in discharge, classification of employees or applicants in a manner that deprives individuals of employment opportunities, discrimination in apprenticeship and on-the-job training programs, and retaliation for opposition to an unlawful employment practice.

In *Robinson v. Shell Oil Company*, ___ U.S.___, 117 S. Ct. (843, 136 L. Ed. 2d 808 (1997), the U.S. Supreme Court resolved an issue involving employer retaliation and title VII

law. The Court ruled that a former employee could sue an employer for illegal retaliation based on conduct that occurred after the employee was discharged. In so ruling, the Court agreed with the statutory interpretation favored by six circuit courts of appeal.

Charles T. Robinson, Sr., was fired by Shell Oil Company in 1991. Shortly after his discharge, Robinson filed a charge with the Equal Employment Opportunity Commission (EEOC), alleging that Shell had fired him on the basis of his race. While this complaint was pending, Robinson applied for work with another company. That company contacted Shell for an employment reference. Robinson filed another charge with the EEOC, alleging that Shell gave him a negative reference in retaliation for his having filed the original EEOC charge.

Robinson later sued under section 704(a) of title VII, alleging retaliatory discrimination. This section makes it unlawful "for an employer to discriminate against any of his employees or applicants for employment" who have either availed themselves of title VII's protections or assisted others in doing so. Shell filed a motion with the court, asking it to dismiss the action because section 704(a) does not apply to former employees. The district court dismissed Robinson's action on this basis, and the Fourth Circuit Court of Appeals reaffirmed its prior interpretation of the law by affirming the trial court's decision (70 F.3d 325 [1995]).

The Supreme Court took the case to resolve a conflict in the courts of appeal over the interpretation of section 704(a). Six other circuits (Second, Third, Seventh, Ninth, Tenth, and Eleventh) had held that the term "employees" in the provision did include former employees. Justice Clarence Thomas, writing for a unanimous Court, held that the statute did cover former employees, thus allowing Robinson to sue for employer retaliation.

Thomas noted that in interpreting a statute, a court must determine whether the language "at issue has a plain and unambiguous meaning with regard to the particular dispute in the case." If the court decides that the language is unambiguous and the statutory scheme is "coherent and consistent," the court must cease its inquiry and apply the plain meaning of the statutory provision. Thomas stated that the inquiry into the plainness or ambiguity of statutory language is guided by three principles: "the language itself, the specific context in which that language is used, and the broader context of the statute as a whole."

Applying these principles, Thomas concluded that the term "employees" in section 704(a) was ambiguous as to whether it excluded former employees. He noted that there was no "temporal qualifier" in the law that would make plain that section 704(a) protects only persons still employed at the time of the retaliation. If the statute had used either of the terms "former employees" or "current employees," the meaning would have been plain. However, neither term is used in title VII, even where the specific context demonstrates an intent to cover current or former employees.

Thomas also found that title VII's definition of "employee" was silent as to whether it applied to either current or past employment. Section 701(f) defines "employee" for purposes of title VII as "an individual employed by an employer."

Another consideration was the number of other provisions in title VII that used the term "employees" to mean something more inclusive or different than "current employee." Thomas pointed out a number of such examples, including section 717(b), which requires federal agencies to have an employment rule that includes a provision "that an employee or applicant for employment shall be notified of any final action taken on any complaint of discrimination." If the complaint involves discriminatory discharge, the "employee" who must be notified is "necessarily a former employee."

Thomas acknowledged that title VII contains sections which, when viewed in context, refer unambiguously to a current employee when using the term "employee." For example, provisions addressing salary and promotions are clearly intended to apply to current employees. However, Thomas concluded that these examples may only demonstrate that the term "'employees' may have a plain meaning in the context of a particular section—not that the term has the same meaning in all other sections and in all other contexts." Based on this analysis, the Court found that the term "employees," standing by itself, was "necessarily ambiguous." Its meaning could only be established by analyzing its use in each section of the statute to determine if the particular context would give "employees" a "further meaning that would resolve the issue in dispute."

Thomas then examined the possible meanings of "employees" in section 704(a). Shell argued that the word "his" before "employees" narrowed the scope of the provision. Thomas disagreed, finding that "his employees" could include "his" former employees but still exclude persons who have never worked for the employer. Shell also contended that the inclusion of "applicants for employment" was equivalent to the phrase "future employees." Therefore, Congress must have intended to limit section 704(a) to current and future employees. Thomas disagreed with this argument as well. He found that the term "applicant" was not synonymous with "future employees," because it covered many persons who would not become employees. Unsuccessful applicants and those who turned down job offers were applicants but not future employees.

Having found that the term "employees" was ambiguous, Thomas looked to other sections of title VII to provide context for the use of the term. He identified several sections that "plainly contemplate that former employees will make use of the remedial mechanisms of Title VII." For example, section 703(a) includes discriminatory discharge as an unlawful employment practice. A former employee would necessarily bring a charge of unlawful discharge. Therefore it was "far more consistent to include former employees within the scope of 'employees' protected by § 704(a)."

In addition, the Court was persuaded that to exclude former employees from the statute's protection would undermine the effectiveness to title VII by "allowing the threat of post-employment retaliation to deter victims of discrimination from complaining to EEOC, and would provide a perverse incentive for employers to fire employees who might bring Title VII claims." It was important to provide victims of illegal discrimination with "unfettered access" to the provisions of title VII. Therefore, the Court endorsed the inclusive interpretation of "employees" in section 704(a), allowing former employees like Robinson to prosecute their complaints of discrimination.

**CROSS REFERENCES**
Civil Rights; Civil Rights Acts; Employment Law

# ENDANGERED SPECIES

A species that is in danger of extinction throughout all or much of its territory; a species that is deemed valuable by society, but which faces daily threats to its population and ecosystem by hunters, poachers, developers, and commercial industries.

A *threatened species* is any species likely to become an endangered species within the foreseeable future (50 C.F.R. 424.02). Congress has passed a body of statutes and regulations to protect threatened and endangered species in the United States, and, to a lesser extent, around the world. The Endangered Species Act (ESA) is probably the most well-known body of law on this subject (16 U.S.C.A. § 1531 et seq).

The ESA is not the only such body of law, however; Congress has passed a number of other laws to regulate the hunting, fishing, trapping, and taking of certain species that are neither endangered by immediate extinction nor threatened by likely future extinction. Some of these species have previously faced extinction, but through national efforts have since been restored to healthier population numbers. On the other hand, some species have received Congressional protection merely because they are considered valuable by American citizens and lawmakers.

Though not statistically threatened with immediate or future extinction, some species face daily threats to their populations and ecosystems from hunters, poachers, developers, and certain commercial industries. In this sense, then, these species are endangered as well. The laws passed by Congress to regulate this area of wildlife help preserve and stabilize ecosystems, and forestall the problems incurred by species that are presently designated by the ESA as endangered or threatened.

An example of legislation designed to forestall extinction is the Marine Mammal Protection Act of 1972 (MMPA), (16 U.S.C.A. § 1361 et seq), which Congress passed to protect marine mammals from the adverse effects of human activities. To achieve this goal, Congress established a moratorium on the "taking" of marine mammals but provided that certain marine mammals may be taken incidentally in the course of commercial fishing operations and that permits may be issued for such operations. Partly because of their highly evolved physiology, and its similarity to the physiology of humans, marine mammals are considered sufficiently valuable in and of themselves without regard to their status under the ESA.

Certain provisions of the MMPA relate to marine mammals located outside the territorial waters of the United States. These provisions help foster concerted international efforts to protect a variety of valued marine mammals. For example, in 1997 Congress passed the International Dolphin Conservation Program Act, legislation amending the MMPA to support the International Dolphin Conservation Program (IDCP) in the eastern tropical Pacific Ocean. (Pub. L. 105-42) Specifically, the legislation gives effect to the Declaration of Panama, signed October 4, 1995, by the governments of Belize, Colombia, Costa Rica, Ecuador, France, Honduras, Mexico, Panama, Spain, the United States, Vanuatu, and Venezuela. The declaration established the IDCP, the protection of dolphins and other species and the conservation and management of tuna in the eastern tropical Pacific Ocean. It recognizes that nations fishing for tuna in the eastern tropical Pacific Ocean have achieved significant reductions in dolphin mortality and eliminates the ban on imports of tuna from nations in compliance with the IDCP.

Continuing on the international front, Congress also passed the Asian Elephant Conservation Act in 1997 (Pub. L. 105-96). The act is designed to perpetuate healthy populations of Asian elephants, to encourage participation in international Asian elephant conservation programs, and to provide financial resources for those programs. In passing the act, Congress made a number of findings, including, (1) Asian elephant populations have continued to decline to the point that the long-term survival of the species is in serious jeopardy; (2) resources to date have not been sufficient to cope with the continued loss of habitat and the consequent diminution of Asian elephant populations; and (3) threats to the long-term viability of Asian elephant populations must be effectively reduced, and will require the joint commitment of the international community.

Other acts Congress has passed to protect species at home and abroad include the Bald and Golden Eagle Protection Act (16 U.S.C.A. § 668 et seq.); the African Elephant Conservation Act (16 U.S.C.A. § 4201); the Migratory Bird Treaty Act (16 U.S.C.A. § 701 et seq.); the Wild Free-Roaming Horses and Burros Act (16 U.S.C.A. § 1331 et seq.), and the Lacey Act, which prohibits any person from knowingly causing or permitting the importation of wild animals and birds under inhumane and unhealthful conditions. (16 U.S.C.A. § 1371 et seq.).

### Constitutional Authority

Congress enacted the Endangered Species Act of 1973 (ESA) (16 U.S.C.A. § 1531 et seq.) pursuant to its power under the Commerce Clause in the U.S. Constitution Article I, section 8, Clause 3. This power authorizes Congress, or a federal agency exercising its administrative power, to regulate activities that substantially affects interstate commerce. When evaluating the effect that an activity will have on interstate commerce under the ESA, Congress and the federal agencies may take into account the cumulative impact that an activity will have on interstate commerce over time, even if the activity may have only a negligible impact at any one time or place.

For example, in *National Association of Home Builders v. Babbitt*, 130 F.3d 1041, (D.C.Cir. 1997), the U.S. Court of Appeals for the District of Columbia ruled that application of the ESA's prohibition against the taking of endangered wildlife to a species of fly found only in a limited area of California was a constitutional exercise of congressional Commerce Clause power to regulate activities substantially affecting interstate commerce. The court said that the prohibition, in the aggregate, prevented the destruction of bio-diversity in the country as a whole, thereby protecting current and future interstate commerce related to wildlife.

## Endangered Habitat

In addition to protecting species that are threatened or endangered, the ESA protects the critical habitat of endangered species. *Critical habitat* refers to the geographical area that is occupied by an endangered species, which possess physical or biological qualities essential to the preservation of the species, and which may require special management considerations or protection. In certain instances critical habitat may refer to habitat located outside the geographical area that is occupied by an endangered species if the habitat is deemed essential to the conservation of the species. However, critical habitat may not include the entire geographic area that is occupied by a species. At the same time, critical habitat may not be restricted to the geographical area necessary for a minimum viable population of an endangered species.

Habitat will not necessarily receive designation as critical merely because it is occupied by wildlife that has been included on the endangered species list. According to the regulations promulgated pursuant to the ESA, critical habitat designation is not appropriate when one or both of the following situations exist: (1) the species is threatened by human activity, and a designation of critical habitat would likely increase the degree of threat to the species; or (2) a designation of critical habitat would not be beneficial to the species (50 C.F.R. § 424.12).

The decision to designate habitat as critical is made by the secretary of the interior, based on a cost-benefit analysis in which the preservation of endangered species weighs most heavily. The secretary of the interior's decision to include or exclude an area from the list of critical habitat is subject to judicial review, but the decision will not be overturned unless it is arbitrary and capricious. However, the secretary must carefully balance all the competing considerations, and decisions based on a cursory or incomplete analysis of the relevant factors will not be upheld, *Natural Resources Defense Council v. U.S. Department of Interior*, 113 F.3d 1121 [9th Cir. 1997].

Once an area has been properly designated as critical habitat, each federal agency is required to ensure that any action authorized, funded, or carried out by the agency is not likely to jeopardize, destroy, or adversely modify the designated habitat. The ESA requires federal agencies to consult the secretary of the interior prior to commencing action that might affect critical habitat. After consultation, the secretary must provide a written opinion to the agency detailing how the proposed action affects a species' critical habitat, and recommending reasonable alternatives when a proposed action threatens that habitat.

## Enforcement

A lawsuit to enforce the ESA may be initiated by the federal government, a state government, or a private citizen. Both state and federal courts have jurisdiction to hear suits commenced pursuant to the ESA. As with any other lawsuit brought in state or federal court, parties initiating an action under the ESA must have standing to sue, which means they must have a personal stake in the outcome of the case or controversy. Although the standing requirements under federal law are fairly relaxed, courts still occasionally dismiss ESA actions for lack of standing.

For example, in 1997 the U.S. District Court for the Southern District of Texas ruled that an association of commercial shrimp trawling vessels and its executive director lacked standing to challenge the federal government's alleged failure to enforce provisions of the ESA so as to prohibit the illegal taking of sea turtles in recreational fishing areas (*Texas Shrimp Association v. Daley*, 984 F. Supp. 1023 [S.D. Texas 1997]). The court found no evidence that failure to regulate recreational areas increased regulation of commercial shrimpers, or that regulation of recreational areas resulted in less regulation of commercial shrimpers.

**CROSS REFERENCES**
Commerce Clause; Constitutional Law; Endangered Species Act

# ENTRAPMENT

The act of government agents or officials that induces a person to commit a crime he or she is not previously disposed to commit.

## Ninth Circuit Allows Evidence of Prior Good Acts

In January 1998, the Ninth Circuit Court decided the question of whether a criminal defendant has the right to present evidence of prior good acts when asserting the defense of entrapment. Entrapment occurs where law enforcement agents induce a person to commit a crime that he had not previously contemplated for the purpose of prosecuting him for the crime.

*United States v. Thomas*, a drug case against Bourne Bobby Thomas began in 1992, when U.S. immigration officials seized the car of Cristobal Crosthwaite-Villa, a friend of Thomas, who had been trying to cross the border between Mexico and the United States illegally, was in Tijuana trying to gain the return of his car when he met a childhood friend, Albert Barruetta. Crosthwaite was unaware that Barruetta had become a professional informer for the U.S. Drug Enforcement Agency (DEA).

When Crosthwaite told Barruetta about the seizure of his car, Barruetta offered to help him get the car back and obtain a permit for Crosthwaite and his family to live in the United States. Barruetta set a price for the services at $1,000, and Crosthwaite gave Barruetta a $400 down payment.

Throughout October 1992, Crosthwaite contacted Barruetta to discuss Barruetta's progress. In the course of their conversations, Barruetta discovered that Crosthwaite used drugs. Although Barrueta had no knowledge that Crosthwaite was involved in drug dealing, he nevertheless told DEA Agent Bruce Goldberg that Crosthwaite distributed multiple pounds of methamphetamine every month. Goldberg arranged a sting operation using Barrueta as an informant. Barruetta asked Crosthwaite to find some methamphetamine, and for some time Crosthwaite looked but could not find the drug.

In time, Crosthwaite contacted Thomas, who had once sold Crosthwaite a couple of doses of methamphetamine for $20 apiece. Crosthwaite eventually introduced Thomas to Barruetta. According to Thomas, Barruetta stated that if Thomas would arrange a drug deal for him, Crosthwaite would be able to get his car and legal entry into the United States. Thomas also testified at trial that Barruetta insisted on getting Thomas to take part in various marijuana, cocaine, or methamphetamine deals and that Barrueta had offered him drugs as incentive. Barruetta denied the claims at trial.

In early December 1992, Thomas, seeking to help his friend, Crosthwaite, arranged a sale of methamphetamine to Barruetta. When the transaction took place, DEA agents arrested Thomas, along with Crosthwaite and José Solorio, a courier who had delivered the methamphetamine.

Thomas was tried twice and convicted both times. The first conviction was overturned on appeal because the trial court failed to give the jury an instruction on the defense of entrapment. As he had done in the first trial, Thomas argued in the second trial that Barruetta had entrapped him and that until he met Barruetta he was not disposed to arranging the sale of methamphetamines. The court allowed the prosecution to prove Thomas's predisposition with evidence that Thomas was an occasional methamphetamine user and that in the past he had sold two doses of the drug to Crosthwaite. However, the court prevented Thomas from presenting evidence to rebut the predisposition evidence offered by the prosecution: specifically, the court forbade Thomas to testify that he had never been arrested and had no record of past criminal behavior that suggested he was predisposed to selling drugs. Thomas was convicted of conspiracy to possess methamphetamine with the intent to distribute, and aiding and abetting the possession of methamphetamine with intent to distribute, and sentenced to 151 months in prison.

In his second appeal, Thomas argued that he should have been allowed to testify to his own good character and his clean record. The question raised by Thomas's argument—whether a defendant asserting entrapment has the right to present favorable character evidence—had never been answered in the Ninth Circuit Court.

In a 2–1 decision, the appeals court reversed Thomas's convictions and granted Thomas the right to a new trial. "Where the issue is predisposition," stated the majority, "the evidence that the defendant has no record of prior bad acts is clearly relevant" (*United States v. Thomas*, 134 F. 3d 975 [9th Cir. 1998]). The majority opined that "it is reasonably likely that a jury would give significant weight to the government's evidence of the earlier $20 sales, even though that evidence was relatively weak and insubstantial as to the question of Thomas's predisposition." The majority concluded that Thomas was prejudiced by the exclusion of the evidence, and the majority ordered a new trial.

Judge Otto R. Skopil, Jr. , dissented. Skopil argued that Thomas's lack of a prior criminal record was not relevant. "Thomas's proffered evidence," Skopil wrote, "in light of his admitted criminal activity, simply means that until now he had eluded arrest and conviction."

**CROSS REFERENCES**
Drugs and Narcotics

# EQUAL PROTECTION

The constitutional guarantee that no person or class of persons shall be denied the same protection of the laws that is enjoyed by other persons or other classes in like circumstances in their lives, liberty, property, and pursuit of happiness.

## M. L. B. v. S. L. J.

Since the 1950s the U.S. Supreme Court has issued a series of decisions requiring the government to provide legal counsel to indigent persons. In addition, state and federal courts may waive filing fees and other court-related costs for persons who cannot afford to pay. These efforts are meant to guarantee a person access to the courts regardless of her income. Nevertheless, the Court has never ruled that states must waive costs in all cases. Typically, the Court has given the most consideration to indigent criminal defendants charged with felonies.

The Supreme Court again faced the issue of equal access to justice in *M. L. B. v. S. L. J.*, __U.S.__, 117 S. Ct. 555, 136 L. Ed. 2d 473 (1996). *M.L.B.* involved Mississippi statutes that required a person who wished to appeal to the Mississippi Supreme Court to pay in advance for the preparation of the trial court transcript. M. L. B. sought to appeal the termination of her parental rights but could not afford to pay for the transcript. The Mississippi Supreme Court denied her application to have the state pay for the transcript, which resulted in her forfeiting

her appeal rights. The U.S. Supreme Court held that the Mississippi statutes violated the Equal Protection and Due Process Clauses of the Fourteenth Amendment.

The case involved M. L. B. and her former husband, S. L. J. After their divorce in 1992, S. L. J. was awarded custody of their two children. Three months later S. L. J. remarried. In 1993 he sought to terminate M. L. B.'s parental rights and have his new wife adopt the children. After taking evidence, a Mississippi chancery court filed a decree in 1994 that terminated M. L. B.'s parental rights and ordered the stepmother's name to be shown as the mother of the children on their birth certificates. Though the court stated that the relationship between M. L. B. and her children had eroded, it did not make specific findings as to the causes of this erosion. The court merely stated that S. L. J. and his wife had met their burden of proof by "clear and convincing evidence."

In January 1995 M. L. B. filed an appeal, paying the $100 filing fee. Within a few days, the chancery court estimated that the cost of preparing the transcript of the trial record would cost almost $2,400. Under Mississippi law (Miss. Code Ann. §§ 11-51-3, 1-51-29 [Supp. 1996]), a civil litigant has the right to appeal, but that right is conditioned on prepayment of costs. Relevant portions of the transcript must be ordered and paid if the appellant (the appealing party) "intends to urge on appeal that a finding or conclusion is unsupported by the evidence or is contrary to the evidence" (Miss. R. App. P. 10(b)(2) [1995]). M. L. B., who intended to challenge the sufficiency of the evidence, filed a motion with the state supreme court asking to appeal *in forma pauperis*. If granted, this type of motion, which in Latin means "as a pauper," allows a person to proceed without paying court costs and filing fees. However, the Mississippi Supreme Court denied M. L. B.'s request, ruling that the right to proceed *in forma pauperis* exists only at the trial level. M. L. B. then appealed to the U.S. Supreme Court.

The Court, on a 6–3 vote, held that the inability to pay for a transcript should not prevent a person from appealing a termination of parental rights. Justice Ruth Bader Ginsburg, writing for the majority, based the decision on a line of cases that began with *Griffin v. Illinois*, 351 U.S. 12, 76 S. Ct. 585, 100 L. Ed. 891 (1956). In *Griffin* the Court struck down an Illinois rule that conditioned an appeal from a criminal conviction on the defendant's purchase of a transcript of the trial proceedings. The rule deprived most defendants lacking the means to pay for the transcript of any access to appellate review. Although the U.S. Constitution guarantees no right to appellate review, once a state provides that right, the state may not, in the words of Justice Felix Frankfurter, "bolt the door to equal justice." The *Griffin* decision concluded that the Due Process and Equal Protection Clauses of the Fourteenth Amendment required the state to provide a criminal defendant with a transcript for an appeal.

Ginsburg acknowledged that the *Griffin* line of cases dealt with criminal, not civil cases. However, Ginsburg said, *Griffin*'s "principle has not been confined to cases in which imprisonment is at stake." In *Mayer v. Chicago*, 404 U.S. 189, 92 S. Ct. 410, 30 L. Ed. 2d 372 (1971), the Court ruled that Illinois had to provide free transcripts to non-felony criminal defendants who did not face incarceration. The Court reasoned that there are "serious collateral consequences" that flow from petty criminal offenses and justify a defendant's unconditional right to appeal.

Ginsburg also noted that the Court had recognized a narrow category of civil cases in which the state may not restrict access on the ability to pay court fees. In *Boddie v. Connecticut*, 401 U.S. 371, 91 S. Ct. 780, 28 L. Ed. 2d 113 (1971), the Court held that a state could not deny a divorce to a married couple based on their inability to pay about sixty dollars in court costs. In *Lassiter v. Department of Social Services of Durham County*, 452 U.S. 18, 101 S. Ct. 2153, 68 L. Ed. 2d 640 (1981), the Court held that the character and difficulty of the case warranted the appointment of counsel for indigent persons seeking to defend against the state's termination of their parental rights. The Court said that the termination of parental rights works "a unique kind of deprivation."

Ginsburg also cited *Santosky v. Kramer*, 455 U.S. 745, 102 S. Ct. 1388, 71 L. Ed. 2d 599 (1982), which also involved termination of parental rights. The Court in *Santosky* noted that a termination decree is "*final* and irrevocable," and that the parent's interest is "far more precious than any property right."

Based on these decisions, Ginsburg concluded that the transcript fee for an appeal unconstitutionally denied M. L. B. access to justice. The state action she was attempting to reverse "is barely distinguishable from criminal condemnation in view of the magnitude and permanence of the loss she faces." Ginsburg agreed with M. L. B. that her parental termination appeal should be treated the same as the petty criminal offense appeal endorsed by the *Mayer* decision.

Ginsburg based the decision on equal protection and due process grounds. The equal protection concern "relates to the legitimacy of fencing out would-be appellants" based only on their inability to pay court costs. The due process concern centers on the "essential fairness of the state-ordered proceedings." Ginsburg noted that the judge's termination order in this case did not describe any evidence that demonstrated M. L. B. was unfit to be a parent: "Only a transcript can reveal to judicial minds other than the Chancellor's [trial judge] the sufficiency, or insufficiency, of the evidence to support his stern judgment."

Ginsburg rejected Mississippi's contention that providing free transcripts for those indigent persons challenging a termination of parental rights would impose a financial burden on the state. In reviewing Mississippi appellate case filings, Ginsburg concluded that only a handful of parental terminations reach the court each year. The few appellants who would require a free transcript would impose a minimal cost on the state. She also made clear that the court's decision was strictly limited to parental termination appeals and could not be applied to other types of civil cases.

Chief Justice William H. Rehnquist and Justices Antonin Scalia and Clarence Thomas dissented. In a dissenting opinion, Thomas attacked the *Griffin* line of decisions and questioned the equal protection analysis of the majority.

**CROSS REFERENCES**
Appeal; Fourteenth Amendment; Parent and Child

# EVERS, MEDGAR WILEY

## Beckwith Conviction Upheld

On December 22, 1997, the Mississippi Supreme Court upheld the conviction of Byron De La Beckwith for the 1963 murder of civil rights leader Medgar Evers *De La Beckwith v. State*, 1997 WL 781301. The decision appeared to close the thirty-four year-long legal odyssey involving the seventy-seven year-old Beckwith, who had faced three trials and filed state and federal appeals. After his conviction in 1992, he appealed on the ground that he had been denied his right to a speedy and fair trial. The Mississippi Supreme Court rejected that claim by a 4–2 vote, with three justices not participating. Writing for the majority, Justice Mike Mills called the decision a signal to "miscreants" that "justice, slow and plodding though she may be, is certain in the state of Mississippi."

In 1963, at the age of thirty-seven, Evers had a prominent place in the civil rights movement. Having been the first black man to seek admission to the University of Mississippi, he was serving as the field secretary of the National Association for the Advancement of Colored People (NAACP) in Jackson, Mississippi, working to end segregation. On June 12, a sniper hiding in bushes killed him in the driveway of his home. Substantial evidence pointed to Beckwith, a twenty-four year-old fertilizer salesman. His fingerprint was found on the scope of the rifle believed to be the murder weapon, and several people said he had bragged at a Ku Klux Klan meeting about killing Evers. Quickly arrested and indicted by a grand jury, he maintained that he had been ninety miles away from Jackson at the time of the killing. In February and April of 1964, two trials ended in hung juries. Many white Mississippians rejoiced; former state governor Ross Barnett even embraced Beckwith in the courtroom.

Over the next three decades, civil rights leaders remained convinced that Beckwith had escaped justice. Then, in 1989, new evidence emerged. The *Jackson Clarion-Ledger* revealed that state officials of the Mississippi State Sovereignty Commission had improperly helped Beckwith's attorneys by privately giving them information about the beliefs of prospective jurors. At the urging of Evers' widow, Myrlie Evers, national chair of the NAACP, the case was reopened in 1990 and Beckwith was again indicted. He sought to prevent the case from going to trial, arguing that too many years had passed to retry him. In 1992 the Mississippi Supreme Court rejected this argument (Beckwith v. State, 615 So.2d 1134 [Miss. 1992]), and the U.S. Supreme Court refused to hear the case. Convicted on December 16, 1992, by a jury of eight blacks and four whites, he was sentenced to life in prison.

At the heart of Beckwith's appeal was the contention that he had been denied a fair and speedy trial. He argued that the delay from 1964 to 1990 had violated the due process, equal protection, and fundamental fairness provisions of the state and federal constitutions. The appeal also alleged more than twenty errors at trial, including improper instructions to the jury, the admission of irrelevant and inflammatory evidence, and the influence of adverse media coverage on the jury.

The court rejected all of Beckwith's claims. In the majority opinion, Justice Mills ruled that Beckwith could fairly be retried because the original cases had ended in mistrials. Moreover, the majority held that Beckwith himself was partly responsible for the long delay between trials. Beckwith had bragged about his "power and connections" among state officials and therefore had "complicity in thwarting the aims of fair and impartial justice" caused by the improper assistance given to his defense team in 1964 by the Mississippi State Sovereignty Commission. Upon a thorough review of the evidence, the majority concluded that Beckwith had indeed killed Evers.

In a strongly worded dissent, Chief Justice Dan Lee blasted prosecutors and the majority on the court. Prosecutors had waited for a favorable political climate in which to convict Beckwith, he wrote, thus giving them an advantage. "The state delayed prosecution of Beckwith for some 9,706 days, and, with the legal equivalent of a 'straight face,' asked us to ignore Beckwith's constitutional rights." By upholding the conviction, the majority had caused "a total eradication of the guarantee of a speedy trial from the constitutional lexicon."

Civil rights leaders celebrated the decision while Beckwith planned to file a federal appeal.

*Byron De La Beckwith's conviction for the murder of Medgar Evers was upheld by the Mississippi Supreme Court.*

GAMMA LIAISON

*Bill Cosby puts his arm around Autumn Jackson in this 1991 home video image shot by Jackson's grandmother, Lois Maxfield, on the set of* The Cosby Show.

AP/WIDE WORLD PHOTOS

## EXTORTION

The obtaining of property from another induced by wrongful use of actual or threatened force, violence, or fear, or under color of official right.

### Bill Cosby Extortion Case

A New York jury convicted a twenty-two-year-old woman of attempting to extort $40 million from celebrity Bill Cosby. Autumn Jackson, who claimed to be the illegitimate child of the well-known entertainer, was arrested in an FBI sting operation in January. Prosecutors said she had threatened Cosby: unless he paid her, she would sell a tabloid newspaper a story that contradicted his wholesome public image. Defense attorneys argued that Jackson had merely conducted lawful negotiations. On July 25, 1997, following a two-week trial, jurors found her guilty of extortion, conspiracy, and crossing state lines to commit a crime. Also convicted were her two co-conspirators. After the trial ended, however, new paternity claims emerged, and legal commentators argued over the correctness of the verdict.

In the 1970s, Cosby had a sexual affair with Jackson's mother, Dawn Upshaw, and he admitted it was possible Jackson was their daughter. Cosby gave Jackson financial gifts over the years, including a car, trust fund, and support for her college education, but he cut her off when she dropped out of school. Between November and December 1996, Jackson, saying she was homeless, asked him for money. She returned in January with a bigger demand: unless he paid her $40 million, she would go to *The Globe* with her "story of desperation." Helped by Jose Medina, 51, and Boris Sabas, 42, Jackson

called and wrote to Cosby, his associates, and his employers over a three-week period. The letters denounced Cosby as a hypocrite for playing the charitable character, Cliff Huxtable, on "The Cosby Show."

On January 16, in an unrelated tragedy, Cosby's only son, Ennis, was murdered on a California highway. Shortly thereafter, Jackson made another demand, and Cosby went to the FBI. Two days later, federal agents set up a sting operation. Jackson and Medina traveled to Los Angeles for what they believed was the payment, signed papers for $24 million, and were arrested. They subsequently arrested Sabas and charged the trio with three felonies. They were tried simultaneously in New York in July.

The question of Cosby's alleged paternity shadowed the trial. No DNA tests had been made to establish whether Cosby was Jackson's father. Robert M. Baum, an attorney with the federal Legal Aid Society, argued that Jackson had been raised to believe she was Cosby's daughter. Baum told jurors that as a result, she "felt that she possessed certain legal and moral rights." However, in instructions to the jury, U.S. District Court Judge Barbara Jones twice ordered them to ignore the issue. Paternity was irrelevant to the case, Judge Jones said, the real issue being extortion—the crime of taking property under actual or threatened force (18 U.S.C.A. § 871 et seq.).

Prosecutor Paul A. Engelmayer, a southern district assistant U.S. attorney, told jurors that the issue of paternity did not matter because "There is no 'father exception' to extortion." Saying the defendants were driven by greed, Engelmayer introduced into evidence letters and tapes, including a telephone message Jackson left for Peter Lund, the former CEO of the television network CBS, in which she hinted at the impact her story would have on the network, Cosby's employer. Some evidence was clearly intended to play for juror sympathy—in particular, a recording of her increasing her fee for *The Globe* after the murder of Cosby's son.

The defense tried to characterize the money requests as legal negotiations. In his summation, defense attorney Baum told the court, "Don't lawyers do the kinds of things Autumn Jackson did every day in this city and this country?" Baum blamed Cosby for initiating what he called a "game" of giving money to Jackson. But jurors were unswayed. In less than an hour, they convicted Jackson and Medina on all three counts, which carry a maximum prison sentence of twelve years. They spent two days on their decision to acquit Sabas of extortion but convict him of conspiracy and crossing state lines to commit a crime.

After the verdict, two men came forward claiming to be the real father. Jerald Jackson, a truck driver, had been named as the father on Jackson's birth certificate. Jesus Vasquez, a former busboy, also claimed paternity. Meanwhile, the legal community debated whether the jury's verdict had been fair. Harvey A. Silvergate, a lawyer and columnist in the *National Law Journal*, speculated that Jackson would probably not have committed a crime if she had hired an attorney to negotiate for her.

**CROSS REFERENCES**
Conspiracy; Paternity

# EXTRADITION

The transfer of an ACCUSED from one state or country to another state or country that seeks to place the accused on TRIAL.

### Felon Who Fled Under Duress Not Fugitive

Timothy Reed, a convicted felon from Ohio, challenged his extradition from New Mexico to Ohio. Reed claimed that he was not a fugitive from justice, and therefore was not subject to extradition. A state district court and the New Mexico Supreme Court agreed. The State Supreme Court held that Ohio's egregious conduct forced Reed to "flee the state under duress, in fear of death or great bodily harm at the hands of government officials."

In 1982 and 1983, Reed pleaded guilty in Ohio to three charges of theft of drugs and aggravated robbery. He was sentenced to concurrent terms of up to twenty-five years imprisonment. Reed, part Lakota Sioux and known as Little Rock Reed, became a jailhouse lawyer and an outspoken advocate for the right of incarcerated Native Americans to practice traditional religious beliefs. While in prison in Lucasville, Ohio, Reed helped inmates prepare petitions for writs of habeas corpus and wrote numerous articles on Native American prison issues. His activism attracted national attention and earned him the animosity of prison officials. Reed claimed that he was mistreated and was denied parole because of his activities.

Shortly before Reed's scheduled release on parole in late 1990, he was asked to sign a contract required of all parolees. Reed altered the wording before signing the contract because he believed it compelled him to waive certain constitutional rights.

Reed met with the chairman of the Parole Authority shortly after his parole. The chairman told Reed that his parole was being rescinded due to his refusal to sign the parole contract as written. According to Reed's unchallenged testimony, the chairman swore at him, told him he would serve twenty-five years, and said that he did not "give a damn" about Reed's constitutional rights. Reed returned to prison in Lucasville.

Reed was again released in May 1992, with a one-year parole term. This time Reed signed the original parole contract, planning to challenge it later in court. He worked as the director of the Native American Prisoners' Research and Rehabilitation Project in Cincinnati, Ohio, became a full-time college student, and continued to publish articles and give speeches. He also corresponded with various officials of the Ohio Department of Corrections, criticizing the lack of Native American religious services and offering to mediate disputes between prison officials and religious organizations. Reed's persistent activism angered some. The warden at Lucasville wrote to Reed that he "personally resent[ed]" Reed's "continued attacks" and attempts to force changes in prison operations.

In the fall of 1992, Reed met with his parole officer, Ron Mitchell. Mitchell told Reed that for the first time in Mitchell's thirteen-year career, the chief of the Parole Authority had personally contacted him. The chief ordered Mitchell to forbid Reed from speaking in public again about the Department of Corrections or the Parole Authority, and to cease writing articles and letters to officials. If Reed refused, his parole would be revoked and he would be returned to the penitentiary, Mitchell informed him.

Reed agreed not to travel for the remainder of his parole term or write to prison officials. However, he planned to continue to speak and to publish his writings, and send videotaped presentations to out-of-town conferences. He canceled various speaking engagements and did not testify as planned before the U.S. Senate Select Committee on Indian Affairs.

In February 1993, Reed had a minor accident with a car he had borrowed from Dinah Devoto, a volunteer at the Native American Project where Reed worked. In mid-March, Steve Devoto (Dinah Devoto's husband) and

Reed argued over the phone. Devoto's husband apparently resented his wife's volunteer work, and remarked to others that he would like to severely hurt Reed. During the conversation Devoto ordered Reed to stay away from his family. He also threatened to "blow off" Reed's head.

The Devotos lived in Kentucky, just across the Ohio border from Cincinnati. On evening, March 18, 1993, Reed was served with a summons and complaint for "terroristic threatening" under Kentucky law. The misdemeanor charge stemmed from his argument with Steve Devoto over the telephone. Upon learning of the charge, Dinah Devoto immediately prepared an affidavit swearing that her husband's allegations were false. In it she stated that she and her husband wanted to meet with Reed's parole officer and that Steve Devoto would drop his complaint.

Reed contacted his parole officer early on Friday, March 19, to explain the events of the previous evening. Mitchell told Reed to report to his office for arrest the following Monday at 9 a.m. and to say "your goodbyes to your family and friends … You're going back to Lucasville." Mitchell refused to listen to Reed's protestations of innocence and would not meet with the Devotos. He told Reed he could present evidence of his innocence to the Ohio Parole Board after he was back in prison. Reed testified that Mitchell "assured me that I was going to have no hearing whatsoever. I was going back to Lucasville without any due process."

Reed and some of his supporters made many calls between Friday and Sunday in an effort to prevent the revocation of Reed's parole without a hearing. Dinah Devoto later prepared an affidavit recounting her conversation with Mitchell, during which he told her Reed would have to serve the remainder of his sentence because certain high-ranking officials held Reed in contempt. Steve Devoto telephoned the regional supervisor of the Parole Authority and admitted he had falsely accused Reed. Harold Pepinsky, a lawyer and criminal justice professor at Indiana University, spoke with Mitchell and became convinced that Reed's rights were going to be ignored. Officials from various government agencies told Pepinsky that Reed's only recourse was to petition the Parole Authority, although it was the very agency Reed claimed was denying him his rights.

Inmates inside Lucasville had previously informed Reed that certain prison authorities had expressed an intent to cause him death or great bodily harm if he ever returned to Lucasville. Furthermore, Reed believed that a riot would soon take place in Lucasville, spurred on by the warden's policies. Warden Tate had forced members of the Black Panthers and the Aryan Brotherhood to integrate. Indeed, a riot occurred on April 11, 1993, lasting eleven days and resulting in eight deaths. One of the dead was Dennis Weaver, a Native American writer and advocate for prisoners' rights.

Reed did not report as ordered for his arrest. Instead, he fled Ohio and eventually took up residence in Taos, New Mexico. He found work at the Center for Advocacy of Human Rights, and continued to publish and speak on Native American and prison issues. Ohio declared him to be a "parole violator-at-large."

Contrary to his earlier assertions, Steve Devoto pursued his complaint of terroristic threatening. In June 1993, Reed was tried and found guilty in absentia in Kentucky and received a thirty-day suspended sentence.

On September 27, 1994, the acting chief of the Ohio Parole Authority executed a warrant for Reed's arrest for violating parole, and executed a request for extradition requisition asking Ohio's governor to petition for Reed's extradition from New Mexico. Within a month Reed was arrested in New Mexico as a fugitive from justice pursuant to the extradition warrant. A few days later he appeared in district court in Taos and stated he would challenge the constitutionality of his arrest by filing a petition for writ of habeas corpus. After hearings, the district court ruled in Reed's favor and ordered him released from custody.

Upon appeal, the State Supreme Court first determined that under New Mexico extradition law, a defendant has a right to a habeas corpus hearing to show how the process of extradition has resulted in an unconstitutional imprisonment. A writ of habeas corpus is provided for in Article I of the U.S. Constitution and is used to release a person from unlawful imprisonment. Its purpose is not to determine a prisoner's guilt or innocence but only whether the prisoner has been restrained of his or her liberty with due process.

The Extradition Clause of the U.S. Constitution (Article IV, section 2) mandates that a person charged with treason, a felony, or other crime in one state who flees from justice shall on demand be delivered to the state having jurisdiction over the crime. In this way no state can become a sanctuary for fugitives from other states.

At the hearings on the petition for habeas corpus, the state asserted that the trial court could only consider four questions: (1) whether the extradition documents are in order; (2) whether the demanding state has charged the defendant with a crime; (3) whether the defendant is the person named in the extradition request; and (4) whether the defendant is a fugitive. These criteria were established in the U.S. Supreme Court case *Michigan v. Doran*, 439 U.S. 282, 99 S. Ct. 530, 58 L. Ed. 2d 521 (1978). Based upon the *Doran* case, New Mexico contended that virtually all Reed's evidence and legal arguments were beyond the scope of permissible inquiry of an extradition proceeding. In other words, the state argued that most of Reed's evidence was irrelevant. Consequently the state did not dispute any of the facts Reed introduced, nor did it introduce contrary evidence.

The district court found that the extradition documents were not in order and that Reed was not a fugitive from justice because he left Ohio "under duress and under a reasonable fear for his safety and his life." Upon appeal, the New Mexico Supreme Court quickly determined that the state had sufficiently established each of the first three elements required under *Doran*. Reed did not dispute that he was the person named in the warrant for extradition. Therefore, only the question of his fugitive states remained.

The U.S. Supreme Court case of *Morrissey v. Brewer*, 408 U.S. 471, 92 S. Ct. 2593 33 L. Ed. 2d 484 (1972), held that the Due Process Clause of the U.S. Constitution entitles a parolee to a preliminary hearing to determine whether probable cause exists for revocation of parole. Furthermore, a parolee is entitled to a second, final hearing once a finding of probable cause has been made. Reed's undisputed evidence demonstrated that he would be denied a prerevocation hearing. "Had Ohio's agents obeyed their own laws, Reed would not have been forced to flee," the New Mexico Supreme Court reasoned. "[T]he agents of Ohio's penal system intended to deny Reed this basic due process guarantee."

The New Mexico Supreme Court determined that the proper definition of "fugitive from justice" a person who seeks "to avoid the maintenance and administration of what is just." The court concluded that Reed demonstrated conclusively that Ohio's conduct toward him was not just. In unequivocal language, the court called Reed "a refugee from injustice." The court found that Reed's quest to escape Ohio's unconstitutional conduct was incompatible with a finding that he was a fugitive from justice.

The New Mexico Supreme Court next addressed the significance of the threat of death or great bodily harm to Reed if he had remained in Ohio. The question was whether Reed's flight from Ohio could be excused because he "acted under threats or conditions that a reasonable man would have been unable to resist," or in other words, whether he acted under duress. The court held that "in extradition cases, duress may be raised as a defense to the fugitivity element if the individual was incited to cross state lines—and would otherwise never have done so—by the illegal actions of the demanding state." Reed essentially had to choose between death and flight, the court found, and was justified in fleeing. The court was persuaded by findings that Reed's unlawful behavior was provoked by Ohio, that he reasonably feared death or harm from state officials, that there was no relief available in Ohio, that he used no force or violence during or after his flight, and that he acted as a reasonable person would have under similar circumstances. Moreover, the court noted that a belated offer of a revocation hearing, after he was found in New Mexico, could not then transform Reed into a fugitive if he had never been one in the first place.

In its lengthy and strongly worded decision the court emphasized repeatedly that the uncontroverted, singularly compelling facts of Reed's case justified the unusual outcome. The court declared that "there is no right more fundamental than the right to one's own life." The chief justice, author of the majority opinion, characterized the case as a decision between ignoring or preventing a violation of Reed's constitutional rights.

Two justices agreed with the majority opinion. One justice concurred with the outcome of the majority opinion, but believed that relief should have been granted for different reasons. One justice dissented, reasoning that the majority exceeded its authority under the law, and arguing that the decision would make New Mexico a haven for those fleeing what they believe is unjust treatment in other states.

On June 8, 1998, the U.S. Supreme Court overruled the Supreme Court of New Mexico (*New Mexico ex rel. Ortiz v. Reed*, ___U.S.___, ___ L.Ed.2d___, 118 S. Ct. 1860). The Court held that the U.S. Constitution's Extradition

Clause overrode the clause in New Mexico's Constitution guaranteeing the right to seek and obtain safety. The Extradition Clause compelled New Mexico to return Reed to Ohio to face proceedings. The Court also ruled that New Mexico's Supreme Court had exceeded its jurisdiction by considering issues not open to consideration by an asylum state in an extradition case. Issues relating to deficiencies in Ohio's penal system must be tried in the state of Ohio, the demanding state, and cannot be tried in New Mexico, the asylum state.

**CROSS REFERENCES**
Parole; Prisoners' Rights

## FETAL RIGHTS

The rights of any unborn human fetus, which is generally a developing human from roughly eight weeks after conception to birth.

### Suit Over Stillbirth

On December 2, 1997, the Supreme Court of Louisiana ruled that a fetus is not a person under state law for purposes of certain lawsuits (*Wartelle v. Women's and Children's Hospital, Inc.* 704 So.2d 778). Two parents had sued a hospital alleging that its error contributed to the death of their child before birth. They sought damages on behalf of the fetus and, separately, for the trauma they had suffered as witnesses to the stillbirth. At trial, the first claim failed but the second succeeded. Subsequently, an appeals court ruled that they could recover on both claims and increased the size of the damage award. But the state supreme court overruled the appellate decision. It held that a stillborn fetus does not possess "legal personality"—the dead fetus is not regarded as a person under state law—and denied the parents' claims.

Patrick and Kristine Wartelle were expecting their first child. Mrs. Wartelle went into labor and was admitted to Women's and Children's Hospital in Louisiana, where, according to standard practice, a fetal heart monitor was attached to her. Later, the monitor was temporarily removed. When it was reattached, the medical staff determined that the fetus had died. The stillborn fetus was then removed by cesarean section. Afterwards, the Wartelles sued on the ground that hospital negligence in failing to monitor the fetus's heartbeat contributed to the death. In a court-approved settlement, the hospital paid them $100,000.

Next, the Wartelles sued the hospital and the Louisiana Patients' Compensation Fund for damages in excess of $100,000 pursuant to the state's Medical Malpractice Act (La. Rev. Stat. ann. sections 40:1299.41–1299.48 [west]). Their suit asserted three claims. First, they sought damages in a so-called survival action on behalf of the fetus. This type of claim is brought by the survivors of a deceased person—typically, relatives or others in the deceased's estate—who seek damages for the harm done to the deceased person. Second, they alleged that the fetus suffered a wrongful death. And third, they brought a *bystander* action, seeking compensation for their own emotional distress and mental anguish at witnessing the delivery of their dead child.

The trial judge dismissed the survival action, ruling that the fetus could not be considered a person under state law because it was stillborn. The Wartelles were awarded a lump sum of $250,000 under the wrongful death action and the bystander claim. Both sides appealed. The appeals court affirmed the general damage award of $250,000, interpreting it as compensation for the wrongful death of the stillborn child. It set bystander damages to $25,000 for each parent. Reversing the trial court and allowing the survival action, it awarded the Wartelles $50,000 on this claim. The total damage award after the first appeal was $350,000.

This decision prompted an appeal by the Louisiana Patients' Compensation Fund. The state supreme court granted review to determine three questions: (1) whether a survival action

*Facial features can be discerned in this ultrasound image of a nearly full-term fetus.*

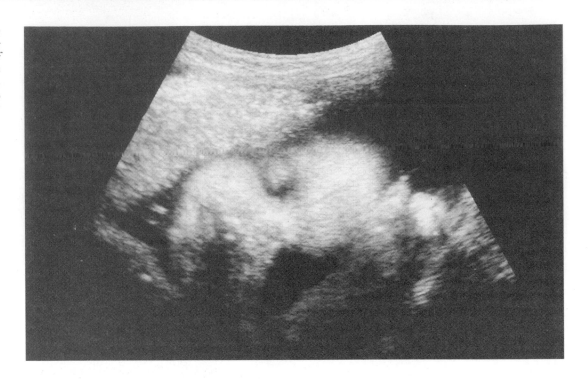

could be pursued in connection with the death of a stillborn fetus; (2) whether the plaintiffs had a valid claim for bystander damages; and (3) whether the amount of damages awarded was excessive. The first and second questions depended directly on whether a stillborn fetus is considered a person under state law.

Instead of a philosophical inquiry into the nature of life, the Louisiana Supreme Court delivered a narrow reading of state law. Initially, the court observed that book I, title I, of the state civil code defines a natural person as a human being, with a natural "legal personality" commencing from the moment of live birth and terminating at death. Accordingly, wrote Justice Walter F. Marcus, Jr., the civil code establishes "the general rule that an unborn fetus is not recognized as possessing legal personality." This view "constitutes no moral or philosophical judgment on the value of the fetus, nor any comment on its essential humanity" but is instead used solely for the purposes of defining legal rights and duties, Marcus wrote.

The court analyzed two exceptions to the general rule that an unborn fetus is not a person. First, article 26 of the civil code holds that an unborn child is considered a person from the moment of conception only as regards its legal interests—its well-being and safety. But if the child is born dead, the law states that "it shall be considered never to have existed as a person, except for purposes of actions resulting from its wrongful death." This exception does not apply

to survival actions, the court ruled, but merely covers "matters that advance the interests of the fetus" while it is alive. If born dead, wrote Marcus, the fetus's "fictional personality is erased." Thus, because the stillborn fetus is not a person and has no rights, it cannot transmit any rights to parents who would wish to bring a survival action.

The second exception under analysis dealt with wrongful death actions. In such claims a stillborn fetus can be considered a person even if it is born dead; the exception thus allows plaintiffs to sue the parties who caused the fetus's wrongful death, as in the case of malpractice claims against doctors. In their brief the Wartelles argued that a survival action fit within this exception. Disagreeing, the court cited a "long established tradition" in Louisiana dating to 1855 of maintaining the distinction between a survival action and an action for wrongful death: the first claim arises from circumstances occurring before death, and the second from circumstances after death. Noting that the state's civil code was extensively revised in 1987, the court said the legislature observed the traditional judicial distinction. The legislature had declined to add survival actions to the exceptions to the general rule that stillborn fetuses do not have a legal personality.

Using a similar analysis, the court also rejected the Wartelles' bystander claim. Since 1991 Louisiana law had permitted claims by bystanders who suffer emotional distress and mental anguish through witnessing injury to another person or coming upon the scene soon thereafter (La. Civ. Code ann. art. 2315 6 [West E]). But the court had already held that a stillborn fetus is not a person, and it found no exceptions in the civil code pertaining to bystander actions. Although the plaintiffs argued that their bystander claim resulted from the fetus's wrongful death, a bystander action "has no necessary relation to death," Marcus wrote. Given the state legislature's unwillingness to create an exception in this context, the court was also unwilling to do so.

In reviewing the damage award, the supreme court held that the trial record was unclear: it was impossible to ascertain how the trial judge had allocated the original damages between the bystander claim and wrongful death claim. Nor, the supreme court reasoned, could the appeals court adequately determine the breakdown. Given this problem, the supreme court sent the case back to the trial court to determine damages based on its decision to disallow both the survival action and the bystander claim.

In dissent, Justice Harry T. Lemmon contended that the court should have upheld both claims. If an unborn fetus can be considered a person for the purposes of a wrongful death action, he argued, then it also should be considered a person for survival and bystander claims. The Wartelles' fetus was viable; if not for medical malpractice, it would have been born alive. Thus, wrote Lemmon, the fetus would have been entitled to full legal personality under Louisiana law "if it had lived for one second longer."

**CROSS REFERENCES**
Medical Malpractice; Wrongful Death

## FIRST AMENDMENT

The First Amendment to the U.S. Constitution reads:

> Congress shall make no law respecting an establishment of religion, or prohibiting the free exercise thereof; or abridging the freedom of speech, or of the press; or the right of the people peaceably to assemble, and to petition the Government for a redress of grievances.

### Bad Frog Beer

In *Bad Frog Brewery, Inc. v. New York State Liquor Authority*, 134 F.3d 87 1998, the Court of Appeals for the Second Circuit ruled that a beer label showing a frog with its middle finger raised was entitled to First Amendment protection. In 1997 the brewery sued the state liquor authority, which had banned the product. Initially, a lower court upheld the ban on the grounds that the state had an interest in protecting children, 973 F.Supp. 280 (1997). But the appeals court held that the frog trademark deserved full protection as commercial speech under the First Amendment.

The illustrated label on Bad Frog Beer is intended as risqué humor: it shows an impertinent frog extending an unwebbed finger alongside various slogans, including "He just don't care" and "The Beer So Good ... It's Bad" (photograph at www.badfrog.com). Since introducing the beer in 1994, the Michigan-based brewery had previously won approval to market it from fifteen states as well as the Federal Bureau of Alcohol, Tobacco and Firearms. At least seven states, however, including Ohio, New Jersey, and Pennsylvania, rejected it. So did the New York State Liquor Authority (NYSLA), whose licensing powers allow it to ban alcohol products based on the content and message of their labels. In turning down Bad Frog Beer, the NYSLA ruled that "the gesture of 'giving the finger' to someone is a confrontational, obscene gesture known to lead to fights, shootings and homicides."

After the initial denial, the brewery attempted a second time to meet the NYSLA's guidelines. It altered the beer's label, replacing the phrase, "He's Mean, Green, and Obscene," with "Turning Bad to Good." But the liquor authority rejected the proposed changes, too. The NYSLA cited its regulation prohibiting signs that are "obscene or indecent" or "obnoxious or offensive to the commonly and generally accepted standards of fitness and good taste".

The brewery brought suit in district court. Asserting that the state had violated its First Amendment right to freedom of speech, it sought an injunction to prevent the NYSLA from enforcing the ban. In reply, the state moved for summary judgment. New York Attorney General Dennis C. Vacco argued that the frog's extended digit was the "visual equivalent of saying 'fuck you,'" and that state law clearly empowered the NYSLA to reject such messages on labels in order to protect children. The court agreed. On July 28, 1997, U.S. District Judge Frederick Scullen, Jr., granted the motion for summary judgment.

Afterwards, Attorney General Vacco traded public barbs with James Wauldron, the brewery's owner. On July 29, Vacco issued a press release calling the decision a "slam-dunk victory for decency" and warning the brewery "to hop back to its lily pond and return to New York when it develops some respect for our children." In a press release of his own, Wauldron replied that New York was rife with crime and wondered, "Where do they get the time and money to worry about our little FROG?"

On appeal, the parties disputed the legal nature of the brewery's speech. The brewery asserted that the label was parody, poking fun at typical beer advertising. As parody, the brewery argued, the frog artwork was a form of noncommercial speech and therefore entitled to the added protection that expressive speech receives over commercial speech. The U.S. Supreme Court has been reluctant to restrict messages intended as parody. In reply, the state conceded that the frog conveyed no useful commercial information, but still maintained that the artwork should be assessed by the reduced standards applicable to commercial speech. Its brief argued that the NYSLA had properly invoked its powers under New York law to ban obscenity for the purpose of protecting minors.

Writing for the court, Judge Jon O. Newman concluded that the brewery had failed to prove that the frog artwork was parody. The artwork functioned "like a trademark," he wrote, and was therefore a form of commercial speech. Next the court applied the so-called Central Hudson test, established by the U.S. Supreme Court in *Central Hudson Gas & Electric Corp. v. Public Service Commission of New York*, 447 U.S. 557, 100 S. Ct. 2343, 65 L. Ed. 2d 341 (1980). This test guides courts in assessing the constitutionality of governmental restrictions on commercial speech. It asks two questions: 1) whether the speech concerns lawful activity and is not misleading, and 2) whether the asserted government interest is substantial.

Applying the test, the appeals court concluded that the consumption of beer is legal in New York, and that "the labels cannot be said to be deceptive even if they are offensive." Although the state had a substantial interest in protecting children, the ban on the frog label could not realistically reduce children's exposure to vulgarity in 1998. Judge Newman noted "the wide currency of vulgar displays throughout contemporary society, including comic books targeted directly as children." The court found the ban to be an ineffective and excessive exercise of government authority and therefore unconstitutional. However, the court ruled that state officials were immune from damage claims brought by the brewery.

The decision disappointed New York officials and satisfied the company. George F. Carpinello, the company's attorney, noted that the court had underscored the limited power of government to determine what is tasteful in commercial advertising. Meanwhile, the brewery was considering suing other states that had banned its frog.

### Glickman v. Wileman Brothers & Elliott, Inc.

The U.S. Supreme Court has developed a large body of law concerning the interpretation of the First Amendment, establishing rules that protect political, religious, and artistic speech. Commercial speech also is subject to First Amendment protection in some situations.

In *Glickman v. Wileman Brothers & Elliott, Inc.*, ___U.S.___, 117 S. Ct. 2130 138 L. Ed. 2d 585 (1997), the Court ruled that federal regulations requiring California fruit growers to contribute to an advertising fund that promotes California fruit in general did not violate the First Amendment. In so ruling, the Court rejected the contention of the growers that the issue involved free speech, finding that the financial contribution requirement was one part of a set of economic regulations mandated by Congress and that therefore prior court decisions on the First Amendment and commercial speech had little relevance in the analysis of the legal issues at stake.

The government regulations at issue were authorized by the Agricultural Marketing Agreement Act of 1937 (AMAA) (7 U.S.C.A. § 601 et seq.), which Congress enacted to establish and maintain orderly marketing conditions and fair prices. The provisions of the AMAA are implemented by a "marketing order," an economic regulation that has replaced competition with collective action in a number of discrete, agricultural markets. These marketing orders, which are exempted from antitrust laws, seek to avoid unreasonable fluctuations in supplies and prices. They may include mechanisms that provide a uniform price to all producers in a particular market, limit the quantity of the commodity that may be marketed, and determine the grade and size of the commodity. Each marketing order must be approved by a vote of either two-thirds of the producers of the commodity producers who market at least two-thirds of the volume of the commodity. The approved orders are implemented by committees, appointed by the secretary of agriculture, composed of producers and handlers of the regulated commodity. These committees recommend rules to the secretary governing marketing matters. The expenses of Administration, including advertising and promotion, are paid by the affected producers, and the committees assess the amount that producers must pay annually.

At issue in the case was the constitutionality of 7 U.S.C.A. § 608c(6)(I), which authorizes marketing orders to include "any form of marketing promotion including paid advertising." Wileman Brothers & Elliott, along with other California producers of peaches, plums, and nectarines, objected to paying their assessments for a generic advertising campaign whose central message was that "California summer fruits"

are wholesome and delicious. They filed an administrative action challenging the advertising assessments.

After the Department of Agriculture ruled against the producers, they filed suit in federal district court. The court affirmed the constitutionality of the regulations, but on appeal, the Ninth Circuit Court of Appeals reversed, finding that the mandatory advertising fees violated the First Amendment rights of the producers (58 F.3d 1367 [1995]).

The Supreme Court, on a 5–4 vote, reversed the court of appeals decision. Justice John Paul Stevens, writing for the majority, concluded that the appeals court had incorrectly applied First Amendment commercial speech rules to the AMAA marketing order concerning advertising and promotion assessments.

*The Supreme Court ruled that California fruit growers' rights were not violated by their forced participation in a generic advertising campaign.*

INGA SPENCE/THE PICTURE CUBE, INC.

Stevens emphasized that the Court refused to consider the factual assumption made by the court of appeals that generic advertising may not be the most effective method of promoting the sale of these fresh fruits. The key issue, in the Court's view, was whether "being compelled to fund this advertising raises a First Amendment issue for us to resolve, or rather is simply a question of economic policy for Congress and the Executive to resolve." He noted that the producers who were compelled to fund generic advertising did so as "part of a broader collective enterprise in which their freedom to act independently is already constrained by the regulatory scheme."

The producers and the court of appeals contended that the advertising regulation should be reviewed under the Court's heightened standard for First Amendment cases. Stevens disagreed, concluding that the Court must apply standards appropriate for the review of economic regulation, which give Congress more latitude in crafting legislation.

Stevens cited three characteristics of the agricultural marketing scheme that distinguished it from laws that the Court had found to abridge freedom of speech protected by the First Amendment. First, the marketing orders did not impose any restraints on a producer's freedom to communicate "any message to any audience." A producer was free to advertise its particular brand. The Court rejected the producers' argument that compelling them to pay for generic advertising reduced their financial ability to pay for their own advertising. Stevens pointed out that this argument would be equally true of assessments "to cover employee benefits, inspection fees, or any other activity that is authorized by a marketing order." An economic regulation that may indirectly reduce a producer's advertising budget "does not itself amount to a restriction on speech."

A second characteristic of the marketing order was that it did not compel any person to engage "in any actual or symbolic speech." The assessments did not force the producers to "repeat any objectionable message out of their own mouths," but "merely required [them] to make contributions for advertising." Stevens noted that the producers did not disagree with any of the messages conveyed by the generic advertising.

A third characteristic was that the marketing order did not compel the producers to endorse or to finance any "political or ideological

views." Stevens concluded that none of the producers was faced with a "crisis of conscience" over the payment of the advertising assessment. The generic advertising of the California fruits was germane to the purposes of the marketing orders, and the assessments were not used to fund ideological activities.

Based on these three characteristics of the regulatory scheme, the Court concluded that the court of appeals had incorrectly applied the First Amendment commercial speech test contained in *Central Hudson Gas & Electric Corp. v. Public Service Commissioner of New York*, 447 U.S. 557, 100 S. Ct. 2343, 65 L. Ed. 2d 341 (1980). In *Central Hudson*, the Court required that the government's asserted interest in the regulation be substantial, that the regulation directly advance this interest, and that it be no more extensive than is necessary to serve that purpose.

The court of appeals had ruled that the generic advertising scheme did not directly advance the purposes of the marketing orders because the secretary of agriculture could not demonstrate that generic advertising was any more effective in stimulating consumer demand than independent advertising by individual producers. Stevens found this an "odd burden of proof," because the generic advertising assessment was part of a "policy displacing unrestrained competition with government supervised marketing programs." Instead, the Court ruled that economic regulations enjoy "the same strong presumption of validity that this Court accords to other policy judgments made by Congress." In this case, the purposes and goals of the statute were legitimate. Therefore, the courts had no reason to "override the judgment of the majority of market participants, bureaucrats, and legislators that such programs are beneficial."

In a dissenting opinion, Justice David H. Souter argued that the *Central Hudson* test was the appropriate standard of review. He concluded that, based on this test, the advertising assessment violated the First Amendment.

### Government Can't Ban Advertising by Non-Indian Casinos

A federal district court ruled that the government cannot ban broadcast advertising for non-Indian casinos in New Jersey (*Players International, Inc. v. United States*, 988 F. Supp. 497 [D.N.J.1997]). In ruling for a group of casinos, radio stations, and their trade associations, the U.S. District Court for New Jersey held that Federal Communications Commission (FCC) regulations violated constitutional guarantees of free speech. The plaintiffs had demanded the same right to advertise on radio and television enjoyed by Indian casinos, whereas the government maintained that the ban was necessary to protect citizens from the social ills of gambling. Subsequently, the FCC announced that it would drop the regulation.

The FCC took its authority from 18 U.S.C.A. § 1304, the federal law banning gambling advertisements on television or radio. It implemented the law through 47 C.F.R. § 73.121, prohibiting broadcast advertising of any "lottery, gift enterprise, or similar scheme." However, the regulation permitted several exceptions, for state-run lotteries and nonprofit organizations, and for "any gaming" conducted by an Indian tribe pursuant to the Indian Gaming Regulatory Act (25. U.S.C.A. et seq.).

The plaintiffs in the lawsuit represented a cross-section of the gambling and broadcast industries: Players International, Inc., a casino developer and operator, was joined by a national association of broadcast licensees, nine state associations of broadcast licensees, and two radio stations. Seeking to overturn the broadcast ban, the plaintiffs sued the federal government and the FCC, alleging violation of their First Amendment rights to free speech.

The plaintiffs made four arguments. First, the regulation had deprived broadcasters of ad revenues through the loss of business to non-broadcast competitors, such as newspapers. Second, FCC enforcement led to a confusing and arbitrary set of exceptions to the ban—in particular, the exception granted to Indian casinos. Third, the regulation did not achieve its goal of countering the social harm caused by gambling

*As a result of* Players International, Inc. v. United States, *non-Indian casinos in New Jersey are now able to broadcast advertisements.*

RAFAEL MACIA/PHOTO RESEARCHERS, INC.

because of the FCC's own broad exceptions. Fourth, the ban ran contrary to the U.S. Supreme Court's decision in *Forty-Four (44) Liquormart, Inc. v. Rhode Island*, 517 U.S. 484, 116 S. Ct. 1495, 134 L. Ed. 2d 711 (1996).

The government argued in defense that one century's worth of federal efforts to discourage the public from gambling had formed the basis for 18 U.S.C.A. § 1304, which would be harmed by a ruling for the plaintiffs. The law, its corresponding regulation, and the exceptions were all constitutionally sound. The government defended the exceptions as embodying the concerns of legislators for certain groups' economic well being. In particular, the Indian exception stemmed from the federal government's "unique Constitutional and trust obligation toward the Indian tribes."

District Judge Joseph H. Rodriguez issued his opinion on December 19, 1997. In analyzing the First Amendment claim, he used the so-called Central Hudson test. This four-part analytical framework for determining whether government regulation unfairly limits commercial speech was established in 1980 by the U.S. Supreme Court in *Central Hudson Gas & Electric Corp. v. Public Service Commission of New York*, 447 U.S. 557, 100 S. Ct. 2343, 65 L. Ed. 2d 341 (1980). Under the test, regulation is constitutional if the government shows 1) the regulated speech accurately informs the public about the lawful activity; 2) the governmental interest behind the regulation is substantial; 3) the regulation directly advances the interest asserted; and 4) the regulation is no more extensive than necessary. A challenged regulation must satisfy each part, or prong, of the test.

As the parties did not dispute the first prong, the court moved directly to the second. It found that the government had a substantial interest in protecting the public from social ills—including addiction and organized crime—by reducing participation in gambling. Specifically, Judge Rodriguez recognized a substantial interest in the use of this power to protect non-casino states from receiving broadcasts of casino ads.

But the government failed on the third and fourth prongs. The Supreme Court had warned in *Liquormart* against constraints upon commercial speech that were engineered to protect consumers against social ills: such bans rarely achieved their goal, and lawmakers should seek alternative forms of protection that do not threaten constitutional rights. Judge Rodriguez

concluded that the government had provided "no evidentiary support beyond a mere assumption" for its claim that the broadcast advertising ban directly advanced the interests of reducing social ills. Moreover, the numerous exceptions to the ban also "subverted" those interests. Finally, the regulation was more extensive than necessary, amounting to a "blanket ban" that harmed speech rights.

Judge Rodriguez granted the plaintiffs' motion for summary judgment—a ruling in their favor without a trial because no material fact was disputed and the law favored plaintiffs. His decision applied specifically to the plaintiffs' right to conduct broadcast advertising for casinos in New Jersey. Less than two weeks later, on December 31, the FCC responded in order to clarify its position on the regulation. After consulting with the Justice Department, the commission decided to stop enforcing the ban in New Jersey.

### Hitman Instruction Manual

A federal appellate panel ruled that a publisher can be sued for liability in three murders incited by its book (*Rice v. Paladin Enterprises*, 128 F.3d 233 [4th Cir. (Md.)]). The decision by a three-judge panel of the U.S. Court of Appeals for the Fourth Circuit allowed a civil lawsuit to go forward against Paladin Enterprises, Inc., publisher of *Hit Man: A Technical Manual for Independent Contractors*. Previously, a lower court had quashed the lawsuit. But the appellate panel revived it, holding that the First Amendment does not offer Paladin a complete defense against being sued. The ruling appeared to limit the rights of publishers when their work provides "integral" instructions on committing crimes. It stunned free speech advocates, but was hailed by victims' rights groups.

The case stemmed from a triple murder in Silver Spring, Maryland, in 1993. James Perry, a novice assassin, embarked on his new career a year after purchasing the 130-page *Hit Man* and a second book, *How to Make a Disposable Silencer, Vol. II*. He was hired by Lawrence Horn to kill Horn's family. Horn's stood to receive $2 million from a trust fund, payable upon the deaths of his quadriplegic son and ex-wife. On the night of March 3, 1993, Perry strangled the boy, Trevor Horn, and shot his mother, Mildred Horn, and the boy's private nurse, Janice Saunders. Police found a copy of *Hit Man* in his apartment. Perry was found to have meticulously followed its instructions and was convicted of the murders (*Perry v. State*, 344 Md. 204, 686 A.2d 274, 278 [1996], cert. denied,

___U.S.___, 117 S. Ct. 1318, 137 L. Ed. 2d 480 [1997]).

Perry had ordered the books from mail-order publisher Paladin Enterprises, Inc. Founded in 1970 by two former servicemen, the Boulder, Colorado-based publishing house sells how-to books and videos on guerrilla warfare, weaponry, assassination, espionage, and related subjects. It bills itself as "the unquestioned leader in the 'action' market" with more than 750 titles.

Subsequently, the survivors of the victims sued Paladin and its president, Peter Lund. The suit argued that they were liable for the deaths in three ways: (1) aiding and abetting the murders; (2) showing reckless disregard for human life; and (3) inciting and producing "imminent" lawless action. The third argument referred to the U.S. Supreme Court's seminal decision on speech that advocates lawlessness, *Brandenburg v. Ohio*, 395 U.S. 444, 89 S. Ct. 1827, 23 L. Ed. 2d 430 (1969). *Brandenburg* held that the First Amendment protects speech that advocates abstract lawlessness; but it does not protect speech that incites specific crimes or violence. In essence, the plaintiffs' lawsuit sought to strip the publisher of any First Amendment protection while advancing the broader claims that its publication had played a critical role in the murders.

In September 1996, the U.S. District Court of Maryland granted Paladin's motion for summary judgment—a finding that, given the facts, Paladin should prevail as a matter of law. Judge Alexander Williams, Jr., dismissed the claim of aiding and abetting as an unprecedented extension of that tort under Maryland case law. Additionally, he ruled that the plaintiffs had cited no authority for their "novel" claim of reckless disregard for human life, noting that such a standard had never been applied in First Amendment cases. Finally, he swept aside the suggestion that the book had incited the murders. Judge Williams concluded that "[n]othing in the book says 'go out and commit murder now!' Instead, the book seems to say, in so many words, 'if you want to be a hit man this is what you need to do.'"

The plaintiffs appealed. All parties stipulated that the sole issue for the appellate panel was whether the First Amendment offered Paladin a complete defense, with other legal and factual issues to be decided in subsequent proceedings. Filing amicus, or friend-of-the-court, briefs on Paladin's behalf was a broad coalition of mainstream publishers and free speech advocates, ranging from the *New York Times* to the American Civil Liberties Union. The National Victim Center and other victims' rights groups filed briefs on behalf of the plaintiffs. Precedent appeared to favor the defense: courts have been reluctant to abridge publisher's speech rights unless the case involved commercial speech (such as advertisements), which generally receives less protection than non-commercial speech.

On November 10, 1997, the three-judge panel ruled that a jury could hold Paladin liable for the killings. Quoting extensively from *Hit Man*, Judge J. Michael Luttig's decision noted that Paladin had made "extraordinary stipulations" about intending the book to be used for committing murders. The decision noted the precedent in *Brandenburg*, but went beyond it. Instead, the panel found that the book was an "integral part" of criminal conduct and, as such, enjoyed no protection under the First Amendment. "The justifications for free speech that apply to speakers do not reach communications that are simply means to get a crime successfully committed," Judge Luttig wrote. A jury could conclude that Paladin marketed the book "directly and even primarily to murderers and would-be criminals," and in turn hold Paladin liable for Perry's murders. Thus the panel restored the lawsuit and ordered a jury trial.

The decision pleased victims' rights groups, who generally favor a broad reading of the law in order to limit the rights of criminals. Free speech advocates criticized the decision, arguing that it discarded the test established in *Brandenburg*, chilled free speech, and opened the floodgates for lawsuits against publishers. Paladin said it would ask the full Fourth Circuit to review the ruling and, if necessary, appeal to the U.S. Supreme Court.

## Turner Broadcasting System v. Federal Communication Commission

Since the 1970s, cable television systems have been required by the Federal Communications Commission (FCC) to dedicate some of their channels to local broadcasting television stations. For many years cable operators did not challenge the constitutionality of these "must-carry" provisions, believing compliance was necessary to obtain operating licenses. With the dramatic growth in the cable industry, however, cable operators argued that they should be able to use these channels for other, more profitable, programming. Challenges by cable operators in the late 1980s resulted in the courts striking

*Ted Turner and other cable operators sued the FCC over the constitutionality of the Cable Television Consumer Protection and Competition Act of 1992.*

ANDREW INNERARITY/AP/WIDE WORLD PHOTOS

down must-carry rules as a violation of the First Amendment.

Congress responded by including in the Cable Television Consumer Protection and Competition Act of 1992 (47 U.S.C.A. § 151 et seq.), a provision requiring that cable systems with twelve or fewer channels must carry at least three local broadcast signals, and that larger systems must carry all local signals up to a maximum of one-third of the system's total number of channels.

A group of cable operators filed suit, attacking the constitutionality of the new law. They asserted that their First Amendment rights had been restricted by the congressional must-carry provision. In *Turner Broadcasting System v. Federal Communications Commission*, 520 U.S. 180, 117 S. Ct. 1174, 137 L. Ed. 2d 369 (1997), the Supreme Court, on a 5–4 vote, upheld the statute and rejected the cable operators' First Amendment claims.

The 1997 decision was the second ruling made by the Supreme Court involving these parties. In 1993 a federal district court held that the must-carry provisions of the Act were constitutional. On direct appeal, the Supreme Court, in *Turner Broadcasting System v. Federal Communications Commission* 512 U.S. 622, 114 S. Ct. 2445, 129 L. Ed. 2d 497 (1994), held that the must-carry provisions constituted a content-neutral regulation and could be constitutional. The Court then ordered the district court to deter-

mine whether the government could demonstrate that the provisions reasonably advanced an important governmental interest. On remand, a divided district court held that Congress had before it "substantial evidence" from which to conclude that the must-carry provisions were necessary to protect the local broadcast industry, 910 F.Supp. 734 (D.D.C. 1995).

Justice Anthony M. Kennedy, writing for the majority, noted that in its previous opinion the Court had concluded the must-carry provisions were content-neutral regulations. Therefore, the courts must apply an "intermediate" level of scrutiny. Under this analysis, legislation that affects speech but does not favor the message of one speaker over another can be constitutional if the legislation furthers an important governmental interest and does not burden more speech than necessary to advance that interest (*United States v. O'Brien*, 391 U.S. 367, 88 S. Ct. 1673, 20 L. Ed. 2d 672 [1968]).

Justice Kennedy reaffirmed the Court's earlier finding that the must-carry provisions were designed to serve three important governmental interests: preserving the benefits of free, over-the-air local broadcast television; promoting the widespread dissemination of information from many sources; and promoting fair competition in the television programming market. (Justice Stephen G. Breyer, the fifth vote, accepted the first two interests but rejected the government's interest in promoting fair competition.) Protecting non-cable households from the loss of regular broadcasting service due to competition from cable systems was an important and legitimate legislative purpose because "40 percent of U.S. households still rely on over-the-air signals for television programming." In addition, there was a governmental purpose "of the highest order" in seeking to ensure public access to a "multiplicity of information sources." Finally, the government had an interest in eliminating restraints on fair competition even when the regulated parties were engaged in protective expressive activity.

The government had argued that these interests would be affected by the loss of even a few broadcast stations. The cable operators contended that these interests were not threatened by the abandonment of the must-carry provisions. They argued that these interests would be relevant if the government could show the entire broadcasting industry would fail. In addition, they limited the interest in assuring a multiplicity of information sources to the preservation of a minimum amount of broadcast service.

Justice Kennedy rejected the arguments of both sides, concluding that they were inconsistent with Congress' stated interests in enacting the must-carry provisions. The congressional findings reflected concern that, "absent must-carry, 'a few voices' would be lost from the television marketplace." Justice Kennedy noted Congress' "expressed clear concern" about the dramatic shift of market share from broadcast television to cable television services. This shift in market share:

> resulting from increasing market penetration by cable services, as well as the expanding horizontal concentration and vertical integration of cable operators, combined to give cable systems the incentive and ability to delete, reposition, or decline carriage to local broadcasters in an attempt to favor affiliated cable programmers.

The Court found that when local broadcasters are denied cable access, audience size and advertising revenues decline, station operations are restricted, and bankruptcy may result. Congress' interests would not be satisfied "by the preservation of a rump broadcast service industry providing a minimum of broadcast service to Americans without cable."

Conversely, the Court determined that the must-carry provisions had not burdened cable operators, with the vast majority unaffected in a significant manner. Most systems had enough channels to accommodate local stations and their own programming. Therefore, Congress had not overstepped the First Amendment in mandating the must-carry requirement.

Justice Kennedy emphasized that Congress had the authority to make judgments about "how competing economic interests are to be reconciled in the complex and fast-changing field of television." The cable operators had not raised significant First Amendment concerns that warranted judicial intervention. Rather, Kennedy characterized their challenges to the must-carry provisions as "little more than disagreement over the level of protection broadcast stations are to be afforded and how protection is to be attained." Because the must-carry provisions were "grounded on reasonable factual findings supported by evidence that is substantial for a legislative determination," the Court would not displace the judgment of Congress.

Justice Sandra Day O'Connor, in a dissenting opinion, contended that the Court had failed to discharge its duty in reviewing the case. The majority should have exercised its "independent duty to identify with care the Governmental interests supporting the scheme," assess the reasonableness of congressional findings, and examine "the fit between its goals and its consequences." In her view, such review would have required the Court to strike down the must-carry provisions.

**CROSS REFERENCES**

Federal Communications Commission; Freedom of the Press; Freedom of Speech; Liquormart v. Rhode Island; Obscenity; Souter, David Hackett; Stevens, John Paul; Trademarks; Victims of Crime

# FRAUD

A false representation of a matter of fact—whether by words or by conduct, by false or misleading ALLEGATIONS, or by concealment of what should have been disclosed—that deceives and is intended to deceive another so that the individual will act upon it to her or his legal injury.

## Fife Symington Conviction and Resignation

In September 1997, Arizona Governor John Fife Symington III resigned from office following his conviction on seven felony counts. The two-term Republican governor had been the subject of a federal probe of his shaky real estate empire since his election to office in 1991 on a pro-business, law-and-order ticket. Investigators spent nearly seven years pursuing him, but their efforts to brand him a major white-collar criminal fell short at sentencing. On February 3, 1998, a federal judge sentenced Symington to pay a $60,000 fine and serve two-and-a-half years in prison with five years' probation—well below the punishment recommended by federal sentencing guidelines. Meanwhile, he awaited the result of an appeal filed in 1997.

Symington achieved prominence in Arizona through his finance and real estate dealings. In 1982 he entered state Republican politics as party finance chair, then mounted a bid for governor in 1989. The difficult race led to a run-off election, which Symington narrowly won in 1991. In his campaign Symington had promised to be tough on crime and to run Arizona like his own successful businesses.

Almost immediately after Symington took office his business empire began to crumble. An investigation of a failed savings and loan led to allegations that he had violated federal banking laws. The accusations followed congressional hearings into the collapse of the Phoenix-based Southwest Savings and Loan, on whose board of directors Symington sat from 1972 to 1984. Southwest Savings had failed in 1989 under $941 million in bad loans and investments; its largest debit was a $25.9 million joint venture to develop real estate for Symington.

A rising star in Republican circles, Symington dismissed the allegations as politically motivated. But in December 1991, the Resolution Trust Corp. (RTC)—the federal corporation created to clean up after the multibillion-dollar savings and loan scandal in the 1980s—became involved. The RTC filed a $197 million suit against Symington and eleven other Southwest Savings officials, alleging that questionable loan practices had caused the thrift's collapse. Concurrently, in early 1992, the U.S. attorney's office in Los Angeles launched a criminal investigation.

By 1994, with most of his major development projects lost to foreclosure or sold at bargain prices, Symington announced that he was broke. He escaped civil liability, however when the RTC settled its lawsuit for $12.1 million— none of which was paid by Symington, who was not required to admit any wrongdoing.

Although Symington won reelection that year, his financial and legal situations worsened.

*Arizona Governor John Fife Symington III resigned from office September 5, 1997, after he was found guilty of seven counts of bank fraud.*

CHERYL EVANS/REUTERS/ARCHIVE PHOTOS

In August 1995, a Maricopa County Superior Court judge ordered him to pay $11.4 million to a union pension fund for reimbursement of one of his development loans. One month later, Symington, shortly after vacationing in Europe, filed for bankruptcy: he listed $25 million in debts—most of them owed on failed real estate developments—and $61,000 in assets.

On June 13, 1996, a federal grand jury returned a twenty-three count indictment against Symington that included charges of false statements to a federally insured institution, lying under oath in a bankruptcy proceeding, wire fraud, and attempted extortion. Symington, prosecutors claimed, had lied about his personal worth—inflating it to secure loans and later deflating it to win refinancing on more favorable terms.

At trial Symington blamed his troubles on accountants and his own mistakes but claimed he had done nothing illegal. However, forty prosecution witnesses and more that fourteen hundred pages of evidence convinced the federal jury, which convicted him on September 3, 1997, on seven counts of bank and wire fraud. He resigned from office hours later. U.S. District Judge Roger Strand later threw out one conviction without explanation.

Symington became the second Arizona governor in a decade to leave office in scandal. In 1988 Governor Evan Mecham was impeached on charges of obstructing justice and misusing state money. Removed from office, Mecham was later acquitted of other charges at trial.

**CROSS REFERENCES**
Savings and Loan Association

# FREEDOM OF INFORMATION ACT

A federal law (5 U.S.C.A. § 552 et seq.) providing for the disclosure of information held by ADMINISTRATIVE AGENCIES to the public, unless the documents requested fall into one of the specific exemptions set forth in the statute.

### John Lennon FBI File

In September 1997, the Federal Bureau of Investigation (FBI) surrendered long-classified documents on the late rock star John Lennon. The file mainly addressed Lennon's activities as a spokesperson against the Vietnam War. Its release was a victory for University of California history professor Jonathan M. Wiener in his fourteen-year legal battle with the agency. Since Wiener brought suit in 1983, the FBI had devoted five different attorneys to the case, appealed an earlier ruling to the U.S. Supreme Court, and insisted that the files were vital to national security. In the end, it paid $204,000 in legal costs and turned over most of its spy reports, which dated from the period 1971–72 when it suspected the former member of The Beatles of engaging in what it called "revolutionary activities." The FBI's refusal to declassify the remaining ten pages of the file, however, prompted yet another lawsuit.

Wiener's pursuit of the documents began in 1981, a few months after Lennon was slain by a deranged fan. Wiener, history professor at the University of California at Irvine, filed a Freedom of Information Act request for academic research on his book *Come Together: John Lennon in His Time* (University of Illinois Press,

1984). But the FBI released only limited portions of its file, citing exemptions under the law that allowed it to withhold the vast bulk of its records. After exhausting internal agency appeals, Wiener filed suit in 1983 alleging violations of the Freedom of Information Act. In court the FBI maintained that releasing the files would compromise its confidential sources and thus endanger national security.

Wiener's lawsuit took several turns, including being thrown out and reinstated on appeal. In 1991 the Ninth Circuit Court of Appeals ruled that the FBI had improperly withheld the file (*Wiener v. FBI*, 943 F.2d 972). The FBI appealed the ruling to the U.S. Supreme Court, which refused to hear the case and returned it to the district court in 1992. As the lawsuit progressed, the agency released dozens of pages from its file, but many of these documents were heavily censored with black felt pen. Then in

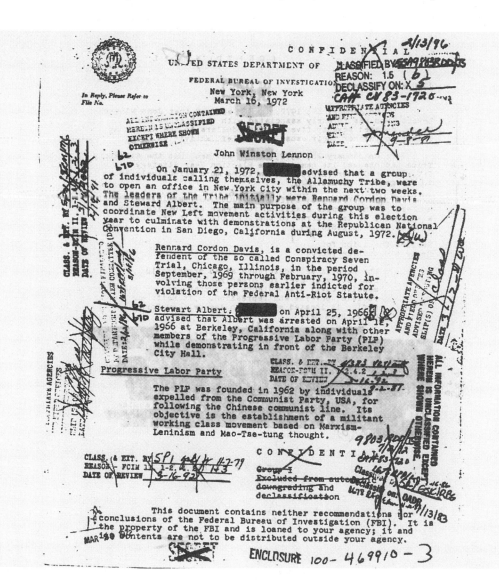

*After a request under the Freedom of Information Act, the Federal Bureau of Investigation released previously censored files on former Beatle John Lennon.*

HO/REUTERS/ARCHIVE PHOTOS

December 1995, U.S. District Judge Robert Takasugi ordered the FBI to comply with Wiener's discovery demands. Instead of fighting further, the agency agreed to settle the case. It paid attorneys' fees to the American Civil Liberties Union (ACLU) of Southern California, which had represented Wiener, and released both new and previously censored documents.

The file revealed that the FBI's investigation of Lennon began shortly after his emigration from west Britain to New York in 1971. His involvement in antiwar protests quickly aroused the suspicion of FBI Director J. Edgar Hoover, who, for years, had been devoting FBI resources to spying on celebrities. On Hoover's orders, FBI bureaus, informants, and spies in the antiwar movement began intensive surveillance of Lennon, amassing about three hundred pages of reports in one year. The campaign would ultimately involve the FBI, the U.S. Attorney general's office, and even the White House.

As the probe advanced, federal officials became worried about two possibilities: Lennon might appear with protesters at the 1972 Republican National Convention, and he might launch a concert tour to encourage young people to register to vote and thus hurt President Richard M. Nixon's reelection chances. The source of these suspicions was a 1972 memo written by Senator Strom Thurmond (R-S.C.) to Attorney General John N. Mitchell. Rather than taking any risks before the convention, Thurmond recommended that the White House deport Lennon as a "strategic countermeasure." FBI Director Hoover supported the idea, but the effort failed. Lennon did not appear at the convention, and the surveillance ended in 1972.

The file cast doubt on the FBI's claim that it had conducted a criminal investigation within the proper scope of its authority. Joe Krovisky, a Justice Department spokesperson, defended the spying, saying that Lennon had offered to give $75,000 to a group planning to disrupt the Republican convention. Wiener noted that the FBI's own files showed that Lennon had insisted on a peaceful demonstration. Denouncing the FBI for abusing its power, Wiener also criticized the agency for wasting taxpayers' money to report that Lennon was teaching a pet parrot to swear and that Lennon's wife, Yoko Ono, failed to "remain on key" while singing. Wiener said he and the ACLU would sue for the release of the final ten pages of the file.

**CROSS REFERENCES**
Federal Bureau of Investigation

# FREEDOM OF SPEECH

The right, guaranteed by the FIRST AMENDMENT to the U.S. Constitution, to express beliefs and ideas without unwarranted government restriction.

## Public Access to School Newspaper

The case of *Yeo v. Town of Lexington*, 131 F.3d 241, 122 Ed. Law Rep 924 (1st Cir. Mass.), tested the editorial freedom of high school students along with the speech rights of an adult. The long string of events that led to *Yeo* began in 1992, when the Lexington School Committee in Lexington, Massachusetts, adopted a policy making condoms available to students at the high school without parental permission. Douglas Yeo, a Lexington resident and parent, opposed the measure. Yeo assumed the lead in a group called "Lexington Citizens for Responsible School Policy," a group that sought to defeat the condom distribution plan.

The school newspaper, *The Lexington High School Musket*, ran articles and editorials on the condom policy. In March 1993, local voters approved the condom distribution policy, and in May of the same year Yeo founded another group, the Lexington Parents Information Network (LEXNET). LEXNET's goal was to inform parents about public education through newsletters and meetings. Over the course of the next two years, Yeo and LEXNET attempted to place advertisements encouraging celibacy in both the school yearbook and the *Musket*.

The editors of the yearbook and the *Musket* refused to publish the advertisements. The yearbook and the *Musket* had an unwritten policy that they would not run political or advocacy advertisements. Yeo sued the town of Lexington, the Lexington school committee, the superintendent, the principal, and faculty advisers in the federal trial court for the district of Massachusetts, claiming that his civil rights to free speech and equal protection under 42 U.S.C.A. § 1983 had been violated by the refusal to print the advertisements. Yeo's theory was that the decisions were the result of state action or action by the government.

At trial, the district court granted summary judgment to the defendants on the grounds that the students were not state actors and that the town and other officials could not be held responsible for the students' actions. On appeal to the First Circuit appeals court, a panel of judges reversed, holding that the student publications were public forums, and that the rejection of

Yeo's advertisements constituted impermissible viewpoint discrimination. The defendants asked for a review of the matter by the full court of appeals, and the court, sitting en banc, withdrew its panel opinion and affirmed the decision of the district court.

The appeals court identified three issues in the case: (1) Was there state action because the decisions were actually made or controlled by the school officials? (2) If the officials were not in fact making the decisions, were they required to intervene? and (3) Even if the decisions were made independently by the students, can the decisions be attributed to the state because they were made in a public school setting? The majority of the appeals court answered in the negative on all three questions.

There was nothing in the record, the court declared, to support the proposition that the school officials had any control over the students' decisions. The school did not profit from the decisions, and the school publications were not governmental functions that government officials had delegated to the students.

On the second issue, the court decided that the school officials had no duty to intervene in the matter of the advertisements. According to the court, First Amendment rights do not require the government to take control where there is otherwise no action by a government official.

Lastly, the court held that the school officials could not be held responsible for the independent decisions of the students. The court noted that the students and the faculty and other officials were often at odds over the issue, and that the decisions appeared to have been made by the students alone. Having rejected the theory that the conduct alleged in the suit constituted state action, the court had no need to address the issue of whether Yeo's free speech rights had been violated.

Two judges concurred in the judgment. Chief Circuit Judge Juan Torruella would have reversed the decision of the panel because the speech was political, a type of speech that the government may filter out when it solicits advertising for a nontraditional public forum. Circuit Judge Norman Stahl also concurred, but he did not concur in its reasoning. According to Stahl, the court only needed to know that the defendants had not caused the conduct of the students and that the students were not parties to the case. Regarding the issue of state action, Torruella maintained that the student decisions on advertising constituted government action. "[T]o the extent public school students solicit funds to support a public enterprise in their capacities as officials of that enterprise," Torruella wrote, "they act under color of state law."

**CROSS REFERENCES**
First Amendment; State Action

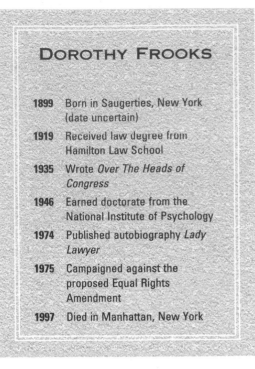

**DOROTHY FROOKS**

**1899**  Born in Saugerties, New York (date uncertain)

**1919**  Received law degree from Hamilton Law School

**1935**  Wrote *Over The Heads of Congress*

**1946**  Earned doctorate from the National Institute of Psychology

**1974**  Published autobiography *Lady Lawyer*

**1975**  Campaigned against the proposed Equal Rights Amendment

**1997**  Died in Manhattan, New York

## FROOKS, DOROTHY

Dorothy Frooks, a lawyer, activist, suffragist, and pioneer of humanitarian law reforms, died in Manhattan on April 13, 1997, at the age of about 100. Frooks' remarkable life spanned the twentieth century. Famous as a child for speeches on behalf of women's suffrage, she earned degrees in law and psychology, served in both World Wars, and was decorated by President Woodrow Wilson. In the 1920s, as an attorney for the Salvation Army, she established free legal clinics, and then turned to lobbying efforts that resulted in major reforms for the benefit of the underprivileged in New York.

Frooks was probably born on February 12, 1899, in Saugerties, New York. The exact date is unknown: she obscured her age to such an extent that, upon her death, even surviving family members was unsure of it. Her father, Reginald, was a wealthy businessman, her mother, Rosita, an international society figure, and Frooks was the seventh of their nine children. By the age of eleven, her precocious talent for speechmaking had emerged, and over the next several years she campaigned widely in New York and London for the right of women to vote. Turning this talent to military recruitment, she enlisted some 30,000 servicemen in World War I. For that effort President Wilson awarded her a gold medal for patriotic services and appointed her chief yeoman in the U.S. Navy—the highest ranking position held by a woman in the service at that time.

In 1919 Frooks received her law degree from Hamilton Law School in Chicago. She entered practice at the approximate age of twenty-one for the Salvation Army in New York City. As the charitable organization's first full-time lawyer, she organized free legal clinics for the poor while also conducting lobbying efforts in city and state government. Her belief that the poor needed means to collect small debts, led her to persuade New York Mayor Fiorello H. LaGuardia to open the city's first small claims courts. Her subsequent criminal defense work, which brought her into contact with needy families, led her to successfully petition the state legislature to establish aid to dependent children.

Frooks was seemingly tireless. She ran for Congress several times, wrote a column for twelve years in *The New York World*, founded two newspapers, ran a publishing house, taught in Puerto Rico, and even operated a flying school. During World War II, she served in the U.S. Army's Judge Advocate's office and later organized a national group for women veterans. She attended several universities throughout her life, earning, in 1946, a doctorate from the National Institute of Psychology. No modern feminist, however, she campaigned passionately in 1975 against the proposed Equal Rights Amendment, which offended her traditional views.

Frooks' passion for ideas led to exchanges with some of her most prominent contemporaries, including a correspondence with George Bernard Shaw and a feud with Eleanor Roosevelt. Known for her wit, she once remarked, "Women should be in the home, have adorable husbands, and be the only wife." Her seven books include *Over the Heads of Congress* (Nelson, 1935) and an autobiography, *Lady Lawyer* (Speller, 1974). She died of unreported causes.

**CROSS REFERENCES**
Equal Rights Amendment; Women's Rights

## FULL FAITH AND CREDIT CLAUSE

The clause of the U.S. Constitution that provides that the various states must recognize legislative acts, public records, and judicial decisions of the other states within the United States.

### Baker v. General Motors Corp.

The Full Faith and Credit Clause of the U.S. Constitution (Article IV, Section 1) requires states to honor the "public Acts, Records, and judicial Proceedings of every other State." Through this clause, the Framers of the Constitution sought to ensure that states would co-operate with each other and enforce judgments from the courts of other states. There are, however, limits on full faith and credit. The U.S. Supreme Court, in *Baker v. General Motors Corp.*, __U.S.__, 118 S. Ct. 657, 139 L. Ed. 2d 580 (1998), placed another limitation on full faith and credit, ruling that an injunction barring a former employee from testifying as a witness against the employer could not be enforced in another state.

Ronald Elwell worked for General Motors (GM) from 1959 until 1989. Beginning in 1971, Elwell studied the performance of GM vehicles, most particularly vehicles involved in product liability litigation. From his research on vehicular fires, Elwell suggested changes in fuel line designs and assisted GM lawyers engaged in defending GM against product liability actions. Beginning in 1987, the Elwell-GM employment relationship soured. GM and Elwell first negotiated an agreement under which Elwell would retire after serving as a GM consultant for two years. When the time came for Elwell to retire, however, there were new disagreements.

In 1991 Elwell testified in a Georgia lawsuit involving a GM pickup truck fuel tank that burst into flames just after a collision. He gave testimony that differed markedly from testimony he had given when serving as an in-house expert witness for GM, testifying in Georgia that the GM pickup truck fuel system was inferior to competing products. Soon after giving this testimony, Elwell sued GM in Michigan state court for wrongful discharge. GM counterclaimed, saying he had breached his fiduciary duty to GM by disclosing privileged and confidential information and misappropriating documents. Eventually Elwell and GM agreed to a settlement, with Elwell receiving an undisclosed amount of money. In return, Elwell agreed to the entry of a permanent injunction by the Michigan trial court that barred him from testifying, without the prior written consent of GM, either upon deposition or at trial, about GM vehicle design and manufacture. The agreement did state, however, that if a court compelled his testimony, Elwell was not in violation of the agreement.

The injunction came into question when Elwell was subpoenaed to appear at a deposition and trial in Missouri. Kenneth and Steven Baker filed a wrongful death product liability action against GM, alleging that a faulty fuel pump in a 1985 Chevrolet S-10 Blazer caused an engine fire that killed their mother, Beverly Garner.

Though GM objected to Elwell testifying, the federal district court ruled that it did not have to enforce the Michigan injunction. At trial Elwell testified in support of the Bakers' claim that the alleged defect in the fuel system contributed to the fire. In addition, he identified and described an internal GM memorandum that discussed the risk of fuel-fed fires. The jury awarded the Bakers $11.3 million in damages.

GM successfully appealed the judgment to the Eighth Circuit Court of Appeals. The court ruled that Elwell's testimony should not have been admitted because the district court should have honored the Michigan injunction under the Full Faith and Credit Clause (86 F.3d 811 [1996]).

The Supreme Court reversed the court of appeals, concluding that the Full Faith and Credit Clause was not controlling in this situation. Justice Ruth Bader Ginsburg, writing for the Court, noted that its precedent "differentiates the credit owed to laws (legislative measures and common law) and to judgments." The clause does not compel a state to substitute the laws of other states for its own laws dealing with subjects that may be legislated in that state. Judgments, however, are different, Ginsburg stated. A final judgment made by a court in one state "qualifies for recognition throughout the land." A judgment of the rendering state, therefore, "gains nationwide force."

Though states must give full faith and credit to judgments from other states, Ginsburg said that this does not mean that states "must adopt the practices of other States regarding the time, manner, and mechanisms for enforcing judgments." An order commanding action or inaction by one state will have no effect in the other state if the order seeks to accomplish an official act that is within the "exclusive province" of the other state, or if the order interferes with litigation over which the ordering state has no authority.

Ginsburg noted that the Michigan judgment at issue in the case contained the prohibition against Elwell's testimony about GM products. This judgment also settled Elwell's claim of wrongful discharge. The Michigan judgment could not, however, "reach beyond the Elwell-GM controversy to control proceedings against GM brought in other States, by other parties, asserting claims the merits of which Michigan has not considered." Ginsburg believed the essential point was that Michigan lacked the authority to control courts in other states by precluding these courts from determining which witnesses should testify.

The Michigan judgment operated against Elwell to prevent him from volunteering his testimony. But Ginsburg ruled that a Michigan court could not, through its injunction against Elwell, "dictate to a court in another jurisdiction that evidence relevant in the Bakers' case—a controversy to which Michigan is foreign—shall be inadmissible." In her view GM had recognized the "interference potential" of the consent decree it negotiated with Elwell by stip-

ulating that if Elwell were ordered to testify, his testimony would "in no way" make him open to a lawsuit in Michigan for violating the injunction.

Because Michigan lacked the authority to shield a witness from another jurisdiction's subpoena power, the district court had properly allowed Elwell's testimony.

**CROSS REFERENCES**
Ginsburg, Ruth Bader; Injunction; Jurisdiction; Subpoena

## GAMING

The act or practice of gambling; an agreement between two or more individuals to play collectively at a game of chance for a stake or wager, which will become the property of the winner and to which all involved make a contribution.

### Card Counter Couldn't Sue Casino

A New Jersey appeals court quashed a $1.5 million jury award to a skilled gambler who had previously won a unique discrimination lawsuit against a casino (*Campione v. Adamar of New Jersey*, 302 N.J.Super. 99, 694 A.2d 1045). A three-judge appellate panel of the New Jersey Superior Court ruled that gamblers do not have a cause of action to sue a casino for violating state gambling regulations. Sole jurisdiction belonged to the state's Casino Control Commission, the panel said. The court reversed a damage award made by a jury to Anthony Campione, who had sued the TropWorld Casino and Entertainment Resort in 1995 for limiting his bets upon determining that he was counting cards to increase his odds of winning. The court decision observed that New Jersey gambling regulations properly allow casinos to foil skilled players.

Campione was a seasoned gambler. Since the opening of casinos in Atlantic City in the late 1970s, he had polished his game through study and practice, even attaining a diploma certifying him as a master blackjack player. Among his skills was cardcounting, the difficult practice of tracking the cards dealt in a blackjack game so as to better calculate the player's odds on a given hand. TropWorld Casino ranked among his favorite casinos. In April 1989, however, he filed a complaint against TropWorld with the New Jersey's Casino Control Commission, alleging discrimination because he had not been allowed to play two hands of blackjack simultaneously. The commission rejected the complaint.

On November 10, 1989, Campione was having a bad day at one of TropWorld's blackjack tables, where the table limit was a minimum bet of $25 and a maximum of $1,000. Suddenly, he placed a $350 bet, but the casino intervened. Michael Imperatrice, a floor supervisor whose duties included monitoring the gambling of cardcounters, noticed that Campione had a so-called "favorable count"—a good likelihood of winning. So he told Campione that his maximum bet could be only $100. Then Imperatrice told the only other player at the table that he was allowed to bet up to $1,000. Campione insisted that he would reclaim his losses and, shoving his $350 in chips back into the betting circle, instructed the dealer to "double down" his cards (which doubles the stakes), played his hand, and won. Observing the limit set by Imperatrice, however, the dealer only paid him $200.

A confrontation ensued. Refusing to relinquish his cards, Campione said he wanted them as evidence. Imperatrice threatened him with arrest before summoning David Duffield, lieutenant of security. Duffield called Patrick Scully, the sergeant of security, and they both told Campione he was under arrest. The two men escorted him to the booth of the Casino Control Commission, where he pleaded his case to

*Men and women play blackjack in a casino.*
BILL BACHMANN/PHOTOEDIT

Ronald Hungridge, an employee of the Division of Gaming Enforcement. But instead of helping Campione, Hungridge typed out a complaint against him on behalf of the casino. Campione was detained for an hour before being released.

Both sides pursued legal action. As a result of the casino's complaint, Campione was tried in Atlantic City Municipal Court on charges of public annoyance and defiant trespass. He was cleared, the judge noting that he had a legitimate reason for trying to protect his bet. Next, Campione sued TropWorld, Imperatrice, and Scully, alleging discrimination, breach of contract, and malicious prosecution. In 1995 a jury awarded Campione a total of $1,519,873 in damages: $300,625 against Tropworld and Imperatrice for discriminating against him because he was a cardcounter; $219,034 against Tropworld and Scully as compensatory damages for malicious prosecution; and $1,000,213.50 for punitive damages against Tropworld on the malicious prosecution claim.

In February 1997, the New Jersey appellate division heard an appeal by the defendants. The defendants argued that the trial judge should have dismissed Campione's case because he had no cause of action under the state's Casino Control Act (N.J.S.A. 5:12-1 to -152). They maintained that the law gave full power over state regulations to the Casino Control Commission, and that the trial judge had overstepped his authority by allowing the jury to interpret the commission's rules. In reply, Campione asserted

that he was not challenging the regulations but TropWorld's implementation of them. Moreover, as the commission had denied him a hearing and maintained that it had no power to compel a casino to pay him, he had no administrative remedy to pursue. Campione also cross-appealed on the issue of damages, but died while the appeal was pending. The appeals court regarded his cross-appeal as moot.

The panel first considered the issue of discrimination against cardcounters in historical terms. Under the commission's regulations, there was no doubt that such discrimination was acceptable. In fact, several anti-counting rules had been put in effect following the New Jersey Supreme Court's decision in 1982 in *Uston v. Resorts International Hotel, Inc.*, 89 N.J. 163, 445 A.2d 370 (1982), which forbade casinos from excluding patrons solely on the basis of their cardcounting. Forced to live with cardcounters, the gambling commission promulgated a variety of rules that allowed casinos to shuffle cards, introduce new decks, limit the number of wagers per player, and so on—countermeasures all designed to confound players who used math to beat the odds.

Next the panel examined the trial court's initial finding that Campione had a cause of action on grounds of discrimination, which allowed the lawsuit to proceed in court. Rejecting this determination, the panel expressed "grave reservations" about how it was at odds with the purpose of anti-counting measures: they were adopted in order "to hobble cardcounters because of their perceived threat to the mathematical advantage the casino industry must enjoy to remain vital." Disparate treatment of cardcounters was exactly what the regulations allowed, and, as such, the trial court erred in hearing the discrimination claim.

The panel ruled that the proper forum for hearing Campione's claim was the Casino Control Commission. Its exclusive jurisdiction over all civil violations of the gambling law was found in N.J.S.A. 5:12-63b and f. The decision in *Uston* had noted that the state legislature intended the Commission's control over the rules as well as their implementation to be comprehensive. "Granting authority to trial courts and juries in twenty-one counties to interpret and apply game rules," concluded the panel, "would be fatal to the legislative intent." Thus the panel reversed the discrimination judgment awarding Campione damages. In a small victory for the plaintiff, it concluded that the commission's responses to him had taken too narrow a view of the board's authority, which, properly understood, included the power to order a casino to pay restitution.

On the malicious prosecution claims, the panel found that the trial court's instructions to the jury had been prejudicial to the defendants. It ordered a new hearing on that claim alone, instructing the trial court to consider whether summary judgment for the casino might be appropriate.

**CROSS REFERENCES**
Damages; Jurisdiction

# GANGS

Any company of persons who go about together or act in concert; in modern use, the term is mainly applied to persons associated for criminal purposes.

Since the late nineteenth century, much of the juvenile crime in the United States has been a group or gang activity. The establishment of juvenile courts and juvenile law in the early 1900s was, in part, directed at breaking down gang relationships, which often provided young people with a supportive social group. By the 1990s, however, increasing gang-related criminal activity, especially violent crime and the selling of illegal narcotics, led federal, state, and local authorities to crack down on gangs. Their efforts, which have included new laws and new forms of police work, have been justified by the

*The 18th Street Gang marked their territory on the back of this stop sign in the Franklin Park area of Los Angeles.*
SUSAN STERNER/AP/WIDE WORLD PHOTOS

need to restore public safety in troubled neighborhoods and to combat illegal activities. However, opposition has arisen to some of these efforts. Some critics, such as the American Civil Liberties Union, have charged that many of these new laws and enforcement tactics violate the civil liberties of individuals and rob them of their First Amendment right of free association. Others have complained that anti-gang initiatives waste public resources because they fail to solve the underlying issues. Courts around the United States have begun to consider the constitutionality of these initiatives, resulting in divergent and conflicting decisions.

## Types of Gangs

Gangs can be divided into four types. Delinquent youth gangs are groups of troubled youths who associate with each other and base that association on delinquent behavior such as vandalism, truancy, curfew, and other "status" offenses (behavior that is illegal only because the offender is not an adult). They are loosely held together and identified through similar clothing, gang names, and the crimes they commit. While not involved for the most part in serious crimes, they begin their criminal activity through acts of vandalism such as drawing graffiti, or "tagging."

Traditional, turf-based gangs are composed of young adults and juveniles who are more sophisticated in identifying themselves through clothing, names, gang colors, and signs. They will typically have an identifiable leader and a

# DO ANTI-GANG LAWS VIOLATE THE CONSTITUTION?

The national aversion to gangs has sparked debate over First Amendment rights of gang members versus citizens' safety at home and on the streets. Anti-gang injunctions and the enactment of anti-gang loitering ordinances are the two most prominent legal weapons currently employed against gangs. Critics of these efforts, most notably the American Civil Liberties Union (ACLU), contend that these initiatives violate the First Amendment's right of free association. Defenders of anti-gang initiatives reply that society's rights to peace and quiet and to be free from harm outweigh the gang members' First Amendment associational rights.

Critics reject the idea that public safety allows the government to tell citizens they may not associate with each other. As long as citizens are not committing a crime, the state cannot tell them not to stand on a street corner to-

gether or walk down the street. The Supreme Court has recognized that freedom of association is on par with freedom of speech and freedom of the press.

The Court has allowed municipalities to require permits for parades, sound trucks, and demonstrations, in the interest of public order. However, the courts have been careful not to abridge the right of unpopular assemblies or protests. In 1977, the largely Jewish suburb of Skokie, Illinois, enacted three ordinances designed to prevent a march through the city by the American Nazi Party. The ACLU sued the city, and a federal court ruled that Skokie had violated the First Amendment by denying the Nazis a permit to march (*Collin v. Smith*, 578 F.2d 1197 [7th Cir. 1978]).

IN FOCUS

Critics of anti-gang laws also argue that just because gang members are un-

popular to a large segment of society does not give society the right to restrict their right to association. Why, for example, should the Ku Klux Klan be allowed to march through an African-American neighborhood while persons in that neighborhood cannot congregate on a playground to talk or play sports?

Critics believe there are better alternatives to controlling illegal gang activity than loitering laws and community injunctions. The ACLU contends that anti-gang injunctions do not work and may even make things worse. The resources of law enforcement are concentrated in one area, causing the shift of criminal activity into other neighborhoods. In addition, arresting a gang member for violating a loitering ordinance will not change the underlying dynamic of gang activity in urban areas. Critics argue that these anti-gang efforts are a cynical, political ploy that has more to do with creating a tough-on-

neighborhood that they claim as theirs and defend against rival gangs. They use graffiti to identify their turf, but they also engage in assaultive behavior that may result in shootings and homicides.

Gain-oriented gangs are composed of juveniles and adults who identify themselves in similar fashion to traditional turf-based gangs but have moved into criminal activity for profit. Typical crimes include robbery, theft, and the sale of drugs.

Hate gangs are composed of adults and juveniles who identify themselves with a name and leader but go beyond the traditional turf or material aspect of other gangs and engage in violence toward particular groups. Crimes associated with this type of gang include arson, assault, and homicide.

The rise in the number of gangs has been dramatic. The U.S. Department of Justice (DOJ) estimated that 95 percent of the largest cities in the United States and 88 percent of

smaller cities suffer gang-related crime. Cities with an emerging gang problem report that up to 90 percent of the gang members are juveniles. With the advent of hard drugs like crack cocaine and the proliferation of assault weapons on our streets, gangs have become violent street families for many young people.

## Anti-gang Initiatives

During the 1990s, federal, state, and local policy makers have given law enforcement officials more tools to deal with gang activities. At the federal level, the DOJ has provided millions of dollars in federal funds to law enforcement agencies that have targeted gang-related violence, drug problems, and intimidation. In 1996 the DOJ's Office of Community Oriented Policing Services (COPS) announced the Anti-Gang Initiative grant program. COPS awarded grants to fifteen jurisdictions that proposed new gang suppression and intervention strategies. In 1997 the Clinton administration proposed additional federal legislation that would provide $200 million over two years to fund new local

crime appearance than with effective law enforcement.

As an alternative, critics would emphasize community policing, increased resources for law enforcement, and efforts to improve the economic status of urban areas. They note that crime prevention and effective enforcement of criminal laws will do more to make a community safe than telling a suspected gang member to leave a street corner. In time, they believe, both the public and law enforcement will realize that solid, everyday police work produces better results.

Defenders of anti-gang initiatives contend that although First Amendment rights should be protected as much as possible, no constitutional right is absolute. In the case of gangs, the violence and criminal activity in certain parts of urban areas have reached a stage where normal law enforcement techniques do not work. Although the ACLU may say that individual rights must be protected, such a claim rings hollow when a gang can take over a neighborhood through violence and intimidation and yet evade law enforcement. In a crisis situation, additional steps must be taken to restore public confidence in the police and local government.

Restricting gang activity is not unconstitutional, argue defenders of the laws, because the Supreme Court has made it clear that no group of persons has the right to associate for wholly illegal aims. Moreover, associations engaging in both legal and illegal activities may still be regulated to the extent they engage in illegal activities. Defenders emphasize that the mere existence of an association is not sufficient to bring all that association's activities within scope of the First Amendment. Therefore, nonexpressive gang activities can be regulated.

Defenders also emphasize that injunctions and loitering ordinances are constitutional because they serve significant, and often compelling, government interests by reducing the threat to public health and safety caused by gang activities. They note that in the case of an injunction, gang members are free to conduct their expressive activities outside of the geographic area defined in the injunction. Thus, the injunction is likely to be upheld because it is narrowly tailored.

Though defenders believe these anti-gang initiatives will become important weapons for law enforcement, they acknowledge the danger of guilt by association. They believe, however, that this problem can be avoided if law enforcement officials adhere to constitutional standards in determining who should be subjected to anti-gang provisions. Judges must also carefully review evidence for each defendant to make sure the person has not been unfairly prosecuted.

Despite criticisms leveled by the ACLU and others, proponents of anti-gang laws adamantly support their use. While some of these initiatives may prove ineffective, law enforcement should be given the chance to test new ways of addressing destructive elements within their communities. Modifications can be made, and new initiatives plotted, but proponents insist that the law is necessary to protect the health and safety of citizens.

prosecutor positions dedicated to gang-related crimes and to provide funds for other initiatives. The funds would go directly to state, county, and local prosecutors to enable them to develop initiatives such as anti-gang units and anti-gang task forces and to purchase equipment to share information about gang members and their activities.

Law enforcement agencies have recognized that they must share with one another information they collect about gangs and gang members. The DOJ has funded a National Gang Tracking Network to help federal, state, and local law enforcement exchange information about gangs. As state and local agencies have entered information into a central computerized database, they have gained the ability to track people who try to avoid detection by moving around.

Information about individuals is entered into these criminal gang databases when the individuals meet objective criteria. The state of Minnesota has adopted a gang identification system developed in Fresno, California. Other jurisdictions have similar systems. The Fresno model uses a ten-point system. A person who meets at least three of the following ten criteria is classified as a criminal street-gang member:

1. Admits gang membership or association
2. Is observed to associate on a regular basis with known gang members
3. Has tattoos indicating gang membership
4. Wears gang symbols to identify with a specific gang
5. Is in a photograph with known gang members or using gang hand signs
6. Is named on a gang document, hit list, or in gang-related graffiti
7. Is identified as a gang member by a reliable source
8. Is arrested in the company of identified gang members or associates
9. Corresponds with known gang members or knows or receives correspondence about gang activities

**10.** Writes about gangs on walls, books, or papers

Persons listed in the database must be fourteen years old and must have been convicted of a felony or gross misdemeanor, in addition to displaying at least three of the criteria. A person's name stays in the database for three years after his last conviction.

Aside from identifying gang members, this type of system creates a record that can be used against the person if she is charged and convicted of a crime. In Minnesota, for example, a 1991 law elevates a crime from a misdemeanor to a gross misdemeanor, or from a gross misdemeanor to a felony, if the crime was done for the benefit of a gang. In addition, state sentencing guidelines provide that a conviction for a crime benefiting a gang adds a year to the presumed sentence. Judges are also permitted under the guidelines to require convicted gang members to stay away from their associates when they are released from prison.

### Legal Challenges to Anti-gang Initiatives

Some of the enforcement strategies instituted against alleged gang members have been challenged in state courts. In *People v. Acuna*, 14 Cal. 4th 1090, 929 P.2d 596, 60 Cal. Rptr.2d 277 (1997), the California Supreme Court upheld the right of the city of San Jose to restrict the rights of alleged gang members to protect an embattled community. In 1993 San Jose pursued a comprehensive solution to its gang problem by asking a court to enforce the state's civil nuisance laws. These laws allow courts to intervene when the risk of harm is great and normal remedies do not work. The court complaint accused 38 named and 100 unnamed gang members.

The court responded by issuing a broad preliminary injunction against eleven defendants who had protested the complaint. It ordered them not to perform, "directly or indirectly," behaviors in twenty-four highly detailed categories. At its broadest, the order banned them from appearing in public in their four-square-block neighborhood with each other or any other known gang members, as well as from bothering neighborhood residents and engaging in several criminal behaviors. The court order also forbade a number of otherwise legal behaviors: carrying electronic pagers or sharp objects such as pens and screwdrivers, using gang hand gestures or verbal phrases, "encouraging" drug use, conversing with the occupants of cars, and even climbing trees. Violations carried penalties of $1,000 and up to six months in jail.

The defendants appealed the order, claiming the injunction was unconstitutionally broad and vague, violating the First Amendment's right to free association. Though an appeals court sided with the defendants, the California Supreme Court reversed that appellate decision. The court concluded that there was ample reason for enforcing statutes in a broad way. The neighborhood was an "urban war zone" of "occupied territory," where the gang's behavior made residents "prisoners of their own homes." The loss of liberty suffered by the gang members was justified by the community's gains in safety and pursuit of happiness.

The Illinois Supreme Court reached a different conclusion in analyzing the constitutionality of an anti-gang ordinance enacted by the city of Chicago. In *City of Chicago v. Morales*, 687 N.E.2d 53, 227 Ill. Dec. 130, 177 Ill. 2d 440 (1997), the court struck down the gang loitering ordinance, which gave broad discretion to police officers to identify persons they reasonably believed to be gang members and to order such persons, and anyone with them, to disperse. Anyone who disobeyed the order was in violation of the ordinance. Each violation was punishable by a fine of $500, imprisonment for up to six months, and the requirement to perform 120 hours of community service.

In three related cases, seventy defendants were charged with violations of the law. The trial courts in two of the cases held the law unconstitutional. However, the third case proceeded to trial, and the six defendants in the case were given jail terms. The Illinois Supreme Court ruled that the ordinance violated the Due Process Clauses of the Fifth and Fourteenth Amendments, because a criminal statute must clearly define the conduct proscribed. In this case the ordinance did not adequately define the prohibited conduct because persons waiting to hail a taxi, pausing on a corner while jogging, or stepping into a doorway to avoid rain could all be charged with loitering under the ordinance. In addition to finding unconstitutional vagueness, the court found that the ordinance invited arbitrary and discriminatory enforcement and deprived persons suspected of gang activity of the rights to walk the streets and associate with friends. By arbitrarily infringing on personal liberties, the law violated substantive due process. The court noted that "gang membership itself is not a crime, and standing in a public place with no apparent purpose is not a crime. ...

Adding these actions together does not make them any more criminal. When you add nothing to nothing you get nothing."

**CROSS REFERENCES**
Due Process of Law; Freedom of Association; Hate Crime; Juvenile Law; Nuisance

## GAY AND LESBIAN RIGHTS

The goal of full legal and social equality for gay men and lesbians sought by the gay movement in the United States and other Western countries.

### California Human Rights Law Doesn't Protect Gay Scoutmaster

The legal controversy over not admitting gays to the Boy Scouts of America continues to produce different results around the United States. The California Supreme Court, in *Curran v. Mount Diablo Council of the Boy Scouts of America*, 17 Cal.4th 670 M Cal.Rptr.2d 410, 952 P.2d 218 (1998), ruled that the state's human rights act did not apply to the Boy Scouts of America because the organization was not a business establishment, and therefore was not a public accommodation. The California decision was the opposite of the New Jersey court ruling in *Dale v. Boy Scouts of America*, 308 710d. 706 A.2d 270 Super. 514, (A.D. 1998).

The situation in Curran was similar to that in *Dale*. Timothy Curran was a Boy Scout from 1975 to 1979, when he was fourteen to eighteen years of age. He had a distinguished scout career, attaining the rank of Eagle Scout and earning numerous scout honors. When Curran turned eighteen, he was no longer an official member of the Boy Scouts, but he maintained contact with his local troop. Like James Dale in New Jersey, Curran drew the attention of Boy Scout officials when he featured prominently in an Oakland newspaper series on gay teenagers. When Curran later applied to be an assistant scoutmaster, scout officials denied his application because of his homosexual lifestyle.

In 1982, Curran filed suit in state court, contending that the rejection of his scoutmaster application violated California's public accommodation statute, commonly known as the Unruh Civil Rights Act, Civ. Code, § 51. Due to a series of events, the trial did not take place until 1990. The trial court ruled that the Boy Scouts were not a business establishment under the Unruh Act and thus not a public accommodation. Therefore, the judge dismissed Curran's claims. The California Court of Appeals af-

firmed this decision, leading Curran to appeal to the California Supreme Court.

Chief Justice Ronald M. George, writing for the court, affirmed the appellate court decision. He emphasized at the beginning of the decision that "the resolution of this matter does not turn on our personal views of the wisdom or morality of the actions or policies that are challenged in this case." Instead, the court was bound to analyze the narrow legal issue of whether the Unruh Civil Rights Act, as interpreted by prior decisions of the supreme court, classified the Boy Scouts as a public accommodation. If so, the membership policies of the Boy Scouts would be subject to the act.

Justice George reviewed many of these prior decisions, pointing out that courts had examined on a case-by-case basis whether organizations were business establishments. If they were, they were a public accommodation and subject to the Unruh act. The court had classified a private golf club as a business establishment because it allowed nonmembers to use the course and facilities on certain days of the week. A Santa Cruz Boys' Club was a business establishment and a public accommodation because admission to the club "was equivalent to admission to a place of public amusement."

Turning to the Boy Scouts, Justice George concluded that the scout organization was not a place of public accommodation. Although the Boy Scouts conducted extensive business activities involving nonmembers through its retail shops and stores, and through the licensing of its insignia, Justice George ruled that these business activities differed from those of the country club or Boys' Club. The Boy Scouts are an "expressive social organization whose primary function is the inculcation of values in its youth members, and whose small social-groups structure and activities are not comparable to those of a traditional place of public accommodation or amusement." Unlike the country club, the Boy Scouts did not sell to nonmembers "access to the basic activities or services offered by the organization." Nonmembers could not purchase entry to scout meetings, overnight hikes, the national jamboree, or to training and education programs.

As for the Boy Scout retail stores, Justice George ruled that while these were business establishments, the business transacted at these stores was "distinct from the Scouts' core functions" and did not demonstrate that the organization had become a "commercial purveyor of

the primary incidents and benefits of membership of the organization." Therefore, the Boy Scouts were not a public accommodation subject to the antidiscrimination provisions of the Unruh Civil Rights Act.

### Cincinnati Removes Antidiscrimination Protections

Gay and lesbian rights advocates have sought the passage of legislation that prohibits discrimination in employment, housing, public accommodations, or public service on the basis of sexual orientation. Many U.S. cities have passed gay rights ordinances that accomplish these objectives, and in the 1990s a backlash has developed in some communities from these ordinances. The efforts of the city of Cincinnati, Ohio, to remove gays, lesbians, and bisexuals from the protections of municipal antidiscrimination ordinances led gay rights advocates to file a lawsuit against city. In *Equality Foundation of Greater Cincinnati, Inc. v. City of Cincinnati*, 128 F.3d 289 (1997), the U.S. Court of Appeals for the Sixth Circuit ruled that the city charter amendment that removed the protections was constitutional because it was rationally related to the city's valid interest in conserving public costs that accrued from investigating and adjudicating sexual orientation discrimination complaints. In so ruling, the appeals court concluded that the city amendment was distinguishable from the Colorado state constitutional amendment that prohibited state and local governments from enacting any law, regulation, or pol-

icy that would, in effect, protect the civil rights of gays, lesbians, and bisexuals. The U.S. Supreme Court struck down the Colorado amendment in *Romer v. Evans*, 517 U.S. 620, 116 S. Ct. 1620, 134 L. Ed. 2d 855 (1996), as unconstitutional.

In 1991 the Cincinnati city council passed an equal opportunity ordinance (No. 79-1991) that mandated that the city could not discriminate in its own hiring practices on the basis of sexual orientation. In 1992 the council enacted an ordinance (No. 490-1992) that prohibited private discrimination in employment, housing, or public accommodation for reasons of sexual orientation. Opposition to this action led to the formation of Equal Rights Not Special Rights, a group that sponsored an initiative petition that appeared on the November 1993 election ballot. The initiative, which was enacted by 62 percent of the ballots cast, became an article in the city charter. This amendment to the charter stated in part:

> The City of Cincinnati and its various Boards and Commissions may not enact, adopt, enforce or administer any ordinance, regulation, rule or policy which provides that homosexual, lesbian, or bisexual orientation, status, conduct, or relationship constitutes, entitles, or otherwise provides a person with the basis to have any claim of minority or protected status,

quota preference or other preferential treatment.

Before the charter amendment took effect, the Equality Foundation of Greater Cincinnati, Inc. , filed suit in federal district court, claiming that the amendment was unconstitutional. The court agreed and entered a permanent injunction restraining the implementation of the amendment. On appeal, the Sixth Circuit reversed and vacated the injunction. Following the *Romer* decision, however, the Supreme Court vacated the appeals court decision and remanded it for reconsideration based on the analysis contained in *Romer*.

Circuit Judge Robert B. Krupansky, writing for a unanimous three-judge panel, reaffirmed its prior decision that the charter amendment did not violate constitutional principles. Krupansky noted that in *Romer*, the Supreme Court had not analyzed the Colorado constitutional amendment under either a "strict scrutiny" or an "intermediate scrutiny" standard. These standards of constitutional review require the state to meet a high burden of proof that demonstrates there is a legitimate state interest for the law or policy. Instead, the Supreme Court had employed a "rational relationship" standard, which will uphold the constitutional validity of a statute or ordinance if it rationally furthers any conceivable, valid, public interest. This standard is comparatively easy for the state to meet, though not in the case of *Romer*.

The appeals court pointed out that the Colorado amendment was invalidated because it was found to be invidiously discriminatory and not rationally connected to the advancement of any legitimate state objective. Comparing the Colorado and Cincinnati amendments, the court declared that the two cases involved "substantially different enactments of entirely distinct scope and impact, which conceptually and analytically distinguished the constitutional posture of the two measures." The court then set out these differences in more detail.

Judge Krupansky pointed out that the Colorado amendment was objectionable because it removed municipally legislated special legal protection from gays and precluded the re-legislation of special legal rights at every level of state government. The amendment did more than simply repeal city human rights ordinances; it barred all legislative, executive, or judicial action destined to protect gays or lesbians. In addition, the Supreme Court observed that the amendment could be read to divest homosexuals of all

state law government protection available to all other citizens.

In contrast, the appeals court concluded that the Cincinnati charter amendment was more restricted, as compared with the actual and potential sweep of the Colorado amendment. Read in its full context, the city amendment "merely prevented homosexuals, as homosexuals, from obtaining special privileges and preferences (such as affirmative action preferences or the legally sanctioned power to force employers, landlords, and merchants to transact business with them) from the City." Where the Colorado amendment "ominously threatened to reduce an entire segment of the state's population to the status of virtual non-citizens," the Cincinnati amendment had no sweeping or "conscience-shocking effect."

Krupansky justified this conclusion by asserting that the Cincinnati amendment applied only at the lowest (municipal) level of government and thus could not take away from gay Cincinnatians any rights derived from any higher level of state law and enforced by a superior apparatus of state government. In addition, the amendment's narrow, restrictive language could not be construed to deprive homosexuals of all legal protections even under municipal law but instead "eliminated only 'special class status' and 'preferential treatment' for gays as gays under Cincinnati ordinances and policies, leaving untouched the application, to gay citizens, of any and all legal rights generally accorded by the municipal government to all persons as persons."

The Cincinnati amendment's comparatively narrow scope appeared obvious to the appeals court. Krupansky noted that persons could seek local repeal of the amendment through ordinary municipal political process, just as the proponents had done in securing passage of the initiative. Opponents of the amendment could also seek relief from higher levels of Ohio state government, including the county, state agencies, the Ohio legislature, or the voters themselves through a statewide initiative.

Another point of contrast with the Colorado amendment was the local nature of the charter amendment. The Colorado amendment interfered "with the expression of local community preferences in that state." The Cincinnati charter amendment constituted "a direct expression of the local community will on a subject of direct consequence to the voters." This amendment was entitled to the "highest degree of deference from the courts" because it did not impinge on any fundamental rights or the interests of a protected class of people, and because it was "designed in part to preserve community values and character." Direct legislation by the people held a special place in U.S. constitutional tradition and jurisprudence and "must not be cavalierly disregarded."

The appeals court concluded that *Romer* should not be interpreted to forbid local electorates from using the initiative process to "instruct" local officials to withhold "special rights, privileges, and protections from homosexuals." Moreover, unlike Colorado, the Cincinnati measure was legally justified because it had a rational basis. The city's voters had a clear and direct interest "in the potential cost savings and other contingent benefits which could result from the law." The exclusion of gays, lesbians, and bisexuals from human rights protections was not, on its face, animated by an "impermissibly naked desire" of the city's voters to injure an "unpopular group of citizens." Krupansky found that the removal of these groups from the antidiscrimination ordinances would eliminate "substantial public costs that accrue from the investigation and adjudication of sexual orientation complaints." This cost savings was of sufficient weight to provide a rational basis for the passage of the initiative, thereby making the amendment constitutional.

### Maine Repeals Gay Rights Law

Gay and lesbian organizations have sought legislation at the state and local level that bans discrimination in housing, public accommodations, credit, and employment on the basis of sexual orientation. Though some states and cities have passed gay rights laws, such legislation has often led to organized opposition. On February 17, 1998, Maine voters repealed the state's gay rights law by a narrow margin, marking the first time a state has repealed a gay rights law. The law, which never went into effect, was repealed by a "people's veto" referendum that was initiated by a petition campaign.

The repeal thwarted the twenty-year effort of Maine's Lesbian-Gay Political Alliance to secure civil rights protections. In May 1997 the Maine legislature passed the amendment to the Maine Human Rights Act (5 Me. Rev. Stat. Ann. § 4552 [West 1997]). The amendment banned discrimination in housing, employment, public accommodations, and credit based on sexual orientation. Governor Angus King, a strong supporter of the legislation, signed the bill into law in May.

The new law aroused immediate opposition. A conservative group led by members of the Christian Civic League of Maine and the state chapter of the Christian Coalition organized volunteers to collect signatures on petitions calling for a state referendum on the law. A total of 51,131 voter signatures were required to force the referendum. On September 19, 1997, one day before the law was to take effect, opponents of the law presented the secretary of state with petitions containing almost 59,000 signatures.

Opponents of the law argued that the law conferred special rights on homosexuals. Michael Health, executive director of the Christian Civic League, stated that the law "threatened the civil liberties of business owners, parents, and even charitable organizations that decline to celebrate homosexuality."

Supporters of the law organized a new group, Maine Won't Discriminate, to defeat the referendum. Leaders were cautiously optimistic because in 1995 Maine voters had narrowly defeated a referendum that sought to outlaw civil rights protections for homosexuals. However, the February 1998 vote went the other way, with opponents of the law winning by a margin of 51 to 49 percent.

The repeal of the Maine law leaves ten states, covering almost 24 percent of the U.S. population, with laws banning discrimination based on sexual orientation: California, Connecticut, Hawaii, Massachusetts, Minnesota, New Hampshire, New Jersey, Rhode Island, Vermont, and Wisconsin.

### New Jersey Law Protects Gay Scoutmaster

Gays and lesbians have used the legal system to challenge discrimination in employment, housing, and association. In *Dale v. Boy Scouts of America*, 308 N.J. Super-516, 706A.2d 270 (1998), the New Jersey Superior Court ruled that a gay scoutmaster could not be expelled from a New Jersey Boy Scout organization on the basis of his sexual orientation because the Boy Scouts of America (BSA) and its New Jersey council were public accommodations under New Jersey's Law Against Discrimination (LAD) (N.J.S.A. 10:5-1 et seq.). LAD prohibits discrimination based on several categories, including affectional or sexual orientation, which encompasses male or female heterosexuality, homosexuality, or bisexuality. In so ruling, the New Jersey court rejected the BSA's contention that it was a private association that was entitled to regulate the type of boys and men admitted into its ranks.

James Dale became a Cub Scout at the age of eight and went on to become an exemplary member, eventually becoming an Eagle Scout. In 1989, after he turned eighteen, Dale applied for adult membership and was approved. He then served as an assistant scoutmaster in a Matawan, New Jersey, troop during the periods he was not attending Rutgers University. On August 5, 1990, Dale received a letter from the Monmouth scout council, informing him that his registration had been revoked. Registration was a prerequisite for service as an adult volunteer.

After Dale asked for the grounds of the decision, he was told that the BSA forbids "membership to homosexuals." The Monmouth scout director noted that Dale had been in a newspaper photograph taken at Rutgers, where he was copresident of the university gay and lesbian campus organization. Dale was also quoted in the newspaper as "only admitting his homosexuality during his second year at Rutgers." According to the scout director, Dale had demonstrated his inability to live by the Scout Oath and Law by publicly avowing that he was homosexual.

Dale filed suit in New Jersey state court, alleging that the BSA's revocation of his membership and his expulsion as an assistant scoutmaster violated the LAD. He asked for reinstatement and damages. The trial court, however, dismissed his suit, ruling that the BSA had consistently excluded any self-declared homosexuals. The trial court found that homosexuality, from biblical and historical perspectives, was not only morally wrong, but also criminal. The BSA had implicitly subscribed to this historical view since its inception. The trial court found that the LAD did not apply in Dale's case because the BSA was not a place of public accommodation and because the BSA, as a private association, could not be compelled to accept a gay scoutmaster because this would violate the freedom of association guaranteed by the First Amendment.

On appeal, the New Jersey Superior Court rejected the assumptions and legal reasoning of the trial court. Presiding Judge James M. Havey, writing for the three-judge panel, concluded that the BSA was a "place of public accommodation" under the LAD. Havey rejected a narrow interpretation of the concept, noting that the LAD was a remedial statute that must be

*James Dale, who had been dismissed from the Boy Scouts of America for his sexual orientation, won his discrimination suit in the New Jersey Superior Court.*

ELIZABETH LIPPMAN/GAMMA LIAISON

"read with an approach sympathetic to its objectives." The court pointed out that a prior New Jersey decision had held that Little League baseball was a place of public accommodation. If activities and facilities were offered to and dependent upon the broad-based participation of members of the general public, then these were the types of accommodations that were intended to be covered by the LAD. The LAD's reach did not turn on whether there was a fixed "place."

Turning to the BSA, the court concluded that it was a public accommodation. The BSA invited the public at large to join its ranks, and it was dependent upon the broad-based participation of its members. The New Jersey BSA alone had more than 100,000 members, demonstrating its mass public appeal. In addition, the BSA used advertising and public promotion to encourage new membership. A variety of other details supported the conclusion that the BSA was a public accommodation and therefore subject to LAD's prohibition against discrimination based on sexual orientation.

The court rejected the BSA's defense that it was an educational facility operated by a religious or sectarian institution, and thus exempt from the LAD provisions. Havey noted that the BSA is "expressly nonsectarian." The requirement that members profess a belief in God did not make the BSA a religious organization.

Havey also rejected the trial court's conclusion that the First Amendment's freedom of association allowed the BSA to avoid the reach of the LAD. He cited the U.S. Supreme Court's ruling in *Roberts v. United States Jaycees*, 468 U.S.

609, 104 S. Ct. 3244, 82 L. Ed. 2d 462 (1984), which distinguished between freedom of intimate association and freedom of expressive association. Freedom of intimate association shields against unjust government intrusion into an individual's choice to maintain intimate or private associations with others. Intimate associations include marriage, child bearing, education, and cohabitation with relatives. Havey concluded that intimate association was not implicated in this case because the BSA had a membership of five million.

Freedom of expressive association is linked to the right of freedom of speech. Generally, overtly political organizations or organizations formed to advance gender or race-based interests are most likely to demonstrate successfully a genuine relationship between their discriminatory practices and their objectives. Though freedom of association presupposes a freedom not to associate, the *Roberts* decision made clear that the government could regulate an association if the state had a compelling interest, unrelated to the suppression of ideas, that could not be achieved in a less restrictive way.

Havey, noting that many types of organizations, such as the Rotary and the Jaycees, had been forced to abandon discriminatory membership practices because they violated civil rights laws, concluded that the BSA had failed to meet the burden of demonstrating "a strong relationship between its expressive activities and its discriminatory practice." Havey ruled that the application of the LAD to the BSA did not impede "the BSA's ability to express its collective views on scouting, or to instill in the scouts those qualities of leadership, courage, and integrity to which the BSA has traditionally adhered." The application of the LAD "leaves in place the integral workings of the BSA and its constitutional right to carry out its mission." In so ruling, Havey rejected the BSA's contention that it had a long and clear policy against homosexual members. The BSA had only adopted statements against homosexual membership after Dale had started his lawsuit. The court also pointed out that many church groups affiliated with the BSA disagreed with the BSA over its rejection of gay members.

In the court's view, Dale had lived up to the BSA's code of conduct by being honest about his sexual orientation and by being courageous enough to admit it. Havey found a patent inconsistency in the notion that a gay scout leader who keeps his "secret" hidden may remain in scouting and the one who adheres to the scout laws by being honest and courageous enough to declare his homosexuality publicly must be expelled:

> We also cannot accept the proposition that the BSA has a constitutional privilege of excluding a gay person when the sole basis for the exclusion is the gay's exercise of his own First Amendment right to speak honestly about himself.

**CROSS REFERENCES**
Civil Rights; Discrimination; First Amendment; Freedom of Association; Human Rights; Lobbying Organizations: Christian Coalition; Referendum; Roberts v. United States Jaycees

# GUARDIAN AND WARD

The legal relationship that exists between a person (the GUARDIAN) appointed by a court to take care of and manage the PROPERTY of a person (the WARD) who does not possess the legal CAPACITY to do so, by reason of age, comprehension, or self-control.

## Sterilization of Developmentally Disabled Ward

A guardian manages the everyday affairs of her ward without consulting the court that granted the guardianship and appointed her the guardian. However, in circumstances where the guardian wishes to take an action that will have a major effect on the life of the ward, the guardian must file a petition with the court and request an order authorizing the action. Such a procedure ensures that the ward will be given due process.

In a case that reflected concerns about the power of guardians and courts to make decisions for developmentally disabled persons, the Michigan Supreme Court ruled in *Wirsing v. Michigan Protection and Advocacy Service*, 456 Mich. 467, 573 N.W.2d 51 (1998), that probate courts had authority to approve the sterilization of a ward for birth control purposes. In so ruling, the court overturned a Michigan court of appeals decision that had concluded that a probate court had no statutory authority to issue such an order.

The case involved Lora Faye Wirsing, who in 1981, at the age of eighteen, was adjudicated to be a developmentally disabled person as a result of retardation since birth. The Michigan probate court appointed Donna L. Wirsing to act as her daughter's guardian. In 1986 Donna Wirsing petitioned the probate court for authorization to have a tubal ligation performed on Lora Wirsing for birth control purposes. The Michigan Protection and Advocacy Service (MPAS) was allowed to intervene in the court proceeding. MPAS argued that Michigan law did not give the probate court the right to authorize the sterilization of developmentally disabled persons.

Following an extensive fact-finding hearing, the probate court found that the guardian had the best interests of her daughter at heart, that Lora Wirsing had no ability to understand the relationship between sexual intercourse and pregnancy, and that Wirsing did not have the ability to consent to the process herself. In addition, the court stated that there was no Michigan statute concerning developmentally disabled persons. On the basis of these findings, the probate court judge authorized the guardian to consent to the tubal ligation for the ward. MPAS appealed this decision to the Michigan Supreme Court, which remanded the case to the court of appeals to determine "whether probate judges possess the power to authorize a guardian to consent to the sterilization of a developmentally disabled citizen" (441 Mich. 886, 495 N.W.2d 388 [1992]).

The court of appeals reversed the probate court (214 Mich. App. 131, 542 N.W.2d 594 [1995]). The court of appeals reasoned that the 1974 revision of the Mental Health Code (M.C.L. § 330.1600 et seq., M.S.A. § 14.800(600) et seq.) eliminated the authority of the probate court to authorize a guardian to consent to the sterilization of a ward. On appeal again to the supreme court, the court reversed the court of appeals.

Justice Michael F. Cavanagh, writing for a unanimous supreme court, acknowledged that Michigan, like most states, had only abandoned forced sterilization of developmentally disabled persons in the 1970s. In 1913 the Michigan legislature had passed a law that allowed sterilization of "mentally defective" persons who were supported by public expense in a public institution. Though the statute was ruled unconstitutional in 1918, in 1923 the legislature passed a similar law, which was upheld by the Michigan Supreme Court. In 1929 this law was repealed and replaced by 1929 P.A. 281, which allowed sterilization of insane and mentally ill persons to prevent them from procreating. Although this act authorized a parent to apply for sterilization of a child, most of the applications came from the administrators of various institutions for the sterilization of the wards under their care.

This law remained in effect until 1974, when the legislature completely revised the Mental Health Code (M.C.L. § 330.1600 et seq., M.S.A. § 14.800(600) et seq.). The revised code did not refer to sterilization in any manner. However, in 1977 the legislature passed M.C.L. § 330.1629, M.S.A. § 14.800(629), which gave immunity to guardians of developmentally disabled persons for medical treatment approved by the guardian, including extraordinary medical procedures. In 1978 the legislature amended this law to include sterilization as an extraordinary medical procedure.

Donna Wirsing argued that these recent changes in the law gave the probate court the power to authorize the guardian of a developmentally disabled ward to allow surgical sterilization of the ward. This authority is implied because the legislature would not refer to sterilization as an extraordinary medical procedure from which the guardian is immune if the legislature did not intend to allow a probate court to authorize a guardian to allow such sterilization.

MPAS contended that the jurisdiction of the probate court cannot arise by implication but must be specifically set forth by statute. The failure of the legislature to enact statutory authorization for sterilization of developmentally disabled persons in the revised 1974 code demonstrated the intent not to allow the probate court to grant such requests. In addition, it agreed with the court of appeals that "adequate safeguards are not provided by statute to assure that the ward has the guarantee of due process."

Justice Cavanagh agreed with Wirsing, finding "the statute to plainly contemplate the probate court's authorization of a guardian to consent to extraordinary medical procedures, specifically including sterilization." The court of appeals had erred by failing to distinguish between "the unfortunate history of forced eugenic sterilization and the separate concept of voluntary sterilization." Eugenic sterilization refers to the now-discredited theory that the human race can be improved by imposing genetic control over persons who do not meet standards of "normality," such as mentally ill or developmentally disabled persons. The eugenics movement had intellectual and popular support in the United States until Nazi Germany began killing "mental defectives," homosexuals, gypsies, and Jews under the banner of racial purity.

Critics note that as many as 70,000 individuals have been sterilized pursuant to state laws authorizing involuntary sterilization. Of that number, only a handful of reported cases disclose that a developmentally disabled male was sterilized, demonstrating that sterilization practice is entwined with the larger issues of control of female reproductive rights and female sexual expression.

Defenders of involuntary sterilization point out that many improvements have been made in legal procedures since the 1970s. Moreover, they contend that theories concerning developmentally disabled persons, which tainted the issue of sterilization for decades, have been totally discredited. Guardians do not seek to have their ward sterilized because of eugenic principles or general social interests. Instead, the guardian, who is usually the parent, is acting in the best interests of the child.

Cavanagh stated that the court's decision was based on the concept of voluntary sterilization and that nothing in the decision "should be interpreted as an endorsement of a return to the routine sterilization system of the past, as MPAS argues may occur." In the court's view, the probate courts would limit "extraordinary procedures to only those situations in which they are appropriate." The legislature may have halted "the routine involuntary sterilization of the past," but it had never explicitly forbade voluntary sterilization.

Under the guardianship case law of Michigan, where a ward is unable to exercise an important right, a "substituted judgment analysis" may be used. In Lora Wirsing's case, she was unable to choose for herself whether she wished to become pregnant. Cavanagh reasoned that depriving her of the option of sterilization "would make the choice for her, and make the same choice for each ward, regardless of the circumstances." This option did not comport with the statute or the interests of the individual ward.

The court found that the legislature had provided a mechanism that encouraged the guardian to apply to the probate court for an order authorizing consent for an extraordinary procedure such as sterilization. If the probate court agrees that it is in the best interests of the ward, it shall order the authorization of consent. In Lora Wirsing's case, the guardian had articulated reasons for the procedure and had provided evidence to support the request. Under the laws of guardian and ward, "where a ward cannot exercise personal judgment, the decision passes to the guardian." In this case the court acted appropriately in evaluating the evidence to make sure the decision was made in Lora Wirsing's best interests.

**CROSS REFERENCES**
Disabled Persons

# GUN CONTROL

Government regulation of the manufacture, sale, and possession of firearms.

### Printz v. United States

The congressional enactment in 1993 of the Brady Handgun Violence Prevention Act (107 State. 1536) marked the first significant federal gun control legislation since the Gun Control Act of 1968 (GCA) (18 U.S.C.A. § 921 et seq.). The GCA established a federal regulatory scheme governing the distribution of firearms, which includes a provision prohibiting firearms dealers from selling handguns to any person under twenty-one years of age, nonresidents, and convicted felons.

The Brady Act amended the GCA. It requires the U.S. attorney general to establish a national instant background check system by November 30, 1998, and immediately put into place certain interim provisions until the federal system becomes operational. Under the interim provisions, a firearms dealer who sought to transfer a handgun was required to obtain from the proposed purchaser a statement, known as a Brady Form, that contained the name, address, and date of birth of the purchaser along with a sworn statement that the purchaser was not among those classes of persons prohibited from purchasing a handgun. The dealer was then required to verify the purchaser's identity and provide the "chief law enforcement officer" (CLEO) within the jurisdiction with a copy of the Brady Form. With some exceptions, the dealer was required to wait five business days before completing the sale, unless the CLEO notified the dealer that there was no reason to believe that the transfer would be illegal.

If the CLEO discovered that a person was ineligible to purchase a firearm, the would-be purchaser was entitled to a written statement from the CLEO providing the reasons for the negative determination. If the purchaser was eligible to secure a firearm, the Brady Act required the CLEO to destroy all records relating to the transfer, including the Brady Form. Any person who violated these interim provisions was criminally liable.

*The Brady Handgun Violence Prevention Act strictly regulates the sale of firearms.*

W.B. SPUNBARG/THE PICTURE CUBE, INC.

A number of CLEOs objected to these interim provisions. Jay Printz, the CLEO for Ravalli County, Montana, and Richard Mack, the CLEO for Graham County, Arizona, filed separate actions in federal court challenging the constitutionality of this part of the Brady Act. In both cases, the district court held that the provision requiring the CLEOs to perform background checks was unconstitutional. However, the Ninth Circuit Court of Appeals consolidated the two cases and reversed these decisions, finding none of the Brady Act's interim provisions unconstitutional.

The U.S. Supreme Court, in *Printz v. United States*, ___ U.S. ___, 117 S. Ct. 2365, 138 L. Ed. 2d 914 (1997), disagreed with the Ninth Circuit and on a 5–4 vote reversed the decision, ruling that the interim provisions were unconstitutional. Therefore, CLEOs were not required to accept Brady Forms from firearms dealers.

Justice Antonin Scalia, writing for the majority, agreed with the CLEOs' contention that Congress did not have the authority to compel state officers to execute federal laws. Scalia observed that "there is no constitutional text speaking to this precise question," yet concluded that the Court could review the constitutionality of the law based on historical understanding and practice, the structure of the Constitution, and prior decisions of the Court.

Scalia reviewed the history of congressional power to determine whether Congress had previously required state officers to enforce federal laws. He noted that there was no evidence in early U.S. history that Congress had sought to command the states' executive power in the absence of express constitutional authorization. Scalia found this lack of evidence critical, because early congressional enactments provide contemporaneous evidence of the Constitution's meaning. These enactments, if unchallenged for a long period, fix the construction given to pertinent provisions of the Constitution. Therefore, the early Congresses' avoidance of this "highly attractive power" led Scalia to conclude that Congress did not think it had the power to order state officials to enforce federal laws. In doing so, he dismissed the fact that early laws required state judges to enforce federal laws. He reasoned that courts, unlike legislatures and executives, "applied the law of other sovereigns all the time." In addition, the Constitution generally required such enforcement "with respect to obligations arising in other States."

Scalia then turned to the structure of the Constitution, finding in it a vital principle: dual sovereignty. When the original thirteen states agreed to abandon the Articles of Confederation and adopt the Constitution, the states surrendered many of their powers to the new federal government. The states, however, retained a "residuary and inviolable" sovereignty that Scalia saw at work throughout the Constitution. Thus, the state and federal governments exercise concurrent authority over the people. Congress was not given all governmental powers but was limited to discrete and enumerated ones in the Constitution. Likewise, the Tenth Amendment stated that the "powers not delegated to the United States by the Constitution, nor prohibited by it to the States, are reserved to the States respectively, or to the people."

Scalia concluded that the concept of dual sovereignty was one of the Constitution's "structural protections of liberty." The Brady Act's interim provisions shifted the balance of constitutional power, allowing the federal government to "impress into its service—and at no cost to itself—the police officers of the 50 states."

The Court also believed that the interim provisions disturbed the separation and equilibrium of powers between the three branches of the federal government. Under the Constitution, the president is to administer the laws enacted by Congress. The Brady Act "effectively transfers this responsibility to thousands of CLEOs in the 50 States," leaving the president with no meaningful way of controlling the administration of the law. Scalia concluded that presidential power would be "subject to reduction, if Congress could act as effectively without the President as with him, by simply requiring state officers to execute its laws."

The federal government contended that the interim provisions were constitutionally valid under the Necessary and Proper Clause. In its view, the law was necessary and proper to execute Congress's Commerce Clause power to regulate handgun sales. Scalia was unpersuaded by this interpretation, concluding that a law that violates state sovereignty was not a "proper" law and hence the Necessary and Proper Clause had no effect.

Scalia also found no justification for the interim provisions in previous decisions of the Court. In *New York v. United States* (505 U.S. 144, 112 S. Ct. 2408, 120 L. Ed. 2d 120 [1992]) the Court ruled unconstitutional a federal law that required the states either to enact laws providing for the disposal of radioactive waste generated within their borders, or to take title to and possession of the waste. The law impermissibly sought to require the states either to legislate pursuant to a congressional directive, or to implement an administrative solution. The Court in *New York* stated that the federal government "may not compel the States to enact or administer a federal regulatory program." Therefore, Congress could not force CLEOs to administer the interim Brady Act provisions.

## Whether Drug Trafficker "Carried" a Gun

A drug trafficker who hid a gun in the truck he was driving did not "carry" the weapon during his arrest, a federal appeals court ruled on January 5, 1998 (*United States v. Foster*, 133 F.3d 704 [9th Cir.]). The decision concerned a critical question in federal drug prosecutions: what constitutes carrying a gun? The answer is important because federal law adds an additional five years in prison for offenders who carry a firearm during a crime involving violence or drug trafficking (18 U.S.C.A. § 924(c)(1)). Courts around the country are divided in their answers. In *Foster* the U.S. Court of Appeals for the Ninth Circuit joined a few jurisdictions that use a narrow definition: the gun must be available for immediate use, not merely transported. In a lengthy dissent, three members of the court chastised the majority for dwelling on linguistic nuances while ignoring the apparent purpose of the law.

The case dated to a 1989 drug bust. Leon Foster and Sandra Ward manufactured methamphetamine, a strong form of speed known as "crystal" on the street. Police stopped Foster while he was driving his pickup truck, arrested him, and discovered a gun in his truck. The loaded 9mm semiautomatic pistol was in a zipped bag stored under a snap-down tarp. Alongside the bag was a bucket that contained a scale, plastic baggies, and some handwritten notes with prices. Foster and Ward were convicted of conspiracy to manufacture and distribute methamphetamine in violation of 21 U.S.C.A. §§ 841(a)(1) and 846, and Foster was also convicted of carrying a firearm during and in relation to a drug trafficking crime.

The Ninth Circuit considered Foster's gun conviction twice with different results. In 1995 it affirmed his conviction (*United States v. Foster*, 57 F.3d 727). Subsequently, the U.S. Supreme Court issued a decision narrowing another provision—that addressing use of a gun—in the gun-carrying law (*Bailey v. United States*, 516 U.S. 137, 116 S. Ct. 501, 133 L. Ed. 2d 472 [1995]). In light of the Supreme Court's decision to strictly define what constitutes use of a gun under the law, the appeals court reconsidered Foster's gun-carrying conviction. This time a three-judge panel held that he did not carry the gun (*United States v. Foster*, 96 F.3d 1177 [1996]) within the meaning of the law. The entire court of appeals then revisited the case to clear up its own conflicting interpretations of carrying a firearm when the gun is found in a vehicle.

Writing for the majority, Justice Kozinski observed that the word *carry* "seems like a simple English word, which is precisely the problem." The word can mean *transport* or *hold*. In relation to weapons, the court said that the first sense of the word leads to a broad definition, whereas the second leads to a narrow definition. But choosing between them was akin to solving a puzzle. The Ninth Circuit first adopted the broad definition in 1979 in *United States v. BarberBarber, United States v.*, 594 F.2d 1242, but switched to the narrow decision after the Supreme Court's decision in 1995 in *Bailey*. It held that carrying a gun in drug trafficking required that the gun must be "immediately available for use by the defendant" (*United States v. Hernandez*, 80 F.3d 1253 [1996]).

Acknowledging that deciding between the broad and narrow definitions is "a close call," the majority chose the latter for four main reasons. The narrow definition (1) closely fit the dictionary definition of *carry*, (2) followed the Supreme Court's decision in *Bailey*; (3) "harmonized" with the statute, and (4) most closely fit the statute's purpose. Finally, the majority invoked the rule of lenity, whereby a court assumes that a statute did not intend to punish conduct that is not clearly prohibited by the language of the statute.

In a scathing dissent joined by two other justices, Justice Stephen S. Trott chastised the majority: "This is not a 'puzzle,' and we do not need 'clues' to solve it," he wrote. "It's 'carry,' that's all, and it's carry in a vehicle during and in relation to a drug trafficking crime." Trott charged that the majority's decision had ignored the proper standard for review, damaged the law, and helped criminals escape prosecution.

For emphasis, he wrote a lengthy monologue in the imaginary first-person voice of a drug trafficker who rejoices over the majority's decision. This unusual passage read in part:

> So imagine my surprise and delight when I read the majority opinion in this case and learned that although I "carried" my gun to the car "during and in relation to a drug trafficking crime, "I was no longer "carrying" the gun as I secretly transported it to the sale because it wasn't "immediately available. " Thanks for the distinction. And for the cover. Now we know how to beat 18 U.S.C.A. § 924(c)(1).

The dissent also attacked the majority's use of the rule of lenity as being unnecessary and inappropriate.

The Ninth Circuit's decision put it in a minority of jurisdictions using the narrow definition of *carry*. The Second and Sixth Circuits also follow the narrow definition, whereas the broader definition is used by the First, Fourth, Seventh, and Tenth Circuits.

On June 8, 1998, the U.S. Supreme Court held that the phrase "carries a gun" in 18 U.S.C.A. § 924(c)(1) applies to a person in knowing possession of a gun in a vehicle, even if the gun is locked in a trunk or otherwise out of the immediate reach of the defendant (*Muscarello v. United States*, ___U.S.___, ___L.Ed.2d.___, 118 S Ct 1911) This decision effectively overruled *Foster* and established the rule for interpreting this statutory provision.

**CROSS REFERENCES**
Commerce Clause; Drugs and Narcotics; Scalia, Antonin

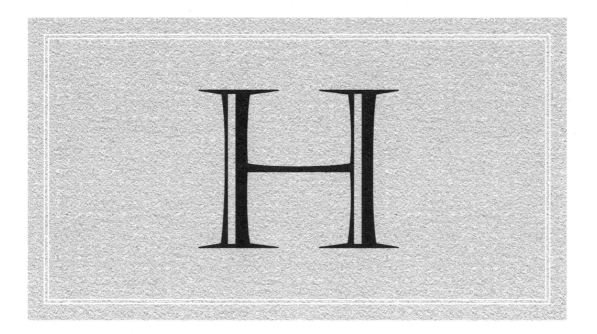

## HABEAS CORPUS

[*Latin, You have the body.*] A WRIT (court order) that commands an individual or a government official who has restrained another to produce the prisoner at a designated time and place so that the court can determine the legality of CUSTODY and decide whether to order the prisoner's release.

### Lindh v. Murphy

Courts of law are regularly called upon to interpret the meaning of legislative statutes. Courts apply various rules of statutory construction to aid them in their interpretations, but they often come to opposite conclusions as to what the provisions mean.

Such a conflict developed in the federal circuit courts of appeal over amendments to the federal habeas corpus statute by the Antiterrorism and Effective Death Penalty Act of 1996 (AEDPA) (110 Stat. 1214, 28 U.S.C.A. § 2254 (d) [Supp. 1997]). The circuits were divided over whether the new section of the statute dealing with petitions for habeas corpus governed applications in noncapital cases that were already pending when the AEDPA was passed.

The U.S. Supreme Court resolved the issue in *Lindh v. Murphy*, __U.S.__, 117 S. Ct. 2059, 138 L. Ed. 2d 481 (1997), ruling that the legislative changes did not apply to an inmate's pending noncapital case. The decision, on a 5–4 vote, revealed that the Court had difficulty interpreting the effect of the changes and discerning the intent of Congress.

The case involved Aaron Lindh, who was convicted by a Wisconsin jury of multiple mur-

ders. Lindh had used an insanity defense and had been examined by a psychiatrist immediately after the killings. Before Lindh's trial, however, the psychiatrist became the subject of a criminal investigation concerning the sexual exploitation of his patients. At trial Lindh was denied the opportunity to question the psychiatrist about the investigation; he had hoped to suggest to the jury that the doctor had slanted his testimony to curry favor with prosecutors.

After Lindh lost his direct appeal in state court, he filed a habeas corpus application in state court, alleging that his inability to cross-examine the psychiatrist about the doctor's criminal investigation violated his constitutional right to confront witnesses. Habeas corpus is the last opportunity for independent federal courts to review state court convictions and sentences to determine whether serious violations of the U.S. Constitution occurred. If the federal court does find a serious violation, it must reverse the state court and direct that the person be retried or resentenced.

After the district court denied Lindh's habeas request, he appealed to the Seventh Circuit Court of Appeals. While the appeals court was considering, however, the AEDPA was enacted, amending the habeas statute. The Seventh Circuit court concluded that the new statute did apply to Lindh's case, and on the authority of the new statute, it denied Lindh relief (96 F.3d 856 [1996]).

The Supreme Court took Lindh's appeal to resolve conflicts over this issue in the various circuit courts of appeal. Justice David H. Souter, writing for the majority, held that the Seventh

Circuit court decision had incorrectly interpreted the provisions of the AEDPA. The Seventh Circuit court had applied the holding of the Supreme Court in *Landsgraf v. USI Film Products*, 511 U.S. 244, 114 S. Ct. 1483, 128 L. Ed. 2d 229 (1994). *Landsgraf* held that if a new statute does not attach new legal consequences to events preceding enactment ("retroactive effect"), the statute may be applied to pending cases.

Souter concluded that *Landsgraf* was not controlling in this case. Instead, he stated, in determining the retroactive effect of a new statute, "normal rules of construction apply." In particular, Souter pointed to the use of the rule of negative implication, which holds that the expression of one thing signifies the exclusion of another thing.

Examining the provisions of AEDPA, Souter noted that the act revised chapter 153 of title 28 for all habeas proceedings. Section 107 of the AEDPA created an entirely new chapter 154 for habeas proceedings in capital cases, with special rules favorable to those states that meet certain conditions. Section 107(c) expressly applied chapter 154 to pending cases. Souter concluded that the negative implication was that the chapter 153 amendments were meant to apply only to cases filed after enactment. If Congress was concerned enough to explicitly state that chapter 154 applied to pending cases, it must have had a different intent for chapter 153 by not enacting a similar provision.

Souter's review of the AEDPA's legislative history confirmed for him the congressional intent to treat the two chapters differently as to their effective dates. He noted that the two chapters had not evolved separately and then been joined carelessly in the legislative "rough-and-tumble." To the contrary, the chapters were introduced as a single bill, and the language-making chapter 154 effective upon enactment was inserted afterward. The insertion of this language strengthened the rule of negative implication, because it suggested that Congress knew it was creating different effective dates for the two chapters. Therefore, the Court held that the new provisions of chapter 153 applied only to habeas cases filed after the AEDPA became effective and did not apply to pending noncapital cases like Lindh's.

Chief Justice William H. Rehnquist, writing for the dissent (which also included Antonin Scalia, Anthony M. Kennedy, and Clarence Thomas), contended that the majority ignored precedents on this issue. He opined that the Court has generally applied new procedural rules and other non-substantive law changes to pending cases.

### Lisa Michelle Lambert Released, Returned to Prison

In 1992 Lisa Michelle Lambert went to prison for life for slitting the throat of another high school girl. In prison she was raped repeatedly by a guard before obtaining a writ of habeas corpus that allowed her to successfully challenge her conviction in April 1997 (*Lambert v. Blackwell*, 962 F. Supp 1521). Following a dramatic three-week hearing, U.S. District Court Judge Stewart Dalzell declared her innocent, released her, and criticized police and prosecutors in East Lampeter, Pennsylvania, for framing her. Their misconduct, he wrote, "shocks our conscience." In December a federal appeals court overruled him (*Lambert V. Blackwell*, 134 F.3d 506 [3rd Cir]). In February 1998 Lambert was rejailed pending her appeals in state court even as her attorneys feared that she would commit suicide.

In late December 1991, the murder of fifteen-year-old Laurie Show shocked the small community of East Lampeter, Pennsylvania. The granddaughter of a prominent local physician, she was found by her mother, Hazel, as she lay near death in their condominium. Her throat was slashed, but her mother said she managed to utter with her dying breath, "Michelle did it."

Police swiftly arrested seventeen-year-old Lisa Michelle Lambert, the victim's alleged romantic rival. At a bench trial in 1992, prosecutors painted a lurid picture: Lambert, they said, hated Show for briefly dating her onetime boyfriend, twenty-year-old Lawrence Yunkin. Lambert allegedly had stalked, plotted to kidnap, and on one occasion publicly accosted and struck Show. Ultimately, they contended, she had killed her rival with the help of Yunkin and another friend, Tabitha Buck, age seventeen. Lambert claimed that the other two had wanted to beat up Show for having accused Yunkin of rape and that, when they attacked her, she fled outside. No physical evidence pointed to Lambert's involvement: unlike Buck and Yunkin, she had no cuts or bruises. The blood found on the victim's ring was not Lambert's type.

Nonetheless, Judge Lawrence F. Stengel found Lambert guilty of first-degree murder and sentenced her to life in prison. The linchpin of his decision, he said, was the victim's dying words. In a separate trial, Buck was convicted of second-degree murder and also got a life sentence. Yunkin admitted to having driven the girls to Show's condominium but claimed he left them there. He pleaded guilty to second-degree murder and received ten to twenty years in prison.

Lambert's conviction was upheld on appeal (*Commonwealth v. Lambert*, 450 Pa. Super. 714, 676 A.2d 283 [1996]). The case might have ended there but for events that occurred while Lambert was imprisoned by the Pennsylvania Department of Corrections. First, for a period of eighteen months, she was repeatedly raped by a prison guard. The guard was later convicted of sexual assault, and Lambert was transferred to a correctional facility in New Jersey. Second, she managed the difficult task of obtaining a writ of habeas corpus, a legal petition that entitles the convicted person to a hearing challenging the conviction on due process grounds. Chiefly, Lambert's petition alleged that she was innocent of murder and that she was the victim of widespread prosecutorial misconduct. In 1996 the U.S. District Court for the Eastern District of Pennsylvania granted her writ and appointed her counsel from the Philadelphia firm of Schnader, Harrison, Segal, and Lewis.

Over three weeks in April 1997, U.S. District Judge Stewart Dalzell heard opposing arguments. Christina Rainville, one of eight attorneys for Lambert, alleged that Lancaster County police and prosecutors were guilty of extensive corruption in an all-out effort to convict Lambert illegally. This may have occurred, she contended, because Lambert had been gang-raped by three police officers six months before the murder. Prosecutors and police officers denied the allegations and stuck to the statements they had made originally at trial. But Rainville presented compelling evidence. Perhaps the most striking was expert medical testimony that Laurie Show's injuries were too severe to have allowed her to speak at all before death, thus casting severe doubt on the claim that she had identified her murderer. Additional expert testimony established that it was unlikely that Show was even conscious when her mother found her.

Then on April 16 a surprise interrupted the proceedings: Hazel Show, the victim's mother, had a startling recollection while listening to the testimony of Lancaster County District Judge Ronald Savage, a former detective who investigated the murder. Show was brought into Judge Dalzell's chambers, where she testified that, in 1991, then detective Savage had told her to forget one of her memories of the murder. This

was her memory of seeing Yunkin leaving the crime scene in his car and pushing the head of a blonde-haired passenger out of view. Savage told her not to dwell on the memory because police had established that Yunkin's car was elsewhere at the time. Significantly, the new testimony comported completely with Lambert's version of events— that it was she and Yunkin leaving in the car.

On April 17 Judge Dalzell told a packed courtroom that there had been remarkable developments in the case. He declared Lambert innocent, released her, and ordered prosecutors not to retry her. This decision was unprecedented: customarily, a judge in Dalzell's position would order a new trial. Then he accused Savage of perjury and recommended that the Pennsylvania Supreme Court immediately suspend him from judicial duties. But most dramatically, Dalzell found twenty-five incidences of police and prosecutorial misconduct that included obstruction of justice, witness tampering, the suppression of evidence that could have exonerated Lambert and perjured testimony. He called for a federal probe of the case. "I invite you to look for any case in any jurisdiction in the English-speaking world where there has been as much prosecutorial misconduct as here," he said, "because I haven't found it."

In a ninety-page opinion issued on April 21, Dalzell wrote that he had considered 3,200 pages of evidence before concluding that Yunkin—rather than Lambert killed Laurie Show. As reason for his unprecedented decision to release Lambert and forbid prosecutors to retry her, he pointed to Lancaster County District Attorney Joseph Madenspacher's agreement that Lambert was entitled to some relief. Moreover, expecting Lambert to exhaust her state remedies would result in an injustice, he wrote. He praised Hazel Show for her courage in testifying at the hearing, despite her belief that Lambert was her daughter's killer. And, in stark language, he criticized the East Lampeter community for regarding Lambert as "trailer trash," saying it had "closed ranks behind the good family Show and exacted instant revenge against this supposed villainess."

The commonwealth appealed the case and won. On December 29, 1997, a three-judge panel of the Court of Appeals for the Third Circuit reversed Judge Dalzell's decision, holding that he had erred in granting Lambert unconditional release. Without reaching the merits on the case, the panel ruled to dismiss Lambert's habeas corpus petition and held that she must first exhaust her remedies in state court. On appeal Lambert asked for a full hearing by all thirteen justices of the Third Circuit. But on January 26, 1998, by an 8–4 vote with one judge abstaining, the appeals court refused to reopen the case. Justice Carol Los Mansmann's majority opinion said that Dalzell should have immediately dismissed Lambert's petition because its legal issues were mixed—some had been addressed by state courts, but other issues had never been raised in federal court. In a dissent joined by three judges, Justice Jane R. Roth called the majority's decision "profoundly disturbing" and a "miscarriage of justice."

In desperation, Lambert's attorneys filed emergency motions throughout late January and early February 1998 asking for her reincarceration to be stayed. If imprisoned she could commit suicide, the motions said, based on the evaluation of a doctor who was treating her for trauma caused by being repeatedly raped in prison. But the Supreme Court of Pennsylvania refused to intervene in the absence of pending proceedings before any state court. Then the U.S. Supreme Court refused to grant her motion. On February 4, she was returned to prison.

As Lambert's attorneys prepared her state appeal, a federal investigation by the U.S. attorney's office in Philadelphia was underway to probe the prosecutorial misconduct identified by Dalzell. Meanwhile, the East Lampeter community remained furious at the judge. The murder victim's father, John Show, headed an impeachment campaign that amassed 37,000 signatures calling for his removal, and a local group calling itself Citizens for Judicial Responsibility publicly denounced attorney Rainville. Not all local reaction was against Rainville and Dalzell, however: both received numerous complaints from prisoners of misconduct by East Lampeter officials.

**CROSS REFERENCES**
Discretion in Decision Making; Judiciary

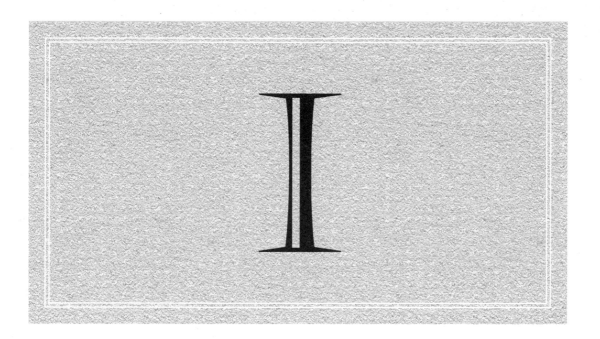

## IMMUNITY

Exemption from performing duties that the law generally requires other citizens to perform, or from a penalty or burden that the law generally places on other citizens.

### Bogan v. Scott-Harris

Under 42 U.S.C.A. § 1983, a person may sue a government official for damages for depriving that person of a constitutional right. This constitutional tort action has proved to be a powerful tool for redressing constitutional violations, but the U.S. Supreme Court has limited the law's reach by granting absolute immunity from section 1983 damage suits to judges, prosecutors when performing the traditional functions of an advocate, and state and regional legislators. In *Bogan v. Scott-Harris,* ___U.S.___, 118 S. Ct. 966, ___L. Ed. 2d___ (1998), the Supreme Court extended absolute immunity to local legislators (city council members, county commissioners, etc.) when they act in their legislative rather than administrative capacities.

The case involved the elimination of Janet Scott-Harris's position as administrator of the Department of Health and Human Services (DHHS) for the city of Fall River, Massachusetts. Scott-Harris, after receiving a complaint about Dorothy Biltcliffe, an employee temporarily under her supervision, prepared termination charges against Biltcliffe. Biltcliffe had been accused of making repeated racial and ethnic slurs about her colleagues. Biltcliffe used her political connections to press her case with city officials, including Marilyn Roderick, the vice

president of the Fall Rivers City Council. The council held a hearing on the charges and ultimately Biltcliffe accepted a settlement proposal that included her suspension without pay for sixty days. The mayor of Fall River, Daniel Bogan, then substantially reduced the punishment.

While the charges against Biltcliffe were pending, Bogan prepared a proposed budget for the next fiscal year. Anticipating a reduction in state aid, he proposed freezing the salaries of municipal employees and eliminating 135 city positions. Included in this proposal was the elimination of DHHS, of which Scott-Harris was the sole employee. A city council committee chaired by Roderick approved the elimination of DHHS and the city council approved the ordinance 6–2, with Roderick voting for the legislation. Mayor Bogan signed the ordinance into law.

Scott-Harris then filed suit under 42 U.S.C.A. § 1983, against the city, Bogan, Roderick, and several other city officials. Scott-Harris alleged that the elimination of her position was motivated by racial animus and a desire to retaliate against her for exercising her First Amendment rights in filing the complaint against Biltcliffe. Bogan and Roderick sought to dismiss the lawsuit on grounds of legislative immunity but the district court denied their motions.

The case went to trial and the jury found no racial discrimination by the defendants, but did find the city, Bogan, and Roderick liable for violating Scott-Harris's First Amendment rights. On appeal, the Third Circuit Court of Appeals set aside the verdict against the city but affirmed the judgments against Bogan and Roderick, __F. 3d__ (1997). The court acknowledged that legislative activities of Bogan and Roderick were protected by absolute immunity, but that in this case their conduct was administrative because the city officials relied on facts relating to a particular individual in the decision-making process.

The Supreme Court reversed the appeals court. Justice Clarence Thomas, writing for a unanimous Court, noted the well-established rule that federal, state, and regional legislators are entitled to absolute immunity from civil liability for their legislative activities. He agreed with Bogan and Roderick that as "local officials performing legislative functions, [they] are entitled to the same protection." In addition, their "acts of introducing, voting for, and signing an ordinance eliminating the government office" held by Scott-Harris were legislative activities, thus entitling them to immunity in this case.

Justice Thomas reiterated the principles that make legislators absolutely immune from liability for their legislative activities. An important factor was the existence of absolute immunity for local legislators at the time section 1983 was enacted in 1871. Therefore, Congress would have expected absolute immunity to apply to local legislators. Nothing in the legislative history suggested otherwise.

Thomas stated that "regardless of the level of government, the exercise of legislative discretion should not be inhibited by judicial interference or distorted by the fear of personal liability." In addition, the time and energy that officials would have to expend in defending themselves would have an impact at the local level, "where the part-time citizen-legislator remains commonplace." The threat of personal liability might discourage persons from serving in local government, "where prestige and pecuniary rewards may pale in comparison to the threat of civil liability."

Having established that absolute immunity attaches to legislative activities at any level of government, Thomas turned to the specific acts surrounding the enactment of the Fall River budget. He concluded that the appeals court had erroneously relied on Bogan and Roderick's subjective intent in determining whether the act was legislative. Whether an act is legislative "turns on the nature of the act, rather than on the motive or intent of the official performing it." To hold otherwise would rob absolute immunity of any value, because legislators could be subjected to a trial and a jury verdict against them based upon a "jury's speculation as to motives."

Thomas noted that Roderick's acts of voting for the budget ordinance were "in form, quintessentially legislative." Likewise, Mayor Bogan's introduction of a budget and his signing of the ordinance were also "formally legislative, even though he was an executive official." His actions were legislative because they were "integral steps in the legislative process."

The Court was unwilling to look beyond the formal actions of Roderick and Bogan to consider whether the ordinance was legislative in substance. Thomas found that the ordinance bore all the marks of traditional legislation and that the city council, in eliminating DHHS, governed in a field where legislators traditionally have power to act. Therefore, the actions of Roderick and Bogan were legislative, resulting in the dismissal of the lawsuit based on their absolute immunity.

### Kalina v. Fletcher

The U.S. Supreme Court has made clear that when criminal prosecutors perform the traditional functions of an advocate, they are absolutely immune from money damage lawsuits. Absolute prosecutorial immunity, however, does not extend to functions that are not associated with advocacy. In *Kalina v. Fletcher*, __U.S.__, 118 S. Ct. 502, 139 L. Ed. 2d 471 (1997), the Supreme Court ruled that a prosecutor was not entitled to absolute immunity with respect to her actions in making an allegedly false statement of fact in an affidavit supporting an application for an arrest warrant.

Rodney Fletcher sued Lynne Kalina, a deputy prosecuting attorney for King County, Washington, for violating his constitutional rights. Fletcher used the Civil Rights statute 42 U.S.C.A. § 1983, which permits the recovery of money damages for deprivations of constitutional rights. Kalina had started a criminal proceeding against Fletcher by filing three documents in state court. Two of the documents, one charging Fletcher with burglary (stealing computer equipment from a school) and the other, a motion for an arrest warrant, were unsworn pleadings. Under the criminal rules of Washington, however, an arrest warrant must be supported by an affidavit of sworn testimony that establishes the grounds for issuing the warrant. To satisfy this requirement, Kalina prepared a "certification for determination of probable cause," in which she summarized the evidence supporting the charge. In addition, she personally vouched for the truth of the facts set forth in the certification under penalty of perjury. Based on Kalina's certification, the court found probable cause and ordered that an arrest warrant be issued.

Fletcher was arrested and spent a day in jail, but the burglary charge was dismissed about a month later. After his arrest, it was discovered that Kalina's certification statement contained two inaccurate factual statements. The certification noted that Fletcher's fingerprints had been found on school property and asserted that Fletcher had never been associated with the school and had never had permission to enter the school. In fact, Fletcher had installed partitions in the school and had been authorized to enter the school. Kalina's claim that an electronics store employee said that Fletcher had sought an appraisal of a computer stolen from the school also proved to be false.

Fletcher's section 1983 lawsuit sought damages for Kalina's alleged violation of his constitutional right to be free from unreasonable seizures. He focused his case on the false statements made by Kalina in the certification. Kalina sought dismissal of the suit, contending that she was entitled to absolute prosecutorial immunity. The federal district court rejected her claim, and she appealed to the Ninth Circuit Court of Appeals, which affirmed the lower court (93 F. 3d 653 [1996]).

The Supreme Court agreed with the court of appeals. Justice John Paul Stevens, writing for the Court, noted that its decision in *Imbler v. Pachtman*, 424 U.S. 409, 96 S. Ct. 984, 47 L. Ed. 2d 128 (1976), relied on common-law precedent, and more importantly, policy considerations, in holding that a prosecutor who "acted within the scope of his duties in initiating and pursuing a criminal prosecution" was immune from a section 1983 suit. Those policy considerations "included both the interest in protecting the prosecutor from harassing litigation that would divert his time and attention from his official duties and the interest in enabling him to exercise independent judgment when 'deciding which suits to bring and in conducting them in court.'" Therefore, *Imbler* and later decisions made it clear that protecting the office of prosecutor is more important than protecting its occupant.

Stevens pointed out that later decisions gave prosecutors absolute immunity for their actions before grand juries and in support of applica-

tions for search warrants, and for their presentation of evidence at these hearings. In addition, a prosecutor's actions in preparing for the start of judicial proceedings or for trial, and actions that are taken in the role of advocate, are entitled to absolute immunity.

Nevertheless, Stevens emphasized that a prosecutor loses absolute immunity when performing different functions. For example, giving legal advice to police during their pretrial investigation of the facts is protected only by qualified immunity, which requires the prosecutor to demonstrate to a trial court good faith and a reasonable basis for the actions in question.

Turning to the facts of the case, Stevens concluded that Kalina enjoyed absolute immunity for her work in preparing and filing the information and the motion for an arrest warrant. The preparation and the filing of the certificate were also part of the advocate's function, and Kalina thus was immune for that legal work. Her problem, however, came with her personal attestation that the facts contained in the certificate were true. The critical question became whether Kalina "was acting as a complaining witness rather than a lawyer when she executed the certification '[u]nder penalty of perjury.'"

The Court concluded that Kalina's personal attestation of the certificate made her a witness. Stevens noted that neither state nor federal law made it necessary for the prosecutor to make the certification. Kalina had performed an act "that any competent witness might have performed." Though King County prosecutors may have routinely followed this practice, they were in the minority both in Washington and around the United States. Federal prosecutors, for example, have law enforcement agents attest to facts in similar applications of arrest warrants.

Stevens rejected Kalina's contention that, viewed as a whole, the execution of the certificate was one incident in a presentation that was the work of an advocate. The preparation of each of the three documents "involved the exercise of professional judgment," but "that judgment could not affect the truth or falsity of the factual statements themselves," Stevens said. Testifying about the facts that implicated Fletcher were the "function of a witness, not of the lawyer." When a lawyer gives sworn testimony, no matter how brief, the only function performed is that of witness.

Therefore, the Court ruled that Kalina was not entitled to absolute immunity and that Fletcher could proceed with his lawsuit.

CROSS REFERENCES
Discrimination; First Amendment; Section 1983

# INDEPENDENT COUNSEL

An attorney appointed by the federal government to investigate and prosecute federal government officials.

### Investigation of Agriculture Secretary's Chief of Staff

In August 1994, U.S. Attorney General Janet Reno sought and received the appointment of an independent counsel to investigate Secretary of Agriculture Alphonso Michael ("Mike") Espy. Under 28 U.S.C.A. § 592(c)(1), the attorney general may request an independent counsel to investigate high-level government officials. For this particular investigation, Reno sought to discover whether Espy had accepted gifts from organizations and individuals with business pending before the Department of Agriculture and whether Espy had committed any crimes connected to or arising out of the investigation, such as obstruction of justice and false testimony or statements. The jurisdictional grant given to the independent counsel by the Special Division for the Purpose of Appointing Independent Counsels of the U.S. Court of Appeals for the District of Columbia (Special Division) included the authority under 28 U.S.C.A. § 594 to fully investigate and prosecute suspected conspirators of Espy and all matters and individuals whose acts might be related to the subject matter of the investigation of Espy.

In January 1996, the independent counsel for the case, Donald C. Smaltz, applied to the Special Division for the authority to investigate Espy's chief of staff, Ronald Blackley. To broaden an investigation under the independent counsel statute, an independent counsel must show the Special Division that the broadened investigation is related to the factual circumstances that gave rise to the appointment. Although Smaltz was commissioned to investigate Espy, Smaltz contended that the suspected activity by Blackley was related to the pattern of conduct involving payments or gifts to Espy, and that the expanded investigation was authorized under 28 U.S.C.A. § 594(e). The Special Division agreed with Smaltz, and in April 1996, it granted him the authority to investigate Blackley.

In April 1997, a federal grand jury in the District of Columbia indicted Blackley on three criminal counts. Blackley was charged with failing to report the receipt of $22,025 in payments on his public financial disclosure report for 1993 in violation of the Ethics in Government Act (18 U.S.C.A. § 1001); making a false statement to an investigator regarding the receipt of the payments; and making a false sworn statement in an investigation about whether he should retain his top-secret security clearance.

At trial in the U.S. District Court for the District of Columbia, Blackley asked the court to dismiss the indictment. Blackley argued that the prosecution was not related to the investigation of Espy, that the charges related only to the completeness of his 1993 disclosure statement, and that the matter was outside the jurisdiction of the independent counsel. Blackley noted that Attorney General Reno had opposed the expansion of the investigation to include Blackley, and he argued that the prosecution was unconstitutional and contrary to the independent counsel statute because Smaltz was not complying with the policies of the Department of Justice, as the statute required. According to Blackley, Smaltz's authority did not extend beyond charges concerning interventions in subsidy applications, appeals, and requests to the Department of Agriculture, and federal criminal violations related to such interventions.

The district court disagreed with all of Blackley's arguments. On the issue of whether there was a sufficient connection between the offense charged and the jurisdiction given to the independent counsel by the Special Division, the district court noted previous prosecutions in which the charges arose from facts that were culled from an expanded investigation. These cases included two other criminal prosecutions brought about by Smaltz in connection with the Espy investigation. In those cases the district court had held that corporate defendants charged with making illegal campaign contributions to Espy's brother Henry in exchange for government favors were not outside Smaltz's jurisdiction (*United States v. Crop Growers Corp.*, 954 F. Supp. 335 [D.D.C. 1987] and *United States v. Sun-Diamond Growers of California*, 941 F. Supp. 1262 [D.D.C. 1996]).

In the instant case, the court noted that the income received by Blackley in 1993 was allegedly given by Charles Fuller and Charles ("Buddy") Cochran, both of whom had sought and received subsidies from the Department of Agriculture in 1993. "An endeavor to conceal payments received from a Department of Agriculture subsidy applicant," the district court ex-

# SHOULD THE INDEPENDENT COUNSEL ACT BE SCRAPPED?

Independent Counsel Kenneth W. Starr's long-running investigation of President Clinton's involvement in the Whitewater affair has sparked renewed debate about alleged shortcomings in the 1978 Independent Counsel Act, (28 U.S.C.A. §§ 591-599). Critics of the act contend that the actions of Starr and other independent counsel demonstrate that the law gives these special prosecutors unlimited power and authority to investigate the lives of government officials. Moreover, the law, as written, provides no effective means of reining in an overly aggressive independent counsel. Defenders of the act believe, however, that the system currently lacks a good alternative to an independent counsel who is shielded from political pressures. The act expires in 1999, giving opponents a ready-made opportunity to either amend or scrap the law.

IN FOCUS

Defenders of the act are quick to point out that the triggering event for the enactment of the statute was the "Saturday Night Massacre," of October 20, 1973, which deepened the Watergate scandal of President Richard M. Nixon. Nixon, who was fighting in court to keep secretly recorded and highly incriminating White House audio tapes out of the hands of special prosecutor Archibald Cox, ordered his attorney general, Elliot L. Richardson, to fire Cox. Because Cox was appointed by the attorney general, it was within Nixon's power to have Cox dismissed. Richardson and his deputy attorney general, William D. Ruckelshaus, resigned rather than carry out the order. Cox was fired that night by solicitor general Robert Bork. The national outrage over this incident led Congress to enact the Independent Counsel Act, which provides that a three-judge panel appoints a counsel after the attorney general certifies that a counsel is needed. Once appointed, the counsel may be removed by the attorney for cause, but this decision can be reviewed by a federal district court.

Defenders of the act acknowledge that the nineteen independent counsels who have investigated executive branch officials accused of wrongdoing have spent large amounts of money and often spent several years on their investigations. However, no counsel has been found to lack the prosecutorial independence needed in searching for evidence of official corruption. Without independence, these special prosecutors would be open to the same pressures Nixon applied to his attorney general and special prosecutor in 1973.

Finally, defenders of the independent counsel statute note the importance of public confidence in the investigation, prosecution, and punishment of official wrongdoing without regard to the political power and influence of the wrongdoer. Public opinion polls have shown an erosion in confidence about the U.S. political system. It is important, say the defenders, to preserve a nonpartisan, independent system of oversight for an executive branch that has grown steadily more powerful since the 1930s.

Critics of the Independent Counsel Act admit that the legislation appeared to be a good idea in 1978, in the aftermath of Watergate. Over time, however, flaws have been revealed that demonstrate that the law gives too much authority to one individual, an authority that cannot be effectively curtailed or revoked by the attorney general.

Critics contend that beyond the enormous expenditures of money (more than $140 million for eighteen investigations and still rising) and time, the independent counsel law has created an unhealthy dynamic in which a prosecutor becomes preoccupied with a narrow area of investigation in order to validate the investigation itself. This zeal to find wrongdoing distorts the traditional role of a regular federal prosecutor, leading to excessive action that would not be taken in the ordinary course of federal investigation. Justice Antonin Scalia expressed this concern in his dissenting opinion in *Morrison v. Olson*, 487 U.S. 654, 108 S. Ct. 2597, 101 L. Ed. 2d 569 (1988), a decision that upheld the constitutionality of the act.

The critics of the act argue that the need for an independent counsel to validate the investigation leads to even more time and money being spent, without regard to the relevance or seriousness of the charges leveled against a government official. They note that the Whitewater investigation was originally directed at a failed real estate deal in Arkansas that took place before Bill Clinton was elected president in 1992. Kenneth Starr's investigation began in 1994, yet by early 1998 he had failed to implicate Clinton in the land deal. However, he had moved on to investigate possible obstruction of justice charges against the president, involving an alleged extramarital affair with a White House intern. Critics argue that Starr illustrates the worst case for an independent counsel: a politically motivated prosecutor with unlimited funds and a willingness to use his power in ways that are out of the ordinary.

In theory the attorney general may remove an independent counsel for cause, yet critics note that political reality makes this impossible. An attorney general who fired an independent counsel would invite comparisons to the Saturday Night Massacre and suggest a cover-up. In effect, the prosecutor is accountable to no one.

Despite the problems with the act, many critics agree that independent prosecutors are necessary to investigate official wrongdoing. One suggestion is that an assistant attorney general be appointed, subject to Senate confirmation, who would head the Justice Department's Public Integrity Section. This official could not be a member of the president's party or a recent holder of high office. Such an approach would, proponents contend, institutionalize the office and make it more accountable.

plained, "could be a causal consequence of possible intervention in the application process on behalf of those from whom he received payment" (*United States v. Blackley*, 986 F. Supp. 607 [1997]). The court concluded that it was logical and reasonable to assume that Blackley would cover up receipt of the payments if they were received in exchange for improper government favors, and this brought the matter within the purview of Smaltz's investigation.

The district court also rejected Blackley's argument that the prosecution was invalid because it was against the policy of the Department of Justice, citing as precedent the case of *United States v. Poindexter*, 725 F. Supp. 13 (D.D.C. 1989). In *Poindexter* the defendant, national security assistant Vice Admiral John M. Poindexter, argued for dismissal of the prosecution based on the same argument, and the district court had rejected it, stating that "that Independent Counsel statute explicitly provides that [the independent counsel] is required to follow Department of Justice policies 'only to the extent possible.'"

In deciding to follow the *Poindexter* ruling, the district court explained that the independent counsel statute was enacted in the wake of the Watergate scandals to restore public faith in government. "[A]dherence to an executive branch policy that directs a prosecutor to not pursue indictments against executive branch officials for their criminal ethical violations," the district court held, "is in direct contravention with the task with which an Independent Counsel is charged."

Finally, the court dismissed Blackley's argument that the prosecution violated the U.S. Constitution because it was contrary to the Department of Justice policy and therefore infringed upon the executive branch's exclusive power to enforce the laws of the United States. That constitutional argument had already been spurned by the District of Columbia Circuit Court in *In re Espy*, 80 F.3d 501 (1996), and the district court was not empowered to sit in review of that judgment. Ultimately, the district court declined to dismiss the indictments against Blackley, and the prosecution against Blackley moved forward.

## INSURANCE

A CONTRACT whereby, for a specified CONSIDER-ATION, one party undertakes to compensate the other for a loss relating to a particular subject as a result of the occurrence of designated hazards.

### Car Insurer Liable for Shooting Death

In South Carolina, a state appeals court ruled that an insurance company's policy for accidental injury covers the shooting and killing of a car's driver (*State Farm Mutual Automobile Insurance Co. v. Moorer*, 330 S.C. 465 496 S.E. 2d 875 (1998). The decision by the Court of Appeals of South Carolina rejected the claim of State Farm Mutual Automobile Insurance Co. that it had no liability because the insured party's decision to shoot the victim was not accidental. Basing its decision on case law as well as a close reading of the policy, the appeals court disagreed: it ruled that since the victim had not expected or intended to die, the shooting was, from his posthumous point of view, an accident.

On May 17, 1992, Eddie Lee Moorer was driving alone in his Chrysler LeBaron on Highway 70 in Orangeburg County. Another car came up behind him, accelerated, and began to pass on Moorer's left side. Suddenly, gunshots were fired at Moorer. One bullet struck him fatally in the head.

Shelton Richardson was driving the vehicle from which the shots were fired. Seated next to him was Sam Neals, the shooter; in the back seat were Michael Anderson and Mono T. ("Tiny") Preston. They drove off and kept silent about what Neals had done.

Because investigators found no weapons and no witnesses, the case remained unsolved for more than a year. But in June 1993, Orangeburg police got a break when an acquaintance implicated Richardson and the others in a written statement. Police arrested four and charged them with murder, but no trial followed. Richardson, Anderson, and Preston cut a deal with prosecutors, agreeing to testify against Neals in exchange for being allowed to plead guilty to a lesser felony. Neal ultimately pleaded guilty to voluntary manslaughter.

Sheila Moorer, the widow of the slain Eddie Lee, filed civil lawsuits. Her wrongful death and survival actions targeted Neals, Anderson, Preston, Richardson, and his mother, Stella Richardson, who owned the car. State Farm had issued four automobile liability policies covering Sam Neals, which were held by his grandmother, Earline Neals. Each policy was worth $50,000. The insurance company asked the Circuit Court of Orangeburg County for a declaratory judgment finding that it was not liable under the polices issued to Earline Neals.

The court's master-in-equity—a court official specializing in insurance liability—held that coverage was due under the policies. First, the master determined that the State Farm policies provided coverage for Sam Neals's use of a non-owned vehicle, the use in which he was engaged while in the Richardson car. In such an instance, liability coverage was not limited to an accident per se. Instead, coverage was triggered by the mere use of a non-owned vehicle that resulted in an injury. Although the policy only covered accidents, the master ruled that an accident is defined from the point of view of the victim, not the insured party. Second, the master ruled that the four policies could be "stacked," allowing for the recovery of damages under more than one policy until all of the damages are satisfied or until the total limits of all policies are exhausted. By stacking the policies, Sheila Moorer stood to recover a total of $200,000. State Farm appealed.

The appeals court began its analysis with the liability issue. State Farm contended that the policy explicitly limited coverage to accidents. Moorer countered that the policy did not specifically state that an accident is required to trigger coverage, and as such, any ambiguity should be resolved in favor of coverage. Examining the policy, the court found a section labeled "Coverage for the Use of Other Cars," which provided that coverage "for owned and non-owned vehicles is limited to 'accidents.'" On this simple matter, the court agreed with State Farm's interpretation.

The appeals court next turned to the question of whether the policy excluded coverage of intentional acts. According to State Farm's argument, it did, and Neals' shooting and killing of Eddie Lee Moorer was just such an excluded intentional act. State Farm asserted that because buying liability coverage for non-owned vehicles is *voluntary* for drivers, an insurer may exclude coverage for intentional acts.

The court dismissed this argument, noting that State Farm had not chosen to exclude them. The master-in-equity had noted in his order and State Farm had conceded that the policy did not include an explicit intentional acts exclusion.

The issue of liability therefore turned on the definition of "accident." The appeals court agreed with the master-in-equity that an accident should be viewed from the standpoint of the person suffering the harm or injury, follow-

*Aside from covering damage to vehicles, automobile insurance may cover personal injury.*

TONY FREEMAN/PHOTOEDIT

ing *Chapman v. Allstate Insurance Co.*, 263 S.C. 565, 211 S.E.2d 876 (1975). *Chapman* established a general rule for instances where an intentional and unforeseen injury is done to an insured party: unless a policy provision explicitly excludes liability, the insured party is considered to have been accidentally injured and the insurer is liable. In the present case, Moorer's shooting death had not been expected, nor had he intended it. Accordingly, it affirmed the master's decision that liability coverage was available under State Farm's policies.

The appeals court, however, rejected the master's finding that the four policies could be stacked. The court noted that the general rule is that stacking is permitted unless limited by statute or by a valid policy provision. Its review of the policies found that their language unambiguously prohibited the stacking of coverage for non-owned vehicles: "If two or more vehicle liability policies issued by us to you apply to the same accident," the policy read, "the total limits of liability under all such policies shall not exceed that of the policy with the highest limit of liability." Moorer was entitled to recover under the limits of only one of the $50,000 policies.

### Providing Cigarette Did Not Create Liability for Fire

A California appeals court ruled that two separate illegal acts—buying cigarettes for a minor and trespassing on private property—did not make a seventeen-year-old legally responsible for an accidental fire in a lumber yard. The trial court had found liability, but the Court of Appeal for the Fourth District reversed (*Wawanesa Mutual Insurance Co. v. Matlock*, 60 Cal.App. 4th 583, 70 Cal. Rptr. 2d 512 [4 Dist.]).

One day in April 1993, Timothy Matlock, then age seventeen, bought two packs of cigarettes. He gave one to his friend, Eric Erdley, age fifteen. As they smoked, they entered the grounds of a private storage facility in Huntington Beach, California, belonging to the Woodman Pole Co., where they had often trespassed in order to climb a stack of some two hundred telephone poles. They climbed the stack and were eventually joined by two younger boys, about ten or eleven years old. Matlock began teasing the younger boys, telling them the poles were going to fall. One of the boys bumped Erdley's right arm causing him to drop his lit cigarette between the poles where it landed on a bed of sand. He tried, but failed, to retrieve it. The poles caught fire and witnesses saw Matlock and Erdley running from the scene.

The Woodman Pole Co. suffered considerable property damage. Eric Erdley was insured under a $100,000 policy with Wawanesa Mutual Insurance Co. It paid $89,000 to Woodman, $10,000 to the Orange County Fire Department, and $1,000 to the Huntington Beach Fire Department. Then the insurance company filed suit against Timothy Matlock and his father, Paul Matlock, seeking contribution for its losses.

At trial, Wawanesa won. Judge H. Warren Siegel of the Superior Court of Orange County held that Timothy Matlock had unlawfully given cigarettes to a minor, in violation of state law (Penal Code § 308). He awarded Wawanesa damages of $44,500, which included $25,000 against Paul Matlock based on a statute which makes a custodial parent liable for the willful misconduct of a minor (Civ. Code § 1714.1, subd. (a)). Unusually, Judge Siegel opined that the exact theory under which the Matlocks were held liable for damages was "not important." Although the insurance company had advanced several different theories in its lawsuit, the judge ruled that they all would lead to a finding of *liability*.

The Matlocks appealed. They argued that there was no basis on which to hold Timothy liable for the damage caused when Eric Erdley dropped the cigarette. In response, Wawanesa Mutual maintained that the trial judge found both teenagers had intended to commit the wrongful acts of illegally smoking and trespassing, and, therefore, it made no difference who started the fire.

The California Court of Appeal for the Fourth District unanimously overturned the decision. From the outset, Justice David G. Sills's opinion took aim at the trial court for asserting that the precise theory of liability was unimportant. Examining the separate theories of liability advanced by Wawanesa Mutual, he found each of them lacking in merit.

The first theory was *negligence per se*. Negligence involves breaching one's duty to act as a reasonable person would to prevent harm to others. Under negligence per se the duty is established by statute. In this case, the statutory violation was giving cigarettes to a minor. But, noted the appeals court, the mere violation of a law does not automatically make the violator liable for damages that can be traced back to the violation. To create liability, the statute must be designed to protect against the kind of harm that occurred. Penal Code § 308 "has nothing to do with fire suppression," Justice Sills wrote. Instead, the California Supreme Court had recognized as recently as 1994 that the statute was primarily concerned with protecting the health of minors (*Mangini v. R. J. Reynolds Tobacco Co.*, 7 Cal.4th 1057, 1061, 31 Cal.Rptr.2d 358, 875 P.2d 73).

The second theory was ordinary negligence. Wawanesa asserted that the fire damages would not have occurred if Matlock had not given the cigarette to Erdley, accompanied him onto Woodman Pole Company grounds, and caused the younger children to rush off the wood pile with the effect of causing Erdley to drop the lit cigarette that started the fire. Justice Sills called this argument a "Rube Goldbergesque system of linkages"—a reference to the early twentieth-century cartoonist whose drawings featured bizarre, improbable chains of events. Wawanesa's claim was based on too many thin connections. Even the unlawful act of giving a cigarette to a minor did not make Matlock "an insurer of any property which the cigarette may by some happenstance ignite."

The appeals court also rejected Wawanesa's three remaining theories of liability—conspiracy, joint venture, and trespass. It observed that the teenagers had gone onto private land where one was jostled into dropping a cigarette, and a fire started. Calling this scenario a conspiracy or joint venture was "a gross overstatement of what common sense reveals really went on," wrote Justice Sills. The teens had never conspired to start a fire. Likewise, the court dismissed trespass as a farfetched basis for liability; it knew of no legal authority to support the proposition that merely trespassing makes a person liable for all damage that can be linked to a fellow trespasser. Holding that Timothy Matlock was not liable for damages, it refused to address his father's potential liability and thus ordered the trial court to enter judgment in the Matlocks' favor.

**CROSS REFERENCES**
Conspiracy; Joint Venture; Tort Law; Trespass

## INTERNAL REVENUE SERVICE

The federal agency responsible for administering and enforcing all internal revenue laws in the United States, except those relating to alcohol, tobacco, firearms, and explosives, which are the responsibility of the Bureau of Alcohol, Tobacco and Firearms.

### Senate IRS Hearings

In September 1997, the Internal Revenue Service (IRS) came under sharp political attack. Over three days of televised hearings, the U.S. Senate Finance Committee heard a litany of horror stories: taxpayers gave accounts of ruined lives, and IRS agents described a culture of lawlessness that included forgeries, spying, shakedowns, and cover-ups. The dramatic testimony capped a six-month committee probe into IRS misconduct. At its end, an apologetic IRS immediately suspended several managers, and the White House suggested additional oversight. Republican lawmakers, however, rallied around the prospect of sweeping reform, vowing to overhaul the agency.

Although the IRS is perennially unpopular, it is rarely subjected to such scrutiny. The oversight function of Congress usually amounts to perfunctory, closed-door work. In 1997, however, Republicans went much further. Through simultaneous probes by the Finance Committee and the Joint Committee on Taxation, they pried into the IRS on two fronts. The Finance Committee examined alleged abuse of taxpayers, and the Joint Committee examined IRS audits of GOP leaders and conservative organizations, including the National Rifle Association and groups formerly led by GOP Chair Haley Barbour and House Speaker Newt Gingrich (R-Ga.). Republicans alleged that the White House was using the IRS to harass political enemies.

From September 23 to 25, the Finance Committee held open hearings. First to testify were taxpayers, from business owners to an el-

*Former IRS historian Shelly Davis, left, along with author Robert Schriebman, center, and author David Burnham, right, are sworn in on Capitol Hill September 24, 1997, prior to testifying before the Senate Finance Committee hearing on the IRS.*

JOE MARQUETTE/AP/WIDE WORLD PHOTOS

derly priest, who told the panel how unfair IRS audits had led to divorce, bankruptcy, and, in some cases, years of fighting inflexible rules to correct the agency's mistakes. Others said they paid the IRS large sums rather than fight and risk jeopardizing their businesses. Tom Savage, a 69-year-old Delaware construction company owner, told lawmakers that he paid $50,000 in fines despite the fact that the Justice Department told the IRS that levying him was wrong. Another taxpayer, Nancy Jacobs of California, said that the IRS mistakenly assigned her husband a taxpayer identification number belonging to someone else but that she and her husband paid the agency $11,000 to stop enforcement actions in order to save her husband's optometrist practice.

IRS whistleblowers also testified. Sitting behind screens with their voices garbled electronically to conceal their identities, they accused IRS management of several questionable practices: illegally snooping on private tax data, preying on vulnerable taxpayers, and unduly focusing collection efforts on lower- and middle-class taxpayers. Their chief allegation was that management evaluated employees based on their collection performance. Agents were pressured, they said, to seize as much taxpayer property and assets as possible—in violation of IRS policy and federal law. One employee testified to personally knowing of dozens of taxpayers that were driven into financial ruin, and even homelessness, due to unnecessary seizures. "If the public ever knew the number of abuses covered up by the IRS," one anonymous employee told the panel, "there could be a tax revolt."

Acting IRS Commissioner Michael P. Dolan apologized before the committee for alleged abuses, describing his experience over the three days as painful. But federal privacy laws prevented Dolan from addressing allegations related to specific cases. He promised swift action nonetheless, and the following week the IRS announced the suspension of several district-level managers pending further review of their cases.

Politicians were not satisfied with either the apology or the suspensions. By the end of September, both Democrats and Republicans promised major legislation to reform the IRS. President Bill Clinton also suggested reform: he backed the appointment of a citizen oversight panel to review allegations against the IRS. But as lawmakers of both parties seized upon the issue, Clinton found himself outflanked by calls for more sweeping changes.

# INTERNATIONAL TRADE

## Fast-Track Authority

The process of negotiating and implementing international trade agreements can take months under established congressional approval procedures. Under the U.S. Constitution, both the legislative and executive branches have authority to formulate foreign trade policy. Article I, Section 8, Clause 3 of the Constitution provides Congress with the power to regulate commerce with foreign nations, while Article II, Section 2, Clause 2, gives the president the authority to enter into treaties on behalf of the United States. As a result, the two branches of government must cooperate in order to implement trade agreements.

During the first 150 years of the nation's existence, Congress controlled international trade. In 1930 Congress passed the Tariff Act

*California rice is loaded onto a ship bound for Japan.*

GARY WAGNER/STOCK BOSTON, INC.

of 1930 (also known as the Smoot-Hawley Act) (19 U.S.C.A. § 1304 et seq.), which set the highest tariff levels in U.S. history. Retaliation by foreign countries helped fuel a worldwide depression. In response, Congress passed the Reciprocal Trade Agreements Act of 1934 (19 U.S.C.A. § 1351 et seq.), which gave the president greater power to negotiate trade agreements and raise and lower tariffs. During the next 40 years, the president continued to assume greater negotiating authority in the area of international trade.

In 1973 President Nixon proposed legislation that would allow the executive branch to negotiate trade agreements and put them into effect without congressional amendment. Congress rejected the proposal. In 1974, however, in response to complaints from U.S. trading partners that the United States could not negotiate credibly when Congress could change completed agreements, Congress enacted procedures to expedite approval of foreign trade agreements.

These procedures, known as fast track, were incorporated into the Trade Act of 1974 (19 U.S.C.A. § 2101 et seq.). Under the fast-track process, the president must notify Congress of his intention to enter into a trade agreement 90 days before doing so and must consult with the House Ways and Means Committee, the Senate Finance Committee, and any other committee that has jurisdiction over the issue. After entering into the agreement, the president must give Congress a copy of the agreement along with other documents explaining proposed administrative action and the reasons why the agreement benefits U.S. commerce. Congress has 60 days to either approve or veto an agreement, and legislative debate is limited to 20 hours in each house of Congress.

Because fast track prevents Congress from amending trade agreements, the president is able to assure foreign countries that trade agreements will not be changed once they are completed. Critics of fast track claim it diminishes Congress's role in setting foreign trade policy to a simple yes or no, and concentrates control over foreign trade policy in the executive branch. Advocates of fast track point out that in return for giving the president greater control over foreign trade, Congress has demanded more influence over the process and greater consultation with the president.

Because fast track is a rule of congressional procedure, Congress has the constitutional authority to modify or retract the procedure at any time (19 U.S.C.A. § 2903). Since the 1974 Trade Act was enacted, Congress has extended fast-track authority several times. The Trade Agreements Act of 1979 (19 U.S.C.A. § 2501 et seq.) authorized fast track for the Tokyo round of the General Agreement on Tariffs and Trade (GATT) and extended fast-track procedures for nine years; the Trade and Tariff Act of 1984 (19 U.S.C.A. § 2101 et seq.) authorized the president to negotiate with Israel; the Omnibus Trade and Competitiveness Act of 1988 (19 U.S.C.A. § 2411 et seq.) granted fast-track authority for three years and provided for a two-year extension. This extension was granted to President Bush in 1991, allowing him to negotiate the North American Free Trade Agreement (NAFTA) and the Uruguay round of the GATT. Most recently, in June 1993, Congress amended the Omnibus Trade and Competitiveness Act of 1988 to authorize President Clinton to use fast-track procedures to complete the Uruguay round of trade negotiations.

Clinton's fast-track authority expired in April 1994 and since that time Congress has become increasingly reluctant to renew it. In October 1997, Congress began considering legislation proposed by Clinton titled the Reciprocal Trade Agreements Act of 1997 (H.R. 2621, S. 1269), which would renew the president's fast-track authority. Although the Senate supported the legislation, a majority of House Democrats opposed him on the measure. Organized labor, led by the AFL-CIO, lobbied heavily against the legislation claiming that it would lead to more imports from low-wage countries that would cost American jobs. Environmental groups argued that the legislation would lead to problems such as those associated with trade with Mexico under NAFTA, including pollution, child labor, hazardous work conditions, and unsafe agricultural products. Despite extensive lobbying by the White House and the support of Republican leaders, Clinton was not able to secure enough Democratic votes for passage. Rather than risk the embarrassment of losing an important vote, the president had the bill withdrawn from consideration in the House. According to the White House, Clinton will resubmit the fast-track proposal to Congress later in 1998.

Although Congress's refusal to extend Clinton's fast-track authority weakened the president's power to negotiate international trade agreements, observers point out that the unilateral dismantling of trade barriers is occurring worldwide, with many countries opening their markets of their own accord.

## INTERNET

A worldwide telecommunications network of business, government, and personal computers.

### Domain Names

The new frontier of the Internet presents a number of novel legal problems, including many intellectual property issues. One of the biggest concerns for registered trademark and service mark holders is protection of the mark on the Internet. As Internet participants establish sites on the World Wide Web, they must create *domain names*, which are names that designate the location of a Web site. Besides providing a name to associate with the person or business that created the site, a domain name makes it easy for Internet users to find a particular home page or Web site. As individuals and businesses devise domain names in this new medium, they find that they are creating names that are similar to, or replicas of, registered, protected trademarks and service marks. In 1996 and 1997 a few cases were decided by the federal courts that reveal the direction of jurisprudence on this issue, and it does not appear to favor trademark and service mark holders.

In *Interstellar Starship Services, Ltd. v. Epix, Inc.*, 983 F.Supp. 1331 (D.Or.1997), Interstellar Starship Services, Ltd. (Interstellar Starship), a circuit analysis consulting business in Oregon, sued Epix, Inc. (Epix), a Delaware corporation that manufactures and sells video imaging hardware and software. Interstellar Starship sought a declaratory judgment that its domain name epix.com did not infringe on the Epix registered trademark, EPIX. Interstellar Starship used the Internet to advertise its association with the Clinton Street Cabaret, a Portland Oregon theater group producing the *Rocky Horror Picture Show*. Epix, Inc., which had used its mark in commerce since 1984, counterclaimed for damages, alleging that Interstellar Starships use of the domain name did infringe on its trademark.

Both parties moved for summary judgment and the federal trial court in Oregon held for Interstellar Starship. After reviewing the facts and the applicable law, the court concluded that consumers and potential consumers of printed circuit boards and computer programs would not be confused by the use of epix.com as an Internet site to publicize the *Rocky Horror Picture Show*.

In another domain name case, *Juno Online Services, L.P. v. Juno Lighting, Inc.*, 979 F.Supp. 684 (N.D. Ill. 1997), a federal court in Illinois held that Juno Online, an online service provider, could not prevent Juno Lighting, Inc., a manufacturer and retailer of recessed and track lighting products, from using its federal trademarks as a domain name. Juno Online had registered with Network Solutions, Inc. (NSI), the nation's exclusive registrar of Internet domain names, in 1994, and began serving customers in 1996. Juno Lighting, Inc., had been operating in Illinois since 1976 and held two trademarks for the name Juno.

In July 1995, a company related to Juno Online applied to the U.S. Patent and Trademark Office for federal service mark and trademark protection for the word Juno. Juno Lighting sent a letter to Juno Online in June 1996, notifying Juno Online that it objected to the trademark applications. Juno Lighting also sent a letter to NSI asking that NSI terminate Juno Online's domain name juno.com. Pursuant to its policy, NSI terminated Juno Online's domain name because NSI was unable to produce its own trademark registration for the name. However, NSI reversed this action when Juno Online brought suit against NSI and Juno Lighting. Juno Online then dropped its action against NSI, leaving only Juno Lighting as a defendant. Juno Lighting then registered its own domain name with NSI, juno-online.com.

Juno Online's amended complaint contained four counts. Count I moved for a declaratory judgment that the use of the domain name juno.com did not violate Juno Lighting's trademarks. Count II asked for damages for trademark misuse by Juno Lighting. Count III sought damages for Juno Lighting's registration of juno-online.com, and Court IV alleged damages based on unfair competition and deceptive trade practices by Juno Lighting. Juno Lighting counterclaimed, alleging trademark infringement and dilution, unfair competition, and violations of Illinois state law by Juno Online.

The court found in favor of Juno Lighting after hearing oral argument. The court was reluctant to hold that Juno Lighting had misused its own trademark because misuse of trademark is typically not an affirmative claim against the trademark holder but a claim by the trademark holder. Furthermore, because Juno Online had the same remedies it sought in Count II available to it through its other claims, the court dismissed Count II.

Count III alleged that Juno Lighting had violated section 43(a) of the Lanham Act of 1946 (15 U.S.C.A. § 1051 et seq.) by registering its name with NSI. Under this provision of the Lanham Act, any person who uses, in commerce and in connection with goods or services, a mark, symbol, or other device or word that is likely to cause confusion or to deceive customers or potential customers is liable in civil court. According to the court, Juno Lighting had not violated the Lanham Act by registering juno-on-line.com with NSI because Juno was simply storing the name and had not actually used it in connection with the Internet.

Count IV, which alleged that Juno Lighting had violated provisions of the Illinois Consumer Fraud and Deceptive Business Practices Act, (815 I11.Comp.Stat. 505/2), also was dismissed by the court. After analyzing the actions of Juno Lighting and the wording of the applicable statutes, the court concluded that Juno Lighting had done nothing wrong in sending Juno Online a letter objecting to the trademark application and registering its trademark with NSI.

The court denied all claims for monetary damages asserted by Juno Online. Conspicuous in its absence was a challenge by Juno Lighting to Count I, which requested a declaration by the court that Juno Online's use of juno.com did not violate Juno Lighting's trademarks. The court offered some insight on this issue, however, when it stated that its ruling on monetary damages did not hinder Juno Online's "ability to ask for sanctions pursuant to Rule 11 should it become apparent that [Juno Lighting's] claim of infringement and dilution is frivolous."

NSI, the nation's sole registrar of Internet domain names, has been able to stay out of the disputes over domain names. In *Lockheed Martin Corp. v. Network Solutions, Inc.*, 985 F.Supp. 949 (C.D. Cal. 1997), Lockheed Martin Corp., a manufacturing company, sued NSI over NSI's registration of Internet domain names that used the phrase "skunk works" in one form or another. For more than fifty years, Lockheed Martin and its predecessors had operated an aerospace development and production facility called Skunk Works. The company also owns service mark for SKUNK WORKS.

Lockheed Martin brought several claims against NSI, but the U.S. District Court for the Central District of California held in favor of NSI on all of them. The court found that NSI's use of domain names was connected to its technical functions and not to a trademark function of identifying goods and services. As a result, NSI was not liable for direct infringement or unfair competition claims. The acceptance of a domain name was not a commercial use under the Federal Trademark Dilution Act, 15 U.S.C.A. § § 1114(1) and 1125(a), so Lockheed Martin's claim under that statute also was unavailing. The court held further that NSI had not contributed to infringement of the SKUNK WORKS mark because Lockheed Martin could not establish that NSI'S domain name registration service was being used to infringe the mark. The court expressed dismay over the Internet addressing functions, noting that "they still operate on the 1960s and 1970s technologies that were adequate when the Internet's function was to facilitate academic and military research. …The solution to the current difficulties faced by trademark owners on the Internet," the court observed, "lies in … technical innovation, not in attempts to assert trademark rights over legitimate non-trademark uses of this important new means of communication."

At least one mark holder was successful in court in 1996. In *Panavision International, L.P. v. Toeppen*, 945 F.Supp. 1296 (C.D. Cal. 1996), the owner of the marks for Panavision and Panaflex brought suit against Dennis Toeppen, an individual engaged in the business of registering federally protected trademark names with NSI as domain names. Toeppen's business theory was that when the companies and organizations eventually sought to create a presence on the Internet, they would prefer to pay Toeppen for the right to the domain name rather than take him to court. Panavision International, L.P., a theatrical motion picture, television camera, and photographic equipment business, decided to sue Toeppen rather than pay his $13,000 "fee."

According to the court, Toeppen had violated federal and California dilution statutes by registering the protected trademarks of others on the Internet. In contrast to other trademark statutes that prohibit the use of infringing trademarks within the same market as the infringed mark, dilution statutes are intended to protect trademarks from damage caused by their use in noncompeting commercial endeavors. The court concluded that Toeppen had made commercial use of the marks by charging Panavision for the domain name, that he had injured Panavision "by preventing Panavision from exploiting its marks," and that he had harmed consumers "because it would have been difficult to locate Panavision's web site if Panavision had established a web site under a name other than its own." The court also found that Toeppen diluted Panavision's marks by preventing Panavision from using the marks on the Internet. The court ultimately held in favor of Panavision and enjoined Toeppen from further violations of the trademark and service mark dilution laws. The court did, however, reject Panavision's claim that Toeppen had intentionally interfered with prospective economic advantage, and the court also held that Panavision was not a third-party beneficiary to the domain name registration contract between Toeppen and NSI.

### E-mail Hate Crime

In February 1998 a jury in California delivered the first federal conviction for a hate crime on the Internet (*United States v. Machado*, N.Y.L.J. 5 (1998)). Watched closely by legal experts for its impact on the evolving area of cyberspace law, the case stemmed from a September 1996 incident: Richard Machado, then a nineteen-year-old University of California student, sent a mass e-mail to fifty-nine Asian students threatening to kill them. Machado was subsequently indicted on ten counts of violating a 1960s-era federal civil rights law. At trial, both sides focused on the question of intent. Prosecutors said the death threat was real, but the defense characterized it as prank that was never intended to be taken seriously. After a mistrial was declared in November 1997, prosecutors narrowed their case against Machado, retried him in February 1998, and won a conviction.

Machado sent the e-mail on September 10, 1996. He was a newly naturalized U.S. citizen from El Salvador attending classes at the University of California at Irvine—a campus where more than half of the seventeen thousand students are of Asian descent. His nine-line, profanity-laced message began with the words "I hate Asians." It blamed them for campus crimes and warned that if they did not withdraw from the school, "I personally will make it my life's work to find and kill everyone [*sic*] of you personally. OK? That's how determined I am." After campus police traced the e-mail, Machado claimed to have meant no harm. He said he had written the message out of boredom to see what response it would get. Asians were his target, he told police, because they were out-performing him in school. He later met with student leaders and apologized.

Federal prosecutors said Machado had violated the students' civil rights. No federal law addresses hate speech on line, but Machado was charged with violating 18 U.S.C.A. § 245, a civil rights law enacted to advance school desegregation in the South. Under the law it is a federal offense to use race, ethnicity, or nationality to interfere with a federally protected activity such as attending school. In mid-November a federal grand jury returned a ten-count indictment against Machado; he faced up to ten years in prison and a fine of up to $1 million.

At trial in federal district court in Santa Ana, California, the key issue in disagreement was Machado's intent. Assistant U.S. Attorney Mavis Lee contended that Machado was evidently hateful. Lee told jurors that Machado had made a death threat to kill fifty-nine people "solely because of their race, the color of their skin and their nationality." The defense denied this. Deputy Federal Public Defender Sylvia Torres-Guillen called the e-mail a "stupid prank" and acknowledged its offensiveness. However, she said, Machado never intended to carry out the threat; he had merely been bored and seeking attention. Torres-Guillen appealed to the jury not to let federal authorities curtail free speech on the Internet simply because of Machado's unpopular politics.

Both sides introduced expert testimony on the nature of Internet culture. The defense called Sara B. Kiesler, an expert in computer communications from Carnegie-Mellon University. Kiesler characterized Machado's e-mail as a common practice on the Net known as "flaming"—the sending of rude messages. The defense hoped this testimony would downplay the seriousness of the e-mail, but the prosecution introduced testimony bolstering its view that Machado meant exactly what he had written. Robert Anderson, a member of the Santa Monica-based Rand Corp., a think tank, testified that messages on the Net commonly offer typographical cues—such as symbols that signify smiling faces—to show that they are flames and hence not to be taken seriously. Machado's e-mail did not.

On November 21, 1997, jurors reported that they were deadlocked in a 9–3 vote for acquittal. U.S. District Court Judge Alicemarie H. Stotler declared a mistrial. Prosecutors subsequently reduced the charges against Machado to two counts of civil rights violations, specifically, basing his threats on the ethnicity of the students and obstructing their right to attend the university. On February 10, 1998, the jury returned a guilty verdict.

Machado's sentencing was delayed until late spring 1998. As a result of his lesser conviction, he faced up to one year in prison, but defense attorneys were expected to ask for leniency on the basis of his having already spent nearly a year behind bars. In the wake of the conviction, legal commentators predicted similar prosecutions in the future.

### Internet Junk Mail or "Spam"

Opponents of Internet junk e-mail won a legal victory against a major supplier of unsolicited commercial messages in *Earthlink Networks, Inc. v. Cyber Promotions, Inc.* In a $2 million consent judgment against Cyber, the Los Angeles Country Superior court fined the company and ordered it to stop sending the unsolicited messages—known popularly as "spam"—to one of the nation's largest Internet service providers, Pasadena-based Earthlink. Earthlink was the last of several Internet service providers (ISPs) to bring suit against Cyber, a pioneer in the controversial practice. The conclusion to the case came as state and federal lawmakers considered legislation to prohibit spam.

The Internet has revolutionized communications though e-mail. Home, business, and academic users send millions of pieces of e-mail daily. By the mid-1990s, spammers had staked a foothold in this conduit: they saw the same opportunities for profit long ago realized by traditional junkmail companies. However, the new spam industry met with resistance from ISPs and their users who objected to the unsolicited messages. Unlike traditional junkmailers who pay postage to send letters, e-mail spammers used the ISPs' networks for free. Freeloading alone was not the real issue: the technological underpinnings of the Net buckled under these mass mailings, resulting occasionally in service delays and even outages that financially harmed the ISPs.

ISPs fought back technologically and legally. With mixed success administrators tried to block the passage of spam through their networks, going as far as to cut off links to other services that tolerated the transmission of spam. Spammers, however, struck back through diversification and enhanced technology. They developed software programs capable of collecting E-mail addresses and sold lists of thousands to anyone interested, along with programs that enabled average computer users to create their own mass mailings. They also devised means to disguise the point of origin of their spam messages. Lawsuits followed. Among the leading targets of litigation was Cyber, a pioneer in the spam business founded by California promoter Stanford Wallace. A turning point in these cases

was a ruling by the U.S. District Court for the Eastern District of Pennsylvania that Cyber had no First Amendment right to spam America Online's customers (*Cyber Promotions, Inc. v. America Online, Inc.*, 948 F. Supp. 436 [E.D. Pa., 1996]). Several ISPs later won judgments against Cyber.

On March 30, 1998, the resolution of the Earthlink lawsuit, which had characterized Cyber's spamming as electronic "trespass," represented the largest monetary judgment reported to date. Under the terms of a consent decree, Cyber agreed to pay $2 million to Earthlink. It also specified that Earthlink can collect $1 million from Wallace personally for any future violation of several prohibited actions—including spamming individual Earthlink subscribers, distributing their e-mail addresses, trespassing on Earthlink's network, fabricating e-mail messages to make them appear as if they originated from Earthlink, or disguising the origin of messages sent to Earthlink. Wallace also agreed to write a letter of apology to Earthlink's customers.

On the Internet reaction to the case was largely celebratory, even though the practice of spamming seemed unlikely to end any time soon. "The most important benefit of this judgment is the message we've sent to spammers that illegally tap our resources and clog up the Internet with this trash," Garry Betty, president and CEO of Earthlink, said in a press release.

Wallace expressed his disappointment, but looked forward to building a network of his own for spam. Meanwhile, anti-spam legislation efforts continued. On March 25, 1998, the state of Washington became the first to enact a law specifically proscribing spamming on private computer networks and providing minimum penalties of $500 for offenses. Other bills remained under consideration in California and in Congress.

### New York's Disseminating Indecent Material to Minors Law

In *People v. Barrows*, 174 Misc. 2d 367, 664 N.Y.S. 2d 410 (1997), a New York trial court ruled that the state of New York has the authority "to punish anyone who sends sexually explicit material over the Internet to a minor ... and then seeks to lure that child to perform a sexual act." In essence, the ruling on the New York statute accomplishes what Congress could not when it passed the Communications Decency Act of 1996 (CDA) which was rapidly struck down in *Reno v. American Civil Liberties*

*Union*, U.S.,117 S. Ct. 2329, 138 L. Ed. 2d 874 (1997). The U.S. Supreme Court in *Reno* struck down federal statutes prohibiting "indecent transmissions" and "patently offensive displays" over the Internet, ruling that the laws violated freedom of expression guarantees of the First Amendment.

James Barrows, known on the Internet as "Captain Jake," logged onto the Internet from Connecticut on August 21, 1996, entered a chat room, and then checked into a private "preteen" room. The preteen room is designed for people who want to trade in pictures of preteen children. Meanwhile, an investigator from the Kings County District Attorney's Office Squad in Kings County, New York, also logged onto the Internet and entered the preteen room. While on the Internet, the investigator adopted the persona of "Tori 83," a thirteen-year-old female from Brooklyn, New York. Captain Jake engaged Tori 83 in an instant message conversation, asking her whether she was interested in older men, whether she was a virgin, what she was wearing, and whether she was a cop. Tori 83 responded that she was not yet 14.

Tori 83 and Captain Jake had a number of Internet conversations over the next few months. During one sexually explicit conversation between the two, Captain Jake told Tori 83 he was not just "into cyber," but that he would like to meet her. During another episode Captain Jake asked Tori 83 what kind of sex acts she liked, engaged her in sexually explicit talk and suggestions, and sent her two explicitly sexual stories and three photo files. This evidence, depicting males and apparently preteen females in sexual acts, was downloaded and eventually placed into evidence before the grand jury.

Captain Jake was arrested at a meeting he and Tori 83 had arranged. Police searched his car and found a brown paper bag containing a rope, a sexual lubricant, and numerous paper towels. Captain Jake was charged with obscenity, promoting an obscene sexual performance by a child, and attempted dissemination of indecent material to a child.

The statute, Disseminating Indecent Material to Minors (N.Y. Penal Law 235.22), has two sections; both must be satisfied in order to obtain a conviction. First, a person must intentionally use a computer to transmit to a minor, a communication depicting nudity, sexual conduct, or sadomasochistic abuse harmful to minors. If a person then "importunes, invites or induces a minor" to engage in sexual activities, he is guilty of disseminating indecent material to minors in the first degree. The statute had only been in effect for about two months before Barrows was arrested, and Barrows challenged its constitutionality on the grounds that was void for vagueness and overbroad.

The court determined that the first element of the offense, intentional transmission of a harmful communication, standing alone, is constitutionally suspect for vagueness and overbroadness, based upon the *Reno* decision. But an analysis of the second element of the offense, the "luring" requirement, saved the statute from constitutional infirmity, the court concluded. The court stated that "an Internet user need have no fear about the nature or content of transmissions under the statute, so long as it is not coupled with an attempt to lure a minor into sexual conduct." The law, read in its entirety, was not constitutionally vague or overbroad as were the challenged statutes in *Reno*. "Freedom of expression is not abridged by a law prohibiting an attempt to engage in a sexually deviate act with a child," the judge wrote in his decision.

## Online Services Liability

In a decision with potentially broad implications for Internet speech, a federal appellate panel ruled that online computer services are not liable for defamatory statements made by subscribers or other third parties. The ruling came in a November 12, 1997, decision by a three-judge panel of the U.S. Court of Appeals for the Fourth Circuit. The panel affirmed a district court decision dismissing a lawsuit against the nation's largest online service, America Online, Inc. (*Zeran v. America Online* 129 F. 3d 327 [4th Cir. (Va.)]). It held that the service could not be sued for failing to promptly remove defamatory statements made in a malicious hoax against a Seattle man in 1995. Absolving online services of a duty to monitor and remove defamatory statements, the ruling gave the services wide latitude in how they regulate speech online.

The hoax originated on America Online (AOL), a private computer service used by approximately 10 million subscribers for entertainment, business, and access to the Internet. On April 25, 1995 an anonymous message was posted to an AOL bulletin board one of the service's many proprietary areas where members can read and write text messages that remain available for weeks. Advertising "Naughty Oklahoma T-shirts," the message glorified the bombing of the Alfred P. Murrah Federal Building in Oklahoma City, which had occurred six days earlier. It offered T-shirts with slogans including "Visit Oklahoma … It's a BLAST!!!" and "Putting the kids to bed … Oklahoma 1995." The message instructed interested parties to call "Ken" at a Seattle, Washington, telephone number.

The phone number belonged to Kenneth Zeran, an independent businessman who was not an AOL subscriber. Deluged with angry calls, Zeran immediately notified AOL of his predicament. An AOL employee told him the message would be removed, but that it was the service's policy not to post a retraction. Over the next four days, however, additional anonymous messages appeared on AOL advertising bumper stickers and key chains with other offensive slogans. The author of the message could not be identified. Unable to change his telephone number because he relied upon it for his home business, Zeran was swamped with abusive calls and death threats. After an Oklahoma radio station broadcast the messages and urged its audience to dial the phone number, he received threatening calls at a rate of one every two minutes.

On April 23, 1996, Zeran sued AOL for negligence. His suit argued that once he notified AOL of the hoax, AOL had a duty to remove the defamatory posting promptly, to notify its subscribers of the message's false nature, and to screen future defamatory material. AOL responded by arguing that lawsuits such as Zeran's were barred by a section of the Communications Decency Act of 1996 (CDA) (47 U.S.C.A. § 230), which reads: "No provider or user of an interactive computer service shall be treated as the publisher or speaker of any information provided by another information content provider." AOL argued that this provision prevents it from being treated as a publisher and, as such, excuses it from liability for messages posted by its subscribers. The Eastern District Court of Virginia agreed and dismissed Zeran's suit, *Zeran v. America Online, Inc.*, 958 F. Supp. 1124 (E.D. Va. 1997).

On appeal, Zeran argued that the CDA did not absolve AOL of all liability. He maintained that the law eliminated only one form of liability for online services, that of publishers, while leaving intact their liability as distributors. This distinction comes from defamation law, which allows both publishers and distributors to be sued. Zeran asserted that AOL was not a publisher; instead, he argued, it was a traditional distributor like a news vendor or bookseller. Generally, distributors can be held liable only if they are proven to have actual knowledge of the ex-

*A woman uses an airport e-mail retrieval center.*

ELENA ROORAID/PHOTOEDIT

istence of defamatory statements. Zeran contended that he had provided AOL with sufficient notice of the defamatory statements on its bulletin boards.

The appellate court disagreed. Calling Zeran's argument "artful," it nonetheless found that AOL was legally a publisher and thus protected in that role by the CDA. The court noted that Congress had enacted section 230 of the law in order "to maintain the robust nature of Internet communication and, accordingly, to keep government interference in the medium to a minimum." Online services are not liable for material produced either by their subscribers or other services, the panel ruled, because it would be impossible for them to screen millions of messages. Moreover, they have no liability even if notified of the existence of defamatory messages. To allow such liability would lead to an explosion of lawsuits, the panel concluded.

The ruling appeared to give online services carte blanche in governing speech on their services. Previously, the services had been wary of self-regulation following the 1995 decision in *Stratton Oakmount, Inc. v. Prodigy Services Co.*, 1995 WL 323710 (N.Y. Supp.), where the New York Supreme Court held the online service Prodigy liable for defamatory statements made by an unidentified party on its bulletin boards. Prodigy was found liable because it had practiced regular monitoring and censorship of its bulletin boards; the decision left other online services worried that similar practices would open them up to liability. Yet in *Zeran*, the appellate court noted that Congress had responded to the decision in *Stratton* with section 230 of the CDA. Lawmakers intended to "encourag[e] service providers to self-regulate the dissemination of offensive material over their services."

### Reno v. American Civil Liberties Union

The dramatic growth of the Internet during the 1990s raised many issues for U.S. law, especially the role of government in policing what is communicated in cyberspace. In 1996 Congress responded to concerns that indecent and obscene materials were freely distributed on the Internet by passing the Communications Decency Act (CDA) (47 U.S.C.A. § 223(a) et seq.). This law, which was enacted as part of the Telecommunication Competition and Deregulation Act of 1996 (110 Stat. 56), forbade the "knowing" dissemination of obscene and indecent material to persons under the age of eighteen through computer networks or other telecommunications media. The act included penalties for violations of up to five years imprisonment and fines of up to $250,000.

The American Civil Liberties Union and on-line Internet services immediately challenged the CDA as an unconstitutional restriction on free speech A special three-judge federal panel in Pennsylvania agreed with these groups, concluding that the law was overly broad because it could limit the speech of adults in attempting to protect children (*American Civil Liberties Union v. Reno*, 929 F. Supp. 824 [1996]).

The government appealed to the U.S. Supreme Court *Reno v. American Civil Liberties Union*, but the Court affirmed the three-judge panel, on a 7–2 vote, finding that the act violated the First Amendment (117 S. Ct.2329, 136 L. Ed, 2d 436 [1997]). Though the Court recognized the "legitimacy and importance of the congressional goal of protecting children from harmful materials," it ruled that the CDA abridged freedom of speech and therefore was unconstitutional.

Justice John Paul Stevens, writing for the majority, reviewed the startling growth of the Internet as a means of telecommunication. Written text represents a significant portion of the Net's content, in the form of both electronic mail (e-mail) and articles posted to electronic discussion forums known as Usenet news groups. Persons can communicate directly with each other by typing messages in "chat rooms." In the mid-1990s, the appearance of the World Wide Web made the Internet even more popular. The Web is a multimedia interface that allows for the transmission of what are known as Web pages, which resemble pages in a magazine. In addition to combining text and pictures or graphics, the multimedia interface makes it possible to add audio and video components. Together these various elements have made the Internet a medium for communication and for the retrieval of information on virtually any topic.

Stevens acknowledged that the sexually explicit materials on the Internet range from the "modestly titillating to the hardest core." he concluded, however, that though this material is widely available, "users seldom encounter such content accidentally." In his view, a child would have to have "some sophistication and some ability to read to retrieve material and thereby to use the Internet unattended." He also pointed out that systems for personal computers have been developed to help parents limit access to objectionable material on the Internet and that many commercial Web sites have age-verification systems in place.

Turning to the CDA, Stevens found that previous decisions of the Court that limited free speech out of concern for the protection of children were inapplicable. The CDA differed from the laws and orders upheld in the previous cases in significant ways. The CDA did not allow parents to consent to their children's use of restricted materials, and it was not limited to commercial transactions. In addition, the CDA failed to provide a definition of "indecent," and its broad prohibitions were not limited to particular times of the day. Finally, the act's restrictions could not be analyzed as forms of time, place, and manner regulations because the act was a content-based blanket restriction on speech.

Stevens ruled that the special factors recognized in some of the Court's decisions as justifying regulation of the broadcast media are not present in cyberspace. Unlike radio and television, the Internet does not have a history of extensive government regulation. More importantly, the Court found that the Internet is not as invasive as radio or television. Users seldom encounter content by accident.

The Court was most troubled by the CDA's "many ambiguities concerning the scope of its coverage." The act's undefined terms "indecent" and "patently offensive" would provoke uncertainty about how the two standards related to each other and just what they meant. The vagueness of this content-based regulation, along with its criminal penalties, led Stevens to conclude that the CDA would have a "chilling effect" on free speech.

The government contended that the term "patently offensive" in the CDA made it constitutional. The term comes from *Miller v. California*, 413 U.S. 15, 93 S. Ct. 2607, 37 L. Ed. 2d 419 [1973], which applied a three-part test to judge whether material was obscene. Stevens rejected this argument, noting that the CDA excluded important elements of the *Miller* test. For one thing, *Miller* requires that the proscribed material be "specifically defined by the applicable state law." Stevens viewed this element as reducing the vagueness in defining the term "patently offensive." In contrast, the CDA did not contain this element, making "patently offensive" an open-ended term.

Another important element of the *Miller* test is the requirement that the material "taken as a whole, lacks serious literary, artistic, political, or scientific value." Stevens found that this "societal value" requirement allowed appellate courts "to impose some limitations and regularity on the definition by setting, as a matter of law, a national floor for socially redeeming value." The failure of the CDA to include this element meant that the law posed a serious threat to censor speech that was outside the statute's scope. Its vagueness undermined the likelihood that Congress had narrowly tailored the CDA to attain its goal of protecting minors from potentially harmful materials.

The government also contended that the CDA was needed to help foster the Internet's growth. Stevens was unpersuaded: "The dramatic expansion of this new forum contradicts the factual basis underlying this contention: that the unregulated availability of 'indecent' and 'patently offensive' material is driving people away from the Internet."

The Court was persuaded that less restrictive alternatives would be as effective as the CDA, finding that technology created to help parents screen on-line content is simply more effective than government regulation. It agreed with the lower-court finding that "currently available user-based software suggests that a reasonably effective method by which parents can prevent their children from accessing material which the parents believe is inappropriate will soon be widely available."

Justice Sandra Day O'Connor, in an opinion that concurred in part of the judgment and dissented in other areas, contended that the Court should not foreclose future regulation of the Internet. She viewed the CDA as "little more than an attempt by Congress to create 'adult zones' on the Internet. Our precedent indicates that the creation of such zones can be constitutionally sound." In her view, technological barriers can be built in cyberspace to keep children out of pornographic areas while letting adults enter freely. The development of "gateway" technology could someday be used to write zoning laws for the Internet. O'Connor concluded that "the prospects for the eventual zoning of the Internet appear promising."

## Web Page Jurisdiction

In a decision with significance for Internet litigation, a federal appeals court ruled on December 2, 1997, that the Constitution limits jurisdiction in lawsuits against owners of Web pages *Cybersell Inc. v. Cybersell Inc.*, 130 F. 3d 414 [9th Cir.]. The decision concerned personal jurisdiction, that which determines the geographical limits on where a party may be sued. The Constitution's due process guarantees prevent a plaintiff from forcing a defendant into court in a state that is different from the state where the defendant resides unless the plaintiff can establish that that court has personal jurisdiction over the defendant. Courts have only recently begun grappling with jurisdictional issues involving the Internet, which, by its nature, challenges definitions of geographic boundaries. In *Cybersell*, the U.S. Court of Appeals for the Ninth Circuit ruled that a Florida-based company's page on the World Wide Web was not a sufficient basis for it to be sued in Arizona.

The plaintiff in the lawsuit was Arizona-based Cybersell, Inc., a corporation providing advertising and marketing services on the Internet. In 1995 Cybersell's owners became aware that a rival company in Florida was using its registered name on that company's Web page. In January 1996, Cybersell filed suit in Arizona district court against the Florida-based company, alleging trademark infringement, unfair competition, fraud, and other violations. On October 21, 1996, the district court granted a defense motion by the Florida company to dismiss the case for lack of personal jurisdiction. The plaintiff appealed.

Since the late 1950s, the U.S. Supreme Court has stressed that plaintiffs must meet a strict test in cases against nonresident defendants. The Ninth Circuit uses a three-part test: (1) the nonresident defendant must do some act or consummate some transaction within the state, thereby invoking its benefits and protections; (2) the plaintiff's claim must arise out of these activities; and (3) the court's exercise of jurisdiction must be reasonable. Each part of the test must be met, or the lawsuit cannot proceed. Cybersell of Arizona contended that the test was met because the alleged trademark infringement occurred on a Web page that could be accessed from Arizona. In reply, Cybersell of Florida contended that a party should not be subject to nationwide—and potentially worldwide—jurisdiction simply for using the Internet.

In upholding the trial court's decision, the appeals court ruled that Cybersell of Arizona failed the first part of the test and therefore could not establish personal jurisdiction. The defendant had conducted no commercial activity in Arizona. The court stressed the "essentially passive" nature of its home page on the Web. Unlike an interactive Web page on which business can be conducted, Cybersell of Florida simply listed a telephone number and allowed an interested party to request further information. Judge Pamela Ann Rymer's opinion distinguished between passive and interactive Web pages: "The court's finding that the Constitution limits personal jurisdiction in the former does not apply to the latter, which 'present somewhat different issues.'"

Although the decision is only binding in the Ninth Circuit, legal analysts emphasized that it was rooted in the Constitution's due process guarantees. Thus it may carry more weight with courts seeking guidance on this evolving area in Internet law than an earlier decision by the Second Circuit, which was based on the narrower guidelines of state law (*Bensusan Restaurant Corp. v. King*, 937 F. Supp. 295 [S.D.N.Y. 1996], *aff'd* 126 F.3d 25 [2d Cir. 1997]). However, some critics doubted the opinion's broader applicability because it is limited to passive, non-interactive Web pages at a time when the trend is toward greater interactivity on Web pages.

**CROSS REFERENCES**
Censorship; Civil Rights; Defamation; First Amendment; Freedom of Speech; Intent; Jurisdiction; Lanham Act; Libel and Slander; Negligence; Telecommunications; Trademarks

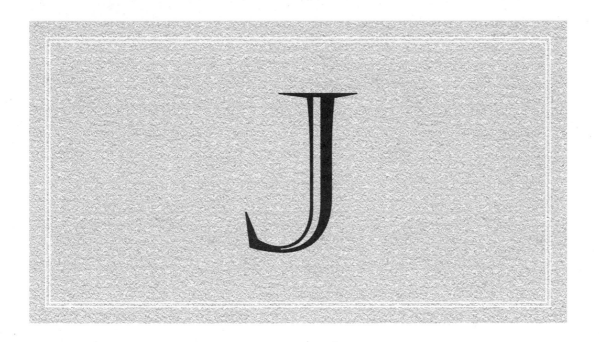

## JUDICIAL IMMUNITY

A judge's complete protection from personal LIA-BILITY for exercising judicial functions.

### Congress Overturns Pulliam v. Allen

The U.S. Supreme Court has made clear that judges have absolute immunity from lawsuits for damages based on the judges' official actions. However, in *Pulliam v. Allen* 466 U.S. 522, 104 S. Ct. 1970, 80 L. Ed. 2d 565 (1984), the Court ruled that a judge will not be given judicial immunity in cases in which a plaintiff, alleging that the judge has acted unconstitutionally, seeks an injunction ending the unconstitutional practice. More importantly, the Court held that a judge will be forced to pay the plaintiff's attorneys' fees and court costs under a federal civil rights statute.

Since *Pulliam*, judges, acting individually and through their various judicial associations, have sought congressional action that would overturn the ruling. Gladys Pulliam, a Virginia state court magistrate, had jailed two men for failure to post bail following their arrest for abusive language and public drunkenness. Under Virginia law, they could not receive a jail sentence if convicted of these offenses. The men sued Pulliam under the federal civil rights statute 42 U.S.C.A. § 1983 and obtained an injunction forbidding her to require bail for nonjailable offenses. Using the 1977 Civil Rights Attorneys' Fees Awards Act (42 U.S.C.A. § 1988), the court also awarded the two men attorney's fees amounting to almost eight thousand dollars. The Supreme Court affirmed the lower court, finding that there was nothing in the wording or legislative history of section 1988 to indicate that Congress exempted judges from paying attorneys' fees.

The Conference of State Chief Justices, the Judicial Conference of the United States, the American Bar Association, and the American Judges Association lobbied Congress to amend the law and overturn *Pulliam*, but they were opposed by the American Civil Liberties Union and the Legal Defense Fund, Inc. Finally, in the Federal Courts Improvement Act of 1996, statutory language was inserted that overturned the decision.

A new clause inserted in section 1983 prohibits injunctive relief against "a judicial officer for an act or omission taken in such officer's judicial capacity" unless "a declaratory decree was violated or declaratory relief was unavailable." In addition, language added to section 1988 precludes the award of costs and attorneys' fees against judges acting in their official capacity, Pub.L 104-317 (1996). The law restores absolute immunity, both in theory and fact, to judges for actions taken in their official capacity. It does not, however, remove their exposure to lawsuits outside their judicial function. For example, an employee of the judge can still sue for sexual harassment by the judge.

**CROSS REFERENCES**

Judge; Section 1983

## JUDICIARY

The branch of government that is endowed with the authority to interpret and apply the law, adju-

# SHOULD JUDICIAL POWER BE STRICTLY LIMITED?

The role of the judiciary and the scope of judicial power has been debated since the drafting and ratification of the Constitution. Alexander Hamilton, in the *Federalist Papers*, called for an independent judiciary that would serve as a check on the executive and legislative branches of government. He also propounded the idea of judicial review, which authorizes the courts to rule on the constitutionality of legislation. On the other hand, Thomas Jefferson and James Madison raised concerns about an unelected federal judiciary whose members were granted lifetime appointment and could only be removed by impeachment. An independent judiciary could thwart the desires of the electorate and its representatives, making the judiciary a potentially undemocratic institution.

Both sets of views continue to be articulated by U.S. politicians and pundits. Critics of judicial power believe judges are too quick to ignore the written law and impose their personal beliefs on the parties who appear before them. Because federal judges have been politically insulated since the early 1800s, modern critics believe Congress must find ways of limiting judicial power and ending a period in U.S. history that has seen judges become *de facto* legislators. However, proponents of an independent judiciary argue that such proposed limitations and restrictions strike at the heart of a vital constitutional check on the popular will.

IN FOCUS

Without an independent, forceful judiciary, the Constitution would soon be ignored by those bent on political power.

Some critics of the judiciary in the 1990s hold important seats in Congress. The foremost critic is Representative Tom DeLay (R.,Tex.), who has suggested that impeachment proceedings should be brought against activist judges who make decisions based on their political ideologies and policy preferences rather than on a plain reading of the law. According to DeLay, "The system of checks and balances so carefully crafted by our Founding Fathers is in serious disrepair" because activist judges are assuming the legislature's lawmaking power. Therefore, Congress should not be afraid to impeach a judge for something other than clearly illegal actions.

Another proposal to limit judicial power is to change federal law to allow each party in a federal case to request that another judge be assigned to the case without having to give any reason for the requested change. This option would allow parties to avoid judges who are known to engage in improper courtroom behavior or who let their biases guide their decisions. Another suggestion is to allow the televising of federal criminal and civil trials and appeals, subject to the judges' approval. Advocates believe that once U.S. citizens watch their federal courts in action, they will discuss the proper limits of federal judges.

dicate legal disputes, and otherwise administer justice.

### Judge Requires Church Attendance

In *In re Quirk*, a Louisiana judge came under scrutiny for his unusual practice of sentencing defendants to attend church. (*In re Quirk*, 705 So. 2d 172 [La.]). The Louisiana Judiciary Commission recommended four types of disciplinary action be taken against Judge Thomas P. Quirk, alleging that Judge Quirk's church sentences violated the First Amendment's ban on the establishment of religion. The Louisiana Supreme Court, however, disagreed, ruling that the judge's actions fell short of judicial misconduct. The court declined to rule on the constitutionality of church-attendance sentences.

Judge Quirk served in Lake Charles City Court, where he heard municipal cases involving traffic offenses and misdemeanors. Between 1993 and 1994, he sentenced 540 defendants to attend a church of their choosing once a week as a condition of their probation. Any church function satisfied the requirement, not just services, and Quirk did not require that they profess any belief in religion. He offered the sentences to defendantes whom he perceived to be unable to afford a fine or court costs, in lieu of jail time or other probationary conditions. The sentencing applied to an estimated 3 percent of his docket. No defendant objected at the time of sentencing. The judge explained that the practice was an attempt to find alternatives that would not only punish defendants, but help them to become good citizens.

In November 1994, a complaint challenging the practice was filed against Judge Quirk with the state Judiciary Commission, which serves as the state's watchdog over judicial ethics and reports to the state supreme court. At the same time, the American Civil Liberties Union (ACLU) filed suit alleging that he had violated the First Amendment's Establishment Clause by ordering Gregory Thompson to attend church

Since the Republican party gained control of Congress in 1994, they have made efforts to attack substantive areas of the law that have, according to the majority, been controlled too closely by federal judges. One example is the Prison Litigation Reform Act (PLRA) of 1995 (28 U.S.C.A. § 1932), which imposes substantive and procedural limitations on the ability of federal courts to issue injunctions mandating prison reform. The act also restricts the courts' ability to employ special masters to assist in prison condition cases. Congress acted to restrict federal judicial power in large part because the states perceived judicial oversight as a usurpation of states' rights. Other proposals seek to limit the jurisdiction of federal courts, curbing the federalization of crimes that have traditionally been the concern of state and local governments.

Finally, opponents of judicial activism have sought to block the confirmation of judicial nominations. President Bill Clinton has been unable to fill many judicial vacancies due to the resistance of congressional Republicans who believe that liberal appointments to the bench will only continue the problem of

activist judges. Nevertheless, Chief Justice William H. Rehnquist called on Congress in 1998 to move quickly to confirm the appointments, as the federal court case backlog continued to grow.

Defenders of an independent judiciary contend that critics of the judiciary oversimplify the issues and fail to see that every judge must, at some point, make rather than interpret law. Indeed, judges cannot avoid making law in some cases because the law does not always provide clear answers to questions that come before the courts. Constitutional and statutory provisions and other legal rules tend to be expressed in general terms, and the courts must decide how these general provisions and rules apply to specific cases.

Defenders point to the Americans with Disabilities Act of 1990 (ADA), (104 Stat. 327), which requires employers to reasonably accommodate the needs of employees with disabilities. The ADA does not, however, say exactly what employers must do to "reasonably accommodate" such persons. This general wording meant that the federal courts had to decide, on a case-by-case basis, what this phrase meant.

In addition, in some cases the court has no relevant law or precedent to follow, yet it must render a decision. For example, courts have continued to struggle with new kinds of legal issues stemming from new communications technology, including the Internet. Proponents of an independent judiciary note that until legislative bodies establish laws governing these issues, it is up to the courts to fashion the law that will apply, even though to do so means the courts are making policy.

As to the recent threats of impeachment, defenders of the judiciary contend that DeLay and others have misread history. The idea of an independent judiciary cannot be sustained if judges are subject to political pressures. The system of checks and balances would be in greater peril if DeLay's proposal was implemented. Finally, it would be difficult to establish a standard for impeachment, since judicial activism has no precise meaning. Defenders believe that limiting judicial independence would cause more damage to the workings of the U.S. justice system than has been caused by activists on the bench.

---

on an no-contest plea to drunken driving in 1993 (*Thompson v. Quirk*, [USDC No. 94-2132]). Judge Quirk subsequently began to offer church attendance as a sentence only to the approximately 969 defendants who specifically requested it.

On December 12, 1995, the commission charged Judge Quirk with four counts of judicial misconduct. Charges one and two related to church attendance in sentencing, which the commission had determined was unconstitutional based on a review of state and federal case law. Charge three accused Judge Quirk of improper representation by an attorney before the Judiciary Committee who was representing the city in a case challenging the constitutionality of one of the judge's sentences (*City of Lake Charles v. Thompson*, No. 94-1451). Charge four accused the judge or writing letters in his official capacity to a judge in Tennessee seeking mercy on behalf of his brother-in-law.

The commission held hearings in September 1996 and issued its findings in April 1997. It found that charges one, three, and four had been proven and constituted violations of the state's Code of Judicial Conduct. It recommended a penalty of twelve months' suspension without salary and payment of investigative costs totaling $6,835. Additionally, the commission recommended that Judge Quirk be ordered to take two immediate steps: stop sentencing church attendance, and begin tape recording all of his court proceedings for inspection by the Judicial Commission and the Louisiana Supreme Court.

On December 12, 1997, the state supreme court reviewed the case. This review was the court's first time considering the issue of when legal error by a judge constitutes judicial misconduct, and, as such, it proceeded carefully in order not "to trammel the exercise of judicial discretion and stifle the independence of the judiciary." After a lengthy review of how other jurisdictions have answered the question, the court noted that the purpose of the Code of Judicial Conduct is to protect the public rather than to discipline a judge. This view informed its announcement of a new standard to be applied in Louisiana: a judge may be found to have committed judicial misconduct when a legal ruling or action is contrary to clear and determined law about which there is no confusion, and where the judge's legal error was egregious, made in bad faith, or made as part of a pattern of legal error.

Under the new standard, the court found Judge Quirk innocent of misconduct. The court found that no court in a jurisdiction binding on Judge Quirk had ruled directly on the constitutional issue. It therefore concluded that the sentences were not clearly illegal at the time they were rendered, and to punish Judge Quirk would weaken the principle of judicial independence. Thus the court rejected charges one and two.

The court also rejected the recommendation for charge three because the commission had failed to give Judge Quirk fair notice of allegations of unethical conduct, and because the court lacked jurisdiction to rule on the charge as it was written. Finally, the court observed that it was unnecessary for it to reach the merits on charge four, noting that Judge Quirk had already complied with a discipline agreement made with the Judiciary Commission.

**CROSS REFERENCES**
First Amendment; Religion; Sentencing

# JURISDICTION

The geographic area over which authority extends; legal authority; the authority to hear and determine CAUSES OF ACTION.

### Arizonans for Official English v. Arizona

Article III, section 2 of the U.S. Constitution requires that federal courts decide only cases or controversies, which means that federal courts have the power to hear cases arising under federal law and controversies involving certain types of parties. The U.S. Supreme Court has interpreted this section of the Constitution to mean that the federal courts may not render advisory opinions, and this interpretation is the most fundamental application of the philosophy of judicial restraint.

The federal doctrine of standing to sue is one aspect of the case or controversy requirement. Standing focuses on whether a prospective plaintiff can show that the defendant has invaded some personal legal interest. It is not enough that a person is merely interested as a member of the general public in the resolution of the dispute. The person must have a personal stake in the outcome of the controversy. Most standing issues arise over the enforcement of an allegedly unconstitutional statute, ordinance, or policy. One may challenge a law or policy constitutional grounds if she can show that enforcement of the law or implementation of the policy infringes on an individual constitutional right, such as freedom of speech.

The U.S. Supreme Court, in *Arizonans for Official English v. Arizona*, ___U.S.___, 117 S. Ct. 1055, 137 L. Ed. 2d 170 (1997), untangled a lawsuit beset by procedural complications, illustrating the fact that substantive and controversial issues may not proceed in federal court without a plaintiff who has standing. In addition, the Court chastised the lower federal courts for wasting eight years on litigation that should have been dismissed early in the proceedings for lack of standing. The Court also noted that the state supreme court rather than a federal court should have decided the substantive issue.

The case arose from an amendment to the Arizona state constitution that declared English "the official language of the State of Arizona"—"the language of … all government functions and actions" (Arizona Constitution, Article XXVIII, Section 1(1), 1(2)). The amendment, which was promoted by the group Arizonans for Official English and passed by voters in 1988, was viewed by many Arizonans as an attempt to curtail the growing use of Spanish in government and public life.

Maria-Kelly E. Yniguez, an Arizona state employee, filed a lawsuit in federal court challenging the constitutionality of the amendment. Specifically, she charged that the amendment violated her First and Fourteenth Amendment rights. An insurance claims manager, Yniguez is fluent in Spanish and English. She used her bilingual skills to communicate with her clients. Her lawsuit alleged that the English-only requirement, if read broadly, might cause her to lose her job or face sanctions if she did not refrain from speaking Spanish while serving the state.

The federal district court agreed with

Yniguez that the amendment was overbroad and unconstitutional. The court saw the amendment as imposing a sweeping ban on the use of any other language than English by state and local government employees.

The procedural problems with the case then began. Arizona Governor Rose Mofford, who had opposed the enactment of the amendment, announced that she would not appeal the district court decision. The state attorney general, Robert K. Corbin, who had earlier been dismissed from the lawsuit at his request, then sought to reenter the case and appeal on behalf of the state. He also asked the court to certify the question of constitutionality to the Arizona Supreme Court. Under this certification process, a federal district or appellate court asks the highest court in which it is located to determine a matter of state law. Once the state high court gives an interpretation, the federal court applies the decision to the case at hand. The court rejected both of Corbin's requests.

The district court also rejected the request of Robert D. Park, the head of Arizonans for Official English (AOE), to allow AOE and himself personally to intervene and represent the state's interest on appeal. The court ruled that AOE and Park did not have standing to sue or defend in a federal court.

AOE and Park appealed this adverse decision to the Ninth Circuit Court of Appeals (939 F.2d 727 [1991]). The Ninth Circuit court looked at standing differently. It ruled that AOE and Park did have standing. AOE, as the principal sponsor of the amendment, had a stake in the outcome of the case. The court also concluded that Yniguez could reasonably expect Park to bring an enforcement action against her for violating the amendment. In addition, the appeals court held that the state attorney general could not reenter the case as a party but could argue before the court.

The procedural issues became even murkier when the state discovered that Yniguez had left state employment in April 1991, almost three months before the appellate decision. The state then moved for dismissal of the case, claiming that Yniguez could not now be affected by the amendment, thus making her case moot. One year later the Ninth Circuit three-judge panel rejected the claim that the case was moot (975 F.2d 646 [1992]), and in December 1994 it affirmed the lower court, finding the amendment unconstitutional (42 F.3d 1217). The full Ninth

Circuit court agreed to rehear the case, and it affirmed and reinstated the three-judge panel's decision. In doing so, it preserved Yniguez's standing by reading her complaint to also call for the award of nominal (token) damages.

On appeal to the U.S. Supreme Court, the Court instructed the parties to discuss two threshold questions: should Park and AOE be allowed to proceed in the action as parties? And did Yniguez have standing to satisfy the "case or controversy" requirement? Justice Ruth Bader Ginsburg, writing for a unanimous Court, answered both questions in the negative. Consequently, the Court ordered that the Ninth Circuit court decision be vacated and the district court case dismissed.

The Court was unpersuaded that Park and AOE had Article III standing. They had argued that because AOE had sponsored the ballot initiative that placed the amendment before the voters and had spent large sums of money on garnering voter support, it had a quasi-legislative interest in defending the constitutionality of the measure. Ginsburg rejected this claim, stating that "we are aware of no Arizona law appointing initiative sponsors as agents of the people of Arizona to defend, in lieu of public officials, the constitutionality of initiatives made law of the State."

The Court also rejected AOE's claim that it had representational or associational standing: "An association has standing to sue or defend in such capacity, however, only if its members would have standing in their own right."

More importantly, the Court ruled that Yniguez did not have standing to pursue her claim. The Court pointed out that to qualify as a case in federal court, the controversy must exist at all stages of review, not just at the time the complaint is filed. Yniguez's complaint rested on her concerns as a state employee. Once she left the employ of the state, she had no stake in the lawsuit. In addition, the Ninth Circuit court's decision to read into her complaint a request for nominal damages was nothing more than an ill-advised effort to preserve Yniguez's standing.

The Court also was troubled by the fact that although the state was no longer a party to the lawsuit, the nominal damage award was levied against it.

Because of these procedural and jurisdictional errors, the Court took the extreme step of not only reversing the Ninth Circuit court decision but also vacating the district court decision and instructing that the case be dismissed. Ginsburg chastised the lower courts for "premature adjudication of constitutional questions." She stated that the better course would have been to follow the advice of the attorney general and certify the constitutional question to the Arizona Supreme Court for a definitive answer.

## KEYCITE

An interactive computer-assisted citator service that allows legal researchers to verify the validity of a case and to find all references that have cited that case as authority.

Every day lawyers are asked by their clients to persuade judges to rule in their favor. One way lawyers try to accomplish this task is by citing prior legal decisions, sometimes called precedent, that support their clients position. Depending on its factual similarity to a pending legal dispute, a relevant precedent can control or influence the outcome of a case. Consequently, lawyers look for ways to make precedents appear more persuasive, while courts look for ways to determine which precedents are relevant, important, or controlling in their jurisdiction.

KeyCite is designed to expedite the process of assessing a case's presidential value. Released by West group in July 1997, KeyCite was initially available only through WESTMATE®, an online software package that allows subscribers to WESTLAW, West's computer-assisted research service, to dial through their personal computer modems over a telephone line into a central mainframe computer located in Eagan, Minnesota. By the end of 1997, however, KeyCite was also made available to customers over the Internet and through West Group's CD-ROM software package called PREMISE®.

KeyCite uses graphical markers to signify the status or history of a case. A red flag warns that a case is no longer good law for at least one of the points it contains, meaning that a case has been reversed, vacated, superseded, overruled, or abrogated in some respect. A yellow flag warns that a case has some negative history, meaning that a point of law contained in a case has been amended, modified, limited, or called into doubt, but not completely eviscerated. A blue H indicates that a case has some history, but no known negative history, which generally means that a case contains a point of law that has been appealed, affirmed, discussed, relied on as precedent, or otherwise cited as relevant authority.

KeyCite also employs graphical markers to signify the extent to which courts have subsequently relied on a case. Stars are used to reveal how much one case discusses another: four stars indicate that a case has been "examined," meaning that the cited case has received more than a printed page of treatment in another decision; three stars indicate that a case has been "discussed," meaning that the cited case has received more than a paragraph of treatment in another decision, but less than a full printed page; two stars indicate that a case has been "cited," meaning that the cited case has received less than a paragraph of treatment in another decision; and one star indicates that a case has been "mentioned," meaning that the cited case has been briefly referenced in another decision.

Quotation marks are used in KeyCite displays to signify that a cited case has been quoted by another court. Based on the idea that cases cited more frequently tend to be more significant, KeyCite tallies citation counts for every case within its coverage. However, KeyCite coverage is not comprehensive. Beginning coverage for state case citations varies according to jurisdiction, and citator coverage is not provided for state or federal statutes.

KeyCite integrates many of the features already found on WESTLAW. KeyCite results can be limited to a particular date range, so that only the most recent cases citing a particular precedent are displayed. KeyCite results can also be restricted by jurisdiction, so lawyers in one state can focus on legal authority in their home jurisdiction, without being sidetracked by cases from foreign jurisdictions. Finally, KeyCite allows headnotes (summaries of legal rules and principles established by courts that are added by West Group editors to case published in the National Reporter Systems®) from particular cases to be traced through subsequent opinions.

**CROSS REFERENCES**
Citator; WESTLAW

## LABOR LAW

An area of the law that deals with the right of employers, employees, and labor organizations.

### Illegal Aliens Protected in Unionization Effort

In *National Labor Relations Board v. A.P.R.A. Fuel Oil Buyers Group, Inc.*, 134 F.3d 50, a seven-year-old labor grievance reached an ironic conclusion when a federal appeals court ordered an employer to reinstate and pay restitution to two illegal aliens the employer had fired. In the decision by the U.S. Court of Appeals for the Second Circuit, a three-judge panel addressed the question of whether an employer who knowingly hires illegal aliens can later use federal immigration law as a defense for firing them when its true purpose was union-busting. By a 2–1 vote, the court held that the policies underlying federal labor and immigration laws protect illegal aliens from retaliatory firing for attempting to unionize.

In 1990, the A.P.R.A. Fuel Oil Buyers Group, Inc. (APRA), hired Jose Ciudad and Jorge Bianey Diaz. Both men told the Brooklyn, New York-based company that they were illegal aliens.

APRA hired them anyway, as a boiler mechanic and truck mechanic, respectively, going to some trouble to do so. The company gave them new names in order to fool investigators, and one was even given another man's social security card. Ciudad became Victor Benavides, and Diaz became Alberto Guzman.

In fall 1990, however, APRA took offense when the men participated in a lawful effort to unionize the company. In early 1991, a company official ordered them to sign prepared affidavits disavowing their intent to be represented by a union. Threatened with losing their jobs, both men signed. As part of other efforts to stop workers from organizing, the company also pressured one of the men to reveal who was leading the unionization effort. Ultimately, it fired Guzman on January 14, 1991, and Benavides on February 3, 1991.

The men took their case to the National Labor Relations Board (NLRB), the agency that enforces federal labor statutes, and won in 1992, *A.P.R.A. Fuel Oil Buyers Group, Inc.*, 309 N.L.R.B. 480 (1992). The board found that the company's union-busting attempt aimed at Guzman, Benavides, and other employees had violated the National Labor Relations Act, 29 U.S.C. §§ 151-168 (1994). In particular, the dismissal of the two men constituted an unlawful retaliatory discharge under Section 8(a)(3) of the Act, which protects unionization activities. The company appealed, but the Second Circuit upheld the ruling 28 F.3d 103 (2d Cir.1994). Because the NLRB had not yet determined a remedy, that issue was severed from the case.

In 1995, the NLRB ordered APRA to reinstate the two men, conditioned upon their obtaining proper work status from immigration officials, 320 N.L.R.B. 408. Additionally, as a penalty, the board ordered the company to pay the men back-salary— dated from the time of their unlawful dismissal until their rehiring, or, alternatively, until the time their efforts to obtain the required work status failed.

APRA appealed, claiming it should not be held liable because the men were illegal aliens.

They argued that immigration law, including the Immigration Reform and Control Act (IRCA), (Pub.L. No. 99-203, 100 Stat. 3359), restricted the power of the labor board to rule on the matter.

On December 5, 1997, the appeals panel ruled that APRA could not hide behind immigration laws that it had knowingly violated. Writing for the majority, Circuit Judge James L. Oakes first considered the interaction of labor and immigration law. Congress, he wrote, had similar goals in mind when enacting the National Labor Relations Act in 1935 and, three decades later, the Immigration Reform and Control Act in 1996: protecting U.S. labor markets from the effects of illegal immigration while also protecting the rights of illegal workers. The 1996 law contained more severe punishments for "unscrupulous employers" who employed undocumented workers. But the law did not reduce protections or remedies for those workers.

In this context, the immigration law did not diminish the board's power to fashion remedies for violations of labor law. Because the reinstatement order required Guzman and Benavides to seek legal status as workers, it "quite clearly tailors the remedy for the violation of the NLRA to the restrictions of the other law," Judge Oakes wrote. He also approved of the manner in which the remedy left compliance with immigration law to immigration officials, keeping the labor board out of this area. Finally, on the question of back pay, the panel saw an obvious reason to enforce such a penalty: employers might simply "compare the expense of the IRCA's fines to the expenses of the back pay and the advantage gained in resisting unions, and decide that the IRCA's penalties were worth incurring." The panel thus rejected the company's appeal and upheld the labor board's remedy.

**CROSS REFERENCES**

Aliens; Labor Union

# LIBEL AND SLANDER

Two TORTS that involve the communication of false information about a person, a group, or an entity such as a corporation. Libel is any DEFAMATION that can be seen, such as a writing, printing, effigy, movie, or statue. Slander is any defamation that is spoken and heard.

## John Dean Libel Suit

On the twenty-fifth anniversary of the Watergate scandal, another chapter was added to its long history with the settlement of a $150 million libel suit. In July 1997, John W. Dean III, former White House counsel to President Richard M. Nixon, settled his six-year lawsuit against St. Martin's Press. Dean had sued the publisher over its best-selling 1991 book *Silent Coup*, a radical reinterpretation of the events that toppled Nixon's presidency. At the heart of the book's controversial allegations was the charge that Dean himself had engineered the break-in of Democratic National Committee (DNC) headquarters in the Watergate hotel in 1972. Separate from his settlement with St. Martin's, Dean continued to pursue libel suits against the book's authors and former Watergate conspirator G. Gordon Liddy.

Although notoriously complex in detail, the broad outlines of Watergate were well known for years before the publication of *Silent Coup*. In June 1972, the arrest of burglars attempting to plant listening devices in the DNC headquarters led to the discovery that they had acted on orders from the Attorney General, the presidential campaign staff, and high-ranking officials in the White House. Most historians believe their goal was to get damaging information about the DNC's chairman. Exposure of a White House cover-up forced the resignation of President Nixon on August 8, 1974, just as he was about to be impeached. Watergate established itself as the gravest political scandal in modern U.S. history.

*Silent Coup* presented an original view of the scandal's origins. Previously, Dean had been regarded as a minor player—and most significantly, as the only White House official to have freely cooperated with congressional investigators. His blunt testimony helped sink Nixon, a fact that infuriated Nixon and his supporters. For his role in the cover-up, Dean later pleaded guilty to obstruction of justice and served four months in prison. But authors Len Colodny and Robert Gettlin charged that the break-in and cover-up were conceived and orchestrated by Dean. They alleged that he planned the break-in to protect his then-girlfriend and future wife, Maureen Biner, from embarrassment. According to the book, Biner's roommate ran a prostitution ring used by top Democrats, and Dean allegedly wanted a photo of Biner to be retrieved from a desk in the DNC's offices.

An immediate sensation, the book remained on the *New York Times* bestseller list for twelve weeks and sold an estimated 100,000 copies. Former President Nixon sent a note congratulating the authors, and former President Gerald R. Ford issued an endorsement. Convicted Watergate conspirator G. Gordon Liddy used his Fairfax, Virginia radio talk show to promote the book and reissued his best-selling memoir, *Will*, with a new chapter incorporating the allegations. But other reviews dismissed *Silent Coup* as fanciful and irresponsible. *The Washington Post Book World* blasted its "wild charges and vilifications" while *The New York Times Book Review* criticized its "ignorance" of the Nixon administration.

Shortly after publication, Dean denounced the book as "absolute garbage" and "fraud full of twisted details." In 1992 he filed three separate libel suits against St. Martin's Press, the book's authors, and Liddy. His action against the publisher asked for $150 million in damages. In July 1997, Dean and St. Martin's agreed to a confidential out-of-court settlement. St. Martin's Press lawyer David Kaye declined to reveal whether the settlement involved any money, but he told the *Washington Post* that the company was returning publishing rights to *Silent Coup* to the authors. Dean said he was satisfied.

The two other lawsuits continued to wind through court. Attorneys for *Silent Coup* co-author Colodny said they were waiting for Dean's response to their motions to dismiss the suit in U.S. District Court in Washington. Much media attention was paid to the suit against Liddy, Dean's longtime enemy. Liddy, who professed to having considered killing Dean in 1973, has regularly used his radio show to criticize him. Meanwhile, St. Martin's continued to publish a hardcover edition of Liddy's memoir; however, unlike an earlier paperback edition, Dean noted that it no longer contained derogatory references to his wife.

### Oprah Winfrey Beef Lawsuit

On February 26, 1998, television talk show host Oprah Winfrey defeated a $10 million libel suit in Amarillo, Texas. The trial pitted Winfrey's speech rights against the commercial interests of aggrieved cattle ranchers, who accused her of slandering their industry on a broadcast in 1996. They sued Winfrey and vegetarian activist Howard Lyman for allegedly making false and disparaging comments about beef raising practices. But the plaintiffs suffered a serious setback when U.S. District Judge Mary Lou Robinson threw out key elements of the lawsuit, refusing to allow them to use the state's "food disparagement" law. The trial's publicity

*John W. Dean III agreed to an out-of-court settlement in his libel suit against St. Martin's Press, publisher of* Silent Coup.

MARK GODFREY/THE IMAGE WORKS

highlighted controversy over this and similar laws nationwide, which have pitted the food industry against free speech activists.

On April 16, 1996, *The Oprah Winfrey Show*, a highly popular syndicated daytime talk show, examined the issue of beef contamination in the United States. Britain had then recently suffered a devastating outbreak of mad cow disease, the popular term for bovine spongiform encephalopathy. Transmitted through beef to humans, it causes a fatal brain illness called Creutzfeld-Jakob disease. In Britain at least twenty people died from the disease and 1.5 million cows were destroyed in efforts to stop it. No cases have been reported in the United States.

Winfrey's guest, Lyman, warned that U.S. outbreak was possible. A former cattle rancher who is now a program director for the Humane Society of the United States, he accused the U.S. beef industry of feeding its cattle ground-up cattle parts. This practice, he said, could lead to an epidemic of mad cow disease that would "make AIDS look like the common cold." Winfrey asked the audience: "Now doesn't that concern you all a little bit, right here, hearing that? It has just stopped me cold from eating another burger!"

Beginning the day of the broadcast, cattle prices fell for two weeks in what beef traders dubbed the "Oprah Crash" of 1996. In Texas, several ranchers, alleging that Winfrey and Lyman had maliciously attacked the cattle industry, brought suit against the pair as well as Winfrey's production company, Illinois-based Harpo Productions, Inc., and the show's distributor, Delaware-based King World Productions. They sought more than $10 million in damages for losses suffered when beef prices fell. Winfrey's ability to influence the public was not in doubt; books that are discussed on her show often become best-sellers. Moreover, her pockets are deep: she has an estimated net worth of $550 million.

The plaintiffs sued under a Texas law forbidding the false disparagement of agricultural products, Texas Civil Practice and Remedies Code § 96.002. Because perishable foods have a short life span, producers stand to suffer severe losses if consumers are scared away, even briefly. Texas is one of thirteen states to have passed such laws in the 1990s, which came about in the wake of a 1989 controversy over a CBS *60 Minutes* broadcast alleging that apples sprayed with a particular pesticide could cause cancer in children. Claiming losses as a result of journalistic irresponsibility, the food industry lobbied hard for these so-called food disparagement statutes. To make suing easier, all of the laws lower the burden of proof required at trial. Texas's law is perhaps the weakest: unlike twelve other states, it does not shift the burden of proof from the plaintiff to the defendant. The food industry defends the laws as simply codifying the common-law tort of business and product disparagement. First Amendment activists argue that the laws chill free speech.

Heard before a jury for six weeks from January to February 1998, the trial became a media spectacle. Winfrey moved her talk show from Chicago to Amarillo, and throngs of her fans demonstrated outside and packed the courtroom. Winfrey said that she initially doubted whether she could get a fair trial in Texas, but that she had changed her mind upon seeing an outpouring of support for her.

Issues at the trial ranged from the truthfulness of the defendants' comments on the show to the damages suffered by the cattle industry. Testifying over three days, Winfrey said that she had only been trying to inform the public about a potential danger. Both sides presented expert testimony disputing cattle prices in April 1996. The plaintiffs' witnesses maintained that cattle ranchers had lost money, while the defendants' witnesses argued that the ranchers could actually have made money if not for their own mistakes. By the trial's end, closing arguments by both sides focused upon the issue of free speech. De-

*Arthur L. Liman*
DOUG MILLS/CORBIS-BETTMANN

fense attorney Charles Babcock called Winfrey an "angel" for helping the national interest. Plaintiffs' attorney Joe Coyne appealed to the necessity of responsible speech: "America," he told the jury, "does not stand for the right to lies."

The turning point in the trial came in mid-February, when defense attorneys moved to throw out the suit. Although Judge Robinson stopped short of doing so, she dealt the plaintiffs a serious blow. Throwing out the elements of their suit that relied on the state's food disparagement law, she held that they had not offered sufficient evidence to sue under it. Instead, they were forced to proceed under a general business disparagement claim, which requires a higher standard of proof: they had to show that Winfrey and Lyman had deliberately and maliciously attacked the industry.

This proved too high a burden for the plaintiffs. On February 26, after a half day of deliberation, the jury of four men and eight women returned a verdict of not guilty. Winfrey celebrated outside the courtroom with a raised fist, declaring that free speech "not only lives—it rocks!" Lyman's organization, the U.S. Humane Society, took out a full-page advertisement in the *New York Times* attacking food disparagement laws as censorship and vowing to fight against their passage in other states. Cattle rancher Paul Engler, one of the plaintiffs, said that he would appeal but that the lawsuit had already achieved the end of reaffirming that U.S. beef is safe. Jurors told reporters that they had decided to protect speech rights.

Those who hoped the case would create precedent on food disparagement laws were disappointed that that claim was dismissed. Some critics hoped that the lawsuit's failure would deter other states from passing their own laws. In early 1998 eight states had bills pending on food disparagement.

**CROSS REFERENCES**
First Amendment; Freedom of Speech; Nixon, Richard Milhous; Watergate

## LIMAN, ARTHUR L.

Arthur L. Liman, one of the nation's leading trial attorneys and a fierce investigator of government wrongdoing, died on July 17, 1997, at the age of 64, in New York. Liman's law career spanned four decades. He was widely sought after by blue-chip corporations, financiers, and other powerful clients for his defense work. Publicly, he was best known for his probing of official malfeasance, both in the aftermath of the riot at the Attica Correctional facility in 1971 and the Iran-Contra Affair in 1987.

Liman was born on November 5, 1932, to teachers Celia and Harry K. Liman and was the younger of two children. He demonstrated early prowess in the law; after graduating magna cum laude from Harvard in 1954, he finished first in his class at Yale Law School in 1957. Turning down an offer to teach at Yale, he joined the prestigious New York law firm of Paul, Weiss, Rifkind, Wharton, and Garrison, where he would practice throughout his career.

Attracted by his reputation for penetrating cross-examination and mastery of detail, Liman's clients usually were high-profile individuals and companies. He represented Michael R. Milken, the junk bond merchant, and John Zaccaro, the real estate mogul and husband of the 1984 Democratic nominee for vice-president, Geraldine A. Ferraro. Liman's many prominent corporate clients included CBS, Time-Warner, Calvin Klein, and Pennzoil. He had an unusual yet pivotal role in Pennzoil's 1985 litigation with Texaco, in which his testimony on the witness stand led to Pennzoil's being awarded $10 billion in damages.

Liman divided his career between private practice and public service, sometimes taking extended leaves from his firm. Beginning in 1961 he began a two-year stint as a U.S. assistant attorney prosecuting white-collar crime. Then in 1972 New York Governor Hugh L. Carey appointed Liman to probe the bloody Attica prison riot of 1971, in which forty-three inmates and guards died. The deaths occurred in part as a result of an assault by state troopers to reclaim the prison. As chief counsel to the state panel's year-long investigation, Liman produced a 470-page report identifying official mistakes that was widely praised.

Liman's most ambitious and historically important role came in 1987 during the height of the Iran-Contra Affair. This scandal involved the United States' secret sale of arms to Iran and the funneling of proceeds to the Contra rebels fighting the government of Nicaragua. Liman served as chief counsel to the Senate committee investigating the role of President Ronald Reagan and several of his aides. During televised hearings, Liman interrogated such figures as National Security Council staff member Lieutenant Colonel Oliver L. North and retired General Richard V. Secord, seeking to ascertain what the president knew about the arms sales.

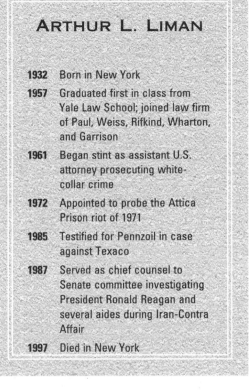

## ARTHUR L. LIMAN

**1932** Born in New York

**1957** Graduated first in class from Yale Law School; joined law firm of Paul, Weiss, Rifkind, Wharton, and Garrison

**1961** Began stint as assistant U.S. attorney prosecuting white-collar crime

**1972** Appointed to probe the Attica Prison riot of 1971

**1985** Testified for Pennzoil in case against Texaco

**1987** Served as chief counsel to Senate committee investigating President Ronald Reagan and several aides during Iran-Contra Affair

**1997** Died in New York

The Iran-Contra scandal was both a high and a low point for Liman's career. His relentless pursuit of the facts led to criminal convictions of North, national security adviser John M. Poindexter, and others, but all were reversed on appeal. Liman received anti-Semitic hate mail from the supporters of the immensely popular North and was criticized for being too hard or too soft on witnesses and for not adequately following evidence that led to President Reagan. Liman replied that the committee had thoroughly researched all that could be learned about the scandal.

Two factors had hampered Liman's investigation, the destruction of evidence by the conspirators and the decision by Congress to grant them immunity from prosecution in exchange for testifying.

In addition to his well-known activities, Liman served the New York bar. As president, he helped revive the New York Legal Aid Society in the 1980s, pursued the goal of prison reform, chaired New York's Capital Defender Office, and served on state commissions devoted to justice administration and sentencing procedures.

**CROSS REFERENCES**
Iran-Contra

## LOBBY

See Lobbying Organizations in this volume's Appendix

## LOSS, LOUIS

Louis Loss, hailed as the father of securities law, died on December 13, 1997, at the age of eighty-three. As an attorney, author, and professor, Loss made groundbreaking contributions to the regulation of the securities and financial markets. From the late 1930s until 1952, he served first as a staff lawyer and later as associate general counsel of the federal Securities and Exchange Commission (SEC). During these years Loss developed the expertise that would define his authoritative 1951 treatise *Securities Regulation*, since revised and still the leading book on the subject. From his writing to his teaching at Harvard Law School, he left an important legacy: courts cited his work widely, his students became Supreme Court justices, and his ideas led to new applications of antifraud provisions in the federal securities laws.

Born on June 11, 1914, in Lancaster, Pennsylvania, Loss was the son of Russian immigrants. Already determined to become a lawyer by his teenage years, he spent his free time watching attorneys in practice at the county courthouse. He earned his undergraduate degree from the University of Pennsylvania in 1934 and his law degree from Yale Law School in 1937. Yet despite his qualifications, the prospect of being hired by a large Wall Street firm was unlikely: as a Jew, Loss knew such doors were closed to him in an era rife with anti-Semitism.

Instead, Loss joined the SEC, then a fledgling organization only three years old. Created under authority of the Securities Exchange Act of 1934 (15 U.S.C.A. § 78a et seq.), the SEC's mission was to provide full disclosure to investors and protect them against malpractice in the securities and financial markets. In the SEC's early years, as it struggled to apply the broadly worded federal law, the young staff attorney soon brought innovations. By 1939 he had helped to establish what became known as the "shingle theory," a principle that held that brokerage firms could be sanctioned for failing to treat their customers fairly. In 1952, he left the SEC, having risen to the rank of associate general counsel.

Loss's contributions to securities law continued during the next three decades. While working at the SEC and teaching part time at

## LOUIS LOSS

| | |
|---|---|
| 1914 | Born in Lancaster, Pennsylvania |
| 1937 | Earned law degree from Yale Law School |
| 1937 | Joined the Securities Exchange Commission (SEC) |
| 1939 | Helped to establish the "shingle theory" |
| 1951 | Published *Securities Regulation* |
| 1952 | Left the SEC; became a professor at Harvard |
| 1961 | Declined offer to become chairman on the SEC; updated *Securities Regulation* |
| 1989 | Updated *Securities Regulation* with Joel Seligman |
| 1997 | Died in Cambridge, Massachusetts |

Yale and George Washington law schools, he began writing his first major work, *Securities Regulation*. Published in 1951, the treatise was the first comprehensive analysis of existing securities law, and in time became a classic in its field; he updated it in 1961 and again in a 1989 edition co-authored by Joel Seligman, dean of the University of Arizona law school. So consuming and ambitious was this work that a colleague once jokingly remarked that Loss had given up his rights under the Thirteenth Amendment—the constitutional amendment that ended slavery.

Although Loss regarded *Securities Regulation* as his greatest accomplishment, his career had many achievements. In 1952 he became a professor at Harvard and shortly thereafter helped draft a uniform securities law that was adopted by thirty states. In 1961 he declined an offer by President John F. Kennedy to become chairman of the SEC. He remained at Harvard, becoming the William Nelson Cromwell Professor of Law, and teaching such students as future U.S. Supreme Court Justices Ruth Bader Ginsburg, Anthony M. Kennedy, Antonin Scalia, and David Souter. In the 1970s, Loss directed an attempt to completely revise federal securities law under one comprehensive statute:

the effort ultimately produced a seven-hundred-page bill that Congress failed to approve, but to which courts have frequently referred in order to interpret the maze of existing laws. Indeed, citations to his various works appear in more than one thousand court decisions.

Loss's impact on securities regulation extended beyond his authoritative treatises and attempts at codifying laws. One of his most significant contributions came in the area of antifraud enforcement: he helped develop theories that led to the first prosecutions of insider trading—the offense of buying or selling corporate stock by exploiting access to information that is not available to the public. Yet even with such endeavors behind him, his imagination was restless. At the age of sixty-nine, he served as co-editor of a treatise on Japanese securities regulation.

He died in Cambridge, Massachusetts.

**CROSS REFERENCES**
Securities and Exchange Commission

## MURDER

The unlawful killing of another human being without justification or excuse.

### Diane Zamora Case

A jury in Fort Worth, Texas, closed one chapter in a long-running, high-profile murder case involving former military academy cadets. Diane Zamora was convicted of capital murder after confessing to the killing of sixteen-year-old Adrienne Jones in a crime of sexual revenge committed with her fiancé, David Graham. Nine months passed before Zamora and Graham, both eighteen years old, admitted to killing Jones. However, at trial, Zamora recanted her confession and blamed Graham. This tactic failed, and she received a life sentence.

In 1995 the couple had high profiles among Fort Worth teens. Their scholastic and athletic gifts were noted in the local press, and each had won a coveted place in a military academy—Zamora at the U.S. Naval Academy, and Graham at the U.S. Air Force Academy. They were engaged to be married. But after Graham had sex with a sophomore girl and confessed the infidelity to his fiancé, they agreed that it was necessary to restore "purity" to their relationship. Graham took Jones on a date with Zamora hidden in the trunk of his car. When they stopped in a desolate field, Zamora emerged and she and Graham attacked Jones.

According to nearly identical statements given to police, the plan quickly went awry. Graham lunged for Jones's neck, but "realized too late that all those quick, painless snaps seen in the movies were just your usual Hollywood stunts." Zamora took over, cracking the girl's skull with a barbell weight. Bloody but still alive, Jones crawled out the window of the car, quickly pursued by Graham with a pistol. He fired twice, once between the eyes. Later, the coroner could not tell whether the cause of death was the blows or the shot.

The pair hid the murder for almost nine months, going away to their respective military academies. But, in a late-night talk in August 1996 with her dormitory roommates, Zamora described the murder. After her roommates told school officials, police interrogated the couple. Zamora at first insisted the story told to her roommates was false, and then traveled to visit Graham. He backed her up, subsequently failed a polygraph test and, on September 6, confessed. Arrested the same day, Zamora also confessed. Police searched the attic of Graham's family home where they recovered the handgun and the barbell weights.

Zamora then changed her story, alleging that Graham had not only committed the murder but had pressured her into taking the blame for him. NBC television created a movie titled *Love's Deadly Triangle: The Texas Cadet Murder*, scheduled for broadcast in February 1997. Zamora's attorneys sought to bar its broadcast in Fort Worth on grounds that it would jeopardize a fair trial, but a judge rejected the plea.

In early 1998, Zamora was tried on charges of capital murder, kidnapping, assault, and false imprisonment. She focused her defense on her fiancé's character in order to establish him as the killer. Defense attorneys painted Graham as

abusive, alleging that Graham choked Zamora and stuck a gun between her legs during sex. In tearful testimony, she denied participating in the killing. Prosecutors, however, said she was a "sociopath," and built their case on the confessions and evidence seized from Graham's home.

Lead prosecutor Mike Parrish showed jurors two daily planners found in Zamora's dormitory room. In one, the date of Jones's murder had been circled; her name and address appeared in the other.

On February 17, after six hours of deliberation, the seven-man, five-woman jury returned a verdict of guilty on the most serious charge, but not guilty on the lesser charges. Jones's parents and two brothers spoke in court about their loss. Prosecutors had not sought the death penalty, so Zamora automatically received a life

sentence with eligibility for parole in forty years.

Meanwhile, Graham's own capital murder trial was pending.

### Louise Woodward Case

The murder trial of nineteen-year-old English nanny Louise Woodward in Boston drew international attention. Woodward was accused of shaking to death the eight-month-old infant she was baby-sitting. Her conviction for second degree murder in October 1997 provoked outrage. Woodward's supporters, particularly in England, denounced the verdict and criticized the jury. In November, Middlesex County Superior Court Judge Hiller Zobel provoked further controversy through his extraordinary intervention. Correcting what he called a miscarriage of justice, Zobel reduced Woodward's conviction to involuntary manslaughter and commuted her sentence. Both sides appealed.

A resident of the small town of Elton, England, Woodward came to the United States in November 1996 to work as a nanny. Two Boston physicians, Sunil and Deborah Eappen, hired her to care for their sons Matthew, an infant, and Brendan, age two. On February 4, 1997, Woodward called the police to report that Matthew was having trouble breathing. Paramedics arrived to find that the baby had a fractured skull and that his eyes were bulging—a sign exhibited by infants who have been vigorously shaken. Four days after being placed on life support, Matthew died from internal bleeding. The autopsy also revealed a month-old wrist fracture. Woodward was arrested and charged with second-degree murder. She was held without bond in a women's detention center after prosecutors said she was likely to skip bail.

At trial in October, both sides presented different theories of what had caused the death. Prosecutors painted a portrait of a normal, healthy infant who had been killed by his enraged caretaker when he would not stop crying. They introduced forensic evidence showing that the injuries were consistent with abuse, as well as a police report stating that Woodward had admitted to shaking and dropping the baby and tossing him on a bed. Woodward took the stand, where she denied making the admission to police and testified to having only been "a little rough" with the infant. The defense proposed alternative explanations for the skull fracture. Forensic expert and attorney Barry Sheck advanced two possibilities: Eappen may have had a preexisting medical condition, Sheck said, or his two-year-old brother many have inflicted the injury.

As the trail ended, defense attorneys took a controversial legal gamble that ultimately backfired. They persuaded Judge Zobel—over the strenuous objection of prosecutors—not to allow the jury to consider the lesser charge of manslaughter. Confident of their case, defense attorneys believed that this all-or-nothing strategy would succeed because a reasonable doubt existed as to Woodward's motives in handling the baby. Under Massachusetts law, a conviction for second-degree murder requires finding that the defendant acted with malice; the lesser charge of manslaughter does not. But on October 30, the jury returned a verdict of guilty.

An uproar followed. Marchers outside the courtroom, carrying signs reading "IQ tests for

jurors," faced off in confrontations with anti-Woodward protesters. The trial also sparked public discussion over standards in child care, including numerous debates in the media and a well-publicized national conference.

In early November, both sides made presentencing motions. Defense attorneys assailed prosecutors for withholding until late in the trial the existence of autopsy photographs, which were never shown to jurors. The photos revealed that the fatal skull fracture had occurred prior to February 4 and hence was not caused by anything Woodward did that day, they argued. If the photos had been divulged earlier, they might not have put Woodward on the stand; however, they acknowledged that their risky strategy regarding jury instructions had been a mistake. For these reasons, and because of prejudicial pretrial publicity, they moved for the court to acquit Woodward, hold a new trial, or reduce the verdict. Prosecutors opposed the motions, saying Woodward should not receive a second chance. Criticizing her for showing no remorse over the killing, prosecutor Gerard Leone, Jr., recommended the maximum state sentence of fifteen to twenty years in prison.

On November 10, the judge announced his surprising decision to reduce Woodward's conviction. In his view she had caused the baby's fatal bleeding by handling him roughly. But he did not believe that she had done so with malice. "I view the evidence as disclosing confusion, fright, and bad judgment," he wrote, "rather than rage or malice." Consequently he ruled that she was guilty of involuntary manslaughter, the offense of using excessive and unjustified force that result in death. He also commuted Woodward's sentence, ruling that she already served her debt to society by spending 279 days in jail since her arrest.

As authority for changing the verdict, Zobel invoked Massachusetts Rule of Criminal Procedure 25(b)(2). This little-used rule allows judges to change a guilty verdict to a similar finding of guilty on any offense charged in the indictment. Noting that it is designed to redress unfair verdicts, Zobel acknowledged that precedent required that it be used sparingly and cautiously as a "safety valve" when "a lesser verdict more comports with justice." The decision, which quoted John Adams and Oliver Wendell Holmes, Jr., also seemed designed to rebut the sharp criticism directed at the U.S. justice system over the trial.

Both sides immediately announced that they would appeal—defense attorneys in an attempt to exonerate Woodward completely, and prosecutors to see her murder conviction reinstated. State authorities kept Woodward's passport to ensure that she would remain in the country pending the outcome. Reaction in the legal community was mixed, with judges and scholars divided over the appropriateness of Zobel's decision. The Eappen family and prosecutors criticized it severely, whereas defense attorneys and relatives of Woodward praised its courage. On June 16, 1998, the Massachusetts Supreme Judicial Court upheld Zobel's decision and allowed Woodward to return to her native England.

## NATIVE AMERICAN RIGHTS

### Alaska v. Native Village of Venetie Tribal Government

The legal status of Native Americans and the land on which they live has generated controversy since the early nineteenth century. The U.S. Supreme Court has had to make numerous decisions on Native American rights. Its most recent decision, *Alaska v. Native Village of Venetie Tribal Government*, __U.S.__, 118 S. Ct. 948, __L. Ed. 2d__ (1998), resolved questions surrounding the Alaska Native Claims Act (ANCSA) (42 U.S.C.A. § 1601 et seq.), a 1971 law that conveyed 44 million acres of land to more than 200 native villages. The ruling made clear that Alaskan tribes, with one exception, do not have the legal status they formerly possessed when they resided on Indian reservations. Therefore, the tribes cannot assert governmental jurisdiction over their lands.

The village of Venetie is located above the Arctic Circle and is the home of the Neets' aii Gwich'in Indians. In 1943 the U.S. government created a reservation for the tribe out of land surrounding Venetie and another village, Arctic Village. The land, about the size of Delaware, remained a reservation until ANCSA was enacted in 1971. ANCSA revoked all but one Indian reservation in Alaska and completely extinguished all aboriginal claims to Alaska land. In return, Congress authorized the transfer of almost one billion dollars and 44 million acres of Alaska land to state-chartered private corporations that were to be formed pursuant to the law. All shareholders of these corporations were required to be Native Alaskans. The ANCSA corporations received title to the transferred land in fee simple. No federal restrictions were placed on this land, and the corporations were free to sell the land to non-natives as they wished.

Two native corporations were established for Venetie and Arctic Village. In 1973 the Neets' aii Gwich'in, acting through these corporations, elected to take title to former reservation lands in return for foregoing monetary payments and transfers of non-reservation land authorized by ANCSA. The United States conveyed title in fee simple to the corporations, which then transferred title to the land to the Native Village of Venetie Tribal Government (the Tribe.)

In 1986 the Tribe notified the state of Alaska and the private contractor that was constructing a state-funded, public school in Venetie that they owed the Tribe $161,000 in taxes for conducting business activities on the Tribe's lands. Alaska filed suit in federal court, challenging the tax assessment. The district court ruled in favor of the state, finding that the Tribe's ANCSA lands were not Indian country within the meaning of 18 U.S.C.A § 1151(b), which provides that Indian country includes all "dependent Indian communities within the borders of the United States." Therefore, the Tribe did not have the power to impose a tax upon nonmembers of the Tribe. The Court of Appeals for the Ninth Circuit reversed, applying a balancing test that led the court to conclude that the land was Indian country (101 F.3d 1286 [9th Cir. 1996]).

The Supreme Court reversed the Ninth Circuit, rejecting the appellate court's balancing test approach. Justice Clarence Thomas, writing for a unanimous Court, stated that the key issue was whether the Tribe's land fell within the "dependent Indian communities" part of Section 1151. Since the enactment of Section 1151 in 1948, the Supreme Court had not been called on to interpret the term "dependent Indian communities." The Court now held that the term 'refers to a limited category of Indian lands that are neither reservations nor allotments." (Allotments are parcels of land created out of a diminished Indian reservation and held in trust by the federal government for the benefit of individual Indians.)

To be considered a dependent community, the lands must have been set aside by the federal government for the use of the Indians as Indian land and must be under federal superintendence. Thomas justified this interpretation by pointing out that in drafting Section 1151, Congress had copied virtually verbatim from the Court's decision in *United States v. Sandoval*, 231 U.S. 28, 34 S. Ct. 1, 58 L. Ed. 107 (1913). Therefore, the Court concluded that Congress believed a federal set-aside and a federal superintendence requirement must be met to qualify as a "dependent Indian community." The federal set-aside requirement ensures that the land is occupied by an Indian community, and the federal superintendence requirement guarantees that the Indian community is sufficiently dependent on the federal government that the federal government and "the Indians involved, rather than the States, are to exercise primary jurisdiction over the land in question."

Thomas rejected the Tribe's argument that the terms "dependent Indian communities" refer to political dependence, and that Indian country exists wherever a federally recognized tribe owns land. Thomas found that prior decisions of the Supreme Court dealing with Indian country indicated both that the federal government "must take some action setting apart the land for the use of the Indians 'as such,' and that it is the land in question, and not merely the Indian tribe inhabiting it, that must be under the superintendence of the Federal Government."

Turning to the Tribe's ANCSA lands, the Court ruled that neither of the two requirements was satisfied. After ANCSA, the Tribe's lands are not set apart for the use of Indians nor are they under the superintendence of the federal government. As to the federal set-aside requirement, ANCSA revoked the existing Venetie Reservation and all but one other reservation in Alaska. Thomas saw this congressional action as a marked departure "from its traditional practice of setting aside Indian lands." The transfer of the lands to the two Native corporations was done without placing any significant restrictions on how the land was to be used. These Native corporations, "can immediately convey former reservation lands to non-Natives, and such corporations are not restricted to using those lands for Indian purposes." Therefore, the federal set-aside requirement was not met.

Thomas also found that the Tribes could not meet the federal superintendence requirement. ANCSA had revoked the Venetie Reservation and Congress had stated its intent to avoid a "lengthy wardship or trusteeship" § 1601(b). After ANCSA, the federal government's protection of the Tribe's land was, in the Court's view, "essentially limited to a statutory declaration that the land is exempt from adverse possession claims, real property taxes, and certain judgment as long as it has not been sold, leased, or developed." These protections did not, however, reach the "level of superintendence over the Indians' land that existed in our prior cases." In those cases, the federal government "actively controlled the land in question, effectively acting as a guardian for the Indians." Finally, Thomas pointed out that the federal government had transferred ANCSA lands to state-chartered and state-regulated private business corporations, "hardly a choice that comports with a desire to retain federal superintendence over the land."

The Tribe had argued that federal superintendence did exist because the federal government provided health, social, welfare, and economic programs to the Tribe. Thomas rejected this argument, ruling that the "mere provisions" of social programs cannot support a finding of Indian country. The health, education, and welfare benefits were "merely forms of general aid" that were not land-related protections indicating sufficient federal government control over the Tribe's lands. Finally, the Court noted that one of the primary purposes of ANCSA was to foster greater tribal self-determination and to renounce the past paternalistic policies of the Bureau of Indian Affairs.

Following the decision, Alaska Governor Tony Knowles announced the formation of a commission to examine Indian self-government issues. The litigation had produced divisions in the state, for if the appeal had been in the Tribe's favor, other Alaska tribes would have sought to assert jurisdiction over hunting, fishing, law enforcement, and environmental regulations within their lands. The states feared that such an outcome would have produced a "crazy quilt of jurisdictional enclaves."

## Indian Gaming

Native American gaming rights have been controversial since 1987, when the U.S. Supreme Court limited the power of the states to apply their gambling laws to Indian gaming (*California v. Cabazon Band of Mission Indians*, 480 U.S. 202, 107 S. Ct. 1083, 94 L. Ed. 2d 244) In *Cabazon*, the Court addressed whether the Cabazon and Morongo bands of Mission Indians could conduct high stakes bingo games on their reservation in violation of California law. The Court held that the tribe's activities were beyond the reach of state law, since "[s]tate regulation would impermissibly infringe on tribal government."

The High Court's decision was based on the fact that Congress had not acted to specifically apply state gambling laws to Indian lands. In 1988, in response to *Cabazon*, Congress enacted the Indian Gaming Regulatory Act (IGRA) (25 U.S.C.A. § 2701 et seq.), creating a framework for the state regulation of gambling on Indian land. One of the stated purposes of the IGRA is to provide a basis for the "operation of gaming by Indian tribes as a means of promoting tribal economic development, self-sufficiency, and strong tribal government."

The IGRA requires that states conduct good faith negotiations with Indian tribes to allow them to operate gambling that is not otherwise prohibited by state law. The IGRA separates gaming into three classes, which is subject to varying degrees of regulation. Class I gaming include social games for prizes of minimal value or gaming in connection with tribal ceremonies. Class II gaming includes card games, bingo and bingo-like games. Class III gaming includes slot machines, casino games, banking card games, dog racing, and lotteries. Class III gaming can only be conducted on Indian lands pursuant to a gambling compact between the tribe and the state. The IGRA also established the National Indian Gaming Commission (NIGC), which oversees all Indian gaming, as part of the U.S. Department of the Interior. Tribes wishing to open casinos or operate slot machines or horse and dog racing tracks must first obtain approval from the NIGC.

As envisioned by the IGRA, gaming has been a successful means of economic development for certain Indian tribes. The NIGC estimated that in 1995, Indian gaming revenues nationwide exceeded $5 billion dollars a year and were growing by $1 billion dollars annually. Casinos on reservations located near large metropolitan areas generally enjoy the most success. For example, one of the nation's largest casinos, Mystic Lake, is operated by Minnesota's Mdewakanton Dakota tribe just twenty-five miles south of the Minneapolis–St. Paul metropolitan area. Opened in 1992, the Mystic Lake Casino has been hugely profitable, with income for each of the approximately one hundred and fifty tribal members estimated at $600,000 per year. Operating a casino does not ensure financial success for a tribe, however. In 1997 the General Accounting Office estimated that although approximately two hundred tribes operated nearly three hundred gaming facilities, eight of those facilities accounted for forty percent of annual tribal gaming revenue.

The success of Indian gaming for some tribes has created conflict with non-Indians who believe that the tribes are unfairly refusing to share their revenue with local and state government. Recent disputes involve attempts at the state and federal levels to tax Indian gaming revenues; gambling compacts between tribal and state governments; and tribal removal of off-reservation lands from local property tax rolls.

Indian casinos built on reservations or on land belonging to a particular tribe are not required to pay federal, state, or local taxes on gaming revenues, although tribal casino employees pay state and federal income taxes. In June 1997, U.S. Representative Bill Archer (R-Tex.), chairman of the House Ways and Means Committee, introduced a five-year, $85 billion tax cut proposal (eventually passed by Congress as H.R. 2014), which included a five-year $1.9 billion tax on Indian tribes' commercial ventures, including casinos. Archer's proposal was defeated after a coalition of Republican and Democratic opponents argued that the bill violated the tribes' constitutional right to tribal sovereignty.

In most states, tribal agreements with state governments do not require revenue sharing, although some tribes make payments to local governments for support services. For example, Connecticut is expected to receive about $247 million in 1998 from its two tribes, in return for the exclusive right to run casinos in that state. In 1997 Michigan tribes paid state and local governments about $44 million or ten percent of their gambling revenues. In contrast, Minnesota's eleven tribes pay only $150,000 per year to the state, and until 1998, Wisconsin's eleven

tribes gave the state only $350,000 per year. Wisconsin tribes operate under seven-year gambling compacts that began to expire in 1998. Wisconsin Governor Tommy Thompson announced that in renegotiating the compacts with the tribes, the state would seek yearly gambling fees of up to $85 million, or about one-third of the tribes' casino profits. Wisconsin state senator Robert Welch (R-Redgranite) threatened to levy a fifty percent tax on winnings at Indian casinos if Wisconsin tribes did not resolve their differences with the state on new gaming compacts.

In February 1998, Wisconsin reached agreements on two compacts under which the Mole Lake Band of Lake Superior Chippewa tribe agreed to give the state $1.29 million over five years and the Lac Courte Oreilles Band of Chippewa agreed to pay $2.1 million over five years. The governor also sought to include nongambling issues such as treaty fishing rights and environmental regulation in the negotiations but later agreed to discuss treaty rights separately from the gaming compacts.

Government officials argue that the success of tribal casinos has created new burdens for local governments, which must rely on voluntary payments from the tribes to pay for additional police and other services. For example, officials of Scott County, Minnesota, in which the Mdewakanton Dakota's Mystic Lake Casino is located, asked the tribe to contribute $2.3 million

annually to defray the costs of increased road repair and law enforcement caused by activity at the casino. At one point, the county considered building tollbooths on county roads leading to the casino. The tribe eventually agreed to pay $200,000 a year, which the county grudgingly accepted. Although county officials have accused the tribe of greed, tribal officials counter that the casino employs nearly four thousand local residents and brings about $100 million to the area's economy annually.

Conflict between the Mdewakanton Dakota tribe and local officials escalated further when the tribe outbid non-Indian developers for valuable off-reservation real estate in the area, which the tribe said it would use for a shopping center and other development. The tribe has petitioned the Bureau of Indian Affairs (BIA) to put this land in trust, which would take it off local property tax rolls and exempt it from local zoning restrictions. The BIA frequently approves tribal requests to put off-reservation lands in trust but such lands are generally used for building housing.

In February 1998, the U.S. Supreme Court heard arguments in a case addressing the extent to which Indians should be able to take property off local tax rolls (*Leech Lake Band of Chippewa Indians v. Cass County, Minn.*, 108 F. 3d 820 [8th Cir. 1997], *cert. granted, Cass County, Minn. v. Leech Lake Band of Chippewa Indians,* ___U.S. ___, 118 S. Ct. 361, 139 L. Ed. 2d 281

[1997]). The case began when the Minnesota Leech Lake Band of Chippewa bought back twenty-one parcels of land that had been taken from them as part of a federal government movement to break up reservation lands in the 1800s. Some of the reacquired land was left undeveloped by the tribe, while other parcels were used for tribal facilities. In 1993 Cass County officials decided to tax the land in the amount of $64,000. The band paid the taxes under protest and then sued to recover the funds and obtain an order protecting itself from future taxation. The U.S. District Court for the District of Minnesota ruled in the county's favor, and the tribe appealed. A three-judge panel of the U.S. Court of Appeals for the Eight Circuit reversed the lower court's ruling as to eight of the parcels, which had been reacquired by the tribe after being sold to non-Indians for lumbering or distributed to non-Indians as homestead lands. The county appealed, arguing that Indian-held land should be considered taxable if it can be sold. Although land held in trust for tribes cannot be sold without federal government approval, the tribe argued that placing land in trust is a complex process that can take years, and that the property should not be subject to taxes in the meantime. A decision in the case is expected in mid-1998.

Technological advances in gambling have created new frontiers in Indian gaming. For example, in September 1997, Wisconsin Attorney General James Doyle filed a lawsuit against UniStar Entertainment, Inc., a company that provides Internet gambling services to the Coeur d'Alene, an Idaho-based Indian tribe. UniStar operates the Internet game, U.S. Lottery, for the tribe. The game is available to residents of thirty-three states and the District of Columbia.

Doyle brought the lawsuit in Wisconsin's Dane County Circuit Court, claiming that Wisconsin's anti-gambling laws prohibit accepting bets through the Internet and that Indian gaming laws require that the game be located on reservation land. The tribe claimed it is authorized to conduct the game under its compact with the state of Idaho and that the actual Internet servers and other computer and telephone equipment involved are located on reservation land.

The defendants moved the suit to federal court on the grounds that the game in question is regulated by the IGRA. In February 1998, U.S. District Judge John C. Shabaz dropped the Coeur d'Alene tribe from the lawsuit, ruling that Wisconsin has no control over Internet gambling by Indian tribes because they are sovereign nations (*State of Wisconsin v. Coeur d'Alene*, 97-C-711-S [W.D. Wis.]). The court retained UniStar as a defendant in the suit, however, finding that the company has sufficient connection with Wisconsin to be tried in federal court there. Missouri Attorney General Jeremiah Nixon began similar litigation against the Coeur d'Alene tribe in 1997.

Critics of Indian gaming on the Internet say that the federal government will have to step in and end the practice. In 1997 U.S. Senator John Kyl (R Ariz.) introduced a bill that would ban all gambling on the Internet (S. 474). The legislation was under consideration in 1998.

**CROSS REFERENCES**
Gaming

## PAROLE

The conditional release of a person convicted of a crime prior to the expiration of that person's term of imprisonment, subject to both the supervision of the correctional authorities during the remainder of the term and a resumption of the imprisonment upon violation of the conditions imposed.

### Spencer v. Kemna

A prisoner who has been released on parole may be returned to prison for violating conditions of the parole. However, the prisoner must be given due process through a parole revocation proceeding. If the parole is revoked, the prisoner may seek judicial review of the decision. The U.S. Supreme Court, in *Spencer v. Kemna, Superintendent, Western Missouri Correctional Center*, __U.S.__, 118 S. Ct. 978, __L. Ed. 2d__ (1998), made clear, however, that if the prisoner's sentence expires before the court rules on the revocation decision, the legal action must be dismissed.

In October 1990, Randy G. Spencer began serving concurrent three-year sentences in Missouri for felony stealing and burglary convictions. In April 1992 he was released on parole but in September 1992 the Missouri Board of Probation and Parole, after a hearing, issued an order revoking Spencer's parole. The order concluded that Spencer had violated three of the conditions for his parole by failing to obey all laws, possessing a controlled substance, and possessing a dangerous weapon. Spencer had been arrested by Kansas City police officers in June 1992 for allegedly smoking crack cocaine and sexually assaulting a woman by threatening her

with a screwdriver. Spencer admitted smoking crack cocaine but did not respond to the allegation of rape.

A parole revocation report summarizing the police report recommended that Spencer be placed in a drug treatment center rather than returned to prison. However, a second report, prepared after the prosecutor declined to file charges on the June 1992 incident, concluded that Spencer had violated the conditions of his parole and that parole should be revoked. The parole revocation order did not mention the second report.

After being returned to prison, Spencer sought to invalidate the revocation order, claiming that he had failed to receive due process. Missouri state courts rejected his appeals, and Spencer filed a petition for a writ of habeas corpus in Missouri federal district court on April 1, 1993, just over six months before the expiration of his three-year sentence. Over Spencer's objections, the state of Missouri was granted extensions to file its response to the petition, not filing it until mid-July. Spencer then filed a motion asking the court to expedite the process. In August 1993, Spencer was re-released on parole and on October 16, 1993, his term of imprisonment expired. The district court, in February 1994, finally noted Spencer's July 1993 motion but did nothing until August 1995, when it dismissed the habeas petition because Spencer's sentence had expired.

Spencer appealed to the Eighth Circuit Court of Appeals, asking that his case be reinstated and that the court rule on the merits of his due process claims. The Eighth Circuit affirmed the district court, concluding that Spencer's case was moot because he had suffered no "collateral consequences" of the revocation order, 91 F.3d 1114 (8th Cir. 1996). (By the time the appeals court considered Spencer's appeal, he was back in prison, serving a seven-year sentence for attempted felony stealing. He is scheduled to be released on parole in January 1999.) Absent such collateral consequences, Spencer did not have standing to press his case because the Constitution's case-or-controversy requirement mandates that a litigant has a stake in the outcome of the case the litigant brings. Once Spencer's sentence expired, the court found he had nothing at stake.

The U.S. Supreme Court took Spencer's appeal because the Second and Ninth Circuits did not agree with the Eighth Circuit's ruling, finding that there were "collateral consequences" in a parole revocation that permitted a person to continue the lawsuit after the expiration of the criminal sentence.

Justice Antonin Scalia, writing for the majority, held that the Eighth Circuit's reading of the Supreme Court's decision in *Lane v. Williams*, 455 U.S. 624, 102 S. Ct. 1322, 71 L. Ed. 2d 508 (1982), was the correct interpretation. Prior to *Lane*, the Court had established that a convict or parolee who was challenging his conviction, must show, once the sentence has expired, some concrete and continuing injury other than the now-ended incarceration or parole, in order to continue the lawsuit. These injuries—collateral consequences—have been easy to show, with the Supreme Court going beyond obvious injuries such as the deprivation of the right to vote, to hold office, to serve on a jury, or to engage in certain businesses, to more generalized and hypothetical consequences.

The *Lane* decision, however, refused to extend the presumption of collateral consequences to the revocation of parole. Justice Scalia noted that, under *Lane*, "it was not enough that the parole violations found by the revocation decision would enable the parole board to deny respondent's parole in the future." In fact, parole violations cannot be used against a person unless that person again violates the law, is returned to prison, and becomes eligible for parole.

Based on the *Lane* holding, the Court reaffirmed that a presumption of collateral consequences allowed Spencer to go forward with this habeas petition. Spencer was required to specify concrete injuries-in-fact that were attributable to his parole revocation. Justice Scalia

reviewed and rejected four asserted injuries advanced by Spencer. First, Spencer claimed that the revocation could be used against him in a future parole hearing. The Court found this assertion "a possibility rather than a certainty or even a probability." Under Missouri law, the prior revocation would be just one factor for the parole board to consider in making its decision. In addition, the board had almost unlimited discretion in whether to grant parole release. Therefore, this alleged collateral consequence was uncertain at best.

Spencer also argued that the revocation order could be used to increase his sentence in a future sentencing proceeding. Scalia rejected this argument, noting that it was contingent upon Spencer "violating the law, being caught and convicted." Thus, Spencer was able to prevent this possibility by obeying the law.

Scalia rejected Spencer's other two claims: that the parole revocation could be used to impeach him should he be a witness in a future criminal or civil proceeding; or could be used against him directly, should he appear as a defendant in a criminal proceeding. Justice Scalia concluded that it is "purely a matter of speculation whether such an appearance will ever occur." In addition, it was far from certain that a prosecutor or examining attorney would use the parole revocation to impeach Spencer. There was uncertainty in Missouri law that such information could be legally admitted into evidence. Based on the speculative nature of Spencer's assertions, the Court found no collateral consequences. The dismissal of his appeal was correct.

Justice John Paul Stevens, in a dissenting opinion, argued that the rape allegation contained in the factual findings gave Spencer a stake in the outcome of the lawsuit that continued after the expiration of his sentence. He could not agree that "an interest in vindicating one's reputation is constitutionally insufficient to qualify as a 'personal stake' in the outcome."

**CROSS REFERENCES**
Criminal Law; Due Process of Law; Standing

# PATERNITY

The state or condition of a father; the relationship of a father.

## Claim Over Extramarital Child

In January 1998, the Minnesota Court of Appeals ruled on an unusual paternity battle (*In *re the Paternity of B.J.H.*, 573 N.W.2d 99). Commonly, paternity lawsuits are brought by women to establish that a man has fathered her child and thus has a financial responsibility to the child. Yet in an odd twist, the Minnesota case involved a husband and wife *opposing* the paternity claim brought by the wife's ex-lover. They argued that the husband should be adjudicated father of the child despite biological evidence that clearly established the ex-lover as the father. The appeals court sided with the ex-lover.

Almost a year after her marriage, the wife began a romantic relationship with A.J.S. (as is common in paternity cases, the court referred to the parties only by their initials). One year into this affair, the wife gave birth to a child. Shortly thereafter, A.J.S. underwent blood tests that showed his paternity index exceeded 99 percent. All was well for a time, with A.J.S admitting the deed to his family and even bringing them into contact with the child and the wife. Back in the marital home, the husband cared for the child as if it were his own.

For reasons that were disputed, the wife later cut off contact with A.J.S. and refused to allow him to see the child. A.J.S. filed suit to establish paternity. He cited the blood test results as meeting the burden of proof under Minnesota law, which states that a man whose paternity index equals or exceeds 99 percent is presumed to be the biological father (Minn. Stat. § 257.55, subd. 1[f]).

Opposing A.J.S.'s suit, the wife and husband sought to have the husband declared the child's father. They cited Minn. Stat. § 257.55, subd. 1(a), which declares that the husband of a woman who conceives or gives birth to a child is presumptively the child's father. They also cited the so-called "best interests" factors, which guide courts in evaluating what would be best for the child (Minn. Stat § 518.17, subd. 1[a]). As the court battle ensued, the district court appointed a *guardian ad litem*—a trained appointee charged with overseeing the child's welfare and making recommendations to the court. The *guardian ad litem* recommended that A.J.S. be adjudicated the child's father.

The district court applied the best interests of the child and other factors, but found in favor of A.J.S. Although the wife was awarded sole legal and physical custody of the child, A.J.S. was adjudicated the child's father and granted visitation rights.

The couple appealed. On appeal, the couple argued that the district court had erred by favoring biological evidence over the child's best interests. Instead, they argued, it should have sought to promote stability for the child. Moreover, they claimed that preference should have been given to the husband because he was the primary parent and had a more intimate relationship with the child. Additionally, the court's decision was based on speculation, they argued. Finally, they asserted that it erred on various issues relating to evidence including the gathering of evidence, or discovery.

The Minnesota Court of Appeals dismissed each claim in the appeal. First, it ruled that the district court had not preferred A.J.S. to the husband based on biological criteria alone, but weighed many factors, including the child's best interests. In any event, it said, the best-interests factors were never intended to be *dispositive*—sufficient to settle such a dispute. Indeed, noted the court hypothetically, if it were to follow the couple's emphasis on promoting stability for the child, it would settle all paternity disputes by presuming that a woman's husband is her child's father. But it was impossible for it to automatically favor one paternity presumption over another.

The appeals court was also held that the district court had properly discounted the husband's role as primary parent and his intimacy with the child. If these factors were determinative, custodial parents would simply terminate a putative father's contact with the child as the wife had done to A.J.S. Nor would the appeals court agree that the district court's decision was based on speculation. To the contrary, A.J.S. had been proven the biological father to a high degree of certainty.

Finally, the appeals court found no basis for the couple's several complaints about discovery and evidence. Most notably, it ruled that no error had been committed when the district court denied the couple access to A.J.S.'s medical and financial data. This denial was proper because it did not impact on the court's inquiry into the child's best interests; would have led to undue delay and costs; was unlikely to have produced evidence admissible in the paternity stage of the trial; and the court, in any event, ordered him to produce financial information for the support stage of the proceedings.

### Court Bars Evidence Disproving Paternity

A state court refused to allow blood test evidence that proved a man was not a child's biological father (*William L., III, v. Cindy E.L.*, W. Va.___, 495 S.E.2d 836 [1997]). The validity of the evidence was not in doubt. Its admissibility,

however, was part of a broader question: can a man who knew he might not be the father of his wife's son, yet who acted as the boy's father for a period of four years, later disprove paternity? The West Virginia Supreme Court of Appeals ruled he could not. The court determined that allowing the man to disprove paternity was not in the child's best interests.

The issues in the case arose out of a divorce action. William L., III, married Cindy E.L. in 1984, and a son, James L., was born in 1987. The couple divorced in 1992. At this point, William L. filed suit alleging that the paternity of the child was uncertain. Blood test results subsequently established that he was not the boy's father. To evaluate the case, the circuit court of Kanawha County, West Virginia, appointed a family law master—a special representative of the court who conducts inquiries and issues a recommendation. Although finding that Cindy E.L.'s testimony was often conflicting and not trustworthy, the family law master nonetheless recommended against allowing William L. to introduce the evidence.

The circuit court agreed. Based on the length of the couple's relationship as husband and wife—during which William L. did not contest his paternity—the court disallowed the blood test evidence and permitted the presumption of William L.'s paternity to stand. He appealed, arguing that the family law master's recommendation was in error.

On appeal, the Supreme Court of Appeals of West Virginia first noted its own strict standard for review of a family law master's recommendation: only "clearly erroneous" recommendations, reached through an abuse of discretion, are subject to reversal. Next, the court turned to its own precedent. In 1989, it had held that a trial judge should refuse to admit blood tests if the man in question "has held himself out to be the father of the child for a sufficient period of time" such that disproof of paternity "would result in undeniable harm to the child." But an exception existed in cases where fraudulent conduct prevented the putative father from questioning paternity. William L. argued that his ex-wife had fraudulently and intentionally refused to identify the actual father, preventing him from challenging paternity.

On December 17, 1997, the court ruled against William L., in part because he did not present a transcript including the family law master's recommendations, without which the court was unwilling to find them clearly erroneous. More importantly, William L. had known he might not be the child's biological father for four years before he acted to contest paternity. The Supreme Court of Appeals found that preventing William L.'s attempt to deny paternity after accepting fatherhood for years best preserved the child's interests.

In dissent, Justice Elliott E. Maynard argued that despite "scholarship coupled with compassion," the majority's opinion was overly broad and would produce harsh results. Justice Maynard concluded that fairness required allowing the admission of blood tests regardless of how long the nonbiological father had cared for the child. Rebutting that view in an opinion that concurred with the majority, Chief Justice Margaret L. Workman contended that the dissent viewed "the law solely in shades of black and white" whereas the majority had more subtly enforced principles of sound public policy by protecting the interests of children.

**CROSS REFERENCES**
Child Custody; Children's Rights; Child Support; Visitation Rights

## PHYSICIANS AND SURGEONS

### Informed Consent

On December 9, 1997, the Washington Court of Appeals ruled that a surgeon was not required to disclose his inexperience with a surgical procedure before an operation (*Whiteside v. Lukson*, 89 Wash. App. 109, 947 P.Zd 1263 [Div. 3]). The issue on appeal concerned *informed consent*: the legal requirement that a surgeon inform a patient of the nature and risks of a given medical procedure. The plaintiff sued partly on the grounds that the surgeon had failed to tell her he had previously practiced the technique only on pigs. The trial court rejected her claim, and the appeals court affirmed the decision. The court followed a traditional model of analysis for determining informed consent, refusing to adopt a broader method of analysis used in other jurisdictions.

In November 1990, Dr. Robert J. Lukson informed his patient, Rosetta Whiteside, that she needed to have her gallbladder removed. A month later, Dr. Lukson obtained Whiteside's consent to perform a procedure called laparoscopic cholecystectomy. At that time, Lukson had never performed the procedure on a human being. He had, however, studied it during a two-day class in November that included hands-on participation using three pigs. He did not inform her of this fact. The operation was delayed, during which time Dr. Lukson performed the procedure on two other patients without problem. However, during Whiteside's operation, Lukson misidentified and consequently damaged her bile duct, causing Whiteside to suffer a number of complications.

Whiteside sued Lukson for malpractice and lack of informed consent. The jury rejected the first claim. On the second claim, it determined that Lukson had failed to obtain Whiteside's informed consent because he did not tell her about his inexperience performing a laparoscopic cholecystectomy. However, the trial court intervened and reversed the jury verdict. It granted Lukson's motion for judgment notwithstanding the verdict—a judicial reversal used when a judge determines that the verdict had no reasonable support in fact or was contrary to law. Whiteside appealed.

The appeals court limited its review to one question: does a physician have a duty to disclose to the patient information about the physician's experience in providing a proposed treatment? Under Washington state law, a physician must advise the patient of material facts relating to the proposed treatment in order to secure informed consent (RCW 7.70.050(1)[a]). Washington's courts determine whether a fact is material by using the objective "reasonable patient" standard: the physician must disclose those facts a reasonable person would consider in deciding whether to consent to the proposed treatment, including the foreseeable risks, the availability and risks of alternative treatment, and the risk of no treatment at all. This standard considers only material facts related to the medical procedure itself.

As the court noted, however, other jurisdictions in the nation have taken a more expansive view of material facts. For example, courts in California and Louisiana have construed material fact to include the physician's conflicts of interest; Maryland has included the physician's HIV status; and Wisconsin has considered the physician's physical impairment and lack of experience as relevant. Citing law review articles from the 1990s, the court opined that a broad range of additional factors could theoretically be seen as material facts—from the physician's financial situation to medical school grades.

Washington courts, however, have not yet adopted the more expansive approach to determining the physician's duty, and the appeals court declined to be the first to do so. Instead, its decision was based on what it deemed the "traditional approach." It cited a 1992 Washington case in which the court expressly excluded the physician's duty to disclose his or her qualifications (*Thomas v. Wilfac, Inc.*, 65 Wash. App. 255, 828 P.2d 597, review denied, 119 Wash. 2d 1020, 838 P.2d 692 [1992]). Based on that decision, the appeals court held that a surgeon's lack of experience in performing a particular surgical procedure is not a material fact in determining liability and, as such, rejected Whiteside's appeal.

**CROSS REFERENCES**
Informed Consent; Malpractice

# PORNOGRAPHY

The representation in books, magazines, photographs, films, and other media of scenes of sexual behavior that are erotic or lewd and are designed to arouse sexual interest.

### Child Pornography Prevention Act

A child pornography law survived its first court challenge in *The Free Speech Coalition v. Reno*, 1997 WL 487758 (N.D. 1997). U.S. District Judge Samuel Conti of San Francisco upheld the constitutionality of the Child Pornography Prevention Act (CPPA) (Omnibus Consolidated Appropriations Act of 1997, Pub. L. No. 104-208, § 121, 110 Stat. 3009. Passed in 1996, the CPPA criminalizes sexually explicit images that appear to be of minors, even if the models in the images are adults. It was challenged by a sex industry lobbying group, The Free Speech Coalition, with support from leading civil liberties organizations. In rejecting the lawsuit, Judge Conti ruled that the law protects minors and society without harming free speech. The case was then appealed.

Congress enacted the CPPA in response to concerns that computer technology was increasing the production and distribution of child pornography. By 1995 federal child porn investigations reached an all-time high, and lawmakers believed that computers were to blame. First, home computer software had made it possible for images of adults to be merged with images of children, creating so-called virtual child porn. Second, the worldwide computer network known as the Internet had allowed for easy dissemination of images. In response, Senators Edward Kennedy (D-Mass.) and Orrin Hatch (R-Utah) proposed a novel solution: criminalizing any sexually explicit images that merely appeared to depict minors. With broad bipartisan support—including that of the Clinton administration—the CPPA was passed as part of the annual federal appropriations act.

The law provoked a court challenge from The Free Speech Coalition, a lobbying group representing six hundred adult entertainment producers and distributors. The group argued that the law's vagueness and broadness violated the First and Fifth Amendments to the U.S. Constitution. The suit further claimed that the law banned materials before they were even published—a form of censorship known as prior restraint that the U.S. Supreme Court has found unconstitutional. As a result, it would ban "materials that involve no actual children and that traditionally and logically have never been considered to be child pornography." The Electronic Frontier Foundation and the American Civil Liberties Union (ACLU) filed amicus, or friend of the court, briefs on the coalition's behalf. The ACLU's brief acknowledged that child porn is illegal but argued that "there is nothing inherently wrongful about using a computer to create sexually explicit images."

The Justice Department defended the law as a necessary protection for children, especially in light of technological advances in photographic manipulation. In support of the government, the National Law Center for Children and Families, a nonprofit group in Fairfax, Virginia, argued that the CPPA would lead to more child porn convictions by eliminating arguments about the age of a model in a film or photo. Federal attorneys moved for summary judgment—a decision in their favor without a trial because no issues of material fact were in dispute and they were entitled to judgment as a matter of law.

Judge Conti granted the Justice's Department's motion, dismissing the challenge to the law. In his opinion, Conti applied the test enunciated by the U.S. Supreme Court in *Ward v. Rock Against Racism* 491 U.S. 781, 109 S. Ct. 2746, 105 L. Ed. 2d 661, *reh'g denied*, 492 U.S. 937, 110 S. Ct. 23, 106 L. Ed. 2d 636 (1989). Under this test restrictions on speech imposed by the government are constitutional provided that (a) the restrictions do not concern the content of the speech; (b) they are narrowly tailored to serve an important governmental interest; and (c) they leave open alternative channels for communication of the information.

Conti found that the CPPA did not regulate the particular content of speech; that is, it did not prohibit a particular message but instead acted to prevent the "secondary effects of pornography"—exploitation of children and encouragement of pedophilia. He also found that because the law did not ban non-pornographic photography depicting children or prevent photographers from using adult models, it was narrowly tailored and allowed alternative avenues of communication.

The Free Speech Coalition appealed the ruling. Washington, D.C., attorney William Bennet Turner filed an amicus brief in support of the appeal on behalf of the ACLU and others. Turner criticized the court's secondary effects rationale, arguing that it had no limits and could be used to justify any kind of speech restriction.

**CROSS REFERENCES**
American Civil Liberties Union; Freedom of Speech; Internet; Prior Restraint

## PRESIDENTIAL POWERS

The executive authority given to the PRESIDENT OF THE UNITED STATES by Article II of the Constitution to carry out the duties of the office.

### Raines v. Byrd

Of all the powers that a U.S. president possesses, the authority to veto congressional legislation is one of the most important. Article I, Section 7, of the U.S. Constitution states that "every bill" and "every order, resolution or vote to which the concurrence of the Senate and the House of Representatives may be necessary" must be presented to the president for approval. A veto occurs when the president disapproves of the legislation and declines to sign the bill, returning it unsigned to Congress. Congress may override the veto by a two-thirds vote in both houses.

The passage in 1996 of the Line Item Veto Act (2 U.S.C.A. § 691 et seq.), however, shifted the rules concerning presidential vetoes. The line-item veto gives the president the authority to selectively delete certain types of items from appropriation and budget bills, many of which are hundreds of pages long. The popularity of the line-item veto (43 states give their governor this power) is based on the desire to eliminate "pork"—appropriations or programs included by a legislator as a political gift to constituents—and other vote-influencing expenditures.

Under the federal law, the president can sign a bill in its entirety and then, within five days, delete a specific item, such as funding for a public works project or a narrowly targeted tax break. The law allows the president to delete specific dollar amounts of discretionary spending, which are normally found in annual appropriations bills and in new or expanded entitlement programs or other mandatory spending that does not rely on annual appropriations. The president may also use the line-item veto to excise tax breaks that would go to one hundred or fewer beneficiaries.

After the president exercises the line-item veto, Congress has 30 days to consider passing a separate disapproval bill to restore funding for the specific project. If this disapproval bill is passed, the president may veto it, forcing Congress to override the veto by a two-thirds vote of both houses in order to assure that the money is spent.

Not all members of Congress were pleased with giving the president the line-item veto. The day after President Bill Clinton signed the act into law, Senator Robert C. Byrd (D-W.Va.), joined by five other senators and representatives who had voted against the bill, filed suit in federal district court, asking that the court strike down the law as unconstitutional. Congress had anticipated the court challenge by authorizing any member "adversely affected" by the act to bring an action. The act provided that an expedited appeal of the district court decision would go to the U.S. Supreme Court, bypassing the court of appeals.

Byrd alleged that the line-item veto disrupted the historic balance of powers between the legislative and executive branches and that it violated Article I, Section 7, of the U.S. Constitution. The district court agreed with Byrd, finding that the law was an unconstitutional delegation of legislative power to the president. The government then appealed to the Supreme Court.

In *Raines v. Byrd*, ___U.S.___, 117 S. Ct. 2312, 138 L. Ed. 2d 849 (1997), the Court refused to rule on the merits of the issue. Instead, the Court held that Byrd and his fellow legislators lacked legal standing to file suit because they could show no personal injury from the new power. The Court ruled for the first time on whether legislators have a right to sue for "institutional injury." It indicated great reluctance to permit legislators to take their losing fights from Congress to the courts.

Chief Justice William H. Rehnquist, writing for the majority, noted that Article III, Section 2, of the U.S. Constitution requires that federal courts only decide cases or controversies. The federal doctrine of standing to sue is one aspect of the case or controversy requirement. Standing focuses on whether a prospective plaintiff can show that the defendant has invaded some personal legal interest. The person must have a personal stake in the outcome of the controversy, demonstrating that he is the proper party to bring the lawsuit.

Rehnquist noted that a federal court cannot have jurisdiction unless there is a case or controversy. It is a "bedrock requirement." He emphasized that a plaintiff must have suffered a personal injury that is "particularized, concrete, and otherwise judicially cognizable." Finally, he pointed out that the Court had "always insisted on strict compliance with this jurisdictional standing requirement."

The Court acknowledged that it had never had occasion to rule on the legislative standing question presented in this case. Byrd and his fellow plaintiffs had not been singled out for unfavorable treatment but claimed that the act caused a type of "institutional injury" that damaged all members of Congress equally. The plaintiffs based their claim on a loss of political power, not on the loss of something to which they were personally entitled.

Byrd argued that the Court's holding in *Coleman v. Miller*, 307 U.S. 433, 59 S. Ct. 972, 83 L. Ed. 1385 (1939), allowed them to claim standing based on an institutional injury. In *Coleman* the Court stated that state legislators "have a plain, direct and adequate interest in maintaining the effectiveness of their votes." Members of the Kansas legislature, who had been locked in a tie vote that would have defeated the ratification of a proposed federal constitutional amendment, contested the tie-breaking vote of the lieutenant governor. Though they eventually lost on the merits of their case, the Court found that the legislators had established standing by arguing that their votes were nullified.

Rehnquist saw no basis for using *Coleman* as a precedent in the line-item veto case. Unlike the situation in Kansas, the plaintiffs did not allege that their votes on the line-item bill were not given full effect. Instead, "they simply lost the vote." In addition, the plaintiffs did not argue that the act would nullify their votes in the future the same way that the votes of the Kansas legislators had been nullified. In the future, a majority of both houses of Congress can pass or reject appropriation bills. The act did not affect this process. Rehnquist also noted that Congress could repeal the line-item veto or exempt certain bills from its application.

The plaintiffs contended, however, that the line-item veto made their votes less effective than before and changed their meaning. Under normal procedures a bill would come into law as passed by Congress and all of the projects in the bill would go into effect, or it would not become law and none of the projects in the bill would go into effect. Either way, "a vote for the appropriations bill meant a vote for a package of projects that were inextricably linked." The line-item veto, however, created a third possibility: the bill becomes law but the president selectively cancels some of the projects.

Rehnquist rejected this theory, characterizing it as the "abstract dilution of institutional legislative power." He noted that the granting of standing on this basis would go against more than 200 years of constitutional history. The federal courts have always been reluctant to become entwined in disputes between the legislative and executive branches.

Therefore, the Court ruled that the plaintiffs "have alleged no injury to themselves as individuals; the institutional injury they allege is wholly abstract and widely dispersed and their attempt to litigate this dispute at this time and in this form is contrary to historical experience." The Court reversed the judgment of the district court and dismissed the case. Rehnquist did state, however, that the Court's decision did not foreclose a constitutional challenge by someone—most likely from outside Congress—who can claim to have been hurt in a specific and personal way by a line-item veto.

In a dissenting opinion, Justice John Paul Stevens contended that the plaintiffs had standing and concluded that the act was unconstitutional.

# PRESIDENT OF THE UNITED STATES

The head of the EXECUTIVE BRANCH, one of the three branches of the federal government.

## Clinton v. Jones

In *Nixon v. Fitzgerald*, 418 U.S. 683, 94 S. Ct. 3090, 41 L. Ed. 2d 1039 (1974), the Supreme Court held that the president of the United States enjoyed absolute immunity against private civil suits for official acts. President Bill Clinton, faced with a civil lawsuit for alleged actions that occurred before he became president in 1993, sought to use the immunity doctrine to postpone litigation of the lawsuit until he left office in 2001. The Supreme Court, in *Clinton v. Jones*, ___U.S.___, 117 S. Ct. 1636, 137 L. Ed. 2d 945 (1997), rejected Clinton's position, ruling that Paula C. Jones's lawsuit should be allowed to proceed.

In her lawsuit, Jones alleged that on May 8, 1991, while Clinton was still governor of Arkansas and she was an employee of the Arkansas Industrial Development Commission, she worked at an official conference at a Little Rock hotel. Clinton made a speech at the conference. Jones alleged that she was persuaded by a member of the Arkansas State police to visit the governor in a business suite at the hotel, where he made sexual advances that she rejected. Jones also claimed that because she rejected Clinton's advances, her superiors dealt with her in a rude and hostile manner and changed her job duties. She charged that the state police officer who allegedly sent her to Clinton's suite had defamed her by stating that Jones had accepted the governor's overtures and that various persons authorized to speak for President Clinton had publicly called her a liar by denying that the incident took place. Jones, who filed her lawsuit in 1994, based her case on Clinton's alleged violations of the federal civil rights laws (42 U.S.C.A. § 1983 and § 1985), as well as violations of state and common law. She sought actual damages of $75,000 and punitive damages of $100,000.

President Clinton's lawyers immediately went into federal court in Little Rock and informed the judge that Clinton intended to file a motion to dismiss on the grounds of presidential immunity. The court granted Clinton's request to defer all other pleadings and motions until the immunity issue was resolved. In Clinton's motion to dismiss, the president requested that Jones's lawsuit be dismissed without prejudice and that she be allowed to refile it after he was no longer president.

The district court denied the motion to dismiss on immunity grounds and ruled that discovery in the case could go forward, but ruled that any trial would be postponed until the end of Clinton's presidency. Both Clinton and Jones appealed these rulings to the Eighth Circuit Court of Appeals. The Eighth Circuit held that the district court properly rejected the motion to dismiss, but it reversed the order to postpone the trial because a postponement would appear to be the "functional equivalent" of a grant of temporary immunity (72 F.3d 1354 [1996]).

President Clinton, represented by a private attorney, and the U.S. government, represented by the solicitor general, requested that the Supreme Court reverse the appeals court decision. The solicitor general argued that the decision was "fundamentally mistaken" and created "serious risks for the institution of the Presidency."

The Court agreed to hear the appeal, but unanimously affirmed the Eighth Circuit's conclusion that the president was not entitled to immunity or a postponement of the trial until after he left office in 2001. Justice John Paul Stevens, writing for the Court, rejected the claim that the Constitution affords the president temporary immunity from civil damages litigation arising out of events that occurred before he took office. Stevens found no constitutional or historical precedents that justified temporary presidential immunity.

Stevens noted that only three sitting presidents (Theodore Roosevelt, Harry S Truman, and John F. Kennedy) had been defendants in civil litigation involving their actions prior to taking office. However, none of these cases reached the Supreme Court or shed "any light on the constitutional issue" before the Court.

Turning to the question of immunity, Stevens stated that the principal reason public officials are given immunity from suits for money damages arising out of their official acts was inapplicable to unofficial conduct. Immunity "serves the public interest in enabling such officials to perform their designated functions effectively without fear that a particular decision may give rise to personal liability." It was upon this basis that the Court, in *Nixon v. Fitzgerald*, granted the president "absolute immunity from damages liability predicated on his official acts."

This reasoning, however, provided no support for an immunity for unofficial conduct. Stevens stated that the Court had never suggested that the president or any other public official has an immunity that "extends beyond the scope of any action taken in an official capacity." The Court has based its immunity doctrine on a functional approach, extending immunity only to "acts in performance of particular functions of his office." Thus, a judge's absolute immunity does not extend to actions performed in a purely administrative capacity.

The Court was likewise unpersuaded by President Clinton's argument that the separation-of-powers doctrine required federal courts to postpone all private actions against a sitting president until he leaves office. Stevens acknowledged the "unique importance" of the presidency in the constitutional system, but he concluded that it does not follow that allowing

*After the Supreme Court denied President Bill Clinton's claim of immunity, a district court judge threw Paula Jones's civil suit against Clinton out of court.*

CRAIG FUJII/AP/WIDE WORLD PHOTOS

Jones's action to proceed would violate the doctrine. The doctrine of separation of powers is concerned with the allocation of official power among the three branches of government. This means that Congress may not exercise the judicial power to revise a final court judgment, nor may the president exercise the legislative power to seize private property for public use.

In Clinton's case, however, the federal courts were not usurping the executive power. Stevens concluded that Jones was merely asking the courts to exercise their core Article III jurisdiction to decide cases and controversies. Whatever the outcome of this case, there is no possibility that the decision will curtail the scope of the official powers of the Executive Branch.

Stevens also rejected the president's contention that defending the lawsuit would impose unacceptable burdens on the president's time and energy. It seemed unlikely to the Court that Clinton would have to be occupied with the Jones lawsuit for any substantial amount of time. The Court also expressed skepticism that denying immunity to the president would generate a "deluge of such litigation." In the history of the presidency, only three other presidents had been subject to civil damage suits for actions taken prior to holding office.

Based on this reasoning, the Court ruled that the district court's decision to postpone the trial was an abuse of discretion. There was noth-ing in the record to enable a judge to "assess whether postponement of trial after the completion of discovery would be warranted." Therefore, the Court directed the district court to proceed with the case.

In a concurring opinion, Justice Stephen G. Breyer agreed with the outcome but contended that if a president could demonstrate to the court that a lawsuit would be damaging to the work of the office, the court should be able to postpone the litigation until the president left office.

On April 1, 1998, U.S. District Court Judge Susan Webber Wright, an appointee of President George Bush, surprised attorneys on both sides of the case by throwing Jones's suit out of court. Judge Wright held that even if Jones's allegations were true, the record in the case failed to support a claim of criminal sexual assault because none of the alleged conduct constituted forcible compulsion. She therefore granted the president's motion for summary judgment.

Jones's attorneys said Jones would consider appealing the decision.

**CROSS REFERENCES**
Immunity; Presidential Powers

# PRISON

A public building used for the confinement of people convicted of serious crimes.

## Attica Prison

In early September 1971, inmates at Attica Correctional Facility in Attica, New York, set in motion a series of events that made the prison infamous. The events of that September also became the topic of one of the longest-running federal cases in U.S. history.

Throughout the spring and summer of 1971, the inmates at Attica had been negotiating with prison administrators over a litany of complaints. Among the grievances listed by the inmates were inhumane conditions, abuse by prison guards, arbitrary release dates, a lack of racial diversity among the prison guards, and the prison's failure to give inmates a reasonable opportunity to exercise their freedom of religion. On September 9, 1971, the talks broke down and dozens of inmates revolted. Inmates managed to overtake prison guards, take hostages, and gain control of the prison facilities. One prison guard and two inmates were killed in the initial uprising.

*New York state police and prison guards stand among the remains of inmates after the 1971 uprising at Attica Correctional Facility.*
UPI/CORBIS-BETTMANN

Over the next three days, the inmates met with a host of attorneys, among them Herman Schwartz and William M. Kunstler. The inmates communicated with state officials through the attorneys and submitted a list of more than two dozen demands. They also took steps to protect the hostages from more hostile inmates by forming a human ring around the hostages.

On a Monday morning, September 13, 1971, Russell Oswald, the commissioner of the New York State Department of Corrections, submitted a settlement offer to the inmates and gave them one hour to respond. Oswald promised that if the inmates did not respond within one hour, the state would regain control of the prison by military force. After nearly two hours had passed, Governor Nelson A. Rockefeller gave the final approval for a forcible takeover. Officials shut off the electricity to the prison, state police dropped tear-gas canisters from helicopters, and state troopers emptied their rifles into inmates in the prison yard. By the time state law enforcement officials were finished retaking the prison, thirty-nine inmates and hostages were dead and eighty-eight were wounded. A total of forty-three deaths were ultimately attributed to the events from September 9 through 13, making the ordeal the largest massacre of Americans by Americans since the Civil War. "Attica" became a catchword for state-sanctioned brutality.

Several dozen prisoners were charged with crimes in the wake of the riot, but all the inmates ultimately prevailed in the prosecutions. Many inmates complained that prison guards increased their torture of inmates after order was restored, and more than one thousand inmates and former inmates filed suits in the U.S. District Court for the Western District of New York. Citing civil rights violations suffered at the hands of prison guards and law enforcement officers during and after the riot, the inmates sought a total of more than $2.8 billion in damages.

The civil cases dragged through the federal court system for more than twenty years. In June 1997 the first jury verdict on the Attica riots was reached in favor of Frank ("Big Black") Smith, a key player in the uprising. The jury believed Smith's claims that he had been tortured after the riots and awarded him $4 million. Smith claimed that he was forced to run through a gauntlet of baton-swinging prison guards, that guards threatened him with castration, that they placed a gun to his head and played Russian roulette, and that former deputy warden Karl Pfeil tried to whip his face with a chain.

Smith called the jury verdict "a message—just because you're in prison, they can't beat you like a dog and get away with it." Smith implored the state to settle with the other plaintiffs before most of them died. Mike Zabel, a spokesperson for New York State Attorney General Dennis C. Vacco, told reporters that the state attorney general's office would explore all its options in the case, including a settlement with the other plaintiffs.

### Richardson v. McKnight

Due to the growing costs associated with running state prison systems, some states have contracted with for-profit businesses to manage their prisons. Though private prison management may save money, the privatization of a typically public function has raised legal questions, especially regarding the status of privately employed prison guards. The foremost issue is whether a privately employed prison guard should be accorded the same legal protections that a publicly employed prison guard receives.

The U.S. Supreme Court confronted this issue in *Richardson v. McKnight*, ___U.S.___, 117 S. Ct. 2100, 138 L. Ed. 2d 540 (1997). The Court ruled that privately employed prison guards are not entitled to qualified immunity from liability when they are sued under the federal civil rights law, 42 U.S.C.A. § 1983. (Under Section 1983 state and local government employees can be held civilly liable for violating an individual's civil rights as long as the officer acted "under color of law.") In so ruling, the Court determined that there was not a "firmly rooted tradition of immunity" applicable to privately employed prison guards and that the purposes of the immunity doctrine did not warrant extending immunity to privately employed prison guards.

The case arose in Tennessee, which had contracted with a private company to run its South Central Correctional Center (SCCC). Ronnie Lee McKnight, a prisoner at SCCC, filed a section 1983 federal constitutional tort action against two prison guards, Daryll Richardson and John Walker. He alleged that the guards had placed him in extremely tight physical restraints, subjecting him to the deprivation of a right secured by the Constitution.

The guards asked the court to dismiss the action on the ground that they were entitled to qualified immunity. Unlike absolute immunity, which protects judges, legislators, and prosecutors from civil lawsuits arising out of their official duties, qualified immunity requires the government employee to meet an objective test: would a reasonable official have known that his actions violated the constitutional rights of the Section 1983 plaintiff? If not, the defendant official will not be liable in damages for his constitutional violation. Immunity allows a public official to escape liability early in litigation, before the time and money to mount a defense have been expended.

The federal district court denied the guards' motion, ruling that because they were private rather than public employees, they could not use qualified immunity. The guards appealed to the Sixth Circuit Court of Appeals, which affirmed the lower court (88 F. 3d 417 [1996]). Because other circuit courts of appeals had taken a different position on this issue, the Supreme Court agreed to hear the guards' appeal.

The Court affirmed the Sixth Circuit court on a 5–4 vote. Justice Stephen G. Breyer, writing for the majority, concluded that neither history nor public policy justified the extension of qualified immunity to privately employed prison guards. Justice Antonin Scalia, writing for the four dissenters, argued that the Court employed the wrong analysis. He stated that the Court should have applied a function test: if the privately employed prison guard performs the same functions as a publicly employed guard, then the privately employed guard is entitled to the same immunity as the public guard.

Breyer used the case of *Wyatt v. Cole*, 504 U.S. 158, 112 S. Ct. 1827, 118 L. Ed. 2d 504 (1992), as the authority for his analysis. In *Wyatt*, the Court considered whether private defendants in a section 1983 action were entitled to qualified immunity. It held that they were not. Breyer highlighted four points in *Wyatt* that were relevant in *Richardson*: private actors may sometimes be liable under section 1983; immunity from suit is distinct from other kinds of defenses; immunity will be granted where it has been historically granted under the common law and where it serves strong public policy interests; and, finally, *Wyatt* did not address whether employees of a private prison management firm enjoyed qualified immunity. The key question in *Richardson*, therefore, was whether history or public policy justified giving the guards qualified immunity.

Breyer concluded that history did not provide justification. Though government–employed prison guards "may have enjoyed a kind of immunity defense arising out of their status as public employees at common law," correctional facilities "have never been exclusively public." Private contractors were commonly involved in prison management in the nineteenth century; southern states like Tennessee leased their entire prison systems to private individuals or companies. These private concerns regularly took complete control over prison management, including prisoner labor and discipline.

In his review of correctional history, Breyer found evidence that common law provided mistreated prisoners in prison-leasing states with remedies against mistreatment by their private lessors. He did not, however, find any evidence that the law gave these private companies or their employees any special immunity from lawsuits. Therefore, history did not provide the privately employed prison guards with any significant support for their immunity claim.

Turning to public policy, Breyer noted that one of the immunity doctrine's most important purposes is to preserve the ability of government officials to perform their work and to make sure that talented individuals are not deterred from entering government out of fear of being exposed to civil lawsuits. Immunity also encourages officials to vigorously exercise their authority and to make decisions out of principle rather than out of fear.

The guards contended that these purposes apply whether their employer is a public or a private organization. In addition, they argued that since they performed the same work as publicly employed prison guards, they must be given the same immunity from suit. Breyer rejected the application of a functional test, concluding that the Court has applied this test "only to decide which type of immunity—absolute or qualified—a public officer should receive." In this case the question was whether immunity should be given.

Breyer also identified three factors that convinced the majority that immunity was not warranted. First, a private company operating a prison is subject to market pressures. A firm whose guards are too aggressive will face damages that raise costs, thereby threatening its replacement, whereas a firm whose guards are too timid will risk replacement "by other firms with records that demonstrate their ability to do both a safer and a more effective job." These competitive pressures serve the same purpose as qualified immunity.

The company running SCCC clearly faced these pressures. Its first contract was set to expire after three years, which meant that it was subject not only to state review but also to "pressure from potentially competing firms who can try to take its place."

Second, the privatization of prison management helps to ensure that talented candidates are not discouraged from taking jobs as guards for fear they will be sued. The company was required to purchase insurance to compensate victims of civil rights torts. Breyer concluded that the insurance increased "the likelihood of employee indemnification," thus reducing the "employment-discouraging fear of unwarranted liability potential applicants face."

Third, the risk that these lawsuits would distract employees from their duties was not sufficient grounds, standing alone, for granting qualified immunity. Though the Court rejected qualified immunity, Breyer pointed out that it had not considered whether the defendants, as private employees, were liable under section 1983. That issue was returned to the district court for further proceedings.

Justice Antonin Scalia, in a dissenting opinion, argued that immunity is determined by function, not status, and that private status does not disqualify a person from claiming immunity.

**CROSS REFERENCES**
Breyer, Stephen G.; Immunity; Prisoners' Rights; Scalia, Antonin; Section 1983

## PRISONERS' RIGHTS

The nature and extent of the privileges afforded to individuals kept in CUSTODY or confinement against their will because they were convicted of performing an unlawful act.

### Federal Law Limits Suits Over Prison Conditions

Since the late 1960s, prisoners have filed lawsuits in federal district courts alleging that the conditions of their confinement violated the Eighth Amendment's prohibition against cruel and unusual punishments. In many cases federal judges have agreed with their contentions, entering orders that set minimum living conditions for state prisons and that sometimes mandated increased funding. A backlash against this type of litigation led Congress to pass the Prison Litigation Reform Act of 1995 (PLRA) (18 U.S.C.A. § 3626) [Supp. 1997]), which imposes substantive and procedural limitations on the ability of federal courts to issue injunctions mandating prison reform.

The federal courts have just begun to confront the issues posed by the enactment of the PLRA. In *Inmates of Suffolk County Jail v. Rouse*, 129 F. 3d 649 (1st Cir. 1997), a federal court of appeals ruled that the new law required a district court to vacate a 1979 consent decree that set conditions for confinement of pretrial detainees in Suffolk County, Massachusetts. In its decision the court rejected the inmates' contention that the PLRA was unconstitutional because it violated the separation of powers principle, and the Due Process and Equal Protection Clauses of the Fourteenth Amendment.

The controversy over the Suffolk County Jail began in 1971, when pretrial detainees held in the jail brought a class action civil suit alleging that the conditions of their confinement violated the Eighth Amendment. A prime issue was double bunking, the housing of two prisoners in space designed for just one. After years of negotiation, the parties agreed in 1979 to a settlement that was embodied in a consent decree signed by the federal district court. The decree contained a plan for a new facility featuring single-occupancy cells and a commitment by the county to phase out the old jail. Growth in the prison population and delays in construction (the new jail was not completed until 1990) led the parties to modify the consent decree by court order in 1985, 1990 and 1994. The last of these orders permitted limited double bunking.

Following the passage of the PLRA, the county and the state of Massachusetts went back into court, requesting that the court vacate the consent decree. Section 3626(b)(2) of the act states that a defendant in a prison condition lawsuit is:

> entitled to the immediate termination of any prospective relief if the relief was approved or granted in the absence of a finding by the court that the relief is narrowly drawn, extends no further than necessary to correct the violation of the Federal right, and is the least intrusive means necessary to correct the violation of the Federal right.

Under the act prospective relief includes all relief other than compensatory monetary damages. This definition meant that provisions of the consent decree dealing with the housing of prisoners could be terminated.

The district court upheld the constitutionality of the provisions of the PLRA and ruled that it would no longer enforce the consent decree. Nevertheless, it declined to vacate the consent decree or terminate its obligations because those obligations represented "consensual undertakings of the defendants with court approval" (952 F. Supp. 869 [D. Mass. 1997]). Both sides appealed.

A three-judge panel of the U.S. Court of Appeals for the First Circuit ruled that the PLRA provisions were constitutional and that

the law mandated termination of the consent decree unless the district court makes specific findings that are necessary to keep the consent decree alive. Judge Bruce M. Selya, writing for a unanimous panel, acknowledged that the PLRA "is not a paragon of clarity." Congress had mistakenly described a consent decree as a form of relief rather than a judgment that engenders relief. Nevertheless, a review of the PLRA's legislative history convinced the court that Congress sought, in part, to "oust the federal judiciary from day-to-day prison management." Therefore, the court felt "duty bound" to interpret the PLRA as mandating the termination of the consent decree unless the district court makes specific findings to keep it alive.

The court rejected the prisoners' claims that the termination provisions of the act were unconstitutional. The prisoners contended that the PLRA infringed upon the constitutional principle of separation of powers. The courts, as the third branch of government, have been independent. The prisoners argued that the reopening by Congress of final judgments of the court, such as a consent decree, was forbidden. The PLRA required a court to rescind relief that the court had already granted.

Selya rejected the separation of powers argument. The consent decree at issue was not a "final judgment" for the purpose of separation of powers analysis. He noted that the Supreme Court had "carefully carved out an exception" for legislation that altered the prospective effect of injunctions entered by the courts. If forward-looking judgments were inviolate, either the

> legislature would be stripped of the ability to change substantive law once an injunction had been issued pursuant to that law, or an issued injunction would continue to have force after the law that originally gave the injunction legitimacy had been found wanting. … The first of these possible results would work an undue judicial interference with the legislative process, while the second would create an intolerable tangle in which some laws applied to some persons and not to others. Since the separation of powers principle is a two-way street, courts must be careful not to embrace a legal regime that promotes such awkward scenarios.

The court also rejected the prisoners' contention that the law violated the Due Process Clause. They claimed that the consent decree was a final judgment that vested property rights in the parties which could not be taken away by Congress. In addition, they posited that the consent decree was a contract and that due process limits the ability of the federal government to enact laws that have a harmful effect on preexisting contracts. Selya found the two arguments unpersuasive. The consent decree was not the same as a money judgment. A money judgment was final and could not be disturbed, but a consent decree with prospective relief was "necessarily impermanent" and could be modified. The PLRA had changed the standard by which courts can continue forward-looking relief, and this "profound change in the relevant underlying law entitles the defendant to termination of the decree."

As to the contract rights argument, the court applied the rational basis test to determine whether the law unconstitutionally impaired an existing contract. Selya found that Congress had a rational basis for enacting the PLRA. The law's termination provisions forged a "practical commonsense linkage between a changed circumstance—the district courts' newfound inability to grant or enforce prospective relief absent a violation of a federal right—and an existing consent decree."

The court also dismissed the prisoners' claim that the termination provisions violated the Equal Protection Clause. The prisoners argued that singling out a certain class of citizens for "disfavored legal status or general hardship" was unconstitutional. Selya found this argument ill conceived because the PLRA did not abridge a fundamental right or operate against a suspect class. He noted that the PLRA limited a district court's ability to provide prospective relief to pretrial detainees unless they suffered a violation of a federal right. In the present case, the PLRA did not permit relief for detainees because no federal right had been violated. Therefore, the PLRA's "denial of relief does not imperil pretrial detainees' fundamental rights."

Having upheld the constitutionality of the provisions, Selya applied them to the consent decree. He found no grounds for exempting the decree from the termination provisions, and therefore the court ordered that the consent decree be terminated.

### Young v. Harper

Prison overcrowding has led federal courts to intervene on behalf of inmates and impose strict controls over the management of state prison systems. Overcrowding has been exacerbated by legislative changes to criminal codes that lengthen prison sentences. In states where overcrowding is acute, prison officials are often forced to release prisoners and place them on parole to free up spaces for incoming convicts.

Typically, when an inmate is released before the end of her sentence, she is placed on parole. If she violates the conditions of her parole, she may be returned to prison. However, states with prison overcrowding have developed other programs for releasing convicts before the completion of their sentences. In Oklahoma, a pre-parole program was created, which frees a prisoner from confinement before the governor acts on the recommendation of parole by the state parole board.

The U.S. Supreme Court was called upon in *Young v. Harper*, ___U.S.___, 117 S. Ct. 1148, 137 L. Ed. 2d 270 (1997), to decide what level of due process a pre-parole prisoner was entitled to before being returned to prison after the governor denied his parole. After reviewing the essential features of the pre-parole system and the program's written rules and conditions that were communicated to participants, the Court ruled that, before being returned to prison, pre-parole prisoners must be given the same amount of due process given to a prisoner whose parole is revoked.

In 1990 Ernest E. Harper had served fifteen years of a life sentence for two murders. In that year the Oklahoma Pardon and Parole Board recommended him for parole and released him under the pre-parole program. This program was in effect whenever the population of the prison system exceeded 95 percent of its capacity. An inmate was eligible for the pre-parole program after completing one-third of his prison sentence. The parole board determined who could participate in the pre-parole program, but the governor, based on the parole board's recommendation, decided whether a prisoner would be paroled.

Harper spent five uneventful months outside the prison. However, the governor denied his parole. Harper's parole officer telephoned him, informed him of the governor's decision, and told him to return to the prison. Harper returned later that day but filed a petition for a writ of habeas corpus in Oklahoma state court, arguing that his summary return to prison had deprived him of liberty without due process of law. The state court system rejected his petition, finding that the pre-parole program impinged only on Harper's degree of confinement, an interest not afforded procedural protections.

Harper then filed his petition with the federal courts. Though the federal district court rejected his claim that he was entitled to a hearing before being returned to prison, the Tenth Circuit Court of Appeals was more sympathetic. The appeals court ruled that the pre-parole program closely resembled parole or probation and that Harper was entitled to due process before being reincarcerated (64 F. 3d 563 [1995]).

Oklahoma appealed the decision to the Supreme Court. The Court unanimously affirmed the Tenth Circuit Court. Justice Clarence Thomas, writing for the Court, noted that the case of *Morrissey v. Brewer*, 408 U.S. 471, 92 S. Ct. 2593, 33 L. Ed. 2d 484 (1972), was central to the issues of this case. *Morrissey* held that paroled inmates were entitled to due process protections before being returned to prison. Therefore, if pre-parole was similar to parole, *Morrissey* must be applied to pre-parole programs.

Thomas pointed to the following language in *Morrissey*, "The essence of parole is release from prison, before the completion of sentence, on the condition that the prisoner abide by certain rules during the balance of the sentence." The liberty interest a parolee has in remaining free includes the ability to be gainfully employed and to be with family and friends. Though the state imposes restrictions on a parolee, her condition is markedly different from that of confinement in a prison. The parolee relies on the implicit promise that parole will be revoked only if she fails to meet the parole conditions.

Thomas concluded that this analysis could be applied to Harper as well. He had been released from prison before completing his sentence and had kept his own residence, obtained and maintained a job, and lived a life different from the one he lived in prison. The restrictions placed on him (no consumption of alcohol, no incurring of debt, and no travel outside the county without permission) and the requirement of regularly reporting to a parole officer were similar to those placed on parolees.

Oklahoma disputed the idea that pre-parole and parole are analogous, if not almost identical. The state contended that the reincarceration of Harper was nothing more than a transfer "to a higher degree of confinement" or a "classification to a more supervised prison environment." Transfers within a prison setting involve no liberty interest and require no due process protections.

Thomas was troubled by Oklahoma's identification of several aspects of the pre-parole program that the state claimed rendered it different from parole. He reviewed several "phantom differences." The state claimed that the purposes of parole and pre-parole are different: parole is designed to reintegrate the inmate into society whereas pre-parole is nothing more than a device to reduce prison overcrowding. Thomas dismissed this claim, noting that parole also reduces the prison population and pre-parole inmates are required to integrate themselves into the community.

Another phantom difference was the state's claim that a pre-parole inmate continues to serve his sentence and receives earned credits whereas a paroled inmate does not. The state said that if the parolee's parole is revoked, he is not entitled to deduct from his sentence the time spent on parole. Thomas disputed this supposed difference, concluding that state law allows parolees to deduct from their sentences all time spent on parole.

Thomas dismissed other supposed differences between parole and pre-parole as being indistinguishable. Both parolees and pre-parolees remain within the custody of the department of corrections, and both are required to report to parole officers. Violation of either the parole or pre-parole requirements subject inmates to re-incarceration.

Thomas acknowledged some real differences between parole and pre-parole. First, he said, the parole board orders participation in pre-parole, but the governor confers parole. Second, pre-parolees who flee the state can be prosecuted as though they had escaped from prison, whereas parolees who flee are subject only to parole revocation. Finally, a pre-parolee cannot leave Oklahoma under any circumstances, but a parolee can leave the state with the permission of the parole officer.

Nevertheless, Thomas concluded that these differences were not substantial and that the pre-parole program "was a kind of parole as we understood parole in *Morrissey*." Therefore, Harper was entitled to due process. The Court did note, however, that Oklahoma had modified its pre-parole procedures after Harper filed suit, mandating due process for a pre-parolee who is denied parole and whose return to higher security is sought by the department of corrections.

**CROSS REFERENCES**
Class Action; Due Process of Law; Eighth Amendment; Equal Protection; Fourteenth Amendment

# PRIVILEGES AND IMMUNITIES

Concepts contained in the U.S. Constitution that place the CITIZENS of each state on an equal basis with citizens of other states in respect to advantages resulting from citizenship in those states and citizenship in the United States.

## Lunding v. New York Tax Appeals Tribunal

The Privileges and Immunities clause of the U.S. Constitution, Article IV, Section 2, seeks to place citizens of the various states, upon the same footing. Therefore while states may tax nonresidents who work, own a business, or derive income in the state, they may not subject them to heavier taxes than those imposed on citizens of the state. The U.S. Supreme Court, in *Lunding v. New York Tax Appeals Tribunal*, __U.S.__, 118 S. Ct. 766, 139 L. Ed. 2d 717 (1998), ruled that a New York tax law that effectively denied only nonresident taxpayers an income tax deduction for alimony paid violated the Privileges and Immunities Clause.

Christopher H. Lunding and his wife were residents of Connecticut in 1990. During that year, Lunding earned a substantial income from the practice of law in New York. During that year he paid alimony to his former wife and deducted a prorated share of the alimony he paid on his New York nonresident income tax form he filed with his spouse. This share was based on the determination that approximately 48 percent of Lunding's business income was attributable to New York. In making this pro rate deduction, the Lundings followed a practice allowed by New York until 1987.

The New York Department of Taxation and Finance denied their deduction because New York Tax Law § 631 (b)(6), which was enacted in 1987, had effectively denied nonresident taxpayers from deducting alimony payments, while allowing residents a deduction. The new law set up a computational formula that in practice made it impossible for a nonresident to deduct alimony. The tax department recalculated the Lundings' tax liability, assessing them more than $3,700 in New York income taxes plus interest. The Lundings appealed to the New York Division of Tax Appeals, arguing that the law discriminated against nonresidents in violation of the Privileges and Immunities Clause. After this administrative appeal failed, the Lundings filed suit in New York state court. The New York Supreme Court (New York's appellate level court) held that the law

violated the Privileges and Immunities Clause but the New York Court of Appeals (New York's highest court) disagreed, reversing the lower court's decision and upholding the constitutionality of section 631 (b)(6). The court reasoned that because New York residents are subject to the burden of taxation on all of their income regardless of source, they should be entitled to receive the benefit of full deduction of expenses. The court concluded that where deductions represent personal expenses of a nonresident taxpayer, they are more appropriately allocated to the state of residence (89 N.Y.2d 283, 653 N.Y.S.2d 62, 675 N.E.2d 816 [1996]).

The Lundings appealed to the U.S. Supreme Court, which reversed the New York Court of Appeals. Writing for the majority, Justice Sandra Day O'Connor noted that the Privileges and Immunities Clause does not prevent a state from taxing a nonresident who has earned income in the state. As a practical matter, the clause "affords no assurance of precise equality in taxation between residents and nonresidents of a particular State." There may be inherent differences in "any taxing scheme," and state legislatures have a substantial amount of discretion in formulating tax policy. Nevertheless, the Supreme Court has consistently required "reasonable grounds for diversity of treatment." A state may defend itself from a privileges and immunities claim by demonstrating a substantial reason for the difference in treatment and that the discrimination practiced against nonresidents "bears a substantial relationship to the State's objectives."

O'Connor did not find New York's reasons substantial enough to justify the discriminatory taxing scheme. She first dismissed the reasoning for the law offered by the New York Court of Appeals, concluding that its analysis borrowed from a case that had no relation to the type of tax provision at issue in this case.

O'Connor then turned to the state's claims. New York claimed that because it only had jurisdiction over nonresidents' in-state activities, its limitation on nonresidents' deduction of alimony was valid. It argued that it should not be required to consider expenses linked entirely to personal activities outside New York. O'Connor ruled that although alimony may be of a "personal" nature, "it cannot be viewed as geographically fixed in the manner that other expenses, such as business losses, mortgage interest payments, or real estate taxes, might be." Alimony is a personal obligation that "generally correlates with a taxpayer's total income or wealth." As such it "bears some relationship to earnings regardless of source."

The law violated the Privileges and Immunities Clause because it required nonresidents to pay more tax than "similarly situated residents solely on the basis of whether or not the nonresidents are liable for alimony payments." The law did not meet the "rule of substantial equality of treatment." O'Connor suggested that New York return to its pre-1987 taxing scheme, which allowed nonresidents a pro rata deduction for alimony payments.

**CROSS REFERENCES**
Taxation

# PRODUCT LIABILITY

The responsibility of a manufacturer or vendor of GOODS to compensate for injury caused by a defective good that it has provided for sale.

### Apportioning Damages to Successive Companies

In *Class v. American Roller Die Corp.*, 308 N.J. Super. 47, 705 A.2d 390 (1998), a state appeals court addressed the thorny question of how product liability passes between successive owners of a company. Product liability concerns the responsibilities of a company to the purchasers and users of its products. In American Roller Die, the company that manufactured the product causing injury had been sold several times. The question before the court was who, then, was responsible for damages. Sometimes contractual agreements decide this issue. At other times, courts must do so. The Appellate Division of the New Jersey Superior Court fashioned a mathematical formula to determine liability based on the length of time the successors had manufactured the products.

On November 10, 1988, Ramon Class injured himself while operating a punch press at his job. The punch press was an old piece of machinery made in 1954 by the *American Roller Die* Corporation (Ardcor). Class wanted to bring a product liability lawsuit based on claims of product defects and the manufacturer's failure to provide sufficient warning about the danger of using its product. However, Ardcor no longer existed, having been sold three times over a seven-year period.

Class sued all three buyers of Ardcor, referred to as the *initial purchaser*, the *interim successor*, and the *ultimate successor*. The initial purchaser was Lee Wilson Engineering Company,

Inc., which bought Ardcor's assets and the right to use its name in 1963, and then continued to make the punch presses for five years. In 1968 it sold the Ardcor line to the interim successor while continuing to service previously sold Ardcor machinery. The interim successor was P & F Industries, Inc. Never a manufacturer, P & F only stored the presses in a warehouse for a period of fourteen months; moreover, it stipulated contractually that it was not assuming any of the seller's obligations or liabilities. In 1970 P & F sold its stock of machinery to the ultimate successor, American Roll Tooling, Inc.

Although the lawsuit might have appeared to present an uphill struggle for Class, all three defendants entered an initial settlement with Class for the sum of $875,000. Wilson, P & F, and American each settled for $250,000, and the latter for an additional $125,000 on a separate claim. This amount was not all that Class might be owed, however. Pursuant to the settlement, the companies retained the right to have a court determine their additional liability as successors. On June 12, 1996, the Superior Court issued a decision that excused P & F from any successor liability: as the interim successor, it had derived no benefit from the assets it sold after holding them for fourteen months (*Class v. American Roller Die Corp.*, 294 N.J.Super. 407, 683 A.2d 595). However, the court ruled that Wilson and American were subject to liability to be divided equally between them.

On appeal, Wilson and American agreed on one aspect of the decision: P & F had been correctly absolved of liability. Otherwise, the two companies pointed to each other. Wilson contended that it should not be held liable because American was still manufacturing the presses, whereas its own manufacturing had ended years earlier and it had dissolved as a company in 1994. At the very least, it asserted, equal liability was unfair. Finally, it contested having to pay attorney fees and defense costs to P & F. On a cross-appeal, American argued that only Wilson should be held liable. Alternatively, if both it and Wilson were to be found responsible successors, then they both should pay an equal share of the plaintiff's damages.

The three-judge appellate panel first upheld the trial court's finding that both companies were liable. It further held that American's current manufacturing did not absolve Wilson of liability, as Wilson had been in business when Ramon Class was injured in 1988. It had even had a $1 million dollar insurance policy covering product defects. American, too, was liable because it operated the Ardcor business from 1970 until the settlement of the plaintiff's claim.

In apportioning damages, the appeals court looked to the principle behind the concept-of-successor liability: successor companies benefit from trading on the predecessor's name, accumulated goodwill, business reputation, and established customers. Therefore, they should share in compensating someone injured by a machine produced by the predecessor. The court apportioned damages based on a mathematical ratio: the number of units produced by Wilson and American during the period of time each manufactured the product up to the date of the plaintiff's accident, compared to the total units produced by both.

Because the number of units produced by each company was unknown, the panel replaced *product units* with *years* in the equation. Damages would be apportioned by each company's number of years manufacturing the product line up to the 1988 accident, compared to the total number—23 years—that both manufactured the product line until the accident. For Wilson, that meant a 5/23 share of liability, and for American an 18/23 share. This method was "not without its faults," the panel acknowledged, but it bore "a reasonable relationship to the benefits received by each corporation." Many, if not all, judicial methods for apportioning damages lack precision, the panel said. Support for its approach could be found in the principles of the so-called market share theory of liability, a legal theory that imposes liability based upon a manufacturer's share of a particular market.

Lastly, the panel reversed the order requiring Wilson to indemnify P & F for attorney fees and defense costs. No indemnification agreement had existed, it ruled, merely an agreement that P & F would not assume liabilities. But that agreement did not guarantee to P & F that it would not be sued "on a judicially created theory of liability established after the parties' agreement."

## Vehicle Manufacturers Not Liable to Negligent Drivers

Deaths in high-speed crashes were the basis for two unsuccessful product liability lawsuits against vehicle manufacturers in 1997. One case involved a Honda motorcycle (*Halbrook v. Honda*, 224 Mich. App. 437, 569 N.W.2d 836 [1997]). The second involved a Ford Explorer sports utility vehicle (*Timmons v. Ford*, 982 F.Supp. 475 [S.D.Ga. 1997]). Separately, both sets of plaintiffs argued a novel claim. In the Honda case, the plaintiffs alleged that the manufacturer was liable for wrongful death because it had built a fast, quickly accelerating motorcycle and deliberately advertised its speed. In the Ford case, the plaintiffs argued that the manufacturer had failed to design a vehicle in which occupants could survive a high-speed collision. The courts rejected both claims, essentially saying that manufacturers are not responsible for the risks incurred by drivers and passengers at excessive speeds.

The Honda case arose from a collision between a car and a motorcycle in Commerce Township, Michigan, March 1990. The crash killed two children in the car, Stephen and Stephanie Loder, as well as the motorcyclist, James Bondie, who was driving a Honda. The children's parents and Karen Halbrook, as personal representative of Bondie's estate, sued each other for negligence. They also separately brought product liability claims against the Honda Motor Company, which were consolidated into one case by the trial court.

The product liability lawsuit had two main allegations. First, it argued that Honda created and sold a vehicle that could travel and accelerate too fast. Neither the inexperienced driver nor other drivers on the road could appreciate the bike's capabilities, the lawsuit claimed, and therefore it was unsafe and unsuitable for public highways. Second, the suit claimed that Honda deliberately marketed the bike to young male riders with special emphasis on speed. But before the case could go to trial, the court granted summary disposition for the defendant—a ruling that the defendant, as a matter of law, owed no legal duty to the plaintiffs. Honda, it said, was not responsible for Bondie's reckless acts.

On appeal, the Michigan appeals court affirmed the trial court's decision. In the main body of her opinion, Judge Marilyn J. Kelly analyzed the question of Honda's legal duty according to six criteria: (1) the foreseeability of the harm, (2) the degree of certainty of injury, (3) the closeness of connection between the conduct and injury, (4) the moral blame attached to the conduct, (5) the public policy of preventing future harm, and (6) the burdens and consequences of imposing a duty and the resulting liability for breach.

Analyzing these factors, Kelly first found that it is foreseeable to vehicle manufacturers that motorists speed and that excessive speed causes accidents. But in every other factor, she ruled in favor of the defendant. The judge found that the degree of certainty of injury depends partly on how the driver handles the vehicle. She held that the accident was more closely connected to the drivers' behavior in the accident than the ability of the motorcycle to accelerate quickly and exceed the speed limit. In determining moral blame, she held that the Honda Motor Company did not cause Bondie to disobey the law by speeding nor cause Loder to ignore the oncoming motorcycle. She declined to impose new policy requirements on manufacturers for limiting maximum speed of their vehicles, a responsibility properly left to the legislature. Finally Judge Kelly held that imposing a burden on manufacturers to protect motorcyclists who misuse their products would lead to too much litigation: "manufacturers," she wrote, "are not insurers."

The judge also undertook two other inquiries. First, she examined whether Honda Motor Company was unreasonable in manufacturing, designing, marketing, and distributing a vehicle that could accelerate quickly and exceed the speed limit. Her answer was no: manufacturers can limit defects in their products, but they are not responsible for consumer misuse. Second, she found that Honda bore no liability for its advertising campaigns. Citing the Michigan Supreme Court's decision in *Buczkowski v. McKay*, 441 Mich. 96, 490 N.W.2d 330 (1992), she noted that manufacturers only incur a legal duty through marketing when products are marketed to children. Bondie, however, was twenty-six years old and licensed to drive a motorcycle. Judge Kelly concluded that there was no evidence that Honda's advertising caused the accident.

Unlike the Honda case, the accident in the Ford case stemmed from drunken driving. On June 26, 1996, at approximately 2:00 A.M., Dwayne Franklin Carr, who was heavily intoxicated, drove his pickup truck across the center line of the Georgia State Road directly into the path of an oncoming Explorer. The combined speed of the vehicles at impact was estimated at between 102 and 130 miles per hour. The collision killed him and four of the Explorer's five occupants: Cynthia Timmons, Lenora Bailey, Edward Bailey, and Desiree Hicks. The Explorer's engine was pushed rearward into the passenger compartment and a fire started in the vehicle. The four passengers' deaths were attributed to trauma from the collision and smoke inhalation.

The descendants of the Explorer's occupants brought suit against the Ford Motor Company under principles of strict liability in tort, negligent design, design defect, and failure to warn consumers of danger. Specifically, they argued that the four occupants' deaths were the result of defects in the fuel and seat systems of the Explorer—the engine should not have been pushed into the passenger compartment, and the fuel system should not have caught fire. Additionally, they asserted that the manufacturer had a duty to warn drivers that these results would occur in an accident. The Ford Motor Company moved for summary judgment, agreeing with the facts presented to the court and asserting that, given those facts, Ford should prevail as a matter of law.

On Sept. 29, 1997, U.S. District Court Judge Dudley H. Bowen granted Ford's motion. Judge Bowen analyzed the manufacturer's liability for product defect using the so-called "Risk-Utility" standard adopted by the Georgia Supreme Court in *Banks v. ICI Americas, Inc.*, 264 Ga. 732 450 S.E.2d 671 (1994). This standard determines the reasonableness of a product's design by considering numerous factors, the most important of which is whether an alternative design exists. Bowen ruled that a reasonable juror could not find that the Explorer's design was defective "in light of the extreme impact speeds and resulting forces of this terrible collision." As a matter of law, the manufacturer was under no obligation to design and build a vehicle that could ensure safety at head-on collision speeds in excess of 100 miles per hour. Thus, Ford had no duty to warn consumers about the dangers inherent in such crashes. "Such a warning," wrote the judge, "be seen by anyone as a foolish restatement of an obvious fact."

Bowen held that the plaintiffs had failed to establish that the Explorer was the proximate cause of the victims' deaths, as required under George law (O.C.G.A. § 51-1-11). They had argued that Ford should be aware that high-speed collisions could and do occur. But as Judge Bowen observed, a great disparity existed between the speed at which the federal government requires vehicles to be tested and the collision speeds in this case. Accordingly, it would be unreasonable to require manufacturers to conduct crash testing at speeds over 100 miles per hour. Thus the plaintiffs had failed to show that Ford should have known or was actually aware of the probable consequences when its product was involved in this type of high-speed accident. Instead, concluded Judge Bowen, Mr. Carr's drunk driving was the sole proximate cause of the deaths in the collision.

**CROSS REFERENCES**
Negligence; Tort Law; Torts; Wrongful Death

## RAILROAD

### Amtrak Legislation

After debating for more than a year, Congress in November 1997 passed a bill to save Amtrak, America's financially struggling passenger railroad. The Amtrak Reform and Accountability Act of 1997, P.L. 105-134, was signed into law by President Bill Clinton in December 1997.

The Amtrak act accomplishes a number of goals. Most importantly, the act temporarily saves the railroad from financial ruin. In 1997 Amtrak was $83 million in debt and was becoming unable to pay its creditors. The act releases $5 billion for operating and capital expenses to Amtrak each year through the year 2002. The act also authorizes $2.3 billion in capital investment funds set aside in the Taxpayer Relief Act of 1997 to help Amtrak modernize equipment and facilities as spelled out in Amtrak's strategic business plan. The new expenditures will ultimately reduce Amtrak's expenses and help increase revenues and ridership. The funds also are intended to help Amtrak decrease the railroad's impact on the environment.

The federal funding of Amtrak, however, comes with a catch; Congress stated in the bill that federal financial aid to Amtrak for operating losses should be eliminated by the year 2002. Essentially, Congress intends that Amtrak wean itself from federal funds for operating support by the year 2002. To help counter the financial challenges Amtrak may face in the future, the act increases the liability protections that Amtrak already receives.

The Amtrak act orders the dissolution by March 30, 1998, of the existing Amtrak board of directors, which was appointed by President Clinton without congressional participation. The act declares that the new board nominees must be made in consultation with Congress. The consultation effectively gives Congress the power to reject an Amtrak board nominee made by the president.

Other changes made by the act include provisions regarding labor relations and other employee issues. The act gives Amtrak greater flexibility in negotiating with its employees' unions and diminishes Amtrak employees' protections against layoffs. Under the Amtrak act, Amtrak can lay off workers due to rerouting and schedule changes. Layoffs due to contracting out by Amtrak are subject to collective bargaining between Amtrak and the affected employees' unions.

Amtrak is the official intercity passenger railroad of the United States, serving more than 65 million customers at 510 stations in 44 states, using more than 22,000 miles of tracks. The railroad also contracts for local commuter service. Amtrak employs more than 23,000 people nationwide, and 21,000 of those workers are represented by unions.

## RECOVERED MEMORY

The remembrance of traumatic childhood events, usually involving SEXUAL ABUSE, many years after the events occurred.

*Congress passed the Amtrak Reform and Accountability Act of 1997 to save the financially struggling passenger railroad.*

MICHAEL OKONIEWSKI/AP/WIDE WORLD PHOTOS

### Pennsylvania Supreme Court Rejects Recovered Memory

In *Dalrymple v. Brown*, (549, Pa. 217, 701A. 2d 164) the Pennsylvania Supreme Court rejected a sexual assault claim based on the controversial theory of recovered memory. This theory holds that psychological therapy can help patients remember certain traumatic events from their past—in some cases, many years after they have repressed such memories. The *Dalrymple* case posed a legal question that many states have faced: can a plaintiff who "recovers" memories of childhood abuse sue her alleged assailant long after the legal time limit for filing such a claim has expired? Bucking the trend in other jurisdictions, the Pennsylvania court said no.

As the basis for numerous allegations of sex abuse in the 1980s and 1990s, the theory of recovered memory has provoked fierce debate in the fields of psychology and law. Apart from the theory's validity, which came under increasing fire, there was also a specific legal problem.

Plaintiffs who repressed memories of abuse can only sue once they remember what was done to them; yet statutes of limitations, which bar the commencement of a lawsuit after a certain period of time has passed, typically begin to run from the time of injury. (For minors, the limitations period begins when they reach the age of majority.) Without some change in the law, most recovered memory cases would be barred. By 1997, a majority of jurisdictions allowed the suits even after the limitations period had expired.

The Pennsylvania case was not unusual. In December 1992, Linda Parisano Dalrymple filed a complaint in the Pennsylvania Court of Common Pleas alleging that Eugene Brown had sexually assaulted her. The assaults, she said, had occurred in 1968 and 1969 when she was a child; her memory of the events had only returned on August 25, 1990. She sought punitive damages on three counts: battery, assault, and intentional infliction of emotional distress.

Brown denied assaulting Dalrymple, alleging that her accusations were unfounded and made in bad faith. Moreover, he argued that the statute of limitations had already run out on her claims. Under Pennsylvania law she only had two years in which to sue (42 Pa. Cons. Stat. § 5524). Based on this argument, the court granted Brown's motion for summary judgment—a decision in his favor without a trial. The court ruled that Dalrymple's claim was barred by the statute of limitations because she had failed to file her claims within two years of reaching her eighteenth birthday.

After losing on appeal to the Pennsylvania Superior Court, Dalrymple took her case to the state supreme court. Her appeal asserted that she could not have known of her injury until she recovered her repressed memory. Accordingly, she invoked the so-called *discovery rule*. This court-made rule is an exception to the statute of limitations, designed to benefit plaintiffs. It holds that if the injured party does not originally know an injury, then the limitations period does not begin until the discovery of the injury is reasonably possible. Typical examples of the discovery rule are found in medical malpractice cases, where a doctor's error is unknown to the patient until its effects become physically evident.

On August 25, the supreme court affirmed the lower court ruling. Justice Ralph J. Cappy's opinion did not recognize the validity of the theory of repressed and recovered memory. Instead it focused solely on the applicability of the discovery rule in belated lawsuits such as Dalrymple's. Cappy observed that courts must apply the discovery rule carefully in order not to undermine the statute of limitations. Nationally, he noted, jurisdictions allowing its use in recovered memory cases have adopted a subjective standard, whereas Pennsylvania, in five superior court cases in the 1990s, had consistently adhered to an objective standard in disallowing its use. That standard was traceable to *Bailey v. Lewis*, 763 F. Supp. 802 (1991), in which the Federal District Court for the Eastern District of Pennsylvania held that the discovery rule was unavailable when the failure to promptly sue was due to the plaintiff's own incapacity—the disability of repressed memory.

Cappy then considered Dalrymple's attempt to distinguish her case from the precedents. Unlike earlier plaintiffs, she claimed that her repression was *not* an incapacity. Instead, she argued, it was a natural reaction of a young child to sexual trauma. In other words, her repressed memory was part of the injury itself, and thus the discovery rule should apply. The court characterized this argument as "original," "creative," and "ingenious," but dismissed it. Noting that the discovery rule applies only when the nature of the injury is such that plaintiffs cannot detect it, Cappy concluded that "it would be absurd to argue that a reasonable person, even assuming for the sake of argument, a reasonable six year old, would repress the memory of a touching so that no amount of diligence would enable that person to know of the injury."

The decision closed the possibility of using the discovery rule in recovered memory cases brought in Pennsylvania. The court acknowledged that its approach put it in the minority among state courts, but it maintained that its objective standard was preferable to the subjective analysis used in other states.

**CROSS REFERENCES**
Sex Offenses; Statute of Limitations

# RELIGION

## Agostini v. Felton

The Establishment Clause of the First Amendment states, "Congress shall make no law respecting an establishment of religion." The clause applies to state governments as well, prohibiting the creation and support of state churches, which exist in Europe. Since the late 1940s, however, the U.S. Supreme Court has gone beyond the simple prohibition against established churches to set narrow limits on permissible government assistance to religion.

In *Agostini v. Felton*, ___U.S.___, 117 S. Ct. 1997, 138 L. Ed. 2d 391 (1997), the Supreme Court overruled its decision in *Aguilar v. Felton*, 473 U.S. 402, 105 S. Ct. 3232, 87 L. Ed. 2d 290 (1985), which held that the Establishment Clause prohibits public school employees from providing remedial education to students at parochial schools. On a 5–4 vote, the Court ruled that *Aguilar* no longer had force because subsequent decisions of the Court had eroded the reasons supporting it.

Under Title I of the Elementary and Secondary Education Act of 1965 (20 U.S.C.A. § 6301 et seq.), all educationally and economically disadvantaged children are entitled to publicly funded remedial education services, regardless of whether they attend public or private schools. Before the Court's decision in *Aguilar*, many school systems provided these services to children attending religious schools by having public school teachers conduct remedial education training at the private schools. In *Aguilar* the Court ruled that New York City's practice of providing Title I services at private schools violated the Establishment Clause because it created excessive entanglement between the public and religious school systems and therefore violated the requirement that church and state remain separate.

As a result, New York City spent more than $100 million between 1986 and 1994, providing computer-aided instruction, leasing sites and mobile instructional units, and transporting students to those sites. With costs escalating, the New York City school board and a group of parents of parochial school children filed suit in federal court in 1995, asking that the permanent injunction issued in response to the *Aguilar* decision be lifted so that Title I services could once again be offered on site, in parochial schools. The district court denied the motion, and the Second Circuit Court of Appeals affirmed the lower court (101 F. 3d 1394 [1996]).

On appeal the Supreme Court reversed the Second Circuit, agreeing with the plaintiffs that *Aguilar* was no longer good law. The result was not surprising. In *Board of Education of Kiryas Joel Village School District v. Grumet*, 512 U.S. 687, 114 S. Ct. 2481, 129 L. Ed. 2d 546 (1994), five justices already had criticized the separation of church and state principles contained in *Aguilar* and were ready to change the way the Court analyzes Establishment Clause cases.

The analysis of Establishment Clause cases has been guided by a three-part test first announced in *Lemon v. Kurtzman*, 403 U.S. 602, 91 S. Ct. 2105, 29 L. Ed. 2d 745 (1971). Under the *Lemon* test, a program will be upheld if it has a secular purpose, has a primary effect that neither advances nor inhibits religion, and does not excessively entangle government with religion. In *Agostini* the Court focused on the last part of the test in reaching its decision, as the first two parts of the test were satisfied.

The plaintiffs relied on rule 60(b) of the Federal Rules of Civil Procedure, a rarely used

provision that permits parties to seek relief from an earlier court order that is no longer supported by law. Justice Sandra Day O'Connor, writing for the majority, acknowledged that the Court's decisions since *Aguilar* had varied as to whether providing public services to students attending parochial schools was constitutional under the Establishment Clause. In *School District of Grand Rapids v. Ball*, 473 U.S. 373, 105 S. Ct. 3216, 87 L. Ed. 2d 267 (1985), as in *Aguilar*, the Court held that a remedial education program violated the Establishment Clause. However, in *Witters v. Washington Department of Services for the Blind*, 474 U.S. 481, 106 S. Ct. 748, 88 L. Ed. 2d 846 (1986), the Court upheld a program that permitted a student to use a state vocational tuition voucher to attend a Christian college. In *Zobrest v. Catalina Foothills School District*, 509 U.S. 1, 113 S. Ct. 2462, 125 L. Ed. 2d 1 (1993), the Court held that a student in a religious high school could use a state-employed sign language interpreter.

O'Connor stated that in *Aguilar* the Court had relied on three fundamental presumptions concerning public aid to parochial schools: Permitting public school teachers to work in religious schools inevitably results in the state-sponsored indoctrination of religion; permitting public employees to work within religious schools necessarily constitutes a symbolic union between church and state; and any government aid that enhances the educational function of religious schools impermissibly violates the separation of church and state.

O'Connor expressly rejected all three of these presumptions. In doing so, the Court shifted its inquiry from whether the New York City program might lead to a violation of the Establishment Clause to whether the program actually did violate it. O'Connor found no evidence that the program, which she referred to as "neutral" and "carefully constrained," actually violated the Establishment Clause. She stated:

> [A] federally funded program providing supplemental remedial instruction to disadvantaged children on a neutral basis is not invalid under the Establishment Clause when such instruction is given on the premises of sectarian schools by government employees pursuant to a program containing safeguards such as those present here.

The Court, by rejecting the three presumptions articulated in *Aguilar*, altered its approach to Establishment Clause cases. The Court shifted its focus on the actual, rather than potential, effect of government programs. If programs actually result in state-sponsored religious indoctrination, they apparently still will violate the First Amendment under the *Lemon* test. Programs that create only the possibility of such indoctrination, however, will likely be found constitutional.

The Court's shift in analysis is a significant change in Establishment Clause law. The difference, however, between actual and potential entanglement may be derived from personal perspective rather than objective measurement.

Justice David H. Souter, in a dissenting opinion, contended that the Court had misapplied rule 60(b) and that the majority had misread the most recent Establishment Clause cases to suggest that the "underpinnings" of *Aguilar* had been removed. Souter argued that the presumptions drawn in *Aguilar* and *Ball* were reasonable and that the Court's decision authorized "direct state aid to religious institutions on an unparalleled scale," in violation of the Establishment Clause.

### City of Boerne v. Flores

Though the First Amendment protects religious freedom, this does not mean that religious institutions are free from all government regulations. In 1990 the U.S. Supreme Court caused consternation within the religious community for its decision in *Employment Division, Department of Human Resources of Oregon v.*

*The landmark commission of Boerne, Texas, denied St. Peter Catholic Church's request to expand, prompting the* City of Boerne v. Flores *suit.*

*Smith*, 494 U.S. 872, 110 S. Ct. 1595, 108 L. Ed. 2d 876. The Court upheld an Oregon state law of general application criminalizing peyote use, which was used to deny unemployment benefits to Native American Church members who lost their jobs because of such use. The Native Americans ingested peyote for sacramental purposes.

In upholding the state law, the Court declined to apply a balancing test that asked whether the law at issue substantially burdens a religious practice and, if so, whether the burden was justified by a compelling government interest. This balancing test weighed the government's interest against the individual's religious liberty interest in the context of each particular case.

Having abandoned the balancing test, which it had used since its decision in *Sherbert v. Verner*, 374 U.S. 398, 83 S. Ct. 1790, 10 L. Ed. 2d 965 (1963), the Court in *Smith* held that neutral, generally applicable laws may be applied to religious practices even when they are not supported by a compelling government interest. Members of Congress expressed alarm at the *Smith* decision and enacted legislation to overturn it. The stated purpose of the Religious Freedom Restoration Act of 1993 (RFRA) (42 U.S.C.A. § 2000bb et seq.) was "to restore the compelling interest test" and "to guarantee its application in all cases where free exercise of religion is substantially burdened."

In *City of Boerne v. Flores*, __U.S.__, 117 S. Ct. 2157, 138 L. Ed. 2d 624 (1997), the Supreme Court held that Congress could not constitutionally enact the RFRA and the higher standard for determining whether a law impermissibly infringes on a person's right to exercise her religion. The Court, on a 6–3 vote, struck down the RFRA, ruling that Congress had exceeded its powers under section 5 of the Fourteenth Amendment to adopt laws to enforce individual rights.

The case arose in 1993, when St. Peter Catholic Church in Boerne, Texas, applied to city officials for permission to expand the size of the church. The city's landmark commission denied the church's request on the grounds that the church's facade was within the city's historic district. After the city council rejected the church's appeal, the church sued in federal court, claiming that the local ordinance establishing the city's historic district was unconstitutional and violated the RFRA.

The trial court rejected the church's argument and ruled that the RFRA was unconstitutional because it infringed on the authority of courts to establish standards for evaluating constitutional issues. On appeal, the Fifth Circuit Court of Appeals reversed, holding that the RFRA was constitutional because the law did not usurp the judiciary's power to interpret the Constitution. The court ruled that the RFRA simply created rights and protections in addition to the constitutional rights already recognized by the courts (73 F. 3d 1352 [1996]).

The Supreme Court disagreed with the Fifth Circuit's ruling. Justice Anthony M. Kennedy, writing for the majority, held that Congress had exceeded its authority under section 5 of the Fourteenth Amendment when it passed the RFRA. Congress used its Fourteenth Amendment enforcement power to impose the RFRA's requirements on the states. Defenders of the RFRA contended that section 5 could be used to protect one of the liberties guaranteed by the Fourteenth Amendment's Due Process Clause, the free exercise of religion, beyond what is necessary under *Smith*.

Kennedy stated that, although section 5 is a "positive grant of legislative power," that power is not unlimited. Congress's power under section 5 extends only to enforcement of the provisions of the Fourteenth Amendment. Kennedy wrote that:

> Congress does not have the power to decree the substance of the Fourteenth Amendment's restrictions on the states. Legislation which alters the meaning of the [First Amendment's] Free Exercise Clause cannot be said to be enforcing the Clause. Congress does not enforce a constitutional right by changing what the right is.

Kennedy admitted that the "line between measures that remedy or prevent unconstitutional actions and measures that make a substantive change is not easy to discern," but stated that the distinction must be observed. Therefore, the Court ruled that although legislation designed to prospectively prevent violations of individual freedom can in some instances be considered "enforcement" under section 5 (and therefore constitutional), the sweep of the legislation may not be disproportionate to the nature of the violations.

In coming to this conclusion, Kennedy relied on his reading of the legislative history of the drafting of the Fourteenth Amendment and its interpretation by the Supreme Court since the 1880s.

Kennedy then turned to the RFRA itself. Supporters contended that the RFRA was a reasonable means of protecting the free exercise of religion as defined in *Smith*. The RFRA invalidated any law that imposed a substantial burden on a religious practice unless it was justified by a compelling government interest and was the least restrictive means of accomplishing that interest. Supporters of the law noted that Congress could prohibit laws with discriminatory effects to prevent racial discrimination in violation of the Equal Protection Clause of the Fourteenth Amendment. Therefore, they argued, Congress can do the same to promote religious liberty.

The Court was unpersuaded. Kennedy stated that the "appropriateness of remedial measures must be considered in light of the evil presented." Strong measures appropriate for one harm may be "an unwarranted response to another, lesser one." Kennedy contrasted the RFRA and the Voting Rights Act of 1965 (VRA) (42 U.S.C.A. § 1973 et seq.) to make this point. Congress and the courts saw a long history of racially discriminatory conduct by the states in the regulation of voting. In contrast, Kennedy said, the RFRA's legislative record "lacks examples of religious bigotry." The history of religious persecution described in the legislative record, includes no examples occurring after the 1950s. One congressional witness admitted that deliberate religious persecution was not the usual problem in the United States. Instead, the congressional testimony emphasized laws of general applicability that place incidental burdens on religion. The Court concluded, therefore, that the RFRA swept too broadly, especially in light of the fact that there was no evidence that states were making widespread efforts to restrict religious freedom.

The Court made clear that Congress may not enact legislation that provides freedoms or rights above and beyond those set forth in the Constitution. In addition, the Court firmly established itself as the only branch of government with the authority to interpret the Constitution. Kennedy reaffirmed the Court's holding in *Smith*, stating, "When the exercise of religion has been burdened in an incidental way by a law of general application, it does not follow that the persons affected have been burdened any more than other citizens, let alone burdened because of their religious beliefs."

Justice John Paul Stevens, in a concurring opinion, stated that the RFRA violated the Establishment Clause of the First Amendment by creating a government preference for religion. Justice Sandra Day O'Connor, in a dissenting opinion, argued that the Court's decision in *Smith* was incorrect and should not be used as a basis for evaluating the constitutionality of the RFRA.

## Kendall v. Kendall, Parish of Advent v. Diocese of Massachusetts

The delicate relationship between law and religion presents courts with thorny issues of church and state. Two cases decided by the Supreme Judicial Court of Massachusetts within a period of eight days reflect the tension between religious rights and freedoms and the power of courts to resolve disputes and uphold the law.

In the first case, *Kendall v. Kendall*, 687 N.E.2d 1228, 426 Mass. 238 (1997), the court was asked to determine the extent to which a divorced father could expose his children, who had been raised Jewish, to his fundamentalist Christian beliefs. In the second case, *Parish of Advent v. Protestant Episcopal Diocese of Massachusetts*, 688 N.E.2d 923, 426 Mass. 268 (1997), the court was asked to resolve a dispute between a church and its members. In one sense, the two cases presented distinct questions of law and fact. In another sense, however, both cases required the legal system to draw a line separating permissible court regulation of matters concerning religion from impermissible regulation of religious decisions that must be left to the discretion and conscience of the parties involved.

The *Kendall* dispute stemmed from a 1996 divorce judgment awarding Jeffrey Kendall and Barbara Kendall joint legal custody of their three minor children, Ariel, Moriah, and Rebekah. Before their marriage in 1988, Jeffrey, then Catholic, and Barbara, then Jewish, agreed to raise any children they might conceive in the Jewish religion. But in 1991 Jeffrey converted from Catholicism to a fundamentalist Christian faith, and three years later Barbara adopted orthodox Judaism. At the end of 1994, Barbara filed for divorce.

The court appointed a (GAL), an official appointed by the court to represent the interests of the child, to address the religious conflict between the parties and their children. Based on the report made by the GAL, the court found that the children would be substantially harmed were each parent allowed to expose the children to his or her religion without limitation.

The court then issued an order and judgment, providing that each parent would be entitled to share his or her religious beliefs with the children, except that (1) neither could indoctrinate the children in a manner that alienated them from either parent; (2) the father could not take the children to his church, whether for church services, Sunday school, or church educational programs; (3) the father could not engage the children in prayer or Bible study if it promoted rejection rather than acceptance of their mother or their Jewish identity; and (4) the father could not share his religious beliefs with the children if those beliefs caused the children significant emotional distress.

More specifically, the court ordered the father not to take the children to any church service where they would be taught that non-Christians are destined to burn in hell. The court said that nothing in the order prevented the father from hanging pictures of Jesus Christ in his home or taking the children to family gatherings at Christmas or Easter. In making this order, the court was cognizant of its limited powers concerning the subject of religion.

Parents, the court said, enjoy a fundamental right to religious expression, including freedom to rear their children in accordance with the dictates of their consciences and deeply held beliefs. This right is not absolute, however, and may be overcome by a compelling countervailing interest. The welfare of a minor child, the court ruled, is one such compelling interest. To prove that the welfare of a minor child would be substantially harmed by the exercise of a parent's religious freedom, the court continued, is not a burden that is easily met. This burden can only be satisfied by "clear evidence," which is something greater than the uncorroborated testimony of one parent.

In this case the court said that there was ample evidence to support the restrictions imposed on the parties, especially the father. The court relied on the GAL's report indicating that in early 1995 the father upset Ariel by threatening to cut the fringe off his *tzitzitz* (a religious garment with four long knotted strands) if he did not tuck it into his pants. The GAL's report also revealed that in the summer of 1995 the father shaved off Ariel's *payes* (sideburns grown in accordance with Jewish tradition). Finally, the GAL's report offered evidence that the father had taken his children to a fundamentalist Christian service that distorted the Jewish religion.

The court said that Ariel demonstrated a strong identity with the Jewish faith and culture and should be allowed to maintain and develop that identity if he so desired. Moriah, the court observed, suffered from emotional stress due to the conflict between her parents, and her sister Rebekah was likely to become emotionally unbalanced if the status quo were preserved. Nonetheless, the court stressed the importance of "frequent and continuing contact" between children and their divorced parents. In light of these conflicting considerations, the court said that the divorce decree properly struck a balance between the best interests of the children and the religious freedom of the parents.

The court was careful not to violate the tenants of the Establishment Clause of the First Amendment. In *Lemon v. Kurtzman*, 403 U.S. 602, 91 S. Ct. 2105, 29 L. Ed. 2d 745 (1971), the U.S. Supreme Court devised a test for courts to apply in rendering decisions under the Establishment Clause. The so-called *Lemon* test prohibits courts from issuing orders that have the primary purpose of advancing or inhibiting religion. Instead, *Lemon* requires court orders to have a secular purpose. Finally, *Lemon* forbids courts from becoming excessively entangled in religious matters.

In *Kendall* the court said that the divorce decree had the secular purpose of advancing the best interests of the children. The order neither advanced Judaism nor inhibited Christianity, the court reasoned, but merely recognized a preference originally made by the parents as to their children's religious upbringing. At the same time, the divorce decree did not foster excessive government entanglement with religion, the court said, because any necessary judicial proceedings in the future would center on the emotional or physical harm to the children rather than on the merits of the parties' respective religious teachings.

If the court tried to avoid excessive entanglement with religion in *Kendall*, then it attempted to avoid any entanglement in *Parish of Advent*. The dispute in *Parish of Advent* stemmed from a lawsuit initiated by thirteen members of the Episcopalian Parish of Advent, a religious corporation located in the Beacon Hill section of Boston. Advent had been duly incorporated under the laws of Massachusetts.

The lawsuit challenged the authority of the Massachusetts diocesan bishop for the Protestant Episcopal Church in the United States (the highest ecclesiastical authority for adjudicating matters concerning the Episcopal Diocese of Massachusetts) to determine how members of the church vestry (the elective body in an Episcopal Church) would be elected. The lawsuit also questioned whether an Advent member was in "communion" with the parish and whether the religious corporation's constitution could be amended unilaterally in violation of canonical mandates.

The court held that these issues are matters of internal church governance, matters better decided by established and recognized ecclesiastical authorities within the parish or religious organization. The court said that for it to resolve competing claims of loyalty to the Episcopalian faith or doctrine would be an "impermissible intrusion" into the affairs of the church. Consequently, the court dismissed the case and each of the issues raised by the parties.

In making this decision, the court said that the First Amendment to the U.S. Constitution prohibits civil courts from disturbing the highest ecclesiastical authority within a hierarchical church polity. Unlike congregational churches that are independent of higher ecclesiastical authority, the court wrote, hierarchical churches are subordinate members of a larger organization to which they have acceded control over a variety of issues, including internal disputes between members of the parish, or disputes between the parish and its parishioners. By acceding this control, civil courts must defer to the internal dispute resolution procedures offered by a church's hierarchy, unless a particular dispute involves no consideration of doctrinal matters.

The court compared the facts in *Parish of Advent* to the facts in other church disputes over which civil courts had legitimately exercised jurisdiction. In *Jones v. Wolf*, 443 U.S. 595, 99 S. Ct. 3020, 61 L. Ed. 2d 775 (1979), the U.S. Supreme Court ruled that it was permissible for a state court in Georgia to assert jurisdiction over a dispute concerning the ownership of church property, because such disputes can be resolved by scrutinizing corporate documents in "purely secular terms," without regard to the religion of the parties.

By contrast, the Court had earlier ruled that it was inappropriate for a state court in Illinois to assert jurisdiction over a dispute involving a decision by a hierarchical national church to remove a local bishop and reorganize a particular parish (*Serbian Eastern Orthodox Diocese for the United States & Canada v. Milivojevich*, 426 U.S. 696, 96 S. Ct. 2372, 49 L. Ed. 2d 151 [1976]). In such contexts, the Court said, civil courts are bound to accept the decisions of the highest authorities in the religious organization.

More difficult questions are presented when lawsuits involve mixed questions of secular and canon law. For example, a bishop's decision to merge two parishes could be considered strictly an ecclesiastical question of church organization, a secular question governed by the law of antitrust and unfair competition, or a mixed question requiring application of both secular and ecclesiastical law. In *Fortin v. Roman Catholic Bishop of Worcester*, 416 Mass. 781, 625 N.E.2d 1352 (1994), the Supreme Judicial Court of Massachusetts held that a bishop's decision to merge two parishes involved primarily secular issues. However, in asserting jurisdiction over the case, the court applied property and trust law to resolve the dispute, not the law of antitrust and unfair competition.

In *Kendall* the court found it necessary to interject the legal system into the continuing relationship between divorced parents and their children, carefully outlining the manner and extent to which the parents could expose their children to conflicting religious faiths. In *Parish of Advent*, the court steered clear of entangling itself in a religious dispute between a church and its members, denying jurisdiction and leaving the parties to resolve their claims pursuant to established ecclesiastical procedure and authority.

### Prayer at Tennessee State University

Tennessee State University in Nashville, Tennessee, had long offered Christian prayers before certain school functions. The prayers expressed devotion and thanks to Jesus Christ.

Dr. Dilip K. Chaudhuri, a tenured professor of mechanical engineering at the school and a follower of the Hindu religion, had repeatedly objected to the practice. In 1988, Chaudhuri filed a complaint with the school, which responded by advising individuals offering the prayers to omit mention of Jesus Christ. A portion of the prayer before commencement exercises in 1991 provides an example of the type of prayer offered:

> Let us pray. Most Heavenly Father, we're thankful for the opportunity to gather here in honor of this class of 1991 … [a]nd so Most Heavenly Father, we thank you for allowing those that have come from such a long distance so that they too might be a part of this celebration today. … These and all blessings we ask from a God that we know, let us all say … Amen.

In January 1991, Chaudhuri filed an action in the U.S. District Court for the Middle District of Tennessee against the state of Tennessee, Tennessee State University, and several Tennessee State administrators. Chaudhuri claimed that the defendants had violated Title VII of the Civil Rights Act of 1964 (42 U.S.C.A. § 2000 et seq.) by failing to promote him based on his Hindu religion and his Indian origin. Chaudhuri also charged that the prayers at Tennessee State functions violated rights protected by the Establishment and Free Exercise Clauses of the First Amendment to the U.S. Constitution. The complaint asked for compensatory damages as well as an order preventing the defendants from offering prayers.

As the case continued, Chaudhuri asked the court for an injunction preventing Tennessee State from offering a prayer at upcoming commencement exercises. Tennessee State President Dr. James Hefner then announced that the school would not offer a prayer at commencement, but would have only a moment of silence. The court denied the request for injunctive relief based on the existence of the new moment-of-silence policy. At commencement, the moment of silence was broken by many persons who recited the Lord's Prayer in unison and cheered.

Chaudhuri again applied for injunctive relief, but was denied. Hefner told the court that the moment of silence would replace prayers wherever prayers had been offered. Hefner also stated that faculty attendance at university functions was not mandatory. At the next graduation ceremony, in August 1993, the moment of silence again was thwarted by persons who recited the Lord's Prayer.

At trial, the defendants asked the court for summary judgment in their favor. The trial court granted their motion as to the claims brought under the Establishment Clause and Free Exercise Clause. Chaudhuri appealed the summary judgment to the U.S. Court of Appeals for the Sixth Circuit, but the appeals court affirmed the decision.

At the outset of its analysis, the appeals court stated that it would not address the issue of injunctive relief, forbidding the offering of Christian prayers at Tennessee State functions. The issue was, according to the majority, moot. The appeals court then identified the U.S. Supreme Court case of *Lemon v. Kurtzman*, 403 U.S. 602, 91 S. Ct. 2105, 29 L. Ed. 2d 745 (1971) as the controlling case in this area of the law. In *Lemon* the High Court created a three-part test for deciding whether a religion-oriented state-sponsored activity is valid under the Establishment Clause. First, the action must have a secular purpose. Second, the principal or primary effect of the action must be one that neither ad-

vances nor inhibits religion. Third, the action must not foster excessive government entanglement with religion.

According to the appeals court, Tennessee State's actions met each prong of the *Lemon* test. The court acknowledged that the prayers were religious and that they did have a monotheistic flavor that was not embraced by Hinduism. However, the court felt that the prayers had a secular purpose in that they "solemniz[ed] public occasions, express[ed] confidence in the future, and encourag[ed] the recognition of what is worthy of appreciation in society."

The court then decided that the prayers neither advanced nor inhibited religion. To complete the *Lemon* test, the court found that the prayers and moments of silence did not create excessive government entanglement. According to the court, there is nothing inherently religious about a moment of silence.

The appeals court also examined *Lee v. Weisman*, 505 U.S. 577, 112 S. Ct. 2649, 120 L. Ed. 2d 467 (1992), a Supreme Court case in which the High Court held that it was unconstitutional to offer nonsectarian prayers at public middle school and high school graduation exercises. The appeals court decided that the obligatory nature of a high school graduation was the dominant factor controlling the *Lee* decision, noting that the *Lee* court had explicitly reserved the question of the constitutionality of prayers at ceremonies for adults.

The appeals court distinguished college graduation ceremonies from high school graduation ceremonies. While attendance at high school graduation ceremonies may not have been mandatory, the court stated that "the youth of the audience and the risk of peer pressure and 'indirect coercion'" made the ceremonies virtually mandatory. Conversely, Chaudhuri was not so obliged to attend the graduation ceremonies at his own school. Furthermore, the court found no risk that adult listeners would be indoctrinated by exposure to the prayers.

The court concluded by rejecting Chaudhuri's claim that the prayers and moments of silence violated his right to the free exercise of religion under the First Amendment, stating that Chaudhuri had failed to show that his practice of Hinduism was impeded.

Circuit Judge Nathaniel R. Jones concurred in part and dissented in part. Jones agreed that the moments of silence did not violate the Establishment Clause, but he disagreed with the majority that the issue of injunctive relief preventing the recitation of Christian prayers at Tennessee State was moot. According to Jones, Tennessee State should revert to offering prayers instead of a moment of silence since merely omitting the name Jesus Christ would not make an otherwise Christian prayer neutral.

### Religious Symbols in the Courtroom

The First Amendment's Establishment Clause prohibits any unit of government from endorsing or promoting religious beliefs. The separation of church and state, which has been a hallmark of U.S. government, has never been absolute. The courts have been called upon to decide whether certain government activities violate the Establishment Clause.

A controversy in the state of Alabama over the Establishment Clause drew national attention. Judge Roy S. Moore of the Etowah County Circuit Court posted a copy of the Ten Commandments on the wall of his courtroom and had prayers conducted at the beginning of court sessions. The American Civil Liberties Union (ACLU) and the Alabama Freethought Association (AFA) challenged these practices, but the Alabama Supreme Court ruled that legal technicalities prevented it from ruling on the merits of the case (*Alabama v. American Civil Liberties Union of Alabama*, So. 2d___, 1998 WL 21985 [1998]). In ruling this way, the court allowed Moore to continue his religious activities.

The events leading to the lawsuit began in 1993, when the ACLU wrote Sonny Hornsby, then the chief justice of the Alabama Supreme Court, telling the judge of complaints about the conducting of prayers in courtrooms around the state. The ACLU asked the chief justice to put a stop to the prayers because they clearly violated federal court decisions concerning the separation of church and state. Hornsby did not respond to that letter or to a similar letter from the ACLU in 1994.

In 1995 the AFA filed suit in federal court, alleging that Judge Moore's conduct violated the Establishment Clause. Alabama Governor Fob James, Jr., and Attorney General Jeff Sessions, on behalf of the state, responded by filing a complaint in state court, naming as defendants the ACLU, the AFA, Judge Moore. The complaint alleged that for many decades judges had begun the commissioning of jurors with a prayer, including "a call on God to save the Court and an expression of thanks for due process of law." The complaint also noted that the U.S. Supreme Court and other courts in the United States open their sessions with a prayer requesting God to save the court.

The state's complaint also pointed out that Moore's display of the plaque with the Ten Commandments was just one of several important U.S. historical documents on the walls of his courtroom. Other documents included the Declaration of Independence and the Mayflower Compact. The state noted that the U.S. Supreme Court's chamber contained a depiction of Moses with the Ten Commandments.

The state defended Moore's actions, stating that the judge believed "it impossible to sit in judgment of others without the guidance of God." Moore believed the display of the Ten Commandments and the use of prayer was "a logical necessity and a reasonable acknowledgment of the presupposition upon which the American government and civilized society are based." The state contended that Moore did not proselytize from the bench, that Moore's conduct served "legitimate secular purposes," and that his actions were not understood as conveying government approval of particular religious beliefs. Therefore, his actions did not amount to the establishment of religion, which is prohibited by the First Amendment.

Finally, the state argued that it was state policy to allow judges to preside over their courtrooms "in the manner they see fit." There was no state policy either requiring or prohibiting the opening of court with a prayer or the depiction of the Ten Commandments on the walls of a courtroom.

Based on these arguments, the state asked the court to declare that the conduct of Moore and other circuit judges did not violate the Establishment Clause.

While this state action was pending, the federal district court dismissed the lawsuit filed by the AFA (*Alabama Freethought Association v. Moore*, 893 F. Supp. 1522 [N.D. Ala. 1995]). The court ruled that the plaintiffs lacked standing as either citizens or taxpayers to maintain the action. Standing is a doctrine that focuses on whether a prospective plaintiff can show that the defendant has invaded some personal legal interest. It is not enough that the plaintiff is merely interested as a member of the general public in the resolution of the dispute. The plaintiff must have a personal stake in the outcome of the controversy. In this case the judge concluded that the plaintiffs could not demonstrate the likelihood that they would be called as jurors or participants into Moore's courtroom. Therefore, they could not demonstrate the possibility of being injured by the judge's conduct.

In May 1996, the ACLU and the AFA filed a counterclaim in the state lawsuit. They asked the court to prohibit all judges, including Moore, from opening court with a prayer and from displaying the Ten Commandments in the courtroom. In addition, they made a claim against Alabama Supreme Court Chief Justice Perry O. Hooper, Sr., in his official capacity as chief justice and chief administrator of the state's courts, to prohibit the religious actions at issue.

In November 1996, the trial court ruled that the practice or policy of permitting courtroom prayers violated the Establishment Clause. The court also ruled that the display of the Ten Commandments, "intermingled with the historical and/or educational items," did not violate the First Amendment. The ACLU asked the court to reconsider the Ten Commandments issue. In February 1997, the court changed its holding, finding that the display of the Ten Commandments did violate the Establishment Clause.

The Alabama Supreme Court, in ruling on the case, acknowledged that the issue had aroused a public controversy that was national in scope. The court had received "a considerable amount of correspondence from private persons expressing support for one side or the other." Nevertheless, the narrow question of whether this was a justiciable controversy became the threshold issue. The court found that the controversy was not properly before it.

Justice Ralph D. Cook, writing for the court, defined justiciability as a "component concept, composed of a number of distinct elements." The key element was, as the federal court found earlier, standing, but with a new twist in the state action. Cook noted that Alabama precedent made a controversy nonjusticiable when the state as a plaintiff sues a "straw man defendant," a person whose position is not adverse to that of the plaintiff and "one against whom the judgment would be ineffective in any event." The state had no standing to start the lawsuit because it had suffered no injury and could not, therefore, seek a remedy.

The present case fell within this precedent. Cook found there was not even "facial adverseness" between the state and the defendant Moore. The court pleadings showed that the state and the judge supported one another. The state had not asked that Moore's conduct be declared incorrect in any respect but instead had extolled the judge's conduct and sought a "judgment declaring that his practices are eminently correct and must be sanctioned." The state had failed to show it had been harmed in any way by Moore's practices. Cook also noted that Moore had expressly agreed with all of the state's substantive allegations; the state and Moore were not adversaries. The court declined to become a "political foil or a sounding board for topics of contemporary interest," and therefore dismissed the state's lawsuit.

The court also dismissed the counterclaims of the ACLU and AFA as nonjusticiable. The claim against Chief Justice Hooper in his capacity as administrator was fatally flawed because the office of chief justice "is unable to provide the relief they seek." The court ruled that the chief justice had no authority to act unilaterally to control the conduct of a circuit judge. Instead, authority is vested with the Alabama Supreme Court. Because the ACLU and AFA could not receive the relief from the chief justice, and because they had not sued the Alabama Supreme Court, their counterclaims were nonjusticiable.

The supreme court vacated the trial court decision and dismissed the proceedings. The practical result was that Moore and other Alabama judges could continue to ask local clergy to offer prayers and to display the Ten Commandments.

**CROSS REFERENCES**
American Civil Liberties Union; First Amendment; Native Americans; Schools and School Districts; Standing

## SARGENT, JOHN GARIBALDI

John Garibaldi Sargent served as attorney general of the United States under President Calvin Coolidge.

Sargent was born October 13, 1860, in Ludlow, Vermont, to John Henmon and Ann Eliza Hanley Sargent. He was schooled locally and then entered Tufts College in Boston, receiving a bachelor's degree in 1887. Early in his college years, Sargent became active in the Zeta Psi Kappa Society; through the fraternity's activities he was introduced to many of Boston's oldest and most influential political families, including the Coolidges.

After college, Sargent returned to Ludlow, where he married Mary Lorraine Gordon in 1887. Sargent studied law with attorney, and future Vermont governor, William Wallace Stickney. Following Sargent's admission to the Vermont bar in 1890, he joined Stickney in the practice of law.

Sargent's first political appointment came in 1898 when he was named state's attorney for Windsor County, Vermont. He served until 1900 when he was appointed secretary of civil and military affairs for the state of Vermont by his law partner, who was then serving his first term as governor. After completing the two-year assignment, Sargent returned to the firm and resumed the practice of law. From 1902 to 1908, he argued the majority of his cases in federal court, and he established a national reputation as a trial lawyer.

In 1908 Sargent was named attorney general of Vermont. While in office, he was in-volved in one of the leading cases in the history of Vermont's highest court. In *Sabre v. Rutland Railroad Co.*, 86 Vt. 347, 85 Aik. 693 (1912), attorneys for the railroad argued that the powers enjoyed by Vermont's Public Service Commission (which regulated railroads) violated the Vermont Constitution by commingling legislative, executive, and judicial functions. Sargent, arguing for Sabre and the state, disagreed. His position was that the separation of powers was only violated when one branch exercised all of the powers of another branch. The court agreed with Sargent and recognized the quasi-judicial powers of executive-branch state agencies. The decision led the way for commissions and boards across the country to wield courtlike powers.

While serving as Vermont's attorney general, Sargent also returned to school, he receiving master's degree from Tufts College in 1912. When Sargent returned to his law firm in 1913, he turned his attention to partisan politics. He supported Republican party candidates in Vermont and throughout the Northeast and campaigned vigorously for Warren G. Harding in 1920 and Calvin Coolidge in 1924.

Sargent was named attorney general of the United States on March 17, 1925, but only after the president's first choice, financier Charles B. Warren, withdrew after the Senate questioned his willingness to enforce antitrust laws. Sargent proved to be a safe and noncontroversial alternative. He was confirmed in just one day, and he served from March 18, 1925, until March 4, 1929.

Sargent was not known as a leader in the fight for racial equality, but he did ask the pres-

*John Garibaldi Sargent*
UPI/CORBIS-BETTMANN

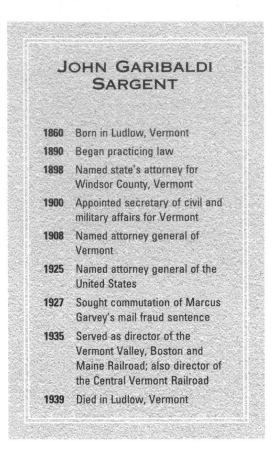

**JOHN GARIBALDI SARGENT**

| | |
|---|---|
| 1860 | Born in Ludlow, Vermont |
| 1890 | Began practicing law |
| 1898 | Named state's attorney for Windsor County, Vermont |
| 1900 | Appointed secretary of civil and military affairs for Vermont |
| 1908 | Named attorney general of Vermont |
| 1925 | Named attorney general of the United States |
| 1927 | Sought commutation of Marcus Garvey's mail fraud sentence |
| 1935 | Served as director of the Vermont Valley, Boston and Maine Railroad; also director of the Central Vermont Railroad |
| 1939 | Died in Ludlow, Vermont |

ident to commute the sentence of Marcus M. Garvey in 1927. Garvey was a political activist from Jamaica who had been convicted of mail fraud for his efforts to recruit black Americans for his Universal Negro Improvement League and African Communities Association (*Garvey v. United States*, 267 U.S. 604, 45 S. Ct. 464 [1925]). The tainted proceeding against Garvey was orchestrated by an overzealous, young Justice Department attorney named J. Edgar Hoover.

Sargent was outspoken in his disapproval of Hoover's tactics in the Garvey case, and he was among the first attorneys general to condemn the gathering of evidence through wiretapping, a tactic approved by Hoover when he was director of the Federal Bureau of Investigation. Testifying before a congressional committee, Sargent said, "Wire tapping, entrapment, or use of any illegal or unethical tactics in procuring information will not be tolerated … )."

In 1930 Sargent returned to Vermont and again took an active role in his law firm. In his later years, Sargent devoted his time and energy to local businesses and community organizations. When years of political infighting finally forced the reorganization of Vermont's railroads

in the early 1930s, Sargent was appointed to oversee the process.

Sargent died at his home in Ludlow, Vermont, on March 5, 1939, at the age of 79.

## SCIENTIFIC EVIDENCE

EVIDENCE presented in court that is produced from scientific tests or studies.

### General Electric Company v. Joiner

How to handle scientific evidence poses a serious concern for courts. Judges and juries must assess competing scientific theories, methodologies, research, and conclusions in order to render verdicts in civil actions. Courts are assisted in this process by rules of evidence, which establish standards for the acceptance of scientific evidence. In *General Electric Co. v. Joiner*, ___U.S.___, 118 S. Ct. 512, 139 L. Ed. 2d 508 (1997), the U.S. Supreme Court clarified the amount of discretion afforded federal trial courts in ruling on the admissibility of scientific evidence from expert witnesses and the proper scope of appellate review of such decisions.

Robert K. Joiner began work as an electrician in the Water & Light Department of Thomasville, Georgia, in 1973. This job required him to work with and around the city's electrical transformers, which used a mineral-based dielectric fluid as a coolant. Joiner often had to stick his hands and arms into the fluid to make repairs. The fluid would sometimes splash onto him, occasionally getting into his eyes and mouth. In 1983 the city discovered that the fluid in some of the transformers was contaminated with polychlorinated biphenyls (PCBs), which are widely considered to be hazardous to human health. Congress, with limited exceptions, banned the production and sale of PCBs in 1978, (15 U.S.C.A. § 2605(e) (2) [A]).

Joiner was diagnosed with lung cancer in 1991. The following year he sued three corporations: Monsanto, which manufactured PCBs from 1935 to 1977, General Electric, and Westinghouse Electric, both of whom manufactured transformers and dielectric fluid. Joiner linked his development of cancer to his exposure to PCBs and their derivatives, polychlorinated dibenzofurans (furans) and polychlorinated dibenzodioxins (dioxins). However, Joiner had been a smoker for eight years, his parents had both been smokers, and there was a history of lung cancer in his family, suggesting the possibility of a heightened risk of developing lung cancer eventually. The suit alleged that his exposure to PCBs "promoted" his cancer: but for his exposure to these substances, his cancer would not have developed for many years, if at all.

The three defendants moved the federal district court to dismiss Joiner's case. They contended that there was no evidence that Joiner suffered significant exposure to PCBs, furans, or dioxins, and that there was no admissible scientific evidence that PCBs promoted Joiner's cancer. Joiner argued that numerous disputed factual issues of his suit required resolution by a jury. He relied on the testimony of expert witnesses, who in depositions had testified that PCBs alone can promote cancer and that furans and dioxins can also promote cancer. They testified that since Joiner had been exposed to PCBs, furans, and dioxins, such exposure was likely responsible for Joiner's cancer.

The district court ruled that there was a genuine issue of material fact as to whether Joiner had been exposed to PCBs, yet it dismissed the case because there was no genuine issue as to whether Joiner had been exposed to furans and dioxins and the testimony of Joiner's experts had failed to show that there was a link between exposure to PCBs and small cell lung cancer. The court believed that the testimony of respondent's experts to the contrary did not rise above "subjective belief or unsupported speculation." (864 F. Supp. 1310, 1326 [N.D. Ga. 1994]). Their testimony was therefore inadmissible.

The Court of Appeals for the Eleventh Circuit reversed 78 F.3d 524 (1996). It held that "[b]ecause the Federal Rules of Evidence governing expert testimony display a preference for admissibility, we apply a particularly stringent standard of review to the trial judge's exclusion of expert testimony." Applying that standard, the court of appeals held that the district court had erred in excluding the testimony of Joiner's expert witnesses. The district court had improperly excluded the experts' testimony because the court "drew different conclusions from the research than did each of the experts." The court of appeals concluded that a district court should limit its role to determining the "legal reliability of proffered expert testimony, leaving the jury to decide the correctness of competing expert opinions." The district court had also incorrectly held that there was no genuine issue of material fact as to whether Joiner had been exposed to furans and dioxins. The court of appeals believed otherwise, because testimony in the record supported the proposition that there had been such exposure.

The Supreme Court disagreed with the court of appeals. Chief Justice William H. Rehnquist, writing for the Court, ruled that the court of appeals had incorrectly applied a standard of review when examining the district court's decision. The court of appeals had applied a "particularly stringent" standard of review rather than the traditional "abuse of discretion" standard. Under the abuse of discretion standard, an appellate court may not overturn a lower court decision unless it is "manifestly erroneous." This standard prevents an appellate court from second-guessing trial decisions.

The court of appeals had justified its more stringent review on the basis of the Supreme Court's decision in *Daubert v. Merrell Dow Pharmaceuticals, Inc.*, 509 U.S. 579, 113 S. Ct. 2786, 125 L. Ed. 2d 469 (1993). *Daubert* had set out standards for the admission or exclusion of expert scientific testimony, and the court of appeals surmised that *Daubert* had altered the general rule that an abuse of discretion standard be applied to a district court's decision to exclude scientific evidence. Justice Rehnquist rejected this conclusion, stating that "*Daubert* did not address the standard of appellate review for evidentiary rulings at all." Though *Daubert* made it easier to admit a broader range of scientific evidence, the opinion made clear that the trial judge had a duty to insure that "testimony or evidence admitted is not only relevant, but reliable." The "gatekeeper" role of the trial judge in screening scientific evidence remained a critical component in such cases. The court of appeals had, in Justice Rehnquist's view, "failed to give the trial court the deference that is the hallmark of abuse of discretion review."

Justice Rehnquist then applied the abuse of discretion standard of review to the facts in the case. He concluded that the district court had not abused its discretion in ruling that Joiner's experts had not provided creditable scientific evidence that linked exposure to PCBs to Joiner's cancer. Animal studies that linked PCB exposure to cancer in mice were not relevant because the mice were injected with high amounts of PCBs, while Joiner had come into contact with much smaller amounts of PCBs.

Justice Rehnquist also agreed with the district court that four epidemiological studies on which Joiner relied failed to make a clear link between exposure to PCBs and lung cancer and were not a sufficient basis for the experts' opinions. Justice Rehnquist stated that it was proper for a court to "conclude that there is simply too great an analytical gap between the data and the opinion proffered.... That is what the District Court did here, and we hold that it did not abuse its discretion in so doing."

Justice Rehnquist noted, however, that the district court had never explicitly considered whether there was admissible evidence on the question of whether Joiner's alleged exposure to furans and dioxins contributed to his lung cancer. Therefore, the Court remanded that portion of the case for further proceedings.

In a concurring opinion, Justice Stephen G. Breyer noted that judges are being called on to make "subtle and sophisticated determinations about scientific methodology." Yet "judges are not scientists and do not have the scientific training that can facilitate the making of such decisions." Justice Breyer urged judges to use several techniques that will improve the decision-making process, including pretrial conferences to narrow the scientific issues in dispute, pretrial hearings where potential experts are subject to examination by the court, and the appointment of special masters and specially trained law clerks.

**CROSS REFERENCES**
Evidence; Matter of Fact; Witnesses

## SEALE, BOBBY

Bobby Seale cofounded the Black Panther Party for Self-Defense in 1966. The Panthers were a radical, militant black group that drew upon the rhetoric of Malcolm X, Mao Tse-tung, Karl Marx, Vladimir Lenin, and others. The group's revolutionary stance and armed patrols of black neighborhoods engendered widespread publicity and fear, although the group was also involved in numerous community service projects.

*Bobby Seale*
CAMERA PRESS/ARCHIVE PHOTOS

Seale was born October 20, 1936, in Dallas, Texas. His family moved and settled in Oakland, California. After leaving high school without earning a diploma, Seale joined the U.S. Air Force and became an aircraft sheet-metal mechanic. Court-martialed and given a bad conduct discharge for disobeying orders, he finished high school, worked sporadically, and then enrolled in Merritt Junior College in Oakland.

In 1962 Seale met fellow student and activist Huey P. Newton. The men grew increasingly disenchanted with what they perceived as the ineffectiveness of Merritt's Afro-American Association, a black separatism and self-improvement organization. The assassination of Malcolm X in 1965 propelled Seale and Newton to found the Black Panther Party for Self-Defense in late 1966. Seale was the party's chair, and Newton its minister of defense. They devised a ten-point platform which included: the black community's fulfillment of its own destiny, reparations for slavery, exemption from military conscription for all African American men, education to teach African Americans their complete history and expose the decadence of the United States, a denunciation of police brutality, and a call to revolution if African Americans could not otherwise obtain justice and peace.

The Panthers' community ventures contrasted starkly with their revolutionary activities. On the one hand, Seale and his fellow Panthers served free breakfasts to children, provided senior citizen escort services, operated health clinics, and distributed free clothing and shoes. On the other hand, the Panthers intimidated many people when, taking advantage of California laws permitting citizens to carry unconcealed weapons, they patrolled black neighborhoods in an effort to prevent police abuse. This militant stance aroused the ire of numerous law enforcement agencies; arrest and conflict with police were common. On May 2, 1967, Seale led thirty armed Panthers into the California State Assembly to protest proposed gun control legislation. He served five months in jail for the incident, bringing the group national notoriety. In 1967 FBI Director J. Edgar Hoover targeted the group for infiltration, exposure, and disruption.

Seale's contacts with white protesters against the Vietnam War led to his participation in a large demonstration at the 1968 Democratic National Convention in Chicago. Seale spoke to the crowd but then returned immediately to California. After Seale and other impassioned leaders spoke, protesters clashed with police. As a result, Seale and seven white men were charged under a recently enacted federal law making it illegal to cross state lines to incite a riot or to instruct in the use of riot weapons.

The joint trial of the defendants, known as the Chicago Eight, began in late September 1969. The other defendants were Abbie Hoffman, Jerry Rubin, Tom Hayden, Lee Weiner, Rennie Davis, David Dellinger, and John Froines. Two weeks before the trial started, Seale requested a delay so that his lawyer could convalesce following major surgery. U.S. District Judge Julius J. Hoffman denied the request, and attorney William M. Kunstler then entered his appearance on Seale's behalf. Upon advice from his original attorney, Seale fired Kunstler and asked to represent himself. Hoffman refused, ruling that Kunstler and his colleagues, who were also representing the other defendants, provided sufficient representation for Seale.

Thus the stage was set for a sensational trial in which the judge and the defendant were simultaneously the harasser and the harassed. Seale repeatedly demanded the right to cross-examine witnesses. In the face of the judge's unwavering denials, Seale's behavior steadily disintegrated from refusing to rise when the judge entered the courtroom to calling the judge a racist, fascist, bigot, and pig.

In the sixth week of trial, Hoffman ordered Seale bound and gagged. Seale was chained to his chair by leg irons and handcuffs, and a gag covered his mouth. Even these degrading restraints did not deter Seale from his relentless courtroom disruption: he rattled his chains so loudly that they had to be replaced by leather straps. He also managed to mutter muffled oinks and obscenities through his gag and at one point managed to free himself from the gag to renew his diatribe at full volume.

The judge's need to maintain an orderly courtroom, Seale's constitutional right to be present at trial, and the very possible prejudice to him caused by the jury seeing him heavily restrained, eventually resulted in the inevitable. In November Hoffman declared a mistrial on Seale's behalf. In a highly controversial move, the judge also found Seale guilty of 16 counts of contempt of court and imposed 16 consecutive three-month prison sentences on him.

The conspiracy charges were ultimately dropped, and Seale was released in 1972. During his incarceration he stood trial in New York on conspiracy to kidnap and murder a man believed to be an FBI informant within the Black Panthers. With the jury deadlocked in trying to reach a verdict, Seale again obtained a mistrial. He was not tried again.

In the 1970s Seale tried to steer the Panthers away from revolutionary conduct toward the development of community improvement programs. He wrote *Seize the Time*, a book that downplayed the widely held perception that the Panthers were racists and police killers. Some were skeptical of Seale's new attitude, but he was

## BOBBY SEALE

| | |
|---|---|
| 1936 | Born in Dallas, Texas |
| 1962 | Met fellow student and activist Huey P. Newton |
| 1966 | With Newton, founded the Black Panther Party for Self-Defense |
| 1967 | Led thirty armed Panthers into the California State Assembly; served five months for the incident |
| 1968 | Charged with inciting a riot during the Democratic National Convention in Chicago |
| 1969 | Tried as a member of the "Chicago Eight"; despite a mistrial, found guilty of 16 counts of contempt of court |
| 1972 | Conspiracy charges dropped; Seale released |
| 1974 | Quit Panthers; started Advocates Scene |

sufficiently convincing to win second place in a race for mayor of Oakland in 1973.

In 1974 Seale quit the Panthers and started Advocates Scene, an organization directed toward helping poor people to form grass roots political organizations. In the 1980s Seale's ideology may have been unrecognizable to his 1960s colleagues when he became an outspoken advocate of handgun control. He also served as the African American studies liaison at Temple University and lectured throughout the country. In 1987 he published a cookbook, *Barbecuing with Bobby*.

## SEARCH AND SEIZURE

(1) In INTERNATIONAL LAW, the right of ships of war, as regulated by treaties, to examine a merchant vessel during war in order to determine whether the ship or its cargo is liable to seizure.

(2) A hunt by law enforcement officials for property or communications believed to be evidence of

crime, and the act of taking possession of this property.

### Chandler v. Miller

The Fourth Amendment generally prohibits the government from undertaking a search and seizure absent individualized suspicion of wrongdoing. However, there are certain exceptions to this rule that are based on special needs beyond normal law enforcement crime detection. When special needs are alleged in justification of Fourth Amendment intrusion, the courts must undertake context-specific reviews, examining the competing private and public interests advanced by the parties.

Drug testing has become a "special needs" area that the courts have examined regarding Fourth Amendment issues. Federal, state, and local government agencies have established mandatory drug testing for certain categories of government employees and for student athletes. The U.S. Supreme Court has issued a series of rulings on these special needs exceptions, the most recent involving a Georgia statute that required candidates for certain state offices to certify that they had taken a drug test and that the drug test was negative. In *Chandler v. Miller*, ___U.S.___, 117 S. Ct. 1295, 137 L. Ed. 2d 513 (1997), the Court struck down the Georgia law as an unjustified intrusion on personal privacy that did not advance a compelling state interest.

In 1990 the Georgia legislature enacted the law (Ga. Code Ann. § 21-2-140), which ordered each candidate for state office to "certify that such candidate has tested negative for illegal drugs." To qualify for a place on the ballot, a candidate had to present a certificate from a state-approved laboratory that the candidate submitted to a urinalysis drug test within thirty days prior to qualifying for nomination or election and that the results were negative. The statute listed illegal drugs as marijuana, cocaine, opiates, amphetamines, and phencyclidines. The offices covered by the law included the governor, lieutenant governor, secretary of state, and attorney general and all judgeships, district attorneys, and members of the state legislature.

In 1994 Walker L. Chandler, the Libertarian party's nominee for lieutenant governor, along with two other of the party's candidates for state office, filed suit in federal court, asserting that the drug-testing law violated their rights under the First, Fourth, and Fourteenth Amendments of the U.S. Constitution. They named as defendants Governor Zell D. Miller and two other state officials charged with administering the law. The plaintiffs sought a preliminary injunction barring enforcement of the law, but the district court denied the request. Chandler and the others then submitted to drug tests and obtained the required certificates, and their names appeared on the ballot. Nevertheless, they continued to seek a permanent injunction. The district court again declined to grant the relief, and a subsequent appeal to the Eleventh Circuit Court of Appeals reaffirmed the constitutionality of the statute (73 F. 3d 1543 [1996]).

The Supreme Court, however, reversed the lower courts. On an 8–1 vote, with Chief Justice William H. Rehnquist the lone dissenter, the Court held that its previous decisions upholding special needs exceptions to the Fourth Amendment did not apply to the Georgia statute. In addition, it held that the state did not have the right under the Tenth Amendment to make the drug test a qualification for office.

Justice Ruth Bader Ginsburg, writing for the majority, noted that government-ordered collection and testing of urine intrudes upon reasonable expectations of privacy and is clearly a search under the Fourth Amendment. The key question in analyzing the claim for a special needs exception is whether the drug test was reasonable. Courts determine whether the test is reasonable by examining the competing private and public interests advanced by the parties.

Ginsburg reviewed three prior Supreme Court cases that upheld the right of government to require a person to submit to a drug test: *Skinner v. Railway Labor Executives' Association*, 489 U.S. 602, 109 S. Ct. 1402, 103 L. Ed. 2d 639 (1989), *National Treasury Employees Union v. Von Raab*, 489 U.S. 656, 109 S. Ct. 1384, 103 L. Ed. 2d 685 (1989), and *Vernonia School District 47J v. Action*, 515 U.S. 646, 115 S. Ct. 2386, 132 L. Ed. 2d 564 (1995).

In *Skinner* Federal Railroad Administration regulations required that employees involved in train accidents submit to blood and urine tests. Ginsburg noted that the drug-testing program came in response to evidence of drug and alcohol abuse by some railroad employees, the safety hazards posed by such abuse, and the documented link between drug- and alcohol-impaired employees and the incidence of train accidents. The Court upheld the drug testing due to important safety interests. Because employees could not forecast the timing of accidents or safety violations that would trigger testing, the testing requirement served as an important deterrent. In addition, the ability of the government to test employees without the need for individualized suspicion aided the government's efforts to determine the cause of the accident and identify individuals who may have caused the accident.

In *Von Raab* the Court upheld a U.S. Customs Service program that made drug tests a condition of promotion or transfer to positions directly involving drug interdiction or requiring the employee to carry a firearm. The Court was persuaded that the unique mission of the agency as the "first line of defense" against illegal drug smuggling required testing. The tests worked to prevent employees who were drug users from being placed in positions where they would be susceptible to bribery or blackmail. In addition, there was no practical way to subject employees to the daily scrutiny that is typical of more traditional office environments.

Ginsburg also reviewed the *Vernonia* decision, in which the Court upheld a random drug-testing program for high school students involved in interscholastic athletic competitions. The Court justified the intrusion on student privacy on the grounds of a sharp increase in illegal drug use by students and the fact that student athletes were "leaders of the drug culture." The Court also noted that students within the school setting have a lesser expectation of privacy than members of the general population. The importance of deterring student drug use and preventing injuries to drug-using student athletes supported the state's interest in drug testing.

Using these three decisions as guides, Ginsburg concluded that the Georgia drug testing was not warranted by a special need. Georgia argued that the use of illegal drugs draws into question an official's judgment and integrity, threatens the discharge of public functions, including anti-drug enforcement, and undermines public confidence and trust in elected officials. The law was designed to deter unlawful drug users from becoming candidates and holders of high state office.

Ginsburg dismissed Georgia's justifications for the law, noting that "nothing in the record hints that the hazards respondents broadly describe are real and not simply hypothetical for Georgia's polity." Unlike the three special cases upheld by the Court, Georgia had failed to show that there was a problem with state officers being drug abusers.

In addition, Ginsburg found that the certification requirement was not well designed to identify candidates who violate anti-drug laws. The test date—thirty days prior to qualifying for the ballot—was no secret. Therefore, a candidate could abstain for a pretest period sufficient to avoid detection. In contrast in *Skinner, Von Raab*, and *Vernonia*, a drug user could not anticipate the drug-testing program.

The Court also rejected Georgia's contention that its program was akin to the U.S. Customs Service program in *Von Raab*, which was upheld despite the absence of any documented drug abuse problem among service employees. Ginsburg noted the "unique context" of *Von Raab*. Customs officers are routinely exposed to organized crime tied to illegal drug use. Officers are targets of bribery. There was no feasible alternative to protect the integrity of customs employees. In contrast, Ginsburg pointed out that political candidates are "subject to relentless scrutiny—by their peers, the public, and the press. Their day-to-day conduct attracts attention notably beyond the norm in ordinary work environments."

Finding no compelling reason for the drug test, the Court ruled that it did not meet the special need exception. In addition, the Court rejected Georgia's contention that the Tenth Amendment gave the state the authority to set the drug test as a qualification for office. A state may set qualifications, but it "may not disregard basic constitutional protections."

In a dissenting opinion, Chief Justice Rehnquist argued that Georgia should be free to institute drug tests. Although Georgia was the only state to take such action, Rehnquist believed the legislation was reasonable, even if the state could not demonstrate a current problem with political candidates: "But surely the State need not wait for a drug addict, or one inclined to use drugs illegally, to run for or actually become Governor before it installs a prophylactic mechanism." He concluded that the privacy interests of candidates were negligible and that the state had a legitimate interest in preventing individuals who were susceptible to bribery and blackmail from being elected to public office.

### Maryland v. Wilson

The Fourth Amendment to the U.S. Constitution guarantees persons freedom from "unreasonable searches and seizures." In most situations, police are required to obtain a search warrant before performing a search and seizure, but there are exceptions. One important exception involves automobile searches. This exception, which was first announced in *Carroll v. United States*, 267 U.S. 132, 45 S. Ct. 280, 69 L. Ed. 543 (1925), has had a long and often confusing history of court decisions. Nevertheless, the U.S. Supreme Court has given police more leeway in stopping and searching automobiles.

In *Maryland v. Wilson*, ___U.S.___, 117 S. Ct. 882, 137 L. Ed. 2d 41 (1997), the Court gave police even more authority. The Court held that an officer may as a matter of course order passengers of a lawfully stopped car to exit the vehicle, even if the passengers are not suspected of having violated the law. In deciding this way, the Court extended its ruling in *Pennsylvania v. Mimms*, 434 U.S. 106, 98 S. Ct. 330, 54 L. Ed. 2d 331 (1977), which authorized police to order the driver of a lawfully stopped car to exit the vehicle. In dissent, Justices John Paul Stevens and Anthony M. Kennedy raised concerns about the erosion of the protections of the Fourth Amendment.

The case arose when a Maryland state trooper observed a car traveling ten miles faster than the posted speed limit. The car had no regular license tags, and a torn piece of paper displaying a rental car company name was hanging from its rear. After the trooper turned on his vehicle's lights and sirens, the car that he was following continued for a mile and a half before pulling over. During the pursuit, the trooper noticed that the car contained a driver and two passengers.

After being pulled over, the driver exited the car. He was ordered to return and retrieve the rental car documents. As he did so, the trooper observed that the front-seat passenger, Jerry Lee Wilson, was sweating and appeared very nervous. The trooper ordered Wilson out of the car, and when Wilson stepped out, a quantity of crack cocaine fell to the ground.

Wilson was charged with possession of cocaine with intent to distribute. Wilson, however, sought to suppress the evidence, arguing that the trooper's ordering of him out of the car was an unreasonable seizure under the Fourth Amendment. The trial court agreed that the search was unconstitutional, and the Court of Special Appeals of Maryland agreed (106 Md. App. 24, 664 A.2d 1 [1995]). Both courts ruled that *Pennsylvania v. Mimms* only applied to drivers, not passengers.

On appeal, the Supreme Court had to determine whether *Mimms* extends to passengers. On a 7–2 vote, the Court held that the decision should be extended. Chief Justice William H. Rehnquist, in his majority opinion, noted that the *Mimms* decision was based on the reasonableness of the search. Reasonableness in that case was based on determining the balance between the public interest and the individual's right to personal security free from arbitrary interference by police officers. In *Mimms* the Court found that ordering a driver to exit a car was a legitimate precautionary safety measure. In addition, there was "appreciable" danger to the officer when standing by the driver's door, in the path of oncoming traffic. On the other hand, the intrusion into the driver's liberty by ordering her out of the car was minimal. Therefore, in *Mimms* the Court held that "once a motor vehicle has been lawfully detained for a traffic violation, the police officers may order the driver out of the vehicle without violating the Fourth Amendment's proscription of unreasonable seizures."

Rehnquist applied the same balancing test in *Wilson*. Rehnquist pointed out that officer safety is an important public interest, "regardless of whether the occupant of the stopped car is a driver or passenger." In 1994 almost six thousand officers were assaulted and eleven officers were killed during traffic pursuits and stops. These statistics persuaded Rehnquist that the presence of more than one occupant of the automobile increased the possible sources of harm to the officer.

The majority opinion did acknowledge, however, that the personal liberty side of the balance was stronger for the passengers than for the driver. Rehnquist stated that there is "probable cause to believe that the driver has committed a minor vehicular offense, but there is no such reason to stop or detain the passengers." Nevertheless, Rehnquist concluded that, as a practical matter, "the passengers are already stopped by virtue of the stop of the vehicle. The only change in their circumstance, which will result from ordering them out of the car, is that they will be outside of, rather than inside of, the stopped car. Outside the car, the passengers will be denied access to any possible weapon that might be concealed in the interior of the passenger compartment.

The Court concluded that the increased danger to an officer when passengers are in the car and the minimal additional intrusion on the passengers justified ordering passengers from the car pending the completion of the stop.

Justice Stevens, in a dissent joined by Justice Kennedy, argued that the ruling gave the state broad power to make an initial seizure of persons who are not suspected of having violated the law. He noted that the ruling could affect the "literally millions" of traffic stops that take place each year, because it applies to traffic stops "in which there is not even a scintilla of evidence of any potential risk to the police officer." In those cases, he concluded, the Fourth Amendment bars "routine and arbitrary seizures of obviously innocent citizens."

Stevens challenged the majority's use of the 1994 traffic stop assault and murder statistics, arguing that these statistics did not reveal how many of the incidents involved passengers. In addition, the statistics did not show how many assaults involved passengers who remained inside the vehicles or who had exited. Because of this dearth of information, Stevens concluded that "the statistics are as consistent with the hypothesis that ordering passengers to get out of a vehicle increases the danger of assault as with the hypothesis that it reduces that risk."

In assessing the balance between officer safety and the invasion of a person's liberty, Stevens argued that any incremental gain in officer safety was outweighed by the "unnecessary invasion that will be imposed on innocent citizens under the majority's rule." He pointed out that most traffic stops involve "otherwise law-abiding citizens who have committed minor traffic offenses." The number of stops in which an officer is at risk is "dwarfed by the far greater number of routine stops." Though the majority concluded that the intrusion on a citizen's liberty is minimal, Stevens thought otherwise, stating that the "aggregation of thousands upon thousands of petty indignities has an impact on freedom that I would characterize as substantial, and which in my view clearly outweighs the evanescent safety concerns pressed by the majority."

In a separate dissent, Kennedy noted that the U.S. criminal justice system requires "principled, accountable decision making in individual cases." Therefore, before a person is seized, "a satisfactory explanation for the invasive action ought to be established by an officer." Kennedy found the majority decision troubling because even routine traffic stops may take up to thirty minutes. Commanding an innocent person to exit a vehicle "and stand by the side of the road in full view of the public" is not a trivial action. In his view, if the "command to exit were to become commonplace, the Constitution would be diminished in a most public way."

## Miranda Rule Violation

The Wisconsin Court of Appeals refused to weaken defendants' rights when police illegally obtain evidence. In *State v. Kiekhefer*, 569 N.W.2d 316 (1997), the court overturned Scott Kiekhefer's 1995 conviction for possession of 14 pounds of marijuana. Kiekhefer had been convicted after police officers raided his room without a search warrant and failed to properly observe the *Miranda* rule which requires police to give certain warnings and affirm certain rights to suspects upon arrest and before questioning. Before the appellate court, prosecutors acknowledged that police had violated Kiekhefer's rights. Yet the state argued that a 1985 U.S. Supreme Court precedent should be extended so that physical evidence seized in the raid would still be admissible. The appellate panel disagreed.

On March 6, 1995, two police agents staked out Kiekhefer's home in Racine County, Wisconsin. They suspected him of holding a large amount of marijuana and some guns for Darryl Wisneski. After a car apparently driven by Wisneski briefly stopped at the house, police gave chase but could not catch it. They returned to try to do a consensual search of the house. Kiekhefer's mother admitted Deputy Brian Londre and agent Joseph Zbleskwski to the house. They never asked for consent to search, but she agreed to let them speak to her son if she accompanied them. Outside the door to his room, they smelled burning marijuana. They called for backup, and two additional agents soon arrived.

Without announcing their presence, the four agents entered the room. They immediately handcuffed and patted down Scott Kiekhefer and his friend Keith Christensen. Agent Zbleskwski asked if there were any controlled substances in the room. Kiekhefer pointed to a joint, or marijuana cigarette, in an ashtray. Asked if there was more, Kiekhefer responded that there was a bag of pot in his dresser. Zbleskwski asked for permission to search the room and, according to testimony, may have said, "We can do this the hard way or we can do this the easy way." He then told Kiekhefer, "We can get a warrant if we need to." Christensen later testified that the agent said that if they obtained a warrant, the police would "tear this place apart." After Kiekhefer gave consent to search, police found a gym bag containing fourteen pounds of pot and also uncovered two guns. Only at this point did Zbleskwski read Kiekhefer his *Miranda* rights. Two hours later, still in his room, Kiekhefer gave a written confession.

Before trial in October, Kiekhefer filed a motion to suppress all evidence seized from the home, as well as his statements made during the search. This common defense strategy is based on the long-standing *Miranda* rule. Established by the U.S. Supreme Court in 1966, the rule attempts to protect a suspect from being coerced into making self-incriminating statements. It goes into effect prior to any interrogation in which law enforcement officers question a suspect in custody—custody meaning, broadly, any significant deprivation of the suspect's freedom. Police must warn a defendant that (1) he has a right to remain silent; (2) any statement he makes may be used as evidence against him; (3) he has a right to the presence of an attorney; and (4) if he cannot afford an attorney, one will be appointed for him prior to any questioning. Generally, unless these warnings are given or the suspect waives these rights, no evidence obtained in the interrogation is admissible at trial. Kiekhefer's defense motion sought to suppress the evidence because he had not been advised of his rights prior to the interrogation.

The trial court denied the motion. Kiekhefer subsequently sought a lesser sentence by pleading no contest to possession of a controlled substance. He received a three-year prison sentence, was ordered to obtain drug and alcohol counseling, was fined $1,000, and had his driver's license revoked for six months. He appealed on the ground that his Fifth Amendment rights had been violated.

On appeal, prosecutors acknowledged the *Miranda* violation and conceded that Kiekhefer's unwarned statements must be suppressed. However, they argued that the physical evidence found as a result of the unwarned statements should be admissible. As precedent, they cited the U.S. Supreme Court's 1985 decision in *Oregon v. Elstad*, 470 U.S. 298, 105 S. Ct. 1285, 84 L. Ed. 2d 222. *Elstad* belongs to a line of opinions dating from the early 1970s in which the Court granted prosecutors exceptions to *Miranda* violations: essentially, it allows the use of oral statements derived from those violations, but only under certain narrow conditions. Wisconsin prosecutors asked the appellate panel to take *Elstad* one step further by allowing for the admission of physical evidence as well.

In its decision the panel noted that Wisconsin courts had yet to fully address the question of whether *Elstad* applied to physical evidence. In any event, the facts in the case could not support the state's case. First, the panel applied the Supreme Court's *Elstad* analysis to Kiekhefer's statements. Police, it found, coerced these statements. Kiekhefer had not made voluntary statements because police had "made a sobering show of force" and had not informed him of his right to withhold his consent to be searched. Moreover, the agents "had no right to imply that they could sit in Kiekhefer's home for two hours" while obtaining a warrant. Hence they had also compelled him to make his subsequent written statement. None of Kiekhefer's statements—oral or written—was therefore admissible under the Fifth Amendment. Accordingly, the panel ruled to suppress the physical evidence derived from those statements and Kiekhefer's consent to search.

Even without these violations, the panel said, the evidence must be suppressed because police had acted illegally in other ways. They had made a warrant-less entry into the home and a subsequent search and seizure, both in violation of the Fourth Amendment to the U.S. Constitution and article I of the Wisconsin Constitution. The trial court had found that the entry into the bedroom was with consent, but the appellate panel called this finding clearly erroneous: police had not originally asked for permission to search.

Finally, the panel considered the state's two arguments that urgent circumstances justified police actions during the raid. Had the agents not acted, prosecutors argued, Wisneski might have destroyed or reclaimed the drugs; moreover, the police were in physical danger. The panel disagreed. Wisneski had fled and was unlikely to return, there were no sounds of destruction emanating from the room, and the police had the situation well under control. At best, the panel ruled, all the agents legally could have done upon smelling the burning pot was procure a search warrant. Observing that "[S]uch flagrant misuse of authority simply cannot be ignored," the panel suppressed all the seized evidence, overturned Kiekhefer's conviction, and sent the case back to the trial court.

### Richards v. Wisconsin

The Fourth Amendment's prohibition against unreasonable searches and seizures has been the subject of countless court challenges. The courts have developed tests to determine when law enforcement officers have a reasonable basis to make a search or seizure. One troublesome area has been the question of whether police must knock on a suspect's door and announce they have a warrant to enter the premises. It is the general rule that police may make a "no-knock" entry if there are reasonable grounds for such a course of action.

The U.S. Supreme Court, in *Richards v. Wisconsin*, ___U.S.___, 117 S. Ct. 1416 137 L.Ed. 2d 615 (1997), was confronted with a decision of the Wisconsin Supreme Court that announced a blanket exception to the knock-and-announce requirement for felony drug investigations. The U.S. Supreme Court unanimously ruled that such an exception violated the Fourth Amendment and undermined the ability of a reviewing court to determine whether a no-knock entry was reasonable. In making this ruling, the Court rejected the idea that the violent world of those who traffic in illegal narcotics justified a departure from Fourth Amendment jurisprudence.

The issue arose from a drug investigation conducted by the Madison, Wisconsin, police involving Steiney Richards. Richards was suspected of dealing drugs out of hotel rooms in Madison. On December 31, 1991, police officers obtained a warrant to search Richards' hotel room for drugs and drug paraphernalia. Although the police had asked the magistrate to give them advance authorization for a no-knock entry into the hotel room, the magistrate explicitly deleted this authorization from the warrant.

The police officers arrived at Richards' hotel room at 3:40 A.M. An officer dressed as a maintenance man, accompanied by several plainclothes officers and at least one man in uniform, knocked on Richards' door. When Richards asked who was there, the officer stated he was a maintenance man. Richards opened the door but quickly closed it when he saw the uniformed officer. The officers then began kicking and ramming the door to gain entry. At trial they testified they had identified themselves as police officers while kicking in the door. When they broke into the room, the officers caught Richards trying to escape through a window. They found cash and cocaine hidden in plastic bags above the bathroom ceiling tiles.

Richards challenged the constitutionality of the search and seizure. He sought to have the evidence from his hotel room suppressed on the ground that the officers had failed to knock and announce their presence prior to forcing entry into the room. The trial court denied the motion, and Richards was convicted at his trial. Richards appealed his conviction to the Wisconsin Supreme Court, again arguing that the search was unconstitutional.

The Wisconsin court affirmed Richards' conviction (201 Wis. 2d 845, 549 N.W.2d 218

[1996]), reaffirming its decision in *State v. Stevens*, 181 Wis. 2d 410, 511 N.W. 2d 591 (1994), that gave Wisconsin police the blanket authority to execute search warrants involving drugs using a no-knock entry.

The state supreme court's *per se* (categorical) exception to the Fourth Amendment "reasonableness" requirement was based on a review of criminal conduct surveys, newspaper articles, and other judicial opinions. The court concluded that felony drug crimes involve "an extremely high risk of serious if not deadly injury to the police as well as the potential for the disposal of drugs by the occupants prior to entry by the police." The court believed that exigent circumstances justifying a no-knock entry were always present in felony drug cases. Thus, police officers did not have to present specific information about dangerousness or the possible destruction of drugs in a particular case in order to dispense with the typical knock-and-announce requirement.

The U.S. Supreme Court took Richards' appeal to consider the constitutionality of this blanket rule. Justice John Paul Stevens, writing for a unanimous court, rejected the opinion of the Wisconsin Supreme Court. However, the Court did affirm the constitutionality of the search of Richards' hotel room, based on the specific facts presented at trial.

Stevens noted that in *Wilson v. Arkansas*, 514 U.S. 927, 115 S. Ct. 1914, 131 L. Ed. 2d 976 (1995), the Court had ruled that the Fourth Amendment incorporates the common-law requirement that police officers entering a dwelling must knock on the door and announce their identity and purpose before attempting forcible entry. The *Wilson* decision recognized, however, that police could use no-knock entry if they had a reasonable basis for employing such a method. It is up to the lower courts to determine, on a case-by-case basis, "the circumstances under which an unannounced entry is reasonable under the Fourth Amendment." The *Wilson* decision acknowledged that the knock-and-announce requirement could give way when there was the threat of physical violence or where police had reason to believe evidence would likely be destroyed if advance notice were given.

Stevens admitted that physical violence and destruction of evidence were often associated with felony drug investigations. The question was whether these factors justified dispensing with the case-by-case review of the way in which the search was executed. The Court expressed reluctance to abandon the case-by-case review. Stevens rejected Wisconsin's argument that the blanket exception was legitimate in light of a violent drug culture. Creating exceptions based on the culture "surrounding a general category of criminal behavior presents at least two serious concerns."

The first concern was that the exception contained "considerable overgeneralization." Stevens pointed out that not every drug investigation would pose a threat to officer safety and the preservation of evidence. For example, a search conducted at a time when individuals present in the residence are not connected to the drug activity would not pose a threat of violence. In other cases the type or location of drugs would make them impossible to destroy quickly. In these situations "the asserted governmental interests in preserving evidence and maintaining safety may not outweigh the individual privacy interests intruded upon by a no-knock entry."

A second concern was that the creation of one criminal-category exception to the knock-and-announce requirement could easily be applied to other categories. Stevens noted that armed bank robbers are, by definition, likely to have weapons and the "fruits of their crime may be destroyed without too much difficulty." The Wisconsin exception could be applied to "each category of criminal investigation that included a considerable—albeit hypothetical—risk of danger to officers or destruction of evidence." Such exceptions would make the knock-and-announce element of the Fourth Amendment "meaningless."

The Supreme Court preferred to retain the "neutral scrutiny of a reviewing court" in determining whether a no-knock entry was reasonable. Stevens announced that for a no-knock entry to be upheld, "the police must have a reasonable suspicion that knocking and announcing their presence, under the particular circumstances, would be dangerous or futile, or that it would inhibit the effective investigation of the crime." This standard "strikes the appropriate balance between the legitimate law enforcement concerns at issue in the execution of search warrants and the individual privacy interests affected by no-knock entries."

### United States v. Ramirez

The U.S. Supreme Court continued to clarify the standards for police when they execute "no-knock" searches, when it ruled in *United States v. Ramirez*, U.S.___, 118 S. Ct.992, ___

L. Ed. 2d___ (1988), that the Fourth Amendment does not hold officers to a higher standard when a no-knock entry results in the destruction of property. In so ruling, the Court overturned Ninth Circuit Court of Appeals precedent and created a no-knock exception for the federal statute 18 U.S.C.A. § 3109 (1948).

The police actions in question came in response to the escape of Alan Shelby from the Oregon state prison system. Shelby, who had allegedly made threats to kill witnesses and police officers, was thought to have access to large supplies of weapons. A reliable police informant told a federal agent that Shelby was staying at Hernan Ramirez's home in Boring, Oregon. The informant and the agent drove to an area near Ramirez's house, where the agent observed a man working outside who resembled Shelby.

Based on this information, a deputy U.S. marshal received a no-knock warrant granting permission to enter and search Ramirez's house. By this time, the confidential informant had told authorities that Ramirez might have guns and drugs hidden in his garage. In the early morning hours, 45 officers stormed Ramirez's house. They broke a window in his garage and pointed a gun through the opening, in hopes of preventing an occupant from rushing to the weapons that the officers believed might be in the garage.

Ramirez and his family were asleep inside. Awakened by the noise, Ramirez thought his home was being burglarized. He grabbed a pistol and fired it into the ceiling of his garage. The officers fired back and shouted "police." Ramirez, realizing it was the police entering his home, ran to his living room, threw his gun away, and threw himself on the floor. He admitted to police that he had fired the gun and that he owned both that weapon and another that was inside the house. He also admitted he was a convicted felon. Officers then obtained a search warrant, which they used to retrieve the two guns. Alan Shelby, the object of the no-knock search, was not found.

Ramirez was indicted for being a felon in possession of a firearm. However, the federal district court suppressed the two weapons as evidence because the police officers had violated the Fourth Amendment and 18 U.S.C.A. § 3109, which permits federal law enforcement officers to damage property in certain instances. The court ruled that there were "insufficient exigent circumstances" to justify the police officers' destruction of property in their execution of the warrant.

*Police officers survey a house during a drug raid.*

MARK RICHARDS/PHOTOEDIT

The Ninth Circuit Court of Appeals affirmed (91 F. 3d 1297 [1996]). The Court, applying Ninth Circuit court precedent, found that although a "mild exigency" is sufficient to justify a no-knock entry that can be accomplished without the destruction of property, "more specific inferences of exigency are necessary" when property is destroyed. In Ramirez's case, this heightened standard had not been met.

The U.S. Supreme Court unanimously rejected the Ninth Circuit court's conclusions and reasoning. Chief Justice William H. Rehnquist, writing for the Court, noted that under its recent decision in *Richards v. Wisconsin*, 520 U.S.___, 117 S. Ct. 1416, 137 L. Ed. 2d615 (1997), if police officers have a "reasonable suspicion" that knocking and announcing would be dangerous, futile, or destructive to the purposes of the investigation, they may use a no-knock entry. Rehnquist found nothing in *Richards* or prior rulings that addressed the question of whether the lawfulness of a no-knock entry depends on whether property is damaged in the course of entry. He stated that excessive or unnecessary destruction of property during a search might violate the Fourth Amendment, "even though the entry itself is lawful and the fruits of the search not subject to suppression."

Turning to the facts of the case, Rehnquist found that the police actions were "clearly reasonable" because of the information provided by the informant. The manner in which the entry was accomplished was also reasonable, because the police wished to discourage Shelby from seeking out weapons in the garage. Therefore, the no-knock entry did not violate the Fourth Amendment.

Ramirez contended that the evidence should be suppressed because 18 U.S.C.A. § 3109, gives police permission to break a window to execute a search warrant only if the police first give notice and are refused admittance into the house. Therefore, all other property-damaging entries are forbidden under the law. Rehnquist rejected this argument, stating that the provisions of section 3109 prohibit nothing. The statute "merely authorizes officers to damage property in certain instances." The Court settled the issue by holding that section 3109 must be interpreted using the reasonableness standard articulated in prior rulings to include "an exigent circumstances exception." The police met that reasonableness standard in Ramirez's case, so section 3109 was not violated. The Court sent the case back to the district court for a trial on the weapons charge.

**CROSS REFERENCES**
Fourth Amendment; Kennedy, Anthony M; Miranda v. Arizona; Rehnquist, William Hubbs; Search Warrant; Stevens, John Paul

## SECURITIES

Evidence of corporation's debts or property.

### United States v. O'Hagan

Since the 1930s, the federal government has sought to protect the integrity of the nation's stock and commodities markets. The Securities Exchange Act of 1934 ( 15 U.S.C.A. § 1 et seq.) placed national regulations on the sale of securities, created the Securities and Exchange Commission (SEC) to oversee the regulatory process, and empowered the SEC to issue rules that detailed illegal practices. A major concern of the SEC has been the prevention of insider trading, where an insider of a corporation buys or sells stock while in possession of nonpublic information. Insider trading, if successful, allows a person to reap a large profit or avoid a steep loss, depending on the type of information.

The U.S. Supreme Court, in *United States v. O'Hagan*, ___ U.S. ___, 117 S. Ct. 2199, 138 L. Ed. 2d 724 (1997), resolved a long-standing conflict over whether a "misappropriation theory" of insider trading can be used to prosecute an individual for securities fraud. The Court ruled that such a theory could be used to convict a person of insider trading, because the Ex-

change Act and SEC rules gave the government authority to prosecute.

In July 1988, James H. O'Hagan was a partner in the Minneapolis, Minnesota, law firm of Dorsey & Whitney. In July, Grand Met, a British corporation, retained Dorsey & Whitney as local counsel to assist it in the possible acquisition of Pillsbury, a U.S. corporation. O'Hagan did not work on the Grand Met initiative but became aware of what was being contemplated. Beginning in August 1988, O'Hagan purchased 2,500 call options for Pillsbury stock with September, October, and November expiration dates. In September 1988, O'Hagan purchased 5,000 shares of Pillsbury common stock. On October 4, 1988, after Grand Met publicly announced its tender offer for Pillsbury stock, the stock rose from $39 a share to $60 per share. O'Hagan soon exercised his options and then liquidated the stock along with his previously purchased common stock, realizing a profit of more than $4.3 million.

The SEC conducted an investigation into O'Hagan's investment activities. He was indicted and later convicted on 57 counts of mail fraud, securities fraud, and money laundering. His conviction was based on a "misappropriation theory" of insider trading. Historically the courts and the SEC have applied two theories of liability under the proscriptions of section 10 (b) of the Exchange Act for prosecuting insider trading cases. The first theory, termed the "classical theory" of insider trading, involves an insider of a corporation who buys or sells stock while in possession of material nonpublic information.

However, under the classical theory, O'Hagan was not an insider. Therefore, O'Hagan was prosecuted on the misappropriation theory of insider trading, which extends insider trading liability to corporate outsiders who obtain and use material nonpublic information by violating a relationship of trust and confidence. Using the misappropriation theory, the government contended that O'Hagan, as a partner in the law firm retained by Grand Met, breached his fiduciary duties owed to Dorsey & Whitney and Grand Met when he obtained confidential, material, nonpublic information regarding Grand Met's interest in acquiring Pillsbury and used that information to purchase Pillsbury securities.

O'Hagan appealed his conviction to the Eighth Circuit Court of Appeals. He contended that there was no statutory basis for applying the misappropriation theory. Although the Second,

Third, Seventh, and Ninth Circuits had upheld the theory, the Eighth Circuit agreed with O'Hagan, rejecting misappropriation on two grounds (92 F.3d 612 [1996]). The court found that the theory was unsupportable because it imposed liability for a mere breach of fiduciary duty, without requiring that the government show a misrepresentation or nondisclosure, elements that the court ruled were necessary to prove a violation of section 10(b).

Second, section 10(b) requires that the fraud be "in connection with the purchase or sale of any security." However, the appeals court concluded that the misappropriation theory allowed for liability "for a breach of duty owed to individuals who are unconnected to and perhaps uninterested in a securities transaction, thus rendering meaningless the 'in connection with' statutory language." The court also found that the misappropriation theory imposes liability "even though no market participant was deceived or defrauded" and thus flies in the face of the statutory requirement that the fraud be "in connection with the purchase or sale of any security." Because O'Hagan's "misappropriation" of information was from Dorsey & Whitney and Grand Met, not Pillsbury, and was not in connection with the purchase or sale of a security, the court held that there was no valid basis upon which to impose criminal liability under section 10 (b).

The Supreme Court rejected the Eighth Circuit's reasoning and reversed its decision. Justice Ruth Bader Ginsburg, writing for the majority, held that a person who trades in securities for personal profit, using confidential information misappropriated in breach of a fiduciary duty to the source of the information, may be held liable for violating, section 10 (b).

Ginsburg found that misappropriation of information comes within section 10 (b)'s proscription against using any "deceptive device … in connection with the purchase or sale of any security." A misappropriator "deals in deception," pretending loyalty while converting information for personal gain. Ginsburg classified confidential information as property to which the company has a right to exclusive use. In this case O'Hagan's undisclosed misappropriation constituted "fraud akin to embezzlement."

The Court concluded that section 10(b) was not an "all-purpose breach of fiduciary ban" but a statute that focused on conducts that is manipulative or deceptive. Ginsburg pointed out that full disclosure foreclosed liability. If O'Ha-

gan had told Grand Met he intended to trade on the information he obtained, there would have been no "deceptive device" and therefore no section 10(b) violation.

Ginsburg also found support for the misappropriation theory in the basic purpose of the Exchange Act, which is to ensure honest markets and promote investor confidence. If O'Hagan's activities were not illegal, Ginsburg said, "investors likely would hesitate to venture their capital in a market where trading based on misappropriated nonpublic information is unchecked by law." For the Court, it made "scant sense" to make O'Hagan a section 10 (b) violator if he had worked for a law firm representing Pillsbury, the target of the tender offer, but not if he worked for the law firm representing Grand Met, the bidder.

The Court also disagreed with the Eighth Circuit's reading of its precedents in this area, finding that the appeals court had misread *Chiarella v. United States*, 445 U.S. 222, 100 S. Ct. 1108, 63 L. Ed. 2d 348 (1980). *Chiarella* involved securities trades by a printer employed at a print shop that printed corporate takeover bids. The Court overturned his conviction for securities fraud, saying that there is no "general duty between all participants in market transactions to forgo actions based on material, nonpublic information." The Eighth Circuit interpreted *Chiarella* to mean that the only relationship prompting liability is the relationship between a corporation's insiders and shareholders. Ginsburg rejected this interpretation, stating that *Chiarella* "expressly left open the misappropriation theory" before it in *O'Hagan*.

Ginsburg emphasized that the Securities Exchange Act requires that the government prove that a person "willfully" violated the law in order to establish a criminal violation. A defendant may not be imprisoned for such a violation if he proves that he had no knowledge of the law.

## SEGREGATION

The act or process of separating a race, class, or ethnic group from a society's general population.

### Yonkers, New York, Still Segregated

In 1980, the U.S. Justice Department and the Yonkers branch of the National Association for the Advancement of Colored Persons (NAACP) filed a civil lawsuit against the city of Yonkers, the Yonkers School Board, and the Yonkers Community Development Agency,

*Herman Keith stands next to a telephone pole that features two signs promoting segregation in Yonkers.*

YVONNE HEMSEY/GAMMA LIAISON

charging that the city had engaged in systematic segregation for the previous thirty years. Specifically, the plaintiffs alleged that the city government had disproportionately restricted new subsidized housing projects to certain areas of the city already heavily populated by minorities. This practice, claimed the plaintiffs, perpetuated racial segregation in the community and in public schools. The case constituted the first time racial segregation charges were levied against housing and school officials in the same suit.

After several years of preparation and a three-month trial, the U.S. District Court for the Southern District of New York found that the combined actions of the various city agencies had segregated the schools and the housing in the city based on racial identity. *United States v. Yonkers Board of Education* 624 F.Supp. 1276 (S.D.N.Y. 1985). The trial court ordered the

city to designate sites for public housing by November of 1986, but the city refused to comply with the order during the appeals process. The Court of Appeals for the Second Circuit affirmed the ruling as to racial discrimination (837 F.2d 1181 [2d Cir. 1987]), but the issue of compliance with court orders remained unresolved. In January 1988, after the U.S. Supreme Court had denied the city's application for certiorari, the parties agreed to a consent decree establishing a new housing plan. That same month, the Yonkers city council voted to approve the decree and the decree was submitted to, and accepted by, the trial court. The decree stated that the city of Yonkers had agreed to pass, within ninety days, legislation that outlined the construction of housing in Yonkers.

The Yonkers city government, however, did not pass the legislation. The Justice Department and Yonkers NAACP submitted a "Long-Term Plan Order" to the trial court and, after a hearing, the court ordered the city to pass the legislation by August 1, 1988. The order stated that refusal to comply with its terms would result in fines for the city and jail for city council members who remained in contempt of the court order. On August 1, 1988, the Yonkers city council defeated the proposed housing legislation package by a vote of four to three, and the trial court held the city and its council members in contempt of court. The Second Circuit affirmed the contempt orders, and the city and city council members requested from the Supreme Court a stay of the sanctions. The Supreme Court put a halt to the sanctions against the city council members, but not against the city. As the city's fines neared $1 million per day, the city council, by a vote of 5–2, enacted the Affordable Housing Ordinance on September 9, 1988.

Less than two years later, the Supreme Court held that the trial court had not abused its discretion in sanctioning the city, but the High Court also held that the city council members were not individually liable. *Spallone v. United States*, 493 U.S. 265, 110 S. Ct. 625, 107 L. Ed. 2d 644 (1990). Four justices dissented, arguing that the extreme circumstances warranted the creation of a temporary bridge between the separation of powers, allowing the court to sanction individual council members.

Although Yonkers had passed the desired legislation and the Supreme Court had issued an opinion on the matter, the case was not closed. In 1993, the Yonkers Board of Education and the Yonkers NAACP reactivated the case, alleging that while the Yonkers schools were no longer identifiable by race, vestiges of segregation remained. The board and the NAACP included the state of New York in the suit, claiming that the segregation continued because Yonkers was underfunded by the state. The trial court found that, although steps were being taken by the city to remedy the situation, segregation remained in effect in Yonkers. The court also found that Yonkers would need money to achieve desegregation. However, the trial court refused to hold the state fiscally responsible for the segregation in Yonkers because the state had never affirmatively participated in the segregation, *United States v. Yonkers Board of Education*, 880 F. Supp. 212 (S.D.N.Y. 1995).

On appeal, the Second Circuit appeals court vacated the trial court's decision, holding that the state was in fact fiscally responsible for alle-viating the segregation in Yonkers. *United States v. Yonkers Board of Education*, 96 F.3d 600 (2d Cir. 1996), cert. denied 117 U.S. 2479, 138 L. Ed. 2d 988 (1996). Another trial ensued, and the state presented evidence to support its proposition that vestiges of segregation no longer existed in the Yonkers public school system. The trial court found that segregation continued in Yonkers, and ordered the city and the state to share the costs in a second desegregation plan devised by the court and called the "Educational Improvement Plan," *United States v. Yonkers Board of Education*, 984 F. Supp 687, 123 Ed. Law Rep 544 (1997) (S.D.N.Y.).

## SEX OFFENSES

A class of sexual conduct prohibited by the law.

### Kansas v. Hendricks

In the 1990s, a number of states have passed "sexual predator" laws that seek to confine violent sexual offenders beyond the expiration of their prison terms by allowing the state to commit them to mental health institutions. Once committed these offenders, who are almost all males, will not be released until it can be proven that they are no longer a threat to the community.

Offenders who have been committed under these statutes have challenged their constitutionality, arguing that they are being punished in violation of the U.S. Constitution's prohibitions against double jeopardy and *ex post facto* laws. The states have disputed these allegations, noting that a civil commitment procedure is used to judge whether an inmate is a sexual predator under the terms of the pertinent statute.

The U.S. Supreme Court, in *Kansas v. Hendricks*, ___U.S.___, 117 S. Ct. 2072, 138 L. Ed. 2d 501 (1997), upheld Kansas's Sexually Violent Predator Act (Kan. Stat. Ann. § 59-29a01 et seq. [1994]), holding that the civil commitment procedures used to confine dangerous sex offenders do not violate the Constitution. However, the 5–4 vote and the concurring opinion of Justice Anthony M. Kennedy suggested that the Court had serious reservations about this type of procedure.

The Kansas Sexually Violent Predator Act establishes procedures for the civil commitment of persons who, due to a "mental abnormality" or a "personality disorder," are likely to engage in "predatory acts of sexual violence." The legislature passed the act in 1994 as a way of dealing with repeat sexual offenders. It concluded that the way to handle a small but dangerous group of sexually violent criminals was to create special civil commitment procedures for their long-term care and treatment. The procedures provide for procedural due process, including paying for an attorney and an examination by mental health professionals if the person is indigent.

Once a person is confined under the act, he may be released under one of three circumstances: the committing court must conduct an annual review to determine whether continued detention is warranted; the secretary of social and rehabilitation services, who is responsible for the care of the person, may determine at any time that the person's condition has so changed that release is appropriate; and, the person may file at any time a release petition. If the court finds that the state can no longer satisfy its burden under the act, the individual will be freed from confinement.

Leroy Hendricks, an inmate with a long history of sexually molesting children, was scheduled to be released from prison shortly after the act became law. Instead Hendricks became the first person committed under the new law. He appealed to the Kansas Supreme Court, attacking the act's constitutionality. The court invalidated the law, ruling that the act's precommitment condition of a "mental abnormality" departs from the standards for involuntary civil commitment, which require a commitment to be predicated on the finding of "mental illness." The state of Kansas appealed the decision to the U.S. Supreme Court.

The Supreme Court reversed the Kansas Court. Justice Clarence Thomas, writing for the majority, ruled that the act's definition of "mental abnormality" satisfies the "substantive" due process requirement. This requirement refers to the freedom from physical restraint, which the Court has consistently held to be at the core of the liberty protected by the Due Process Clause. Thomas noted that the Court has consistently upheld involuntary commitment statutes that detain persons who are unable to control their behavior and who pose a danger to the public health and safety, provided the confinement takes place according to proper procedures and evidentiary standards.

Thomas agreed that a finding of dangerousness is not enough to justify an indefinite involuntary commitment. The Kansas act, however, links dangerousness with a "mental abnormality" or "personality disorder." Hendricks contended that previous Court rulings mandated that only a finding of "mental illness" could meet the substantive due process requirement for civil commitment and that therefore the Kansas requirements were unconstitutional.

The Court disagreed. Thomas stated that "the term 'mental illness' is devoid of any talismanic significance." He noted that the psychiatric profession disagrees widely on what constitutes mental illness and that the Court itself has used "a variety of expressions to describe the mental condition of those properly subject to civil confinement." Because the Court never required state legislatures to adopt "any particular nomenclature," the states have, over the years, developed "numerous specialized terms to define mental health concepts." The Kansas act establishes criteria that are within the scope of conditions that permit confinement. In Hendricks' case he had been diagnosed as suffering from pedophilia, a condition that the psychiatric profession classifies as a serious mental disorder. Therefore, his diagnosis satisfied both the act's "mental abnormality" requirement and substantive due process.

Thomas then examined whether the act violates the Constitution's double jeopardy provision, which prohibits trying and punishing a person twice for the same crime. Hendricks claimed that though the Kansas law is in the guise of civil commitment, in effect it is criminal in nature. To overcome the "manifest intent" of the Kansas legislature that the law is civil in nature, Hendricks needed to show that the sexual predator act implicates either of the two primary objectives of criminal punishment: retribution or deterrence.

After reviewing the law, Thomas concluded that its purpose is not retributive. It does not affix culpability for prior criminal conduct, it does not make criminal conviction a prerequisite for commitment, and it does not contain a scienter requirement, which forces the state to show that a criminal defendant knowingly committed a crime. Thomas also found no evidence that the act serves as a deterrent, because persons with a mental abnormality or personality disorder are "unlikely to be deterred by the threat of confinement." He concluded that "if detention for the purposes of protecting the community from harm *necessarily* constituted punishment, then all involuntary civil commitments would have to be considered punishment. But we have never so held."

Hendricks also claimed that the law is punitive because it fails to offer any legitimate treat-

*President Bill Clinton signs "Megan's Law," named after the late Megan Kanka of Hamilton Township, New Jersey, May 17, 1996, in the Oval Office. In attendance from left to right are Megan's mother Maureen, her brother Jeremy, New Jersey Representative Dick Zimmer, and America's Most Wanted host John Walsh.*

DENIS PAQUIN/AP/WIDE WORLD PHOTOS

ment. Without such treatment, confinement amounts to little more than disguised punishment. Thomas rejected this claim, ruling that the act is not punitive if it fails to offer treatment where treatment is not possible, or where protection of public safety is a concern that overrides the providing of treatment. Thomas stated that "incapacitation may be a legitimate end of the civil law."

Thomas also rejected the claim that the Kansas act is an *ex post facto* law, which violates the Constitution by punishing a person for conduct that occurred prior to the creation of a law that makes the conduct illegal. The *Ex Post Facto* Clause only applies to criminal statutes. Because the act is not punitive, Thomas said, its application does not raise *ex post facto* concerns. In addition, Thomas ruled that the law has no retroactive effect because it does not criminalize conduct that was legal before its enactment, nor does it deprive Hendricks of any defense that was available to him at the time of his crimes.

Justice Kennedy, in a concurring opinion, noted that the "practical effect of the Kansas law may be to impose confinement for life." He warned that if civil confinement were to become a "mechanism for retribution or general deterrence, or if it were shown that mental abnormality is too imprecise a category to offer a solid basis for concluding that civil detention is justified, our precedents would not suffice to validate it."

Justice Stephen G. Breyer, in a dissenting opinion, agreed that the Due Process Clause permitted Kansas to classify Hendricks as a mentally ill and dangerous person under its civil commitment laws. But he disagreed with the majority's analysis of whether the act constitutes an *ex post facto* law. Breyer concluded that the confinement the act imposes is punishment. The act violated *ex post facto* because it altered the legal consequences that attached to Hendricks's earlier crimes, seriously disadvantaging him.

### Megan's Law—E.B. v. Verniero

Since 1994 most states and the federal government have enacted laws that require convicted sex offenders to register their whereabouts with law enforcement officials. In addition, 35 states require public authorities to tell communities that certain types of sex offenders have moved into their neighborhood. This kind of legislation has become known as Megan's Law, because the New Jersey legislature named its 1994 legislation after Megan Kanka, a seven-year-old girl who was raped and murdered in 1994 by a twice-convicted sex offender who lived across the street (N.J.S.A. 2C:7-1 to 7-11). Megan's parents and neighbors were unaware of Jesse Timmendequas' background and the fact that he was sharing a house with two other men who had been convicted of sex offenses. Timmendequas was subsequently convicted of the charges and sentenced to death.

# SEX OFFENSES: DO OFFENDER LAWS PROTECT PUBLIC SAFETY OR INVADE PRIVACY?

The enactment of state and federal sex offender notification and registration laws came at a furious pace in the 1990s. Legislators and their constituents have endorsed notification and registration as simple but effective ways of protecting public safety. Even though support for such laws has been overwhelming, concerns have been raised by some legal commentators that these laws invade the privacy of released sex offenders and make it difficult for them to rebuild their lives.

Defenders of these laws note that requiring released offenders to register with the police is an easy way for police to keep tabs on potentially dangerous persons. With the release of large numbers of sex offenders into the general population, public safety demands that the police know where these potentially dangerous persons live. In the event of

IN FOCUS

a new sex offense, the police have the ability to quickly round up possible suspects. Registration also gives police in nearby towns and cities the opportunity to share information on suspects and to help locate suspects for questioning.

The law's proponents believe, however, that notification is the most important element. Prior to the passage of Megan's Law in New Jersey, and similar laws throughout the United States, citizens did not know when a released sex offender moved in next door or down the block. Because certain sex offenders are likely to commit criminal acts again, no notification means that offenders can use their anonymity to help conceal their criminal pursuits. Community notification laws rob the released offender of anonymity by letting neighbors know

the offender's criminal history and his place of residence. Public safety is enhanced, and, armed with this information, neighbors can be on guard and assist in the monitoring of the released offender's activities.

Communities also use notification to prevent a released offender from moving into the neighborhood. Once a public hearing is held and information is distributed, landlords often become reluctant to rent housing to a person the community does not wish to have around. Even if the released offender does move into the community, the person will be isolated from his neighbors. Communities are therefore empowered to take control of their neighborhoods and assert their right to safe and secure homes.

Defenders of these laws agree that registration and notification do have an impact on the lives of released sex of-

After New Jersey passed Megan's Law, other states were quick to follow. By May 1996, forty-nine states had adopted sex offender registration laws as well a federal version of Megan's Law requiring mandatory notification (42 U.S.C.A. § 14071 (d)).

Supporters of the law believed its requirements would help law enforcement keep tabs on predatory sex offenders and alert local communities to the possible danger of their new neighbors. Opponents of mandatory registration and notification of sex offenders claimed that the law unfairly subjected offenders who had served their criminal sentences to double jeopardy (punishment twice for the same crime) and *ex post facto* (retroactive application of a criminal law) liability, both of which are forbidden by the U.S. Constitution.

In 1996 the constitutionality of the New Jersey registration law was upheld by the Third Circuit Court of Appeals in *Artway v. Attorney General*, 81 F. 3d 1235 (3rd Cir. 1996). The court in

*Artway* noted that under the law the registrant must provide to the chief law enforcement office of the municipality in which he resides his name, social security number, age, race, sex, date of birth, height, weight, hair and eye color, address of legal residence, address of any current temporary legal residence, and the date and place of employment. The registrant must confirm his address every ninety days, notify the police if he moves, and re-register with the law enforcement agency of any new municipality.

This information is sent to the state police headquarters, which incorporates it into a central registry and notifies the prosecutor of the county in which the registrant plans to reside. The information is available to all state and federal law enforcement agencies. A sex offender who fails to register can be prosecuted. The registration requirement lasts for fifteen years from the date of conviction or the date of release from a correctional facility, whichever is later. After fifteen years, the registrant may apply to state court to terminate the obligation to register.

fenders. However, they believe that society as a whole should have more rights than an individual sex offender. Felons, for example, are not entitled to vote or possess firearms and can suffer other civil disabilities because of their criminal convictions. Registration and notification are legitimate civil disabilities that flow from the underlying criminal act. Public safety mandates that such laws be used effectively.

Critics of registration and notification are troubled by the departure these laws take from the traditional belief that once a person serves a criminal sentence, the person has paid her debt to society and should be allowed to reenter society without significant restrictions on privacy or liberty. According to the critics, released offenders share the same expectations of privacy as other citizens. Though some courts have acknowledged that notification laws infringe upon a sex offender's privacy interest by disseminating in a packaged form, various pieces of the registrant's personal history, the state's strong interest in protecting its citizens through public disclosure substantially outweighs the sex offender's privacy interest. Crit-

ics contend that such rulings are a slippery slope, for they provide future legislatures with the opportunity to broaden the types of crimes that are subject to notification. Society will always have a strong interest in protecting its citizens, thereby allowing more intrusive government actions over an individual's right to privacy.

Critics also believe registration and notification laws constitute cruel and unusual punishments, which are banned by the Eighth Amendment. These laws are penal, because they subject the released offender to additional punishment. Defenders of the laws may claim that notification is merely a way to provide information to the public, but the impact on released offenders clearly can feel like punishment. Critics note that convicted sex offenders now have difficulty finding a place to live. Communities often use this information to prohibit entry or to try to remove the individual from his surroundings. Offenders who do move into the community are subjected to taunts and threats, and their property is sometimes vandalized. It is unfair and unconstitutional, the critics allege, to subject a person

who has served the sentence of the court to another layer of punishment that is indefinite in length or scope.

Opponents further claim that notification has a detrimental effect on rehabilitating a released offender. Public notification may have improved personal safety, but it has also created public hysteria. Sex offenders are now viewed as modern day lepers, increasing the difficulty for them to find and retain jobs. For those released offenders who truly want to make a new life, notification makes such an effort almost impossible.

In addition, critics argue that notification laws undermine a community by promoting fear. Notification may inflame passions, and sometimes lead to mob rule. Instead of providing rehabilitation or deterrence, notification shames convicted offenders in a way that registration and other civil disabilities do not. Though such laws satisfy a public demand that officials crack down on offenders, critics remain skeptical as to whether such laws truly promote public safety enough to justify their intrusiveness.

---

The obligation may be terminated only upon a persuasive showing that the registrant is not likely to pose a threat to the safety of others.

In *Artway*, the appellate court ruled that registration was not a form of punishment and therefore was not a violation of double jeopardy and *ex post facto* prohibitions. The court found that New Jersey had valid public safety reasons for imposing the registration.

The other part of Megan's Law involves community notification. Under this section, once a sex offender registers with the municipality, the county prosecutor must determine whether the sex offender poses a low (tier 1), moderate (tier 2) or high (tier 3) reoffense risk. Every registrant at least qualifies for tier 1 treatment, where notification is extended only to law enforcement agencies likely to encounter the registrant. Tier 2 notification results in a written alert to registered schools, day care centers, summer camps, and other community organizations that care for children or provide support

to women and where individuals are likely to encounter the sex offender. Tier 3 results in community notification, where members of the public likely to encounter the registrant are notified. This notification means that the neighbors of the sex offender will be alerted to his past record and his presence in the neighborhood.

Because the three-tier classification system results in varying levels of notification, the New Jersey law required the attorney general to develop guidelines and objective criteria for county prosecutors to use in assessing the likelihood a registrant will reoffend. The attorney general's guidelines require prosecutors to use a registrant risk assessment scale, a numerical scoring system that seeks to apply objective criteria to the evaluation process. The scale is a matrix of 13 factors grouped into four general categories: seriousness of the offense, offense history, characteristics of the offender, and community support. The more points an offender scores on the scale, the more likely he will be classified as tier 2 or 3.

The type of information distributed is the same regardless of the classification. The information packet includes the registrant's name, a recent photograph, a physical description, the offense of conviction, home address, place of employment and schooling, and a vehicle description and license plate number. Those who are given tier 1 and 2 information are warned that the information is confidential and not to be shared with the general public. Every notification must contain a warning about the criminal consequences of vandalism, threats, and assaults against the registrant.

A group of New Jersey sex offenders challenged in federal court the constitutionality of the notification portion of Megan's Law. The Third Circuit, in *E. B. v. Verniero*, 119 F. 3d 1077 (3rd. Cir. 1997), found the scheme constitutional, basing much of its analysis on reasoning contained in its *Artway* decision.

Judge Walter K. Stapleton, in his majority opinion, held that the notification requirements of Megan's Law do not constitute state inflicted "punishment" on tier 2 and tier 3 registrants for purposes of the Ex Post Facto and Double Jeopardy Clauses. Stapleton applied the *Artway* standard, which requires that for the law to constitute nonpunishment, the measure must pass a three-part test: actual purpose, objective purpose, and effect. Actual purpose examines whether the "adverse effect on individuals results from a desire on the part of the legislature to punish past conduct or is a by-product of a bona fide legislative effort to remedy a perceived societal problem." The objective purpose inquiry "focuses on the operation of the legislative measure and on whether analogous measures have traditionally been regarded in our society as punishment." The last part examines whether the effect, or "sting," of a measure is so harsh as a matter of degree that it constitutes "punishment."

Judge Stapleton concluded, as the court did in *Artway*, that the legislative purpose of Megan's Law was "to identify potential recidivists and alert the public when necessary for the public safety, and to help prevent and promptly resolve incidents involving sexual abuse and missing persons." The legislature's "declared remedial purpose" clearly indicated that public safety rather than punishment was the controlling factor in enacting Megan's Law.

As for objective purpose, Judge Stapleton ruled that the notification law was fully explained by the "nonpunitive, legislative purpose." A reasonable legislator could have been motivated by the goals of "identifying potential recidivists, notifying those who are likely to interact with such recidivists to the extent necessary to protect public safety, and helping prevent future incidents of sexual abuse." The premise of Megan's Law that law enforcement and the public should be aware of potential danger was not unreasonable. In addition, the use of guidelines and the registrant risk assessment scale demonstrated that the legislative goals had not imposed an excessive burden on the registrants. The varying tiers meant that all offenders are not treated the same.

The court rejected the claim that the dissemination of information beyond law enforcement personnel is similar to the historical punishments of public shaming, humiliation, and banishment employed in the colonial period. Stapleton concluded that the "sting" of Megan's Law for tier 2 and 3 registrants "results not from their being publicly displayed for ridicule and shaming but rather from the dissemination of accurate public record information about their past criminal activities and a risk assessment by responsible public agencies based on that information."

As to the effects of the notification law, Judge Stapleton recognized that registrants and their families had experienced "profound humiliation and isolation," yet these indirect effects did not rise to the level of punishment. Stapleton also concluded that while there had been episodes of "vigilante justice," they were not common and registrants did not "live in fear of them."

Based on this three-part analysis, the court found the notification law constitutional. As to the two procedural parts of Megan's Law, however, the court was more sympathetic to the registrants' concerns. If a registrant sought to challenge his tier classification, the law allowed him to challenge it through a court hearing. The law placed the burden of persuasion on the registrant to show that the tier classification was incorrect. The court of appeals rejected this approach, stating that the Due Process Clause required the state to carry the burden of persuasion and prove that its classification was correct. In addition, the court found that the Due Process Clause required the state at such a proceeding to carry the burden of justifying the classification and notification plan by clear and convincing evidence. This evidentiary standard is higher than the preponderance of the evidence standard incorporated into Megan's Law.

The upholding of both parts of Megan's Law, and the refusal of the Supreme Court to hear an appeal of the 1997 decision, meant that the constitutionality of sex offender registration and notification laws has been established. Judge Edward R. Becker, in a dissenting opinion, warned, however, that Megan's Law and others like it create an illusion that notification will enhance the protection of children. Becker believed that the "change in protection secured by notification will be marginal at best." Moreover, he wondered whether this "marginal change" justified the tampering with constitutional rights that are afforded individual citizens. He would have ruled the notification law unconstitutional, because the legislative purpose was to punish sex offenders by subjecting them to punitive public humiliation and shame.

**CROSS REFERENCES**

Double Jeopardy; Due Process of Law; *Ex Post Facto* Laws; Punishment

# SEXUAL HARASSMENT

Unwelcome sexual advances, requests for sexual favors, and other verbal or physical conduct of a sexual nature that tends to create a hostile or offensive work environment.

### Oncale v. Sundowner Offshore Services, Inc.

Sexual harassment in the workplace has been recognized by the courts as conduct prohibited by Title VII of the Civil Rights Act of 1964, 42 U.S.C.A. § 2000e et seq. Unwelcome or uninvited conduct or communications of a sexual nature is prohibited. Many courts have concluded that Title VII's prohibition against discrimination on the basis of sex was limited to claims where the harasser was of one sex and the harassed employee was of the other sex. The U.S. Supreme Court rejected this conclusion in a landmark decision, *Oncale v. Sundowner Offshore Services, Inc.*, __U.S.__, 118 S. Ct.998, __L. Ed. 2d__ (1998). The Court stated forcefully that same-sex sexual harassment was barred under Title VII.

Joseph Oncale filed suit in federal court claiming sexual harassment by three of his former coworkers. Oncale had been employed by Sundowner Offshore Services on an oil platform in the Gulf of Mexico. He was part of an eight-man crew, which included John Lyons, Danny Pippen, and Brandon Johnson. Lyons, the crane operator, and Pippen, the driller, had supervisory authority over Oncale. On several occasions Lyons, Pippen, and Johnson subjected Oncale to sex-related, humiliating actions in the presence of the rest of the crew.

Oncale complained to supervisory personnel, but the company took no steps to end the conduct. Oncale eventually quit, asking that his pink slip reflect that he left due to sexual harassment and verbal abuse. He later testified that he feared he would be raped or forced to have sex if he remained on the platform.

The district court granted summary judgment to Sundowner and Lyons, Pippen, and Johnson, concluding that even if everything that Oncale alleged was true, there was no cause of action under Title VII for harassment of a male worker by male coworkers. Oncale appealed the dismissal of his case to the Fifth Circuit Court of Appeals, but the court concluded that the district court had correctly interpreted the law, 83 F. 3d 118 (1996).

The Supreme Court rejected the Fifth Circuit's decision. Justice Antonin Scalia, writing for a unanimous court, noted that the Court had made clear in its previous decisions that section 2000e-2(a)(1) covered not only terms and conditions "in the narrow contractual sense," but displayed an intent by Congress "to strike at the entire spectrum of disparate treatment of men and women in employment." Title VII is violated when the workplace is filled with "discriminatory intimidation, ridicule, and insult" that reaches a level where an abusive working environment is created.

Justice Scalia pointed out that Title VII's prohibition of discrimination because of sex protects men as well as women. Nevertheless, because some courts were apparently under some misapprehension about the Court's position, Scalia stated that "if our precedents leave any doubt on the question, we hold today that nothing in Title VII necessarily bars a claim of discrimination 'because of ... sex' merely because the plaintiff and the defendant (or the person charged with acting on behalf of the defendant) are of the same sex."

Justice Scalia acknowledged that male-on-male sexual harassment was not the principal problem Congress sought to remedy when it passed Title VII. Nevertheless, "statutory prohibitions often go beyond the principal evil to cover reasonably comparable evils." The Court had to look at the provisions of the law rather than the primary concerns of the legislators who enacted the law.

Responding to the defendants' claim that recognizing same-sex harassment would transform Title VII into what he called a "general civility code for the American workplace," Justice Scalia found that risk no greater for same-sex than opposite-sex harassment. He noted that Title VII does not prohibit all verbal or physical harassment in the workplace but was directed only at sex-based discrimination. Courts and juries had "found the inference of discrimination easy to draw in most male-female sexual harassment situations. The "same chain of inference" would be available to a plaintiff alleging same-sex harassment if there was credible evidence the harasser was homosexual. However, Scalia concluded that "harassing conduct need not be motivated by sexual desire to support an inference of discrimination on the basis of sex." The key issue was whether the conduct at issue was discrimination based on sex and not "merely tinged with offensive sexual connotations."

Justice Scalia emphasized that the statute did not reach "genuine but innocuous differences in the ways men and women routinely interact with members of the same sex and of the opposite sex." The law did not mandate "asexuality or androgyny in the workplace," it only barred behavior "so objectively offensive as to alter 'conditions' of the victim's employment." This requirement prevented courts and juries from mistaking ordinary socializing, "such as male-on-male horseplay or intersexual flirtation," for discriminatory conduct.

Finally, Justice Scalia pointed out that objective severity of harassment must be judged from the perspective of a reasonable person in the plaintiff's position, considering all the circumstances. The social context was critical in judging the conduct in question. Scalia cited the example of a professional football player who is patted by the coach on the buttocks as he heads onto the field. The coach's behavior in this context does not create an abusive work environment, yet "the same behavior would reasonably be experienced as abusive by the coach's secretary (male or female) back at the office." Scalia, noting the "constellation of surrounding circumstances, expectations, and relationships" that are hard to define in words, called for common sense and "an appropriate sensitivity to social context." If these standards are applied by courts and juries, they will be able to "distinguish between simple teasing or roughhousing among members of the same sex, and conduct which a reasonable person in the plaintiff's position would find severely hostile or abusive."

Based on this ruling, the Court sent Oncale's case back to district court, where he will be allowed to prove at trial that the conduct in question rose to the level of sexual harassment in the workplace.

### Record Settlement Against U.S. Affiliate of Swedish Company

On February 4, 1998, an extraordinary case of company-wide sexual harassment ended in a record settlement of $9.85 million. The federal Equal Employment Opportunity Commission (EEOC) settled its case against Astra USA, the U.S. affiliate of the Swedish pharmaceutical company. In agreeing to pay the highest EEOC settlement in history, the company admitted to allowing a hostile work environment in which male executives fondled women employees and pressured them into sexual acts and older and married women employees were replaced with young, single female workers. The settlement award will be shared by 79 women, nearly half of whom left the company, and one man who suffered reprisals for criticizing his employers.

The case was notable partly for the size of the company involved. Based in Westboro, Massachusetts, Astra USA has annual sales of $400 million. The pharmaceutical company makes an ulcer medication called Prilosec, the best-selling prescription drug in the nation, and is also known for asthma and heart medicines. About 40 percent of its 1,500 employees are women.

Problems at the company came to public light in May 1996. With the publication of a cover story entitled "Abuse of Power," *Business Week* magazine revealed that it had conducted a six-month investigation into allegations by women employees of Astra. The magazine concluded that sexual harassment was "rampant" throughout the company, tracing specific allegations to company President and Chief Executive Officer Lars Bildman. Depicting an inebriated Bildman running his hands over and nibbling the neck of a distraught female employee in a hotel ballroom, it alleged that such behavior was commonplace from the top of the organization on down: executives, managers, and even contractors pressured women employees to party with them after work, sometimes expecting sexual favors. One former employee who had settled a lawsuit out of court with the company told the magazine that managers felt free to fondle women's bodies. Male workers confirmed their female colleagues' accounts.

At first the company denied some of the magazine's allegations. And after six former employees took legal action, it called their lawsuit "outrageous." But later in 1996, it fired Bildman for allegedly spending company funds on his personal expenses, including high-priced prostitutes.

In February 1998 Astra USA and the EEOC announced the record settlement. In addition to paying $9.85 million—$8 million more than any previous EEOC settlement—the company agreed to several remedies. These included restructuring its personnel department, establishing a sexual harassment policy, firing or disciplining employees who had committed harassment, and ending contracts with clinics, hospitals, and other places where employees had been harassed. It also apologized. "As a company we are ashamed of the unacceptable behavior that took place," Ivan Rowley, Astra USA's new president, said at a press conference.

Only days earlier, on January 26, Bildman pleaded guilty in Boston to charges of tax evasion and received a twenty-one month prison sentence. Astra USA, meanwhile, announced that it was suing him to recover costs related to the EEOC investigation.

### Sergeant Major Gene McKinney Case

Sergeant Major Gene McKinney, an African American who was once the Army's highest-ranking enlisted soldier, had a spotless record of service spanning twenty-nine years. But early in 1997, a female colleague accused him of sexual harassment in a televised interview. By the time the case came to trial, five other women had also come forward to accuse McKinney not only of harassment but of attempting to intimidate them into silence. In February 1997, in two separate media interviews, Sergeant Major Brenda Hoster said the married McKinney had tried to pressure her into having sex with him in a hotel room. By summer, five other servicewomen leveled related charges at a military hearing that resulted in a nineteen-count indictment, ranging from maltreatment and soliciting adultery, to threats, indecent assault, and obstruction of justice. McKinney denied any wrongdoing. As details of the alleged encounters emerged, critics charged the U.S. military with widespread sexual harassment and senior military officials acknowledged publicly that the service had a problem.

At trial in Fort Belvoir, Virginia, the prosecution faced the difficult task of bringing down a celebrated soldier with proof of sexual misbe-

*Sergeant Major Gene McKinney of the U.S. Army was tried and acquitted of sexual harassment.*

HO-U.S. ARMY/REUTERS/ARCHIVE PHOTOS

havior. Their case faltered when the plaintiffs gave conflicting testimony. Defense attorney Charles Gittins attacked the witnesses' credibility, portraying them as liars and golddiggers. The defense also repeatedly charged that the trial was racially biased because McKinney's six accusers, as well as all eight jurors, were whites.

A significant piece of evidence for the prosecution was a tape recording of a telephone conversation that McKinney had with Sergeant Christine Fetrow, which was played for the eight jury members. On the tape, which formed the basis of the justice obstruction charge, he could be heard instructing Fetrow to tell military investigators that all they had discussed was her career development. The defense called the phone conversation entrapment.

On March 13, 1998, the jury acquitted McKinney on 18 of the 19 charges, finding him guilty only of one count of obstruction of justice. Under military law, the jury could choose from a range of punishments from no sentence at all to five years in prison and a dishonorable discharge. The defense asked for no sentence, and McKinney pleaded that he and his wife be allowed "to move forward with some honor." Prosecutors asked for at least six months in prison. Reconvening three days later, the jury exercised leniency, reducing McKinney's rank by one level and requesting that he be reprimanded. In practical terms, the rank reduction meant a loss in pay for him.

Army Chief of Staff General Dennis Reimer declared the outcome a sign that the service's justice system was functioning fairly and correctly. But the women who had brought the charges disparaged the verdict, some of them telling reporters that their lives had been damaged by the Army's treatment of them during the investigation and trial. Gittins said his client was mostly satisfied with the verdict, yet disappointed by the sentence. He announced that McKinney would bring a $1.5 million libel suit against Hoster for her "false accusations" on national television.

**CROSS REFERENCES**
Civil Rights; Court-Martial; Equal Employment Opportunity Commission; Military Law; Settlement

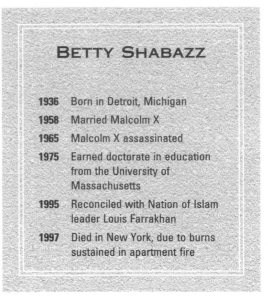

## BETTY SHABAZZ

| | |
|---|---|
| **1936** | Born in Detroit, Michigan |
| **1958** | Married Malcolm X |
| **1965** | Malcolm X assassinated |
| **1975** | Earned doctorate in education from the University of Massachusetts |
| **1995** | Reconciled with Nation of Islam leader Louis Farrakhan |
| **1997** | Died in New York, due to burns sustained in apartment fire |

*Betty Shabazz*
PATRICK J. CUNNINGHAM/AP/WIDE WORLD PHOTOS

## SHABAZZ, BETTY

The tragic death of Betty Shabazz on June 23, 1997, at age sixty-one, provoked grief in the nation's civil rights community. Shabazz, the widow of slain activist Malcolm X, died from complications from burns caused by a fire in her New York apartment. A nurse, educator, and prominent speaker on racial issues, Shabazz had suffered severe burns in a gasoline fire set by her troubled twelve-year-old grandson, Malcolm Shabazz. He later pleaded guilty to two criminal counts related to the fire.

Shabazz, who was born Betty Sanders in Detroit in 1936, rose to prominence through her marriage to the provocative black nationalist leader Malcolm X. He had changed his surname from Little to X to symbolize the African family name that had been taken from his ancestors, as for almost all Africans, who were brought to this country as slaves. After their marriage in 1958, the couple adopted the Muslim name Shabazz. The assassination of her husband in 1965, while she and their daughters watched, pushed Shabazz into the public spotlight. She became an inspirational figure to black women and an important figure in black politics.

In her own right, Shabazz was an accomplished person. Working as a nurse while raising her six daughters, she earned her doctorate in education from the University of Massachusetts in 1975 and then served as an administrator at Medgar Evers College in Brooklyn. In later years she devoted herself to speaking engagements. Shabazz spoke widely on civil rights, urged racial tolerance, and ultimately sought to heal rifts in the African American community related to her husband's death.

Shabazz had long suspected that blame for her husband's murder lay with Nation of Islam leader Louis Farrakhan. Farrakhan had written in 1964 that Malcolm X's political decisions made him "worthy of death." Farrakhan consistently denied involvement. In 1995, Betty Shabazz's daughter, Qubilah Shabazz, was charged in Minneapolis, Minnesota, with attempting to hire a hit man to kill Farrakhan. The defense alleged that a paid FBI informant with a criminal record had set up Qubilah. After much publicity, prosecutors cut a deal requiring only that Qubilah agree to alcohol and psychiatric treatment and sign an affidavit accepting responsibility for her actions. Betty Shabazz later reconciled publicly with Farrakhan.

Because of charges against his mother, Qubilah's son, Malcolm, was removed from her care and sent to live with his grandmother. On June 1, 1997, he set the fire that swept through Shabazz's Yonkers apartment leaving her with burns over 80 percent of her body. She died three weeks later, on June 23. At trial in July in Yonkers family court, psychologists testified that Malcolm suffered from schizophrenia and paranoia, and prosecutors said he had set the fire because he wanted to be returned to his mother. The boy pleaded guilty to two counts—the juvenile equivalents of arson and manslaughter. On August 8, 1997, he was sentenced to be treated for eighteen months in a juvenile detention center, after which his case will be reviewed again. He can be ordered to continue treatment until the age of 18.

**CROSS REFERENCES**
Malcolm X; Nation of Islam

*Sam Reese Sheppard bows his head in silent prayer after the remains of his father, Dr. Sam Sheppard, were exhumed from his grave at Forest Lawn Cemetery in Columbus, Ohio, September 17, 1997.*

NEAL LAURON/REUTERS/ARCHIVE PHOTOS

## SHEPPARD, SAMUEL H.

### Murder Case Update

New scientific evidence revived interest in a famous forty-year-old murder case. The evidence may suggest the posthumous innocence of Dr. Sam Sheppard in the 1954 slaying of his wife, Marilyn Sheppard. Sheppard's case, which loosely served as the basis for the television series and movie, *The Fugitive*, has long been regarded as closed. He was convicted in a chaotic and highly publicized trial in 1954, served ten years in prison, and was later acquitted. But the acquittal never satisfied his son, Sam Reese Sheppard, who, in a long effort to clear his father's name, had the body exhumed in 1997. DNA testing performed on the corpse upholds Dr. Sheppard's claim that another man killed Marilyn Sheppard, argues the younger Sheppard, who has been pursuing a wrongful imprisonment suit against the state of Ohio.

The original Sheppard trial is infamous in U.S. law. Prosecutors and the Ohio media did everything possible to discredit his explanation that a bushy-haired stranger broke into the couple's Cleveland home in July 1954, knocked him unconscious, and then killed his thirty-one-year-old wife. In a campaign of sensationalism, they cast the doctor as a murderous philanderer. Convicted, he remained in prison until the U.S. Supreme Court intervened in 1966 (*Sheppard v. Maxwell*, 384 U.S. 333, 86 S. Ct. 1507, 16 L. Ed. 2ds 600). Likening his trial to a carnival, the

Court ruled that pretrial publicity had tainted the proceedings. Because its decision did not consider guilt or innocence, he was retried and, subsequently, acquitted in November 1966. But amid personal turmoil, he died in 1970 at the age of 46.

The new evidence came as a result of tests performed by a leading DNA expert, Dr. Mohammad Tahir, a supervisor of DNA and serology at the Indianapolis—Marion County Forensic Services Agency, used tissue samples taken from Sheppard's body in 1997. The tests revealed that Sheppard's DNA did not match that of blood found at the murder scene; other tests have shown that the blood was not Marilyn Sheppard's, either. Terry Gilbert, the attorney for Sam Reese Sheppard, told reporters that the results point to the bushy-haired intruder. This suspect he said, could be Richard Eberling, a former window washer at the home who was found to be in possession of a ring belonging to Mrs. Sheppard in 1959. Additional tests by Dr. Tahir found a match between Eberling's DNA type and that of semen taken from vaginal smears from Mrs. Sheppard. Prosecutors never disclosed at trial that crime scene evidence suggested she had been raped. Eberling is now serving a life sentence for murdering an elderly woman in 1984.

The younger Sheppard has spent years trying to uncover a conspiracy. His lawsuit for wrongful imprisonment of his father seeks as much as $2 million in damages. The Cuyahoga County prosecutor's office has attempted to block the suit, which, in 1998, remained before the Ohio Supreme Court. County prosecutor Stephanie Tubbs Jones has argued that the suit is irrelevant because the statute of limitations on wrongful imprisonment have already expired. Sheppard and Gilbert, however, have maintained that improper opposition to the case comes from prosecutors and journalists involved in the original trial who want to shield themselves or their cronies. Among them, allegedly, is Ohio Supreme Court Justice Francis Sweeney, an assistant prosecutor at the time of the trial, who has refused to recuse himself from the case.

**CROSS REFERENCES**
DNA Evidence; Statute of Limitations

## SIXTH AMENDMENT

The Sixth Amendment to the U.S. Constitution reads:

> In all criminal prosecutions, the accused shall enjoy the right to a speedy and public trial, by an impartial jury of the State and district wherein the crime shall have been committed, which district shall have been previously ascertained by law, and to be informed of the nature and cause of the accusation; to be confronted with the witnesses against him; to have compulsory process for obtaining witnesses in his favor, and to have the Assistance of Counsel for his defense.

### Gray v. Maryland

Under the Sixth Amendment, a person on trial for a crime has the right to cross-examine witnesses. The U.S. Supreme Court, in *Bruton v. United States*, 391 U.S. 123, 88 S. Ct. 1620, 20 L. Ed. 2d 476 (1968), ruled that the Confrontation Clause is implicated when two or more defendants are tried jointly and the state introduces the confession of one of them that incriminates both himself and the other. The Court held that the introduction of the confession would allow the jury to use it to convict the nonconfessing codefendant, despite instructions to consider it only against the confessing codefendant. Therefore, the confession could not be used at the joint trial.

The Supreme Court extended the reach of *Bruton* in *Gray v. Maryland*, U.S. , 118 S. Ct. 1151, ___L. Ed. 2d___ (1998). The Court, by a 5–4 vote, ruled that a confession that substituted blanks and the word "deleted" for the nonconfessing defendant's proper name could not be used at a joint criminal trial. The majority concluded that these substitutions, called redactions, did not protect the nonconfessing codefendant and still allowed the jury to draw the conclusion that the nonconfessor was the person whose name had been removed.

The case arose out of the beating death of Stacy Williams in Baltimore, Maryland. Anthony Bell confessed to police that he, Kevin Gray, and a third man had participated in the beating death. The third man later died, but Bell and Gray were indicted for murder and tried jointly, over Gray's objections, in Maryland state court. The judge allowed Bell's confession to be read into the record by a police detective, who said the words "deleted" or "deletion" whenever Gray's name or the third man's name appeared. After reading the redacted confession to the jury, the detective was asked by the prosecutor whether after Bell made the confession, the detective was able to arrest Gray. The detective responded affirmatively. The state produced other witnesses that said six persons, including Bell and Gray, had participated in the beating. Gray testified and denied his participation, but Bell did not testify. The judge instructed the jury that the confession was evidence only against Bell and should not be used as evidence against Gray. The jury convicted both Bell and Gray.

Gray appealed his conviction, contending that the redacted confession should not have been used under the *Bruton* precedent. Maryland's intermediate court of appeals agreed, 107 Md.App. 311, 667 A.2d 983 (1995), but its supreme court reinstated the conviction, 344 Md. 417, 687 A.2d 660 (1997).

The U.S. Supreme Court reversed the Maryland high court, agreeing with Gray that *Bruton* applied to a redaction that replaces a name with an obvious blank space or symbol. Justice Stephen G. Breyer, writing for the majority, noted that the state had "simply replaced the nonconfessing defendant's name with a kind of symbol, namely the word 'deleted' or a blank space set off by commas." Calling this manner of removal of Gray's name "an obvious indication of deletion," Breyer said it so closely resembled *Bruton* that the same result was mandated.

Breyer expressed concern that the jury would realize the redacted confession referred specifically to the nonconfessing defendant. Replacing a name with a blank "will not likely fool anyone." Moreover, the judge's instruction not to consider the confession as evidence against a defendant made obvious the reason for the blanks in the confession. Breyer also concluded that the "obvious deletion may well call the juror's attention specially to the removed name." Such deletions encouraged the jury to speculate about the reference and "may overemphasize the importance of the confession's accusation."

The majority conceded that deleting a name "less obviously refers to the defendant than a confession that uses the defendant's full and proper name." Even so, Justice Breyer found that the blanks and the word "deleted" were similar enough to the use of Gray's name as to put the confession in violation of the Sixth Amendment. To be constitutional, a confession must be edited in such a way as to remove all obvious references to the defendant and to prevent the jury from drawing an obvious conclusion as to the identity of the persons not mentioned by name in the confession.

Justice Antonin Scalia, writing for the dissenters, argued that the Court wrongly extended *Bruton* to confessions "that incriminate only by inference from other evidence." Scalia agreed with the majority that confessions are redacted to omit the defendant's name were more likely to incriminate than confessions redacted to omit any reference to his existence. However, he concluded that the incrimination was not so powerful as to "depart from the normal presumption that the jury follow its instructions." In addition, Scalia expressed concern that the majority endorsed "free-lance editing" of confessions to remove all evidence of the defendant. The risk posed by such editing "seems to me infinitely greater than the risk posed by the entirely honest reproduction that the Court disapproves."

**CROSS REFERENCES**
Confrontation

## SMITH, MARY LOUISE

Mary Louise Smith was a Republican party activist who became the first woman to serve as head of the party's national committee. A political moderate, Smith's advocacy of abortion rights and the Equal Rights Amendment (ERA) during the 1970s ran counter to the ideology of the party's conservative majority. Her outspoken manner disturbed the Republican party leadership, which sought to bar her from the 1996 Republican National Convention.

## MARY LOUISE SMITH

**1914**  Born in Eddyville, Iowa

**1935**  Graduated from Iowa State University

**1964**  Became alternate delegate to the Republican National Convention; became vice-chair of the Iowa presidential campaign of Senator Barry Goldwater; elected to the Republican National Committee

**1974**  Appointed chair of the Republican National Committee

**1976**  First woman to organize and call to order a national presidential nominating convention of a major political party

**1977**  Resigned as chair of Republican party; inducted into Iowa Women's Hall of Fame

**1980**  Appointed to U.S. Civil Rights Commission

**1991**  Created the Women's Archive Project at Iowa State University

**1995**  Iowa State University honored her by creating the Mary Louise Smith endowed chair in women and politics

**1996**  Party leaders sought to exclude her from national convention, but was given entrance at the last minute

**1997**  Died in Des Moines, Iowa

Smith was born on October 16, 1914, in Eddyville, Iowa. She attended Iowa State University, graduating with a degree in social work in 1935. She married Elmer M. Smith, a physician, and moved with him to Eagle Grove, Iowa. Smith raised three children and soon became active in local politics, winning a seat on the Eagle Grove school board.

Smith's life changed when she began to work in the local Republican party organization. Soon she was working at the county and state levels, becoming the leader of the Iowa Feder-

*Mary Louise Smith*
AP/WIDE WORLD PHOTOS

ation of Republican Women. In 1964 Smith became the alternate delegate to the Republican National Convention and vice-chair of the Iowa presidential campaign of the party's nominee, Senator Barry M. Goldwater of Arizona. In that same year, Smith was elected to the Republican National Committee, the party's most powerful leadership organization.

Smith remained a member of the Republican National Committee during the 1960s and early 1970s. After President Richard M. Nixon resigned from the presidency in 1974 because of his involvement in the Watergate scandals, President Gerald R. Ford sought to restore the credibility of the Republican party and separate it from the scandals of the Nixon administration. One step he took to accomplish these objectives was to appoint Smith as chair of the Republican National Committee in 1974. As the first woman to head a major U.S. political party, Smith drew national attention for her commitment to abortion rights and the ratification of the Equal Rights Amendment.

In 1976 Smith was the first woman to organize and call to order a national presidential nominating convention of a major political party. President Ford won the Republican nomination, turning back an attempt by conservatives to nominate Ronald Reagan, then governor of California. However, Democratic nominee Jimmy Carter defeated Ford in the November election, and in 1977 Smith resigned as chair of the party. She did, however, remain on the national committee until 1984.

President Reagan appointed Smith to the U.S. Civil Rights Commission in 1980, but soon regretted his action. Smith publicly criticized Reagan for his policies on civil rights and the lack of women in his administration. Because of her criticisms, Smith was not re-appointed to the commission in 1983.

Smith returned to Iowa and continued to seek a more moderate course for Republican politics, which was dominated by political and social conservatives. Though the ERA failed to be ratified by its 1982 deadline, Smith continued to advocate equal rights for women. She also became an outspoken proponent for gay and lesbian rights.

By 1996 Smith had been pushed to the margins of the Republican party. Party leaders sought to exclude her from the 1996 Republican National Convention because delegates feared she might make public statements that were out of step with party ideology. At the last minute, a party leader secured her entrance to the convention floor by giving her a ticket as a member of the convention's security personnel.

Though outspoken, Smith was an admired figure in Iowa politics. As founder of the Iowa Women's Political Caucus, she was inducted into the Iowa Women's Hall of Fame in 1977. In 1991 Smith created the Women's Archives project at Iowa State University, and in 1995 the university honored her by creating the Mary Louise Smith endowed chair in women and politics.

Smith died on August 22, 1997, in Des Moines, Iowa.

**CROSS REFERENCES**
Republican Party

## SPORTS LAW

The laws, regulations, and judicial decisions that govern sports and athletes.

### Latrell Sprewell Assault Case

During the 1997–98 National Basketball Association (NBA) season, a player's assault on his coach tested the authority of the league to discipline its highly paid players. On December 1, 1997, Latrell Sprewell, a 28-year-old guard for the San Francisco-based Golden State Warriors, allegedly choked, hit, and threatened to kill the team's coach, P. J. Carlesimo. The team fired Sprewell and the NBA expelled him for one year. But in a surprising reversal in March 1998, the league's arbitrator ruled that these punishments were excessive: the team had to fulfill $17.3 million due on a $32 million contract, and the league's suspension was shortened by 14 games. The assault ultimately cost Sprewell $6.4 million in lost salary, a price he declared worthwhile for defending his manhood. The decision infuriated league officials but satisfied the NBA player's union, which had opposed the punishment.

The assault capped tensions that had been building for a month between the all-star player and the coach of the faltering Warriors. During a November game, Sprewell used an obscene term to describe Carlesimo; additional confrontations led to his being temporarily replaced in the starting lineup. Then, at a practice on December 1, a disagreement erupted into violence. According to team officials, Sprewell became enraged when told to make better passes to teammates, choked Carlesimo while threatening to kill him, briefly left the basketball court, and then returned and struck him. Sprewell admitted to scratching but denied choking or hitting Carlesimo, emphasizing that he had allowed the coach to breathe at all times. Explaining the assault to *The San Francisco Chronicle*, he said that he had been unable to tolerate verbal abuse of himself and other teammates.

Disciplinary actions immediately followed. The team initially suspended Sprewell for ten games. Two days later, after Sprewell refused to apologize, it fired him. Sprewell was only in the second year of a four-year contract worth $32 million, meaning that he stood to lose nearly two-thirds of his salary while the Warriors lost the ability to trade him to another team. Then, on December 4, NBA Commissioner David Stern banned Sprewell for one year of play on any team in the league. The punishment was the most severe ever handed down for a non drug-related offense in the NBA. Sprewell subsequently apologized.

One day after the league's suspension, the NBA Players Association filed a grievance on Sprewell's behalf. The ability of the player's union to take this step reflects the unique organizational structure of professional basketball. The NBA is a league consisting of 28 privately owned franchises, all of which are governed by the league's commissioner. Players, however, have specific rights as defined in the collective bargaining agreement between their union and the league. This agreement includes the right to submit disputes to the decision of a professional arbitrator, a quasi-judicial authority who hears both sides and then issues a binding decision.

The league, the team, and the union submitted their arguments in the case to the NBA's grievance arbitrator, John Feerick. A veteran of labor law and the dean of Fordham University Law School, Feerick conducted closed hearings between January 27 and February 16, 1998. Although he imposed a gag order on the participants, the broad outlines of the hearings were made public: the parties disputed the nature of the assault as well as the contractual authority of officials to impose severe discipline upon a player. In particular, the team asserted its right to fire Sprewell under a clause in all NBA players's contracts making "moral turpitude" a cause for dismissal. It asserted that Sprewell's second assault, when he returned from the locker room and punched Carlesimo, was premeditated. The union denied the charge of premeditation and argued that the punishments were excessive.

*Former Golden State Warrior guard Latrell Sprewell publicly apologizes for his attack on Warrior coach P.J. Carlesimo during a press conference held December 9, 1997.*

LOU DEMATTEIS/REUTERS/ARCHIVE PHOTOS

On March 4, Feerick's 106-page decision largely favored the union's contention. He ruled that both attacks had occurred in the heat of argument; neither was premeditated. As such, the firing was a contractual violation. The Warriors had to reinstate Sprewell and honor the remaining two years on his contract, worth $17.3 million. The NBA's one-year suspension was shortened so that Sprewell could begin play immediately at the start of the 1998–1999 season. A penalty of 68 games, instead of 82, was "commensurate with the severity of misconduct," Feerick wrote. The opinion also generally addressed the NBA's authority to impose severe discipline. The attack upon the coach had struck "at the very core" of organized basketball, and the NBA was empowered to impose discipline. But Feerick insisted that such discipline must be fair and uniformly applied to all players.

Sprewell filed a $30 million civil suit against the National Basketball Associations and the Golden State Warriors, alleging violations of his civil rights and of racial discrimination. On July 30, 1998, Federal District Judge Vaughn Walker dismissed his suit.

**CROSS REFERENCES**
Arbitration; Collective Bargaining

## STRATEGIC LAWSUITS AGAINST PUBLIC PARTICIPATION (SLAPPs)

### Restrictive Real Estate Covenants

The phrase Strategic Lawsuit Against Public Participation (SLAPP), coined by University of Denver Professors George W. Pring and

# SHOULD SLAPPS BE PROHIBITED?

The increased use of lawsuits known as Strategic Lawsuits Against Public Policy Participation (SLAPPs) has led to legislative and judicial efforts to prohibit them or to insure that such suits are dismissed quickly. In the debates surrounding legislation and court rules, critics of SLAPPs have charged that this type of lawsuit is an assault on a citizen's right to free speech, to petition the government, and to participate in the political process. Defenders of SLAPPs dispute these charges, arguing that the courts should be open to plaintiffs who believe they have been injured by the statements and actions of an individual or an organization. They contend that hasty efforts to dismiss allegedly frivolous lawsuits labeled SLAPPs prevent plaintiffs from obtaining due process.

IN FOCUS

Critics of SLAPPs acknowledge that it would be difficult to simply prohibit SLAPPs because identifying SLAPPs can be quite difficult. Many lawsuits do not fit into a "good guy–bad guy" scenario, but more importantly, SLAPP complaints often distort or leave out facts to hide the true nature of the suit. A skillful attorney for a SLAPP plaintiff may disguise such a suit by filing a complaint that which demonstrates technical skill rather than objective reality. SLAPPs are often "camouflaged" as ordinary civil lawsuits based on traditional theories of tort or personal injury law. Among the most often used legal theories are defamation, invasion of privacy, malicious prosecution, abuse of process, conspiracy, nuisance, interference with contract, and intentional infliction of emotional distress.

Critics point out that most SLAPPs are ultimately unsuccessful. While most SLAPPs lose in court, they succeed in forcing the defendant to make a substantial investment in time, money, and resources. SLAPPs also divert attention away from the public issue as the defendant shifts her focus to the legal arena. Therefore, critics have sought legislative

and judicial methods to identify and dismiss SLAPPs cases quickly.

Critics of SLAPPs point to a California law that seeks to protect expressive activity. The law (Civ. Code § 425.16) allows a judge to decide at the outset of the suit whether the SLAPP has a "probability" of winning. If the judge finds that it does not, the SLAPP must be dismissed and the SLAPP plaintiff must pay the defendant's attorneys' fees and defense costs. The expressive activity that forms the basis of the suit must be made before a legislative, executive, or judicial proceeding, or made in a place open to the public or a public forum in connection with an issue of public interest.

Critics have also encouraged defendants to file SLAPP-back lawsuits, suing the SLAPP plaintiff for malicious prosecution. Despite the apparent allure of such an action, most commentators have found it is very difficult to prevail in a malicious prosecution lawsuit. Moreover, most defendants are not happy about being in court in the first place. The prospect of spending more time and money on a lawsuit is usually unappealing to the defendant.

The desire to minimize the impact of SLAPPs is based on the fear that SLAPPs threaten democratic principles. If a person cannot exercise his First Amendment rights on a matter of public interest without fear of being sued, freedom of expression will become a hollow principle. In addition, public participation should be encouraged at every level because it legitimizes the government, makes it more responsive, and ensures that it is representative of the people's will. The chilling effect of SLAPPs on citizen involvement must, according to the critics, be minimized.

Finally, critics of SLAPPs counsel citizens to make sure their statements are factually correct. If the statements are accurate, there will be no factual disputes

later on, and will help convince the court, for example, that the lawsuit is a SLAPP rather than a defamation action.

Critics of anti-SLAPP legislation contend that SLAPP opponents have unfairly labeled all lawsuits involving matters of public interest as being frivolous or malicious. These critics point out that not all plaintiffs who file SLAPPs are malicious, any more than SLAPP defendants are all well-intentioned. By seeking to portray the subjective motives of SLAPP plaintiffs—bad faith, frivolousness, and intimidation—SLAPP critics have demonized the often legitimate attempts of plaintiffs to seek redress in a court of law.

The defenders of SLAPPs reject the label itself, contending that such labeling is unfair. Whether, for example, a lawsuit is a defamation action or a so-called SLAPP is in the eye of the beholder. If a person speaks at a public meeting and states that a company is illegally polluting the water supply, the company should be permitted to file a defamation action that challenges the veracity of the statement and seeks compensation for the injury to its good name. Laws such as the one in California give too much discretion to the trial judge to assess the probability of the plaintiff winning the lawsuit. In addition, at this early stage of the lawsuit, the court and the parties will not have developed a detailed factual record. A judge may dismiss a legitimate action merely because the statements in question were made in a public forum. If they were made in a setting not covered by the anti-SLAPPs law, the plaintiff would be allowed to proceed.

Finally, critics of anti-SLAPPs laws believe it is unfair to remove this legal avenue for plaintiffs. If a person or group involved in a public issue is acting irresponsibly, the threat of a lawsuit may make them more responsible. This approach enhances the democratic process, critics maintain, because the First Amendment does not protect slander and libel.

Penelope Canan, describes a lawsuit that attempts to prohibit a range of public speech on issues of public interest through the threat of defamation, libel, business interference, and conspiracy. Typically, parties attempt to limit public speech on such issues as pollution, the actions of public officials, land use, and land development.

Some real estate developers have sought ways to prevent residents of subdivisions from opposing the re-zoning of property adjacent to the subdivision. One method developers have used to attempt to accomplish this is to include in the contract for sale of a subdivision lot an agreement, or *covenant*, stating that the purchaser takes the property on the condition that the purchaser will not oppose any re-zoning plans for adjacent lands acquired by the developer. In the event that a party to the agreement violates the clause by speaking publicly, the covenant can lead to a SLAPP.

Although most SLAPPs are dismissed by the courts, parties continue to file them. Some states have passed anti-SLAPP laws to thwart SLAPPs at their inception and prevent costly litigation fees for defendants of SLAPP suits. Anti-SLAPP statutes make it difficult for parties to enforce SLAPP provisions by creating procedural hurdles. For example, in Minnesota, a court must dismiss a SLAPP claim unless the plaintiff can prove that the target's activities were not directed toward producing favorable government action (Minn. Stat. Ann. § 554.01-05). As of 1997, eleven states had passed anti-SLAPP statutes, and several others had considered passing them.

In 1996 an anti-SLAPP law was passed by the General Assembly of Georgia (Ga. Code Ann. § 9-11-11). The statute requires SLAPP plaintiffs to verify that the suit is grounded in fact and is filed in good faith. A SLAPP plaintiff also must verify that the basis of the suit is not a privileged communication and that the suit is not filed for an improper purpose, such as the suppression of the right to free speech or the right to petition the government. If a SLAPP defendant files a motion to dismiss the case, the court must hear arguments on the motion within thirty days of service of the motion if possible.

Before 1996 the Providence Construction Company (Providence), which owned a subdivision in Cobb County, had included a covenant in its deeds for sale of subdivision lots. The covenant stated that the new owner "agrees not to oppose any application to amend the zoning ordinances or any petition seeking a variance of the zoning laws and regulations" to permit such land uses as public golfing, dining, and recreation. The covenant also stated that "each owner agrees not to oppose any license application or transfer relating to any such permitted land usages in the Development" as well as "any and all contiguous land" surrounding the development acquired by Providence.

When Providence sought a re-zoning of land adjacent to the subdivision, a group of residents publicly opposed the change. The residents circulated petitions, wrote letters to Cobb County officials, and spoke before the county planning commission. Providence sued the residents for breach of contract and tortious interference with contractual relations, but it eventually dropped its suit against all but one defendant, Dave Bauer, a resident of the subdivision who continued to oppose the re-zoning (*Providence Construction Co. v. Bauer*, 494 S.E. 2d 527 [Ga. App. 1997]).

At trial Bauer moved for summary judgment, which the court granted. Providence appealed to the Georgia Court of Appeals, but the appeals court affirmed the lower court, holding that the developer's suit was contrary to public policy and foreclosed by Georgia's anti-SLAPP statute. According to the appeals court, the covenant violated the Georgia Constitution because it was overly broad in seeking to prevent residents from opposing future unspecified re-zoning attempts of any and all contiguous land that Providence might acquire. The covenant was also too vague in its limitation of speech, because it prevented residents from opposing government action that could affect their neighborhood's character and the value of their homes. The court held that "[s]uch a prohibition is contrary to public policy and the public interest."

**CROSS REFERENCES**

Land-Use Control; Zoning

# SURROGATE MOTHERHOOD

A relationship in which one woman bears and gives birth to a child for a person or a couple who then adopts or takes legal custody of the child; also called mothering by proxy.

### Couple With No Biological Tie to Child Declared Legal Parents

Advances in reproductive technology such as artificial insemination, in vitro fertilization,

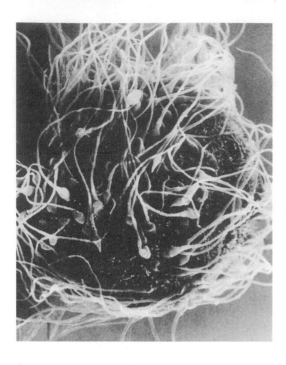

and surrogacy have raised complex and novel legal issues. Litigation is likely to involve a divorcing couple's ownership of frozen sperm and embryos, family members' claims to genetic material from a dead person, or a surrogate mother's claim to maternity rights over the child she was hired to carry.

Surrogacy has become an increasingly popular method used by infertile couples to create children. The number of children born from donated eggs increased from 112 babies conceived at 48 clinics in 1989 to 1,240 babies conceived at 163 clinics in 1994. Experts believe use of the technique has increased substantially since then. Although surrogacy can cost much more than adoption, some couples feel that it gives them more control over the child because they can ensure the health of the surrogate mother and the egg and sperm donors and protect against genetic problems. In addition, only a small percentage of surrogate mothers change their mind and attempt to keep the child.

Although most surrogacy cases involve at least one parent who is biologically related to the child, donating either sperm or egg, many childless couples are arranging to hire surrogate mothers to carry donations of egg and sperm obtained from third parties. In such cases no person other than the surrogate has a biological relationship to the child.

In a closely watched case that legal experts predict will set a benchmark in surrogacy law, a California state appeals court has ruled that a couple who hired a surrogate to bear a child for them are the legal parents of the child, although neither individual has any biological tie to the child (*Buzzanca v. Buzzanca*, 72 Cal. Rptr. 2d 280 61 Cal. App. 4th 1410 [Cal. App. 4 Dist. 1998]). According to legal commentators, the decision will strengthen the rights of infertile couples who want to have children but who fear that courts could grant parental rights to surrogates or egg and sperm donors.

John and Luanne Buzzanca were both thirty-nine years old when they married in May 1989. After trying for several years to have a child, they contacted the Center for Reproductive Alternatives of Southern California in 1994. The center put them in touch with Pamela Snell, a thirty-seven-year-old married mother of two from northern California who had previously served as a surrogate for other couples. The Buzzancas arranged to obtain an egg and sperm from anonymous donors and signed a written contract with Snell and her husband under which Pamela would carry the baby to term for them. Under the contract the Buzzancas agreed to pay Snell monthly expenses of $800 for housing, $500 for food, and $115 for clothes. The contract stated that the offspring would legally be the Buzzancas' child and acknowledged that no established legal guidelines existed for the arrangement.

The contract referenced the well-known California Supreme Court case *Johnson v. Calvert*, 5 Cal. 4th 84, 851 p.2d 776, 19 Cal. Rptr. 2d 494 (1993), *cert. denied, Johnson v. Calvert*, 510 U.S. 874, 114 S. Ct. 206, 126 L. Ed. 2d 163 (1993). In that case Mark and Crispina Calvert had contracted with a surrogate, Anna Johnson, to carry an embryo, created from the couple's own egg and sperm, to term in return for $10,000. After the birth of the child, Johnson sued the Calverts for custody, claiming they had breached the contract with her. In ruling that the Calverts were the child's legal parents, the California Supreme Court became the first state high court to enforce a surrogacy contract. The Buzzancas' contract noted that although the *Calvert* case created a favorable environment for surrogacy in California, the legislature had not endorsed the practice. (In 1992 the California Legislature had attempted to enact legislation stripping a surrogate mother of all rights to a newborn in favor of the couple who intended to raise the child [S. 937]. Governor Pete Wilson vetoed the bill on the grounds that there were too few disputed cases to warrant the legislation.)

In March 1995, a month before Jaycee was born, John Buzzanca filed for divorce, alleging that there were no children of the marriage. Luanne Buzzanca responded that the parties were expecting a child by way of a surrogate contract and later filed a petition in family court to establish herself as Jaycee's mother. John Buzzanca argued that because no court had established that Jaycee was a child of the marriage, no family court could order him to pay child support. He also suggested that the surrogate mother, Snell, might be held legally responsible for the child. At one point in the proceedings, Snell did seek legal custody of Jaycee, claiming that she had contracted to deliver the child to a happily married couple, not one involved in a bitter divorce. Snell later withdrew her custody claim. In February 1996, the family court ruled that it had no jurisdiction to order John Buzzanca to pay child support (Orange County Superior Court, No. 95 D 002992).

Luanne Buzzanca appealed to the Fourth District Court of Appeals in Santa Ana, California. The appeals court determined that the family court did have jurisdiction to hear the case and ordered John Buzzanca to pay child support until the family court could make a final ruling (*Jaycee B. v. Superior Court (John B.)*, 42 Cal. App. 4th 718, 49 Cal. Rptr. 2d 694 [1996]). The appeals court noted that it was not required to determine at that time whether Jaycee was legally John Buzzanca's daughter. "It is enough [to establish jurisdiction] that John admits he signed the surrogacy agreement," wrote the court, "which, for all practical purposes, caused Jaycee's conception every bit as much as if he had caused her birth the old-fashioned way."

The case was returned to the lower court. Although Jaycee ostensibly had as many as six parents—the couple who arranged for her birth, the anonymous egg and sperm donors, and the surrogate mother and her husband—Orange County Superior Judge Robert Monarch ruled in September 1997 that under the law Jaycee had no legal parents. The court said that under California law Luanne Buzzanca was not the lawful mother of Jaycee because she had not given birth to the child, had not donated the ovum that helped to create the child, and had not adopted the child (Cal. Fam. Code § 7610). Therefore, the court said, John Buzzanca could not be the lawful father or owe any child support. The court suggested that Luanne would need to adopt Jaycee, although Luanne contended that under the contract she was Jaycee's intended mother. Luanne also sought clarification on from whom she needed to seek adoption—the anonymous genetic parents or the surrogate mother and her husband.

Both Luanne Buzzanca and the attorneys appointed to represent Jaycee appealed the trial court's decision to the Fourth District Court of Appeals. In October 1997, the appellate court temporarily stayed the lower court's ruling, ordering John Buzzanca to pay child support and granting temporary legal custody to Luanne pending a final decision in the matter.

In March 1998, the appeals court issued its final decision, reversing the lower court. The court relied on California case law and a statute establishing that a husband who consents to the artificial insemination of his wife with another man's sperm is recognized as the legal father of the child (Cal. Fam. Code § 7613; *People v. Sorensen*, 68 Cal. 2d 280, 437 P. 2d 495, 66 Cal. Rptr. 7 [1968]). The court wrote:

> The same rule which makes a husband the lawful father of a child born because of his consent to artificial insemination should be applied here … to both husband and wife. Just as a husband is deemed to be the lawful father of a child unrelated to him when his wife gives birth after artificial insemination, so should a husband and wife be deemed the lawful parents of a child after a surrogate bears a biologically unrelated child on their behalf. In each instance, a child is procreated because a medical procedure was initiated and consented to by intended parents.

According to the court, the fact that Luanne Buzzanca did not give birth to Jaycee was irrelevant. A woman can be declared the legal mother of a child not biologically related to her, said the court, if she consents to a medical procedure that results in a pregnancy and the eventual birth of a child.

The court pointed out that the California legislature has made it clear that public policy favors the establishment of legal parenthood whenever possible. The court cited section 7570 of the California Family Code, which states, "There is a compelling state interest in establishing paternity for all children." According to the court, this legislative policy is applicable to maternity as well.

The court said it was necessary to examine the parties' intent to parent. In *Johnson* the California Supreme Court addressed the very situation presented by the Buzzancas stating:

> In what we must hope will be the extremely rare situation in which neither the gestator nor the woman who provided the ovum for fertilization is willing to assume custody of the child after birth, a rule recognizing the intending parents as the child's legal, natural parents should best promote certainly and stability for the child.

Although John Buzzanca argued that this statement applies only in situations where the intended parents have a genetic tie to the child, the appeals court disagreed, finding that the language applied to any situation in which a child would not have been born but for the efforts of the intended parents.

The court ordered that Luanne have legal custody of Jaycee, that Jaycee's birth certificate be amended to reflect John and Luanne Buzzanca as her lawful parents, and that the lower court enter a permanent order for child support. The court also called on the legislature to sort out parental rights and responsibilities of those involved in artificial reproduction. Although the courts can continue to make decisions on a case-by-case basis, said the court, a broader order imposed by the legislature would bring a degree of predictability to individuals using artificial reproductive techniques.

**CROSS REFERENCES**
Children's Rights; Child Support; Parent and Child; Reproduction

# TAXATION

The process whereby charges are imposed on individuals or property by the legislative branch of the federal government and by many state governments to raise funds for public purposes.

## Refusal to Pay Taxes

In February 1998, the U.S. Bankruptcy Appellate Panel of the Sixth Circuit refused to allow a bankrupt debtor to discharge unpaid taxes. The debtor, Terrance J. Myers, had willfully failed to file tax returns for the years 1980–1983 because he believed that the tax system was unconstitutional and that paying taxes was voluntary.

Myers filed for Chapter Seven bankruptcy in January 1993 and scheduled a debt for federal income taxes for 1980 through 1983. Myers's debts were discharged in June 1993, but the bankruptcy court did not rule on whether Myers's federal tax debts could be discharged. When Myers's debts were discharged by the bankruptcy court, the Internal Revenue Service began pursuing federal taxes from Myers. Myers then returned to the bankruptcy court, asking for a stop to the collection activities, a return of wages garnished by the IRS, interest on the garnished wages, and attorney's fees.

The federal government moved for summary judgment, arguing that Myers's federal tax debt was intentional and therefore nondischargeable. Under various sections of Title 11 of the U.S. Code, a bankrupt debtor may gain a discharge of a federal tax debt, but under 11 U.S.C.A. § 523(a)(1)(C), a bankrupt debtor may not discharge a tax debt for a tax owed from a fraudulent return or from an attempt to evade or defeat the tax.

Myers did not dispute the facts in the case. Myers admitted that he had intentionally refused to file tax returns for the years 1980–1983, but that he had paid taxes since 1985, when his attorney convinced him to abandon his position that the tax system was unconstitutional and voluntary. Myers argued that this turnabout should be given consideration, and that the bankruptcy code did not "forever preclude a rehabilitated taxpayer from the statutory relief available under Title 11," *In re Myers*, 214 B.R. 402 (6th Cir. BAP [Ohio]). Myers urged the court to discharge the taxes under 11 U.S.C.A. § 524 or through the court's equitable powers to discharge owed taxes under 11 U.S.C.A. § 105.

The bankruptcy court granted summary judgment to the government. Myers appealed, but the appeals panel affirmed the ruling. The appeals panel noted that Myers's case went further than the mere nonpayment of taxes: Myers refused to file returns for four years, and the refusal was a voluntary, conscious, and intentional attempt to avoid tax liability. Myers's belief about the tax code "was not based on a misunderstanding of the tax laws; it was admittedly just a restatement of the Debtor's rhetoric that the tax code is unconstitutional." The appeals panel analyzed prior bankruptcy cases and found no precedent that recognized an exception to nondischargeability for bankrupt debtors who had willfully avoided the payment of taxes, including cases in which tax protesters who had refused to file taxes for a time but who eventually decided to "come in from the cold."

**CROSS REFERENCES**
Bankruptcy

## TERRORISM

The unlawful use of force or violence against persons or property in order to coerce or intimidate a government or the civilian population in furtherance of political or social objectives.

### Terry Nichols Convicted for Oklahoma City Bombing

On December 23, 1997, a federal jury convicted Terry Nichols for his role in the Oklahoma City bombing case. (*U.S. v. Nichols*, Criminal Action No. 96-CR-68). Nichols was the second person tried for the 1995 bombing of the Alfred P. Murrah Federal Building, the worst act of domestic terrorism in U.S. history, which claimed 168 lives. Five months before his trial, another jury had convicted the principal terrorist, Timothy McVeigh, of murder and conspiracy to commit murder. Federal prosecutors hoped for a similar result with their identical eleven-count indictment against Nichols, a forty-three-year-old drifter and anti-government extremist. The jury found Nichols guilty of conspiracy and involuntary manslaughter, but acquitted him of murder. As the men began appealing their federal convictions, state prosecutors proceeded with plans to try them in Oklahoma.

Within three days of the bombing on April 19, 1995, the FBI arrested McVeigh; one day later, Nichols surrendered for questioning. Over the next four months, investigators built an elaborate case that posited McVeigh as the chief architect and executor of the bombing with Nichols as his co-conspirator. The charges went before a federal grand jury in Oklahoma City on August 10. The grand jury indicted both men on eleven counts that included the murder of eight federal law enforcement agents. But the government's plans to try the defendants together in Oklahoma were blocked. Prompted by concerns for a fair trial, U.S. District Judge Richard Matsch intervened twice. In February 1996, ruling that pretrial publicity had "demonized" the defendants, Judge Matsch moved the case from Oklahoma to Denver. Then, in December 1996, he ordered separate trials.

In mid-1997, McVeigh was tried first. Prosecutors had a relatively easy time convincing the

jury to convict the twenty-nine-year-old former Army sergeant on all eleven counts. They presented substantial physical evidence supporting their contention that he had planned the bombing as retaliation for past FBI actions against anti-government radicals, rented a Ryder truck, filled it with homemade explosives, and then drove it from Kansas to Oklahoma City where he lit the fuse. Defense attorneys tried to discredit the government's evidence, but they also sought to elaborate upon McVeigh's anti-government views. The jury returned its verdict on June 2, 1997; on June 13, it decided on the death sentence.

Nichols's trial commenced on November 3, 1997. Federal agents who interrogated Nichols for nine hours in April 1996 had failed to write down, record, or videotape his statements—a stark departure from standard law enforcement procedure. Months before the trial, defense attorneys tried, but failed, to have the statements barred as evidence. Even though Judge Matsch allowed the statements to be admitted, the lack of a verifiable record cast doubt on the agents' recollections. Moreover, the evidence against Nichols was largely circumstantial. Phone records showed that he made calls to chemical companies and rented storage sheds; traces of ammonium nitrate had been found in his home, as had bombing caps and a drill bit that allegedly matched one used to break into an explosives shed. But no witnesses could place him at the construction of the bomb or the scene of the crime.

Over twenty days, prosecutors presented ninety-eight witnesses, including Nichols's former wife, Lana Padilla. She testified that Nichols had given her a sealed envelope a few months before the bombing, intended for McVeigh, which read in part, "You're on your own. Go for it!" Other damaging testimony came from FBI agents who had conducted the 1996 interrogation, during which Nichols repeatedly mentioned McVeigh. The agents testified that Nichols said he drove to Oklahoma City to get McVeigh days before the bombing, and then took him to a motel in Kansas City. In the car, McVeigh allegedly told him "something big is going to happen." They also focused on Nichols's admitted knowledge of explosives.

The defense denied that Nichols had any role in the bombing. Although acknowledging that Nichols was close to McVeigh and had helped him gather bomb materials, the defense maintained that he had no knowledge of McVeigh's intentions. Lead defense attorney

Michael Tigar repeatedly attempted to distance his client from the convicted man. He stressed that Nichols was not present at key points in the government's chronology of the case. In fact, he argued, prosecutors had got the wrong man: the bombing was the work of McVeigh and another, unidentified accomplice. Defense witnesses said they had seen another person with McVeigh in Kansas. Others testified that they saw a Ryder truck at the motel prior to the time when prosecutors said McVeigh had rented one.

Tigar's strategy also required attacking the government's key physical evidence. Months before the bombing, prosecutors said Nichols purchased two tons of ammonium nitrate fertilizer—material they contended was used in the bomb, as traces of ammonium nitrate had allegedly been found at the bombing site. But this evidence was no longer in the FBI's possession. Tigar argued that the FBI had mishandled its evidence; moreover, he contended that the bureau had leaped to judgment even before completing its testing of the evidence.

The defense presented ninety-two witnesses in eight days. At the end of his summation, Tigar wept and put his arm on Nichols's shoulder. "This is my brother," he said through tears. "He's in your hands."

The seven-woman, five-man panel had significant difficulty reaching its verdict, requiring a week for deliberations. They found Nichols guilty of conspiring to use a weapon of mass destruction, but acquitted him of actual use of the weapon. Next, they returned verdicts of not guilty of first or second-degree murder for the deaths of the eight federal agents. Instead they convicted Nichols of the lesser charge of involuntary manslaughter. Essentially, the split verdict said that Nichols had helped to plan the bombing, but that he had not participated in it. The jury decided that Nichols's deliberate participation in a conspiracy had led to foreseeable results in the deaths of the federal officers. But it had also somehow concluded that Nichols's role in their deaths was involuntary—without intention.

The confusing verdict had several short-term results. In Oklahoma City, where closed-circuit broadcasts of the trial had been made available by the court, public outrage was immediate. Survivors of the bombing, Mayor Ron Norick, and Oklahoma Governor Frank Keating all denounced the verdict. Some commentators believed the jury had not understood its job; they reported that a few jurors looked surprised when told they would next have to consider sentencing. In Denver, defense attorney Tigar asked the court to block the sentencing phase of the trial due to an inherent conflict in the verdict. In response, Judge Matsch instructed jurors to give more thought to the issue of Nichols's intent.

The judge's instruction seemed only to deepen jurors' confusion. On January 14, 1998, when they remained hopelessly deadlocked after deliberating for thirteen hours, Judge Matsch dismissed them and took over the sentencing phase himself.

The jury's dismissal may have been fortunate for Nichols. Under federal law, he could be given the death penalty for his conspiracy conviction. However, federal sentencing guidelines allow the death penalty only to be meted out by a jury. On June 4 Judge Matsch sentenced Nichols to life in prison without the possibility of parole.

Both Nichols and McVeigh, meanwhile, were separately pursuing appeals of their federal convictions, a lengthy process that could take two to three years. In Oklahoma, prosecutors were also moving forward with state charges against both men. Noting that the federal murder charges had covered only eight deaths, Oklahoma County District Attorney Bob Marcy vowed to prosecute both men on behalf of the other 160 victims of the explosion.

### Unabomber

On January 22, 1998, Theodore Kaczynski admitted in a Sacramento, California, federal court that he was the Unabomber, the person

*Terry Nichols is escorted by U.S. Marshals to a federal courthouse on January 31, 1996, for the second day of the change of venue hearing.*

DAVID LONGSTREATH/REUTERS/
ARCHIVE PHOTOS

responsible for a series of deadly bomb attacks over a seventeen-year period. Kaczynski, diagnosed a paranoid schizophrenic by a government-appointed psychiatrist, agreed to a plea bargain and accepted life in prison without parole to avoid the death penalty that might have resulted from a trial on the charges. He admitted to thirteen separate counts based on two deadly bomb attacks in Sacramento and one in New Jersey. Kaczynski also admitted to eleven uncharged bombings in Utah, Illinois, Tennessee, Connecticut, Washington, and Michigan, and an attack on an American Airlines plane that was forced to land in Virginia.

Between 1978 and 1995, Kaczynski, known as the Unabomber because his first targets were universities and airlines, periodically placed or mailed explosive devices to individuals around the United States. Most of the devices were detonated, resulting in the deaths of three people and the wounding of twenty-nine people, many of them seriously. After sixteen attacks, federal investigators had run out of leads. Then, in 1995, the Unabomber wrote a letter demanding that *The Washington Post* and *The New York Times* publish his 35,000-word antitechnology manifesto or risk further attacks. The newspapers complied, running the manifesto in their September 19, 1995, editions.

The publication of the manifesto proved Kaczynski's undoing. David Kaczynski, his brother, read the manifesto and then compared it with letters he had received from Theodore, who had lived a hermit's existence in a mountain cabin in Montana since 1979. Theodore, who had graduated from Harvard University and gone on to earn a masters degree and a doctorate in mathematics from the University of Michigan, had been emotionally troubled since childhood. In 1969, after two years in a teaching position at the University of California at Berkeley, Kaczynski quit without explanation. In 1971 he began writing antitechnology tracts and moved to land near Lincoln, Montana, where he built a small cabin. Over time, Kaczynski further distanced himself from his family in Illinois and lived a solitary life. He briefly returned to the Chicago area in 1978, but returned to Montana after his brother fired him for harassing a female employee at the factory where they worked. Kaczynski continued to live off the land but still borrowed money from his family to survive.

Based on his suspicions and his knowledge of his brother's past actions, David Kaczynski contacted the Federal Bureau of Investigation (FBI). David later claimed that federal prosecutors agreed to his demand that in return for the tip, they would not seek the death penalty against his brother.

On April 3, 1996, FBI agents arrested Theodore Kaczynski at his Montana cabin and began a thorough search of his residence and the land around it. On April 8, the FBI determined that one of the two live bombs found in Kaczynski's cabin was virtually identical to the explosive device used in one of the Unabomber's recent killings. On April 12, they discovered the original typewritten manuscript of the Unabomber's manifesto, along with an original of a letter he sent to *The New York Times*. They also found Kaczynski's journal, which contained references to the bombs he had sent and the subsequent deaths and injuries they caused. Finally, investigators uncovered hotel records placing Kaczynski in Sacramento on the same days that some of the Unabomber's package bombs were mailed from that city.

The court-appointed defense attorneys for Kaczynski announced they would seek an acquittal based on the insanity defense. He rejected the idea he was, in his words, a "sickie," and refused to be examined by a psychiatrist representing the government. He offered to plead guilty in return for a life sentence, but he placed conditions on his offer, including the right to appeal the constitutionality of the search of his cabin. The government refused and announced they would seek the death penalty.

The trial, which was scheduled to begin in November 1997, was delayed by a series of events. Because of Kaczynski's refusal to be examined by government experts, the defense team in late December was forced to withdraw its insanity plea. Just as the trial was to start on January 5, 1998, Kaczynski asked to make a statement to the judge in private. He protested the presence of his brother David in the courtroom and raised the request of dismissing his attorneys and representing himself. On January 8, Kaczynski attempted to commit suicide in his jail cell, after which he agreed to be examined by a government psychiatrist to determine whether he was competent to stand trial and to represent himself. On January 22, the judge reported that the psychiatrist had found Kaczynski competent to stand trial. However, the judge denied him the right to represent himself. At that point, Kaczynski agreed to plead guilty, without conditions, to the bomb charges in return for a sentence of life in prison without parole.

**CROSS REFERENCES**
Evidence; Insanity Defense; Jury; Victims of Crime

# TRADEMARKS

Distinctive symbols of authenticity through which the products of particular manufacturers or the sal-able commodities of particular merchants can be distinguished from those of others.

### "Wing Flings" Infringed "Wing Dings"

In *Hester Industries, Inc. v. Tyson Foods, Inc.*, 985 F. Supp. 236 (N.D.N.Y.), frozen chicken wings were at the center of an $8.6 million damage award for trademark infringement. Trademarks include a company's registered names or symbols for its products. Infringement occurs when a competitor makes unauthorized use of the trademark—even by using a similar name that can confuse, deceive, or mislead others as to the product's source. Hester Industries, Inc., which makes frozen "Wing Dings," sued Tyson Foods, Inc., over use of the name "Wing Flings." Hester originally filed suit in 1989, after which Tyson agreed to change the name of its product. On July 29, 1997, a federal judge in New York ruled that Tyson had violated the agreement, and awarded Hester all of Tyson's profits on "Wing Flings."

As a pioneer in the chicken wing business, Hester Industries had vigorously defended its trademark. The family-owned West Virginia company first introduced its "Wing Dings" mark in 1964 to great success. Previously, consumers had viewed the chicken wing as a leftover, but the precooked, preseasoned product helped turn wings into a popular snack, and, in time, accounted for 40 percent of Hester's $42 million annual sales. When competitors later launched products called "Wing King" and "Wing Thing," the company successfully fought back through litigation and negotiated settlements.

Hester first sued Tyson Foods for infringement in 1989. The Arkansas-based Tyson, with annual sales of approximately $8 billion, is the largest poultry processor in the world. It had dared to tread on the same ground as Hester's other competitors by marketing "Wing Flings," a raw, unseasoned chicken wing product. Before the case could go to trial in March 1992, Tyson settled. The settlement gave Tyson until December 1992 to exhaust its current inventory of "Wing Flings," after which the company was prohibited from using the name on any products or other materials. Additionally, Hester agreed to allow Tyson to change the product's name to "Wing Flingers." The settlement was approved by the U.S. District Court for the Northern District of New York on April 9, 1992, and incorporated into a dismissal order, the court's legally binding order ending the litigation.

Nearly one year later, in March 1993, Hester officials discovered an advertisement for "Wing Flings" in the *Washington Post*. On March 17, Hester's attorneys wrote a letter of complaint to Tyson about the ongoing use of the infringing name, and demanded an accounting of all its uses after September 1, 1992. Tyson's attorneys wrote back that their client had "better things to do with its time." Hester sued again, this time demanding as damages Tyson's profits on the sale of chicken wing products after the deadline set forth in the settlement. In its defense, Tyson argued that the name "Wing Flings" had survived due to inattention and mistake.

Following a trial, Judge Thomas J. McAvoy ruled in Hester's favor on July 29, 1997. Judge McAvoy swept aside Tyson's defense. He found that the company had "exhibited no more than a callous disregard for the rights of Hester" by using the infringing name after the deadline date on labels, packaging, invoices, price lists, film, advertising, and promotional materials. He noted that trial testimony had shown that compliance with the dismissal order would have taken one day; however, Tyson's violations continued from 1993 through 1996. Accordingly, he held the company in civil contempt for disobeying the court's order.

As penalties, the court awarded Hester the amount that Tyson had earned in profit on its use of the name "Wing Flings" after the settlement. By Judge McAvoy's calculations, Tyson's profit on sales of 13 million pounds of chicken wings came to $8,558,272. He declined to award damages on the use of the name in Tyson's internal documents, however, because this action had neither harmed Hester nor earned profits for Tyson.

**CROSS REFERENCES**
Contempt; Settlement

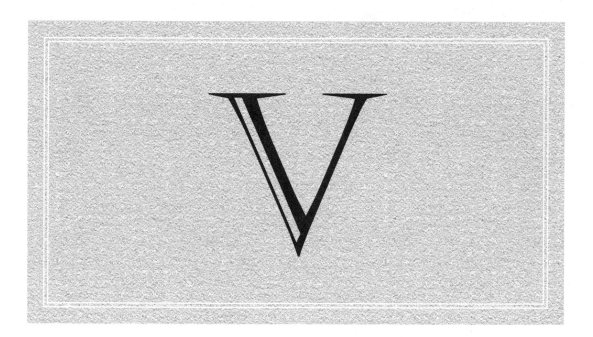

# VETO

The refusal of an executive officer to assent to a BILL that has been created and approved by the LEGISLATURE, thereby depriving the bill of any legally binding effect.

### Federal Judge Strikes Down Line Item Veto Act

Though the U.S. Supreme Court refused to rule on the merits of the 1996 Line Item Veto Act (2 U.S.C.A. § 691 et seq.) in *Raines v. Byrd*, ___U.S.___, 117 S. Ct. 2312, 138 L. Ed. 2d 849 (1997), it made clear in its decision that plaintiffs who could demonstrate that they had been injured by the act would be permitted to challenge its constitutionality. Following President Bill Clinton's first use of the line-item veto in August 1997, two groups of plaintiffs who had been affected by the vetoing of selected legislative provisions filed suit in federal court. In *City of New York v. Clinton*, 985 F. Supp. 168 (D.D.C. 1998), Judge Thomas F. Hogan found that the plaintiffs had standing to sue and ruled that the Line Item Veto Act was unconstitutional because it violated the procedural requirements of Article I of the Constitution and upset the balance of powers prescribed by the Constitution's framers.

The case involved two groups of plaintiffs. The first group included the city of New York, two New York associations, one hospital, and two unions that represented health care employees. The other group was Snake River Potato Growers, Inc., which consisted of approximately thirty potato growers located throughout Idaho.

The New York plaintiffs' claims arose out of a dispute over federal Medicaid payments to the state of New York. Medicaid is a joint state-federal program that provides health care to indigent persons. The federal Health Care Financing Administration (HCFA) of the Department of Health and Human Services provides federal funds to match certain state Medicaid expenditures. These funds are reduced by the revenue the state receives from health-care-related taxes unless the tax revenue meets specified criteria. New York state taxes its health care providers and uses this revenue to help fund Medicaid but exempts certain revenues of some health care providers from the tax. In 1994 HCFA notified New York that these exemptions violated HCFA's requirements. A finding by HCFA that a state's taxes are impermissible leads to the disallowance of the state's Medicaid expenditures and allows HCFA to recoup matching funds that it has already paid to the state.

In New York's case, if HCFA were ultimately to decide that New York's tax exemptions were not permitted, New York would be required to tax the previously exempted health care providers approximately $4 million for each year at issue. More ominous for the state was the possibility that HCFA would demand repayment of the Medicaid matching funds, which totaled $2.6 billion. To escape these possibilities, New York successfully lobbied for a provision that was enacted as part of the Balanced Budget Act of 1997 (Pub. L. No. 105-33). This provision, section 4722 (c), would have removed this exposure to liability by stating that the New York tax exemptions were proper and that the state would not have to return the funds in question.

President Clinton signed the Balanced Budget Act into law on August 5, 1997. However, on August 11, he identified section 4722(c) as an item of direct spending and canceled it using his authority under the Line Item Veto Act. The administration estimated that the cancellation of the provision would reduce the federal budget deficit by $200 million in the 1998 fiscal year. Therefore, New York again was liable for the HCFA funds.

The Snake River Potato Growers, a farmers' cooperative, sued because Clinton used the line-item veto to cancel a provision in the 1997 Taxpayer Relief Act (Pub. L. No. 105-34, 111 Stat. 788). Section 968 of the act amended the Internal Revenue Code to allow the owner of the stock of a qualified agricultural refiner or processor to defer recognition of capital gains on the sale of such stock to an eligible farmers' cooperative without paying tax currently on any capital gain. The stated purpose of this provision was to aid farmers' cooperatives in the purchase of processing and refining facilities.

Clinton identified this provision as a "limited tax benefit" under the Line Item Veto Act and canceled it, citing a potential loss of tax revenue of $98 million during the first five years after enactment and $155 million over the first ten years. Snake River had actively pursued the purchase of a potato processing plant in Blackfoot, Idaho, during the spring and summer of 1997 when section 968 was before Congress. The purchase was to have been structured to

give the seller the advantages conferred in section 968. After the section was canceled, the seller broke off negotiations with Snake River. Thereafter, Snake River filed suit, challenging the constitutionality of the Line Item Veto Act.

Judge Hogan agreed with the New York and Idaho plaintiffs that the act was unconstitutional. However, before he proceeded to the merits of the case, he made a careful examination of the plaintiffs' standing to bring a legal challenge to the legislation. In *Raines*, the Supreme Court had ruled that members of Congress lacked standing to challenge the act in court. Chief Justice William H. Rehnquist had emphasized that a plaintiff must have suffered a personal injury that is "particularized, concrete, and otherwise judicially cognizable."

Hogan concluded that both groups of plaintiffs had met this three-part standing test. He found that the New York plaintiffs had "suffered an immediate, concrete injury the moment that the President" had canceled section 4722(c) and "deprived them of the benefits of the law." The legislation had given the plaintiffs a "valuable protection against any liability that otherwise might befall them." Reduced to its simplest terms, the "plaintiffs had a benefit, and the President took that benefit away. That is injury."

Hogan found that the Snake River plaintiffs had suffered an immediate, concrete injury as well. Section 968 gave them a benefit by "putting them on equal footing with investor-owned businesses." Before section 968 was passed, farmers' cooperatives could not, unlike investor-owned businesses, acquire processing facilities through the exchange of their stock because a cooperative's stock can be held only by its members. Section 968 would have allowed sellers to defer capital gains taxes on sales to farmers' cooperatives, "thus putting co-ops in the same competitive position as investor-owned businesses." Hogan found that it was "highly likely" that Snake River would have been able to take advantage of this provision and that therefore it was a benefit. The cancellation of this benefit constituted an injury because the provision, at minimum, would have given Snake River "some room to negotiate in terms of price."

Having established that both groups of plaintiffs had standing to bring their lawsuits, Hogan turned to the merits of the case. Like the district court in *Raines*, he concluded that the act was unconstitutional. The first problem with the act was its attempt to avoid Article I's dual requirements of bicameral passage of legislation and presentment to the president. Hogan explained that bicameral passage meant that any bill must be passed by both houses of Congress in "exactly the same form." The Line Item Veto Act changed this requirement because the laws that resulted from the president's line-item veto "were different from those consented to by both Houses of Congress."

Hogan found that there was "no way of knowing" whether these "truncated" laws would have received the required support of both houses. Because the laws that emerged after the use of the line-item veto were not the same laws that went through the legislative process, the resulting laws were not valid. In addition, Hogan concluded that once a bill becomes law, it can only be repealed or amended through "another, independent legislative enactment, which itself must conform with the requirements of Article I."

The act was also unconstitutional because it violated the principle of separation of powers. Hogan noted that all legislative authority is vested in Congress. Though Congress may delegate rule-making authority to the executive branch to facilitate the enforcement of laws, it may not give the president the discretion and authority to decide the final form of legislation. Hogan stated that the Line Item Veto Act "impermissibly crosses the line between acceptable delegations of rulemaking authority and unauthorized authority and unauthorized surrender to the President of an inherently legislative function." Therefore, Hogan ruled the act unconstitutional.

Under a provision of the law, the government may take a direct appeal of Hogan's decision to the U.S. Supreme Court. It was expected that the Court would hear the case before the end of its term in June 1998.

**CROSS REFERENCES**
Separation of Powers; Standing

# VISITATION RIGHTS

In a marriage dissolution or custody action, permission granted by the court to a noncustodial parent to visit his or her child or children. May also refer to visitation rights extended to grandparents.

In marriage dissolutions where one parent is awarded sole custody of the child or children, the noncustodial parent is usually given legal permission to visit the children in the court order that ends the marriage. Courts have also considered and granted visitation rights to grandparents. Visitation rights may be withheld if evidence shows it is in the best interest of the child not to see the parent; such withholding will typically occur only where it has been shown the parent used illegal narcotics, abuses alcohol, or is physically or verbally abusive.

As in the case of custody rights, visitation rights may be determined by the agreement of the parties or by court order. If the court believes the parents will genuinely cooperate, a detailed visitation schedule may not be formally drafted. Working out reasonable visitation means the parents must agree to times and terms that work best for both parents and child. Even though courts encourage parents to cooperate and be flexible, a detailed schedule leaves no doubt about the frequency of visitation, days and times of pickup and return, and holiday and vacation schedules.

Visitation schedules are often established as a test, and may be made prior to the final divorce decree. The parents use the arrangements to see how the parent-child relationship will develop. Typically visitation schedules will change over time, and these changes are done without returning to court. Sometimes, however, the court will make a decision if a parent is being deprived of visitation rights.

In most states, courts will consider the wishes of the child when reviewing custody and visitation issues. The child's wishes are typically

*A non-custodial father picks up his child for a weekend visit.*

BOB DAEMMRICH/STOCK BOSTON, INC

granted, but only if the court sees the wishes as being in the best interests of the child. This judgment will depend on the age of the child and the maturity level the court determines the child to possess. A court will not grant visitation rights to the noncustodial parent if the court believes the child's request is based on ignorance or immaturity. The court will also be mindful that the custodial parent is in a position to exert undue influence over the child's decision-making process.

One of the more intractable problems in family law is the situation in which one parent uses visitation to spite the other parent. Examples include a custodial parent refusing visitation, not having the child available for the noncustodial parent at the appointed time for pickup, or a noncustodial parent not returning the child at the prescribed time.

When a drastic change in conduct or circumstances involving the parents occurs, the court can make permanent modifications in visitation rights. One of the parties must present clear evidence to the court of the change in conduct or circumstances. This evidence usually must be completely new to the court. Any issues addressed before in any prior proceedings are generally not grounds for modification. Common grounds for permanent modifications include chronic noncompliance with the visitation schedule, repeated failure to return the child at the designated time, the teaching of immoral or illegal acts to the child, or the parent's conviction for a crime.

When a noncustodial parent encounters problems in exercising visitation rights, the par-

ent may simply stop paying child support. Such a course of conduct is not recognized as legal by the courts. The noncustodial parent's only legal recourse is to ask the court that issued the visitation order for guidance. Some courts order the child support funds to be paid into court until the custodial parent complies with the other's visitation rights.

Grandparents' visitation rights have gained legal recognition in some form in all fifty states. Several states limit visitation to cases in which the parent is deceased, while others specifically extend the right to the case of divorce, annulment, or separation. Twenty-two states allow grandparent visitation without the requirement of death or divorce, and over the objection of the parents in an ongoing family, if such visitation is shown to be in the best interests of the child. However, the highest courts in several states have found that grandparent visitation statutes impose unconstitutional state interference with the privacy rights of the immediate family. Most states, by statute or court decision, hold that the ongoing family is not subject to enforced intrusion by grandparents, if both parents are fit and object to grandparent visitation. A majority of states also hold that any adoption preempts visitation by the grandparents and that grandparents generally have no right to intervene in an adoption proceeding involving their grandchild.

**CROSS REFERENCES**
Divorce; Family Law; Parent and Child

# VOTING

### Abrams v. Johnson

The Voting Rights Act of 1965 (VRA) (42 U.S.C.A. § 1973 et seq.) continues to generate litigation in the federal courts. The VRA, which was extended in 1970 and again in 1982, seeks to prevent voting discrimination based on race, color, or membership in a language minority group. It was enacted at the high watermark of the civil rights movement to end a century of racial discrimination in voting in seven southern states. Section 5 of the VRA applies only to southern states with histories of voter discrimination, whereas section 2 applies to every state in the nation.

Section 5 of the VRA was enacted to address pervasive voting discrimination in the South. It was directed at seven southern states that had used poll taxes, literacy tests, and other devices to obstruct registration by African

Americans. These "covered" states are Alabama, Georgia, Louisiana, Mississippi, South Carolina, Virginia, and parts of North Carolina. A highly controversial provision, section 5 sought to end southern resistance to changes in voting and election laws by preventing these states from changing their laws without the prior approval of the U.S. attorney general and a three-judge federal district court panel in Washington, D.C. To obtain "preclearance," state and local units of government in the seven states have the burden of proving that the proposed changes do not have the purpose or "effect of denying or abridging the right to vote on account of race or color."

Section 2, however, applies to all fifty states and their political subdivisions. It was designed as a way of eradicating voting practices that minimize or cancel out the voting strengths and political effectiveness of minority groups. Section 2 bars state and local governments from main-

taining any voting "standard, practice, or procedure" that "results in a denial or abridgment of the right ... to vote on account of race or color." A private plaintiff or the federal government may bring a lawsuit alleging a violation of section 2.

In the 1990s the U.S. Supreme Court greatly restricted the scope of the VRA (42 U.S.C.A. § 1973 et seq.), forbidding the creation of minority-dominated legislative districts that appeared to be drawn solely on the basis of race. The Court, in *Shaw v. Reno*, 509 U.S. 630, 113 S. Ct. 2816, 125 L. Ed. 2d 511 (1993), ruled that "racial gerrymandering" was unconstitutional under the Equal Protection Clause of the Fourteenth Amendment and that the VRA could not be used to justify such practices. In *Shaw v. Hunt*, 517 U.S. 899, 116 S. Ct. 1894, 135 L. Ed. 2d 207 (1996), the Court reaffirmed its position by striking down a "bizarre-looking" North

Carolina congressional district that contained a majority of African American voters.

In 1997 the Court again interpreted the VRA. By a 5–4 vote, the Court in *Abrams v. Johnson*, ___U.S.___, 117 S. Ct. 1925, 138 L. Ed. 2d 285, affirmed a federal district court reapportionment plan that provided only one African American majority congressional district. It rejected the argument of African American voters that the court should have created two majority-black districts.

The case illustrates the protracted struggle to redistrict congressional districts in Georgia and the competing views of the U.S. attorney general, the Georgia legislature, white and African American voters, and the federal courts. Following the 1990 census, Georgia was awarded an eleventh congressional seat. Under the terms of section 5 of the VRA, Georgia had to obtain "preclearance" from the Department of Justice or the U.S. District Court for the District of Columbia before making changes in the electoral system. In 1991 the state legislature prepared a redistricting plan and submitted it to the attorney general. In January 1992, the attorney general rejected the plan, which contained two majority-black districts, the Fifth and the Eleventh. Previously Georgia had one majority-black district, the Fifth. A second plan, again containing two majority-black districts, was rejected, leading the legislature to adopt a plan that created three majority-black congressional districts. The attorney general precleared this plan. Georgia's Eleventh District, which was described as a "geographic monstrosity," stretched from Atlanta to Savannah.

In November 1992, all three majority-black districts elected African American candidates to Congress. In 1994 five white voters from the Eleventh District filed suit, alleging that the redistricting plan was racial gerrymandering and in violation of the *Shaw v. Reno* holding. The district court agreed, and the Supreme Court affirmed the ruling in *Miller v. Johnson*, 515 U.S. 900, 115 S. Ct. 2475, 132 L. Ed. 2d 762 (1995).

When the Georgia legislature deadlocked over a new plan, a three-judge federal district court panel issued its own congressional redistricting plan. The court maintained the Fifth District as majority-black, but the remaining ten districts were majority-white. African American voters and the Department of Justice appealed to the Supreme Court, contending that the district court should have approved at least two majority-black districts.

Justice Anthony M. Kennedy, writing for the majority, concluded that the district court had acted reasonably in redrawing Georgia's congressional districts. In so ruling, Kennedy rejected a series of challenges based on the Voting Rights Act and prior court decisions.

The African American voters and the government argued that the district court had exceeded its authority in drafting the plan. They cited *Upham v. Seamon*, 456 U.S. 37, 102 S. Ct. 1518, 71 L. Ed. 2d 725 (1982), in which courts drawing voting district lines were instructed to follow the legislative policies underlying the existing plan to the extent they did not lead to a violation of the Constitution or the VRA. In their view, the court should have adopted the three majority-black districts as in the 1992 plan or at least the two majority-black districts of the legislature's 1991 plan.

Kennedy rejected this argument. The Court was disturbed by the pressure that the Department of Justice had placed on the Georgia legislature to create the maximum number of majority-black districts. The department's refusal to preclear the legislature's first two plans led the legislature to create the third plan with three majority-black districts. Kennedy stated that the fact that this plan was based on "an overriding concern with race, disturbed any sound basis for the trial court to defer" to it. The unconstitutional nature of the 1992 plan, as confirmed by the Court in its earlier decision, prevented the trial court from using it as indicative of legislative policy. Kennedy concluded that the trial court had properly exercised its discretion in declining to draw two majority-black districts, which would have required racial gerrymandering.

Kennedy also ruled that the court-ordered plan did not violate section 2 of the Voting Rights Act. Under this section, a violation will occur if it is shown that the political processes leading to election "are not equally open to participation by members of [a racial minority] ...." Kennedy held that the trial court's plan was not based on "impermissible vote dilution," ruling that the voters and the government had failed to meet the three-part test set out in *Thornburg v. Gingles*, 478 U.S. 30, 106 S. Ct. 2752, 92 L. Ed. 2d 25 (1986): the minority population is "sufficiently large and geographically compact to constitute a majority in a single-member district; the minority group is "politically cohesive;" and, the majority "votes sufficiently as a bloc to enable it ... to defeat the minority's preferred candidate." He concluded that the African American population was not sufficiently compact to justify the drawing of a majority-black district solely on the basis of race. More importantly, he endorsed the trial court's finding that there was sufficient crossover voting in Georgia to negate the claim that white voters refused to vote for African American candidates.

In addition, the Court ruled that the redistricting plan did not violate section 5 of the VRA, which requires southern states, including Georgia, to preclear any voting-procedure changes. Kennedy cited *Beer v. United States*, 425 U.S. 130, 96 S. Ct. 1357, 47 L. Ed. 2d 629 (1976), which held that under section 5, a redistricting plan will not be precleared if it "would lead to a retrogression in the position of racial minorities with respect to their effective exercise of the electoral franchise." Though a court-devised plan does not need to be precleared, Kennedy acknowledged that a court should take into account the appropriate section 5 standards in creating such a plan.

The African American voters and the government contended that the court-ordered plan was "retrogressive." Kennedy disagreed, ruling that it was impossible to create a second majority-black district within constitutional requirements. Moreover, he found there was no retrogression because the 1991 and 1992 plans could not be used as benchmarks to measure whether the right to vote in Georgia had decreased. The trial court had properly used the 1982 redistricting plan as the benchmark. The 1982 plan created one majority-black district, as did the court-devised plan. Therefore Kennedy found that the status quo had been maintained and no retrogression had occurred.

Finally, the Court rejected the contention that the plan violated the "one person, one vote," constitutional guarantee. Kennedy ruled that the population variations among the eleven districts were minimal and were based on historically significant state policies that the federal courts have honored. Even if these variations were corrected, there still would be no constitutional basis for creating a second majority-black district.

Justice Stephen G. Breyer, in a dissenting opinion, concluded that the plan was flawed and that a second majority-black district could have been constitutionally established. He disagreed as to the interpretation of the *Gingles* test, pointing out that white voters still voted in blocs. In the 180–member Georgia House of Representatives, 138 members came from majority-white

districts. Only one black person was elected from these districts. Of the forty-two majority-black districts, thirty members were black and twelve were white. For Breyer, this demonstrated that bloc voting must be minimized by creating a second majority-black congressional district, because it was unlikely that an African American could be elected in the ten majority-white districts.

### Reno v. Bossier Parish School Board

In *Reno v. Bossier Parish School Board*, U.S., 117 S. Ct. 1491, 137 L. Ed. 2d 730 (1997), the U.S. Supreme Court resolved the relationship between sections 2 and 5 of the Voting Rights Act of 1965 (VRA) (42 U.S.C.A. § 1973 et seq.), ruling that a redistricting plan could be "precleared" under section 5, even though it appeared to violate section 2.

In *Reno v. Bossier Parish School Board*, sections 2 and 5 came into conflict when the school board of Bossier Parish, Louisiana, proposed a redistricting plan after the 1990 census. The board redrew the election districts to equalize the population distribution. It chose to follow a municipal government redistricting plan that had been precleared by the U.S. attorney general under section 5.

In selecting this plan, the board rejected a proposal by the local chapter of the National Association for the Advancement of Colored People (NAACP). The NAACP, noting that none of the twelve districts in the board's existing or proposed plan contained a majority of black residents (and that no African American had ever sat on the school board), proposed a plan that created two districts, each containing a majority of black voters.

Even though the municipal government had obtained preclearance of the plan, Attorney General Janet Reno objected to it on the basis of the NAACP's proposal, which provided new information that demonstrated that black residents were sufficiently numerous and geographically compact so as to constitute a majority in two districts. In the objection letter, the attorney general asserted that the plan violated section 2 of the VRA because it "unnecessarily limit[ed] the opportunity for minority voters to elect their candidates of choice," as compared with the NAACP alternative. Reno relied on an attorney general regulation, 28 CFR § 51.55(b)(2) (1996), which authorizes the attorney general to withhold preclearance of a redistricting plan if it clearly violates section 2.

The school board filed suit in the district court of the District of Columbia, seeking preclearance for the plan from the three-judge panel. The panel granted the board's request for preclearance, concluding that a political subdivision that does not violate the effect or purpose of section 5 cannot be denied preclearance because of an alleged section 2 violation (907 F. Supp. 434 [1995]).

The attorney general appealed to the Supreme Court, which essentially agreed with the lower court reasoning but vacated its decision and remanded the case to the panel with instructions to consider evidence of a section 2 violation as evidence of discriminatory purpose under section 5. Justice Sandra Day O'Connor, writing for the majority, relied on the Court's decision in *Beer v. United States*, 425 U.S. 130, 96 S. Ct. 1357, 47 L. Ed. 2d 629 (1976). Because of the "retrogression" measurement established by *Beer*, the proposed school board plan could only be compared to the existing districting plan. As long as the new plan did not increase the degree of discrimination, it was not retrogressive and therefore was entitled to section 5 preclearance.

O'Connor rejected the attorney general's argument that a section 2 violation could be used as the basis for denying preclearance under section 5. O'Connor refused to shift the focus on section 5 "from nonretrogression to vote dilution, and to change the section 5 benchmark from a jurisdiction's existing plan to a hypothetical, undiluted plan."

The Court also refused to defer to the attorney general's regulations interpreting the VRA, including 28 CFR § 51.55(b)(2) (1996), which gave the attorney general the authority to bar preclearance if there was a clear section 2 violation. O'Connor agreed that the Court normally gave the attorney general's construction of the VRA "great deference" but concluded that the regulation went against the Court's longstanding interpretation of section 5. She also pointed out that Congress had declined to alter the language of section 5 to overturn the Court's interpretation.

O'Connor dismissed the government's contention that public policy favored the application of section 2 to section 5 actions. The attorney general had argued that it was a waste of government and judicial resources to require the litigation of separate section 5 and section 2 actions. O'Connor thought otherwise, stating that section 2 litigation would effectively become part of every section 5 action.

Though the Court ruled that a section 2 violation may not automatically doom a section 5 preclearance request, it expressed concern that the three-judge panel had refused to consider the "dilutive impact" of the plan in determining whether the school board acted with a discriminatory purpose. Evidence of dilutive impact may reveal retrogressive intent, which violates section 5. Therefore, the Court vacated the lower court's decision and directed the panel to consider section 2 evidence that might show a discriminatory purpose under section 5.

Justice John Paul Stevens, in a dissenting opinion joined by Justice David H. Souter, contended that the Court had misread legislative history and intent concerning the VRA. It was clear to Stevens that the attorney general had ample justification to deny preclearance based on a section 2 violation. Moreover, he concluded that the Bossier Parish School Board's history of discrimination had continued with the adoption of the redistricting plan. Stevens opined that discriminatory purpose was apparent and warranted a denial of preclearance under section 5.

### Young v. Fordice

The issue of preclearance reached the U.S. Supreme Court in *Young v. Fordice*, ___U.S.___, 117 S. Ct. 1228, 137 L. Ed. 2d 448 (1997). At issue was whether Mississippi had made changes in its voter registration system to comply with the 1993 National Voter Registration Act (NVRA) (42 U.S.C.A. § 1973gg et seq.) without first obtaining federal preclearance required by the VRA. The Court held that Mississippi had violated the VRA preclearance provision and that the voter registration changes could not be used until and unless they were precleared.

The case illustrates the legal complexities of harmonizing two federal laws. The NVRA, popularly known as the "motor voter" law, requires states to provide simplified systems for registering to vote in federal elections (elections for federal officials, such as the president, congressional representatives, and U.S. senators). The states must provide a system for voter registration by mail, a system for voter registration at various state offices, and a system for voter registration on a driver's license application. The NVRA specifies how these systems must work and when and how states may remove people from the federal voter rolls.

The legal controversy in Mississippi involved three different voter registration systems. Mississippi used the first system, called the "old system" by the Court, before it tried to comply with the NVRA. The second system, the "provisional plan," was a system aimed at NVRA compliance, which the state tried to implement for six weeks in early 1995. The third system, the "new system," was the system that Mississippi put into place after February 1995 in an effort to comply with the NVRA.

The old system provided for a single registration that allowed the registrant to vote in both federal and state elections. A citizen could register to vote either by appearing personally at a county or municipal clerk's office or by obtaining a mail-in registration form, available at driver's license agencies, public schools and libraries, and mailing it back to the clerk. State law allowed registration officials to purge voters from the rolls if they had not voted in four years.

The Mississippi secretary of state prepared the provisional plan in late 1994. The plan contained a series of changes in voter registration that were designed to achieve compliance with the NVRA and that would apply to both state and federal elections. For example, the new voter registration application that was incorporated into the driver's license form did not require an attesting witness. In addition, the four-year purge of voters was replaced with other methods of obtaining up-to-date voter rolls. The secretary of state provided information and instructions to voter registration officials on the assumption that the Mississippi state legislature would adopt the recommendations in early 1995.

In December 1994, the provisional plan was submitted to the U.S. attorney general for preclearance under the VRA. The submission included administrative changes and the proposed state legislation necessary to make the plan work for state elections.

On January 1, 1995, the provisional plan was implemented. Between that date and February 10, 1995, four thousand voters registered under this system. However, on January 25, the state legislature tabled the bill that would have made the plan applicable to state elections. Therefore, on February 10, the new system was implemented. The system applied the provisional plan only to registration for federal elections. Mississippi maintained the old system for registration for state elections, making it the only state not to modify its voter registration rules so that the NVRA registration registers voters for both federal and state elections.

Unaware that the Mississippi legislature had tabled the state election registration bill, the Department of Justice wrote to Mississippi on February 1 that it did not object to the provisional plan and thereby precleared Mississippi's submitted changes. Upon learning of the new system, the department wrote Mississippi that its earlier preclearance did not approve of the new system and asked that the new plan be submitted for preclearance. Mississippi made no further preclearance submissions.

Four private citizens filed suit in federal court, alleging that the dual voter registration system had not been precleared and therefore violated the VRA. The Department of Justice filed a similar suit, and the two cases were consolidated. However, the three-judge panel dismissed the actions, ruling that the Department of Justice had precleared the administrative changes needed to implement the NVRA for federal elections and that because the state had never ratified the provisional plan, Mississippi's attempt to correct the situation by implementing the new system was not subject to preclearance.

The Supreme Court disagreed with the lower court's reasoning. Justice Stephen G. Breyer, writing for a unanimous Court, reversed and vacated the district court decision. Breyer did agree with the lower court that the provisional plan never became part of the state's voter registration procedures but "instead simply amounted to a temporary misapplication of state law." Therefore, the state was not required to preclear the new system "insofar as it differed from the provisional plan."

Nevertheless, the Court agreed with the plaintiffs that the new system, standing on its own, included changes that must be precleared. The new system included practices and procedures that were significantly different from the old system, and it was these differences that had not been precleared.

Breyer, noting that even minor changes must be precleared, pointed out that the new system contained "numerous examples of new, significantly different administrative practices—practices that are not purely ministerial, but reflect the exercise of policy choice and discretion by Mississippi officials." Examples included revised written materials describing what kind of assistance state agency personnel should offer potential NVRA registrations, which state agencies would be NVRA registration agencies, and instructions on how and in what form registration materials should be forwarded to those who maintain the voting rolls. Breyer concluded that because "they embody discretionary decisions that have a potential discriminatory impact," these practices should be submitted for pre-clearance.

The Court emphasized that implementation of the NVRA gives the states the opportunity to make policy choices. Breyer stated that the "NVRA does not list, for example, all the other information the State may—or may not—provide or request." Therefore, Breyer said,

Mississippi must submit the new system for pre-clearance. The Department of Justice's pre-clearance of the provisional plan had no force or effect because of the failure of the legislature to amend state voter registration laws.

**CROSS REFERENCES**

Civil Rights; Gerrymander; National Association for the Advancement of Colored People; Shaw v. Hunt; Voting Rights Act of 1965

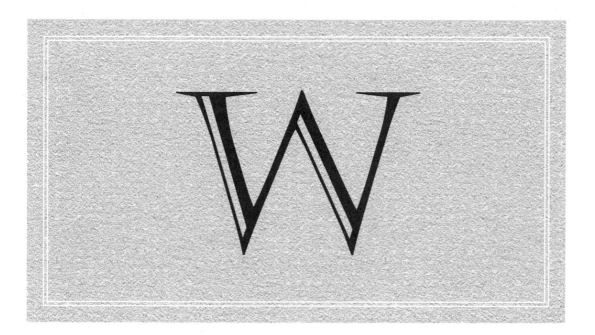

## WATER RIGHTS

### Lake Bounded by National Wilderness and Private Property

In a victory for three resort owners, a federal district court stopped the U.S. Forest Service from restricting motorboat use in a nationally designated wilderness area (*Stupak-Thrall v. Glickman*, 988 F. Supp. 1055 [W.D.Mich.1997]). The decision resolved a lawsuit brought by three landowners in the Upper Peninsula of Northern Michigan. They accused the Forest Service of violating their right to continue using the land as they and their resort guests had historically done by prohibiting power boats and water skiing. The Forest Service asserted its right under federal law to preserve a pristine wilderness environment. In ruling for the plaintiffs, the U.S. District Court for the Western Division of Michigan held that their natural rights as landowners took precedence over the government's authority to manage the land.

The case arose in the Sylvania Wilderness, an 18,327-acre area in the Ottawa National Forest. In 1987 Congress added it to the National Wilderness Preservation System through enactment of the Michigan Wilderness Act (MWA) (Pub. L. No. 100-184, 101 Stat. 1274). This legislative decision took its authority from the Wilderness Act of 1964 (16 U.S.C. § 1131 et seq.), which allows Congress to designate for preservation those "areas where the earth and its community of life are untrammeled by man, where man himself is a visitor who does not remain."

In the Sylvania Wilderness, however, some men and women were more than visitors. Eleven people owned property along the north shore of Crooked Lake, including two sets of resort owners: Kathy Stupak-Thrall, and Michael and Bodil Gajewski. Stupak-Thrall's property had been in her family since 1939, and, in addition to using it for fishing and water skiing, she operated a two-unit rental called Fox's Den. The Gajewskis bought the six-cabin Crooked Lake Resort in 1980.

In 1992 the U.S. Forestry Service (UFS) which administers the Sylvania Wilderness, promulgated amendment number 1 to its Land and Resource Management Plan for the Ottawa National Forest. The amendment prohibited, among other things, sailboats, houseboats, and nonburnable disposable food and beverage containers in the Sylvania Wilderness; it also restricted snowmobiles. Stupak-Thrall and the Gajewskis opposed the amendment, exhausted their administrative appeals with the UFS, and then brought suit. But the district court upheld the amendment, ruling that it had a minimal impact upon the plaintiffs (*Stupak-Thrall v. United States*, 843 F.Supp. 327 (W.D. Mich. 1994). That decision, which became known as *Stupak-Thrall I*, was affirmed by the Sixth Circuit (*Stupak-Thrall v. United States*, 89 F.3d 1269 [6th Cir. 1996], cert. denied, ___U.S.___, 117 S. Ct. 764, 136 L. Ed. 2d 711 [1997]).

Then, in 1995, the plaintiffs sued again after the UFS promulgated a new set of restrictions for Crooked Lake and neighboring waters. In amendment number 5, the service prohibited boat motors exceeding 24 volts or 48 pounds of thrust—the equivalent of a small 4-horse power motor—and also restricted boats to a no-wake

speed. Alleging harm to their businesses, the plaintiffs argued that the UFS lacked either constitutional or statutory authority to restrict their continued use of the entire lake and shore for fishing, gas-powered motorboating, and other recreational purposes including snowmobiling. They contended that these activities were within their *riparian rights*—so-called natural rights that accrue to owners of land on the banks of water. In response, the government asserted that its authority to regulate the Sylvania Wilderness had been fully litigated and upheld in *Stupak-Thrall I*.

Upon review, the district court disagreed that all the issues in the new suit were settled by the previous one. The first lawsuit had chiefly covered the use of sailboats and houseboats, activities in which the plaintiffs had not engaged. By contrast, amendment number five restricted activities that were significant to their livelihood and enjoyment of the lake, the court ruled.

The court concluded that the UFS had overstepped its authority. In section 5 of the Michigan Wilderness Act (MWA), Congress made UFS authority subject to "valid existing rights." The government had contended that the court should dismiss any consideration of the clause, since the legislative history showed that Congress intended to allow reasonable regulation of motorboat use. The court dismissed this argument, holding that no language in the statute suggested that the term *valid existing rights* should be given anything other than its plain meaning. Riparian rights were just such rights, the court ruled, and the plaintiffs were entitled to them. The court also found the motorboat restriction unconstitutional because it deprived the plaintiffs of private property without compensation.

The Court stressed that its ruling was narrow. The decision did not affect the general right of the UFS to regulate the public's use of the Sylvania Wilderness; instead, it applied only to one lake, the plaintiffs, and their customers.

## WELFARE

Government benefits distributed to impoverished persons to enable them to maintain a minimum standard of well-being.

### Blessing v. Freestone

Many federal laws provide federal funds for state and local governments. Historically the federal government has given large amounts of money to the states to help pay for welfare. In return, the states have been required to administer their welfare programs in accordance with a comprehensive set of federal regulations. If a state violates these regulations, it may lose some of its federal money.

Welfare recipients, however, have sought to sue individually for deficiencies in state welfare programs. Individuals seeking to use the federal civil rights statute 42 U.S.C.A. § 1983 have filed numerous lawsuits in federal court to force reforms in the administration of state welfare. The circuit courts of appeal have been in conflict over whether mothers, whose children are eligible for state child-support services under title IV-D of the Social Security Act of 1935 (42 U.S.C.A. §§ 651–669b), may file a section 1983 lawsuit. The key issue in these lawsuits is whether title IV-D creates rights that are enforceable under section 1983.

The U.S. Supreme Court attempted to resolve the conflict in *Blessing v. Freestone*, ___U.S.___, 117 S. Ct. 1353, 137 L. Ed. 2d 569 (1997). Although the Court made clear that it was unpersuaded that title IV-D creates individually enforceable rights under the civil rights statute, it found that the lower-court rulings were insufficiently specific about the particular rights that might be enforceable. Therefore, it remanded the case to the district court for a determination of the particular rights asserted by the plaintiffs. Nevertheless, the Court did make clear that if title IV-D did create individually enforceable rights, there was nothing in the Social Security Act to bar an individual plaintiff from suing under section 1983.

The case arose when Cathy Freestone and four other mothers in Arizona whose children received child support services from the state pursuant to title IV-D sued the director of Arizona's child support services. The plaintiffs claimed that they had a right to have the state's programs achieve substantial compliance with the requirements of title IV-D.

Title IV-D mandates that in return for federal welfare funding, a state must certify that it will operate a child support enforcement program that meets numerous federal requirements. The federal government underwrites two-thirds of the child support efforts, but the state must do more than simply collect support payments. The state must also establish a comprehensive system to establish paternity, locate absent parents, and help families obtain support orders.

In addition, title IV-D requires the state to establish a separate agency to collect and disburse child support. The agency must meet federally mandated staffing levels and set up computer systems that conform to federal specifications. The federal Office of Child Support Enforcement (OCSE) within the Department of Health and Human Services (HHS) oversees compliance by the states, conducting audits at least every three years. If a state does

*A woman applies for welfare as a child looks on.*

STEPHEN FERRY/GAMMA LIAISON

not substantially comply with the requirements, HHS may reduce funding by five percent. HHS may also suspend a penalty if the state takes corrective action.

The five plaintiffs sued the state, alleging that the child support agency never took adequate steps to obtain child support payments from the fathers of their children. The failure to take action was attributed to structural defects in the state system, including staff shortages, high caseloads, unmanageable backlogs, and deficiencies in the state's accounting methods and record keeping. The plaintiffs alleged that these systemic failures violated their federal rights under title IV-D. They asked the court to order the state to comply with the federal law.

The district court dismissed the plaintiffs' case, concluding that title IV-D creates no individual rights enforceable under section 1983. Only HHS could enforce the child support provisions.

On appeal, the Ninth Circuit Court of Appeals reversed the lower court (68 F.3d 1141 [1995]). It ruled that the plaintiffs could sue the state, because they had met prior Supreme Court precedents for establishing an individual right to sue.

The Supreme Court unanimously disagreed with the reasoning and ruling of the Ninth Circuit. Justice Sandra Day O'Connor, writing for seven justices (Justices Antonin Scalia and Anthony M. Kennedy concurred in the decision), acknowledged that "Arizona's record of enforcing child support obligations is less than stellar, particularly compared with those of other States." The state obtained regular child support payments for less than five percent of the parents it served. Federal audits conducted by OCSE identified many shortcomings in Arizona's child support collection system. The federal government penalized the state one percent of its welfare funding but suspended this penalty when Arizona proposed a corrective plan of action.

Though O'Connor recognized that Arizona had problems with child support collection, she noted that to seek redress through section 1983, "a plaintiff must assert the violation of a federal *right*, not merely a violation of federal *law*." The Supreme Court has looked at three factors when determining whether a statutory provision creates a federal right: (1) whether Congress intended that the provision benefit the plaintiff; (2) whether the plaintiff's asserted interests are not so "vague and amorphous" that enforcement "would strain judicial competence"; and (3) whether the statute unambiguously imposes a binding, mandatory obligation on the states. If the plaintiff meets all three factors, the court must then examine whether Congress specifically foreclosed a remedy under section 1983.

O'Connor criticized the appeals court for not specifying "exactly which 'rights' it was purporting to recognize." She explained that a court must break down the plaintiff's complaint "into manageable analytic bites" in order to apply the three factors. Nevertheless, the Court proceeded to analyze the case as best it could.

O'Connor concluded that requiring a state to substantially comply with title IV-D was not intended to benefit individual children and custodial parents and that therefore it did not constitute a federal right. Compliance standards were a "yardstick" for HHS to measure the systemwide performance of the state's title IV-D program. O'Connor noted that even when the state is in substantial compliance, between ten and twenty-five percent of the persons in the program will not be served. In addition, HHS has no authority to force the state "to take any particular action or to provide any services to certain individuals." HHS can only increase the number of program audits and reduce welfare payments by a maximum of five percent.

The Court also pointed out other shortcomings in the Ninth Circuit's ruling. O'Connor dismissed the idea that title IV-D's detailed requirements for the state's data processing system "give[s] rise to individualized rights to computer services." The same reasoning was applied to the staffing levels of the state child support collection agency, which the plaintiffs claimed

were inadequate. O'Connor stated that the link between staffing levels and the services provided to an individual "is far too tenuous to support the notion that Congress meant to give each and every Arizonan who is eligible for Title IV-D" the right to have the state agency staffed at a sufficient level. In addition, the statute gives no guidelines to define "sufficient."

Despite these conclusions, O'Connor stated that "we do not foreclose the possibility that some provisions of Title IV-D give rise to individual rights." Because of the vagueness of the plaintiffs' complaint and the court rulings, the Court sent the case back to the district court "to determine exactly what rights, considered in their most concrete specific form" the plaintiffs were asserting. The tenor of the Court's decision, however, made the possibility of discovering enforceable rights remote.

The Court did rule, however, that if individually enforceable rights were found, there was nothing in the Social Security Act to prevent plaintiffs from using section 1983 as a remedy. Absent an explicit provision in the law prohibiting individual lawsuits or setting forth a comprehensive scheme for exclusive federal enforcement, section 1983 was an appropriate remedy.

**CROSS REFERENCES**
Health and Human Services, Department of

## WESTWOOD, JEAN MILES

Jean Miles Westwood was the first woman to chair the Democratic National Committee (DNC), serving in that position only five months. Westwood, who was a leader of George S. McGovern's 1972 presidential campaign, was driven from the DNC post after President Richard M. Nixon's crushing defeat of McGovern. Westwood, however, continued to be active in Democratic politics.

Jean Miles was born on November 22, 1923, in Price, Utah. She married Richard E. Westwood in 1941, and they were the parents of two children. Westwood attended Carbon College (now the College of Eastern Utah) and also took courses at universities in Utah, Colorado, and California.

In the mid-1940s, Westwood and her husband organized the Westwood Mink Farms, a successful business that they continued until the 1980s. She was secretary of the Utah Mink Show from 1951 to 1954 and also was involved with other business enterprises.

*Jean Miles Westwood*

UPI/CORBIS-BETTMANN

Beginning in the mid-1950s, Westwood became active in the Utah Democratic Party and served in a variety of party positions. In 1965 and 1966, she served as a staff member for Congressman David S. King. She served as a national delegate to the 1964 and 1968 Democratic National Conventions and served as Utah's national committeewoman. In 1968, Westwood served as Hubert H. Humphrey's Utah presidential campaign coordinator.

Westwood became a national figure in 1972, when she became vice-chair of the McGovern-for-President Committee. After McGovern received the Democratic presidential nomination, he named Westwood chair of the DNC. McGovern's campaign proved a disaster. His vice-presidential nominee, Senator Thomas F. Eagleton of Missouri, left the ticket after he revealed he had undergone electric shock treatments for depression. In addition, President Nixon painted McGovern as a left-wing politician who was out of step with the country. Westwood sought to overcome these problems through public statements of optimism, but McGovern's November 1972 election defeat was overwhelming. Nixon won almost 61 percent of the popular vote and carried every state except Massachusetts.

The magnitude of the defeat proved Westwood's undoing. Democratic governors demanded she be removed as chair, but in December 1972 she narrowly survived a no-confidence vote. Nevertheless, Westwood resigned after the vote and was replaced by Texas lawyer Robert Strauss. Westwood returned to Utah and continued as Utah Democratic National Committeewoman until her term expired in 1976.

Westwood moved to Scottsdale, Arizona, in 1976 and resided there until 1995. She remained politically active, working on the presidential campaigns of Terry Sanford, Gary W. Hart, and Bruce Babbitt.

Westwood returned to Utah in 1995, settling in American Fork. She died there on August 18, 1997.

**CROSS REFERENCES**
Democratic Party

## WHITEWATER

*Whitewater*, the name given to the scandal involving President Bill Clinton, First Lady Hillary Rodham Clinton, members of the Clinton Administration, and private individuals and

### JEAN MILES WESTWOOD

| | |
|---|---|
| **1923** | Born in Price, Utah |
| **1941** | Married Richard E. Westwood |
| **1964** | Served as a national delegate to the 1964 Democratic National convention |
| **1965** | Served as staff member for Congressman David S. King |
| **1968** | Served as Hubert H. Humphrey's Utah presidential campaign coordinator |
| **1972** | Became vice-chair of the McGovern-for-President Committee; named chair of the Democratic National Convention; after McGovern was defeated, resigned after Democratic governors demanded her removal |
| **1976** | Moved to Scottsdale, Arizona |
| **1995** | Moved back to Utah |
| **1997** | Died in American Fork, Utah |

public officials in Arkansas, remained in the public spotlight during 1997 and 1998. Whitewater special prosecutor Kenneth W. Starr pursued evidence of wrongdoing that went beyond the failure of the Whitewater resort development in Arkansas. In the process, Starr was criticized by members of the Clinton Administration and some commentators for straying far from his mandate and seeking to bring down President Clinton through unseemly investigations of Clinton's private life. Most of Starr's work has remained confidential, though periodic news leaks provided the public with the probe's direction.

Susan McDougal, convicted of fraud and conspiracy in 1996 for her role in the making of questionable loans through an Arkansas bank connected to Whitewater and the Clintons, was sentenced to two years in prison in August 1996. When Starr granted her immunity to testify before a grand jury on other Whitewater matters, McDougal refused. McDougal, who said she did not trust the prosecutors, was jailed for contempt in August 1996. As of March 1998, she

remained in jail, not having begun her two-year sentence.

In June 1997, the news media reported that Starr's team had been questioning Arkansas state troopers about President Clinton's personal life, including possible extramarital affairs he may have had while governor. These revelations raised questions about the direction of the investigation and its relevance to the Whitewater real estate and banking scandal. Skepticism about the probe mounted when the General Accounting Office disclosed that Starr had spent more than $25 million on his investigation as of March 1997.

In July 1997, Starr released a report that concluded Deputy White House Counsel Vincent Foster's death in July 1993 was suicide. Though earlier investigations had come to the same conclusion, Starr's investigators produced new details that debunked a host of conspiracy theories put forward by critics of the Clintons. Some theorists had speculated that Foster, an Arkansas law partner of Hillary Clinton, had been murdered to prevent him from disclosing damaging evidence about Whitewater. Starr's investigators confirmed, however, that Foster, who had been suffering from depression, had killed himself in a secluded area of a public park using a handgun he owned.

During the fall of 1997, few new details about the investigation were revealed. But dramatic events in January 1998 heightened the scrutiny cast on both President Clinton and Starr. Linda R. Tripp, a former White House staff person who had transferred to the Pentagon, went to Starr with allegations that Clinton had an affair with Monica Lewinsky, a White House intern. Tripp also alleged that Lewinsky had been directed by Clinton and his close friend Vernon E. Jordan, Jr., to deny she had a sexual relationship with Clinton when questioned by the lawyers for Paula Jones. Jones's sexual harassment lawsuit against Clinton was scheduled to go to trial in May 1998, and her lawyers sought information that might be useful when they questioned the president under oath at a January deposition. Lewinsky, in a sworn affidavit, denied having an affair with Clinton, but Tripp provided Starr with audiotapes of more than ten conversations she had with Lewinsky over recent months in which Lewinsky recounted details of a year-and-a-half-long affair she said she had with Clinton. Some of the conversations addressed Lewinsky's testimony and guidance she claimed to have about it. When Clinton was asked about Lewinsky at the Jones deposition, he denied under oath having had a sexual relationship with her.

On January 16, 1998, Starr received permission from the three-judge appeals court panel that supervises his work to expand his investigation into whether Clinton and Jordan encouraged Lewinsky to lie under oath. He was authorized to examine allegations of suborning perjury, false statements, and obstruction of justice. Within days, the story appeared in the news media, sparking debate over whether Clinton should resign or be impeached if the allegations proved true. President Clinton publicly denied having had a sexual relationship with Lewinsky and then refused to answer any more questions until Starr's investigation was completed. During February 1998, Starr subpoenaed numerous persons who work or worked in the White House, seeking information to corroborate Tripp's allegations.

Starr's investigation of the Lewinsky matter led to a concerted attack on him by the White House and other Clinton supporters. Public opinion polls showed Clinton achieving his highest popularity ratings while in office. Starr, on the other hand, saw his credibility drop to almost single digits, as many in the public questioned his tactics and whether the Lewinsky matter had anything to do with the Whitewater real estate deal.

Amid the publicity surrounding Lewinsky, former Arkansas Governor Jim Guy Tucker, convicted of bank fraud in 1996, announced in February 1998 that he was prepared to cooperate with Starr's investigators concerning President Clinton's role in the banking and real estate scandals. In addition, James McDougal, also convicted of bank fraud and conspiracy, had begun talking in late 1997 to investigators about Clinton's alleged activities surrounding Whitewater. However, Starr's investigation was dealt a blow when McDougal died on March 8, 1998.

Throughout the spring of 1998 and into the summer months, President Clinton vehemently denied the existence of a sexual relationship with Monica Lewinsky, and his legal team made every effort to block Starr's subpoenas of secret service agents and presidential aides. A breakthrough occurred, however, on July 28, 1998, when lawyers for Lewinsky and Starr worked out a full immunity agreement for Lewinsky in exchange for her testimony. The next day Clinton agreed to voluntarily testify before the grand jury, leading to widespread speculation as to what his response would be to Lewinsky's testimony.

On August 17, 1998, Clinton testified before the grand jury. Following questioning, he appeared on national television and admitted to having an "inappropriate relationship" with Lewinsky.

**CROSS REFERENCES**
Clinton, Hillary Rodham; Clinton, William Jefferson; Independent Counsel

# WIRETAPPING

A form of electronic eavesdropping accomplished by seizing or over-hearing communications by means of a concealed recording or listening device connected to the transmission line.

## Videotape of Abusive Nanny Admissible

In *State v. Diaz* a New Jersey appeals panel addressed the issue of whether prosecutors could use videotaped evidence of a nanny abusing an infant in her employer's home, 308 N. J. Super. 504, 706 A. 2d 264 (1998). The parents of a five-month-old infant suspected that the child's nanny, Siobhan Diaz, was abusing the child. They installed video taping equipment that confirmed their suspicion. Before trial on two charges, Diaz sought to have the tape's video and audio portions suppressed as a violation of New Jersey's wiretapping law. The trial judge rejected the argument, and so did the appeals panel. In a narrow ruling allowing the evidence to be introduced, the three-judge panel held that the parents had provided the consent necessary under the law through the installation of the recording equipment in their own home.

J.S. and D.S. were the parents of five-month-old T.S. (courts commonly use initials rather than full names in cases involving minors). In January 1996, they hired Diaz as a day-time nanny. Bruises soon appeared on this infant that Diaz could not explain. Out of concern, the parents hired Babywatch, a private company that installs video surveillance equipment. On May 2, 1996, Babywatch installed a video camera with sound recording capability, disguised as part of an air filtration system in the family room. The next day, the tape revealed Diaz slapping the infant's head, twisting her leg, stuffing a blanket into the infant's mouth to squelch her cries, and yelling, "I'll give you something to fucking scream about, bitch!" The audio track also picked up Diaz's end of a telephone conversation.

After the couple turned the videotape over to police, Diaz was indicted on charges of second degree aggravated assault and second degree endangerment of the welfare of a child. At trial, her attorney moved to suppress all of the taped evidence. The defense motion argued that use of either the video or the audio portions of the tape would violate the New Jersey Wiretapping and Electronic Surveillance Act (N.J.S.A. 2A:156A-1 to-34). Similar to other state and federal laws, the New Jersey act bans the use of electronic means to intercept private communication. Enacted in 1969, it was modeled after Congress's wiretapping restrictions found in Title III of the Federal Omnibus Crime Control Act and Safe Streets Act, 18 U.S.C. § 2510 to § 2520, which was enacted in 1968 (Pub. L. No. 90-351, Title III, § 802, 82 Stat. 212).

The trial court denied the motion. The judge ruled that the evidence was permissible under section 156A-4d of the law, which provides an exception to the ban when one party to the communication has given prior consent for the interception of the communication. In this case, the court found "vicarious consent" because the family had installed the videotaping equipment in their own home. Diaz appealed arguing that law required the consent of a party to the conversation, which was not present in this case.

The appeals panel looked to federal law for guidance. Parts of the New Jersey statute under dispute were substantially similar to their federal counterparts (18 U.S.C.A. §§ 2510 and 2511), and a decade earlier, the appellate division had determined that the state's legislative intent in enacting the statute had been similar to that of Congress (*State v. Fornino*, 223 N.J.Super. 531, 543-44 App.Div, 539 A.2d 301, cert. denied, 111 N.J. 570, cert. denied, 488 U.S. 859, 109 S. Ct. 152, 102 L. Ed. 2d 123 [1988]). The panel determined that federal courts appeared to be unanimous in their rulings that videotaping is not subject to the federal wiretap ban. It thus concluded that New Jersey's statute did not ban outright the use in court of videotape images—whether the images of a silent video camera or the video portion of a tape that also included a sound component. Diaz's image on tape was admissible evidence.

The panel also upheld the admissibility of Diaz's speech to the baby, agreeing with the judge's theory of vicarious consent. "[W]e find no basis," it held, "to prevent the admission of otherwise lawful recordings contemporaneously made as part of the same videotape by private parties in their own home." By installing the equipment in their home the parents had established vicarious consent for recording communications involving their infant child. The panel noted that its ruling was specific to this case and was not a ruling as to the admissibility of audio material in all cases involving videotaped surveillance. The court avoided ruling on the admissibility of the audio recording of Diaz's telephone conversation, because the prosecution had indicated it would not introduce the conversation at trial.

Affirming the judge's denial of Diaz's motion to suppress the videotape, the panel sent the case back to court to be tried.

**CROSS REFERENCES**
Evidence

## WITNESSES

Individuals who provide EVIDENCE in legal proceedings before a tribunal. Persons who have sufficient knowledge of a fact or occurrence to TESTIFY about it and who give TESTIMONY under OATH in court, concerning what they have seen, heard, or otherwise observed.

### Expert Testimony Could Not Replace Drug Evidence

In December 1997, a New York appellate court overturned a drug conviction in which prosecutors had used expert testimony to compensate for a complete lack of material evidence, *People v. Colon*, (238 A.D. 2d 18, 667 N.Y.S.2d 692 [N.Y.A.D. 1 Dept.1997]). William Colon's indictment for possessing and selling heroin was difficult to prosecute. Police found no evidence on Colon at the time he was arrested. Prosecutors addressed that problem by calling an expert witness, who testified that drug peddlers commonly do not have drugs or money in their possession when arrested. In ruling that Colon had been denied a fair trial, a five-judge panel of the New York Appellate Division, First Department, ruled that expert testimony cannot substitute for evidence.

The case began with an undercover drug bust in the Bronx, New York. Having observed Colon pass an envelope to a woman, an undercover officer approached him and said, "Uno," meaning "one." Colon then allegedly sold one envelope of heroin to the officer, who paid for it with a marked ten dollar bill. Minutes later, another officer arrested and searched Colon. Colon, however, was found to be carrying only ten dollars in unmarked currency. Neither the marked currency nor any drugs were in his possession. He claimed police had arrested the wrong man. Nonetheless, he was later indicted on two counts of third-degree criminal possession and sale of a controlled substance.

At trial before a jury in the Supreme Court of Bronx County, prosecutors had no physical evidence. Assistant Bronx District Attorneys Jacqueline M. Vernon and Stanley R. Kaplan called a police officer—an expert in street-level narcotics transactions—to testify. The officer gave lengthy and detailed testimony to the jury on how such deals typically work: a "steerer" directs customers to a "pitcher," who retrieves drugs from a "stash man" and passes them to the buyer, whose payment is given to a "money man" while "lookouts," "managers," and "owners" operate behind the scenes.

Colon's court-appointed attorneys objected to the use of expert testimony. They argued that it was unnecessary and would encourage the jury to speculate about Colon's possible but unproven participation in a conspiracy. The court, however, overruled the objection instructing the jury that the testimony was admissible for the limited purpose of explaining why Colon had no money or drugs in his possession at the time of his arrest. He was convicted.

On appeal, Colon successfully argued that the trial court erred in admitting the testimony. By a 4–1 vote, the appeals panel ruled that he had been denied a fair trial. Justice Francis T. Murphy's majority opinion began by defining the limits of expert testimony. Such testimony must be based on facts in the record or personally known to the witness, but cannot reach conclusions by assuming facts that are not supported by evidence. In Colon's case, there was "not a scintilla of proof" that he was a pitcher, stash man, money man, or other participant to a conspiracy. Therefore, the jury could reasonably have concluded police arrested the wrong man. The appeals court flatly rejected the state's argument that expert testimony had been necessary to prevent juror confusion. Instead the court found that the testimony had prejudiced Colon's case, opening it to "a speculative onslaught" by the jury, which made acquittal "highly unlikely." The court overturned the conviction and ordered a new trial.

In dissent, Justice Richard T. Andrias argued that the testimony constituted "nothing more than background information," which served the proper purpose of detailing the defendant's arrest and avoiding jury speculation about the police. Moreover, it was properly admitted to counter Colon's contention that the police arrested the wrong man. As such, Justice Andrias concluded, the testimony's value outweighed any prejudicial harm done to the defendant.

**CROSS REFERENCES**

Conspiracy; Evidence

## VICTORIA CLAFLIN WOODHULL

| | |
|---|---|
| **1838** | Born in Homer, Ohio |
| **1864** | Divorced Canning Woodhull; married Colonel James H. Blood |
| **1868** | Moved to New York City |
| **1870** | Along with sister, Tennessee, started *Woodhull and Claflin's Weekly*, a periodical |
| **1871** | Appeared before the U.S. House of Representatives' judiciary committee arguing for women's right to vote |
| **1872** | Ran for U.S. president, but lost to incumbent Ulysses S. Grant; jailed for libel and shipment of obscene material through the mail |
| **1876** | Divorced Blood |
| **1877** | Moved with sister to England |
| **1883** | Married John Biddulph Martin |
| **1927** | Died in Norton Park, Worcestershire, England |

## WOODHULL, VICTORIA CLAFLIN

U.S. reformer Victoria Claflin Woodhull was involved with a number of causes, including women's suffrage, free love, birth control, and socialism. Woodhull ran for the U.S. presidency in 1872, making her the first woman to do so. A successful spiritualist, stockbroker, and political agitator before the age of forty, Woodhull left the United States in disgrace in 1877 for accusing Henry Ward Beecher, the most prominent clergymen at the time, of adultery.

Victoria Claflin was born on September 23, 1838, in Homer, Ohio. Her parents ran a traveling medicine show and dabbled in fortune-telling and psychic healing. At age fifteen, Claflin married Canning Woodhull. She had two children with Woodhull but soon became disenchanted with his excessive drinking. She divorced Woodhull in 1864 and married Colonel James H. Blood, a Civil War veteran who introduced her to the world of politics. They moved to New York City in 1868, where she and her sister Tennessee practiced fortune-

*Victoria Claflin Woodhull*

telling and spiritualism. The sisters attracted the interest of Cornelius Vanderbilt, the railroad magnate and devotee of spiritualism, who found Victoria's clairvoyance compelling. With Vanderbilt's support, the sisters established a Wall Street stock brokerage. The firm of Woodhull, Claflin, and Co. was successful, earning attention in large part because the sisters were the first women in the United States to own a stock brokerage.

In 1870, after making $700,000 in the brokerage, the sisters started *Woodhull and Claflin's Weekly*, a periodical that espoused women's suffrage, short skirts, spiritualism, free love, vegetarianism, and socialism. Woodhull's socialistic philosophy was heavily influenced by Stephen Pearl Andrews, who rejected conventional marriage and advocated a social order of free love along with communal management of children and property.

Woodhull's beliefs in equal rights for women and a single standard of morality for both men and women spurred her call for women's suffrage. In 1871 she appeared before the judiciary committee of the U.S. House of Representatives to argue for giving women the right to vote. Undaunted by the rejection of her views, in 1872 she announced her campaign for presidency under the banner of the Equal Rights Party, an offshoot of Susan B. Anthony's National American Woman Suffrage Association. Woodhull's running mate was Frederick Douglass, the former abolitionist leader. Her campaign, while drawing publicity, was unsuccessful against incumbent-Republican General Ulysses S. Grant. Woodhull was actually ineligible to run for the presidency since she was only 34 and the Constitution mandates that a candidate must be at least thirty-five years of age.

The presidential campaign marked the high point for Woodhull's political career. By election day, Woodhull was in jail. She and her sister had printed in their periodical rumors of an alleged affair between Henry Ward Beecher and Elizabeth Tilton, the wife of Theodore Tilton. Beecher and Theodore Tilton headed rival suffrage associations and had been friends. News of the alleged adulterous affair created a national scandal and led to the indictment and jailing of Woodhull and Claflin for libel and shipment of obscene materials through the mail. Ironically, the sisters did not condemn Beecher for the affair, but proved the need for a single standard of morality, which would allow women and men to express their sexuality freely. Woodhull was labeled "Mrs. Satan" for views that outraged Victorian morality. Despite the public outcry over their views, the sisters were acquitted of the charges.

Woodhull divorced Blood in 1876 and moved with her sister to England in 1877. Woodhull attracted the attentions of a wealthy banker, John Biddulph Martin, who married her in 1883. She moved within upper crust British society, yet helped her daughter publish *Humanitarian*, a journal devoted to eugenics. Woodhull never returned to the United States. She died on June 10, 1927, in Norton Park, Worcestershire, England.

**CROSS REFERENCES**
Grant, Ulysses Simpson; Women's Rights

There are thousands of organizations in the United States that lobby for and against government policies. Traditionally, lobbying organizations and the lobbyists who represent these groups have sought to influence the outcome of proposed legislation and regulations by providing officials with information about the issues. Organizations representing economic interests, such as banks, insurance companies, utilities, phone companies, labor unions, lawyers, and doctors traditionally have performed this role.

Since the 1960s, however, different types of lobbying organizations have been established that rely on a grassroots network of individuals committed to a specific agenda. The National Rifle Association is committed to the unregulated sale and transfer of firearms, and the American Association of Retired Persons (AARP) represents the interests of senior citizens. Organizations that take a stand on a controversial social issue, such as abortion, have become, over time, skillful players in the political process. These organizations can mobilize their members to write letters, make phone calls, appear at demonstrations, and vote for candidates who are sympathetic to the group's goals.

Many lobbying organizations are organized as nonpartisan, nonprofit institutions under federal tax laws. This means, however, that they cannot endorse or give money to political candidates directly. Organizations can get around this restriction by creating separate entities, called political action committees, which can give money to candidates and political parties. An organization that fails to remain nonpartisan can lose its tax-exempt status and can be subject to criminal and civil penalties. The Christian Coalition, for example, has been embroiled in litigation with the Federal Elections Committee about its alleged direct support of Republican party candidates in the 1992 elections.

A number of prominent lobbying organizations have been involved in the political process for most, if not all, of the twentieth century. The National Association of Manufacturers, the American Bankers Association, the U.S. Chamber of Commerce, the American Farm Bureau, and the American Federation of Labor and Congress of Industrial Organizations (AFL-CIO) have shaped the debate over government regulation of business, agriculture, and labor, U.S. trade policy, and taxation. The AARP, the American Legion, and the Veterans of Foreign Wars are potent lobbying organizations, fighting to enhance and preserve benefits for their membership.

Other lobbying organizations combine legislative efforts with court actions. The National Association for the Advancement of Colored People (NAACP), the American Civil Liberties Union, the Sierra Club, and the National Gay and Lesbian Task Force represent different constituencies, but they have all achieved legal change through the courtroom as well as through the legislative hearing room.

Organizations that seek to change public policy often hire professional lobbyists to represent their interests. The hired spokespersons for large interest groups usually have access to information about any issue that may affect their clients. Legislators, who are always pressed for time, rely on lobbyists they trust to provide them with clear explanations about pending legislation. In addition, if a legislator values an organization for its political support, he will give the group's lobbyist his attention.

Yet a lobbying organization does not always need financial contributions and institutional clout to succeed in moving its agenda forward. A good example is Mothers Against Drunk Driving (MADD), which grew from one small community group into a formidable national organization. MADD drew its strength from moral outrage at the way the legal system treated persons who killed innocent victims while driving intoxicated. State legislatures across the United States have adopted many of MADD's reform proposals.

The following thirty organizations include some of the most powerful and influential lobbying groups in the United States, as well as others, such as the National Organization for the Reform of Marijuana Laws, who have a difficult time garnering widespread support for their agendas. However, politics and policy making are dynamic processes that can quickly shift the fortunes of a lobbying organization from "outsider" to "insider." Public support for a particular issue can help move a lobbying organization from the fringe to the center of the political arena.

## AMERICAN ASSOCIATION OF RETIRED PERSONS

The American Association of Retired Persons (AARP) is a nonprofit, nonpartisan organization dedicated to helping older Americans achieve lives of independence, dignity, and purpose. The AARP, which was founded in 1958 by Dr. Ethel Percy Andrus, is the oldest and largest organization of older Americans, with a membership of more than 33 million. The National Retired Teachers Association, which was founded in 1947, is a division of AARP. Membership in AARP is open to anyone age fifty or older, working or retired. More than one-third of the association's membership is in the work force. The AARP's headquarters are in Washington, D.C. In addition, there are state and regional offices that serve four thousand local chapters. The organization is led by a twenty-one member board of directors and has an administrative staff that carries out the group's day-to-day activities. The organization is funded almost entirely by annual membership dues.

The AARP has been an effective advocate for issues involving older persons, in part because of its large membership and its ability to mobilize its members to lobby for its positions before Congress and government agencies. The organization has concentrated much of its lobbying effort on Social Security, Medicare, and long-term care issues. The AARP has fought zealously to protect the Social Security benefits of senior citizens and has resisted efforts by Congress to change the system itself. Its Advocacy Center for Social Security develops policy proposals and lobbies Congress.

The AARP Advocacy Center for Medicare seeks to ensure the availability of affordable, quality health care to seniors and persons with disabilities. It currently is working to develop ways of maintaining the short-term solvency of the Hospital Insurance Trust Fund and is preparing for the needs of the baby boomers in the longer term. With the dramatic growth in managed health care plans, the AARP has sought to educate its members about this new way of providing services and to empower seniors by telling them what their rights are under this system.

The association also is actively involved in voter education. A major, nonpartisan component of the Association's legislative program is AARP/VOTE, a voter education program that is charged with informing the public about important public policy issues and the positions of candidates for public office. Through issue and candidate forums and voter guides, AARP/VOTE works to promote issue-centered campaigns and a more informed electorate.

The organization also provides many benefits to its members. The AARP licenses the use of its name for selected services of chosen providers. For example, it offers members a choice of insurance plans. Because most of the plans are neither age-rated nor medically underwritten, the association can make health insurance available to many of its members who otherwise would be unable to obtain insurance coverage because of pre-existing conditions. The association receives an administrative allowance or a royalty from the providers and the income realized from these services is used for the general purposes of the association and its members.

The AARP also operates a nationwide volunteer network that helps older citizens. Programs include information and support for grandparents who are raising their grandchildren, legal hotlines, and income tax preparation.

These and other programs are funded, in part, by federal grants.

The association publishes a bimonthly magazine, *Modern Maturity*, and the *Bulletin*, a newspaper published eleven times a year.

Website: www.aarp.org

**CROSS REFERENCES**
Lobbying; Senior Citizens

## AMERICAN BANKERS ASSOCIATION

The American Bankers Association (ABA) is comprised of banks and other financial institutions. It seeks to promote the strength and profitability of the banking industry by lobbying federal and state governments, building industry consensus on key issues, and providing products and services, including public affairs support and legal services, to its member banks. Membership in the ABA includes community, regional, and money-center banks (the nation's major banks) and holding companies, as well as savings associations, trust companies, and savings banks. The ABA, which was founded in 1875, is the largest banking trade association in the United States, with 95 percent of the commercial banking industry as members. Its headquarters are in Washington, D.C.

The ABA places great emphasis on representing the interests of banks before Congress and state legislatures. It takes stands on banking and bank-related bills as they move through Congress, attempts to influence the interpretations of laws and regulations by banking regulators, and is actively involved in state litigation that has implications for the banking industry. In 1995 ABA representatives testified before Congress or regulatory agencies almost twenty-five times, filed more than twenty-four official letters of comment, and sponsored three trips to the nation's capital for state associations. In the 1990s it has fought legislative efforts to regulate the fees banks charge customers to use automatic teller machines and has challenged in court the membership policies used by credit unions to gain customers. BankPac, the banking industry's political action committee and one of the strongest committees nationwide, raised and distributed $2 million for the 1994 congressional elections.

The ABA also operates the American Institute for Banking (AIB), which is the largest provider of banking education. The AIB teaches hundreds of thousands of students annually. The ABA also sponsors approximately twenty-four residential schools with 3,700 students covering specialty areas within banking and the prestigious Stonier Graduate School of Banking. New technology has provided new opportunities as well. American Financial Skylink is a satellite telecommunications network that delivers news, information, and training directly to banks through regular telecasts.

Though the ABA is a nonprofit organization, it operates the for-profit Corporation for American Banking (CAB). CAB was created to facilitate group buying of services, allowing participating banks to receive CAB-arranged discounts on long-distance telephone service, overnight package delivery, office products, and copying products.

The Bank Marketing Association, an ABA affiliate, helps bank marketers and promotes professionalism and creativity in the industry's marketing efforts. The ABA Securities Association, also an ABA affiliate, assists sections of the banking industry that are competing in the securities business.

Website: www.aba.com

## AMERICAN CIVIL LIBERTIES UNION

The American Civil Liberties Union (ACLU) is a nonprofit, nonpartisan organization that seeks to defend individual rights and civil liberties guaranteed by the U.S. Constitution. The ACLU selects legal cases that involve civil liberties and provides legal representation. Representatives of the ACLU appear before the U.S. Supreme Court more than representatives from any other organization except the U.S. Department of Justice.

The ACLU is supported by annual dues and contributions from its 275,000 members, along with grants from private individuals and foundations. The national headquarters are located in New York City, New York. The ACLU has affiliate offices in all fifty states, including most major cities and more than three hundred chapters in smaller towns, as well as regional offices in Denver, Colorado, and Atlanta, Georgia.

The ACLU was founded in 1920 by a group of civil libertarians. Roger Nash Baldwin, the founder and executive director for thirty years, envisioned the ACLU as a public interest law firm that could extend the reach of the Bill of Rights into many areas of U.S. law. The ACLU has been involved in many issues central to U.S. law in the twentieth century, challenging censorship laws, the internment of Japanese Americans during World War II, racial segregation in public schools, and the criminalization of abortion. Because of its stands on controversial issues and its representation of unpopular people and causes (defending the right of Nazis or the Ku Klux Klan to demonstrate, attacking publicly financed nativity scenes), the ACLU has often been attacked by conservative groups as an extremist organization.

The ACLU has more than a dozen national projects devoted to specific civil liberties issues: AIDS, arts censorship, capital punishment, children's rights, education reform, lesbian and gay rights, immigrants' rights, national security, privacy and technology, prisoners' rights, reproductive freedom, voting rights, women's rights, and workplace rights. It has more than sixty staff attorneys, who collaborate with more than two thousand volunteer attorneys. The ACLU either represents a client directly or it files an amicus curiae (friend of the court) brief that seeks to help the court understand the particular constitutional right at stake in the case.

It successfully challenged the constitutionality of the Communications Decency Act of 1996 (47 U.S.C.A. § 223(a) et seq.), which sought to prevent children from accessing "indecent" materials on the Internet. The U.S. Supreme Court ruled in *Reno v. American Civil Liberties Union*, ___ U.S.___, 117 S. Ct. 2329, 138 L. Ed. 2d 874 (1997), that the CDA violated the First Amendment because the law's classification of what is "indecent" was too vague.

Website:www.aclu.org

## AMERICAN FARM BUREAU FEDERATION

The American Farm Bureau Federation (AFBF) is a nonprofit, nonpartisan organization dedicated to promoting, protecting, and representing the interests of U.S. farmers. More than four-and-a-half million families (membership is on a family basis) in fifty states and Puerto Rico belong to the AFBF, making it the largest U.S. farm organization. The AFBF is a federation of 2,800 county farm organizations, which elect representatives to state farm bureaus. The organization maintains its general headquarters in Park Ridge, Illinois and has an office in Washington, D.C. From these offices the AFBF staff offers many services and programs for state and county farm bureaus and members.

The first county farm bureau was formed in Broome County, New York, in 1911. The word *bureau* in farm bureau is used because the first organization was formed as a "bureau" of the local chamber of commerce. Missouri was the first state to form a statewide organization of farm bureaus in 1915. The AFBF was founded in 1919 when a small group of farmers from thirty state bureaus gathered in Chicago, Illinois. The AFBF soon became a voice for agriculture at the national level, lobbying Congress for passage of legislation favorable to farmers.

The AFBF relies on its 2,800 county bureaus for direction and support. Thousands of volunteer leaders serve on county farm bureau boards and committees. Members organize social outings, educational workshops, political action and community forums, and other programs and services for farm families.

State bureaus adopt policies and name delegates to represent them at the AFBF annual meeting. Policies adopted by voting delegates govern the federation. These policies deal with many issues, including the use of natural resources, taxation, property rights, services to the farm community, trade, food safety and quality, and other issues that affect rural America.

The AFBF has historically been a conservative organization, favoring flexible price supports for crops and a minimum of government regulation and oversight. Its government relations division employs a number of registered lobbyists who are specialists on farm policy, trade, budget and taxes, farm credit, labor, transportation, conservation, and the environment. They maintain daily contact with Congress and regulatory agencies and appear before congressional committees.

The AFBF's public policy division is responsible for research, education, and policy support for AFBF and the state farm bureaus. Staff members provide analysis and information on current issues, including property rights, health care, clean water, endangered species, animal welfare, farm programs, dairy policy, ethanol, and trade. The division also coordinates several special farm bureau activities, including commodity advisory committees, annual crop surveys, and various national seminars and conferences on policy issues.

The federation's communication division operates a computerized marketing, news, and weather system, which delivers the latest news, market information, U.S. Department of Agriculture news, and agricultural weather reports to subscribers by satellite.

The American Farm Bureau Foundation for Agriculture, founded in 1967, funds research on agricultural issues. The foundation is funded by gifts from individuals, county and state farm bureaus, corporations, and foundations. The foundation has funded research on animal waste management, pesticide use, new methods of helping endangered species, and animal welfare education.

Website: www.afbf.org

## AMERICAN FEDERATION OF LABOR-CONGRESS OF INDUSTRIAL ORGANIZATIONS

The American Federation of Labor-Congress of Industrial Organizations (AFL-CIO) is a national federation of U.S. labor unions. The AFL-CIO is comprised of seventy-eight national union affiliates, forty-five thousand local unions, fifty-one state central bodies (including Puerto Rico), and a membership of more than thirteen million workers. The organization, which has had enormous political influence since the 1930s, has its headquarters in Washington, D.C.

The AFL was formed in 1886 as a loose confederation of twenty-five autonomous national trade unions with more than 316,000 members. The AFL, renouncing identification with any political party or movement, concentrated on pursuing achievable goals such as higher wages and shorter hours. Members were encouraged to support politicians who were friendly to labor, no matter what their party affiliation.

During the 1930s the AFL became embroiled in internal conflict. The trade unions that dominated the AFL were composed of skilled workers who opposed organizing the unskilled or semiskilled workers on the manufacturing production line. Several unions rebelled at this refusal to organize and formed the Committee for Industrial Organization (CIO). The CIO aggressively organized millions of workers who labored in automobile, steel, and rubber plants. In 1938, unhappy with this effort, the AFL expelled the unions that formed the CIO. The CIO then formed its own organization and changed its name to the Congress of Industrial Organizations. By the 1950s the leadership of both the AFL and CIO realized that a unified labor movement was a necessity. In 1955 the

AFL and the CIO merged into a single organization, the AFL-CIO.

The AFL-CIO is primarily concerned with influencing legislative policies that affect unions. Its staff members conduct research, set policy, and testify before congressional and state legislative committees. More importantly, the organization provides funds and volunteers to labor-endorsed political candidates. Though the AFL-CIO is a nonpartisan organization, it has traditionally supported Democratic party candidates.

With the 1995 election of John J. Sweeney as president, the AFL-CIO has made increasing union membership its highest priority. Membership in U.S. trade unions has fallen since the 1950s, as the manufacturing sector of the U.S. economy has steadily declined. Union membership in 1995 comprised just 14.9 percent of the workforce, compared with a high of 34.7 percent in 1954. Sweeney has pushed the organization to recruit women, minorities, low-paid workers, and white-collar workers.

Website: www.aflcio.org

## AMERICAN ISRAEL PUBLIC AFFAIRS COMMITTEE

The American Israel Public Affairs Committee (AIPAC) is a national advocacy group that lobbies for U.S. support to the nation of Israel. Founded in 1951, AIPAC has grown into a fifty-five-thousand-member organization that is recognized as one of the most influential foreign policy groups in the United States. AIPAC has lobbied Congress for U.S. foreign aid to Israel since 1951, when it helped defeat several efforts to cut aid for the resettling of hundreds of thousands of Holocaust refugees in Israel. In addition, it has lobbied for U.S. military aid to Israel and has helped preserve the special relationship that has existed between the United States and Israel since the United States recognized the nation of Israel in 1948.

AIPAC has its headquarters in Washington, D.C. Members of its staff maintain an active presence in the halls of Congress, attending committee sessions and reviewing legislation that may affect the relationship between the United States and Israel. AIPAC estimates that it monitors two thousand hours of congressional hearings annually. Its research staff members analyze periodicals and documents in five different languages, amassing a large archive of information on hundreds of issues, including foreign aid, antiterrorism initiatives, and programs that promote United States-Israel strategic cooperation. AIPAC staff members also work with key officials in developing legislation and policy, presenting concepts and information that is moved into the legislative process. AIPAC lobbyists hold one thousand meetings annually with congressional offices.

AIPAC also works with aspiring politicians. During the 1994 elections, representatives of AIPAC met with six hundred congressional candidates. Nearly half of the members of Congress have been elected since 1990, and AIPAC has worked to educate these new legislators about the relationship between the United State and Israel and the key issues critical to maintaining that relationship. After the 1994 election, AIPAC staff met with every freshman representative elected.

AIPAC regional staff members travel to more than six hundred communities a year to train AIPAC members to be effective advocates for United States-Israel relations. AIPAC works in every congressional district, especially those districts with little or no Jewish population. AIPAC conducts small meetings and statewide workshops, giving its members the opportunity to become involved in grassroots lobbying.

The influence of AIPAC remains strong. The 1998 foreign aid appropriation bill contained $3 billion in aid to Israel. Of that amount, $1.8 billion was for military aid and $1.2 billion was for economic aid. An additional $80 million was appropriated to help settle Jewish refugees in Israel. AIPAC has also maintained congressional support for Israel's position in the Middle East peace process, arguing that attempts to distance the United States from Israel's position will only encourage its Arab neighbors to ask for unilateral concessions. AIPAC believes that the peace process will only achieve results if the close working relationship between the United States and Israel continues.

## AMERICAN LEGION

The American Legion is a wartime veterans' organization that was chartered by Congress in 1919. The American Legion has almost three million members in nearly fifteen thousand American Legion posts worldwide. These posts are organized into fifty-five departments, one each for the fifty states, the District of Columbia, Puerto Rico, France, Mexico, and the Philippines. The American Legion's national headquarters is in Indianapolis, Indiana, with additional offices in Washington, D.C. Though volunteer members do most of the work of the American Legion, the national organization has a regular full-time staff of about three hundred employees.

Eligibility in the American Legion is based on honorable service with the U.S. armed forces during World War I, World War II, the Korean War, the Vietnam War, and military operations in Lebanon (1982–84), Grenada (1982–84), Panama (1989–90) and the Persian Gulf (1990 to the present). Because membership is based on the period of service, not the place of service, an individual does not have to be stationed in a combat zone to be eligible. Members may participate in a low-cost life insurance program and may receive discounts on moving expenses, car rentals, hotel and motel rentals, eyewear, and prescription drugs. American Legion service officers provide free advice and guidance to veterans who need to deal with the Department of Veterans Affairs (VA) about benefits and other issues.

The American Legion sponsors many community activities and programs. Students showing the highest qualities of citizenship are recognized with an American Legion School Medal Award. In 1996 more than thirty-three thousand students in elementary, junior high, and senior high schools were recognized for their commitment to honor, courage, scholarship, leadership, and service. The organization also awards ten national college scholarships each year. At the state level, forty-nine departments host Boys State programs each summer for outstanding high school juniors. Local posts sponsor nearly twenty-eight thousand young men each year to attend the week-long government education program. Two outstanding leaders from each of these Boys State programs are selected to attend the American Legion Boys Nation in Washington, D.C. The American Legion Auxiliary conducts parallel programs for young women through Girls State and Girls Nation.

Many local posts sponsor Junior Shooting Clubs, which provide training in gun safety and marksmanship for students ages fourteen though twenty. However, the American Legion is probably best known for its sponsorship of youth baseball programs. In 1996 legion posts spent more than $16 million to sponsor 4,800 baseball teams representing more than 89,000 players. Champions from the state level meet on the national level in the American Legion World Series tournament.

The American Legion has always been a strong advocate for U.S. veterans, appearing before congressional committees to submit information and viewpoints on pending legislation. The Veterans Affairs and Rehabilitation Commission (VAR) is a cornerstone of the American Legion, overseeing federally mandated programs provided by the VA for veterans and their dependents. VAR services include assistance with medical care, claims, and appeals, insurance programs, burial benefits, and veterans' employment. Staff members also communicate with administrators of state veterans' affairs programs.

American Legion volunteers give more than one million hours of service to disabled veterans annually. Field representatives from the American Legion's Washington office systematically visit VA medical centers, nursing home care units, and outpatient clinics to evaluate their programs and facilities. The field representatives report resource needs and areas for improvement to the VA headquarters in Washington, D.C.

Website: www.legion.org

## AMERICAN MEDICAL ASSOCIATION

The American Medical Association (AMA) is a federation of state and territorial medical associations. The AMA seeks to promote the art and science of medicine, the medical profession, and the betterment of public health. Its purposes include obtaining, synthesizing, integrating, and disseminating information about health and medical practice; setting standards for medical ethics, practice, and education; and being an influential advocate for physicians and their patients.

The AMA was founded in 1847. At its organizing convention, the AMA adopted the first code of ethics in the United States, a detailed document that addressed the obligations of physicians to patients and to each other, and the duties of the profession to the public at large. The delegates also adopted the first national standards for medical education through a resolution establishing prerequisites for the study of medicine. Since that time, the AMA has grown into a large organization, with great influence over issues involving health care and medicine. Its headquarters are in Chicago, Illinois.

The AMA speaks out on issues important to the medical community. AMA policy on such issues is decided through a democratic process, at the center of which is the AMA House of Delegates. The house is comprised of physician delegates from every state, the national medical specialty societies, the surgeon general of the United States, and sections representing organized medical staffs, resident physicians, medical students, young physicians, and medical schools.

Before the opening of the House of Delegates, which meets twice a year, individual committees consider resolutions and reports in hearings open to all AMA members. Each committee prepares recommendations for the delegates. The house then votes on these recommendations, deciding the AMA's formal position and future action on an issue.

The AMA is the world's largest publisher of scientific medical information. The *Journal of the American Medical Association* is printed in twelve languages and reaches physicians in forty-two countries worldwide, making it the world's most widely read medical journal. The AMA also publishes nine monthly medical specialty journals as well as a newspaper of social and economic health news, *American Medical News*.

The AMA has played a major role in national health care policy. It opposed the creation of Medicare in the 1960s and remains opposed to national health care insurance. It has sought, however, to extend access to the health care system and to contain its costs while improving its quality. The AMA is extremely active in public health campaigns, working vigorously for healthy lifestyles and against tobacco use and violence of all kinds.

Website: www.ama-assn.org

## ASSOCIATION OF TRIAL LAWYERS OF AMERICA

The Association of Trial Lawyers of America (ATLA) is a nonprofit organization that represents the interests of personal injury attorneys. The ATLA is the world's largest trial bar organization, with about sixty thousand members worldwide. The ATLA's goals are to safeguard the interests of people who seek redress for injury and to protect individuals from abuses of power. Any person who is licensed to practice law in any country, state, or jurisdiction, who is committed to the adversary system, and who, for the most part, does not represent the defense of personal injury litigation is eligible for membership.

The ATLA is comprised of a network of U.S. and Canadian affiliates involved in diverse areas of trial advocacy. It provides lawyers with the information and professional assistance needed to serve clients successfully and protect the civil justice system. The ATLA is governed by its membership through a board of governors and national officers, who are elected at the organization's annual convention. ATLA committees help to set policies in critical areas, make recommendations to the board of governors, and oversee staff implementation of ATLA objectives. The ATLA is headquartered in Washington, D.C., and has 160 staff members, including approximately thirty attorneys. It publishes the monthly magazine *Trial*, the *ATLA Law Reporter*, and the *Advocate*.

The ATLA has sections, each of which encompasses an area of litigation practice. Sections include admiralty, aviation, civil rights, products liability, insurance, family law, and workers' compensation law. Services of the sections include the publication of annual directories and periodic newsletters, and information exchange. The ATLA also has organized litigation groups, which are voluntary networks of ATLA members sharing an interest in a particular type of case, many of which involve hazardous products. The groups share timely documents and information, much of it obtained from discovery in similar cases. The litigation groups also organize programs that educate members about recent developments in their special areas.

The ATLA has been a leading opponent of state and federal legislative efforts to restrict the amount of damages a plaintiff can recover for medical malpractice or for injuries caused by a defective product. The organization has lobbied against tort reform bills, rebutting arguments that too many lawsuits have led to excessive costs and delays and that juries can no longer be trusted to render fair verdicts.

In addition to its lobbying efforts, the ATLA provides a specialization certification program for trial skills, statistical compilation, and a placement service. It also conducts seminars and conferences.

Website: www.atlanet.org

## CHILDREN'S DEFENSE FUND

The Children's Defense Fund (CDF) is a nonprofit organization focusing on children's issues. The CDF was established in 1973 by Marian Wright Edelman, a Washington, D.C., lawyer and civil rights leader. The CDF grew out of Edelman's Washington Research Project, an advocacy and research group that lobbied Congress for an expansion of Head Start, a program that encourages the intellectual and social development of poor, at-risk children. The CDF, which has its headquarters in Washington, D.C., has proved to be an effective organization, with a staff of one hundred and an annual budget of almost $11 million. It is supported by foundations, corporation grants, and individual donations and does not accept government funds.

The CDF seeks to provide hope and social change for poor, neglected, and abused children in the United States. It conducts research, drafts legislation, lobbies, and provides education support on issues affecting children. It has lobbied government officials on issues such as childhood diseases and immunizations, homelessness, child abuse, education, and foster care. The CDF has consistently supported increased funding for Medicaid spending, welfare, and Head Start programs.

In 1997 the CDF announced a five-point program that seeks to educate citizens about the needs of children and to encourage preventive investment in children before they get sick, drop out of school, suffer early pregnancy or family breakdown, or get into trouble. It has declared that no child should be left behind and that every child should have a "healthy start," a "head start," a "fair start," a "safe start," and a "moral start" in life with the support of parents and communities.

As part of a healthy start, the CDF seeks to provide all children with access to comprehensive health and mental health services that offer preventive care as well as treatment when they are ill. A head start refers to the CDF's commitment to seeing that child care and early education are available to children, regardless of their economic status. A fair start refers to the CDF's goal of having children grow up in families and communities that are economically secure. As part of this agenda, the CDF has lobbied for an economic system that provides jobs that pay livable wages, the earned income tax credit for persons not making a livable wage, and short-term income support and job training when parents are out of work.

The CDF also has been concerned about child abuse and neglect, as well as teen violence, especially among persons of color. Its call for a safe start refers to ensuring that children have safe families, safe neighborhoods, and safe schools. The CDF has also lobbied for gun control, noting that guns kill fourteen children each day. Finally, the CDF's moral start stresses the need for children to be taught the values of honesty, hard work, discipline, respect for self and others, and responsibility.

Website: www.cdf.org

## CHRISTIAN COALITION

The Christian Coalition is a nonprofit organization that serves as a powerful lobby for politically conservative causes. Under federal tax law, the organization is permitted to lobby for political issues but cannot endorse political candidates. The Christian Coalition has primarily sought the support of born-again evangelical Christians, but since 1996 it has attempted to build alliances with Roman Catholics, members of the Greek Orthodox Church, and Jews.

The Christian Coalition was founded in 1989 by religious broadcaster Pat Robertson. Robertson, who unsuccessfully sought the 1988 Republican party presidential nomination, decided to create an organization of evangelical Christians that would exert influence over the party. The coalition's central goals have been to gain working control of the Republican Party through grassroots organizing and to elect Christian candidates to office. The coalition soon became a potent political force. By 1997 it claimed control of several Republican state central committees and had elected to public office numerous Christian Coalition members and other candidates it endorsed. In the 1994 general election, the coalition distributed thirty-three million voter guides and has been credited with helping the Republican party gain control of Congress.

The Christian Coalition has focused on family and moral issues. It strongly opposes legalized abortion, and in 1998 it began an effort to require all endorsed Republican candidates to oppose partial-birth abortions. The coalition has also campaigned against gay rights, and through its legal arm, the American Center for Law and Justice, it has filed many church-state lawsuits.

Robertson, who served as president until 1997, appears on the *700 Club*, a television show that reaches seven million viewers each week. Robertson has characterized politics as a struggle pitting militant leftists, secular humanists, and atheists against conservative, evangelical Christians. The success of the coalition's grassroots organizing, however, can be attributed to Ralph Reed, who served as executive director until 1997. Reed encouraged coalition members to run for school boards, city councils, and legislatures without revealing their affiliation. This strategy also proved effective within the Republican Party.

The Christian Coalition has two thousand chapters in the United States with 1.7 million members. The coalition's staff of fifty is headquartered in Chesapeake, Virginia. With a budget of more than $27 million, the coalition has the resources to mount nationwide campaigns on public policy issues.

In 1996 the Federal Elections Commission sued the Christian Coalition in federal court, alleging that the organization violated campaign laws by working directly with particular candidates and tailoring its voter guides to favor Republicans. The coalition has denied the allegations, and the lawsuit is pending.

Website: www.cc.org

## ELECTRONIC FRONTIER FOUNDATION

The Electronic Frontier Foundation (EFF) is a nonprofit organization that seeks to ensure that civil liberties are protected as new communications technologies emerge. With the dramatic growth of the Internet and the use of E-mail, the World Wide Web, and other forms of electronic communication, the EFF seeks to balance legitimate public concerns about the distribution of sexually explicit materials, the protection of intellectual property, and the right to privacy with the need for free speech and the open communication of ideas.

The EFF was founded in 1990 by Mitchell D. Kapor, founder of Lotus Development Corporation, and his colleague John Perry Barlow. Kapor and Steve Wozniak, cofounder of Apple Computer, Inc., provided the initial funding for the EFF, but the foundation now derives its income from membership fees and private contributions. The foundation's headquarters are in San Francisco, California.

The EFF's mission is not only to increase public awareness about civil liberties issues arising in the area of computer-based communications but also to support litigation in the public interest. It submits amicus curiae (friend of the court) briefs and finds pro bono counsel when possible for important legal cases. The EFF monitors the on-line community for legal actions that merit EFF support.

The EFF joined numerous other plaintiffs in challenging the constitutionality of the Communications Decency Act of 1996 (CDA) (47 U.S.C.A. § 223(a) et seq.), which sought to prevent children from accessing "indecent" materials on the Internet. The U.S. Supreme Court responded, ruling in *Reno v. American Civil Liberties Union*, ___U.S.___, 117 S. Ct. 2329, 138 L. Ed. 2d 874 (1997), that the provisions concerning indecent and "patently offensive materials" were unconstitutional.

The foundation also produces legal memoranda informing bulletin board operators, telephone companies, and public utility commissions about the civil liberties implications of their actions. The EFF works with EFF members and groups of members on state and local levels to affect local legislation. To raise public awareness, EFF members speak to law enforcement organizations, bar associations, and conferences on the work that the EFF performs and suggests how these groups can get involved.

To ensure the free flow of information, the EFF has lobbied for laws that are based on common carrier principles, which require network providers to carry all speech, regardless of its controversial content. The EFF advocates a new common carrier system, based on minimal regulation, in which system operators are shielded from liability for the actions of users. The EFF also has lobbied Congress for legislation that would promote broader public access to information. On the other hand, the foundation supports efforts to enhance privacy in electronic communications. It believes that the public has a right to use the most effective encryption technologies available.

Website: www.eff.org

## HERITAGE FOUNDATION

The Heritage Foundation is a research and educational institute, popularly known as a "think tank," whose mission is to formulate and promote conservative public policies based on the principles of free enterprise, limited government, individual freedom, traditional values, and a strong national defense. Founded in 1973, the Heritage Foundation has proven to be effective, gaining national influence during the administrations of Presidents Ronald Reagan and George Bush. This influence has grown in the 1990s, as conservative Republicans gained control of Congress in 1994. Speaker of the House Newt Gingrich of Georgia declared just after the 1994 election, "Heritage is, without question, the most far-reaching conservative organization in the country in the war of ideas, and one which has had a tremendous impact not just in Washington, but literally across the planet."

The Heritage Foundation is a nonpartisan, tax-exempt institution and is governed by an independent board of trustees. It relies on the private financial support of individuals, foundations, and corporations for its income and accepts no government funds and performs no contract work. Currently, it receives support from more than 200,000 contributors. Its headquarters are in Washington, D.C.

The staff of the Heritage Foundation includes policy and research analysts who examine issues in a wide variety of fields, including the legislative and executive branches of government, domestic policy, education, corporations, foreign policy, the United Nations, Asian studies, and other areas of public concern. Once the researchers have made their findings, the foundation markets the results to its primary audiences: members of Congress, key congressional staff members, policy makers in the executive branch, the news media, and the academic and policy communities.

The Heritage Foundation also publicizes its work through weekly, monthly, and quarterly periodicals, including *Policy Review*. It also provides public speakers to promote its positions and convenes conferences and meetings on policy issues.

The Heritage Foundation has played an important role in advancing conservative ideas, especially after the election of Republican majorities in the U.S. House of Representatives and Senate in 1994. The Republican "Contract with America" agenda sought major changes in the size and power of the federal government. Heritage Foundation staff played a key role behind the scenes in helping to craft and refine legislative proposals. The overhaul of the system of agricultural subsidies and the first comprehensive rewriting of the telecommunications law embraced free-market approaches advocated by the foundation. Its research and proposals also shaped the 1996 welfare reform bill. It currently is working with Congress on reform of the federal tax system.

Website: www.heritage.org

## MOTHERS AGAINST DRUNK DRIVING

Mothers Against Drunk Driving (MADD) is a nonprofit organization with more than six hundred chapters nationwide. MADD seeks to find effective solutions to the problems of drunk driving and underage drinking, while also supporting those persons whose relatives and friends have been killed by drunk drivers. MADD has proved to be an effective organization, successfully lobbying for tougher laws against drunk drivers.

MADD was founded by a small group of California women in 1980 after thirteen-year-old Cari Lightner was killed by a hit-and-run driver who had previous drunk driving convictions. Although the offender was sentenced to two years in prison, the judge allowed him to serve time instead in a work camp and a halfway house. Candy Lightner, the victim's mother, worked to call attention to the need for more appropriate, vigorous, and equitable actions on the part of law enforcement and the courts in response to alcohol-related traffic deaths and injuries. Lightner and a handful of volunteers campaigned for tougher laws against impaired driving, stiffer penalties for committing crimes, and greater awareness about the seriousness of driving drunk.

As the California group drew public attention, other individuals who had lost relatives or who had been injured by drunk drivers formed local chapters. By 1997 MADD's membership had grown to three million people, making it the largest victim-advocate and anti-drunk-driving organization in the United States and the world. In addition to local chapters, MADD has state offices in twenty-nine of the fifty states. Coordination of the organization is handled by a national headquarters staff of approximately sixty individuals located in Irving, Texas, who direct training, seasonal and ongoing education and awareness programs, national fund-raising, media campaigns, and federal and state legislative activities.

Beginning in 1995, MADD embarked on a five-year plan to reduce the proportion of alcohol-related traffic fatalities by 20 percent by the year 2000. This "20 by 2000" campaign is a comprehensive approach that embraces both previous positions and goals, and new objectives. Five main areas are addressed: youth issues, enforcement of laws, sanctions, self-sufficiency, and responsible marketing and service.

Youth issues include enforcement of the twenty-one-year age requirement for purchasing and consuming alcohol, zero tolerance for underage drivers who drink, and limits on advertising and marketing of alcoholic beverages to young people.

MADD also endorses the use of sobriety checkpoints by law enforcement and the lowering of the blood alcohol count for drunk driving to .08 percent. As for sanctions, MADD advocates administrative revocation of the licenses of drunk drivers, the confiscation of license plates and vehicles, progressive sanctions for repeat offenders, and mandatory confinement for repeat offenders. The organization wants drunk drivers to pay for the cost of the system that arrests, convicts, and punishes them. Funding for enforcement through fines, fees, and other assessments will make this system self-sufficient. Finally, MADD wants businesses that serve alcohol to be more vigorous in preventing customers from becoming intoxicated. MADD seeks the end of "happy hours" and other promotions that encourage irresponsible drinking.

Website: www.madd.org

## NATIONAL ABORTION AND REPRODUCTIVE RIGHTS ACTION LEAGUE

The National Abortion and Reproductive Rights Action League (NARAL) is a nonprofit organization that is primarily concerned with maintaining a woman's legal right to have an abortion. The mission of NARAL, however, has broadened to include supporting policies that enable women and men to make responsible decisions about sexuality, contraception, pregnancy, childbirth, and abortion. NARAL, which was founded in 1969, is comprised of a network of thirty-five state affiliates and has 500,000 members. It has proven to be an effective organization, promoting pro-choice candidates for state and federal offices and lobbying for pro-choice legislation.

Since the U.S. Supreme Court legalized abortion in *Roe v. Wade*, 410 U.S. 113, 93 S. Ct. 705, 35 L. Ed. 2d 147 (1973), opponents of abortion have sought to overturn or limit this decision. NARAL has vigorously defended *Roe* but has also encouraged better sex education and the use of birth control to make abortion less necessary. Through NARAL-PAC, its political action committee, NARAL has been a driving force behind the election of many pro-choice candidates. NARAL-PAC mounts campaigns to elect pro-choice candidates and defeat candidates opposed to legalized abortion, using paid advertising and get-out-the-vote efforts.

The NARAL Foundation, a charitable organization founded in 1977, supports research and legal work, publishes substantive policy reports, mounts public education campaigns and other communications projects, and provides leadership training for grassroots activists. The NARAL Foundation and NARAL employ a computerized state-by-state database, NARAL*STAR (State Tracking of Abortion Rights), which provides up-to-the-minute information for NARAL staff, affiliates, policy makers, media, and coalition partners on state laws related to reproductive rights, pending legislation, state constitutions, and state executive branches.

NARAL and the NARAL Foundation regularly publish *Who Decides? A State-by-State Review of Abortion Rights*, a compilation of abortion-related information in each state, including the position on choice of elected officials, summaries of selected statutes and regulations, and recent legislative activity.

NARAL worked with the Clinton administration to reverse policies of the Reagan and Bush administrations dealing with abortion. It helped remove bans on the testing of RU-486 (a nonsurgical abortion method), the use of fetal tissue in scientific research, and the provision of abortion services at military hospitals. NARAL also played a major role in the passage of the Freedom of Access to Clinic Entrances Act, which places certain restrictions on protestors' ability to obstruct or hinder persons seeking access to abortion services. Since 1996, when Congress enacted a bill banning the practice of partial-birth abortions, NARAL has been on the defensive. Though President Bill Clinton vetoed the bill, many states have since passed laws banning the procedure, and Congress continues to debate the issue.

Website: www.naral.org

## NATIONAL ASSOCIATION FOR THE ADVANCEMENT OF COLORED PEOPLE

The National Association for the Advancement of Colored People (NAACP) is the oldest and largest civil rights organization in the United States, with a membership exceeding 500,000. The principal objective of the NAACP is to ensure the political, educational, social, and economic equality of minority-group citizens of the United States. The NAACP seeks to achieve equality through nonviolence and relies upon the media, the ballot, and the courts to press its point of view. The organization is a network of more than 2,200 branches covering all fifty states, the District of Columbia, Japan, and Germany. The branch offices are divided into seven regions and are managed and governed by a national board of directors. The NAACP is headquartered in Baltimore, Maryland.

The NAACP was established in 1909 but had its roots in the Niagara Movement, which was formed in 1905 by a group of African American intellectuals led by W. E. B. Du Bois. The group demanded full civil rights for African Americans. In 1909 the Niagara Movement joined with white socialists and liberals to form the NAACP. The organization drew national attention in 1915 when it organized a national boycott of D. W. Griffith's film *Birth of a Nation*, which portrayed African Americans in racially derogatory stereotypes.

From its inception, the NAACP has used the courts to fight racial discrimination. It attacked voting discrimination in the southern states and forced the elimination of grandfather clauses and white primaries. The NAACP's most significant achievement, however, was its twenty-year campaign to end racial segregation in public education. This legal battle culminated in the 1954 U.S. Supreme Court decision in *Brown v. Board of Education*, 347 U.S. 483, 74 S. Ct. 686, 98 L. Ed. 873, which prohibited state-imposed racially segregated public schools.

The NAACP underwent a period of turmoil in the 1990s when Benjamin F. Chavis, Jr., its executive director, and members of the board of directors were accused of financial and administrative mismanagement. In 1995 the board elected as chair Myrlie Evers-Williams, who succeeded in recruiting former Maryland Congressman Kweisi Mfume to become president of the NAACP.

The NAACP continues to emphasize legal action dealing with major issues such as employment, housing, voting, and education. It also lobbies Congress on civil rights legislation. In the 1990s it started the Environmental Justice Program, which publicizes industries that are located in minority communities. Nevertheless, president Mfume has acknowledged that the NAACP is at a critical point in its history. He has worked to rebuild the membership and revitalize the organization. The focus for rebuilding the NAACP is based on voter empowerment, educational excellence, and individual responsibility; creation of an infrastructure for economic and social parity; and development of new and effective ways to involve young people.

Website: www.naacp.org

## NATIONAL ASSOCIATION OF BROADCASTERS

The National Association of Broadcasters (NAB) is comprised of representatives of radio and television stations and networks. The NAB, which has a membership of 7,500, seeks to ensure the viability, strength, and success of free over-the-air broadcasters (companies that do not charge customers for service, as do cable and satellite television operators). It serves as an information resource to the industry, and it also lobbies the Federal Communications Commission (FCC) for regulations favorable to the radio and television industry. The NAB is headquartered in Washington, D.C., with a staff of approximately 165 employees.

The organization was founded in 1922, when radio broadcasting was in its infancy. Founded as the National Association of Radio Broadcasters, it changed its name to the National Association of Radio and Television Broadcasters in 1951, when it absorbed the Television Broadcasters Association. In 1958 it changed its name to the NAB. In 1985 it absorbed the Daytime Broadcasters Association, and in 1986 it absorbed the National Radio Broadcasters Association.

The NAB seeks to maintain a favorable legal, governmental, and technological climate for free over-the-air broadcasting. Its legal and regulatory department represents broadcasters before the FCC and other federal agencies, as well as before courts and other regulatory bodies. This department provides legal guidance to NAB members through "counsel memos," legal memoranda that identify and explain current legal issues for broadcasters.

The NAB opposes legislation that would require broadcasters to provide free air time to political candidates. In addition, it is opposed to discounting the commercial rates stations charge to candidates, contending that broadcasters now provide candidates with heavily discounted air time.

Because the NAB represents the interests of free over-the-air broadcasters, it has sought to protect the industry from the inroads made by cable and satellite television. For example, as TV viewers in rural areas began to buy home satellite equipment, Congress passed laws in 1988 and 1994, with the encouragement of the NAB, that restrict access to network programming sent by satellite only to those viewers who live outside the local market of over-the-air network affiliates. By 1997 satellite operators and the NAB were in court, because the NAB sought to end the practice of some operators who flout the law and provide network signals to satellite subscribers who are already served by their local network affiliates.

Aside from lobbying and bringing legal actions, the NAB provides members with other benefits. Its research library contains ten thousand volumes, and its staff includes experts in science and technology and research and planning. For its members, the NAB publishes a monthly newsletter, *NAB World*, as well as the weekly publications *RadioWeek* and *TV Today*. The NAB's annual spring convention is the world's largest showcase for broadcast, postproduction multimedia and telecommunications hardware, software, and services. The convention draws more than 100,000 attendees.

Website: www.nab.org

## NATIONAL ASSOCIATION OF MANUFACTURERS

The National Association of Manufacturers (NAM) is the oldest and largest broad-based industrial trade association in the United States. NAM seeks to enhance the competitiveness of manufacturers by lobbying for legislation and regulations conducive to U.S. economic growth and to increase understanding among policy makers, the media, and the general public about the importance of manufacturing to U.S. economic strength. NAM is comprised of more than fourteen thousand member companies and subsidiaries, including almost ten thousand small manufacturers. NAM members, which represent more than 80 percent of U.S. industry, produce about 85 percent of U.S. manufactured goods and employ more than eighteen million persons. The NAM is headquartered in Washington, D.C., with ten regional offices located across the United States.

NAM was founded in Cincinnati, Ohio, in 1895, in the midst of a deep economic recession. Many major manufacturers saw a need to find new markets for their products in other countries. At its organizing convention, the NAM adopted a number of objectives, including the retention and supply of home markets with U.S.

products, extension of foreign trade, development of reciprocal trade relations between the United States and foreign governments, rehabilitation of the U.S. Merchant Marine, construction of a canal in Central America, and improvement and extension of U.S. waterways.

NAM soon became a dominant influence in U.S. economic and politic affairs. It lobbied for higher tariffs on imported goods and for the creation of the U.S. Department of Commerce in 1903, and it called for states to enact workers' compensation laws. During the 1930s, the NAM vigorously opposed many of President Franklin D. Roosevelt's New Deal proposals. In the 1940s and 1950s, it lobbied for the passage of federal laws restricting the power and internal governance of labor unions.

In the 1990s, NAM has undertaken new initiatives. The Manufacturing Institute was established to provide information on modern industry. This organization distributes monthly mailings to Congress, conducts research on technology and exports, produces research reports, commissions public opinion polls, and disperses books and educational CD-ROMs to schools.

The NAM and the Manufacturing Institute joined forces in the 1990s with key partners in the Partnership for a Smarter Workforce and other efforts to identify the best ways to train employees. In 1997 the institute established the Center for Workforce Success and an awards program for outstanding manufacturing workers. In addition, NAM has lobbied for increased accountability and results in taxpayer-funded training programs.

NAM has increased its lobbying on international economic issues. The association played a key role in a number of trade policy victories during the 1990s, including the North American Free Trade Agreement (NAFTA) and the certification of China as a most favored nation. NAM also lobbied vigorously for a national campaign to facilitate exports.

Website: www.nam.org

## NATIONAL ASSOCIATION OF REALTORS

The National Association of Realtors (NAR) is made up of residential and commercial realtors who are brokers, salespeople, property managers, appraisers, and counselors, and others working in the real estate industry. The NAR began in 1908 with a membership of 120.

In 1998 its membership numbered 720,000, making it the world's largest professional association. Members belong to one or more of 1,700 local real estate associations and boards and fifty-four state and territory associations. The NAR's headquarters are located in Washington, D.C.

The NAR provides a national facility for professional development, research, and exchange of information among its members and to the public and government. More importantly, it plays an influential role in shaping public policies at the local, state, and national level that affect real property. Through its legislative and lobbying efforts, the NAR seeks to protect the real estate industry from what it considers burdensome legislative and regulatory changes and to advocate for legislative and regulatory changes that enhance the conduct of real estate business. At the national level, the NAR analyzes federal issues and lobbies Congress and regulatory agencies.

The NAR's 1998 legislative agenda included rewriting federal law that governs the disclosure of closing costs at the time a real estate purchase is completed. In addition, the NAR supports federal legislation that would give persons more rights to contest a government "taking" of their property through the power of eminent domain.

The NAR also participates in the political process through its Realtor Political Action Committee. This committee contributes to campaign funds to federal political candidates and encourages members to volunteer for candidates. The committee also educates voters on issues that affect home ownership and real estate.

Apart from political involvement, the NAR seeks to make its viewpoint known through legal advocacy. The NAR's Legal Action Committee provides financial support to legal cases that will establish a favorable precedent for real estate brokerage or that preserve the rights to own, use, and transfer real property. The NAR also participates in lawsuits involving real estate by filing amicus curiae (friend of the court) briefs in cases that will set legal precedent.

The NAR has established a code of ethics to enhance the professionalism of its members. In addition, it has created NAR sections, professional institutes, societies, and counsels that allow members to communicate with others in their particular real estate specialty. These speciality groups include Counselors of Real Estate, the Commercial Investment Real Estate Institute, the Institute of Real Estate Management, the Real Estate Brokerage Managers Council, the Residential Sales Council, the Real Estate Buyers Agent Council, and the Appraisal Section. Education and certification in these specializations enable members to receive professional designations, identifying them as highly qualified specialists to business associates and the public.

Website: www.nar.realtors.com

## NATIONAL EDUCATION ASSOCIATION

The National Education Association (NEA) is a nonprofit and nonpartisan professional organization made up of school teachers, administrators, and others interested in public education. The NEA, which was founded in 1857, is the oldest and largest organization dealing with public education. The organization has more than 2.2 million members and is headquartered in Washington, D.C. The NEA has affiliates in every state and in more than 13,000 local communities across the United States. Anyone who works for a public school district, a college or university, or any other public institution devoted primarily to education is eligible to join the NEA. It also has special membership categories for retired educators and college students studying to become teachers.

The NEA is a volunteer-based organization supported by a network of staff at the local, state, and national levels. At the local level, NEA affiliates are active in a wide variety of activities, such as conducting professional workshops on discipline and bargaining contracts for school district employees. At the state level, NEA affiliates regularly lobby legislators for the funds for public education, campaign for higher professional standards for the teaching profession, and file legal actions to protect academic freedom. At the national level, the NEA coordinates innovative projects to restructure how learning takes place and lobbies Congress on behalf of public education.

NEA members nationwide set association policy, meeting at their annual representative assembly every July. NEA members at the state and local levels elect the more than nine thousand assembly delegates, who, in turn, elect the NEA's top officers, debate issues, and set NEA policy.

The NEA has been a vigorous opponent of efforts to privatize education through the use of tuition vouchers. It rejects the arguments of voucher advocates that vouchers improve student learning, provide meaningful parental choice, and increase educational opportunities for low-income students. Instead, the NEA contends that vouchers are costly and that they are not the panacea for the problems in public education.

The NEA has also expressed concerns about laws that allow the creation of charter schools, which are deregulated, autonomous public schools. Advocates of charter schools believe that freeing some public schools from many state and local mandates will encourage educational innovation, create greater parental involvement, and promote improvement of public education in general. The NEA, while not opposing the concept of charter schools, has lobbied for sufficient oversight of these new schools, believing that public accountability is necessary.

## NATIONAL FEDERATION OF INDEPENDENT BUSINESSES

The National Federation of Independent Businesses (NFIB) is the largest U.S. advocacy organization representing small and independent businesses. The NFIB has a membership of 600,000 business owners, including commercial enterprises, manufacturers, family farmers, neighborhood retailers, and service companies. The total membership employs more than seven million people and reports annual gross sales of approximately $747 billion.

Founded in 1943, the NFIB was created to give small and independent business a voice in government decision making. The NFIB is recognized as one the most influential lobbying organizations in the United States, working with state and federal legislators and regulators. Its administrative headquarters are located in Nashville, Tennessee, but its public policy headquarters are in Washington, D.C. The NFIB also has state legislative offices in all fifty state capitals.

The governance of the NFIB differs from that of more traditional lobbying organizations. The NFIB uses the balloting of its membership, rather than a steering committee or a board of directors, to determine NFIB policies. In addition, it seeks to prevent undue influence by one member or group of members by setting a maximum contribution of dues. Minimum dues are

$100, and the maximum is $1,000. The NFIB follows these procedures so that the policies it advances will reflect the consensus of the business community rather than the narrow interests of any particular trade group. Once the ballots are counted—five times a year on federal issues and at least once a year on state issues—NFIB's lobbyists carry the message to Congress and the state legislatures.

The NFIB opposes higher taxes on business and government regulation. At the state level, it works to lower the rates businesses are required to pay for workers' compensation insurance. At the federal level, it has campaigned for cutting the federal deficit, stopped an effort to raise employment taxes, and fought to increase the deductibility of health insurance premiums for the self-employed.

The NFIB has been a critic of the Environmental Protection Agency, the Occupational Safety and Health Administration, and the Internal Revenue Service, believing that these federal agencies stifle the productivity and profitability of business through overregulation. It emphasizes the need for a free-market economy, noting that small business produces 38 percent of the gross domestic product.

As part of its 1998 agenda, the NFIB has begun a campaign to abolish the Internal Revenue Code. It contends that the code cannot be repaired but must be replaced with a simpler, fairer tax code. The NFIB has started a nationwide drive encouraging small business owners to sign a petition calling on the president and Congress to abolish the Internal Revenue Service Code.

Website: www.nfib.org

## NATIONAL GAY AND LESBIAN TASK FORCE

The National Gay and Lesbian Task Force (NGLTF) is a nonprofit organization that supports grassroots organizing and advocacy for lesbian, gay, bisexual, and transgender rights. Founded in 1973, NGLTF works to strengthen the gay and lesbian movement at the state and local levels while connecting these activities to a national agenda. It is recognized as the leading activist organization in the national gay and lesbian movement and serves as a national resource center for state and local organizations. Its headquarters are in Washington, D.C.

NGLTF works to combat antigay violence and antigay legislative and ballot measures. It also lobbies state and federal governments to end job discrimination and repeal sodomy laws. With the arrival of HIV and AIDS in the 1980s, NGLTF has sought government funding of medical research and has campaigned for the reform of the health care system.

In 1997 NGLTF played a major role in the creation of a new national political organization, the Federation of Statewide Lesbian, Gay, Bisexual, and Transgender Political Organizations. The purpose of the federation, which draws its membership from thirty-two state groups, is to strengthen the efforts of these statewide groups through a network that will foster strategizing across state lines, building stronger state organizations, and developing good working relationships between state and national groups. The need for the federation grew out of meetings of statewide activists at NGLTF's annual Creating Change Conference, held each November in a major U.S. city.

The federation consists of thirteen executive committee members, selected from each region of the country, who will develop the federation's mission. NGLTF serves as coordinator of the federation, supporting its work through the creation and dissemination of information and materials, and regular conference calls.

At the federal level, NGLTF was unsuccessful in its opposition to the 1996 Defense of Marriage Act (DOMA), which permits states to bar legal recognition of same-sex marriages performed in other states. In 1988 NGLTF renewed its efforts to have Congress expand the federal mandate for prosecution of hate crimes to include crimes that are committed against people because of their sexual orientation. The Hate Crimes Prevention Act (S. 1529 and H.R. 3081) would add hate crimes based on an individual's real or perceived sexual orientation to the list of bias crimes that the federal government can prosecute.

NGLTF, through its policy institute, conducts research and publishes studies on many topics, including civil rights, workplace discrimination, violence, health, campus activities, and families.

Website: www.ngltf.org

## NATIONAL ORGANIZATION FOR THE REFORM OF MARIJUANA LAWS

The National Organization for the Reform of Marijuana Laws (NORML) is a nonprofit organization dedicated to the legalization of marijuana. Founded in 1970, NORML remains the leading national advocate for legalization. NORML, which believes it should be legal for adults to smoke marijuana privately, seeks the repeal of federal antimarijuana laws. Repeal would allow states to experiment with different models of legalization. During the 1970s, NORML led the successful efforts to decriminalize minor marijuana offenses in eleven states and significantly lower penalties in all others. During the 1980s, however, the decriminalization movement lost political appeal when Presidents Ronald Reagan and George Bush committed their administrations to the "war on drugs."

NORML has a five-person staff at its national headquarters in Washington, D.C. It is governed by a board of directors which, in 1997, included prominent attorneys, scientists, and researchers. NORML provides information to the national news media for marijuana-related stories and lobbies state and federal legislators to permit the medical use of marijuana and to reject attempts to treat minor marijuana offenses more harshly. NORML also functions as the umbrella group for a national network of activists committed to ending marijuana prohibition.

NORML also assists those who are arrested on marijuana charges through a legal committee (NLC) comprised of two hundred criminal defense attorneys. The NLC also sponsors NORML legal seminars, notifies NORML of important judicial decisions and law enforcement trends, and provides NORML with copies of briefs and other legal documents. These lawyers regularly defend victims of marijuana prohibition and sometimes set important legal precedents.

The NORML amicus curiae committee files amicus curiae (friend of the court) briefs in important or novel marijuana-related legal actions at the appellate court level. This committee, which is comprised of experienced NORML criminal defense attorneys from around the country, gives NORML the opportunity to contribute its point of view in cases that may have national importance.

NORML has actively supported efforts to legalize the medical use of marijuana. In 1996 California and Arizona voters passed initiatives that permit the medical use of marijuana, but federal law still prohibits such use. NORML supports legislation to allow physicians to legally prescribe marijuana for those patients suffering from serious illnesses and medical symptoms, including glaucoma, AIDS, multiple sclerosis, quadriplegia and paraplegia, and the side effects of chemotherapy.

Website: www.norml.org

## NATIONAL ORGANIZATION FOR WOMEN

The National Organization for Women (NOW) is the largest organization of feminist activists in the United States, numbering more than 250,000 members. A nonpartisan organization, it has six hundred chapters in all fifty states. It receives its funding from membership dues and private donations. NOW has used both traditional and nontraditional means to push for social change. Traditional activities have included extensive electoral and lobbying work, and the filing of lawsuits. NOW also has organized mass marches, rallies, pickets, counter-demonstrations, and nonviolent civil disobedience. Its headquarters are located in Washington, D.C.

NOW was established in 1966 in Washington, D.C., by people attending the Third National Conference of the Commission on the Status of Women. Among NOW's twenty-eight founders was its first president, Betty Friedan, author of *The Feminine Mystique* (1963). In its original statement of purpose, NOW declared to "take action to bring women into full participation in the mainstream of American society now, exercising all privileges and responsibilities thereof in truly equal partnership with men."

As part of its efforts to pursue economic equality and other rights for women, NOW launched a nationwide campaign in the 1970s to pass the Equal Rights Amendment (ERA) to the U.S. Constitution. Though the ERA ultimately failed to be ratified, NOW's efforts helped the organization. NOW became a huge network of more than 200,000 activists and began operating with multimillion-dollar annual budgets. Leaders organized political action committees, NOW/PAC and NOW Equality PAC, that raised hundreds of thousands of dollars for pro-ERA candidates.

NOW's priorities are economic equality, including an amendment to the U.S. Constitution that will guarantee equal rights for women; championing abortion rights, reproductive freedom, and other women's health issues; opposing racism and opposing bigotry against lesbians and gays; and ending violence against women. The organization has proved effective in many of these areas. NOW points to sweeping changes that put more women in political posts, increased educational, employment, and business opportunities for women, and the enactment of tougher laws against violence, sexual harassment, and discrimination.

Its 1992 "Elect Women for a Change" campaign sent an unprecedented number of feminist women and men to the U.S. Congress. NOW has combated harassment and violence by organizing the first "Take Back the Night" marches and establishing hot lines and shelters for battered women. NOW has also successfully prosecuted lawsuits against antiabortion groups that bombed and blocked clinics and laws that deprived lesbian women of custody of their children. NOW has also consistently sought economic equality for women in the workplace, exposing both the "glass ceiling" that professional women face in advancing in the workplace and the difficult circumstances that poor women face in the United States.

Website: www.now.org

## NATIONAL RIFLE ASSOCIATION

The National Rifle Association (NRA) is a nonpartisan organization that promotes the sport of shooting rifles and pistols in the United States. The NRA's almost 3 million members include hunters, target shooters, gun collectors, firearms manufacturers, and police personnel. Since the 1960s, the NRA has been the leading opponent of any type of gun control legislation, mobilizing its members to lobby Congress and state legislatures. From its headquarters in Washington, D.C., the NRA has been a dominant voice in the debate over gun control.

The NRA was incorporated in 1871 to provide firearms training and encourage interest in the shooting sports. The organization grew steadily and now is directed by a seventy-six-member board of directors elected by its voting members. The NRA has thirty-six standing and special committees, that oversee the organization's various activities, as well as a paid staff of more than three hundred persons at its main headquarters, which are located in Fairfax, Virginia.

The NRA has divisions representing firearms safety, firearms training, law enforcement programs, junior shooting activities, women's issues, hunter services, recreational shooting, competitions, and gun collecting. The NRA staff works with such diverse groups as the Boy Scouts of America, 4-H clubs, The American Legion, Veterans of Foreign Wars, hunting and shooting clubs, schools, and law enforcement organizations. It is nationally known for its opposition to gun control and has a division dedicated to combating such legislation. The NRA believes that the U.S. Constitution's Second Amendment prohibits any government unit from restricting citizens from owning firearms.

The NRA in the 1990s, in addition to fighting gun control, has worked to pass state laws that make it easier for gun owners to carry their weapons in public. The "right-to-carry" movement is based on the idea that any trained, law-abiding citizen has a right to get a permit from the government to carry a firearm. As a result of the NRA's lobbying efforts, fourteen states have passed right-to-carry laws and twenty-four other states have liberalized their statutes.

The NRA has also fought efforts by city and county governments to regulate firearms. It has lobbied for state preemption statutes, which declare that only the state government may pass firearms laws. Through its efforts, Wisconsin, Pennsylvania, and several other states passed preemption laws in 1995.

Despite its longtime success in fighting gun control, the NRA's increasingly belligerent rhetoric became a problem for the organization in 1995. Former President George Bush, a lifetime member, resigned from the NRA to protest a fund-raising letter that contained antigovernment statements.

Website: www.nra.org

## NATIONAL RIGHT TO LIFE COMMITTEE

The National Right to Life Committee (NRLC) is a nonprofit organization that seeks to end legalized abortion in the United States. Founded in 1973, following the U.S. Supreme Court's decision in *Roe v. Wade*, 410 U.S. 113, 93 S. Ct. 705, 35 L. Ed. 2d 147 (1973), that women had a constitutional right to abortion, the NRLC has become the leading antiabortion organization in the United States. It has more than seven million members, with three thousand local chapters in all fifty states. It is headquartered in Washington, D.C., and has an annual budget of more than $9 million. The

*National Right to Life News*, a biweekly newsletter, has a circulation of 135,000.

From its inception, the NRLC has sought the passage of a constitutional amendment banning abortion. Though this effort has not been successful, the NRLC has played an important role in state and federal legislation regulating and restricting abortion and has been instrumental in restricting government funding of abortions to poor women. The NRLC has a political action committee that endorses and campaigns for candidates who support its agenda, which includes opposition to some forms of birth control as well as physician-assisted suicide.

The NRLC has lobbied for federal legislation banning partial-birth abortions. Though Congress passed the Partial-Birth Abortion Ban Act in 1996 and 1997, President Bill Clinton vetoed the measure both times. The act remains the highest priority of the NRLC, which has helped secure state legislation banning the abortion procedure in seventeen states. It also supports legislation that would make it a federal offense to transport an individual age seventeen or under across a state line for an abortion if this action circumvents the application of a state law requiring parental involvement in a minor's abortion.

The NRLC operates four outreach programs: National Teens for Life, American Victims of Abortion, National Pro-Life Religious Council, and Black Americans for Life. National Teens for Life organizes various activities for its teenage members, including speaking in schools and to youth groups, volunteering in crisis pregnancy centers, peer counseling, debating, and helping adult groups work to pass legislation. American Victims of Abortion is comprised of women who have had an abortion. This group lobbies legislators and seeks to educate the media about the physical and emotional risks associated with abortion. The National Pro-Life Religious Council seeks "to articulate the historic Judeo-Christian perspective concerning human life issues," and "to support efforts that discourage and prevent acts that dehumanize and harm women, the unborn, disabled persons, the elderly and those who are medically dependent." Black Americans for Life attempts to discourage African American women from having abortions.

Website: www.nrlc.org

## SIERRA CLUB

The Sierra Club is a nonprofit, member-supported public interest organization that promotes conservation of the natural environment by influencing public policy decisions. In addition, the Sierra Club organizes participation in wilderness activities for its members, including mountain climbing, backpacking, and camping. It is the oldest and largest nonprofit, grassroots environmental organization in the world, with more than 630,000 members. The Sierra Club is comprised of the national organization, located in San Francisco, California, fifty-eight chapters, and 409 local groups.

The organization was founded on June 4, 1892, by a group of 162 California residents. The Sierra Club's first president was John Muir, a pioneer in the promotion of national parks and the protection of the environment. Muir involved the club in political action, leading a successful fight to preserve Yosemite as a national park. Muir and the club also lobbied for the creation of national parks at the Grand Canyon and Mt. Rainier in the late nineteenth century. The Sierra Club drew national attention during the administration of President Theodore Roosevelt, when Muir got the president interested in creating more national parks.

The Sierra Club did not seek members outside of California until 1950, when membership stood at ten thousand. Membership has increased dramatically since that time, due in large part to the club's intense interest in protecting the environment. Since 1970 the club has played a major role in gaining legislative support for many federal environmental protection measures, including the establishment of the Environmental Protection Agency and the Arctic National Wildlife Refuge and the passage of the Endangered Species Act, the Clean Air Act, the Clean Water Act, the National Forest Management Act, and the Alaska National Interest Lands Conservation Act. The Sierra Club has also campaigned for similar state legislation.

During the 1990s, the Sierra Club has filed lawsuits that seek to require the federal government to enforce provisions of the Endangered Species Act and the Clean Air Act. The club's current agenda also includes pushing for toxic cleanup, resolving the problems of solid waste disposal, promoting sustainable population and family planning, and fighting to reverse ozone depletion and global warming.

Website: www.sierrac.org

## TOBACCO INSTITUTE

The Tobacco Institute (TI) is a public relations and lobbying organization that represents the interests of the twelve companies that fund it. The mission of the TI is to increase awareness of the historic role of tobacco and its place in the national economy and to foster understanding of tobacco-related issues. The institute has been a controversial organization: critics of tobacco products have charged it with using sophisticated propaganda techniques and high-powered lobbying to manipulate public opinion and public policy.

The Tobacco Institute was founded in 1958 by the major U.S. tobacco manufacturers and has an estimated annual budget of more than $20 million. It is headquartered in Washington, D.C., and has a staff of fifty. The institute's publications include two annual reports, *Tax Burden on Tobacco* and *Tobacco Industry Profile*. It also publishes historic, economic, and topical material.

The TI was established in response to a growing public health movement in the 1950s against smoking. From its inception, it has stressed the contribution of tobacco to the U.S. economy and the preservation of tobacco farms. It also has stressed the inconclusiveness and inconsistency of antismoking findings and has supported the rights of individual smokers to smoke in public places. The TI has publicized the research findings of the Council for Tobacco Research, an organization funded by the tobacco companies, that dispute critics' claims that tobacco has harmful effects and addictive properties. Historically, the TI has fought efforts to raise the federal cigarette tax and to label tobacco products as being hazardous to health.

The TI's lobbying efforts in Washington, D.C., have proved effective. Aside from informing legislators about tobacco-related issues, the TI has made significant political contributions through its political action committee. In December 1997, it sponsored an all-expense-paid trip to Arizona for members of Congress and their staffs to discuss the proposed $368 billion national tobacco settlement that would compensate states that are suing the tobacco industry for smoking-related health care costs and fund antismoking programs.

Because the TI has a controversial role in defending tobacco companies and disputing claims that smoking causes illnesses, it has become part of the proposed national settlement. If Congress adopts the settlement, the TI will be dissolved and disbanded within ninety days.

## U.S. CHAMBER OF COMMERCE

The U.S. Chamber of Commerce is the world's largest federation of businesses, representing more than three million businesses and organizations in the United States. The chamber states that its mission is to "advance human progress through an economic, political and social system based on individual freedom, incentive, initiative, opportunity and responsibility." The chamber has historically been an influential lobbyist for legislation that favors the free enterprise system. It looks to its membership to help define policy on national issues critical to business. Once a policy is developed, the chamber informs Congress and the administration of the business community's recommendations on legislative issues and government policies.

The U.S. Chamber of Commerce was founded in 1912 at a conference called by President William Howard Taft in Washington, D.C. At the time of the conference, there were many local chambers of commerce throughout the United States. Chambers are now organized at the local, state, and regional levels, and all of them may hold membership in the national organization. The headquarters of the national chamber are in Washington D.C. It is controlled by a large national board of directors, with a chair and president elected by the board each year.

The chamber's policy division provides members with the opportunity to influence pro-business issues in Washington through the use of satellite video conferences and town hall meetings that are broadcast directly from the chamber offices. The division convenes meetings of business leaders and also provides opportunities for chamber members to meet with and question congressional candidates in small, informal gatherings.

The chamber's Small Business Institute (SBI) seeks to provide small business professionals and their employees with self-study training programs and interactive satellite seminars. Subjects include marketing, management, productivity, technology, and forecasting. The chamber also offers an on-line catalog that provides access to books, audio programs, videotapes, and software that deal with business topics.

Several affiliated organizations work closely with the chamber. The Center for International Private Enterprise (CIPE) was formed under congressional mandate in 1983. CIPE has sponsored nearly two hundred programs promoting economic growth and democratic development in more than forty countries worldwide as part of a program called the National Endowment for Democracy. The National Chamber Foundation (NCF) is a public policy research organization that concentrates on economic and business issues. It researches and analyzes issues and provides educational tools to improve understanding of economics and business. The Center for Leadership Development, the educational division of the NCF, conducts training for chamber and association managers and business executives.

The chamber publishes for its members the *Nation's Business*, a monthly magazine aimed at the owners and top management of small businesses. The magazine provides practical information about running and expanding an established business.

Website: www.chamber.org

## VETERANS OF FOREIGN WARS

The Veterans of Foreign Wars (VFW) is a U.S. organization comprised of men who have served overseas in the military services during World Wars I and II, the Korean War, the Vietnam War, and the Persian Gulf War. Veterans who served in expeditionary campaigns such as Grenada and Panama are also eligible to join. Female relatives of veterans and women who have served overseas in the armed forces are eligible to join the Ladies Auxiliary. In 1997, 2.1 million veterans belonged to the VFW, with 1.1 million having served in World War II. Its national headquarters are located in Kansas City, Missouri, but it also has a large office in Washington, D.C.

The VFW was established in 1913, consolidating three organizations created by Spanish-American War veterans. From its inception, the VFW has sought to promote patriotism and national security. Its paramount mission, however, has been ensuring that needy and disabled veterans receive aid. Beginning in 1922, it has sold a paper flower called the "Buddy Poppy," to raise funds for national service programs and relief for needy veterans and their families. The VFW fought for military pensions after World War I, planned the establishment of the Veterans Administration (VA) in 1930, lobbied for the GI Bill of Rights after World War II, and helped develop the national cemetery system for veterans. The VFW has also contributed millions of dollars to cancer research since the 1950s.

The VFW's National Legislative Service office in Washington, D.C., monitors legislation that affects veterans. It alerts the membership to key legislation and lobbies Congress and the executive branch on veterans issues. The office often assists congressional staffs in preparing legislation. In the late 1990s, the VFW legislative goals include a VA budget with sufficient funds to provide adequate veterans health care, a cost-of-living adjustment for VA beneficiaries and military retirees equal to the consumer price index, and vocational training and retraining for veterans.

The VFW has almost 16,000 trained service officers to assist veterans and their dependents in gaining federal or state entitlements. These service officers help with military discharge upgrades, records correction, education benefits, disability compensation, pension eligibility, and other types of veterans issues. Field representatives conduct regular inspections of VA health care facilities, regional VA offices, and national cemeteries.

Historically, the VFW has promoted patriotism through its "Americanism Program." It provides materials and information and sponsors events and activities that are designed to stimulate interest in U.S. history, traditions, and institutions. The "Voice of Democracy" program is a national essay competition that annually provides more than $2.7 million in college scholarships and incentives.

Website: www.vfw.org

| | |
|---|---|
| A. | Atlantic Reporter |
| A. 2d | Atlantic Reporter, Second Series |
| AA | Alcoholics Anonymous |
| AAA | American Arbitration Association; Agricultural Adjustment Act of 1933 |
| AALS | Association of American Law Schools |
| AAPRP | All African People's Revolutionary Party |
| AARP | American Association of Retired Persons |
| AAS | American Anti-Slavery Society |
| ABA | American Bar Association; Architectural Barriers Act, 1968; American Bankers Association |
| ABM Treaty | Anti-Ballistic Missile Treaty of 1972; antiballistic missile |
| ABVP | Anti-Biased Violence Project |
| A/C | account |
| A.C. | appeal cases |
| ACAA | Air Carrier Access Act |
| ACF | Administration for Children and Families |
| ACLU | American Civil Liberties Union |
| ACRS | Accelerated Cost Recovery System |
| ACS | Agricultural Cooperative Service |
| ACT | American College Test |
| Act'g Legal Adv. | Acting Legal Advisor |
| ACUS | Administrative Conference of the United States |
| ACYF | Administration on Children, Youth, and Families |
| A.D. 2d | Appellate Division, Second Series, N.Y. |
| ADA | Americans with Disabilities Act of 1990 |
| ADAMHA | Alcohol, Drug Abuse, and Mental Health Administration |
| ADC | Aid to Dependent Children |
| ADD | Administration on Developmental Disabilities |
| ADEA | Age Discrimination in Employment Act of 1967 |
| ADR | alternative dispute resolution |
| AEC | Atomic Energy Commission |
| AECB | Arms Export Control Board |
| AEDPA | Antiterrorism and Effective Death Penalty Act |
| A.E.R. | All England Law Reports |
| AFA | American Family Association; Alabama Freethought Association |
| AFB | American Farm Bureau |

| AFBF | American Farm Bureau Federation |
| AFDC | Aid to Families with Dependent Children |
| aff'd per cur. | affirmed by the court |
| AFIS | automated fingerprint identification system |
| AFL | American Federation of Labor |
| AFL-CIO | American Federation of Labor and Congress of Industrial Organizations |
| AFRes | Air Force Reserve |
| AFSC | American Friends Service Committee |
| AFSCME | American Federation of State, County, and Municipal Employees |
| AGRICOLA | Agricultural Online Access |
| AIA | Association of Insurance Attorneys |
| AIB | American Institute for Banking |
| AID | artificial insemination using a third-party donor's sperm; Agency for International Development |
| AIDS | acquired immune deficiency syndrome |
| AIH | artificial insemination using the husband's sperm |
| AIM | American Indian Movement |
| AIPAC | American Israel Public Affairs Committee |
| AIUSA | Amnesty International, U.S.A. Affiliate |
| AJS | American Judicature Society |
| Alcoa | Aluminum Company of America |
| ALEC | American Legislative Exchange Council |
| ALF | Animal Liberation Front |
| ALI | American Law Institute |
| ALJ | administrative law judge |
| All E.R. | All England Law Reports |
| ALO | Agency Liaison |
| A.L.R. | American Law Reports |
| AMA | American Medical Association |
| AMAA | Agricultural Marketing Agreement Act |
| Am. Dec. | American Decisions |
| amdt. | amendment |
| Amer. St. Papers, For. Rels. | American State Papers, Legislative and Executive Documents of the Congress of the U.S., Class I, Foreign Relations, 1832-1859 |
| AMS | Agricultural Marketing Service |
| AMVETS | American Veterans of World War II |
| ANA | Administration for Native Americans |
| Ann. Dig. | Annual Digest of Public International Law Cases |
| ANRA | American Newspaper Publishers Association |
| ANSCA | Alaska Native Claims Act |
| ANZUS | Australia-New Zealand-United States Security Treaty Organization |
| AOA | Administration on Aging |
| AOE | Arizonans for Official English |
| AOL | America Online |
| APA | Administrative Procedure Act of 1946 |
| APHIS | Animal and Plant Health Inspection Service |
| App. Div. | Appellate Division Reports, N.Y. Supreme Court |
| Arb. Trib., U.S.-British | Arbitration Tribunal, Claim Convention of 1853, United States and Great Britain Convention of 1853 |
| Ardcor | American Roller Die Corporation |
| ARPA | Advanced Research Projects Agency |
| ARPANET | Advanced Research Projects Agency Network |
| ARS | Advanced Record System |
| Art. | article |
| ARU | American Railway Union |
| ASCME | American Federation of State, County, and Municipal Employees |

| | |
|---|---|
| ASCS | Agriculture Stabilization and Conservation Service |
| ASM | Available Seatmile |
| ASPCA | American Society for the Prevention of Cruelty to Animals |
| Asst. Att. Gen. | Assistant Attorney General |
| AT&T | American Telephone and Telegraph |
| ATFD | Alcohol, Tobacco and Firearms Division |
| ATLA | Association of Trial Lawyers of America |
| ATO | Alpha Tau Omega |
| ATTD | Alcohol and Tobacco Tax Division |
| ATU | Alcohol Tax Unit |
| AUAM | American Union against Militarism |
| AUM | Animal Unit Month |
| AZT | azidothymidine |
| BALSA | Black-American Law Student Association |
| BATF | Bureau of Alcohol, Tobacco and Firearms |
| BBS | Bulletin Board System |
| BCCI | Bank of Credit and Commerce International |
| BEA | Bureau of Economic Analysis |
| Bell's Cr. C. | Bell's English Crown Cases |
| Bevans | United States Treaties, etc. *Treaties and Other International Agreements of the United States of America, 1776-1949* (compiled under the direction of Charles I. Bevans, 1968-76) |
| BFOQ | bona fide occupational qualification |
| BI | Bureau of Investigation |
| BIA | Bureau of Indian Affairs; Board of Immigration Appeals |
| BJS | Bureau of Justice Statistics |
| Black. | Black's United States Supreme Court Reports |
| Blatchf. | Blatchford's United States Circuit Court Reports |
| BLM | Bureau of Land Management |
| BLS | Bureau of Labor Statistics |
| BMD | ballistic missile defense |
| BNA | Bureau of National Affairs |
| BOCA | Building Officials and Code Administrators International |
| BOP | Bureau of Prisons |
| BPP | Black Panther Party for Self-defense |
| Brit. and For. | British and Foreign State Papers |
| BSA | Boy Scouts of America |
| BTP | Beta Theta Pi |
| Burr. | James Burrows, *Report of Cases Argued and Determined in the Court of King's Bench during the Time of Lord Mansfield* (1766-1780) |
| BVA | Board of Veterans Appeals |
| c. | chapter |
| $C^3I$ | Command, Control, Communications, and Intelligence |
| C.A. | Court of Appeals |
| CAA | Clean Air Act |
| CAB | Civil Aeronautics Board; Corporation for American Banking |
| CAFE | corporate average fuel economy |
| Cal. 2d | California Reports, Second Series |
| Cal. 3d | California Reports, Third Series |
| CALR | computer-assisted legal research |
| Cal. Rptr. | California Reporter |
| CAP | Common Agricultural Policy |
| CARA | Classification and Ratings Administration |
| CATV | community antenna television |
| CBO | Congressional Budget Office |
| CCC | Commodity Credit Corporation |
| CCDBG | Child Care and Development Block Grant of 1990 |

| | |
|---|---|
| C.C.D. Pa. | Circuit Court Decisions, Pennsylvania |
| C.C.D. Va. | Circuit Court Decisions, Virginia |
| CCEA | Cabinet Council on Economic Affairs |
| CCP | Chinese Communist Party |
| CCR | Center for Constitutional Rights |
| C.C.R.I. | Circuit Court, Rhode Island |
| CD | certificate of deposit; compact disc |
| CDA | Communications Decency Act |
| CDBG | Community Development Block Grant Program |
| CDC | Centers for Disease Control and Prevention; Community Development Corporation |
| CDF | Children's Defense Fund |
| CDL | Citizens for Decency through Law |
| CD-ROM | compact disc read-only memory |
| CDS | Community Dispute Services |
| CDW | collision damage waiver |
| CENTO | Central Treaty Organization |
| CEQ | Council on Environmental Quality |
| CERCLA | Comprehensive Environmental Response, Compensation, and Liability Act of 1980 |
| cert. | *certiorari* |
| CETA | Comprehensive Employment and Training Act |
| C & F | cost and freight |
| CFC | chlorofluorocarbon |
| CFE Treaty | Conventional Forces in Europe Treaty of 1990 |
| C.F. & I. | Cost, Freight, and Insurance |
| CI NP | Community Food and Nutrition Program |
| C.F.R. | Code of Federal Regulations |
| CFTA | Canadian Free Trade Agreement |
| CFTC | Commodity Futures Trading Commission |
| Ch. | Chancery Division, English Law Reports |
| CHAMPVA | Civilian Health and Medical Program at the Veterans Administration |
| CHEP | Cuban/Haitian Entrant Program |
| CHINS | children in need of supervision |
| CHIPS | child in need of protective services |
| Ch N.Y. | Chancery Reports, New York |
| Chr. Rob. | Christopher Robinson, *Reports of Cases Argued and Determined in the High Court of Admiralty* (1801-1808) |
| CIA | Central Intelligence Agency |
| CID | Commercial Item Descriptions |
| C.I.F. | cost, insurance, and freight |
| CINCNORAD | Commander in Chief, North American Air Defense Command |
| CIO | Committee for Industrial Organizations; Congress of Industrial Organizations |
| CIPE | Center for International Private Enterprise |
| CJ | chief justice |
| CJIS | Criminal Justice Information Services |
| CJ.S. | Corpus Juris Secundum |
| Claims Arb. under Spec. Conv., Nielsen's Rept. | Frederick Kenelm Melsen, *American and British Claims Arbitration under the Special Agreement Concluded between the United States and Great Britain, August 18, 1910* (1926) |
| CLASP | Center for Law and Social Policy |
| CLE | Center for Law and Education; Continuing Legal Education |
| CLEO | Council on Legal Education Opportunity; Chief Law Enforcement Officer |
| CLP | Communist Labor Party of America |
| CLS | Christian Legal Society; critical legal studies (movement), Critical Legal Studies (membership organization) |

| | |
|---|---|
| C.M.A. | Court of Military Appeals |
| CMEA | Council for Mutual Economic Assistance |
| CMHS | Center for Mental Health Services |
| C.M.R. | Court of Military Review |
| CNN | Cable News Network |
| CNO | Chief of Naval Operations |
| CNR | Chicago and Northwestern Railway |
| CO | Conscientious Objector |
| C.O.D. | cash on delivery |
| COGP | Commission on Government Procurement |
| COINTELPRO | Counterintelligence Program |
| Coke Rep. | Coke's English King's Bench Reports |
| COLA | cost-of-living adjustment |
| COMCEN | Federal Communications Center |
| Comp. | Compilation |
| Conn. | Connecticut Reports |
| CONTU | National Commission on New Technological Uses of Copyrighted Works |
| Conv. | Convention |
| COPS | Community Oriented Policing Services |
| Corbin | Arthur L. Corbin, *Corbin on Contracts: A Comprehensive Treatise on the Rules of Contract Law* (1950) |
| CORE | Congress on Racial Equality |
| Cox's Crim. Cases | Cox's Criminal Cases (England) |
| COYOTE | Call Off Your Old Tired Ethics |
| CPA | certified public accountant |
| CPB | Corporation for Public Broadcasting, the |
| CPI | Consumer Price Index |
| CPPA | Child Pornography Prevention Act |
| CPSC | Consumer Product Safety Commission |
| Cranch | Cranch's United States Supreme Court Reports |
| CRF | Constitutional Rights Foundation |
| CRR | Center for Constitutional Rights |
| CRS | Congressional Research Service; Community Relations Service |
| CRT | critical race theory |
| CSA | Community Services Administration |
| CSAP | Center for Substance Abuse Prevention |
| CSAT | Center for Substance Abuse Treatment |
| CSC | Civil Service Commission |
| CSCE | Conference on Security and Cooperation in Europe |
| CSG | Council of State Governments |
| CSO | Community Service Organization |
| CSP | Center for the Study of the Presidency |
| C-SPAN | Cable-Satellite Public Affairs Network |
| CSRS | Cooperative State Research Service |
| CSWPL | Center on Social Welfare Policy and Law |
| CTA | *cum testamento annexo* (with the will attached) |
| Ct. Ap. D.C. | Court of Appeals, District of Columbia |
| Ct. App. No. Ireland | Court of Appeals, Northern Ireland |
| Ct. Cl. | Court of Claims, United States |
| Ct. Crim. Apps. | Court of Criminal Appeals (England) |
| Ct. of Sess., Scot. | Court of Sessions, Scotland |
| CU | credit union |
| CUNY | City University of New York |
| Cush. | Cushing's Massachusetts Reports |
| CWA | Civil Works Administration; Clean Water Act |
| DACORB | Department of the Army Conscientious Objector Review Board |

| | |
|---|---|
| Dall. | Dallas' Pennsylvania and United States Reports |
| DAR | Daughters of the American Revolution |
| DARPA | Defense Advanced Research Projects Agency |
| DAVA | Defense Audiovisual Agency |
| D.C. | United States District Court; District of Columbia |
| D.C. Del. | United States District Court, Delaware |
| D.C. Mass. | United States District Court, Massachusetts |
| D.C. Md. | United States District Court, Maryland |
| D.C.N.D.Cal. | United States District Court, Northern District, California |
| D.C.N.Y. | United States District Court, New York |
| D.C.Pa. | United States District Court, Pennsylvania |
| DC-S | Deputy Chiefs of Staff |
| DCZ | District of the Canal Zone |
| DDT | dichlorodiphenyltricloroethane |
| DEA | Drug Enforcement Administration |
| Decl. Lond. | Declaration of London, February 26, 1909 |
| Dev. & B. | Devereux & Battle's North Carolina Reports |
| DFL | Minnesota Democratic-Farmer-Labor |
| DFTA | Department for the Aging |
| Dig. U.S. Practice in Intl. Law | Digest of U.S. Practice in International Law |
| Dist. Ct. | D.C. United States District Court, District of Columbia |
| D.L.R. | Dominion Law Reports (Canada) |
| DNA | deoxyribonucleic acid |
| Dnase | deoxyribonuclease |
| DNC | Democratic National Committee |
| DOC | Department of Commerce |
| DOD | Department of Defense |
| DODEA | Department of Defense Education Activity |
| Dodson | Dodson's Reports, English Admiralty Courts |
| DOE | Department of Energy |
| DOER | Department of Employee Relations |
| DOJ | Department of Justice |
| DOL | Department of Labor |
| DOMA | Defense of Marriage Act, 1996 |
| DOS | disk operating system |
| DOT | Department of Transportation |
| DPT | diphtheria, pertussis, and tetanus |
| DRI | Defense Research Institute |
| DSAA | Defense Security Assistance Agency |
| DUI | driving under the influence; driving under intoxication |
| DWI | driving while intoxicated |
| EAHCA | Education for All Handicapped Children Act of 1975 |
| EBT | examination before trial |
| E.coli | Escherichia coli |
| ECPA | Electronic Communications Privacy Act of 1986 |
| ECSC | Treaty of the European Coal and Steel Community |
| EDA | Economic Development Administration |
| EDF | Environmental Defense Fund |
| E.D.N.Y. | Eastern District, New York |
| EDP | electronic data processing |
| E.D. | Pa. Eastern-District, Pennsylvania |
| EDSC | Eastern District, South Carolina |
| E.D. | Va. Eastern District, Virginia |
| EEC | European Economic Community; European Economic Community Treaty |
| EEOC | Equal Employment Opportunity Commission |

| EFF | Electronic Frontier Foundation |
| EFT | electronic funds transfer |
| Eliz. | Queen Elizabeth (Great Britain) |
| Em. App. | Temporary Emergency Court of Appeals |
| ENE | early neutral evaluation |
| Eng. Rep. | English Reports |
| EOP | Executive Office of the President |
| EPA | Environmental Protection Agency; Equal Pay Act of 1963 |
| ERA | Equal Rights Amendment |
| ERDC | Energy Research and Development Commission |
| ERISA | Employee Retirement Income Security Act of 1974 |
| ERS | Economic Research Service |
| ERTA | Economic Recovery Tax Act, 1981 |
| ESA | Endangered Species Act of 1973 |
| ESF | emergency support function; Economic Support Fund |
| ESRD | End-Stage Renal Disease Program |
| ETA | Employment and Training Administration |
| ETS | environmental tobacco smoke |
| et seq. | *et sequentes* or *et sequentia* (and the following) |
| EU | European Union |
| Euratom | European Atomic Energy Community |
| Eur. Ct. H.R. | European Court of Human Rights |
| Ex. | English Exchequer Reports, Welsby, Hurlstone & Gordon |
| Exch. | Exchequer Reports (Welsby, Hurlstone & Gordon) |
| Ex Com | Executive Committee of the National Security Council |
| Eximbank | Export-Import Bank of the United States |
| F. | Federal Reporter |
| F. 2d | Federal Reporter, Second Series |
| FAA | Federal Aviation Administration; Federal Arbitration Act |
| FAAA | Federal Alcohol Administration Act |
| FACE | Freedom of Access to Clinic Entrances Act of 1994 |
| FACT | Feminist Anti-Censorship Task Force |
| FAMLA | Family and Medical Leave Act of 1993 |
| Fannie Mae | Federal National Mortgage Association |
| FAO | Food and Agriculture Organization of the United Nations |
| FAR | Federal Acquisition Regulations |
| FAS | Foreign Agricultural Service |
| FBA | Federal Bar Association |
| FBI | Federal Bureau of Investigation |
| FCA | Farm Credit Administration |
| F. Cas. | Federal Cases |
| FCC | Federal Communications Commission |
| FCIA | Foreign Credit Insurance Association |
| FCIC | Federal Crop Insurance Corporation |
| FCRA | Fair Credit Reporting Act |
| FCU | federal credit unions |
| FCUA | Federal Credit Union Act |
| FCZ | Fishery Conservation Zone |
| FDA | Food and Drug Administration |
| FDIC | Federal Deposit Insurance Corporation |
| FDPC | Federal Data Processing Center |
| FEC | Federal Election Commission |
| FECA | Federal Election Campaign Act of 1971 |
| Fed. Cas. | Federal Cases |
| FEMA | Federal Emergency Management Agency |
| FFB | Federal Financing Bank |
| FFDC | Federal Food, Drug, and Cosmetics Act |

| | |
|---|---|
| FGIS | Federal Grain Inspection Service |
| FHA | Federal Housing Administration |
| FHWA | Federal Highway Administration |
| FIA | Federal Insurance Administration |
| FIC | Federal Information Centers; Federation of Insurance Counsel |
| FICA | Federal Insurance Contributions Act |
| FIFRA | Federal Insecticide, Fungicide, and Rodenticide Act |
| FIP | Forestry Incentives Program |
| FIRREA | Financial Institutions Reform, Recovery, and Enforcement Act of 1989 |
| FISA | Foreign Intelligence Surveillance Act of 1978 |
| FJC | Federal Judicial Center |
| FLSA | Fair Labor Standards Act |
| FMC | Federal Maritime Commission |
| FMCS | Federal Mediation and Conciliation Service |
| FmHA | Farmers Home Administration |
| FMLA | Family and Medical Leave Act of 1993 |
| FNMA | Federal National Mortgage Association, "Fannie Mae" |
| F.O.B. | free on board |
| FOIA | Freedom of Information Act |
| FOMC | Federal Open Market Committee |
| FPC | Federal Power Commission |
| FPMR | Federal Property Management Regulations |
| FPRS | Federal Property Resources Service |
| FR | Federal Register |
| FRA | Federal Railroad Administration |
| FRB | Federal Reserve Board |
| FRC | Federal Radio Commission |
| F.R.D. | Federal Rules Decisions |
| FSA | Family Support Act |
| FSLIC | Federal Savings and Loan Insurance Corporation |
| FSQS | Food Safety and Quality Service |
| FSS | Federal Supply Service |
| F. Supp. | Federal Supplement |
| FTA | U.S.-Canada Free Trade Agreement, 1988 |
| FTC | Federal Trade Commission |
| FTCA | Federal Tort Claims Act |
| FTS | Federal Telecommunications System |
| FTS2000 | Federal Telecommunications System 2000 |
| FUCA | Federal Unemployment Compensation Act of 1988 |
| FUTA | Federal Unemployment Tax Act |
| FWPCA | Federal Water Pollution Control Act of 1948 |
| FWS | Fish and Wildlife Service |
| GAL | guardian ad litem |
| GAO | General Accounting Office; Governmental Affairs Office |
| GAOR | General Assembly Official Records, United Nations |
| GA Res. | General Assembly Resolution (United Nations) |
| GATT | General Agreement on Tariffs and Trade |
| GCA | Gun Control Act |
| Gen. Cls. Comm. | General Claims Commission, United States and Panama; General Claims United States and Mexico |
| Geo. II | King George II (Great Britain) |
| Geo. III | King George III (Great Britain) |
| GI | Government Issue |
| GID | General Intelligence Division |
| GM | General Motors |
| GNMA | Government National Mortgage Association, "Ginnie Mae" |
| GNP | gross national product |

| | |
|---|---|
| GOP | Grand Old Party (Republican) |
| GOPAC | Grand Old Party Action Committee |
| GPA | Office of Governmental and Public Affairs |
| GPO | Government Printing Office |
| GRAS | generally recognized as safe |
| Gr. Br., Crim. Ct. App. | Great Britain, Court of Criminal Appeals |
| GRNL | Gay Rights-National Lobby |
| GSA | General Services Administration |
| Hackworth | Green Haywood Hackworth, *Digest of International Law* (1940-44) |
| Hay and Marriott | Great Britain. High Court of Admiralty, *Decisions in the High Court of Admiralty during the Time of Sir George Hay and of Sir James Marriott, Late Judges of That Court* (1801) |
| HBO | Home Box Office |
| HCFA | Health Care Financing Administration |
| H.Ct. | High Court |
| HDS | Office of Human Development Services |
| Hen. & M. | Hening & Munford's Virginia Reports |
| HEW | Department of Health, Education, and Welfare |
| HFCA | Health Care Financing Administration |
| HGI | Handgun Control, Incorporated |
| HHS | Department of Health and Human Services |
| Hill | Hill's New York Reports |
| HIRE | Help through Industry Retraining and Employment |
| HIV | human immunodeficiency virus |
| H.L. | House of Lords Cases (England) |
| H. Lords | House of Lords (England) |
| HNIS | Human Nutrition Information Service |
| Hong Kong L.R. | Hong Kong Law Reports |
| How. | Howard's United States Supreme Court Reports |
| How. St. Trials | Howell's English State Trials |
| HUAC | House Un-American Activities Committee |
| HUD | Department of Housing and Urban Development |
| Hudson, Internatl. Legis. | Manley O. Hudson, ed., *International Legislation: A Collection of the Texts of Multipartite International Instruments of General Interest Beginning with the Covenant of the League of Nations* (1931) |
| Hudson, World Court Reps. | Manley Ottmer Hudson, ea., *World Court Reports* (1934- ) |
| Hun | Hun's New York Supreme Court Reports |
| Hunt's Rept. | Bert L. Hunt, *Report of the American and Panamanian General Claims Arbitration* (1934) |
| IAEA | International Atomic Energy Agency |
| IALL | International Association of Law Libraries |
| IBA | International Bar Association |
| IBM | International Business Machines |
| ICBM | intercontinental ballistic missile |
| ICC | Interstate Commerce Commission |
| ICJ | International Court of Justice |
| ICM | Institute for Court Management |
| IDEA | Individuals with Disabilities Education Act, 1975 |
| IDOP | International Dolphin Conservation Program |
| IEP | individualized educational program |
| IFC | International Finance Corporation |
| IGRA | Indian Gaming Regulatory Act, 1988 |
| IJA | Institute of Judicial Administration |
| IJC | International Joint Commission |
| ILC | International Law Commission |
| ILD | International Labor Defense |

| | |
|---|---|
| Ill. Dec. | Illinois Decisions |
| ILO | International Labor Organization |
| IMF | International Monetary Fund |
| INA | Immigration and Nationality Act |
| IND | investigational new drug |
| INF Treaty | Intermediate-Range Nuclear Forces Treaty of 1987 |
| INS | Immigration and Naturalization Service |
| INTELSAT | International Telecommunications Satellite Organization |
| Interpol | International Criminal Police Organization |
| Int'l. Law Reps. | International Law Reports |
| Intl. Legal Mats. | International Legal Materials |
| IPDC | International Program for the Development of Communication |
| IPO | Intellectual Property Owners |
| IPP | independent power producer |
| IQ | intelligence quotient |
| I.R. | Irish Reports |
| IRA | individual retirement account; Irish Republican Army |
| IRCA | Immigration Reform and Control Act of 1986 |
| IRS | Internal Revenue Service |
| ISO | independent service organization |
| ISP | Internet service provider |
| ISSN | International Standard Serial Numbers |
| ITA | International Trade Administration |
| ITI | Information Technology Integration |
| ITO | International Trade Organization |
| ITS | Information Technology Service |
| ITT | International Telephone and Telegraph Corporation |
| ITU | International Telecommunication Union |
| IUD | intrauterine device |
| IWC | International Whaling Commission |
| IWW | Industrial Workers of the World |
| JAGC | Judge Advocate General's Corps |
| JCS | Joint Chiefs of Staff |
| JDL | Jewish Defense League |
| JNOV | Judgment *non obstante veredicto* (judgment "nothing to recommend it") or (judgment "notwithstanding the verdict") |
| JOBS | Jobs Opportunity and Basic Skills |
| John. Ch. | Johnson's New York Chancery Reports |
| Johns. | Johnson's Reports (New York) |
| JP | justice of the peace |
| K.B. | King's Bench Reports (England) |
| KGB | Komitet Gosudarstvennoi Bezopasnosti (the State Security Committee for countries in the former Soviet Union) |
| KKK | Ku Klux Klan |
| KMT | Kuomintang |
| LAD | Law Against Discrimination |
| LAPD | Los Angeles Police Department |
| LC | Library of Congress |
| LCHA | Longshoremen's and Harbor Workers Compensation Act of 1927 |
| LD50 | lethal dose 50 |
| LDEF | Legal Defense and Education Fund (NOW) |
| LDF | Legal Defense Fund, Legal Defense and Educational Fund of the NAACP |
| LEAA | Law Enforcement Assistance Administration |
| L.Ed. | Lawyers' Edition Supreme Court Reports |
| LLC | Limited Liability Company |
| LLP | Limited Liability Partnership |

| | |
|---|---|
| LMSA | Labor-Management Services Administration |
| LNTS | League of Nations Treaty Series |
| Lofft's Rep. | Lofft's English King's Bench Reports |
| L.R. | Law Reports (English) |
| LSAC | Law School Admission Council |
| LSAS | Law School Admission Service |
| LSAT | Law School Aptitude Test |
| LSC | Legal Services Corporation; Legal Services for Children |
| LSD | lysergic acid diethylamide |
| LSDAS | Law School Data Assembly Service |
| LTBT | Limited Test Ban Treaty |
| LTC | Long Term Care |
| MAD | mutual assured destruction |
| MADD | Mothers against Drunk Driving |
| MALDEF | Mexican American Legal Defense and Educational Fund |
| Malloy | William M. Malloy, ed., *Treaties, Conventions International Acts, Protocols, and Agreements between the United States of America and Other Powers* (1910-38) |
| Martens | Georg Friedrich von Martens, ea., *Noveau recueil ge'neral de traites et autres act es relatifs azlx rapports de droit international* (Series I, 20 vols. [1843-75]; Series II, 35 vols. [1876-1908]; Series III [1909- ]) |
| Mass. | Massachusetts Reports |
| MCC | Metropolitan Correctional Center |
| MCH | Maternal and Child Health Bureau |
| Md. App. | Maryland, Appeal Cases |
| M.D. Ga. | Middle District, Georgia |
| Mercy | Movement Ensuring the Right to Choose for Yourself |
| Metc. | Metcalf's Massachusetts Reports |
| MFDP | Mississippi Freedom Democratic Party |
| MGT | management |
| MHSS | Military Health Services System |
| Miller | David Hunter Miller, ea., *Treaties and Other International Acts of the United States America* (1931-1948) |
| Minn. | Minnesota Reports |
| MINS | minors in need of supervision |
| MIRV | multiple independently targetable reentry vehicle |
| MIRVed ICBM | Multiple Independently Targetable Reentry Vehicled Intercontinental Ballistic Missile |
| Misc. | Miscellaneous Reports, New York |
| Mixed Claims Comm., Report of Decs | Mixed Claims Commission, United States and Germany, Report of Decisions |
| MJ. | Military Justice Reporter |
| MLAP | Migrant Legal Action Program |
| MLB | Major League Baseball |
| MLDP | Mississippi Loyalist Democratic Party |
| MMI | Moslem Mosque, Incorporated |
| MMPA | Marine Mammal Protection Act of 1972 |
| Mo. | Missouri Reports |
| MOD | Masters of Deception |
| Mod. | Modern Reports, English King's Bench, etc. |
| Moore, Dig. Intl. Law | John Bassett Moore, *A Digest of International Law*, 8 vols. (1906) |
| Moore, Intl. Arbs. | John Bassett Moore, *History and Digest of the International Arbitrations to Which United States Has Been a Party*, 6 vols. (1898) |
| Morison | William Maxwell Morison, *The Scots Revised Report: Morison's Dictionary of Decisions* (1908-09) |
| M.P. | member of Parliament |
| MPAA | Motion Picture Association of America |

| | |
|---|---|
| MPAS | Michigan Protection and Advocacy Service |
| mpg | miles per gallon |
| MPPDA | Motion Picture Producers and Distributors of America |
| MPRSA | Marine Protection, Research, and Sanctuaries Act of 1972 |
| M.R. | Master of the Rolls |
| MS-DOS | Microsoft Disk Operating System |
| MSHA | Mine Safety and Health Administration |
| MSSA | Military Selective Service Act |
| N/A | Not Available |
| NAACP | National Association for the Advancement of Colored People |
| NAAQS | National Ambient Air Quality Standards |
| NAB | National Association of Broadcasters |
| NABSW | National Association of Black Social Workers |
| NAFTA | North American Free Trade Agreement, 1993 |
| NALA | National Association of Legal Assistants |
| NAM | National Association of Manufacturers |
| NAR | National Association of Realtors |
| NARAL | National Abortion and Reproductive Rights Action League |
| NARF | Native American Rights Fund |
| NARS | National Archives and Record Service |
| NASA | National Aeronautics and Space Administration |
| NASD | National Association of Securities Dealers |
| NATO | North Atlantic Treaty Organization |
| NAVINFO | Navy Information Offices |
| NAWSA | National American Woman's Suffrage Association |
| NBA | National Bar Association; National Basketball Association |
| NBC | National Broadcasting Company |
| NBLSA | National Black Law Student Association |
| NBS | National Bureau of Standards |
| NCA | Noise Control Act; National Command Authorities |
| NCAA | National Collegiate Athletic Association |
| NCAC | National Coalition against Censorship |
| NCCB | National Consumer Cooperative Bank |
| NCE | Northwest Community Exchange |
| NCF | National Chamber Foundation |
| NCIP | National Crime Insurance Program |
| NCJA | National Criminal Justice Association |
| NCLB | National Civil Liberties Bureau |
| NCP | national contingency plan |
| NCSC | National Center for State Courts |
| NCUA | National Credit Union Administration |
| NDA | new drug application |
| N.D. Ill. | Northern District, Illinois |
| NDU | National Defense University |
| N.D. Wash. | Northern District, Washington |
| N.E. | North Eastern Reporter |
| N.E. 2d | North Eastern Reporter, Second Series |
| NEA | National Endowment for the Arts; National Education Association |
| NEH | National Endowment for the Humanities |
| NEPA | National Environmental Protection Act; National Endowment Policy Act |
| NET Act | No Electronic Theft Act |
| NFIB | National Federation of Independent Businesses |
| NFIP | National Flood Insurance Program |
| NFPA | National Federation of Paralegal Associations |
| NGLTF | National Gay and Lesbian Task Force |
| NHRA | Nursing Home Reform Act, 1987 |
| NHTSA | National Highway Traffic Safety Administration |

| | |
|---|---|
| Nielsen's Rept. | Frederick Kenelm Melsen, *American and British Claims Arbitration under the Special Agreement Concluded between the United States and Great Britain, August 18, 1910* (1926) |
| NIEO | New International Economic Order |
| NIGC | National Indian Gaming Commission |
| NIH | National Institutes of Health |
| NIJ | National Institute of Justice |
| NIRA | National Industrial Recovery Act of 1933; National Industrial Recovery Administration |
| NIST | National Institute of Standards and Technology |
| NITA | National Telecommunications and Information Administration |
| NJ. | New Jersey Reports |
| N.J. Super. | New Jersey Superior Court Reports |
| NLRA | National Labor Relations Act |
| NLRB | National Labor Relations Board |
| NMFS | National Marine Fisheries Service |
| No. | Number |
| NOAA | National Oceanic and Atmospheric Administration |
| NOI | Nation of Islam |
| NORML | National Organization for the Reform of Marijuana Laws |
| North Carolina A&T | North Carolina Agricultural and Technical College |
| NOW | National Organization for Women |
| NOW LDEF | National Organization for Women Legal Defense and Education Fund |
| NOW/PAC | National Organization for Women Political Action Committee |
| NPDES | National Pollutant Discharge Elimination System |
| NPL | national priorities list |
| NPR | National Public Radio |
| NPT | Nuclear Non-Proliferation Treaty of 1970 |
| NRA | National Rifle Association; National Recovery Act |
| NRC | Nuclear Regulatory Commission |
| NRLC | National Right to Life Committee |
| NRTA | National Retired Teachers Association |
| NSI | Network Solutions, Inc. |
| NSC | National Security Council |
| NSCLC | National Senior Citizens Law Center |
| NSF | National Science Foundation |
| NSFNET | National Science Foundation Network |
| NTIA | National Telecommunications and Information Administration |
| NTID | National Technical Institute for the Deaf |
| NTIS | National Technical Information Service |
| NTS | Naval Telecommunications System |
| NTSB | National Transportation Safety Board |
| NVRA | National Voter Registration Act |
| N.W. | North Western Reporter |
| N.W. 2d | North Western Reporter, Second Series |
| NWSA | National Woman Suffrage Association |
| N.Y. | New York Court of Appeals Reports |
| N.Y. 2d | New York Court of Appeals Reports, Second Series |
| N.Y.S. | New York Supplement Reporter |
| N.Y.S. 2d | New York Supplement Reporter, Second Series |
| NYSE | New York Stock Exchange |
| NYSLA | New York State Liquor Authority |
| N.Y. Sup. | New York Supreme Court Reports |
| NYU | New York University |
| OAAU | Organization of Afro American Unity |
| OAP | Office of Administrative Procedure |

| | |
|---|---|
| OAS | Organization of American States |
| OASDI | Old-age, Survivors, and Disability Insurance Benefits |
| OASHDS | Office of the Assistant Secretary for Human Development Services |
| OCC | Office of Comptroller of the Currency |
| OCED | Office of Comprehensive Employment Development |
| OCHAMPUS | Office of Civilian Health and Medical Program of the Uniformed Services |
| OCSE | Office of Child Support Enforcement |
| OEA | Organización de los Estados Americanos |
| OEM | Original Equipment Manufacturer |
| OFCCP | Office of Federal Contract Compliance Programs |
| OFPP | Office of Federal Procurement Policy |
| OICD | Office of International Cooperation and Development |
| OIG | Office of the Inspector General |
| OJARS | Office of Justice Assistance, Research, and Statistics |
| OMB | Office of Management and Budget |
| OMPC | Office of Management, Planning, and Communications |
| ONP | Office of National Programs |
| OPD | Office of Policy Development |
| OPEC | Organization of Petroleum Exporting Countries |
| OPIC | Overseas Private Investment Corporation |
| Ops. Atts. Gen. | Opinions of the Attorneys-General of the United States |
| Ops. Comms. | Opinions of the Commissioners |
| OPSP | Office of Product Standards Policy |
| O.R. | Ontario Reports |
| OR | Official Records |
| OSHA | Occupational Safety and Health Act |
| OSHRC | Occupational Safety and Health Review Commission |
| OSM | Office of Surface Mining |
| OSS | Office of Strategic Services |
| OST | Office of the Secretary |
| OT | Office of Transportation |
| OTA | Office of Technology Assessment |
| OTC | over-the-counter |
| OTS | Office of Thrift Supervisors |
| OUI | operating under the influence |
| OWBPA | Older Workers Benefit Protection Act |
| OWRT | Office of Water Research and Technology |
| P. | Pacific Reporter |
| P. 2d | Pacific Reporter, Second Series |
| PAC | political action committee |
| Pa. Oyer and Terminer | Pennsylvania Oyer and Terminer Reports |
| PATCO | Professional Air Traffic Controllers Organization |
| PBGC | Pension Benefit Guaranty Corporation |
| PBS | Public Broadcasting Service; Public Buildings Service |
| P.C. | Privy Council (English Law Reports) |
| PC | personal computer; politically correct |
| PCBs | polychlorinated biphenyls |
| PCIJ | Permanent Court of International Justice |
| | Series A-Judgments and Orders (1922-30) |
| | Series B-Advisory Opinions (1922-30) |
| | Series A/B-Judgments, Orders, and Advisory Opinions (1931-40) |
| | Series C-Pleadings, Oral Statements, and Documents relating to Judgments and Advisory Opinions (1923-42) |
| | Series D-Acts and Documents concerning the Organization of the World Court (1922 -47) |
| | Series E-Annual Reports (1925-45) |

| | |
|---|---|
| PCP | Phencyclidine |
| P.D. | Probate Division, English Law Reports (1876-1890) |
| PDA | Pregnancy Discrimination Act of 1978 |
| PD & R | Policy Development and Research |
| Pepco | Potomac Electric Power Company |
| Perm. Ct. of Arb. | Permanent Court of Arbitration |
| PES | Post-Enumeration Survey |
| Pet. | Peters' United States Supreme Court Reports |
| PETA | People for the Ethical Treatment of Animals |
| PGA | Professional Golfers Association |
| PGM | Program |
| PHA | Public Housing Agency |
| Phila. Ct. of Oyer and Terminer | Philadelphia Court of Oyer and Terminer |
| PHS | Public Health Service |
| PIC | Private Industry Council |
| PICJ | Permanent International Court of Justice |
| Pick. | Pickering's Massachusetts Reports |
| PIK | Payment in Kind |
| PINS | persons in need of supervision |
| PIRG | Public Interest Research Group |
| P.L. | Public Laws |
| PLAN | Pro-Life Action Network |
| PLI | Practicing Law Institute |
| PLLP | Professional Limited Liability Partnership |
| PLO | Palestine Liberation Organization |
| PLRA | Prison Litigation Reform Act of 1995 |
| PNET | Peaceful Nuclear Explosions Treaty |
| PONY | Prostitutes of New York |
| POW-MIA | prisoner of war-missing in action |
| Pratt | Frederic Thomas Pratt, *Law of Contraband of War, with a Selection of Cases from Papers of the Right Honourable Sir George Lee* (1856) |
| PRIDE | Prostitution to Independence, Dignity, and Equality |
| Proc. | Proceedings |
| PRP | potentially responsible party |
| PSRO | Professional Standards Review Organization |
| PTO | Patents and Trademark Office |
| PURPA | Public Utilities Regulatory Policies Act |
| PUSH | People United to Serve Humanity |
| PUSH-Excel | PUSH for Excellence |
| PWA | Public Works Administration |
| PWSA | Ports and Waterways Safety Act of 1972 |
| Q.B. | Queen's Bench (England) |
| QTIP | Qualified Terminable Interest Property |
| Ralston's Rept. | Jackson Harvey Ralston, ed., *Venezuelan Arbitrations of 1903* (1904) |
| RC | Regional Commissioner |
| RCRA | Resource Conservation and Recovery Act |
| RCWP | Rural Clean Water Program |
| RDA | Rural Development Administration |
| REA | Rural Electrification Administration |
| Rec. des Decs. des Trib. Arb.Mixtes | G. Gidel, ed., *Recueil des decisions des tribunaux arbitraux mixtes, institués par les traités de paix* (1922-30) |
| Redmond | Vol. 3 of Charles I. Bevans, *Treaties and Other International Agreements of the United States of America, 1776-1949* (compiled by C. F. Redmond) (1969) |
| RESPA | Real Estate Settlement Procedure Act of 1974 |
| RFC | Reconstruction Finance Corporation |

| | |
|---|---|
| RFRA | Religious Freedom Restoration Act of 1993 |
| RICO | Racketeer Influenced and Corrupt Organizations |
| RNC | Republican National Committee |
| Roscoe | Edward Stanley Roscoe, ed., *Reports of Prize Cases Determined in the High Court Admiralty before the Lords Commissioners of Appeals in Prize Causes and before the judicial Committee of the Privy Council from 1745 to 1859* (1905) |
| ROTC | Reserve Officers' Training Corps |
| RPP | Representative Payee Program |
| R.S. | Revised Statutes |
| RTC | Resolution Trust Corp. |
| RUDs | reservations, understandings, and declarations |
| Ryan White CARE Act | Ryan White Comprehensive AIDS Research Emergency Act of 1990 |
| SAC | Strategic Air Command |
| SACB | Subversive Activities Control Board |
| SADD | Students against Drunk Driving |
| SAF | Student Activities Fund |
| SAIF | Savings Association Insurance Fund |
| SALT | Strategic Arms Limitation Talks |
| SALT I | Strategic Arms Limitation Talks of 1969-72 |
| SAMHSA | Substance Abuse and Mental Health Services Administration |
| Sandf. | Sandford's New York Superior Court Reports |
| S and L | savings and loan |
| SARA | Superfund Amendment and Reauthorization Act |
| SAT | Scholastic Aptitude Test |
| Sawy. | Sawyer's United States Circuit Court Reports |
| SBA | Small Business Administration |
| SBI | Small Business Institute |
| SCCC | South Central Correctional Center |
| SCLC | Southern Christian Leadership Conference |
| Scott's Repts. | James Brown Scott, ed., *The Hague Court Reports*, 2 vols. (1916-32) |
| SCS | Soil Conservation Service; Social Conservative Service |
| SCSEP | Senior Community Service Employment Program |
| S.Ct. | Supreme Court Reporter |
| S.D. Cal. | Southern District, California |
| S.D. Fla. | Southern District, Florida |
| S.D. Ga. | Southern District, Georgia |
| SDI | Strategic Defense Initiative |
| S.D. Me. | Southern District, Maine |
| S.D.N.Y. | Southern District, New York |
| SDS | Students for a Democratic Society |
| S.E. | South Eastern Reporter |
| S.E. 2d | South Eastern Reporter, Second Series |
| SEA | Science and Education Administration |
| SEATO | Southeast Asia Treaty Organization |
| SEC | Securities and Exchange Commission |
| Sec. | Section |
| SEEK | Search for Elevation, Education and Knowledge |
| SEOO | State Economic Opportunity Office |
| SEP | simplified employee pension plan |
| Ser. | Series |
| Sess. | Session |
| SGLI | Servicemen's Group Life Insurance |
| SIP | state implementation plan |
| SLA | Symbionese Liberation Army |
| SLAPPs | Strategic Lawsuits Against Public Participation |
| SLBM | submarine-launched ballistic missile |

| | |
|---|---|
| SNCC | Student Nonviolent Coordinating Committee |
| So. | Southern Reporter |
| So. 2d | Southern Reporter, Second Series |
| SPA | Software Publisher's Association |
| Spec. Sess. | Special Session |
| SRA | Sentencing Reform Act of 1984 |
| SS | Schutzstaffel (German for Protection Echelon) |
| SSA | Social Security Administration |
| SSI | Supplemental Security Income |
| START I | Strategic Arms Reduction Treaty of 1991 |
| START II | Strategic Arms Reduction Treaty of 1993 |
| Seat. | United States Statutes at Large |
| STS | Space Transportation Systems |
| St. Tr. | State Trials, English |
| STURAA | Surface Transportation and Uniform Relocation Assistance Act of 1987 |
| Sup. Ct. of Justice, Mexico | Supreme Court of Justice, Mexico |
| Supp. | Supplement |
| S.W. | South Western Reporter |
| S.W. 2d | South Western Reporter, Second Series |
| SWAPO | South-West Africa People's Organization |
| SWAT | Special Weapons and Tactics |
| SWP | Socialist Workers Party |
| TDP | Trade and Development Program |
| Tex. Sup. | Texas Supreme Court Reports |
| THAAD | Theater High-Altitude Area Defense System |
| THC | tetrahydrocannabinol |
| TI | Tobacco Institute |
| TIA | Trust Indenture Act of 1939 |
| TIAS | Treaties and Other International Acts Series (United States) |
| TNT | trinitrotoluene |
| TOP | Targeted Outreach Program |
| TPUS | Transportation and Public Utilities Service |
| TQM | Total Quality Management |
| Tripartite Claims Comm., Decs. And Ops. | Tripartite Claims Commission (United States, Austria, and Hungary), Decisions and Opinions |
| TRI-TAC | Joint Tactical Communications |
| TRO | temporary restraining order |
| TS | Treaty Series, United States |
| TSCA | Toxic Substance Control Act |
| TSDs | transporters, storers, and disposers |
| TSU | Texas Southern University |
| TTBT | Threshold Test Ban Treaty |
| TV | Television |
| TVA | Tennessee Valley Authority |
| TWA | Trans World Airlines |
| UAW | United Auto Workers; United Automobile, Aerospace, and Agricultural Implements Workers of America |
| U.C.C. | Uniform Commercial Code; Universal Copyright Convention |
| U.C.C.C. | Uniform Consumer Credit Code |
| UCCJA | Uniform Child Custody Jurisdiction Act |
| UCMJ | Uniform Code of Military Justice |
| UCPP | Urban Crime Prevention Program |
| UCS | United Counseling Service |
| UDC | United Daughters of the Confederacy |
| UFW | United Farm Workers |

| | |
|---|---|
| UHF | ultrahigh frequency |
| UIFSA | Uniform Interstate Family Support Act |
| UIS | Unemployment Insurance Service |
| UMDA | Uniform Marriage and Divorce Act |
| UMTA | Urban Mass Transportation Administration |
| U.N. | United Nations |
| UNCITRAL | United Nations Commission on International Trade Law |
| UNCTAD | United Nations Conference on Trade and Development |
| UN Doc. | United Nations Documents |
| UNDP | United Nations Development Program |
| UNEF | United Nations Emergency Force |
| UNESCO | United Nations Educational, Scientific, and Cultural Organization |
| UNICEF | United Nations Children's Fund |
| UNIDO | United Nations Industrial and Development Organization |
| Unif. L. Ann. | Uniform Laws Annotated |
| UN Repts. Intl. Arb. Awards | United Nations Reports of International Arbitral Awards |
| UNTS | United Nations Treaty Series |
| UPI | United Press International |
| URESA | Uniform Reciprocal Enforcement of Support Act |
| U.S.A. | United States of America |
| USAF | United States Air Force |
| USF | U.S. Forestry Service |
| U.S. App. D.C. | United States Court of Appeals for the District of Columbia |
| U.S.C. | United States Code; University of Southern California |
| U.S.C.A. | United States Code Annotated |
| U.S.C.C.A.N. | United States Code Congressional and Administrative News |
| USCMA | United States Court of Military Appeals |
| USDA | U.S. Department of Agriculture |
| USES | United States Employment Service |
| USFA | United States Fire Administration |
| USICA | International Communication Agency, United States |
| USMS | U.S. Marshals Service |
| USSC | U.S. Sentencing Commission |
| U.S.S.R. | Union of Soviet Socialist Republics |
| UST | United States Treaties |
| USTS | United States Travel Service |
| v. | versus |
| VA | Veterans Administration |
| VAR | Veterans Affairs and Rehabilitation Commission |
| VAWA | Violence Against Women Act |
| VFW | Veterans of Foreign Wars |
| VGLI | Veterans Group Life Insurance |
| Vict. | Queen Victoria (Great Britain) |
| VIN | vehicle identification number |
| VISTA | Volunteers in Service to America |
| VJRA | Veterans Judicial Review Act of 1988 |
| V.L.A. | Volunteer Lawyers for the Arts |
| VMI | Virginia Military Institute |
| VMLI | Veterans Mortgage Life Insurance |
| VOCAL | Victims of Child Abuse Laws |
| VRA | Voting Rights Act |
| WAC | Women's Army Corps |
| Wall. | Wallace's United States Supreme Court Reports |
| Wash. 2d | Washington Reports, Second Series |
| WAVES | Women Accepted for Volunteer Service |
| WCTU | Women's Christian Temperance Union |

| | |
|---|---|
| W.D. Wash. | Western District, Washington |
| W.D. Wis. | Western District, Wisconsin |
| WEAL | West's Encyclopedia of American Law, Women's Equity Action League |
| Wend. | Wendell's New York Reports |
| WFSE | Washington Federation of State Employees |
| Wheat. | Wheaton's United States Supreme Court Reports |
| Wheel. Cr. Cases | Wheeler's New York Criminal Cases |
| WHISPER | Women Hurt in Systems of Prostitution Engaged in Revolt |
| Whiteman | Marjorie Millace Whiteman, *Digest of International Law*, 15 vols. (1963-73) |
| WHO | World Health Organization |
| WIC | Women, Infants, and Children program |
| Will. and Mar. | King William and Queen Mary (Great Britain) |
| WIN | WESTLAW Is Natural; Whip Inflation Now; Work Incentive Program |
| WIU | Workers' Industrial Union |
| W.L.R. | Weekly Law Reports, England |
| WPA | Works Progress Administration |
| WPPDA | Welfare and Pension Plans Disclosure Act |
| WTO | World Trade Organization |
| WWI | World War I |
| WWII | World War II |
| Yates Sel. Cas. | Yates' New York Select Cases |
| YWCA | Young Women's Christian Association |